The Indispensable Guide to C

With Engineering Applications

The Indispensable Guide to C

With Engineering Applications

Paul Davies
Sheffield Hallam University

ADDISON-WESLEY

Harlow, England • Reading, Massachusetts • Menlo Park, California • New York
Don Mills, Ontario • Amsterdam • Bonn • Sydney • Singapore
Tokyo • Madrid • San Juan • Milan • Mexico City • Seoul • Taipei

Addison Wesley Longman Limited
Edinburgh Gate
Harlow
Essex CM20 2JE
England

Cover designed by Chris Eley
and printed by The Riverside Printing Co. (Reading) Ltd.
Typeset by CRB Associates, Lenwade, Norwich
and printed and bound in Great Britain by Biddles Ltd, Guildford and King's Lynn.

First printed 1995. Reprinted 1996 and 1997

ISBN 0–201–62438–9

British Library Cataloguing-in-Publication Data
A catalogue record for this book is available from the British Library.

Library of Congress Cataloging-in-Publication Data applied for

Prologue

A brief history of the development of C

One of the most startling developments to have taken place in the computing arena over the past 10 to 15 years must surely be the almost explosive growth that has occurred in the use of C as a general purpose programming language. Today, there is a seemingly endless supply of low cost, high quality C compilers directed at just about every computer imaginable, from the humblest PC to the largest mainframe. Interest in C and more recently its object-oriented cousin C++ continues to develop unabated, while interest in many other languages has dwindled with time. So why is C now so incredibly popular and what factors influenced its evolution into the language we have today? To fully comprehend this, one has to analyse the historical developments that were taking place in the early 1970s and those that have occurred since.

One of the most influential of these was the announcement by DEC of their new PDP-11 range of mini-computers which at that time represented a significant step forward in processing power and has since come to be regarded as something of a landmark development. Unfortunately, the host operating system did not meet with the same universal acclaim as the machine itself and it was this, amongst other things, that prompted Ken Thompson and Dennis Ritchie of AT & T's Bell Laboratories to transfer the developments of a new operating system, written predominantly in DEC assembly language, from an ageing PDP-7 onto the new PDP-11.

It must have been apparent from the outset that to continue developing in DEC assembly language would have precluded the widespread use of the emerging operating system on other (incompatible) equipment and would similarly have restricted its life expectancy to that of the PDP-11 itself, so a conscious decision was taken to switch development to a more portable, high level programming language, but which one?

Because of the close and intimate relationship that has always existed between an operating system and its host CPU, such a language would not only have to facilitate low level accesses to bits and bytes within the machine, but also be capable of producing fast, compact and efficient code, hence the traditional use of assembly language for this role. At the same time, such a language would have to offer comprehensive support for essential housekeeping operations carried out by operating systems, such as the creation and manipulation of complex file and data structures.

Building upon earlier developments by Ken Thompson of the language B, itself a development of BCPL, Ritchie slowly began to evolve the new language C as a tool for developing systems level applications. By 1973, the new operating system, the first ever to have been written in a high level language, had been completely re-written in C. That operating system was UNIX which remains one of the most popular, influential and widespread operating systems in existence today. Demand for UNIX and C was so great that Brian Kernighan and Dennis Ritchie were eventually forced to define the informal specification for C and its UNIX interface in their book *The C Programming Language* (1978) which led to C compilers of that time being informally designated as K & R compatible.

Because of C's portability, and by implication that of UNIX, computer vendors were generally more than happy to port UNIX on to their new machines, although there was understandable caution on the part of some vendors who had invested considerable time, money and effort in developing and promoting their own systems. But it was seen by many as opening a gateway to a wealth of pre-written software and applications while at the same time lending their products an air of credibility and acceptance in a market-place where compatibility and the adherence to standards, perhaps more than anything else, dictated the success or failure of one's products. In fact, whole new industries evolved based around the need to port C and UNIX applications on to a variety of new computer platforms.

As more and more young programmers and students developed their C skills in a UNIX environment and the range of applications software written in C grew, there was considerable pressure to provide support for C in other non-UNIX environments, most notably in the emerging PC environment dominated by MS-DOS. This too was an important development, for it encouraged companies such as Borland and Microsoft, attracted by the economies of scale present in the huge PC market-place, to develop high quality compilers at very keen prices, further promoting the acceptance of C as a general purpose programming language and helping to shake off the perception of C as a programming language exclusive to UNIX.

Soon C began to emerge as the language of choice for professional and enthusiast programmers working in MS-DOS and UNIX environments alike. Indeed, there can be few commercial applications developed for these two environments that have not been written in C. Evidence for this can be seen by the fact that virtually all the software tools, editors, word processors and desktop publishers needed to create and publish this book were written in C for an MS-DOS environment.

And yet there was one further, very important development in the C language that had yet to take place. Given the widespread acceptance of C in a host of new environments, coupled with a corresponding increase in the availability of new C compilers in the early 1980s, there emerged several notable weaknesses in the original, less than formal specification of the language laid down in K & R's book. This led to some compiler vendors interpreting the specification of the language somewhat differently from others, often to suit a non-UNIX environment, which inevitably led to incompatibilities emerging between compilers.

Not only that, some compilers were beginning to appear with enhanced features and facilities only hinted at in the original specification and there was a genuine fear that C might evolve, in much the same way as BASIC and (to a lesser extent) Pascal had done in the late 1970s, into a number of distinct dialects that could seriously affect the portability of C code.

This fear was finally acknowledged in 1983 when the American National Standards Institute (ANSI) was charged with the task of providing a more formal specification for the C language and thus committee X3J11 was born, comprising professional programmers, academics, compiler vendors and C user groups from around the world.

One of the committee's major objectives was to tighten the original specification and remove many of its ambiguities; more importantly, it was to highlight those parts of the language that were deemed to be 'Implementation Dependent', that is, likely to vary from one compiler/operating system environment to another, and for the first time, in an attempt to encourage the development of a more portable code (or at least the documentation of that code which was non-standard) set about defining the operation of a minimalist set of functions that should be available within the standard library of each and every C compiler.

If that wasn't enough, the committee was also given the task of ensuring that a new 'standard C' would be upwardly compatible from the previous generation 'K & R' compilers (often referred to these days as 'traditional' compilers) while in the process retaining much of that language's original spirit and philosophy. In 1988 the committee published its draft proposals for the C language which were eventually accepted by ANSI in 1989 and thus ANSI, or 'Standard' C, whose discussion forms the basis of this book, was born.

C as a first programming language

It is highly unfortunate that some of the very features of the C language that have led to it being perceived as a 'professional' programming language have not always been those that have most endeared it to academics around the world, charged with the task of turning novice students into competent C programmers. A situation that has not been helped by the image of the traditional C compiler as a less than friendly beast, notorious for generating cryptic error messages whose explanations were often only apparent to other experienced C programmers and offered precious little in the way of help or advice.

For example, it was not uncommon for a novice programmer to be deluged by screenfuls of unhelpful and misleading error messages arising as a result of a simple misplaced or absent semicolon or closing brace within the program. Even worse was the fact that the inherent flexibility of C (like assembly language) allowed programs to be run that were syntactically correct even though they still contained obvious and fundamental flaws leading ultimately to programs that simply crashed or, worse still, gave the wrong results. Hardly the most sympathetic environment for a young inexperienced programmer still struggling to come to terms with the grammar and terse syntax of the language itself.

It's not that these problems don't exist in other languages, it's simply that they seem more prevalent in C and have led to it being perceived as a difficult, blunt language only to be tackled by more experienced programmers who have previously 'cut their teeth' on more 'user friendly' languages, such as BASIC or Pascal. A situation that for many years was not helped by the lack of any good 'teach yourself C' books.

So why is this changing? Why are more and more first time programmers now being taught C, particularly in the fields of science and engineering? It cannot be due to any fundamental change or shift in emphasis within the language itself and must therefore be attributed to other facts. Market forces have undoubtedly played a part in this, with the demands of prospective employers compelling many institutions to adapt their courses to suit the needs of the prevailing market-place[1], but undoubtedly one of the most influential factors has been the widespread adoption by many academic institutions of the IBM-PC as a vehicle for teaching introductory programming and language concepts. Indeed, many students were already familiar with this machine, often possessing one of their own, and generally felt quite at ease with it, .particularly when equipped with a 'Windows' style environment.

Other developments such as Borland's Turbo C compiler also played an important role, offering a friendly, mouse driven, graphical environment with which to write, compile and debug programs while possessing excellent on-line help and documentation. Borland's compiler even offered helpful advice and intuitive (by the standards of a traditional UNIX C compiler) error messages and, it must be said, represents a far less intimidating environment to a student than that on offer from UNIX, where students have traditionally been stuck at the end of a dumb terminal attached to a timeshare mini-computer using an editor such as 'vi' (no disrespect intended). It has additionally accelerated the rapid growth and acceptance of C as a language for first time programmers.

[1] A survey published in the UK by a leading professional computing newspaper revealed that in the twelve month period leading up to August 1994, the twenty computing skills most in demand were headed by C and UNIX accounting jointly for 27% of all advertised job vacancies with 'Windows' experience third. C++, a relatively new language, featured seventh with 6.5% of all adverts while Ada, the only other non-specialist programming language, could only manage last position with 1.3%. Most telling of all was the absence of other popular skills such as Pascal, BASIC and Fortran programming from the ratings.

Preface

About this book

During the past six years, the author has increasingly become involved in the development and delivery of a series of lectures and short courses on C programming directed at professional programmers and undergraduate students alike. A significant feature of these courses was the presentation of a number of highly visual transparencies and example programs projected directly from the screen of a PC, an approach which has proved to be highly effective in delivering complex material in an easy to follow form, and left a lasting impression on those who attended these courses.

With these ideas in mind, the author set about developing a text that would attempt to capture the essential essence of these courses, a development that led ultimately to the book that you see before you. Believing strongly in the old adage that a 'picture paints a thousand words', the book develops a unique approach in presenting its material and examples in a highly visual, almost graphical form which should help students rapidly extract and digest the most important features of the discussion in hand.

In recognition of the wide ranging and diverse skills and interests of the many students now seeking to acquire fluency in C, many of the examples and discussions presented here have been carefully chosen to appeal to a multi-disciplinary audience, most notably in the fields of science and engineering, and are similarly supported by a comprehensive range of graded exercises designed to promote and develop a deeper understanding of the subject material.

With such a transformation in target audience it became necessary to shift the emphasis in the discussion and method of delivery of certain material, compared to more traditional books on C directed at the computer scientist. In particular, material from Chapter 1 has been carefully selected to guide students through what the author considers to be the most salient features of the language, in an easy to comprehend form that will rapidly develop students' knowledge and skills to the point where they feel able to experiment with programs of their own.

Special care has been taken to ensure that each new topic is presented in a logical, progressive manner with fundamental issues being discussed early on before taking a more in-depth look in later chapters. Both are important points if the motivation and interest of a student are to be sustained.

So who is the book aimed at? Well, it would be something of a cliché to say anybody. Suffice to say that the book is intended to appeal to anybody with sufficient interest and motivation to gain a deeper understanding of the C language, and should appeal in particular to the more modern needs of the electronic, computer and micro-systems engineer as well as the traditional needs of the computer scientist; it should serve equally well as a self-study guide to, or as a text in support of, a C programming course reinforced by lectures, for novice and more experienced programmers alike. In addition, the book has been written to promote an easy understanding of the language within the framework of a useful reference guide and should hopefully fulfil its intended role of serving as a lifelong 'Indispensable Guide to C'.

Note to the reader

The book assumes that the reader has access to and is familiar with a particular computer system, editor and 'standard C' compiler and can recognize and can issue commands and options to the host operating system. It also assumes some minor familiarity with basic number systems such as binary, decimal and hexadecimal and, in later chapters, the concepts of memory, addresses and contents.

Knowledge of common design methodologies such as top down, modular design, structured programming and so on, although useful, are not prerequisites for a study of this book as they are implicitly developed in an informal manner.

An instructor's manual, containing the solutions to end-of-chapter problems, is available to instructors and can be obtained by contacting the publisher. Source code from this book is available on disk from the author or via anonymous ftp at: **ftp aw.com** under **aw.computer.science**, in a file entitled **davies**.

Acknowledgements

My heartfelt appreciation goes out to everyone who has offered their support and encouragement in the production of this book, particularly to staff at Sheffield Hallam University and Addison-Wesley for their patience and understanding and of course to my wife Helen for entertaining our three young children, Sam, Jodie and Amy, who didn't always understand why their dad couldn't play football or go swimming at weekends.

P.J. Davies
School of EIT, Sheffield Hallam University
Pond Street, Sheffield S1 1WB
e-mail P.Davies@shu.ac.uk

Contents

1 Introduction and Overview

One of the most difficult aspects of developing a book to teach a programming language is that of keeping the reader motivated by the material currently being delivered. All too often, books launch into a discussion of new material at such a frantic pace and in such detail that the reader loses heart. In fact, it is perhaps not until midway through the book that the reader has grasped enough relevant (and, unfortunately, irrelevant) material to feel able to tackle even a simple program.

The main objective of this first chapter is to introduce new readers to the more useful aspects of the language through a simple overview of its fundamental features in an attempt get them programming and experimenting early. It is important, however, for the reader to appreciate that such an overview is simply a first step towards a greater understanding of each topic, which can only be gained through the study of subsequent chapters. To assist the reader in this, cross-references to additional relevant material in later chapters are presented where appropriate.

Perhaps the most important observation and advice that the author can pass on is that learning to program is not easy. As with learning to drive a car, the requisite knowledge cannot be gained simply by reading a book; it is acquired through exposure to new situations and 'hands-on' experience. The novice programmer must therefore learn to adopt a disciplined and experimental approach to problem solving.

The structure of this book encourages such an approach through its inclusion of sample programs and applications designed to demonstrate the most important features of the topics currently under discussion, while postponing a discussion of the finer detail until later. The examples chosen have been deliberately kept short and simple to reduce the amount of time required to enter them (an important feature in many student environments where 'hands-on' time is often restricted by considerations such as resources, timetabling and student numbers) and to enable the main features under discussion to be presented clearly with the minimum of distraction and fuss.

If you are new to programming, and to C in particular, then over the course of this chapter you will acquire a great deal of new knowledge which will, of course, take time to digest, but do not feel that you have to understand all of this material before progressing to Chapter 2. To help you along, you might like to skip Sections 1.10 and 1.11 until you have gained more confidence. Before we discuss the C language itself, however, let us first take at look at how programs are written, compiled and run, operations that the reader will become intimately familiar with over a very short period of time.

1.1 Creating, compiling and running a program

Before any program can be executed or run, it must first be entered into the computer. This is achieved by the programmer typing in the program at the keyboard using a conventional text editor, before saving that program to a disk file. The file that the programmer enters and saves is known as the **source file**, since it contains the original source of the program's code.

If you are developing your C programs in a UNIX environment, then an editor such as 'vi' or 'emacs' (depending upon what is available on your system) may be used; on an IBM PC running MS-DOS, an editor such as 'edit' may be used. Many C compilers for the IBM PC, such as Borland's Turbo C, for example, are already equipped with an editor as standard, and the use of this is generally preferable to that of 'edit'.

The name of the source file we wish to create is largely irrelevant, because it only serves to identify the disk file, should we wish to compile or modify it later. For example, suppose we were developing a test program. We could run the editor and ask it to open or create a file ready for us to enter our program with an MS-DOS command such as:

If you are using Borland's Turbo C Integrated Design Environment (IDE), choose the 'New' option from the 'File' menu. Note how the above source file name includes the file name extension '.c'. This is important, because it identifies the file as a C source file. If this extension is not used, you may find that you are not able to compile your program later. At this stage, you may enter the program source code into the editor then save it to a disk file (use the 'Save-as' option from the 'File' menu if using Borland's IDE) ready for the next stage in the process, compilation.

Since your computer does not understand raw C code directly, the source file must first be translated, or converted into what is known as **machine code**. This is a complex operation, usually performed with the aid of a **compiler**. In a UNIX environment, compiling a program is achieved using the command shown below, while under Borland's Turbo C IDE, the programmer could simply choose the Compile and Link options from the Compile menu:

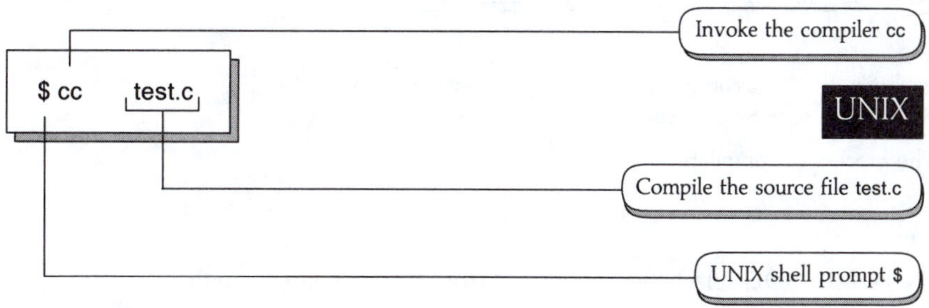

During compilation, various messages may be observed, which bring to the attention of the programmer any **warnings** (which will *not* prevent the program from being compiled and run) and errors (which will) that may be detected. If the program is free of errors, a further file is generally created containing the machine code equivalent version of the C program. This is called the **executable file**. If, however, the compiler reports any errors, the source file will have to be re-edited to correct them and another attempt made to compile it.

With a UNIX based C compiler, the executable file is generally saved to disk under the file name 'a.out', regardless of the name of the original source file that was compiled, but this can be overridden, if required, by the use of the '-o name' option in the command line, for example:

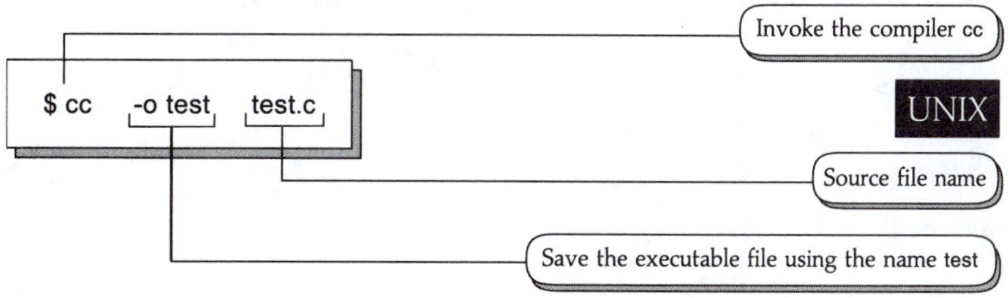

Other compilers, such as those running under MS-DOS, generally save the executable program using a file name derived from the original source file in conjunction with the file name extension '.exe'. This edit/compile sequence is illustrated in Figure 1.1.

Once the executable file has been created, it may be run and tested simply by entering its name at the operating system prompt; that is, 'a.out' in a UNIX environment or 'test.exe' in an MS-DOS environment. Alternatively, if you are

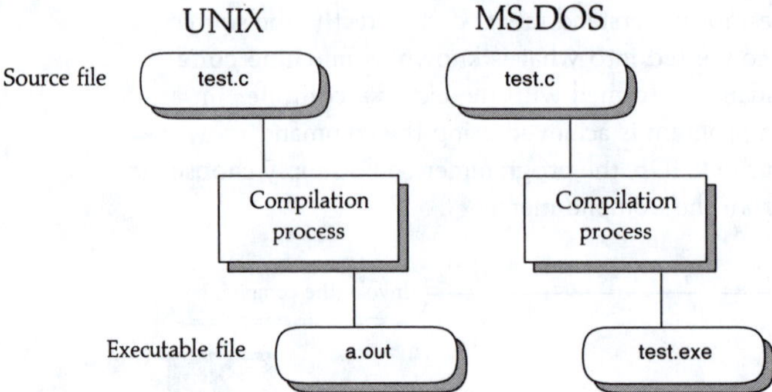

Figure 1.1 The process of compilation.

using Borland's Turbo C IDE, select the Run option from the Compile menu. It is important to appreciate that every modification to the source file requires the program to be re-compiled if the effect is to be observed in the executable program.

1.2 Your first C program

Now that you are familiar with the steps involved in entering and compiling programs, let us take a look at an actual C program. You can enter this yourself, exactly as it is shown in the box below, using an appropriate editor, compile it and then run it. This will give you the opportunity to try out the ideas from the last section and satisfy yourself that you understand the processes involved.

```
#include    <stdio.h>

int main( void )
{
   printf("Welcome !!!!! \n" ) ;
   return 0 ;
}
```

If this program were compiled and run, you would observe the following message displayed on your output screen/terminal:

```
Welcome !!!!!
```

Let us take a closer look at this program and try to figure out what each line of program code does. The first line of the program is shown below. Notice how it begins with the character '#'. This character has special significance when placed at the beginning of a line of C code, because it identifies what is known as a **pre-processor directive** (pre-processor directives are dealt with fully in Chapter 13). The pre-processor can be thought of as part of the compilation process and is responsible for processing the source file prior to its actual compilation. Thus the directive:

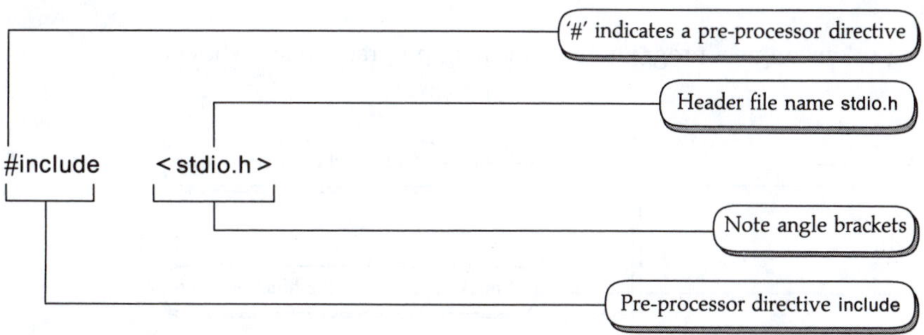

requests the pre-processor to read or include the contents of the disk file 'stdio.h' (a C source file supplied by the compiler vendor; pronounced Standard-IO) at compile time and merge it with the source file being compiled (an operation that does not modify your original source file). Thus the pre-processor replaces the directive '#include <stdio.h>' in the resultant merged file with the contents of the file 'stdio.h'.

This is important, since it is the merged file that is actually compiled; later in the compilation process it will appear as if the programmer had actually typed the contents of the file 'stdio.h' into the source file. The file 'stdio.h' is one of a number of so-called **header** files supplied with every C compiler. It was included in the program because it contains important information relevant to the remainder of the compilation. This will become apparent towards the end of the chapter.

Notice how the file name 'stdio.h' was enclosed by angle brackets '< >'. The use of these brackets is important, because they direct the pre-processor to the location of the file 'stdio.h' on disk. It is worth noting that a header file may be included by enclosing its name within quotation marks. For example:

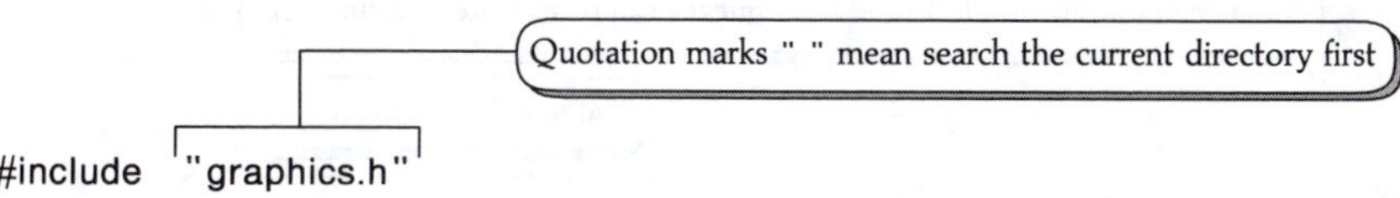

The use of quotation marks forces the pre-processor to search for the header file 'graphics.h' located within the programmer's current (default)

directory, thus permitting the programmer to create and include his or her own header files. In any case, all assumptions about the location of a header file can always be overridden by specifying the exact location using a pathlist. For example, under UNIX we could include the header file 'stdio.h' with the directive:

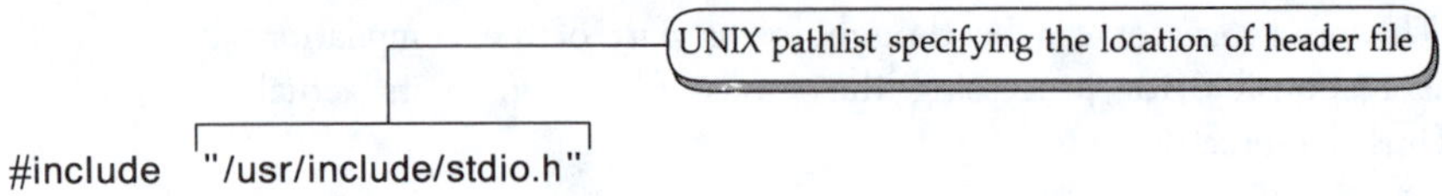

Returning to our original program, the remaining program code is shown below:

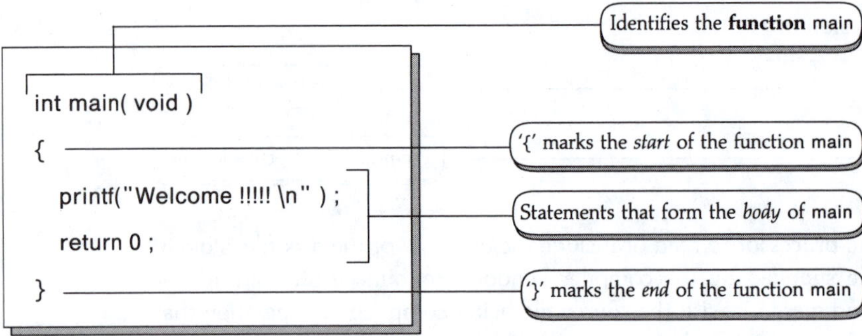

Here, the word 'main', because it is followed by an opening bracket '(' identifies a **function** called main. (Note that this book adopts the convention of placing brackets after a function name, for example 'main()'.) In C, programs are often organized into a number of smaller functions, of which main() is just one example. It is, however, the most important function in the program, since it marks the starting point for the program's eventual execution. It follows from this that a program without a function called main() cannot be run. (Functions are dealt with in more detail in Chapter 6.)

The start and end of every function are marked by the presence of opening and closing braces '{' and '}'. Beneath the opening brace '{' in this example lie two further **statements**, which are executed in sequence, from top to bottom. The first of these two statements is shown below:

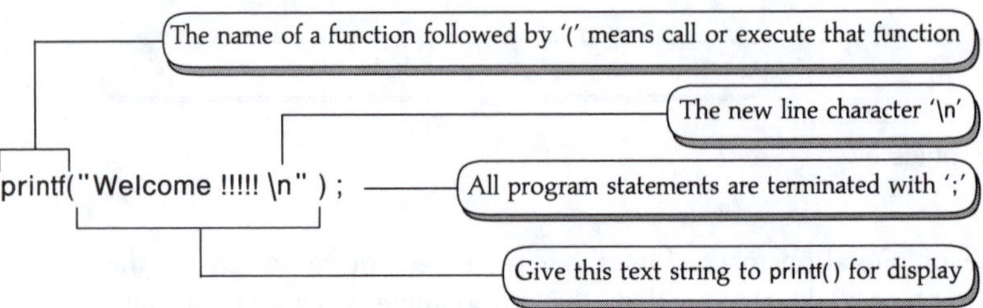

This statement **calls/invokes/runs** another function called printf( ), which is a general purpose output function used extensively by most programs to display text and numeric values. In this instance, printf( ) is being given the text string '"Welcome !!!!! \n"' to display.

Note the use of the '\n' in that text string. This asks printf( ) to begin a new line of text after the message 'Welcome !!!!!' has been displayed. The '\n' character may occur any number of times, at any position within the string. Try experimenting with it. Lastly, notice how the call to the function printf() was terminated with a semicolon ';'. This marks the end of every statement in C. The last remaining statement in the function main( ) is shown below:

Terminate the execution of main( ), and return the value 0 to the host environment

```
return 0 ;
```

This serves to terminate the execution of a function, and in this instance, because it is the function main( ), the program itself. The program's operator is then returned to the host environment from which the program was run, generally the operating system or IDE in the case of Borland C. In this example, a value of 0 was returned to that environment to indicate that the program had terminated successfully, but other values may sometimes be used to indicate an unsuccessful termination. As a useful exercise, we could experiment with this program by placing additional statements inside main( ) as shown below, which now contains two separate calls to the function printf( ):

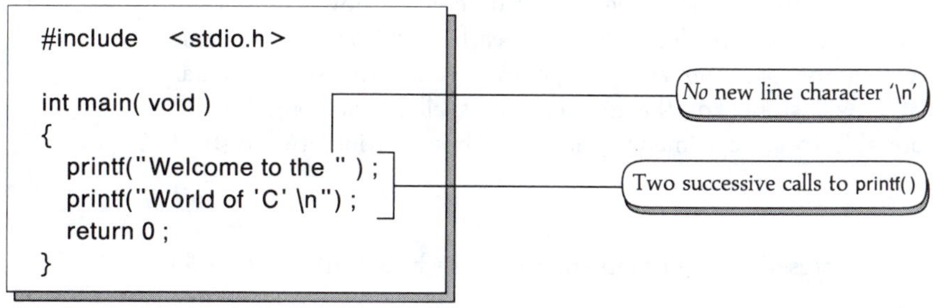


```
#include   <stdio.h>

int main( void )
{
   printf("Welcome to the " ) ;
   printf("World of 'C' \n") ;
   return 0 ;
}
```

If this program were run, the operator would observe the following output displayed on the terminal/screen:

```
Welcome to the World of 'C'
```

1.2.1 *The C standard library*

It is usual at this point in the discussion to pause and consider where the function printf( ) came from. After all, we have called it twice in the above program, but the code for this function does not appear to have been entered into the source file; that is, the function printf( ) has not been **defined** by the program. So where does printf( ) come from? The answer lies with the concept of a **library**.

All C compilers are equipped with a library of useful functions, of which printf( ) is just one example. These functions have been written by the compiler vendor and reside in what is known as the **C standard library** (a full discussion of the functions available in the C standard library can be found in Chapter 18).

At compile time, a search of the standard library is automatically performed to locate any functions whose definitions are missing from the source file (that is, functions that the program calls but does not define) and to ensure that a copy of their compiled code is placed in the executable program. Should the library not contain the missing function(s), errors will be generated. You can verify this for yourself by modifying your source file to replace the call to the library function printf( ) with a call to the non-existent library function print( ).

1.3 Introducing variables and constants

To make our programs more interesting and versatile, we can introduce program **variables** to hold data or the results of calculations – data that will be needed by the program. The concept of a variable is similar to that of the memory facility provided by most calculators. There are important differences, however, since in C you can introduce as many variables as you need, each of which is given a name to identify it within the program and a type to describe the sort of data/ information that it will store. For the moment we shall restrict ourselves to variables that are able to store numeric quantities. These fall into two distinct groups:

- those able to represent whole or integral values, such as 0, 10, 12, 93, −53 and so on;
- those able to represent real or floating point values, such as numbers with decimal points and/or exponents such as 0.0, −2.5, 3.141 59, 1e09 (1.0×10^{09}), −1.3e−12 (1.3×10^{-12}) and so on.

C has several built-in data types to support the creation of integral and real variables. A subset of these types is presented in Table 1.1 (a full description of C's data types is given in Chapter 2).

Table 1.1 A subset of C's data types.

Type	*Main usage*
char	Primarily single text characters and small integral quantities
int	Larger integral values, at least in the range −32 768 to +32 767
float	Floating point or real values, at least in the range $\pm 1.0 \times 10^{\pm 38}$

There are several places where a variable may be introduced or **defined** within a program. For the moment we will restrict ourselves to a class of variables known as **automatic** variables, which are introduced after the opening '{' within a function (for other classes of variables, see Section 2.2).

Several example variable types are given in the program section below (note that the notation '...' used in this example is intended to signify incomplete code; that is, code omitted for clarity, which will of course have to be supplied in order to make the program compile and run):

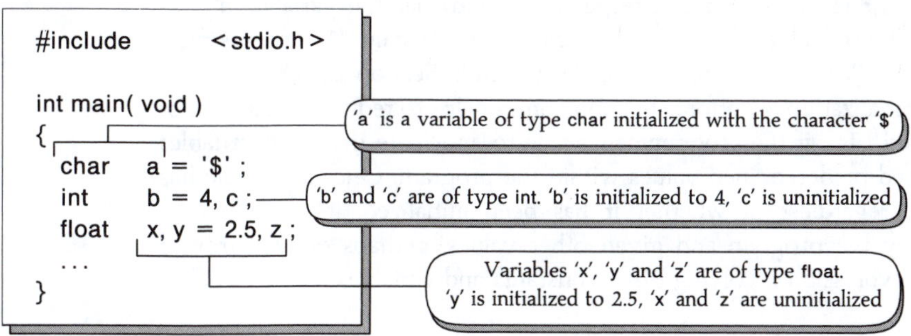

```
#include        <stdio.h>

int main( void )
{
    char    a = '$' ;
    int     b = 4, c ;
    float   x, y = 2.5, z ;
    ...
}
```

'a' is a variable of type char initialized with the character '$'
'b' and 'c' are of type int. 'b' is initialized to 4, 'c' is uninitialized
Variables 'x', 'y' and 'z' are of type float.
'y' is initialized to 2.5, 'x' and 'z' are uninitialized

It is important to appreciate that C is a **case sensitive** language, in that it does differentiate between upper and lower case names within a program. For example, the functions Main(), MAIN() and main() are all unique and individual. However, it is considered bad programming practice to differentiate between variable or function names purely on case alone. The normal convention in C is to use lower case but there are exceptions to this, as we shall see later.

The names given to any variables (and indeed any functions, such as main()) are known generically as **identifiers**. Many compilers use this term when issuing error messages, such as 'identifier missing', which simply means that your program is incorrect and that the compiler was expecting a variable or function name at that point in the program.

C has very strict rules governing the creation of identifiers. In essence, you can use any of the characters a–z and A–Z, the digits 0–9 (although identifiers cannot begin with a digit) and the special underscore character '_' within an identifier name. Furthermore, each identifier should be unique within the first 31 characters of its name. Finally, you cannot create an identifier using any of the names shown in Table 1.2, since these are **key** words that are reserved for constructing the language itself.

Table 1.2 C's key or reserved words.

auto	break	case	char	const	continue
default	do	double	else	enum	extern
float	for	goto	if	int	long
register	return	short	signed	sizeof	static
struct	switch	typedef	union	unsigned	void
volatile	while				

Notice how in the last example program several variables of the same type, such as 'b' and 'c', were introduced/defined with a single statement and that with such a definition, each variable name is separated by a comma ','. Of course, separate statements could have been used to define each if required.

Notice also how some of the variables, such as 'b' and 'y', were initialized during their definition with the integer and floating point **implicit** (that is, implied) constant values 4 and 2.5, respectively, and that the variable 'a' was initialized with the value of the implicit character constant '$' using **single** quotation marks. (Variable initialization is dealt with in Section 2.2.5.)

Such initialization is optional but sometimes helps to reduce the amount of coding required later, if the programmer is able to anticipate that such variables will be assigned predetermined values within the program. Once a variable has been defined, regardless of whether it has been initialized, it may then be manipulated by the program and given other values, perhaps derived from a mathematical expression involving other constants and variables.

1.3.1 *Introducing explicit constants*

An **explicit** constant is introduced in much the same way as a variable, but with its definition prefixed by the word (or type qualifier) 'const'. Such constants should be initialized during their definition, since they cannot be assigned other values later (they are, after all, constants). This allows the program to create symbolic names for known fixed values. For example, the program below defines the floating point constant 'pi' to present the floating point value 3.141 59:

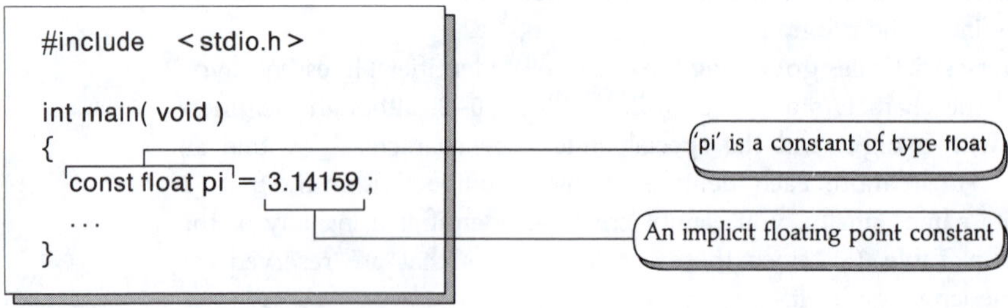
```
#include    <stdio.h>

int main( void )
{
   const float pi = 3.14159 ;
   ...
}
```

Now, instead of always referring to the value 3.141 59 within our programs, we could instead refer to the symbolic name 'pi'. For example, the statement below references the value of the constant 'pi' in determining the circumference of a circle:

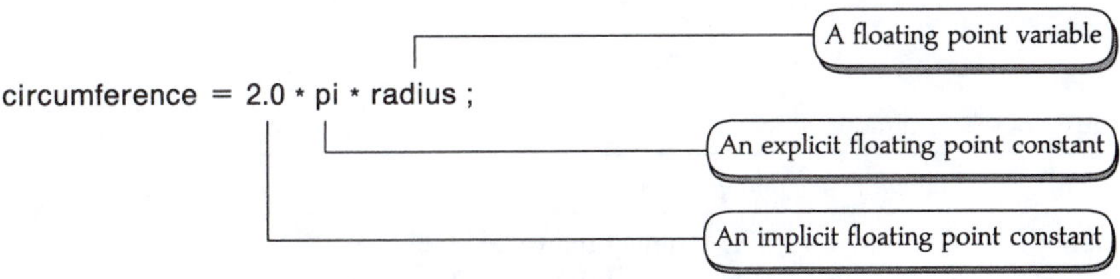

1.3.2 *Pre-processor constants*

Another simple method of introducing symbolic constants involves the use of the pre-processor directive '#define' (see Section 13.2). Traditionally, symbolic constants created in this way are often given **upper case** names and are introduced at the top of the program source code, usually after any '#include' directives. For example, we could introduce the symbolic constant PI with a directive of the form:

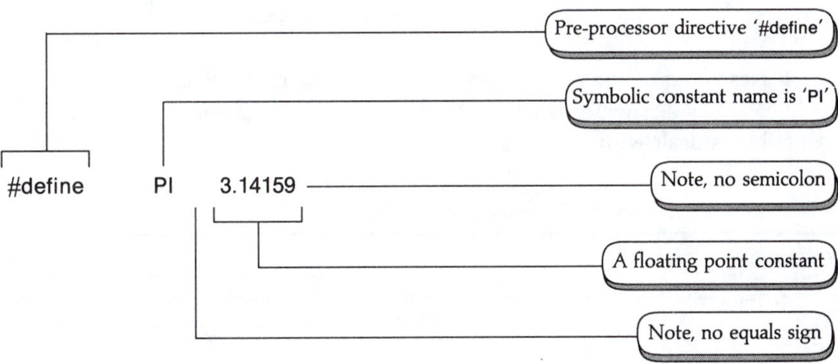

At compile time, the pre-processor ensures that any references to the symbol PI (except where they occur within text strings denoted by quotation marks " ") are replaced by the floating point constant 3.141 59, and thus it will appear to the compiler as if the program had never contained any references to PI in the first place.

1.4 Arithmetic operators and assignment

It is not much use introducing variables and constants into a program unless you can perform calculations based upon them. C therefore provides several arithmetic **operators** to assist in the evaluation of mathematical expressions. A subset of these is shown in Table 1.3.

Table 1.3 A subset of C's arithmetic operators.

Operator	*Operation*	*Example*	*Interpretation*
+	Addition	a = b + c ;	'a' is assigned the value of 'b' plus 'c'
–	Subtraction	a = b – c ;	'a' is assigned the value of 'b' minus 'c'
*	Multiplication	a = b * c ;	'a' is assigned the value of 'b' multiplied by 'c'
/	Division	a = b / c ;	'a' is assigned the value of 'b' divided by 'c'

In addition to the operators listed in Table 1.3, C also provides the '++' and '––' operators specifically to increment (add 1) or decrement (subtract 1) a variable. For example, the following statements increment 'x' and decrement 'y' (operators are discussed in more detail in Chapter 3).

```
x ++ ;        /* Increment the value of 'x' */
y -- ;        /* Decrement the value of 'y' */
```

Increment the value of 'x'

Decrement the value of 'y'

Program 1.1 uses some of these operators to calculate the circumference and area of a circle of radius 2.5, which is complete except for the displaying of the results, an issue that is dealt with in the next section.

Program 1.1 Calculating the area and circumference of a circle.

```
#include   <stdio.h>
#define  PI   3.14159
int main( void )
{
  float  area, circ, radius = 2.5 ;
  area = PI * radius * radius ;
  circ = 2.0 * PI * radius ;
  return 0 ;
}
```

Pre-processor constant PI equivalent to 3.141 59

Multiplication operator '*'

Assignment operator '='

1.5 Simple numeric output: The function printf()

Before we can display the results generated by Program 1.1, we must take a closer look at the function printf(). Although we have used this function already, to display simple text messages, it is capable of much more than this. By placing special '%' format indicators in the text string, we can tell printf() *where* and *how* to display other values, such as variables and constants (a full description of printf()'s capabilities can be found in Chapter 15).

For example, suppose we wished to display the value of the floating point variable 'area', as calculated by Program 1.1. We could call printf() and supply it with a **format string** containing some general literal text, which will be displayed on the operator's screen exactly as it appears in the program, but containing a '%f' format indicator to mark the position where the value of 'area' is to be displayed. To complete the operation, printf() now has to be given the value of the variable 'area' as a second **argument** or **working parameter**. Thus, the following statement placed in Program 1.1 after the calculation of 'circ':

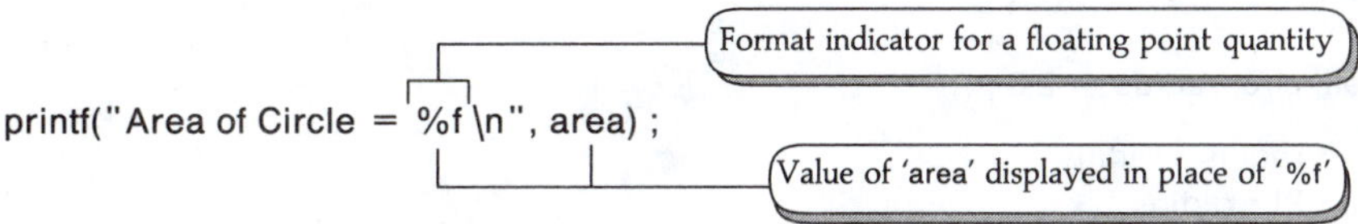
Format indicator for a floating point quantity
printf("Area of Circle = %f \n", area) ;
Value of 'area' displayed in place of '%f'

produced the following display on the author's computer when the program was run:

```
Area of Circle = 19.634937
```

Note how the second argument 'area' is separated from the text string (itself an argument) by a comma ','. Additional data could also be displayed with this call to printf() simply by including additional format indicators in the text string and supplying additional arguments. For example, the following statement included in Program 1.1:

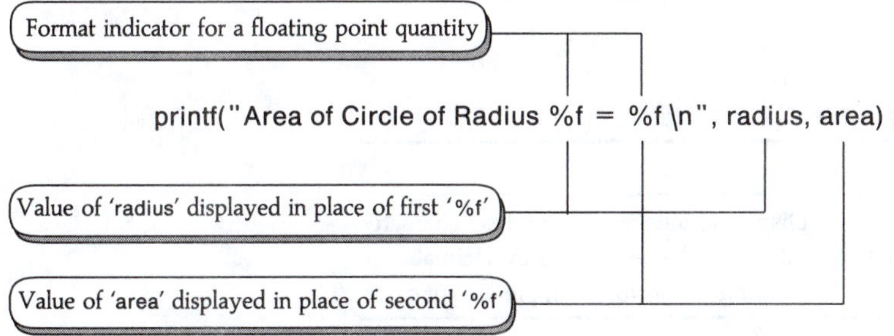
Format indicator for a floating point quantity
printf("Area of Circle of Radius %f = %f \n", radius, area) ;
Value of 'radius' displayed in place of first '%f'
Value of 'area' displayed in place of second '%f'

requests printf() to display the values of the variables 'radius' and 'area' in place of the first and second '%f' format indicators, respectively. On the author's computer, the execution of this statement led to the following display:

```
Area of Circle of Radius 2.500000 = 19.634937
```

Now in order to complete Program 1.1, we could include two calls to printf() as shown in Program 1.2.

Program 1.2 Displaying the area and circumference of a circle.

```
#include  <stdio.h>

#define  PI  3.14159

int main( void )
{
  float  area, circ, radius = 2.5 ;

  area = PI * radius * radius ;
  circ = 2.0 * PI * radius ;

  printf("Area of Circle of Radius %f = %f \n", radius, area) ;
  printf("Circumference of Circle of Radius %f = %f \n", radius, circ) ;

  return 0 ;
}
```

A subset of the '%' formatters recognized by printf() is given in Table 1.4. It is imperative that the correct '%' formatter is used for the type of data/variable that the program intends to display. A very common mistake here is to use, for example, '%d' to display a floating point quantity. This leads to unpredictable program output as printf() misinterprets the argument(s) it has been given. You can verify this for yourself with a little experimentation.

Table 1.4 A subset of printf()'s '%' formatters.

Formatter	*Suitable for*	*Type of output*
%c	Integral values	Displays value as a single text character
%d	Integral values	Integral value expressed in decimal
%f	Real values	Floating point, for example 1.250562

1.5.1 *Simple numeric input: The function* scanf()

It is generally useful to be able to enter data into a program once it is running, rather than have the program assume a value, for example the radius of the circle. Such an operation can be accomplished in C using the function scanf(), which is similar in principle to the output function printf(). Both functions, for example, make use of and recognize a similar range of '%' formatters. A subset of the '%' format indicators recognized by scanf() is shown in Table 1.5 (a full description of scanf()'s capabilities can be found in Chapter 15).

Table 1.5 A subset of the '%' formatters recognized by scanf().

Formatter	*Suitable for reading*
%c	Single text characters
%d	Integral values expressed in decimal, for example 2, 5, −10
%f	Floating point real values, for example 1.24, 0.3, 1.625e3

The most important difference between printf() and scanf(), apart from the fact that one displays data while the other reads/accepts it, is that scanf() requires the memory **addresses** of the variables into which it ultimately stores the data it reads.

As a variable generally lives in memory, the location or address of that variable (often known as and referred to by the compiler as the variable's **lvalue**) may be obtained with the address operator '&'. Thus, to read a floating point value from the keyboard and store this in the floating point variable 'radius' we could call scanf() with the following statement:

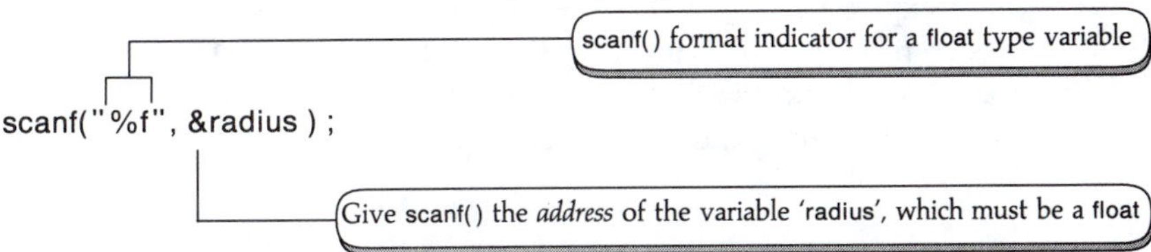

As with printf(), failure to use the correct '%' format indicator for the type of variable into which scanf() will store the entered data is one of the most common mistakes a programmer can make, followed closely by failure to include the address operator '&' with each subsequent argument.

As an example, let us modify Program 1.2 to enable the operator to supply the radius of the circle to the program once it is running. The complete program is shown in Program 1.3.

Program 1.3 Calculation of the area and circumference of a circle.

```
#include  <stdio.h>

#define  PI  3.14159

int  main( void )
{
  float  area, circ, radius ;                              Prompt the operator to enter the 'radius'

  printf("Enter a Value for the Circle's Radius : " ) ;

  scanf("%f", &radius ) ; ------------------------ Pause, read and store a floating value into 'radius'

  area = PI * radius * radius ;
  circ = 2.0 * PI * radius ;

  printf("Area of Circle of Radius %f = %f \n", radius, area) ;
  printf("Circumference of Circle of Radius %f = %f \n", radius, circ) ;
  return 0 ;
}
```

When Program 1.3 was run, the following sample display was produced:

```
Enter a Value for the Circle's Radius : 5 ---------- User supplied input
Area of Circle of Radius 5.000000 = 78.539749
Circumference of Circle of Radius 5.000000 = 31.415899
```

Application 1.1

The current i expressed in amps flowing in the electrical resistor circuit shown in Figure 1.2 is given by the expression i = v1/(r1 + r2), while the voltage potential at point v2 expressed relative to 0v is given by the equation v2 = i × r2, where r1 and r2 are resistance values expressed in ohms. Write a program to read in the values of v1, r1 and r2 and calculate the current i and voltage v2.

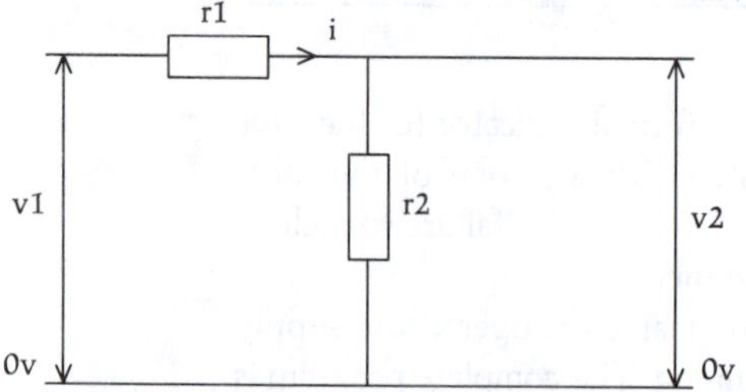

Figure 1.2 An electrical resistor circuit.

Application 1.1 Calculation of current and voltage in a circuit.

```
#include   <stdio.h>

int main( void )
{
  float   r1, r2, v1, i ;

  printf("Enter the Voltage 'v1': ");
  scanf("%f", &v1) ;

  printf("Enter the resistance values 'r1' and 'r2': " ) ;
  scanf("%f %f", &r1, &r2 ) ;

  i = v1/( r1 + r2 ) ;
  printf("Current = %f Amps\n", i ) ;
  printf("Potential at v2 = %f Volts\n", i * r2 ) ;
  return 0 ;
}
```

Prompt the operator for voltage v1

Read and store *one* floating point value or v1

Read and store *two* floating point resistance values for r1 and r2

Result of i × r2 given to printf()

When Application 1.1 was run, the following two sample displays were produced:

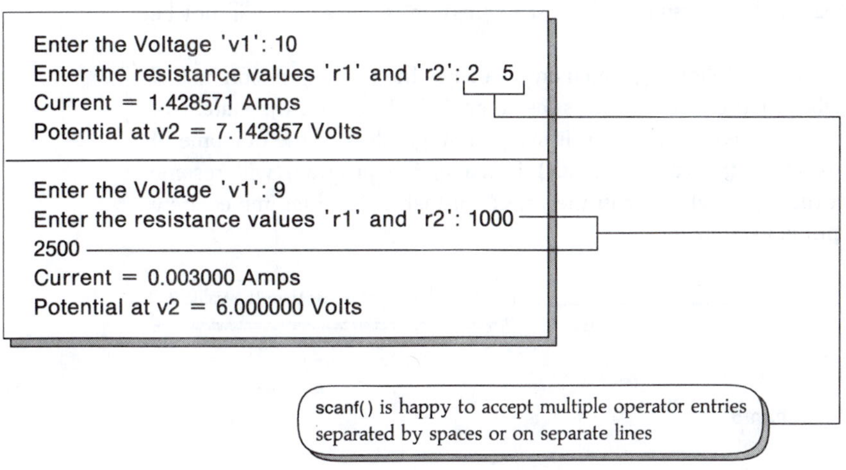

Enter the Voltage 'v1': 10
Enter the resistance values 'r1' and 'r2': 2 5
Current = 1.428571 Amps
Potential at v2 = 7.142857 Volts
Enter the Voltage 'v1': 9
Enter the resistance values 'r1' and 'r2': 1000
2500
Current = 0.003000 Amps
Potential at v2 = 6.000000 Volts
scanf() is happy to accept multiple operator entries separated by spaces or on separate lines

Notice how scanf() was able to read two values from the operator's keyboard using multiple '%' formatters in the format string, and that it waits until it thinks it has got both. This means that operator entries can be separated by **white space** characters such as the space character itself, tabs or carriage returns but *not* by commas or other printable characters.

1.6 Program selection

There comes a point in most programs when a decision about the operations that will be performed next must be made. Statements, as we have already seen, are executed sequentially within a function, one after another. This sequential execution may be interrupted using a **conditional test**, the outcome of which may be used to select one or more alternative paths or routes through a program. In C, the most common form of conditional test involves the use of the if statement, the general form of which is shown below. (A full discussion of the facilities available to control program selection can be found in Chapter 4.)

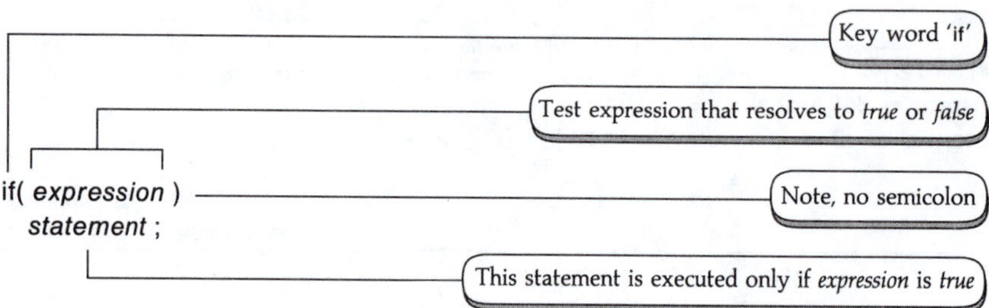
Key word 'if'
Test expression that resolves to *true* or *false*
if(*expression*)
statement ;
Note, no semicolon
This statement is executed only if *expression* is *true*

Here, the 'test' expression inside the brackets '( )' is evaluated at **run time**; that is, while the program is running or executing. If the outcome of that test is considered to be 'true', then the single statement that follows will be executed. Otherwise – that is, if the result of the test expression is 'false' – it will not be executed.

For example, the following statement evaluates the test expression 'a < 5' to determine whether the value of 'a' is less than 5. If it is, then the statement calling printf( ) is executed, otherwise it is skipped. Regardless of the outcome of this test and whether the call to printf( ) is made, the program will resume execution with the next statement in the program; that is, the one immediately following the printf( ) statement.

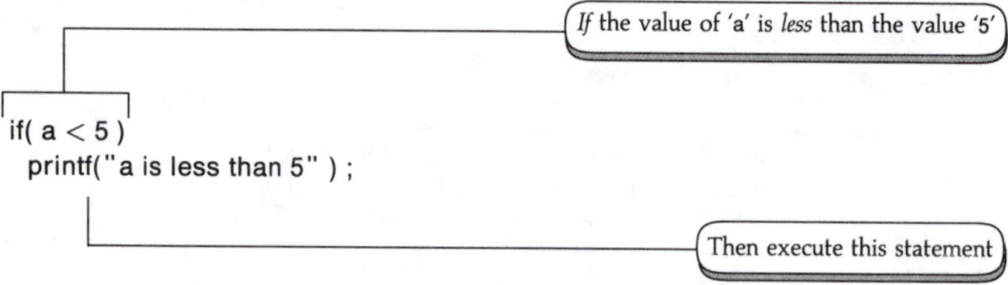
If the value of 'a' is *less* than the value '5'
if(a < 5)
printf("a is less than 5") ;
Then execute this statement

A simple **flowchart** (a graphical illustration of the various possible routes or paths of execution through the whole or part program along with a statement of any conditions required to follow that route) for the basic form of the if test is shown in Figure 1.3.

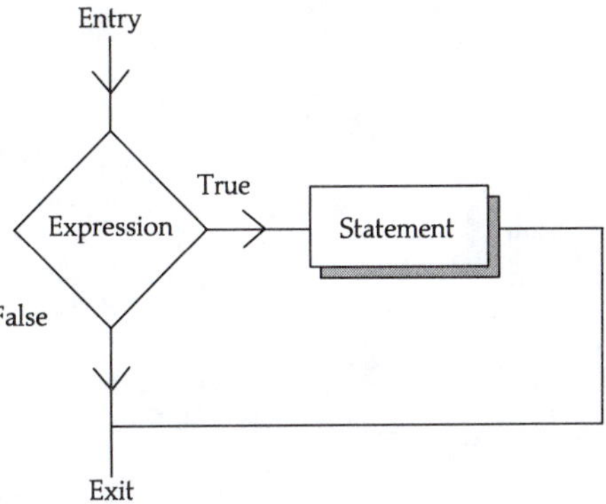

Figure 1.3 Flowchart for the simple if test.

In the previous example, only one statement was associated with and thus affected by the outcome of the if test. If *more* than one statement is to be associated with the test, then those statements must be enclosed by a **statement block**, the start and end of which are marked with opening and closing braces '{ }', as shown below:

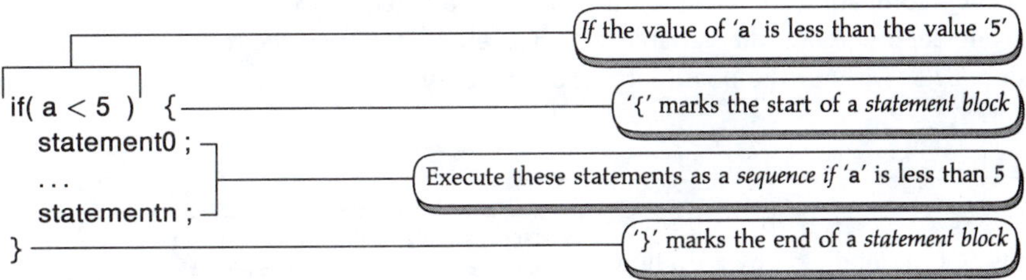

Here, if the test expression is deemed to be true, that is if the value of 'a' is less than 5, then all those statements that lie between the '{' and the '}' following the if test are executed as a sequence, otherwise they will all be ignored or skipped. Program execution then resumes with the statement following the '}' irrespective of the outcome of the test.

A useful and simple variation on the basic if test is the if-else test, the general form of which is shown below:

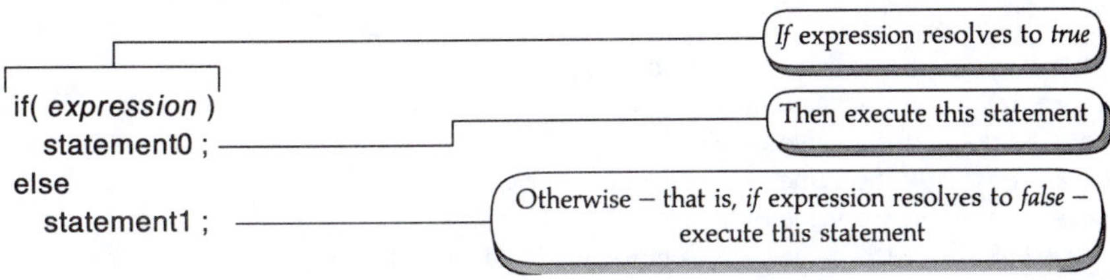

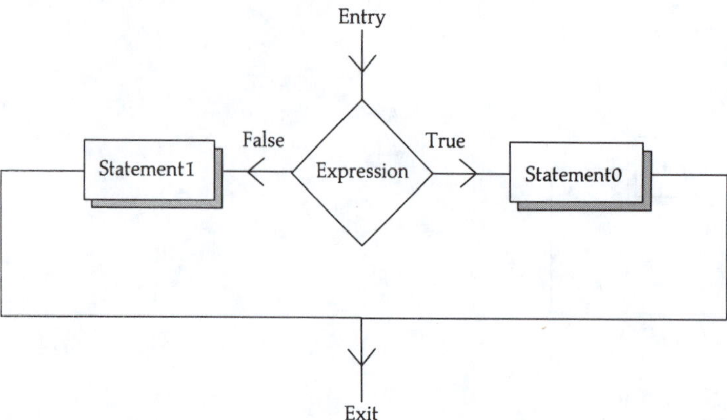

Figure 1.4 Flowchart for a simple if-else test.

Here, if the test expression is deemed to be true, then only 'statement0' is executed, otherwise 'statement1' is executed. In other words, statements 0 and 1 are **mutually exclusive**. A simple flowchart illustrating the flow of program execution for a simple if-else test is shown in Figure 1.4.

As an example, the if-else test shown below checks for a possible divide by zero situation by comparing the value of 'a' with 0. If 'a' is equal to 0, then a call to printf( ) is made, otherwise, the variable 'c' can safely be assigned the result of the expression '5 / a' without the possibility of a divide by zero occurring:

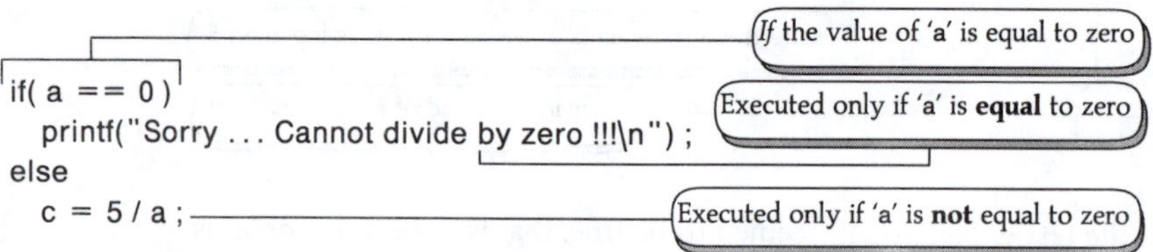


```
if( a == 0 )
   printf("Sorry . . . Cannot divide by zero !!!\n") ;
else
   c = 5 / a ;
```

As with a simple if test, braces '{ }' may be used to associate more than one statement with the if or else parts of the test. Table 1.6 contains a summary of C's **relational operators** that permit two expressions to be compared with each other.

Table 1.6 C's relational operators.

Operator	*Example test*	*Interpretation*
>	if(c > b)	If the value of 'c' is greater than 'b'
>=	if(c >= b)	If the value of 'c' is greater than or equal to 'b'
<	if(c < b)	If the value of 'c' is less than 'b'
<=	if(c <= b)	If the value of 'c' is less than or equal to 'b'
==	if(c == b)	If the value of 'c' is equal in value to 'b'
!=	if(c != b)	If the value of 'c' is not equal in value to 'b'

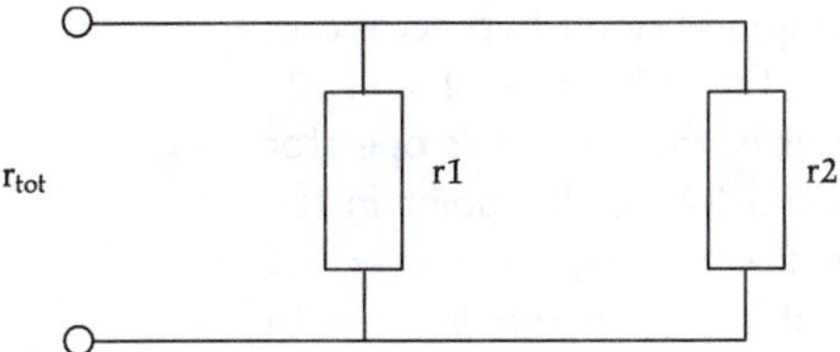

Figure 1.5 A parallel resistor network.

Application 1.2

The combined resistance 'r_{tot}' of the parallel electrical circuit shown in Figure 1.5 is given by the equation '$1/r_{tot} = 1/r1 + 1/r2$'. Write a program to read in the values of 'r1' and 'r2' from the program's operator and calculate and display the value of 'r_{tot}'.

Application 1.2 Combined resistance of a parallel resistor circuit.

```
#include   <stdio.h>
#include   <stdlib.h>  ——— <stdlib.h> included because it contains information relating to exit()

int main( void )
{
  float r1, r2, r3 ;

  printf("Enter the Resistance Values 'r1' and 'r2': " ) ;
                                              Check that scanf() reads two values correctly
  if( scanf("%f %f", &r1, &r2 ) != 2)  {
    printf("Data Entered Incorrectly ... Bye !!\n") ;
    exit( 0 ) ;  ——— Call to exit() always terminates program
  }

  if( r1 != 0 )  {        Statements executed only if 'r1' and 'r2' are not equal to 0
    if( r2 != 0 )  {
      r3 = (1.0/r1) + (1.0/r2) ;
      printf("Total Resistance Rtot = %f ohms\n", 1.0/r3 ) ;
    }
    else
      printf("r2 is a Short Circuit ... \n") ;  ——— Execute this statement if 'r1' is not equal to 0
                                                    and 'r2' equals 0
  }
  else
    printf("r1 is a Short Circuit ... \n") ;  ——— Execute this statement if 'r1' equals 0

  return 0 ;
}
```

In this example, selective execution is put to good use on two occasions. Firstly, scanf( ) is asked to read two numeric values for the resistances 'r1' and 'r2'. If scanf( ) reads and converts them successfully – that is, the program's operator supplied two recognizable numeric values for 'r1' and 'r2' at this point in the program – then scanf( ) should return the answer 2 – that is, the number of conversions that were successfully performed. If not, the program terminates with an error message and a call to exit( ).

Secondly, two **nested** if tests are used – that is, one placed within another – prior to the calculation of 'r_{tot}' (that is, 1.0/r3). This effectively creates a logical AND condition, where the value of 'r_{tot}' is calculated *only* if 'r1' AND 'r2' are not equivalent to zero (that is, short circuits). Three sample outputs produced by the above program are given below:

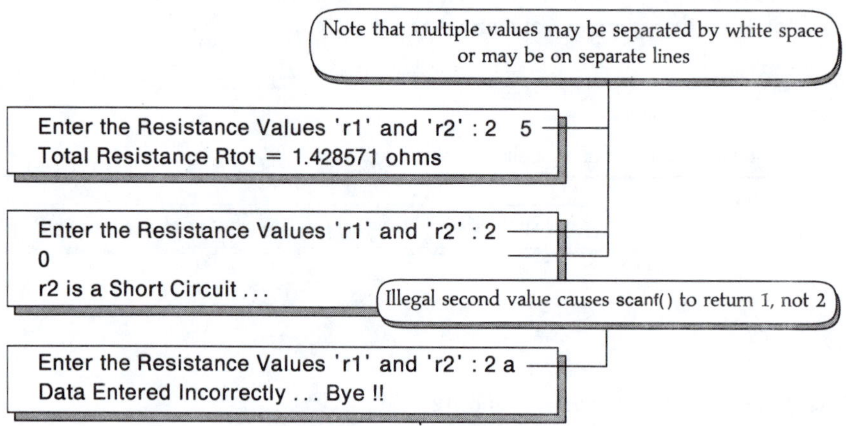

1.6.1 *C's logical operators*

In addition to C's relational operators, listed previously in Table 1.6, C also provides a number of **logical** operators that permit expressions to be cascaded to create a logical AND, OR or NOT operation. These operators and some sample expressions are shown in Table 1.7 (note that the character '|' is usually above the '\' character on a PC-style keyboard).

Table 1.7 C's logical operators.

Operator	*Sample if test*	*Interpretation*
&&	if($expr_1$ && $expr_2$)	If $expr_1$ AND $expr_2$ are both true
||	if($expr_1$ || $expr_2$)	If either $expr_1$ OR $expr_2$ OR both are true
!	if(!$expr_1$)	If $expr_1$ is NOT true – that is, it is false

For example, we could have written a portion of the program code from Application 1.2 in a variety of different ways, some of which are shown below:

If value of 'r1' OR 'r2' OR both are equal to 0

```
if( r1 == 0 || r2 == 0 )
  printf("Either r1 or r2 is a short circuit . . . ") ;
else {
     r3 = (1.0/r1) + (1.0/r2) ;
     printf("Total Resistance Rtot = %f ohms\n", 1.0/r3 ) ;
}
```

Then execute this statement

If 'r1' AND 'r2' are not equal to 0, execute these statements

```
if( r1 != 0 && r2 != 0) {
     r3 = (1.0/r1) + (1.0/r2) ;
     printf("Total Resistance Rtot = %f ohms\n", 1.0/r3 ) ;
}
else
  printf("Either r1 or r2 is a short circuit . . . ") ;
```

If 'r1' AND 'r2' are equal to 0, execute these statements

```
if( !(r1 == 0) && !(r2 == 0) ) {
     r3 = (1.0/r1) + (1.0/r2) ;
     printf("Total Resistance Rtot = %f ohms\n", 1.0/r3 ) ;
}
else
  printf("Either r1 or r2 is a short circuit . . . ") ;
```

1.7 Repetition: The while, do-while and for loops

Another fundamental building block is the repetitive, or looping, construct. Here one or more statements are executed repeatedly **while** some test expression is deemed to be true. When the condition becomes false, the loop will terminate and the program may resume with any statements that follow. (A full discussion of the facilities available to control program repetition can be found in Chapter 5.)

C supports three types of looping constructs in the form of while, do-while and for loops, all of which are closely related. The general form of the while loop is given below:

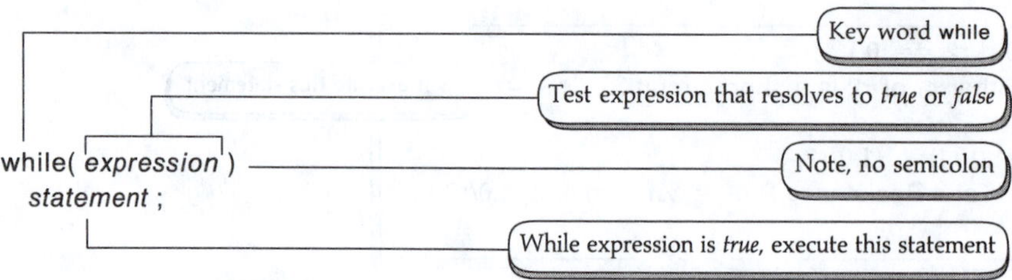

Here, a single statement, known as the **body** of the loop, is repeatedly executed while the result of the test expression is true. The loop only terminates when the test expression resolves to false. A simple flowchart illustrating the flow of program execution for a while loop is shown in Figure 1.6.

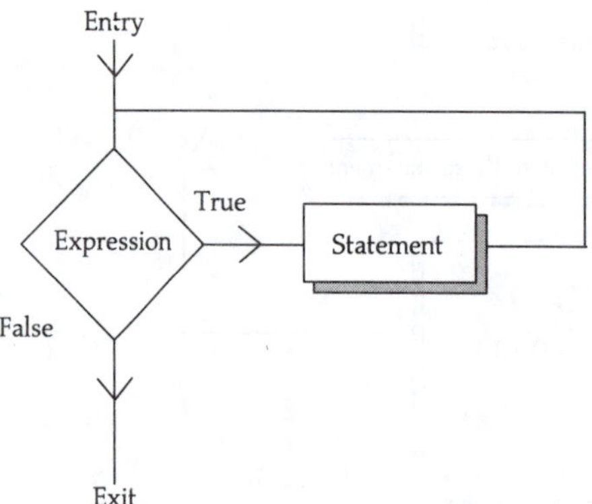

Figure 1.6 Flowchart for the while loop.

As we saw with the if test, a statement block consisting of opening and closing braces '{ }' may be used to associate more than one statement with the body of the while loop.

As a simple example Program 1.4 displays a table of values for 'x' between 0 and 10 along with the values of x^2 and x^3. The heart of the program is a while loop that increments the value of the variable 'x', commencing with 0, while 'x' is less than or equal to 10.

Program 1.4 A simple example of the while loop.

```
#include   <stdio.h>

int main( void )
{
  int x = 0 ;
                                   While the value of 'x' is less than or equal to 10, execute these statements

  while( x <= 10 )  {
    printf("%d %d %d\n", x, x*x, x*x*x ) ;
    x ++ ;
  }
  return 0 ;
}
```

When Program 1.4 was run, the following display was produced on the author's screen. Try to follow the program for yourself. Can you see that the final value of the variable 'x' is 10 and the loop repeats for 11 iterations? Try to imagine what would happen if the '<=' operator was replaced by the '<' operator. What would happen if the order of execution of the statements 'x++' and the call to printf( ) were swapped over?

```
0    0    0
1    1    1
2    4    8
3    9    37
4    16   64
5    25   125
6    36   216
7    49   343
8    64   512
9    81   729
10   100  1000
```

Application 1.3

It can be shown that the exponential function e^x can be written in terms of the following power series:

$$e^x = 1 + \frac{x}{1!} + \frac{x^2}{2!} + \frac{x^3}{3!} + \frac{x^4}{4!} \dots \frac{x^n}{n!}$$

where n! means factorial n. Given that n! may be expressed as $n \times (n-1)!$ and that 0! and 1! both evaluate to 1, write a simple program to calculate the value of e^x for a given value of x by calculating all terms in the series up to $x^{100}/100!$. In order that an overflow does not occur prematurely when evaluating, say, the 100th term of, for example, $e^{23.0}$, the program calculates the $(n+1)$th term in the series as (nth term) $\times\ x/(n+1)$.

Application 1.3 Evaluating the exponential function e^x

```
#include   <stdio.h>

int main( void )
{
   int     i = 1;
   float  x, next = 1.0, e = 1.0 ;

   printf("Enter a Value for x:" ) ;
   scanf("%f", &x) ;

   while( i < 100 )  {
      next = (x / i) * next ;
      e = e + next ;
      i++ ;
   }

   printf(" 'e' raised to the power %f = %f\n", x, e ) ;
   return 0 ;
}
```

While the value of 'i' is less than 100, execute this sequence

When Application 1.3 was run, the following sample display was produced:

```
Enter a Value for x : 5
'e' raised to the power 5.000000 = 148.413177
```

1.7.1 *Repetition: The* do-while *loop*

A useful variation on the while loop is the do-while loop, the general form of which is shown below:

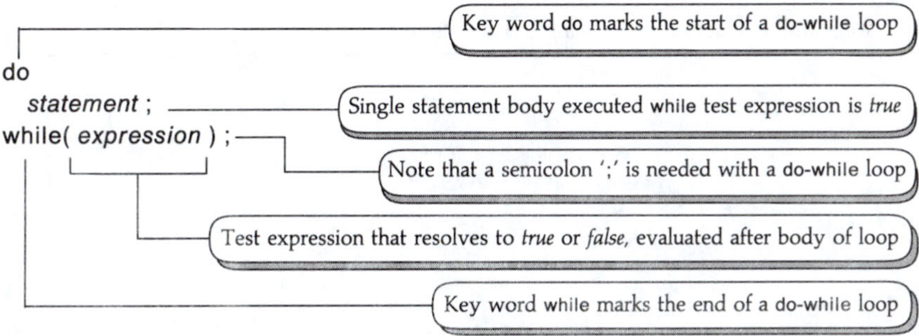
Key word do marks the start of a do-while loop
do
statement ;
Single statement body executed while test expression is true
while(expression) ;
Note that a semicolon ';' is needed with a do-while loop
Test expression that resolves to true or false, evaluated after body of loop
Key word while marks the end of a do-while loop

The only important difference between this and the while loop is that the body of the loop is executed *before* the test expression, thus ensuring that the body is always executed at least once. Figure 1.7 illustrates the flowchart for a simple do-while loop.

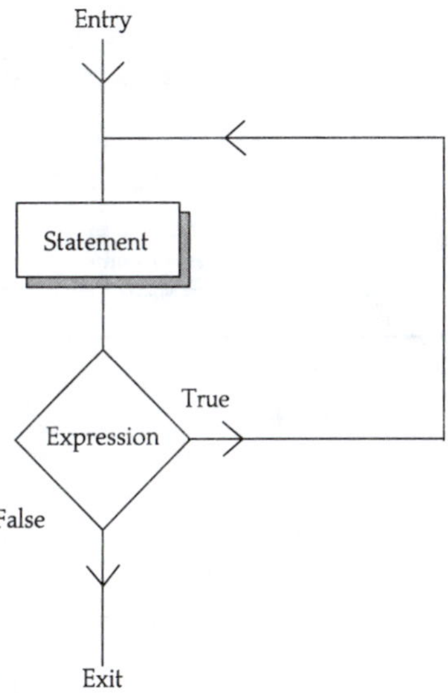
Entry
Statement
True
Expression
False
Exit

Figure 1.7 Flowchart for the do-while loop.

As we saw with the while loop, a statement block consisting of opening and closing braces '{ }' may be used to associate more than one statement with the body of a do-while loop. As an example, we can rewrite the program for Application 1.3 to make use of a do-while loop, thus giving the program's operator the option of re-running the program at the end (Application 1.4). This program also demonstrates the effect of nesting loops within each other.

Application 1.4 Repeated evaluation of e^x using a do-while loop.

```
#include   <stdio.h>

int main( void )
{
   int    response, i;
   float  x, next, e ;

   do  {
      next = 1.0 ;
      e = 1.0 ;
      i = 1 ;
      printf("Enter a Value for x: " ) ;
      scanf("%f", &x) ;

      while( i < 100 )  {
         next = (x / i) * next ;
         e = e + next ;
         i++ ;
      }

      printf(" 'e' raised to the power %f = %f\n\n", x, e ) ;
      printf("Do you wish to try another [1=Yes, 0=No] ? : ") ;
      scanf("%d", &response) ;

   } while( response == 1 ) ;
   return 0 ;
}
```

Make sure 'next', 'e' and 'i' are initialized to 1 each time around

While the value of 'i' is less than 100, execute this sequence

Go back and do program again while response means yes

An example of the display produced by Application 1.4 is given below:

```
Enter a Value for x : 5
'e' raised to the power 5.000000 = 148.413177

Do you wish to try another [1 = Yes, 0=No] ? : 1

Enter a Value for x : 7
'e' raised to the power 7.000000 = 1096.633423

Do you wish to try another [1 = Yes, 0=No] ? : 0
```

1.7.2 *Repetition: The* for *loop*

The final looping construct supported by C is the for loop, which is simply a modified version of the while loop. The general form of this loop is given below:

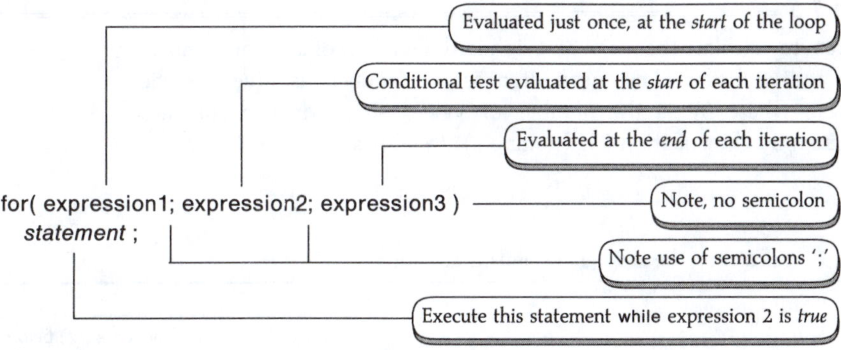
Evaluated just once, at the *start* of the loop
Conditional test evaluated at the *start* of each iteration
Evaluated at the *end* of each iteration
for(expression1; expression2; expression3)
statement ;
Note, no semicolon
Note use of semicolons ';'
Execute this statement while expression 2 is *true*

For most purposes, this is equivalent to a while loop of the form:

```
expression1 ;
while( expression2 )  {
  statement ;
  expression3 ;
}
```

The flowchart for the for loop is given in Figure 1.8.

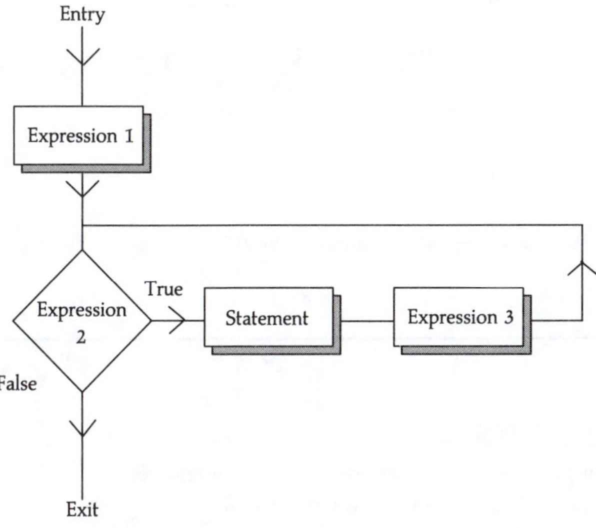
Entry
Expression 1
True
Expression 2
Statement
Expression 3
False
Exit

Figure 1.8 Flowchart of the for loop.

Application 1.5

Write a program to calculate the mean and standard deviation of a set of numbers entered from the keyboard. The mean of a set of numbers is given as the $\sum$ (numbers) / n, where 'n' is the number of values summed. The standard deviation is given by the equation $(\sum(\text{numbers})^2/\text{n} - \text{mean}^2)^{1/2}$.

Application 1.5 Calculating the mean and standard deviation.

```
#include  <stdio.h>
#include  <math.h>

int main( void )
{
  int    s, num ;
  float  sum = 0.0, squares = 0.0 ;
  float  number, mean, stdev ;

  printf("How many numbers ? ") ;
  scanf("%d", &num ) ;

  for( s = 0; s < num ; s ++ )  {
    printf("Enter Number %d : ", s ) ;
    scanf("%f", &number ) ;
    sum = sum + number ;
    squares = squares + number * number ;
  }

  mean = sum / num ;
  stdev = sqrt((squares / num) – (mean * mean)) ;

  printf("\nMean = %f\nStandard Deviation = %f\n", mean, stdev) ;
  return 0 ;
}
```

Included because of function sqrt() below

's' set to zero at start of loop and incremented with each iteration

While 's' is less than 'num', execute these statements

Note how the additional header file <math.h> was included in Application 1.5 because it contains important information relating to the square root function sqrt( ). When the program in Application 1.5 was run, the following sample display was produced:

```
How many numbers ? 5
Enter Number 0 : 3.125
Enter Number 1 : 2.6
Enter Number 2 : 19.12
Enter Number 3 : 27.4
Enter Number 4 : -12.625

Mean = 7.924001
Standard Deviation = 13.987864
```

1.8 Arrays

During program development, the need to record several related items of data of the same type arises frequently. For example, a program designed to record the ages of 30 classroom students, in preparation for later analysis, could obviously elect to introduce 30 separate integer variables to record them.

However, such an approach makes the manipulation of the data as a whole rather difficult since a distinct statement is required to access each student's age. Furthermore, if the size of the class were to change, to, say, 45 students then 15 more variables would have to be introduced, and 15 extra lines of code would be required each time the ages of all students were manipulated.

The solution to this problem lies with an **array** (arrays are dealt with fully in Chapter 7), which in simple terms can be thought of as a collection of items of data sharing a common **type** and **name**. When an array is introduced, the programmer decides how many individual **elements** are to exist within the array. For example, an array of 30 integer elements might be defined using the notation shown below:

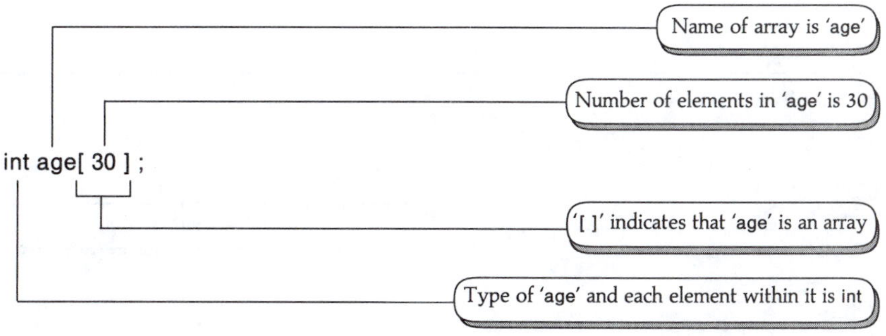

Each element in the array is unique and may be accessed subsequently using the array operator '[ ]' in conjunction with an integer **subscript** to identify the element, where subscript 0 refers to the first element in the array. For example, the statements:

```
b = age[ 9 ] ;
age[ 5 ] = 12 ;
```

'[9]' means access the 10th element in array

6th element in 'age' assigned the value 12

respectively assign the value of the 10th element in the array 'age' (that is, element 'age[9]') to the variable 'b', while the 6th element in 'age' is assigned the integer value 12. Note that the last or 30th element is accessed using the subscript value 29. Because we now have a method of accessing individual elements using an integer value, we can manipulate the array as a whole using a simple loop.

For example, the following for loop calculates the sum of all the elements in the array 'age' using the value of the integer variable 'i' (which is incremented every time around the loop) as a subscript to the array. Note how the loop terminates *before* an attempt to access element [30] is made:

```
for( i = 0 ; i < 30 ; i ++ )
  sum = sum + age[ i ] ;
```

Loop terminates when 'i' reaches 30

Value of 'i' used as the subscript to 'age'

As an example, we could write a program to read five floating point numbers, store them in an array and then display the values of those numbers in tabular form, along with the square and cube of their values, as shown in Program 1.5.

Program 1.5 An example use of an array.

```
#include  <stdio.h>

#define  SIZE  5

int main( void )
{
  int    i ;
  float  v, n[ SIZE ] ;

  for( i = 0; i < SIZE; i ++ )  {
    printf("Enter Number %d : ", i ) ;
    scanf("%f", &n[ i ] ) ;
  }
```

Define an array of five floating point numbers

scanf() given the address of the 'ith' element in array 'n'

```
    for( i = 0; i < SIZE; i ++ )  {
      v = n[ i ] ;
      printf("%15.3f%15.3f%15.3f\n", v, v*v, v*v*v) ;
    }
    return 0 ;
}
```

Output field width set to 15 characters

Precision restricted to three digits after '.'

Notice how the value of the integer variable 'i', which was incremented with each iteration of the loop, served as the subscript to the array. Note also how scanf( ) was given the address of each successive element in the array. Lastly, note how the width of each display field was controlled with printf( ) using the format indicator '%15.3f'. This sets printf( )'s output field width to 15 characters with a maximum of three digits after the decimal point for each displayable field. It also illustrates that printf( ) uses **right justified** text as a default format. When the above program was run, the following sample display was produced:

```
Enter Number 0 : 1.3
Enter Number 1 : 9.6
Enter Number 2 : 2.5
Enter Number 3 : 12.125
Enter Number 4 : 25
          1.300          1.690          2.197
          9.600         92.160        884.736
          2.500          6.250         15.625
         12.125        147.016       1782.564
         25.000        625.000      15625.000
```

1.9 Creating and manipulating text strings

An important feature of all programming languages is the ability to manipulate text and characters. In C, all text strings are represented as arrays of characters. The individual characters of the string are stored as successive elements within the array, with the first character generally stored in element 0. A special NULL character '\0' (note the use of **single** quotatation marks ' ' around individual characters) is used to mark the end or position of the last character in the string, which may not necessarily be the last element in the array. The NULL character is a character with all of its bits set to 0. (Strings are dealt with fully in Chapter 9.)

Implicit text strings are created by enclosing some text within **double** quotation marks " ". Here the compiler creates a **hidden** char array to represent the characters within the text string and ensures that a '\0' termination character is placed after the last character in the string to terminate it correctly. An example of an implicit text string, which is used as the argument to printf( ), is given below:

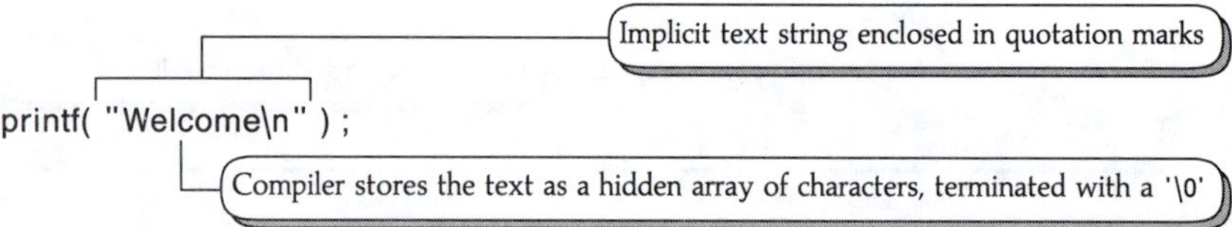

From an illustrative point of view, such a string may be thought of as being represented by the (hidden) array of characters shown in Figure 1.9.

Element	[0]	[1]	[2]	[3]	[4]	[5]	[6]	[7]	[8]
	'W'	'e'	'l'	'c'	'o'	'm'	'e'	'\n'	'\0'

Figure 1.9 The internal representation of a literal text string as a hidden array of characters terminated by a NULL character '\0'.

The concept of a hidden array was used to express the fact that such an array has no name to which the program can refer, neither does the program have any control over the size or number of elements in the array, which was **implicitly** sized by the compiler. Variable text strings, on the other hand, are created by defining an explicit array of char and then initializing it with other text. For example, the following statement:

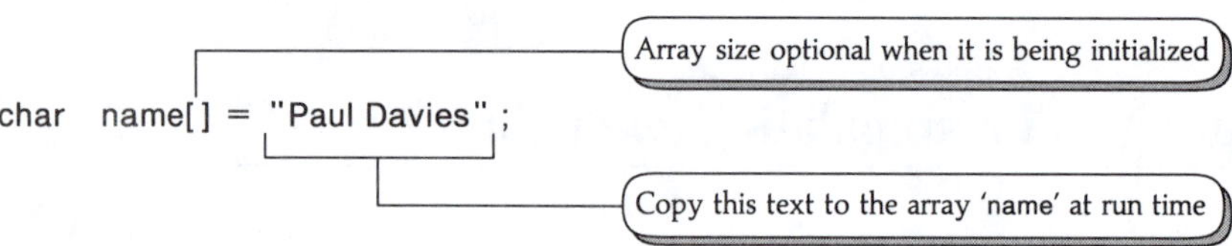

defines the char array 'name' and initializes its individual elements with characters from the implicit text string "Paul Davies". Note that it was not necessary to state the storage requirements or number of elements allocated to the array, since this will be calculated by the compiler. Thus the array 'name' above is 12 elements in size (including space for the '\0' character).

If a specific array size were defined, the compiler would ensure that sufficient storage was allocated to the array to enable it to represent that number of characters. This is extremely useful, as it can be used to leave additional space at the *end* of the array to allow extra text to be appended to it. For example, the statement below defines an array 'name' of 100 characters, where only the first 12 are initialized:

Specifying a larger size leaves space in the array for other text to be appended

```
char   name[100] = "Paul Davies" ;
```

A text string may be read and stored in an array and subsequently displayed using calls to the functions scanf() and printf() in conjunction with the '%s' formatter. Program 1.6 demonstrates this.

Program 1.6 Example string input and output using scanf() and printf().

```
#include   <stdio.h>

int main( void )
{
  char name[ BUFSIZ ] ;

  printf("What is your name ? ") ;
  scanf("%s", name ) ;

  printf("Pleased to meet you %s", name ) ;
  return 0 ;
}
```

Define a char array of BUFSIZ elements

Read a text string using scanf()

'%s' means display array as a text string

Note how the array was defined to be BUFSIZ elements in size. BUFSIZ is a symbolic pre-processor constant created using #define within the header file <stdio.h>, which represents a 'safe' size for an array that will be used to read a line of text entered at the keyboard.

Note also how the address operator '&' was not required with scanf() when reading and storing text in an array. This is because the name of an array in C represents a shorthand notation for the address of the first element in the array. Thus, the following two calls to scanf() are equivalent and may be used interchangeably:

```
scanf("%s", name ) ;
scanf("%s", &name[0] ) ;
```

For programs that are only required to read and/or display single lines of text and are *not* interested in formatting it, the standard library provides two specific string input and output functions in the form of gets() and puts(). In fact, the use of gets() to read a text string from the keyboard is generally preferable to the use of scanf( ) as the latter uses any white space characters contained in the operator's entry to separate data into different fields (as we saw in Application 1.2 when we asked scanf( ) to read two floating point numbers).

You can see this for yourself if you run Program 1.6 and supply both your first name and surname separated by a space character. You should see that scanf( ) only accepts your first name. An example display produced by this program is given below, demonstrating that the author's surname, because it was separated by a space character from his first name, was not read by scanf( ). (The surname is not lost, however, it simply remains inside the operating system's input buffer and can be read with another suitable call to scanf( ).)

```
What is your name ? Paul Davies
Pleased to meet you Paul
```

The function gets( ), however, reads the whole entry up to and including the new line character '\n'; its use, along with that of puts( ), is demonstrated in Program 1.7.

Program 1.7 Example string input and output using gets( ) and puts( ).

```
#include    < stdio.h >

int main( void )
{
   char name[ BUFSIZ ] ;

   printf("What is your name ? ") ;
   gets( name ) ;                          Read a string into the array 'name'

   puts("Pleased to meet you ") ;
   puts( name ) ;                          Display the string in the array 'name'
   return 0 ;
}
```

You should observe several subtle differences between Programs 1.6 and 1.7. Firstly, as has already been pointed out, the use of gets( ) permits a whole line to be read and does not use white space characters in the operator's entry to separate various items of data entry; thus Program 1.7 permits you to enter your whole name. Secondly, the use of puts( ) always results in a new line character '\n' being issued at the end of each line of output whereas printf( ) only issues one when asked. A sample output from Program 1.7 is given below:

```
What is your name ? Paul Davies
Pleased to meet you
Paul Davies
```

1.9.1 *Manipulating text strings*

C does not permit string manipulation operations such as comparison and copying to be achieved through the use of operators such as '==', '+' and '='. If a program wishes to manipulate strings, it must perform these operations for itself on a character by character basis. For example, copying a string from one array to another can be achieved with a simple do-while loop of the form shown below, where the string in array 'a' is copied to array 'b':

```
do {
    b[ i ] = a[ i ] ;
} while( a[ i++ ] != '\0' ) ;
```

Copy respective characters from array 'a' to 'b'

Up to and including the '\0' string termination character

'i' incremented after its value has been used as a subscript to '0'

It is worth mentioning that the standard library defines a number of useful functions such as strlen( ), strcpy( ) and strcmp( ) to perform string manipulation on behalf of the program. A discussion of these may be found in Chapters 9 and 18.

As an example of such manipulation, we shall write a simple program to read a line of text from the operator's keyboard, convert all lower case characters to upper case and vice versa, then redisplay the text in its new converted form. The complete program is given in Program 1.8.

In this example we introduce two further input/output functions in the form of getchar( ) and putchar( ) which respectively read and display a single character from/to the operator's terminal. These functions are analogous to calls to scanf( ) and printf( ), respectively, using the '%c' formatter.

Program 1.8 A case conversion program.

```
#include    <stdio.h>
#include    <ctype.h>

int main( void )
{
    int     i ;
    char  c, name[ BUFSIZ ] ;

    printf("Enter a text String: ") ;

    for( i = 0; (c = getchar()) != '\n'; i++)  {
        if( isupper( c ) != 0)
            name[i] = tolower( c ) ;
```

Included for information about toupper( ), tolower( ) and so on

Read characters and assign to 'c' while 'c' is not equal to a new line character

Store upper case characters as lower case

```
        else if( islower( c ) != 0)
            name[i] = toupper( c ) ;          Store lower case characters as upper case

        else
            name[i] = c ;                     Ignore conversion if not a suitable character
    }

    name[i] = '\0' ;                          Terminate the string with a '\0'

    for( i = 0; name[i] != '\0'; i++ )
        putchar( name[i] ) ;
                                              Display the 'ith' character using putchar()
    putchar( '\n' ) ;

    return 0 ;                                Finally issue a new line character
}
```

The functions toupper() and tolower() are also introduced, which convert their character argument, respectively, into its upper or lower case version before returning it to the program. The functions isupper() and islower() determine whether their character argument is an upper or lower case character, respectively. If so, they return a non-zero value.

When Program 1.8 is run, the following sample display is produced:

```
Enter a text String: This is an Example of String Conversion
tHIS IS AN eXAMPLE OF sTRING cONVERSION
```

As another example, to demonstrate the use of some of the string manipulation functions provided in the standard library, take a look at Program 1.9. The program demonstrates the use of the functions strcpy(), strcat() and strcmp(), which, respectively, copy, append and compare two strings, while strlen() determines the length of a string.

Program 1.9 Example use of string manipulation functions.

```
#include   <stdio.h>
#include   <string.h>       <string.h> contains information about string manipulation functions

int main( void )
{
    char name[BUFSIZ], buff[BUFSIZ] ;

    printf("Hello, what is your name ? ");
    gets( name) ;                         Read operator's name into the array 'name'
```

```
strcpy( buff, "Pleased to meet you ") ;
strcat( buff, name) ;
```

Copy the string "Pleased to meet you" to the array 'buff'

Append the string in array 'name' to the string in array 'buff'

```
printf("%s\n", buff ) ;
printf("I bet you knew there were %d letters in your name ?\n\n", strlen( name)) ;
```

strlen() returns the integer length of the string in the array 'name'

```
printf("Now tell me, what magic 3 letter code will unlock the secret of success: ") ;
gets( buff ) ;
```

Compare the string "abc" with the string in the array 'buff'

strcmp() returns 0 if both strings are identical

```
if( strcmp( buff, "abc") == 0)
    puts("Congratulations, health, wealth and happiness are yours forever ... ") ;
else
    puts("Bad luck loser !!! ... ") ;

return 0 ;
}
```

When Program 1.9 is run, the following sample display is produced:

```
Hello, what is your name ? Paul
Pleased to meet you Paul
I bet you knew there were 4 letters in your name ?

Now tell me, what magic 3 letter code will unlock the secret of success: abc
Congratulations, health, wealth and happiness are yours forever ...
```

1.9.2 *An alternative form of numeric entry*

Reading in numeric data can, as we have already seen, be achieved using scanf(), but there are many reasons why this function is not always the preferred method of reading data from an operator's keyboard, principally because scanf() gets very upset if the operator does not enter the data in the form the programmer has told it to expect.

The remainder of the chapters mainly make use of an alternative form of numeric entry based around the functions atoi() and atof() from the C standard library (except where scanf() is being used to illustrate a point). These functions attempt to convert a previously entered text string into an integer or a floating point number, respectively, which is then returned to the calling program. For example, a call to atof( ) of the form:

```
x = atof( "1.234" ) ;
```

atof( ) given an implicit text string or char array

atof( ) returns the floating point number 1.234, which is assigned to 'x'

asks atof( ) to examine the text string "1.234" and convert this into a floating point representation of the same value, which is returned as the answer; thus 'x' is assigned the value 1.234. As a more useful example let us rewrite Application 1.5 in the form of Program 1.10 to make use of the functions atoi( ) and atof( ) to enter an integer and floating point number, respectively.

Program 1.10 An example use of atoi( ) and atof( ).

```
#include   <stdio.h>
#include   <stdlib.h>
#include   <math.h>

int main( void )
{
  int    s, num ;
  char  buff[ BUFSIZ ] ;

  float  sum = 0.0, squares = 0.0 ;
  float  number, mean, stdev ;

  printf("How many numbers ? ") ;
  num = atoi( gets( buff )) ;

  for( s = 0; s < num ; s ++ )  {
    printf("Enter Number %d : ", s ) ;
    number = atof( gets( buff )) ;
    sum = sum + number ;
    squares = squares + number * number ;
  }

  mean = sum / num ;
  stdev = sqrt((squares / num) – (mean * mean)) ;
  printf("Mean = %f\nStandard Deviation = %f\n", mean, stdev) ;
  return 0 ;
}
```

Included because they contain information about atof( ), atoi( ) and sqrt( )

An array of char into which the operator entry is initially read

Read a string into 'buff' and convert to an int using atoi( )

Read a string into 'buff' and convert to a float using atof( )

Notice how the operator's entry was on each occasion read using a statement of the form shown below. This is an example of a nested function call, where the call to the inner function gets( ) is made first to read a line of text from the operator's keyboard and subsequently store it in the array 'buff'.

Because gets( ) notionally returns the array into which it has placed the text (more on this in Chapter 8), the array returned by gets( ) (that is, buff[ ]) is subsequently used as the argument in the outer function call to atof( ), which then converts the string stored in buff[ ] into a floating point value before it is assigned to 'number'.

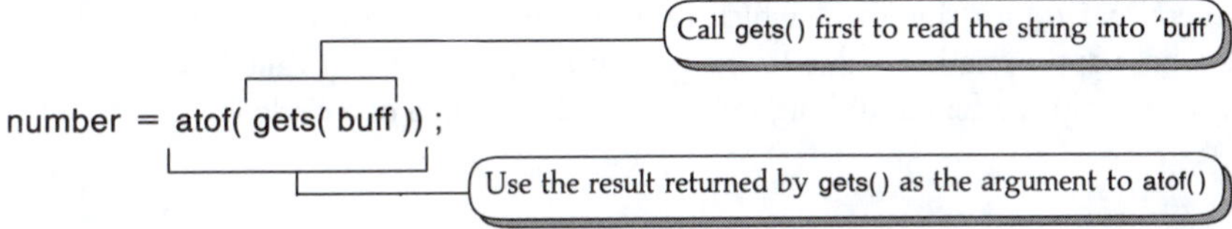

1.10 Defining and using functions

Good programming practice dictates that programs should, wherever possible and practical, be expressed in terms of a number of smaller, separate functions. A function can be thought of as a self-contained section of code written to perform a well-defined action.

The statements within the function may be executed by **calling** or **invoking** the function, an operation that may be performed many times within a program. The general form of a function **definition** is given below; you might like to compare this to the way you have defined the function main( ) so far. (Defining functions is dealt with in Chapter 6.)

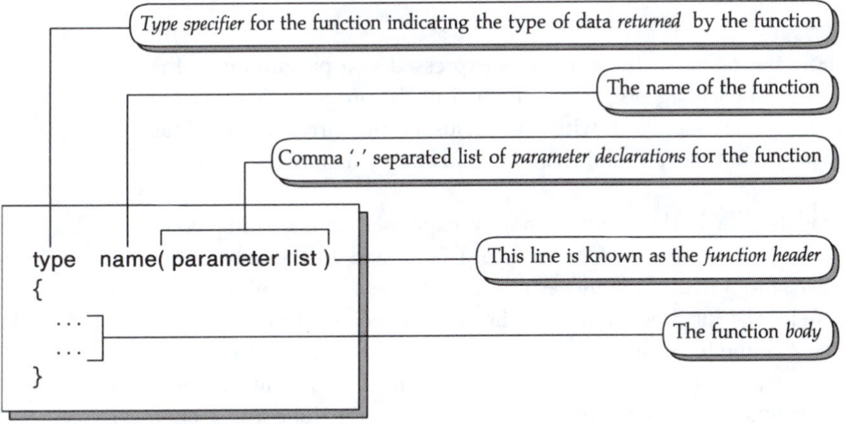

When a function is invoked, it generally expects to be given the number of arguments expressed in the function's parameter list. The compiler checks this wherever possible against the type of the actual data given to the function by the calling program, and notes any inconsistencies as errors. The **type specifier** for the function describes the type of data **returned** by the function. If the function returns no data or expects no arguments then both the type specifier and/or the parameter list may be omitted or defined as void.

Following the function header lie the opening and closing braces '{ }' that mark the start and end of the function. Between these lie a number of statements, depending upon the operations the function was written to perform. The last statement is generally a return statement which returns control of the program execution, and, where appropriate, a value to the part of the program that called the function. As an example, a function designed to calculate the area of a circle is given below:

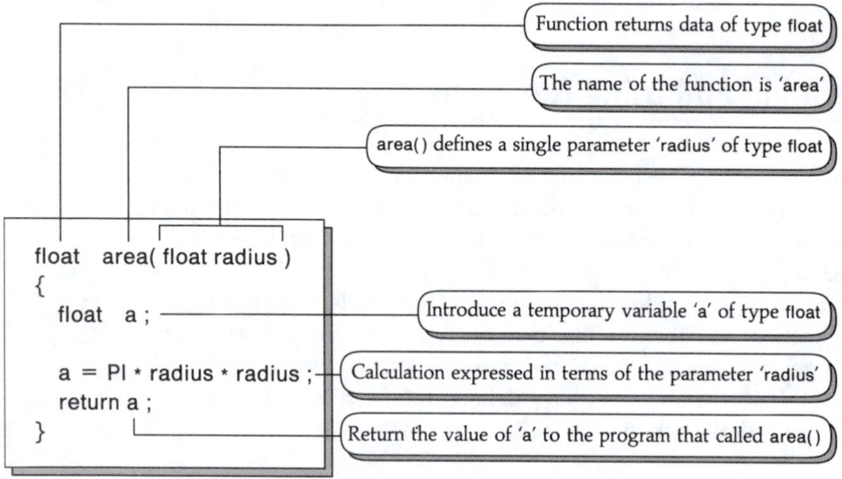

Notice how the radius of the circle was expressed as a **parameter** of the function. This allows the calling program – the part of the program that will call the function area( ) – to supply it with the radius of the circle at run time. This feature makes area( ) more useful than if it had simply assumed a value for 'radius'.

As the radius of a circle is more usefully expressed as a floating point quantity, the parameter 'radius' was defined as a float, and as the subsequent calculation gives rise to a floating point result – that is, the value of 'a', which is returned by area( ) – the function's type specifier was also defined as a float.

A statement of the form shown below will invoke the function area( ) and present it with the value of the variable 'i' as an **argument**. This statement makes a copy of the argument 'i', then presents the copy to the function area( ), whereupon the copy *becomes* the parameter 'radius' within the function area( ). Thus the variable 'i' in the calling program and the parameter 'radius' within area( ) are distinct and separate variables with the same value:

```
x = area( i ) ;
```

Invoke the function area()
The value of 'i' is given to area() and becomes the parameter 'radius'
The value returned by area() – that is, the area of a circle of radius 'i' – is assigned to 'x'

Once the area of the circle has been calculated, area() returns the result to the calling program, where it is subsequently assigned to the variable 'x'. Thus, 'x' is now equal to the area of a circle of radius 'i'. A complete program to demonstrate these principles is shown in Program 1.11, in which the arrows illustrate the flow of program execution.

Program 1.11 Calculating the area of a circle using a function.

```
#include  <stdio.h>
#include  <stdlib.h>

#define  PI  3.14159

float area( float radius )
{
   float  a ;

   a = PI * radius * radius ;
   return a ;
}

int main( void )
{
   char  buff[ BUFSIZ ] ;
   float  radius, circle_area ;

   printf("Enter the Circle Radius : ") ;
   radius = atof( gets( buff )) ;

   circle_area = area( radius ) ;

   printf("Area = %f\n", circle_area ) ;
   return 0 ;
}
```

Call to function area() with the argument 'radius'
Start
End

Notice how the function area() was defined *before* the function main(). This is important, because the compiler needs to know about each function before it encounters any statements that attempt to invoke them – that is, it needs to know in advance that area() expects to be given a single argument of type float, and that it returns a result of type float. This enables the compiler (among other things) to check that the program is calling the function correctly. When Program 1.11 was run, the following sample display was produced:

```
Enter the Circle Radius : 5
Area = 78.539749
```

1.10.1 *Function prototyping*

If a function's definition is not **visible** to the compiler at that point in the compilation when a call to the function is first encountered (this could happen for several reasons, such as calling a function from the standard library), then we must ensure that a **function prototype** is 'visible' to the compiler. A function prototype is easily constructed by making a copy of the function's header and appending a semicolon to it, as shown below for the function area( ) given previously.

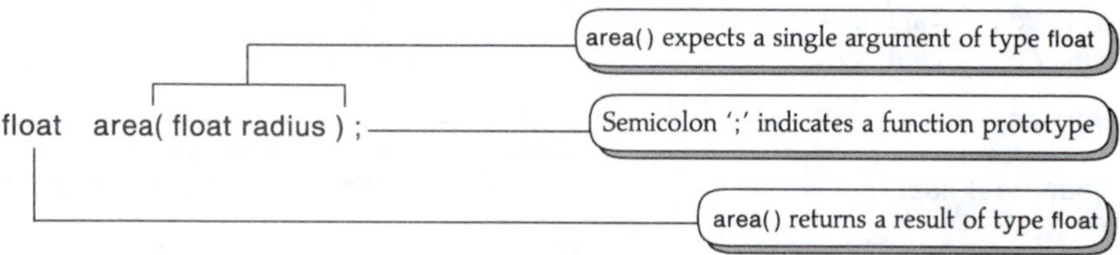

Provided a function's prototype is introduced to the compiler prior to the point where the program first attempts to call that function, the compiler will be able to check that the function is being called correctly by the program. The reader should note that introducing function prototypes into a program does *not* lead to the production of any executable code since they only contain information for the compiler.

Because functions such as printf( ), scanf( ), gets( ), puts( ), getchar( ) and putchar( ) are defined in the C standard library, their definition is never likely to be encountered by the compiler when compiling a program. For this reason, we always include the header file <stdio.h> at the start of any program that calls these functions, because it contains their function prototypes.

For similar reasons, the header file <stdlib.h> is included when making calls to the functions atoi( ) and atof( ). These concepts are demonstrated in Program 1.12, in which Program 1.11 has been rewritten to place the definition of area( ) after main( ) and thus demonstrate the use of a prototype. As an experiment, compile and run this program with and without the function prototype for area( ). You will see that in the latter case, the program's operation is undefined, since it does not calculate the result correctly (more on this in Chapter 6).

A number of useful mathematical functions that the reader may wish to explore are given in Table 1.8. Full descriptions of these and other mathematical functions in the C standard library can be found in Section 18.7, or in your C compiler library reference manual.

Program 1.12 Program 1.11 rewritten to include a function prototype.

```
#include   <stdio.h>
#include   <stdlib.h>

#define  PI  3.14159

int main( void )
{
  char  buff[ BUFSIZ ] ;
  float  radius, circle_area ;
  float  area( float radius ) ;

  printf("Enter the Circle Radius : ") ;
  radius = atof( gets( buff )) ;

  circle_area = area( radius ) ;

  printf("Area = %f\n", circle_area ) ;
  return 0 ;
}

float   area( float radius )
{
  float  a ;

  a = PI * radius * radius ;
  return a ;
}
```

Function prototype for area()

Call to area() occurs after prototype and before definition

Definition of area() not encountered until after it has been called

All arguments and returned data are in the form of floating point values, while all angles are expressed in radians. The header file <math.h> *must* be included in any program that calls any of these functions because it contains essential function prototypes.

Table 1.8 Some useful mathematical functions.

Function name	*Operation*
sin(x), asin(x)	Returns, respectively, the sine and inverse sine of x
cos(x), acos(x)	Returns, respectively, the cosine and inverse cosine of x
tan(x), atan(x)	Returns, respectively, the tangent and inverse tangent of x
sinh(x)	Returns the hyperbolic sine of x
cosh(x)	Returns the hyperbolic cosine of x
tanh(x)	Returns the hyperbolic tangent of x
sqrt(x)	Returns the square root of x
exp(x)	Returns the value of e^x
pow(x, y)	Returns x^y
log10(x), log(x)	Returns, respectively, $\log_{10}$ and $\log_e$ of x
fabs(x)	Returns the absolute positive floating point value of x

1.11 Stream and file manipulation

The ability to manipulate data within disk files is an important aspect of many applications. Word processors, spreadsheets and databases, for example, all rely on the ability of the program to save and recover data to and from more permanent storage on disk. Accessing and manipulating files is not difficult in C. Such operations are accomplished using functions such as fprintf() and fscanf() that are in many ways similar to their equivalent terminal input/output functions printf() and scanf(), which is more than pure coincidence since the functions are more closely related than you might think.

In this section we take a *brief* look at how files are created and manipulated in C. The reader is reminded that this is just an introduction to the subject and consequently provides little more than a limited feel for what can be achieved; there are, however, a number of interesting programs that can be written using only the basic knowledge presented here. A more rigorous treatment of the subject can be found in Chapter 16.

Before any communication can take place with an external device, such as a disk file, the program must first establish a link with the device via the operating system. This is achieved using the function fopen(), which expects to be given the **pathlist/name** of the device/file that the program is attempting to establish communication with, and the **mode** in which it intends to communicate with it, such as for reading, writing, appending and so on.

If the request is successful, the operating system establishes a **stream** through which the program can exchange data with that device/file and results in fopen() returning a special type of variable called a **FILE pointer** to the calling

```
#include   <stdio.h>
#include   <stdlib.h>

int main( void )
{
  FILE  *f1 ;

  if(( f1 = fopen("joe.txt", "w") == NULL )  {
    printf("Error Cannot open 'joe.txt' for writing ... \n") ;
    exit( 0 ) ;
  }
    ...
}
```

program. This file pointer must be saved by the program since it will be used with subsequent read and write requests to identify the stream and hence the device. An example of a FILE pointer variable capable of saving the data returned by fopen( ) is given below. Notice the '*' prior to the variable name 'f1' identifying it as a 'pointer' (see Chapter 8).

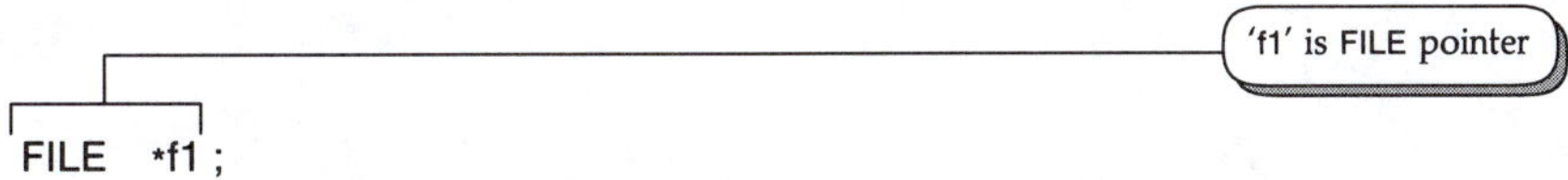

A unique FILE pointer will be required for each device/file that is simultaneously in use by the program. An example section of code to open the disk file 'joe.txt' for writing and to check that the operation has been performed correctly is shown opposite.

Notice how both parameters to fopen( ) are text strings. The FILE pointer returned by fopen( ) is assigned to 'f1' and a test made to establish the validity of the request. If for some reason the request is unsuccessful, fopen( ) will return the value of the symbolic constant NULL (defined in <stdio.h>), which in this instance forces the termination of the program via a call to exit( ).

Having opened the file, the program is now free to write to (but not read from) the file using a number of functions such as fprintf( ), fputs( ) and fputc( ). These are similar to the functions printf( ), puts( ) and putchar( ) that we met earlier. As an example, let us write a simple program to output the sine of all angles in the range 0 to PI in increments of 0.01 radians to the disk file. The solution is presented in Program 1.13.

Program 1.13 Writing to a file using fprintf( ).

```
#include  <stdio.h>
#include  <stdlib.h>
#include  <math.h>

#define  PI  3.14159

int main( void )
{
  FILE  *f1 ;
  float  count ;

  if( (f1 = fopen( "sine.dat" , "w")) == NULL)  {
    printf("Error cannot open file 'sine.dat' for writing ... \n" ) ;
    exit( 0 ) ;
  }
```

Open/create file "sine.dat" for *writing*

Check that file was opened successfully

Exit if unsuccessful

```
for( count = 0 ; count < PI ; count += 0.01 )  {
```

'f1' returned by fopen() used as an argument to fprintf() to identify file

Check for fprintf() failure

```
    if( fprintf( f1 , "%f\n" , sin( count )) == EOF)  {
       printf("Error writing to file 'sine.dat' . . . \n") ;
       exit( 0 ) ;
    }
}
```

```
fclose( f1 ) ;
return 0 ;
}
```

Explicit closure of file 'sine.dat' at the end of the program

---

Here we see the program attempting to open the file at the start of the program. The mode specified was again "w", indicating that the program intends to write to the file 'sine.dat.' The operating system looks in the current (or specified) directory when this request is issued by the program, to determine whether a file with that name already exists. If not, it will be created as a new and *empty* file, otherwise (if it already exists) it will be truncated to zero length, with the loss of all of its data, so be careful!

Once the file has been successfully opened/created, the program proceeds to enter a simple for loop writing values to the previously opened file using fprintf(). Notice how the FILE pointer 'f1' returned by fopen() was given as the first argument to fprintf(). This is essential, since it identifies the previously opened file as the one being written to. Apart from this, fprintf() behaves in exactly the same way as printf().

To ensure the integrity of the write operation, the program compares the values returned by fprintf() with that of the symbolic constant EOF (end of file; defined in <stdio.h>). If for some reason fprintf() had failed, perhaps because the disk had become full or had been removed, then it would return EOF back to the program, which in this case forces its termination.

If no errors arise as a result of writing to the file, the program rounds things off by closing the file using a call to fclose(). In this instance, an explicit closure of the file is optional, since all streams/files are automatically closed by the operating system when the program naturally terminates (or prematurely terminates via a call to exit()).

Having now seen how simple it is to write data to a file, let us see how easy it is to read it back using fscanf(). Again, this function is similar to scanf() but it reads data from a stream instead of just from the operator's keyboard. The solution is presented in Program 1.14.

Again, the program commences by opening the file 'sine.dat' but this time specifying read mode "r", which does not attempt to create or truncate the file. If

Program 1.14 Reading data from a file using fscanf().

```
#include   <stdio.h>
#include   <stdlib.h>

int main( void )
{
  FILE  *f1 ;
  float  svalue ;

  if( (f1 = fopen( "sine.dat" , "r")) == NULL)  {
    printf("Error cannot open file 'sine.dat' for reading ... \n" ) ;
    exit( 0 ) ;
  }

  while( fscanf( f1, "%f", &svalue) != EOF )
    printf("Read value %f from file ... \n", svalue) ;

  fclose( f1 ) ;
  return 0 ;
}
```

Mode is for *reading*

Check that file was opened successfully

Read values until the *end-of-file* is reached

Explicit closure of file 'sine.dat' at the end of the program

successful a simple while loop is entered which repeatedly reads successive floating point values from the file, which are stored on each occasion in the variable 'svalue' before being displayed on the operator's screen. This operation is only terminated if fscanf() returns the value EOF, indicating that all of the data in the file has been read and that the end of the file has been reached.

As an example of character manipulation Program 1.15 demonstrates the use of the functions fgetc() and fputc(), which respectively read and write single characters from/to a disk file. The program was written to convert the text from one file into upper case before writing it to a second file. It commences by prompting the operator for the names of the **source** and **destination** files.

Program 1.15 Example usage of fgetc() and fputc().

```
#include   <stdio.h>
#include   <stdlib.h>
#include   <ctype.h>

int main( void )
{
  int    c ;
  FILE  *f1 , *f2 ;
  char  source[BUFSIZ], destination[BUFSIZ] ;

  printf("Enter source file name ... ") ;
  gets( source ) ;
```

Define two file pointers

```
    printf("Enter destination file name ... ") ;
    gets( destination ) ;

    f1 = fopen( source , "r" ) ;
    f2 = fopen( destination , "w") ;        Open two files for reading and writing, respectively

    if( (f1 == NULL) || ( f2 == NULL) )  {
       printf("Error opening file %s or %s\n", source, destination) ;
       exit( 0 ) ;
    }                                         Check for end-of-file reading

    while(( c = fgetc( f1)) != EOF )   {
       c = toupper( c ) ;                    Check for error writing data
       if( fputc( c, f2 ) == EOF )  {
          printf("Error writing to destination file ... \n") ;
          exit( 0 ) ;
       }
    }

    fclose( f1 ) ;
    fclose( f2 ) ;                           Close the two opened files
    return 0 ;
}
```

If these two files are opened successfully, a while loop commences which reads single characters from the source file before they are written back to the destination file in their upper case version. The program stops if either the end of the source file has been reached (fgetc() returns EOF) or an error occurs while writing to the destination file (fputc() returns EOF).

As you will have gathered by now, reading and writing to disk files is only a little more complicated than reading or writing to the operator's terminal. The program has to open the files in the first place and then ensure that functions such as fprintf(), fscanf() and so on are used, but other than that there is very little difference.

What you may not have appreciated thus far, however, is that the operator's terminal – that is, the screen and keyboard, and for that matter any devices within the system – are all interfaced to the user's program via generic streams and as such can all be treated in a similar way. How does this work?

In brief, whenever a program is run, the operating system automatically opens three external devices on its behalf, as if the program had made three **invisible** calls to fopen() before the function main() began. The three FILE pointers that result from these hidden calls are associated with the program default input, output and error message devices – that is, the operator's terminal – and are known universally as stdin, stdout and stderr. They are defined symbolically within <stdio.h>.

What this means is that calls to printf() and putchar() are translated somewhere along the line (either within their respective library function or replaced at compile time by macros) into equivalent calls to fprintf( ) and fputc( ) in association with the FILE pointer 'stdout'. Likewise, calls to scanf( ) and getchar( ) are translated into equivalent calls to fscanf( ) and fgetc( ) in association with the FILE pointer 'stdin'.

We can verify this quite easily for ourselves. For example, if Program 1.15 were rewritten to use the predefined FILE pointers 'stdin' in place of the FILE pointer 'f1' and 'stdout' in place of 'f2', then instead of converting characters read from one disk file and writing them to another, the program would now convert characters read from the operator's keyboard and write them back to the operator's screen. Likewise, error messages could be displayed using a call to fprintf( ) in conjunction with the FILE pointer 'stderr'. The complete program is shown in Program 1.16. Try it and see.

Since 'stdin', 'stdout' and 'stderr' are assumed to exist already (they were automatically opened by the operating system when the program was run), the calls made previously by Program 1.15 to fopen( ) have been removed. Of course the concept of an EOF condition used to terminate the program input is somewhat artificial for a keyboard in the sense that there is no naturally occurring limit to the amount of data that could be entered by the operator, who could supply data at any time by pressing a key. However, such a condition is designed to be *simulated* whenever the operator presses <control-D> on a UNIX system or <control-Z> on an MS-DOS system. This again is important because it allows a program to be written to be independent of the source of its data.

Of course an alternative way of terminating the program would be to interrupt its execution by (generally) pressing <control-C>, which returns you to

Program 1.16 Example use of 'stdin', stdout', 'stderr'.

```
#include   <stdio.h>
#include   <stdlib.h>
#include   <ctype.h>

int main( void )
{
  int    c ;

  while(( c = fgetc( stdin )) != EOF )  {
    c = toupper( c ) ;

    if( fputc( c, stdout )  == EOF )  {
      fprintf(stderr, "Error writing to destination file . . . \n") ;
      exit( 0 ) ;
    }
  }
  return 0 ;
}
```

Read a character from 'stdin'; that is, from the keyboard

Write a character to 'stdout'; that is, to the operator's screen

Write error messages to 'stderr'; that is, to the operator's screen

the environment from which your program was run, usually the operating system or IDE.

Program 1.16 demonstrates a very powerful feature of C and its host operating system in allowing programs to be written that are more or less independent of the characteristics of the devices with which they communicate. That is to say, a program needs to know very little, if anything, about the device with which it is exchanging data. This fact makes **redirection** of input and output on behalf of the program a simple matter.

In common with UNIX, most operating systems, including MS-DOS, permit all default input, output and error messages for a program to be redirected to alternative devices at run time. Such redirection is handled transparently by the operating system, with the program itself generally unaware that it is taking place. For example, if the following command were issued on a UNIX system:

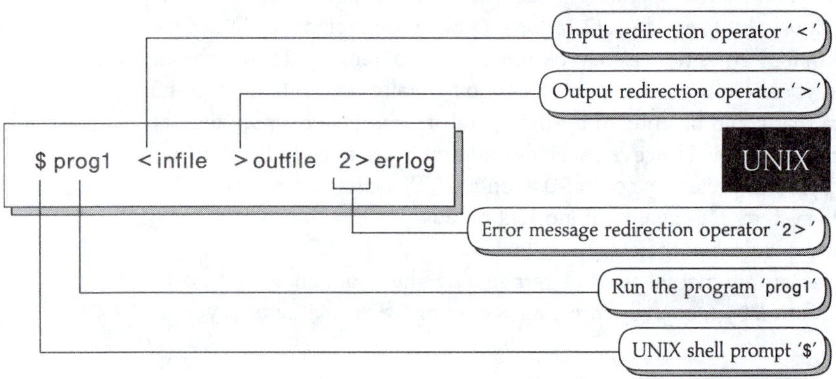

then program 'prog1' would be run, with its input redirected to come from the disk file 'infile', while its output and error messages are redirected to the files 'outfile' and 'errlog', respectively. Any input requests made by the program, as a result of calls made to functions such as scanf(), gets(), getchar() and so on (or fscanf(), fgets() and fgetc() in association with the FILE pointer 'stdin') will actually be supplied from data read from the disk file 'infile' rather than coming from the program operator's keyboard.

Likewise, any output generated as a result of calls made to functions such as printf(), puts() or putchar() (or fprintf(), fputs() and fputc() in association with the FILE pointer 'stdout') would not be displayed on the operator's terminal, but would instead be written to the disk file 'outfile'. Lastly, any calls made to fprintf() in association with the FILE pointer 'stderr' would be redirected separately from program output to the file 'errlog'.

This is an important concept, because it permits the program's operator to choose where the program's data will come from and be written to at *run* time, rather than at *compile* time. As an example, you might like to run Program 1.16 but using the redirection operators '<' and '>' to redirect the program's input and output to a disk file instead.

(Note that if you are using Borland's Turbo C you cannot perform I/O redirection from within its graphical development or 'windows' type environment. You must return to the basic MS-DOS shell to achieve this and run your programs directly from the DOS command line prompt 'c:' or similar.)

1.12 Documenting your programs

As with other programming languages, C lets you document your programs by allowing you to place comments within the source file alongside the program code itself. Such comments are ignored by the compiler, so programmers are free to place them virtually anywhere they wish to aid readability and understanding.

The start of a comment is marked with the character sequence '/*', and a comment is terminated by the sequence '*/' – that is, the same characters but in the reverse order; watch out for this as it is a common mistake. Any text placed between these two sequences (except if they occur as part of an implicit text string) is ignored. Program 1.17 contains a number of comments placed randomly.

Because a comment *must* be terminated, frequently at the end of the line on which it began, it is easy for the programmer to forget to include the comment terminator sequence '*/'. When this occurs, it can be particularly tricky to track down, since the compiler, having lost synchronization with the actual program code, generates errors that are often *unrelated* to the root cause of the problem. The problem is often made worse when the comment spans several lines, so take care.

The author, like many other programmers who have experienced this problem first hand, has adopted a scheme that, wherever possible, attempts to place the opening and closing comments beneath each other, so that the start and end of a comment are simultaneously visible on the screen. This makes it easy to spot when a comment has not been closed correctly when rapidly scanning

Program 1.17 Example program with comments.

```
#include  <stdio.h>

/* This is a comment */

int main( void )                    /* and this is a comment */
{
  printf("Welcome !!!!! \n" ) ;     /* This is a comment also */

  printf(" /* But this is NOT a comment */ " ) ;
  return 0 ;
}
```

Program 1.18 Laying out a program with comments.

```
#include  <stdio.h>

/*
**  This is typically where the function would be documented,
**  usually at the start. Its operation, limitations, expectancies etc. are
**  described here, along with the nature of any calculations and results
**  generated. The programmer may well document which
**  parts of the program make use of this function.
*/

int main( void )
{
  int i = 0 ;                    /* definition of an integer variable 'i' */

/*
**  Now count from 0 to 10 using 'i' and a while loop
*/

  while( i <= 10 ) {
    printf("i = %d\n", i ) ;  /* print out value of 'i' */
    i ++ ;                    /* increment i */
  }

/*
**  End of program, document any returned data here
*/

  return 0 ;
}
```

through a program listing. Much of Program 1.18 has been documented using this approach.

1.13 Program layout and style

The choice of a suitable program style/layout is pretty much left to the discretion of the programmer. The compiler itself is not particularly interested in the position or layout of statements within the program, only in their order and the correct sequence/order of semicolons, braces and so on. Thus, programmers may sprinkle white space characters such as spaces, tabs, line feeds and carriage returns liberally within the program to suit themselves and to aid readability. There are a few occasions where this is not the case, and we shall look at these shortly. Preprocessor directives in particular, such as #include and #define, are more restrictive and care must be taken about using white space with these; they should generally be written on a line of their own (more on this in Chapter 13).

As an example, we could rewrite our introductory program from Section 1.2 in the following manner, where all of the C code has been placed on one line:

```
#include    <stdio.h>
int main(void ){printf("Welcome !!!!! \n");return 0;}
```

You will notice that the use of white space has been minimized, but the syntax is still correct. Consequently, the program will still compile and run but the program code is much more difficult to follow and, for larger programs, almost impossible to maintain and develop. Fortunately, a number of recognized styles have evolved, which can help to improve productivity and reduce the occurrence of bugs. An example of the author's favourite style is shown in Program 1.19.

Program 1.19 Example program layout with 'correct' indentation.

```
#include    <stdio.h>

/*
**  Example program layout using braces and tabs
*/

int  main( void )
{                               /* Start of a function, indent further statements by 1 tab */
    . . .
    . . .
    while( . . . ) {            /* start of a WHILE loop */
        . . .                   /* statements indented by 2 tabs */
        . . .
        if ( . . . )      {     /* start of an IF test */
            . . .               /* statements indented by 3 tabs */
            . . .
        }                       /* end of an IF test, indented by 2 tabs */
        else   {                /* start of an ELSE test */
            . . .               /* statements indented by 3 tabs */
            . . .
            if( . . . ){        /* start of an IF test */
                . . .           /* statements indented by 4 tabs */
                . . .
            }                   /* end of an IF test, indented by 3 tabs */
            else   {            /* start of an ELSE test */
                . . .           /* statements indented by 4 tabs */
                . . .
            }                   /* end of an ELSE test, indented by 3 tabs */
        }                       /* end of ELSE test, indented by 2 tabs */
    }                           /* end of a WHILE loop, indented by 1 tab */
    return 0 ;
}
```

Here, a function begins in the leftmost column, while the opening and closing braces '{' and '}' that mark the start and end of the function align vertically beneath it. All statements associated with the function are indented by a (consistent) number of spaces or, more often, by a single tab stop. This makes the start and end of the function immediately visible when scanning through a program listing.

Whenever an if or if-else test, or a while, do-while or for loop occur, the statement(s) associated with these constructs are indented by further spaces or one more tab stop (note that the size of a tab can be set under Borland's Turbo C using the Tab Size option from the Options window, submenu Environment/Editor), which makes it easy to spot the start and end of a statement block. Eventually, if the program has been entered 'correctly', a 'staircase' effect of closing braces '}' is observed at the end of the function; thus, it is immediately apparent if one too many or one too few closing braces have been used.

1.13.1 *Dealing with long statements*

You may find, from time to time, that a program statement, because of its length, can 'disappear' off the right-hand edge of your terminal's screen. There are several ways of overcoming this. Firstly, you could simply start a new line (not a new statement) at an appropriate point and type the remainder of the statement on that line. For example, the simple statement:

```
result = result + 2 * result ;
```

although not exceptionally long, *could* have been written as:

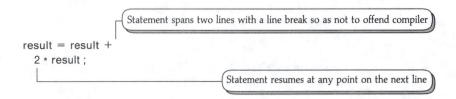

Statement spans two lines with a line break so as not to offend compiler

```
result = result +
  2 * result ;
```

Statement resumes at any point on the next line

Be careful to choose a suitable point for your line breaks because the compiler is not very happy for them to occur midway through a variable/function name or an implicit text string. If this should prove to be a problem then the line continuation character '\' may be placed *anywhere* in a statement to tell the compiler that the current statement resumes at the start of the next line. Be careful not to indent this following line, however, because it will be seen by the compiler as white space and could result in an error. For example, the previous statement could, rather perversely, have been written as:

The line continuation character used to separate a statement midway through a variable name

```
  res\
ult = res\
ult + 2 * res\
ult ;
```

New lines must commence immediately after the '\'

New line begins in left-hand column

If a text string becomes too large to enter as a single line of text, it should be split into two separate text strings (that is, enclosed within separate pairs of quotation marks '" "'. Provided these strings are separated by nothing more than white space (which includes line breaks) the compiler will automatically concatenate them into a single text string. For example, the statement:

```
printf("This is an example of a very long literal text string\n") ;
```

could also have been written as:

Large implicit text strings may be split into separate ones, which are automatically joined

```
printf("This is an example of a "
     "very long literal text string\n") ;
```

1.14 Chapter summary

(1) Program development proceeds as a sequence of edit, compile and test operations.

(2) A function is identified by placing brackets '( )' after its name. All complete programs must contain a function called main( ), of which there must be only one and which serves to mark the point where the program begins.

(3) A statement is a complete line of executable code and is terminated with a semicolon ';'. All statements within a function are executed as a sequence commencing with the statement following the opening brace '{' and ending (if the program gets that far) with the closing brace '}'.

(4) Variables may be introduced or defined immediately after the opening brace '{' of a function. All simple variables are essentially integral or real. Examples of integral data types include char and int and the real (floating point) data type float. Variables may be initialized with values at their point of definition with the assignment operator '='.

(5) Numeric values such as 10 or 3.141 59 are known as implicit constants and are represented by integral and real data types, respectively. Values such as 'a' and "Hello" are implicit character and string constants and are represented by char and arrays of char, respectively.

(6) Explicit constants are introduced like variables but their definition is prefixed with the word const. Such constants should be initialized during their definition if they are to be of any use, because the program will not be permitted to modify them later.

(7) Pre-processor constants may be created with the pre-processor directive #define.

(8) The arithmetic operators '+', '–', '*' and '/' cater for the addition, subtraction, multiplication and division of numeric data. The assignment operator '=' provides a means of assigning a value to a variable. The operators '++' and '--' specifically cater for the incrementing and decrementing of variables. The address operator '&' permits the memory address or location of a variable to be taken.

(9) The functions scanf() and printf() cater for the formatting of and input/output of data from/to the operator's terminal. Both functions rely upon a format string containing a number of '%' format indicators that determine the type, position and format of data to be input/output; scanf() differs from printf() in that it requires the addresses of the variables in which it stores the operator's entered data.

(10) Selective execution is achieved with the if or if-else statements, typically in conjunction with a number of relational operators such as '<', '>', '<=', '>=', '!=' and '==' and logical operators such as '&&', '||' and '!', all of which yield a true or false result.

(11) Repetition is achieved using looping constructs such as the while, do-while and for loops. Each executes one or more statements while some test expression resolves to true.

(12) An array is a collection of items of data of a common type such as an array of int or char. Access to arrays is via the array operator '[]' in conjunction with a single integer subscript. The first element of any array in C is referenced using the subscript 0.

(13) Text strings are internally represented and stored as arrays of char terminated with the special NULL character '\0'. Text strings may be read or displayed using scanf() or printf(), respectively, in conjunction with the '%s' format indicator. The C standard library also provides the functions gets() and puts() specifically for reading and displaying text strings, while the functions getchar() and putchar() allow a single character to be read/displayed.

(14) The functions atoi() and atof() provide string to numeric conversion, which in conjunction with a call to gets() provide an alternative means of entering numeric data, other than via scanf().

(15) A function is a sequence of statements that are executed when the function is invoked. A function may or may not be given data in the form of arguments when it is called or invoked. A copy of these arguments becomes the parameters within the function.

If a program contains the code for a function then it is said to contain that function's definition. Either the definition of a function or its function prototype must have been encountered by the compiler before the function is called by the program or its operation may be undefined.

(17) When a program is run, three FILE pointers – 'stdin', 'stdout' and 'stderr' – are automatically created, referring to the program default input, output and error message streams, respectively. A call to printf() is thus equivalent to a call to fprintf() in association with the FILE pointer 'stdout', while a call to scanf() is equivalent to a call to fscanf() in association with the FILE pointer 'stdin'.

(18) Input, output (and error messages) may be redirected to alternative devices or disk files when the program is run using the shell command line operators '<' and '>'.

(19) A comment begins and ends with the character sequences /* and */, respectively. Everything between these characters is ignored by the compiler.

(20) The line continuation character '\' may be used to start a new line at a convenient place in a statement. Two adjacent literal text strings separated only by white space are automatically concatenated into one text string at compile time.

1.15 Exercises

1.1 What are 'source' and 'executable' files? How are they created?

1.2 What is a function? What is the significance of the function main() in C?

1.3 How are the start and end of a function indicated and how is a function invoked? What is responsible for invoking the function main() in a program and what operation does the statement 'return 0;' at the end of main() perform?

1.4 What is the purpose of the C standard library and how are functions within it called?

1.5 What is a header file and what does the directive #include <stdio.h> achieve? What is the significance of the angle brackets '< >' placed around the header file's name? What happens if quotation marks '" "' are used instead?

1.6 Rewrite Program 1.1 to include the header file my_header.h (one that you have created). This header file should replace the directives #include <stdio.h> and #define PI 3.14159 contained within that program.

1.7 What is meant by the term 'data type' and what are the basic data types discussed in this chapter? Suggest a purpose for each type.

1.8 What is meant by the terms 'variable' and 'constant'? How are they introduced?

1.9 How can constants be created using the #define directive? Describe how this directive works in relation to Program 1.1.

1.10 What is an implicit constant (as opposed to an explicit constant)? Do constants created using #define give rise to implicit or explicit constants? Give examples of implicit character, integral, real and string constants. What happens if you attempt to assign a value to a constant?

1.11 What does the following call to printf() display?

```
printf("The area and circumference of a circle of radius %f = %f and %f respectively\n",
    a, b, c) ;
```

For this statement to work in the manner anticipated, what values do 'a', 'b' and 'c' represent and what should their type be?

1.12 Why does scanf() require the address operator '&' for each variable whereas printf() does not? What does the following statement attempt to do?

```
scanf("%c %f %d", &a, &b, &c) ;
```

1.13 How does scanf() indicate that it has read and successfully converted all of the values it was asked to read? What happens to any operator entered text that is not successfully converted (or read) by scanf()?

1.14 Modify the program presented in Application 1.2 to make two separate calls to scanf() to read the values for 'r1' and 'r2'. By looking at the value returned by scanf() in each case the program should be able to determine if one or both numeric values have been read successfully. By placing each call to scanf() within its own while loop, the program should be able to reject an invalid response. Try it and explain what you see when non-numeric responses are supplied. Now try incorporating the statement 'fflush(stdin) ;' prior to each call to scanf(). What do you think this achieves?

1.15 What is meant by 'program selection' or 'conditional execution'? Given the following variable definitions, list the outcome of the following conditional tests in terms of the results 'true' or 'false':

```
int a = 5, b = 10 ;

if( a < 5 )
if( a <= 5 )
if( a >= 5 )
if( !( a == 5 ))
if((a – 4) >= ( b – a ))
```

```
if(( a > b ) || (a <= 5 ))
if(((b >= 10) && (a < 5)) || (b >= 2*a))
```

Draw flowcharts for the following more complex arrangements of if tests. Check the operation of your flowcharts by testing them against a program written to read in the values for 'a', 'b' and 'c' using scanf( ). Describe the conditions in terms of the values of 'a', 'b' and 'c' that would enable each of the calls to printf( ) to be executed.

(a)

```
if( a != b ) {
  printf("Point 1\n") ;
  if( c != 2 ) {
    printf("Point 2\n") ;
    if((a - c) > b)
      printf("Point 3\n");
  }
  printf("Point 4\n") ;
}
```

(b)

```
if( a > b ) {
  printf("Point 1\n") ;
  if( c < a + b ) {
    printf("Point 2\n") ;
    if( a != 0 )
      printf("Point 3\n") ;
    else
      printf("Point 4\n") ;
  }
  else
    printf("Point 5\n") ;
}
else
  printf("Point 6\n") ;
```

1.16 What is meant by program repetition? Describe the operation of the while, do-while and for loops in C. List their general form and draw flowcharts for each.

1.17 Trace the operation of the following while loops, draw their flowcharts, and describe the displays produced by each. Rewrite each in its equivalent do-while and for loop forms.

(a)

```
int i = 0 ;
while( i < 10 )
  printf("%d\n", i++ ) ;
```

(b)

```
int i = 0, j ;
while( i <= 12 ) {
  j = 0 ;
  while( j <= 12 ) {
    printf("%d * %d = %d\n", i, j, i*j ) ;
    j ++ ;
  }
  i++ ;
}
```

1.18 Rewrite the following example programs and applications to use a do-while loop, so that they prompt the operator with the question, 'Do you want to run the program again [1=Yes, 0=No]?:', as we saw in Application 1.4.

(a) Application 1.5

(b) Program 1.5

(c) Programs 1.8 and 1.9

1.19 Modify the program presented in Application 1.3 such that the while loop and the statements associated with it that are responsible for evaluating e^x are written in the form of a function called e(). This function should expect to be given the value of x (a floating point quantity) as an argument and return the value of e^x (also a floating point value). The function can then be invoked with a statement of the form 'result = e(x);' where 'x' and 'result' are floating point variables. Using this function, verify the following mathematical identities:

(a) $\sinh(x) = (e^x - e^{-x})/2$

(b) $\cosh(x) = (e^x + e^{-x})/2$

(c) $\tanh(x) = \sinh(x)/\cosh(x)$

Hint: Remember to include a function prototype for e(), or alternatively ensure that it is defined before any statements that attempt to invoke it; that is, before main().

1.20 Write functions to evaluate the volume of a sphere of radius r, given by the equation volume $= 4/3\pi r^3$, and that of a cylindrical cone of base radius r and height h, given by the equation volume $= 1/3\pi r^2 h$.

1.21 If a ladder of length l is leant against a house at an angle θ degrees to the horizontal, write two functions called x_distance() and y_distance() to evaluate the distance from the bottom of the house to the foot of the ladder (assuming level ground) and the distance from the bottom of the house to the top of the ladder (assuming a vertical wall).

Note: The functions sin() and cos() in the standard library expect angles expressed in radians, so write an intermediate function called deg_to_rad() that can be called from the two functions you have written to convert between degrees and radians.

1.22 What is an array, and how are arrays defined? Write example statements to define the following arrays:

(a) An array of 20 int.

(b) An array of 32 float.

(c) An array of BUFSIZ char where BUFSIZ is a symbolic constant created using #define within the header file <stdio.h> (examine this header file for yourself to verify this).

1.23 What happens if you attempt to define the number of elements in an array using the value of a variable rather than an implicit constant?

1.24 What is the notation for referencing an element from within an array in terms of the integer subscript i? Given the array of 20 integers defined in Exercise 1.22(a), which of the following integer subscripts refer to the first/last elements in the array: −1, 0, 1, 19, 20, 21?

1.25 Using a for loop, write a program to initialize an array of integers in the manners described below. Use a #define constant to size the array and to control the loop.

(a) To initialize all elements to 0.

(b) To initialize all elements to a random number (see the function rand() described in Section 18.13).

(c) To assign successive incremental values to each element, commencing with 0, for example, 0, 1, 2 and so on.

(d) To assign successive decremental values to each element, for example, 25, 24, 23 and so on.

(e) To assign numbers to each element in an array x such that $x[0] = 0$ and $x[1] = 1$ and $x[i] = x[i - 1] + x[i - 2]$ for all values of i greater than 1 (that is, a Fibonacci sequence).

1.26 How is a text string such as "Hello World" represented in C? Write a program to read a line of text from the operator's keyboard and store it. What happens if scanf() (in conjunction with the '%s' formatter) is used to read a line of text containing many separate words? Explain why the string input function gets() is often preferred for reading lines of text.

1.27 Write a program to read and store an operator's name, for example "paul davies". Modify the operator's entry to convert the initial of each name to upper case before displaying it, for example "Paul Davies". Now modify the program so that the converted name is concatenated to the back end of the string "Hello ". Finally, concatenate the string ", how are you?" to the result and thus display a sample message of the form "Hello Paul Davies, how are you?"

Note: Remember to include the header files <string.h> and <ctype.h>.

1.28 Write a simple program making use of fgetc() and putchar() to list/display the contents of a file on the operator's terminal. The program should prompt for the name of the source file. Modify the program to use fscanf() (in conjunction with the %c formatter) in place of fgetc().

1.29 Modify your program from Exercise 1.28 so that all occurrences of a specified character are filtered (removed) prior to displaying other characters in the file.

1.30 Write a program to count the number of spaces, characters and lines of text in a file.

1.31 What do the FILE pointers 'stdin', 'stdout' and 'stderr' refer to? Modify the program you wrote for Exercise 1.28 to assume that the operator's data will be read from the standard input device. Using the input and output redirection operators '<' and '>', redirect the program's input and output to come from and be written to text files.

1.32 Construct a program to write a sequence of 10 random integer values (using the standard library function rand()) to a disk file using fprintf(). Verify that this has been done by displaying the file on your screen. Now write a second program to read them back using fscanf(). What happens when you come to read the numbers back if:

(a) The numbers are not separated from each other within the file?

(b) The numbers are separated by commas?

(c) The numbers are separated by space characters?

(d) The numbers are placed on separate lines?

What happens if the first program opens the file using fopen() in conjunction with mode 'a' as opposed to 'w' prior to writing the numbers?

2 A Closer Look at Data Types and Storage Classes

In Chapter 1 we introduced and discussed some of the more useful data types supported by C in the form of char, int and float. We restricted ourselves to the use of the **automatic** class of variables, which, as you will recall, is defined within the confines of a function. In this chapter we expand upon both of these topics. Several new and modified data types will be introduced, along with a discussion of how each is represented in memory and how that representation affects the range and accuracy of their values.

Also of interest is a discussion of the related subjects of storage **scope** and **privacy** and how these affect a program's ability to **hide**, or restrict access to, a variable from certain areas of the program, but first let us begin by taking a look at each data type in more detail.

2.1 C's fundamental and modified data types

Along with the data types char, int and float that we met in Chapter 1, the data type 'double' (used to represent real quantities) completes the list of C's fundamental data types, a summary of which is given in Table 2.1.

The reason for introducing a float as well as a double to represent a real quantity boils down to three important issues: speed, storage requirements and accuracy/precision. The double is primarily of use in applications where precision

Table 2.1 C's fundamental data types.

Type	*Suggested usage*
int	Integral numbers such as 1, 2, 3 and so on
float	Low/medium precision real numbers
double	Medium/high precision real numbers
char	Text characters such as 'a', 'b', '@' and so on

Table 2.2 C's modified data types.

Type	*Suggested usage*
short int	Small to medium sized integral numbers such as 1, 2, 3 and so on
long int	Medium to large sized integral numbers such as 12 000, −254 642 and so on
long double	Medium/high value/precision real numbers such as 2.0×10^{2310}

and accuracy are more important than speed, for example in numerical analysis and many CAD applications, although it is probably fair to say that many programmers often use a double rather than a float for all floating point calculations. In addition to these fundamental data types, C also naturally evolved a number of 'modifed' versions of the above data types, as shown in Table 2.2.

Let us begin by taking a closer look at how each of the four fundamental and three modified data types are represented in terms of their memory requirement and what their useful ranges of values are.

2.1.1 *The integral data types:* int, short int *and* long int

The int data type is often referred to as the **default** data type in C, since, as we shall see later, the compiler will in certain situations assume that variables and constants are of type int unless otherwise stated.

The size of an int is not strictly defined by the standard, so the range of values that it may assume is likely to vary from one compiler to another. The rationale behind this was to enable a compiler vendor to select the most appropriate size for an int to suit the architecture of the host computer. You should find, however, that an int is at least 16 bits (2 bytes) in size.

Figure 2.1 illustrates the representation and range of values for various sizes of int. Interestingly enough, most compilers available for the IBM PC

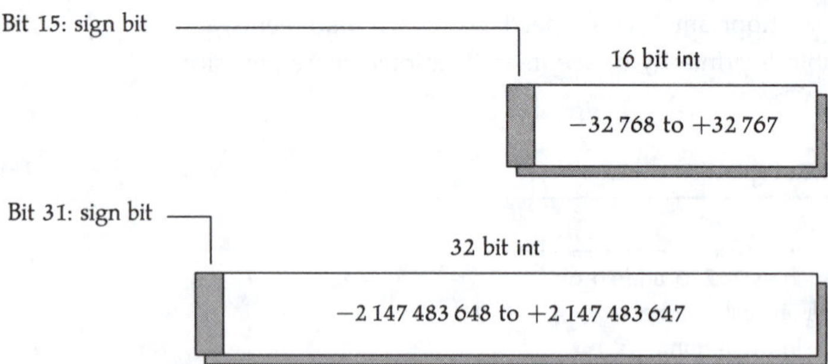

Figure 2.1 Typical representation of a 16 bit and a 32 bit integer.

implement the int data type as a 16 bit quantity to enable compatibility across a broad range of CPUs from the 8088 to the 80486.

By default, an int is always a **signed** quantity, able to assume both negative and positive values. Using two's complement notation (see Section 2.1.2), a 16 bit int could thus assume values in the range −32 768 to +32 767, while a 32 bit int could assume values in the range −2 147 483 648 to +2 147 483 647. Each definition of an int variable could, if required, be prefixed by either of the key words 'signed' or 'unsigned'. The first is rarely used because ints are implicitly signed anyway, while the second has the effect (assuming a two's complement representation of an int) of doubling the positive range of values that an int may assume, at the expense of their ability to represent negative values.

Note that in the absence of any specific int type specifier in the definition of a variable (for example, 'signed a;' or 'unsigned b;'), the compiler assumes such variables to be implicitly signed ints and unsigned ints, respectively. Thus, the shortened or abbreviated form is frequently used.

Because the storage requirements for, and range of values that may be assumed by, an int are likely to vary from one machine to another, and problems that may consequently arise as a result of this if a program written with one compiler in mind is 'ported' (transferred) to a compiler environment assuming different representation, C has evolved modified integral data types in the form of the short int and long int. Both are implicitly signed by default (unless prefixed by unsigned) and their types may be abbreviated to short and long, respectively. Note that neither of these types is required to be any bigger or smaller (in terms of their storage or range of values) than an int.

Tables 2.3 and 2.4, however, show how these data types are typically represented by compilers generating code for 8, 16 and 32 bit CPUs, along with the range of values they are able to assume.

Table 2.3 Typical size and range of integral data types for 8 and 16 bit CPUs.

Data type	*Size*	*Typical range of values*
char	8 bits	−128 to +127
short int	16 bits	−32 768 to +32 767
int	16 bits	−32 768 to +32 767
long int	32 bits	−2 147 483 648 to +2 147 483 647

Table 2.4 Typical size and range of integral data types for 32 bit CPUs.

Data type	*Size*	*Typical range of values*
char	8 bits	−128 to +127
short int	16 bits	−32 768 to +32 767
int	32 bits	−2 147 483 648 to +2 147 483 647
long int	32 bits	−2 147 483 648 to +2 147 483 647

Table 2.5 '%' format indicators recognized by printf( ) for integral quantities.

'%' formatter	*Data type(s)*	*Output displayed in following format*
%d	char, short, int	Decimal
%x	char, short, int	Hexadecimal
%o	char, short, int	Octal
%u	char, short, int	Unsigned decimal
%ld, %lx, %lo, %lu	long int	Decimal, hexadecimal, octal or unsigned decimal

Table 2.6 '%' format indicators recognized by scanf( ) for integral quantities.

'%' formatter	*Appropriate data type(s)*	*Input recognized in following format*
%d, %i, %u, %x, %o	int	Decimal, decimal, unsigned decimal, hexadecimal, octal, respectively
%ld, %li, %lu, %lx, %lo	long int	Decimal, decimal, unsigned decimal, hexadecimal, octal, respectively
%hd, %hi, %hu, %hx, %ho	short int	Decimal, decimal, unsigned decimal, hexadecimal, octal, respectively

Both scanf( ) and printf( ) have evolved additional '%' formatters that allow short, int and long data to be displayed and accepted from the keyboard in both their signed and unsigned forms. These are given in Tables 2.5 and 2.6.

One of the most common mistakes with scanf( ) is to specify an incorrect '%' formatter for the type of variable whose value is being read (and stored). For example, scanf( ) has separate formatters to allow it to distinguish ints from short ints, while printf( ) does not. This is to let scanf( ) implicitly know the size of the integral quantity to be read and stored – that is, whether it is a short or an int quantity.

Note that the standard library defines the function atol( ) to complement the functions atoi( ) and atof( ) that we met briefly in Chapter 1, to facilitate the conversion of a text string into a long int value.

Implicit integer constants

From time to time, our programs will inevitably contain a number of what are known as implicit (or implied in the sense that they cannot be changed by the program) constants. For example, the expression 'a = 5' assigns the value of the implicit integer constant '5' to the variable 'a'. Such constants may be expressed in a number of numeric bases, including decimal, hexadecimal and octal (but not binary).

Any implicit integer constant *not* beginning with 0 is assumed to be expressed in base 10 (decimal). Those beginning with 0 and 0x (or 0X) are assumed to be expressed in base 8 (octal) and base 16 (hexadecimal), respectively. Decimal constants may be constructed using the characters 0–9, hexadecimal constants using the characters 0–9, a–f and A–F, while octal constants may use the characters 0–7. From this it follows that the values 077 and 77 are not the same. The former is octal 77, while the latter is decimal 77. Some examples of implicit hexadecimal, octal and decimal integral constants are shown below:

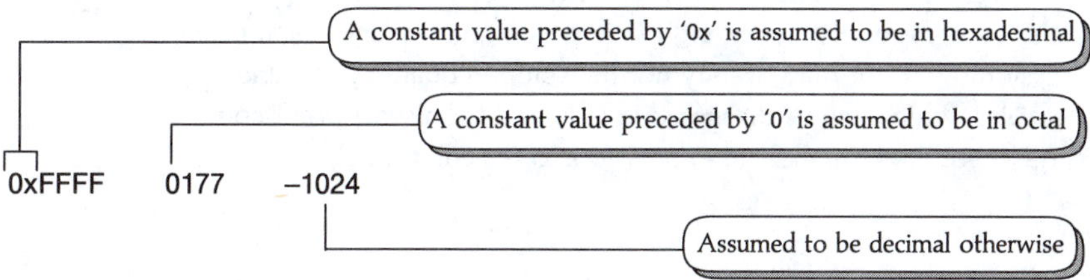

Let us consider now how such constants are actually represented by the compiler. By default, any integer constant expressed in decimal will always be represented by a signed int quantity unless its value is too large (such as the value 56 000 on a compiler that uses 16 bit ints), in which case it will be represented by a signed long int, or ultimately, if it still too large, by an unsigned long int. Good compilers should warn the programmer if an integral constant cannot be represented by a signed int.

An implicit integral constant expressed in hexadecimal or octal will also be represented by a signed int, but if that value is too large (such as 0xFFFF on a compiler that uses 16 bit ints), it will be represented by an unsigned int, or, failing this, a signed long int and ultimately an unsigned long int.

If an implicit integer constant is followed by either of the characters 'l' (lower case 'el') or 'L' it is automatically represented by a signed long int. Similarly, an integer constant followed by either of the characters 'u' or 'U' is assumed to be an unsigned quantity. Thus the decimal integer constant 23UL is represented by an unsigned long int. Table 2.7 presents some examples, where it is assumed that ints and long ints are represented by 16 and 32 bit quantities, respectively.

Table 2.7 Examples of implicit integral constants and their representations.

Value	*Notation*	*Represented as*
23	Decimal	signed int
23U	Decimal	unsigned int
23L	Decimal	signed long int
23UL	Decimal	unsigned long int
45000	Decimal	signed long int
3000000000	Decimal	unsigned long int
0x53	Hexadecimal	signed int
0x8000	Hexadecimal	unsigned int
0x7ffffff	Hexadecimal	signed long int
0x80000000	Hexadecimal	unsigned long int

Note that the use of commas and spaces between digits in any implicit integer constant (or when entering numbers at the keyboard into a running program for scanf()) is not permitted; thus, the integer constant 2,123 is illegal.

Why make such a fuss over how an implicit constant is represented? The difference is important for two reasons. Firstly, other operators that we have not yet met operate differently depending upon whether their operands are signed or unsigned quantities, and, secondly, when signed and unsigned quantities appear in the same expression the result may or may not be a signed quantity, depending upon a number of rules, which will be discussed in Chapter 3. This last point could affect the outcome of some mathematical expressions or calculations.

2.1.2 *Two's complement binary notation for integral quantities*

Two's complement binary notation is probably the most frequently chosen method of representing signed integral quantities on a computer, although other schemes do exist. Using this scheme the most significant bit (MSB) of the integer quantity is used to indicate its sign. A value of 0 here indicates a positive quantity, while 1 indicates a negative quantity. Whatever bits are left are used to represent the value of the quantity. Assuming an integer 'n' bits in size, this gives a range of values for a signed integral quantity of $-2^{(n-1)}$ to $(+2^{(n-1)} - 1)$. For an unsigned integral quantity, where all the bits are used to represent its value, the range of values is 0 to $+(2^n - 1)$.

Tables 2.8 and 2.9 demonstrate how both signed and unsigned 8 and 16 bit quantities are represented using this notation. Notice the sudden change in bit pattern when 1 is subtracted from 0 in a signed quantity. Notice also how an

Table 2.8 Two's complement representation of 8 bit integral quantities.

Signed 8 bit quantity		*Unsigned 8 bit quantity*	
Binary	*Decimal*	*Binary*	*Decimal*
10000000	−128	11111111	+255
10000001	−127	11111110	+254
...		...	
11111110	−2	01111111	+127
11111111	−1	01111110	+126
00000000	0	...	
00000001	+1	00000011	+3
00000010	+2	00000010	+2
...		00000001	+1
01111110	+126	00000000	0
01111111	+127		

Table 2.9 Two's complement representation of 16 bit integral quantities.

Signed 16 bit quantity		*Unsigned 16 bit quantity*	
Binary	*Decimal*	*Binary*	*Decimal*
1000000000000000	−32768	1111111111111111	+65535
1000000000000001	−32767	1111111111111110	+65534
...		...	
1111111111111110	−2	0000000001111111	+127
1111111111111111	−1	0000000001111110	+126
0000000000000000	0	...	
0000000000000001	+1	0000000000000010	+2
0000000000000010	+2	0000000000000001	+1
...		0000000000000000	0
0111111111111110	+32766		
0111111111111111	+32767		

unsigned quantity is able to assume a positive range twice that of its signed counterpart.

Care must be taken with signed quantities to ensure that any arithmetic operations such as addition or subtraction do not generate an overflow or underflow. For example, if the value of a signed int were incremented beyond +32 767 or decremented below −32 768, a change of sign would occur, with possibly disastrous consequences for the program.

(Note that changing the sign of a positive quantity into its equivalent negative value is achieved simply by performing a one's complement of the original integer value (that is, all 0s become 1s and vice versa) and adding 1 to the result, as can be seen from any of the values above.)

2.1.3 *The real data types:* float, double *and* long double

The float and double data types are used to represent floating point or real quantities such as the values 3.141 or 2.718. A float is typically a smaller quantity than a double (in terms of its storage requirement) but is not required to be. Consequently, a float is generally able to represent real numbers with a more restricted range of values and precision than a double. A float is often implemented as a 4 byte quantity and generally possesses a range of values of the order $\pm 1.0e^{\pm 37}$ (that is, $\pm 1.0 \times 10^{\pm 37}$) and is generally able to represent numbers with a precision of seven digits.

A double, on the other hand, is generally implemented as an 8 byte quantity and is thus able to assume values in the range $\pm 1.0e^{\pm 308}$, with typically 14 digits of precision. These two data types and their representations in memory are illustrated in Figure 2.2.

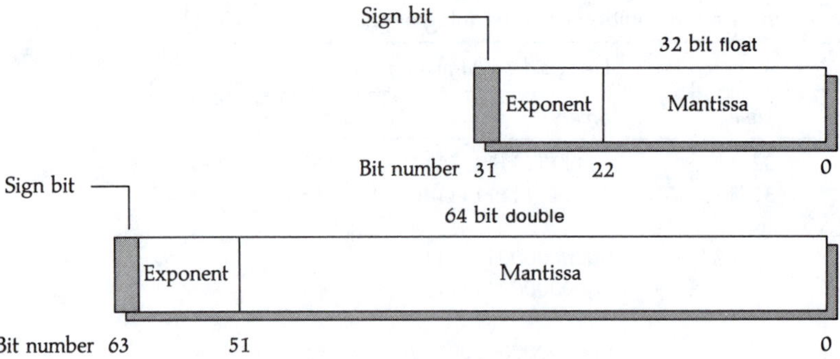

Figure 2.2 Typical representations of float and double.

The long double (a modified version of the double) has been introduced primarily to provide support for real variables with an increased precision and range. On many systems, a long double might require as many as 10 bytes of storage, giving rise to perhaps 19 or more digits of precision and a larger exponent range than either a float or a double.

You may, however, find that your compiler elects to represent a long double in exactly the same way as a double, and thus the two types will often be indistinguishable in use. Check your compiler's reference manual for details of how each type is represented. The simple program presented in Section 2.1.5 (Program 2.2) will allow you to determine this for yourself. Tables 2.10 and 2.11 demonstrate the typical storage requirements and range of values that these three real types are able to assume.

Both scanf() and printf() support additional '%' formatters that allow float, double and long double data to be displayed and entered. These are given in Tables 2.12 and 2.13.

Table 2.10 Typical size and range of real data types for 8 and 16 bit CPUs.

Data type	*Size*	*Typical range of values*	
float	32 bits	$\pm 3.4e^{+38}$ to $\pm 1.1e^{-38}$	(7 digits of precision)
double	64 bits	$\pm 1.7e^{+308}$ to $\pm 2.2e^{-308}$	(15 digits of precision)
long double	64 bits	$\pm 1.7e^{-308}$ to $\pm 2.2e^{-308}$	(15 digits of precision)

Table 2.11 Typical size and range of real data types for 32 bit CPUs.

Data type	*Size*	*Typical range of values*	
float	32 bits	$\pm 3.4e^{+38}$ to $\pm 1.1e^{-38}$	(7 digits of precision)
double	64 bits	$\pm 1.7e^{+308}$ to $\pm 2.2e^{-308}$	(15 digits of precision)
long double	80 bits	$\pm 1.1e^{+4932}$ to $\pm 3.3e^{-4932}$	(19 digits of precision)

Table 2.12 '%' format indicators recognized by printf() for real quantities.

'%' formatter	Appropriate data type(s)	Output format
%f	float or double	Floating point format
%e	float or double	Scientific format
%g	float or double	Shortest of '%f' and '%e'
%Lf, %Le, %Lg	long double	Floating point, scientific, and shortest of '%f' and '%e', respectively

Table 2.13 '%' format indicators recognized by scanf() for real quantities.

Format indicator	Input format
%f, %lf, %Lf	Floating point or scientific format for a float, double or long double, respectively
%e, %le, %Le	Floating point or scientific format for a float, double or long double, respectively
%g, %lg, %Lg	Floating point or scientific format for a float, double or long double, respectively

Again, take care to use the correct '%' formatter for the type of variable whose value you are displaying or reading. '%lf' does not mean the same thing as '%Lf' to scanf(). Note also that some compilers provide the function atold() (although it is not defined by the standard) to complement the function atof(), which we met briefly in Chapter 1, to allow the conversion of strings into long double values.

A complete treatment of both printf() and scanf() can be found in Chapter 15, which readers are invited to study at their leisure. The chapter is fairly easy to read and requires no knowledge other than that covered so far, but its length does reflect the sophistication and complexity of these two functions.

Implicit real constants

Implicit real constants arise as a result of the inclusion of a decimal point '.' or the use of the characters 'e' or 'E' to indicate scientific notation within an implicit constant. By default, such constants are always represented by doubles. Some example real constants are shown below:

```
3.141    0.5    -1.23e-200    354.4e23    3.
```

A C compiler will never resort to using a float representation for a real implicit constant, even if such a value could be represented accurately, unless it is followed by the letters 'f' or 'F'. For example, the implicit constants '2.3f' and '1.6e-09F' demonstrate examples where the compiler would use a float representation of a real implicit constant.

Similarly, any real implicit constants that are too large to be represented by a double, such as the values '1.0e+4000' and '−1.0e+4000', for example, will *not*

Table 2.14 Examples of implicit real constants.

Real value	*Represented by*
23.5	double
3.6e05f	float
23.5F	float
19.5e16l	long double
3.141692653L	long double

automatically be represented by a long double, but instead gives rise to an overflow, resulting in the effective values +INF (plus infinity) and −INF (minus infinity), respectively. If, however, the value of the implicit constant is followed by the character 'l' (lower case 'el') or 'L', then the compiler is forced to represent it using a long double. Some example real constants and their representations are shown in Table 2.14. Note that there is no such thing as an unsigned real quantity.

Note that the use of commas and spaces between digits in any implicit constant (or when entering numbers at the keyboard into a running program for scanf()) is not permitted; thus, the floating point constant 2,145,234.123 is illegal.

Application 2.1

The area under the curve $y = f(x)$ between the two points 'x = a' and 'x = b' may be approximated, using the trapezoidal rule, by dividing the area into 'N' smaller strips, each of width 'h' (Figure 2.3). If a straight line is then used to join two adjacent points on the curve separated by distance 'h' along the x-axis, the

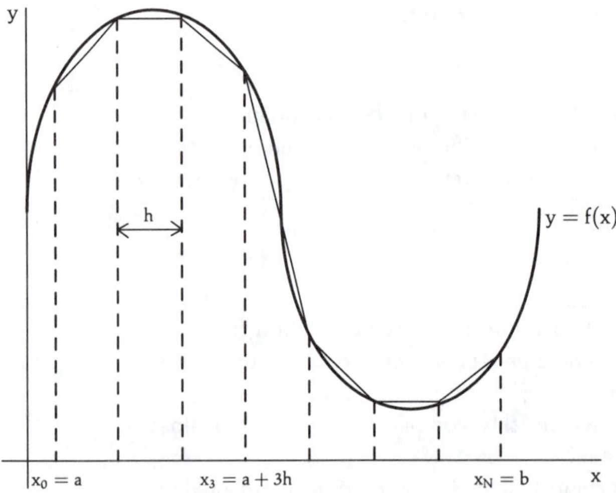

Figure 2.3 Approximation to the area under a curve using the trapezoidal rule.

approximate area under the curve is intuitively equal to the sum of a number of smaller trapezoids. As the value of 'N' is increased (and thus 'h' reduced), the approximation becomes more accurate. This gives rise to the equation:

$$area = h/2(f_0 + f_N) + h(f_1 + f_2 + \ldots + f_{N-1})$$

where f_0 = value of f(a) and f_j = value of $f(a + jh)$.

Write a program to read in the lower and upper bounds of the integration 'a' and 'b' and the value for 'N', and thus deduce the approximate area under the curve $y = x^2$ between the limits 0.5 and 0.6. This is, of course, a fairly trivial example, since the integral of x^2 is $(x^3)/3$ and thus the area is actually equal to $(0.6)^3/3.0 - (0.5)^3/3.0 = 0.033\,333\,3$. It does, however, serve as a good test of the program integrity before moving on to more useful equations.

Application 2.1 The area under a curve using the trapezoidal rule.

```
#include <stdio.h>

/* The function fx() equal to x² */

                                  fx() expects and returns a long double argument/value

long double   fx( long double x )
{
   return (x * x) ;
}

int main( void )
{
   int              i, N ;
   long double   a, b, h ;                      Implicit long double constant
   long double   x, area, sum = 0.0L ;

   printf("Enter Lower bound of Integral: ") ;
   scanf("%Lf", &a) ;
                                        scanf() '%' formatter for a long double

   printf("Enter Upper bound of Integral: ") ;
   scanf("%Lf", &b) ;

   printf("Enter number of sub-divisions: ") ;
   scanf("%d", &N) ;

   x = a ;                                  /* let x equal the value of the lower integral limit */
   h = (b – a ) / N ;
   area = 0.5L * h * (fx(a) + fx(b)) ;      /* calculate first portion of area */

                                                    Implicit long double constant
```

```
    for( i = 1; i < N; i++ ) {              /* now calculate remainder */
        sum = sum + fx(x) ;
        x = x + h ;
    }

    area = area + (sum * h) ;
    printf("Area = %Lg\n", area ) ;
    return 0 ;
}
```

General purpose '%' formatter for a long double quantity

If the program in Application 2.1 were run, the following sample display would be produced:

```
Enter Lower bound of Integral: 0.5
Enter Upper bound of Integral: 0.6
Enter number of sub-divisions: 30
Area = 0.0299801
```

```
Enter Lower bound of Integral: 0.5
Enter Upper bound of Integral: 0.6
Enter number of sub-divisions: 300
Area = 0.0302968
```

```
Enter Lower bound of Integral: 0.5
Enter Upper bound of Integral: 0.6
Enter number of sub-divisions: 30000
Area = 0.030333
```

2.1.4 *The data type* char

One of the more frequent operations performed with any programming language is the manipulation of text strings composed of characters, so it would seem appropriate for C to offer support for characters with their own specific data type, hence the introduction of the data type char. In C, a char is represented by an 8 bit integral quantity but the standard does not dictate whether it should be a signed or unsigned quantity (unlike the other integral data types). The choice is instead left to the compiler vendor, who is free to represent them in whichever way is deemed most appropriate.

With 8 bits of storage, an unsigned char can assume 2^8 possible positive values, in the range 0–255. A signed char, however, uses the most significant bit (assuming two's complement representaion) or bit 7 to represent the sign of the

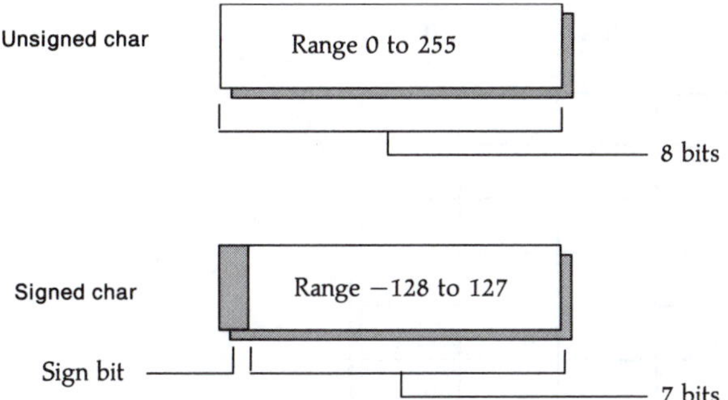

Figure 2.4 Typical representation of a signed and unsigned char.

value. A value of 0 here indicates a positive value, while 1 means negative. The remaining 7 bits (0–6) then represent the value of the char. Most compilers (that the author has encountered) elect to represent chars as signed quantities, which enables a signed char to assume values in the range −128 to +127.

Borland's Turbo C, interestingly enough, permits the programmer to specify whether the compiler should default to signed or unsigned chars at compile time, but, regardless of this, any assumptions about the signedness of a char can be overridden during its definition using either of the type modifiers signed or unsigned, for example, 'signed char c ;'. Figure 2.4 shows how a char is typically represented in both its signed and unsigned forms.

Now, unless your computer is unusual, most of the single character keys on your keyboard (ignoring some ALT and Function code keys on, for example, a PC) generate a unique 7 bit ASCII code to identify each particular key press. For example, the upper case character 'A'. generates the binary code (1000001) or hexadecimal 41, while lower case 'a' generates the binary code (1100001) or hexadecimal 61. Thus a char, being represented by an 8 bit (1 byte) integral quantity, is ideally placed to store and represent ASCII characters with the minimum of overhead and wastage. A complete list of ASCII codes is given in Figure 2.5.

It is worth pausing at this point to study Figure 2.5 in more detail, since the allocation of ASCII codes to individual characters is not as haphazard as it might at first seem and reveals some usful properties, some of which are listed below:

(1) All of the numeric digit characters 0–9 are represented by successive hexadecimal values in the range 0x30–0x39, respectively. This is an important point, since a simple test of the form shown below allows a program to establish whether the value of the character stored within the variable 'c' is a numeric digit:

```
if((c >= '0') && (c <= '9'))   /* test for 'c' equal to a numeric digit */
```

Least significant four bits (0–3) \ Most significant three bits (4–6), bit 7 is always 0 in ASCII	0	1	2	3	4	5	6	7
0	NUL	DLE	Space	0	@	P	`	p
1	SOH	DC1	!	1	A	Q	a	q
2	STX	DC2	"	2	B	R	b	r
3	ETX	DC3	#	3	C	S	c	s
4	EOT	DC4	$	4	D	T	d	t
5	ENQ	NAK	%	5	E	U	e	u
6	ACK	SYN	&	6	F	V	f	v
7	BEL	ETB	'	7	G	W	g	w
8	BS	CAN	(	8	H	X	h	x
9	HT	EM	)	9	I	Y	i	y
A	NL	SUB	*	:	J	Z	j	z
B	VT	ESC	+	;	K	[	k	{
C	NP	FS	,	<	L	\	l	|
D	CR	GS	-	=	M	]	m	}
E	SO	RS	.	>	N	^	n	~
F	SI	US	/	?	O	_	o	DEL

Figure 2.5 A table of ASCII (American Standard Code for Information Interchange) coded characters expressed in hexadecimal.

(2) Furthermore, a numeric character could easily be converted to its equivalent integral representation (for example, the character '9' (value 0x39) could be converted to the integer value 9) by subtracting the value 0x30 from that character, or – looking at it in another way – by subtracting the value of the character '0', as demonstrated by the statement:

```
i = (c - '0') ; /* convert numeric digit in 'c' to equivalent integer value */
```

(3) All lower case characters are represented by successive values in the range (0x61–0x7a) and all upper case characters are represented in the range hexadecimal (0x41–0x5a), making it a simple task to determine whether a character is lower or upper case using the expressions:

```
if((c >= 'a') && (c <= 'z'))   and   if((c >= 'A') && (c <= 'Z'))
```

(4) Conversion from upper to lower case and conversion from lower to upper case is easily achieved by adding or subtracting the value 0x20 to/from the character, or more typically, the value of the space character. For example, the expression (c + ' ') yields the value of the equivalent upper case character currently within the variable 'c', while the expression (c – ' ') yields the value of the equivalent lower case character.

(5) The values of all of the 'control code' characters lie in the range hexadecimal 0–0x1f. The equivalent control code for a character – the code produced by the keyboard when, for example, the character 'a' or 'A' is pressed while holding the control key down – can be generated by simply subtracting the value 0x60 (the value of the character '`') or 0x40 (the value of the character '@') from the equivalent lower or upper case character, respectively. For example, the BELL character (ASCII code 07, represented as <control-G> on the keyboard) can be generated using the expression 'G' – '@'.

Some of these ideas are presented in Program 2.1, which performs various character validation and conversion operations.

Program 2.1 A character validation/conversion program.

```
#include   <stdio.h>

int main( void )
{
  char c;

  printf("Enter a Character: ") ;
  c = getchar() ;

  printf("The ASCII Encoded Hexadecimal Value of Character '%c' is %x\n", c, c) ;

  if((c >= '0') && (c <= '9'))
    printf("'%c' is a Numeric/Decimal Digit Character\n", c) ;

  if((c >= 'a') && (c <= 'z')) {
    printf("'%c' is a Lower Case Character\n", c) ;
    printf("The Upper Case Version of '%c' is '%c'\n", c, c - ' ') ;
    printf("The Hexadecimal Value of <Control-%c> is %x\n", c, c - '`') ;
  }

  if((c >= 'A') && (c <= 'Z')) {
    printf("'%c' is an Upper Case Character\n", c) ;
    printf("The Lower Case Version of '%c' is '%c'\n", c, c + ' ') ;
    printf("The Hexadecimal Value of <Control-%c> is %x\n", c, c - '@') ;
  }
```

```
    if((c >= '0') && (c <= '7'))
      printf("'%c' is an Octal Digit Character\n", c) ;

    if(((c >= '0') && (c <= '9')) ||
        ((c >= 'a') && (c <= 'f')) ||
          ((c >= 'A') && (c <= 'F')))
      printf("'%c' is a Valid Hexadecimal Character\n", c ) ;

    return 0 ;
}
```

A sample of the typical display produced when this program is run is given below:

```
Enter a Character: 5
The ASCII Encoded Hexadecimal Value of Character '5' is 35
'5' is a Numeric/Decimal Digit Character
'5' is an Octal Digit Character
'5' is a Valid Hexadecimal Character
```

```
Enter a Character: A
The ASCII Encoded Hexadecimal Value of Character 'A' is 41
'A' is an Upper Case Character
The Lower Case Version of 'A' is 'a'
The Hexadecimal Value of <Control-A> is 1
'A' is a Valid Hexadecimal Character
```

Now apart from their most common application in representing single text characters, it is important for the reader to appreciate that as far as the compiler is concerned, a **char** is simply a small integral quantity and, as such, the values of **char** type variables and constants may legitimately be used in any mathematical expression alongside other data types such as **int**, **float**, **double** and so on.

In most situations, particularly when **chars** are only being used to represent ASCII encoded characters, the difference between **signed** and **unsigned** **chars** is of little consequence, since all standard ASCII codes are designed to have a positive value in the range 0–127 and can all be correctly represented by either **signed** or **unsigned chars**.

Implicit character and string constants

Implicit character constants, as we have already seen, are created whenever a single character is enclosed within single quotation marks ' '. Interestingly enough, the standard dictates that such constants are represented by **signed int** quantities (not by **chars**, as you might expect), and they consequently might require as much as 32 bits (or more on some machines) of storage to represent them. Some example character constants are shown below:

```
'A'    '@'    '#'    '$'    '9'
```

It is interesting to note that some of the character codes that can be entered at the keyboard or written to the operator's terminal are not by themselves displayable characters but more often serve to control the operation of the output device in subtle ways. Examples of this are the control codes and the backspace, tab and carriage return keys.

Because of their non-displayable features, it is extremely difficult to generate such character constants implicitly within the program code itself using the single character notation ' '. For this reason, a character constant may also be expressed in its equivalent hexadecimal or octal form using the notation shown below. Here, however, the programmer will have to look up the code for the desired character from an ASCII (or other) chart (see Figure 2.5):

'\xnn'   (hexadecimal)
'\ooo'   (octal)

Here 'ooo' is an octal number consisting of up to three digits and 'nn' is a two digit hexadecimal number. Table 2.15 illustrates some example character constants and their equivalent representations in hexadecimal, decimal and octal.

Table 2.15 Various representations of implicit character constants.

ASCII	*Octal*	*Hexadecimal*	*Equivalent decimal value*
'a'	'\141'	'\x61'	97
'@'	'\100'	'\x40'	64
'1'	'\061'	'\x31'	49
'}'	'\175'	'\x7d'	125

Note that because the single quote character ''' and the backslash '\' are effectively reserved by the above notation, the only way that these characters may be entered as implicit character constants by themselves is by preceding them with a further '\' character, for example, '\'' and '\\'. Similarly, when we consider string constants, the double quotation mark character '"' is also reserved and may thus be represented as a character in a similar manner, for example, '\"'.

For those particularly common non-printable character constants, such as new line, tab, backspace and so on, C provides a more convenient way of representing them, which avoids having to look up their equivalent hexadecimal, decimal or octal code each time. These are summarized in Table 2.16.

Table 2.16 Common character constants.

Character	*Interpretation*
'\a'	Internal computer/terminal beep
'\b'	Backspace
'\f'	Form feed (useful for printers)
'\n'	New line: equivalent to carriage return/line feed
'\r'	Carriage return
'\t'	Tab (size of tab depends on terminal set up)
'\v'	Vertical tab
'\?'	Question mark (see 'Trigraph sequences', below)
'\\'	'\' character
'\''	Single quote
'\"'	Double quote
'\0'	NULL character (for strings)

For example, the following call to printf( ) contains examples of some of the character constants from Table 2.16 as part of a text string:

```
printf("Pathlist = \"c:\\dos\\example.c\" \a\n") ;
```

This produces the following text on the operator's display and then sounds the internal computer buzzer, which might be an important consideration for those programming in an MS-DOS environment, where the character '\' is used in general directory pathlists:

```
Pathlist = "c:\dos\example.c"
```

An implicit string constant is created wherever a sequence of characters (perhaps as few as one or even no characters) is enclosed within **double** quotation marks " ". We have already seen this type of implicit constant used as the argument to printf( ), as in the statement:

```
printf( "Hello World\n" ) ;
```

Here, the text string "Hello World\n" was formed by enclosing the text within the double quotation marks " ", which are not part of the string itself, but simply delimit or mark the start and end of it. We saw in Chapter 1 that such a string is represented by a hidden or implicit char array terminated by the NULL character '\0'.

Trigraph sequences

If you are programming on an IBM PC or other modern computer system, you will probably not be too concerned by this section, because it is mainly of interest to those who are forced to write their programs on a machine with a restricted keyboard and/or display which conforms strictly with the ISO 646 standard on character sets. Unfortunately for these people, C uses a number of characters as part of its natural language which are not defined by this standard. These are listed below:

```
#   [   \   ]   ^   {   |   }   ~
```

If you find yourself using a computer that conforms strictly with that standard, then these characters may not be present on your keyboard and may not be displayable. For this reason, each of these characters may be entered using an alternative three character **trigraph sequence** as shown in Table 2.17.

Table 2.17 Trigraph character sequences.

<table>
<tr><th>Character</th><th>Equivalent trigraph sequence</th></tr>
<tr><td>#</td><td>??=</td></tr>
<tr><td>[</td><td>??(</td></tr>
<tr><td>]</td><td>??)</td></tr>
<tr><td>{</td><td>??<</td></tr>
<tr><td>}</td><td>??></td></tr>
<tr><td>\</td><td>??/</td></tr>
<tr><td>|</td><td>??!</td></tr>
<tr><td>~</td><td>??–</td></tr>
<tr><td>^</td><td>??'</td></tr>
</table>

Thus, the statement:

```
#include    <stdio.h>
```

could (less intuitively) be entered as:

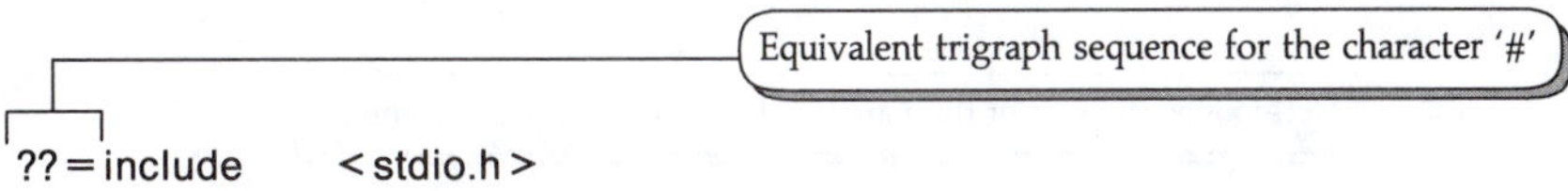

Note that the string "???" is still interpreted as the string "???", but that the string "???)" may be interpreted as "?]". To avoid this confusion, the string should be written as "?\??)" which was the reason why the '\?' form of expressing the question mark (see Table 2.16) was introduced. If your computer does support C's extended characters, you should always use these in preference to a trigraph sequence because the resultant program is far more readable.

2.1.5 *Addressing portability issues: The* sizeof *operator*

With all of these discussions relating to assumptions the compiler makes about the sizes of its data types, you might begin to worry about the issue of writing portable code – that is, code that can be transferred from one compiler to another without modification. After all, if your compiler is assuming 32 bit integers, would your programs still run if they were compiled using a different compiler that assumed 16 bit integers?

The answer depends on what assumptions the programmer has made about the range of values and size of such quantities and whether, in the case of chars, they are signed or unsigned. To be safe, you should not make any assumptions about the signedness of chars but should define each explicitly using the signed and unsigned modifiers. The only real exception to this is when a char is being used to represent an ASCII encoded character. Likewise, the programmer should not assume that the size of an int will be any bigger than 16 bits.

Even bearing these points in mind, however, there are a number of situations where programmers will need to be able to determine the size of each type for themselves in a portable manner. Examples of this arise when dynamically allocating memory using functions such as malloc() and calloc() (see Chapter 8) as well as saving and recovering binary data to/from a file using the stream manipulation functions fread() and fwrite() (see Chapter 16). For this reason, C provides the sizeof operator, to enable the compiler (not the program, since the calculation is done at compile time and resolves to an implicit integer constant) to yield the sizes of the data types it uses. For example, the statement:

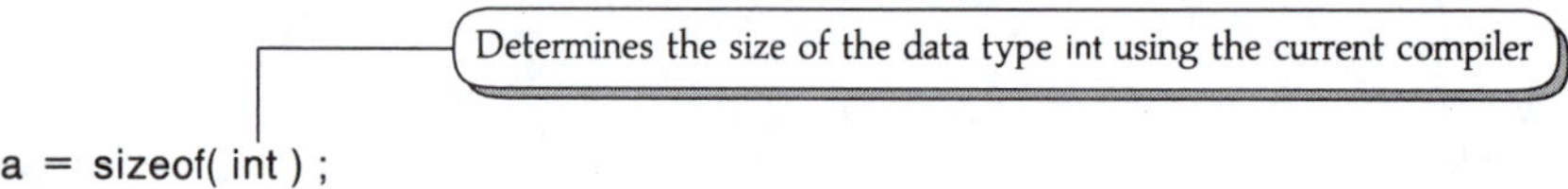

asks the compiler to determine the size in bytes of an int (on that compiler) and would typically yield the result 2 on 8 and 16 bit systems or 4 on a 32 bit system. Likewise, the statement below requests the compiler to determine the storage requirements for the variable 'b':

Determines the size of the variable 'b' using the current compiler

```
a = sizeof b ;
```

Note that parentheses are optional around a variable name (as above), but are obligatory with a data type such as int, char, float and so on. Now, if our programs make judicious use of this operator then many of the portability problems cease to be an issue. For example, the statement below evaluates the storage requirements for an array of 10 integers at compile time:

Size of an array of 10 int determined in a portable manner

```
a = sizeof( int [10] )) ;
```

If this statement were to be re-compiled using a different compiler, it would not need to be altered; it would be correct for all compilers.

In addition to the use of the sizeof operator, many portability problems can be reduced by making use of the symbolic constants defined within the header files <float.h> and <limits.h>. These define the maximum and minimum values that may be assumed by each data type using that compiler. For example, the following for loop counts from 0 to the *maximum* value of an int quantity for any one compiler, where the symbolic constant INT_MAX is defined within <limits.h> and can vary from one compiler to another:

Symbolic constant equal to the maximum value of an int on that compiler

```
for( i = 0; i < INT_MAX; i ++)
  printf("%d\n", i ) ;
```

Further examples of the use of these constants can be found in Sections 18.4 and 18.5, while Program 2.2 demonstrates their use along with that of the sizeof operator in a simple program.

Program 2.2 Size and range of values of fundamental/modified types.

```
#include   <stdio.h>
#include   <limits.h>
#include   <float.h>

int main( void )
{
   printf("%12s%12s%15s%15s\n", "Data Type", "Size Bytes", "Min Value",
      "Max Value") ;
   printf("%12s%12d%15d%15d\n", "char", sizeof(char), CHAR_MIN, CHAR_MAX) ;
   printf("%12s%12d%15d%15d\n", "short int", sizeof(short int), SHRT_MIN, SHRT_MAX) ;
   printf("%12s%12d%15d%15d\n", "int", sizeof(int), INT_MIN, INT_MAX) ;
   printf("%12s%12d%15ld%15ld\n", "long int", sizeof(long int), LONG_MIN,
      LONG_MAX) ;

   printf("%12s%12d%15g%15g\n", "float", sizeof(float), FLT_MIN, FLT_MAX) ;
   printf("%12s%12d%15g%15g\n", "double", sizeof(double), DBL_MIN, DBL_MAX) ;
   printf("%12s%12d%15Lg%15Lg\n", "long double",sizeof(long double), LDBL_MIN,
      LDBL_MAX) ;

   return 0 ;
}
```

The following typical display was produced when Program 2.2 was run:

Data Type	Size Bytes	Min Value	Max Value
char	1	0	255
short int	2	–32768	32767
int	2	–32768	32767
long int	4	–2147483648	2147483647
float	4	1.17549e–38	3.40282e+38
double	8	2.22507e–308	1.79769e+308
long double	10	3.3621e–4932	1.18973e+4932

2.2 Variable scope and privacy

In Chapter 1, we saw how a class of automatic variables could be introduced into our programs by defining them immediately after the opening brace '{' marking the start of a function. This is highly significant, although we did not dwell on the importance of it then, because the place or position where a variable is defined in the source file is very important and directly affects what are known as the variable's **scope** and **privacy**.

Providing a variable with scope permits us to restrict which parts of the program code are permitted to access, and hence modify, the variable. By restricting a variable's scope, we can afford it a degree of privacy and exclude unauthorized sections of the program from accessing it. C provides three different storage classes of variable, listed below, each of which has its own rules relating to scope and privacy:

- Global
- Automatic
- Static

The remainder of this chapter introduces these three basic storage classes. In particular, we shall be examining the program's ability to restrict or limit access to a particular variable through an appropriate choice of storage class. In Chapter 14 we extend the discussion to cover 'external variables', a concept that is best left until the subject of separate compilation is discussed. This is a useful feature of the language that enables a large source file/program to be broken down into many smaller source files, each of which can be compiled separately to produce a relocatable object file (ROF) before being linked to produce the final executable program.

2.2.1 *Global variables*

A global variable may be introduced by defining it outside or between two functions. Such variables have a scope that extends from their point of definition in the program up to the end of the current source file and may thus be accessed by all parts of the program that appear after their definition. (We shall see in Chapter 14, however, that global variables may also be accessed by parts of the program contained in other source files provided an external definition for the variable exists, and thus that access to a global variable can transcend source file boundaries.) It follows from this that a global variable defined at the top of the program is accessible by any statement or function within the current source file that appears after it.

The initialization of all global variables is performed immediately when the program is run, even before the function main() begins. Now, unless the program has *explicitly* assigned them a value, the programmer may safely assume that they will have been initialized to zero. As an example, study the program below. The scope of each global variable is illustrated with the use of boxes, which serve to highlight those parts of the program that may access each variable.

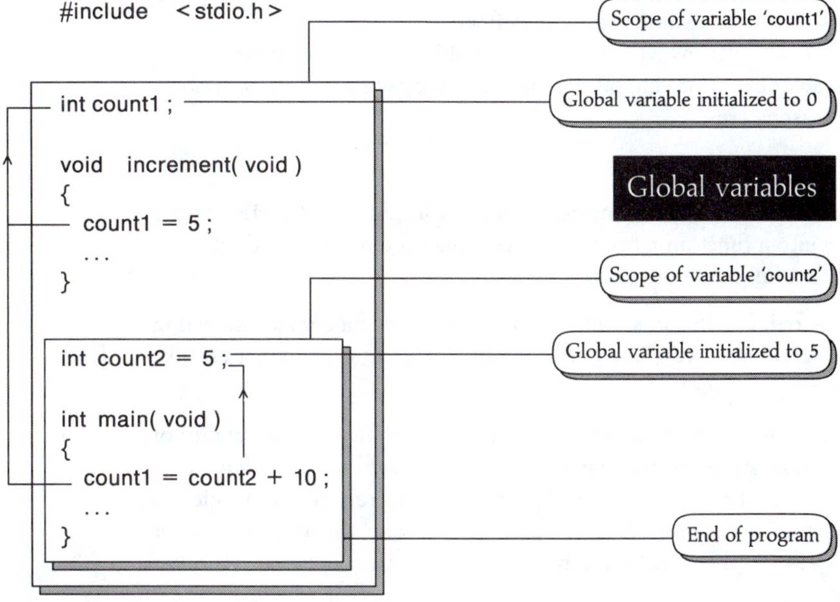

In this example, 'count1' was defined at the start of the program and is thus accessible by both functions, main() and increment(), that are defined after it. On the other hand, 'count2' is not defined until after the function increment() and thus will only be accessible by the function main() (and any other functions that might come after its definition).

2.2.2 *Automatic variables*

Automatic variables, as we have already seen, are introduced by defining them immediately after the opening brace '{' of a **function** or **statement block**. Such variables are allocated storage in an area of memory known as the **stack**, a concept that is dealt with in more detail in Chapter 6. The C language reserves the key word auto for use as a prefix to an automatic variable definition, but this is rarely used because the variable is assumed to be automatic based upon the position of its definition and in the absence of any other overriding information to the contrary.

It is important to appreciate that the scope of an automatic variable is restricted to the block (which commences with an opening brace '{' and terminates with its corresponding closing brace '}') in which it is defined. In other words, only those statements contained within the same block as the automatic variable's definition are able to access it directly.

Unlike a global variable, which is created and initialized conceptually before the program even begins, an automatic variable is created when that part of the program block in which it is defined commences execution, and, similarly, it ceases to exist when that block terminates. Also, in the absence of any explicit initializing value, no implicit initialization of automatic variables is performed by the compiler, and thus their value will be undefined.

There are many reasons why automatic variables are more commonly used than global variables even though, on the face of it, they appear more restrictive. Some of these reasons are:

(1) They provide a convenient means of introducing localized or temporary variables into a function whose results or values are not required once the function has finished execution;

(2) Their use reduces the possibility of two or more functions interacting adversely and unknowingly, by accidentally using the same global variable for different purposes;

(3) Perhaps the most important reasons lies with portability and reusability of code. Because an automatic variable is defined within the confines of a function block, the function itself does not have to rely on other (global) variables that are not an integral part of the function, thus making it easier to place the function into a library and/or reuse it in other applications.

To demonstrate automatic scope, the program below defines two functions, each of which introduces its own automatic variable 'i'. The scope of each variable is again illustrated through the use of boxes around those parts of the program that are permitted access to each variable:

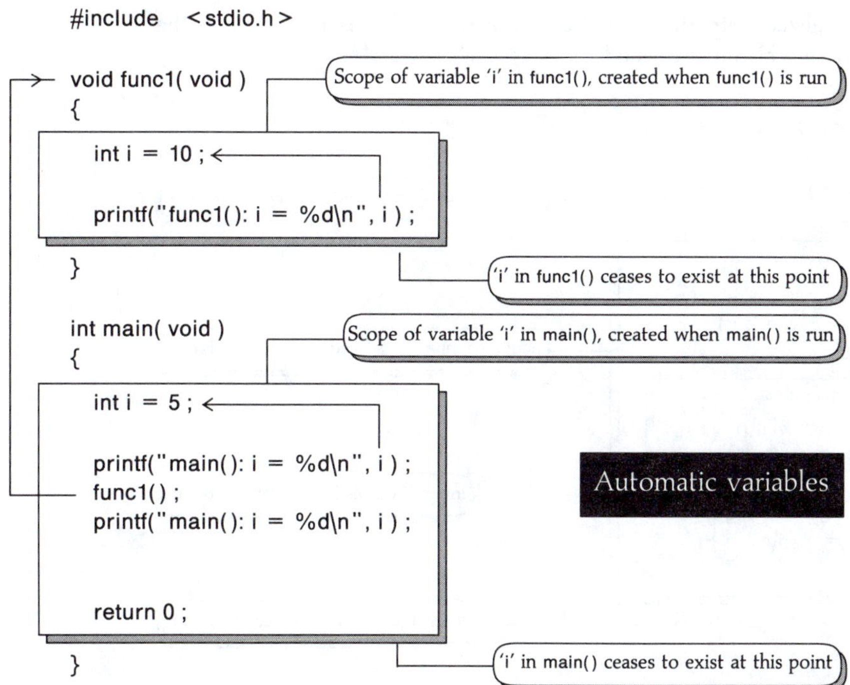

#include <stdio.h>
void func1(void)
{
int i = 10 ;
printf("func1(): i = %d\n", i) ;
}
int main(void)
{
int i = 5 ;
printf("main(): i = %d\n", i) ;
func1() ;
printf("main(): i = %d\n", i) ;
return 0 ;
}
Scope of variable 'i' in func1(), created when func1() is run
'i' in func1() ceases to exist at this point
Scope of variable 'i' in main(), created when main() is run
'i' in main() ceases to exist at this point

Automatic variables

Even though both main() and func1() in the above program define an integer variable 'i', each 'i' is in fact unique, with access to each being restricted to those sections of code contained within the same block as the variable definition.

Note also that even though main() invokes func1() in the above program, the variable 'i' defined by main() is still assumed to exist while func1() is executing (at which point there will be two separate variables called 'i') and will do so until main() terminates, as its value is required by main() after func1()'s termination. If the above program were run, then the following display would be observed on the operator's screen, which demonstrates that assigning 'i' a value of 10 within func1() does not affect the value of 'i' defined in main():

```
main(): i = 5
func1(): i = 10
main(): i = 5
```

As another example, study the program below, which again defines two automatic variables, both called 'i', but this time within the confines of the same function, main(). However, as each is defined within a different block, they are considered to be unique. The first variable 'i' (initialized with the value 5) has a scope that extends from the start to the end of the function main(). The second variable 'i' (initialized with the value 10) has a scope that is restricted to the statement block in which it is defined.

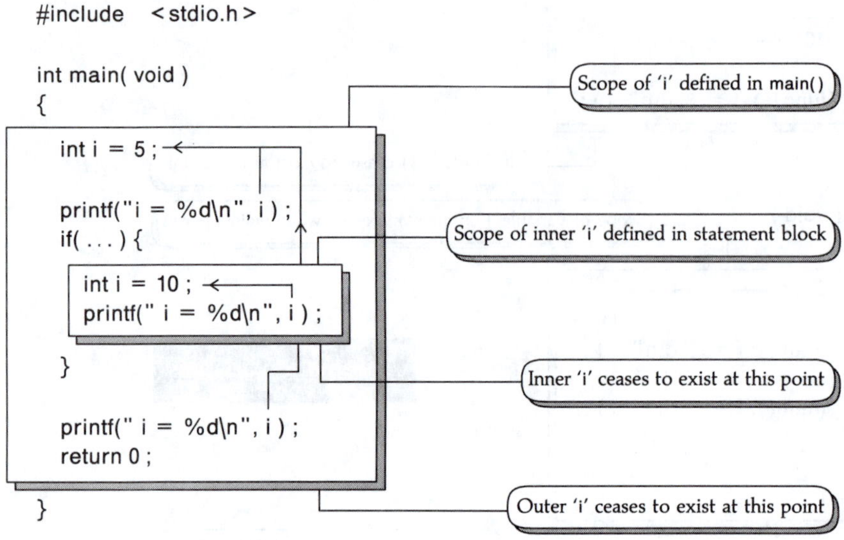

The obvious question here is how the compiler is able to determine which value of 'i' to display with each call to printf(). The answer is simple: the compiler will *always* use the variable most in scope, that is, the most recently introduced variable with that name, if two or more with the same name exist at that time. When the above (completed) program is run, the operator would observe the following output displayed on the screen (assuming that the appropriate if test expression resolves to 'true'):

```
i = 5
i = 10
i = 5
```

Similarly, should the situation arise where both an automatic and a global variable with the same name exist, access to the automatic variable will always take precedence over the global variable in an expression for the same reason outlined above. For example, the function display() below defines an automatic variable 'c1' with the same name as a global variable. When display() is called, it is the value of 'c1' defined within that function that will be referenced while display() is executing, rather than the global variable 'c1', which is effectively excluded and cannot be accessed at all by display().

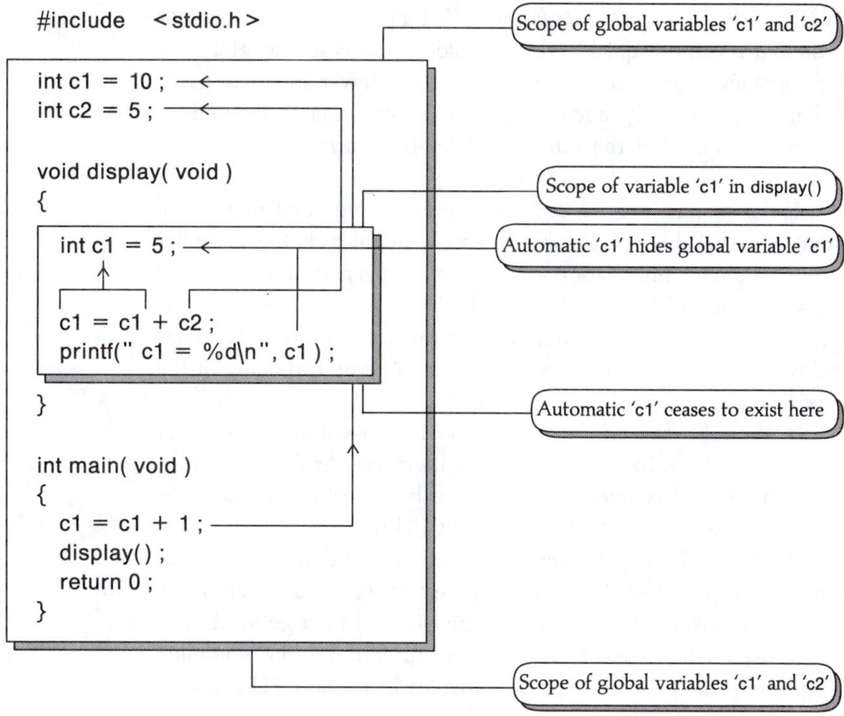
#include <stdio.h>
int c1 = 10 ;
int c2 = 5 ;
void display(void)
{
int c1 = 5 ;
c1 = c1 + c2 ;
printf(" c1 = %d\n", c1) ;
}
int main(void)
{
c1 = c1 + 1 ;
display( ) ;
return 0 ;
}
Scope of global variables 'c1' and 'c2'
Scope of variable 'c1' in display( )
Automatic 'c1' hides global variable 'c1'
Automatic 'c1' ceases to exist here
Scope of global variables 'c1' and 'c2'

2.2.3 *Register variables*

An interesting variation on the automatic variable theme is the **register** variable. Consider for a moment the following variable definition:

```
register int i = 0 ;
```

The compiler interprets the register prefix as a hint or suggestion that, if possible, 'i' should be allocated to a physical register within the CPU, rather than allocated storage in main memory. Other than this, and the fact that you cannot take the address of a register variable (that is, you cannot read in a value for it using scanf( ), for example), they behave in exactly the same way as automatic variables. The attractions of using register variables are numerous, but the most useful and important reasons are highlighted below:

- Program size is reduced since access to a register variable generally requires less code than accessing a variable stored in memory;

- A by-product of the previous observation is that a program using register variables should run more quickly than would be the case had global or automatic variables been used, since there will be fewer instructions to execute. This is particularly apparent if a register variable is used to control a loop, or is used as the subscript/index to an array.

Your C compiler manual should describe the exact type and number of CPU registers that are available for use by register variables. If the compiler adopts the programmer's recommendation and the variable is allocated to a CPU register, it will retain the use of that register for the life of the variable – that is, until the block in which it is defined terminates. For this reason global variables are not permitted with a register prefix, since they would tie up too many of the CPU resources for too long a period.

Considerable thought should be given to the allocation of register variables if maximum benefit is to be derived from their use. As a general rule, the more frequently a variable is referenced/accessed by a section of code, the more beneficial it would be to have it allocated to a CPU register.

Do not get too carried away, however, and attempt to define all of your variables with the register prefix, because only certain types are permitted. Arrays and structures/unions (see Chapter 11) are physically too large to fit, thus any register prefix used with these types will be ignored by the compiler. Furthermore, many compilers allocate register variables to actual CPU registers on a simple first-come, first-served basis, so careful choice is important.

Note, however, that if the compiler cannot accommodate all of the program's register variables, it is not considered to be an error and the prefix will simply be ignored. The effect of this is that they will be treated as if they had been defined as automatic variables (but you still cannot take their address), so make sure that your preferred choices are defined first. The program below demonstrates the use of the register prefix applied to automatic variables and constants:

```
#include   <stdio.h>

int   main( void )
{
    register   double          area, circum, radius = 1.2 ;
    register   const double   pi = 3.1415927 ;

    area = pi * radius * radius ;
    circum = 2.0 * pi * radius ;
    printf("area = %f , circumference = %f\n", area, circum) ;

    return 0 ;
}
```

Scope of register variables

CPU registers released at this point

It is worth noting that the compiler also permits function parameters (see Chapter 6 for more details) to be allocated to registers, as shown below, which can also improve the speed and size of the program code:

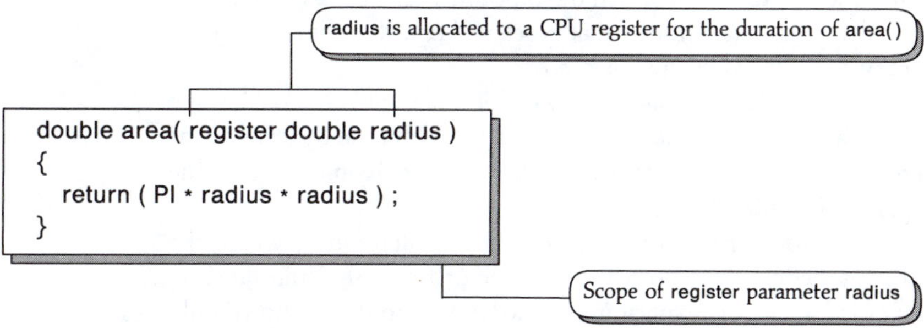

radius is allocated to a CPU register for the duration of area()
double area(register double radius)
{
return (PI * radius * radius) ;
}
Scope of register parameter radius

2.2.4 *Static variables*

We mentioned earlier that one of the main attractions for the use of automatic variables was the degree of privacy they afforded the program, which prevented two possibly unrelated functions from interacting adversely with each other through the use of global variables. However, one possibly major (depending upon the application) drawback to their use was the fact that such variables, and the values they held, ceased to exist at the end of their block.

Suppose, then, that we required a function that could retain the value of a variable defined within it from one call of the function to another. Up until now the only solution to this would have involved the use of a global variable, but this would undermine the variable's privacy and reduce the portability of the function to other applications.

A better solution exists in the form of the **static** storage class. Such variables are defined in much the same way as automatic variables, but with the (optional) key word auto replaced by the key word static, as in the example shown below, where the function count() keeps a record of how many times it has been called:

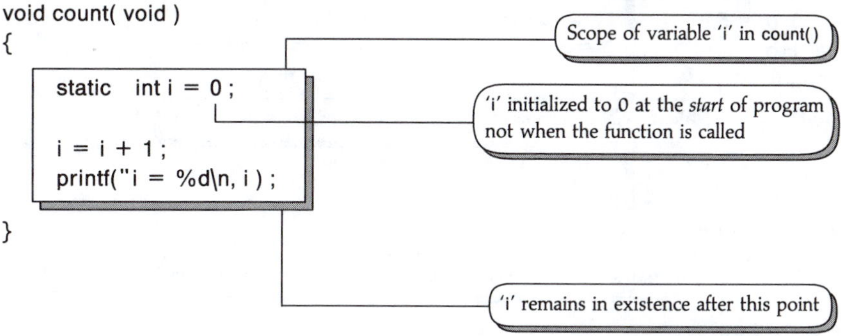

void count(void)
{
static int i = 0 ;
i = i + 1 ;
printf("i = %d\n, i) ;
}
Scope of variable 'i' in count()
'i' initialized to 0 at the *start* of program not when the function is called
'i' remains in existence after this point

Here, 'i' still possesses the same scope and privacy afforded to an automatic variable in the sense that access to it is restricted to statements that exist within the block where 'i' is defined. However, the key feature of a **static** variable is that it *retains* the storage allocated to it even when the block in which it was defined has terminated. Thus subsequent execution of that block will find that the value of the variable from a previous call has been preserved.

It is important to realize that all static variables, like global variables, are initialized only once, at the start of the program, and *not* each time their function/block is executed. Furthermore, any static variables not explicitly initialized by the program are implicitly initialized to zero.

We can see this for ourselves in the function count( ) above, where the static variable 'i' was defined to record the number of times that the function count( ) had been called. Here, the explicit initialization of 'i' to 0 was shown only for illustration since it would have been implicitly initialized with this value anyway. Had 'i' been defined as an automatic variable, then the function would not have worked, since 'i' would have been explicitly initialized to 0 each time count( ) was invoked or called.

2.2.5 *A closer look at variable initialization*

We have seen in previous discussions how a variable may be initialized by the program during its definition. Although this appears straightforward enough, C imposes some simple but important restrictions upon the types of initialization permitted, which are related to the variable's storage class – global, static, auto and so on – and are a reflection of how and when such initialization is performed.

When a global or static variable is initialized with the value of an expression, it is the compiler that evaluates that expression and generates code to ensure that the variable is initialized with that value right at the start of the

```
#include  <stdio.h>
#include  <math.h>

double  a = 2.3, b = 5.6 ;
double  i = a + b ;
double  j = sin( 0.321 ) ;


int main( void )
{
   static  double  x = i + 2 ;
   ...
}
```

Legal: 'a' and 'b' are initialized with implicit constants

Illegal: *global* variables must be initialized with 'constant' data

Illegal: *static* variables must be initialized with 'constant' data

program. Because of this, such variables are only allowed to be initialized with an implicit constant value, such as 10 or 3.12.

For example, given the program section opposite, the initializations of the global variables 'a' and 'b' are legal since 2.3 and 5.6 are implicit real constants. However, the initializations of 'i', 'j' and 'x' are illegal, since none of the expressions 'a + b', 'sin(0.321)' or 'i + 2' is an implicit constant value and cannot be evaluated at compile time.

Of course, such initialization could always be performed once the program is running, but *not* during the definition of the variable.

When an auto or register variable is initialized, it is the program code executed at run time rather than the compiler that evaluates the initializing expression, and thus the expression may be as complex as the programmer wishes and may even invoke other functions in the process. Thus in the program below, the initializations of 'a', 'b', 'i', 'j' and 'x' are all legal:

```
#include   <stdio.h>
#include   <math.h>

int main( void )
{
   double   a = 2.3, b = 5.6, i = a + b, j = sin( a ) ;
   register  int x = i + 2 ;
   ...
}
```

Legal: auto and register variables may be initialized with any expression

2.3 Chapter summary

(1) The fundamental data types are char, int, float and double. Modified versions of int exist in the form of short int and long int, the definitions of which may be reduced to short and long, respectively. A long double is an extended precision real quantity.

(2) All integral quantities except char are implicitly signed to allow them to assume both negative and positive values. A char may be signed or unsigned, depending upon the compiler. Such quantities are generally represented using two's complement notation, where the most significant bit is used to indicate the sign of the quantity. Prefixing the definition of an integral quantity by the words signed or unsigned removes any ambiguity about the signedness of the quantity.

(3) Not all data types are necessarily the same size on every system. The sizeof operator may be used to determine the size of a variable or type at compile time.

(4) Implicit constants includes such quantities as 2 (integer) represented by an int, 3.141 (real) represented by a double, '@' (character) represented by an int and "Hello" (string) represented by arrays of char.

(5) The scope of a variable affects which part of the program may access it. A global variable is created by defining it outside a function and is accessible to all parts of the program that are defined after it. All global variables are initialized at the start of the program to the value zero, unless the programmer supplies an explicit initialization.

(6) Automatic variables are introduced within function or statement blocks immediately following the opening brace '{'; the use of the key word auto in the definition is optional. Only program statements appearing within the same block are permitted to access directly an automatic variable. No *implicit* initialization of automatic variables is performed.

(7) Register variables are defined in a similar manner to automatic variables but their definition is prefixed by the key word register. They have the same scope, privacy and initialization rules as automatic variables but you cannot take the address of a register variable.

(8) Static variables are introduced in a similar manner to automatic variables but with the (optional) key word auto replaced by the key word static. They have similar scope and privacy rules. Unlike automatic variables, however, their storage and value live on after the block in which they were defined terminates. All static variables are initialized at the start of the program to zero unless the programmer supplies an explicit initialization.

(9) Global and/or static variables may only be initialized with implicit constant values. Automatic and register variables may be initialized with the value of any complex expression.

2.4 Exercises

2.1 What are C's fundamental and modifed data types?

2.2 What '%' formatters are provided by printf() and scanf() to deal with quantities of each type?

2.3 What can you say about the size and range of values of C's fundamental data types? Why might this be a problem when it comes to writing portable programs? How can these problems be reduced using the sizeof operator and the standard header files <limits.h> and <float.h>?

2.4 What is meant by two's complement binary notation and which of C's data types use this notation to represent their values?

2.5 What is the difference between a signed and an unsigned quantity and to what data types may these type modifiers be applied? Furthermore, what effect do these modifiers have on the range and size of those data types?

2.6 What is the difference between implicit and explicit constants? What are the sizes and types of the following implicit constants on your compiler?

```
'a'   0    0x27    23L    23U    23UL    45000    4000000000    0x7fff
0.0   2.3   2.6e–19   –234.45e108   19.2e12f   76.34L
```

Use the sizeof operator and printf( ) to verify your assumptions.

2.7 Write a program to display all of the printable characters in the ASCII character set.

2.8 Some characters in the ASCII character set are used to control the output device and format the display, such as carriage return, line feed and tab. Discuss various ways in which these non-displayable characters may be sent to the terminal.

2.9 Discuss what portability issues arise in the following sections of code. Why might they work using some compilers and not others? How could you overcome some of these problems in a portable manner using the header files <float.h> and <limits.h> or by defining different or modified variable types? You may assume the following variable definitions: int i; char c; float f;.

```
for( i = 0; i < 65535; i ++ )              for( i = 0L; i < 45000L; i ++ )
    ;                                          ;

for( c = 0; c < 0xff; c ++ )               for( i = 0; i < 0xffff ; i ++ )
    ;                                          ;

for( c = –100 ; c < 0; c ++ )              for( c = 0; c > –127; c –– )
    ;                                          ;

for( c = 0; c < 255; c ++ )                for( f = 1.0; f < 1.0e308; f = f * 10.0 )
    ;                                          ;
```

2.10 What is meant by the terms 'scope' and 'privacy'? Why does restricting the former also affect the latter?

2.11 What is meant by global and local variables? How are they introduced?

2.12 List the differences between an auto variable and a static variable.

2.13 What is the use of the register prefix in a variable definition and why might it improve program speed and efficiency? Why does C not allow global variables to be made register variables? How many register variables does your compiler support?

2.14 Why is it preferable for a program to use local rather global variables?

2.15 List the rules that govern the implicit and explicit initialization of global, static and automatic variables.

2.16 Rewrite the program presented in Application 1.4 to calculate the value of the exponential function e^x to make use of `doubles` rather than `floats` and thus compare the accuracy of both. Further modify the program to make use of global variables rather than automatic variables.

2.17 Although the trapezoidal rule can give a good approximation to the area under a curve when the number of sub-divisions 'N' is large, the large number of calculations that arise as a result of this can often slow the calculation, particularly if f(x) is quite complex. Simpson's method, on the other hand, offers similar accuracy with smaller 'N' by attempting to fit a parabolic curve, rather than a straight line between two points on the graph (refer to Figure 2.3) and the area is then given by the equation:

$$\text{sum}(h/3 \times [f(x_i) + 4f(x_{i+1}) + f(x_{i+2})])$$

for all *odd* values of 'i' from 0 up to and including 'N−1', provided 'N' is an even number. Using this equation, rewrite Application 2.1 to make use of this equation and hence compare the accuracy of Simpson's method with the trapezoidal rule for a given value of 'N'.

2.18 For Electrical and Electronic Engineers only. The electrical circuit shown below is that of a simple transistor amplifier biased with currents derived from the voltage source Vs. Write a program to read in the values of h_{FE} (the transistor's DC current gain), Vs (the supply Voltage) and Ic (the desired collector current). The program should then calculate the values of Rc, Re, R1 and R2, the currents flowing in, and the voltage dropped across each of the resistors VRc, VRe, VR1, VR2 in the network and the voltage Vout.

The programmer may assume the following general design information. Vbe, the voltage drop across the transistor's base–emitter junction, is constant at 0.7 volts. Re and Rc are designed, respectively, to drop one-tenth and one-half of the supply voltage Vs, and the bias current Ibias flowing through the R1, R2 network is chosen to be 10 times the base current Ib.

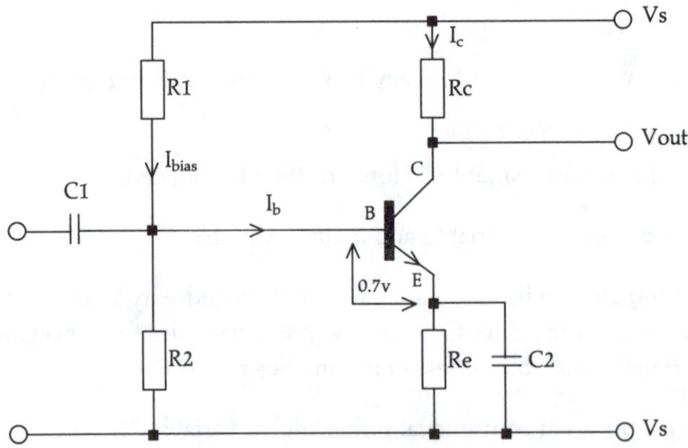

3 A Closer Look at Operators

In this chapter we take a closer look at the range of operators provided by C, some of which were discussed briefly in Chapter 1. Of particular importance to the new reader are the related subjects of operator **precedence** and **associativity**. These describe the order and manner in which each operator is evaluated by the compiler. An understanding of these concepts is essential if the programmer expects the compiler to interpret an expression in the manner intended.

We also take a closer look at what happens when data – that is, variables and constants – of various mixed types appear within the same expression. The C standard defines a set of rules describing how each numerical type (`int`, `float` and so on) may or may not be converted to another type prior to evaluating part or all of an expression, an action which can under some circumstances lead to undesirable side effects if care is not observed.

3.1 The arithmetic operators, assignment and casting

Virtually all of C's operators are classed as either **unary** or **binary** in operation. This simply means that they are required to operate with one or two operands, respectively. C's five basic arithmetic operators, all of which are binary, are summarized in Table 3.1, along with a collection of example statements demonstrating their use. With the exception of the '%' operator, these were all discussed briefly in Chapter 1.

The addition '+', subtraction '–' and multiplication '*' operators require little in the way of explanation since their mathematical interpretation is well known. However, the use of the division '/' and modulus operators '%' requires further explanation, because there are a number of subtle traps into which the novice programmer can fall, as well as a number of interesting applications for the modulus operator.

Table 3.1 C's basic binary arithmetic operators.

Operator	*Interpretation*	*Example C statement*
+	Addition	c = a + b ;
–	Subtraction	c = a – b ;
*	Multiplication	c = a * b ;
/	Division	c = a / b ;
%	Modulus	c = a % b ;

3.1.1 *A closer look at the division and modulus operators: '/' and '%'*

Consider for a moment the division of two real numbers, as shown below:

```
9.0 / 2.5
```

Here, because both operands are real quantities (they are in fact implicit double precision constants, as we saw in the last chapter), the expression will be evaluated using **double precision** arithmetic division to yield the double precision result 3.6. However, had the operands been integers, as shown below:

```
11 / 4
```

then the expression would have been evaluated using an integer form of division to produce the integer result 2 (rather than 2.75, demonstrating that a C compiler truncates the result of an integer division, rather than rounding it up or down). It follows from this that the expression 1/2 produces zero, not 0.5, while division by 0 in any form may lead to unpredictable program behaviour.

The modulus operator '%' (pronounced 'mod') divides its first operand by its second (both of which must be integral) in much the same way as the division operator, but differs in respect of the result it yields, which is defined as the integer **remainder** of the division. For example, the expression:

```
9 % 4
```

yields the value 1 – in other words, 9 divided by 4 is 2 **remainder** 1. The modulus operator may be found useful in situations such as determining whether a number is odd or even or whether a certain year is a leap year. For example, the expression 'years % 4' yields the result 0 if years divides exactly by 4. Another use lies in generating random numbers in the range 0 to 'n–1' using the statement:

```
random_number = rand() % n ;
```

where rand() is a standard library function for generating random numbers.

3.1.2 *A discussion of floating point inaccuracies*

A potential problem when performing any type of floating point calculation relates to accuracy. Since any real quantity is represented by a finite number of bits, it may not be possible to represent a given quantity *exactly*. For example, you might expect the value of the expression:

```
1.0 / 3.0 + 1.0 / 3.0 + 1.0 / 3.0
```

to equal exactly 1.0, but this may not be the case on all systems and the result may, due to rounding errors, be slightly different, a problem that is not unique to C. Furthermore, there is always the possibility of a floating point calculation producing an **overflow** or **underflow**. An overflow occurs when two large numbers are multiplied together, and the result cannot be represented within a given data type. For example, the following expression:

```
2.2e307 * 4.3e34
```

would probably yield a result that could not be represented by a double (on most systems at least), and would be represented as infinity, a fact that can be verified using printf(), which would display the quantity as '+INF'. Consequently, if such a value were used subsequently in further calculations, then they too could give rise to an overflow.

Underflows occur when an expression gives rise to a result that is so small it cannot be represented within a given data type and consequently may be rounded down to zero. For example, the following expression would on many machines give rise to the answer zero:

```
2.2e-307 * 4.3e-34
```

Cancellation errors occur when a relatively small number is added to or subtracted from a relatively large number, as demonstrated below, where the value '2.0' is small in comparison to '4.3e53'. The effect of the operation may be lost due to the limited precision of a floating point quantity:

```
4.3e53 + 2.0
```

3.1.3 *C's unary arithmetic operators: '+' and '–'*

C provides two useful unary operators that serve to change the sign of a variable. These are summarized in Table 3.2, along with some example statements to demonstrate their use.

The unary minus operator (–), preceding an expression, changes the sign of that expression and the effect is similar to multiplying the expression by (–1).

Table 3.2 C's basic unary arithmetic operators.

Operator symbol	*Interpretation*	*Example*	*Equivalent effect*
–	Unary minus	c = –c ;	c = ((–1) * c)
+	Unary plus	c = +c ;	c = ((+1) * c)

The unary plus operator '+' on the other hand serves no obvious purpose, other than providing symmetry for the unary minus operator. The effect is similar to multiplying an expression by (+1).

3.1.4 *Precedence and associativity of C's arithmetic operators*

In any expression involving more than one operator, it is important to be clear about the order in which each operator is evaluated by the compiler. For example, consider the simple expression below:

```
3.0 + 7.0 / 2.0
```

There are in principle two ways in which this expression could be evaluated. Firstly, we could evaluate the sub-expression (3.0 + 7.0) to yield the intermediate result 10.0 before dividing this by 2.0, to produce the final result 5.0. Alternatively, we could evaluate the expression (7.0/2.0) first and then add this to 3.0 to produce the different result 6.5.

To avoid such confusion, all of C's operators are given a **precedence** or priority when more than one of them occur within a complex expression. The higher an operator's precedence, the earlier that operator will be evaluated in an expression. Of the operators discussed so far in this chapter, the unary '+' and '–' operators have equal and highest precedence and as such will be evaluated first.

Multiplication '*', division '/' and modulus '%' all have equal precedence below unary '–' and '+', followed lastly by addition and subtraction. Using this knowledge, we can now predict how the compiler will evaluate the following expression:

```
4.2 + 11.35 / –2.1
```

(1) Evaluate the unary operator '–' to change the sign of 2.1 to (–2.1);

(2) Perform the division of 11.35 / –2.1 to produce the intermediate result –5.404 76;

(3) Add 4.2 to –5.404 76 to produce the final result of –1.204 76.

Of course, programmers can always force their own order of evaluation through the use of parentheses, which have the highest precedence of all and are always evaluated first in an expression. For example, the previous expression is equivalent to, and thus could be replaced by, the expression:

```
4.2 + (11.35 / (–2.1))
```

However, had we wished to perform the addition *prior* to the division, we could have parenthesized the expression in the manner shown below:

```
(4.2 + 11.35) / –2.1
```

If more than one operator with the *same* precedence appears in an expression, the compiler uses built in rules of **associativity** to determine the order in which they will be evaluated. The binary operators, for example, are evaluated in a 'left to right' manner. That is to say, if two operators with equal precedence, such as '*' and '/', appear in the same expression then the compiler evaluates them by traversing the expression from left to right, dealing with each operator as it is encountered. Thus the expression:

```
8.0 / 3.0 / 2.0 * 1.2
```

yields the result 1.6 since it is evaluated as if it had been written as:

```
(((8.0 / 3.0) / 2.0) * 1.2)
```

However, the unary operators '–' and '+' are evaluated from right to left. Thus in the expression below the compiler evaluates the unary '+' operator first, followed by the unary '–' followed lastly by the '*':

```
b * –+a
```

A summary of these operators, their precedence and their associativity rules may be found in Table 3.3 (see also Table 3.13). The higher in the table an

Table 3.3 Precedence and associativity of C's arithmetic operators.

Operators	*Type*	*Order of evaluation*
+ –	Unary	Right to left
* / %	Binary	Left to right
+ –	Binary	Left to right

Table 3.4 Example expressions.

Expression	*Equivalent expression fully parenthesized*
a – b + c	((a – b) + c)
a * b + c	((a * b) + c)
a + b * c – d	((a + (b * c)) – d)
a + b * c / d * e	(a + (((b * c) / d) * e))
–a – –b * –c	((–a) – ((–b) * (–c)))

operator appears, the higher its precedence. Operators with the same precedence are shown on the same level.

Table 3.4 contains some example expressions and the equivalent way in which they could be expressed using parentheses.

3.1.5 *Mixed expression types: Promotion and implicit casting*

In contrast to other more tightly checked languages, C permits operands of different type to be used within the same expression. Where necessary, the compiler performs a number of automatic conversions, variously described as **promotions**, **coercions** or **implicit casts**, in an attempt to ensure that all operands within a given expression are of the same type before evaluating them. Such conversions attempt, wherever possible, to preserve the value, accuracy and precision of the original quantity in its new form, but this is not always possible and some precision may be lost, as we shall see.

Promotion is a term variously used to describe the process of converting a smaller sized quantity (smaller in the sense that it requires fewer bytes of storage to represent it) into a larger quantity of a similar type; for example, promoting smaller integral quantities such as chars or shorts into ints, or promoting smaller real quantities such as floats and doubles into long doubles.

An implicit cast is an operation generally used to describe the process of converting a quantity into a different form, such as converting an integral quantity to its equivalent representation in real form or vice versa. As an example, consider the following variable definitions:

```
int     a = 23 ;
char    b = 19 ;
short   c = 45 ;
float   jim = 3.1415927 ;
```

In evaluating the expression below, the compiler applies the following implicit casts and promotions to each variable and sub-expression:

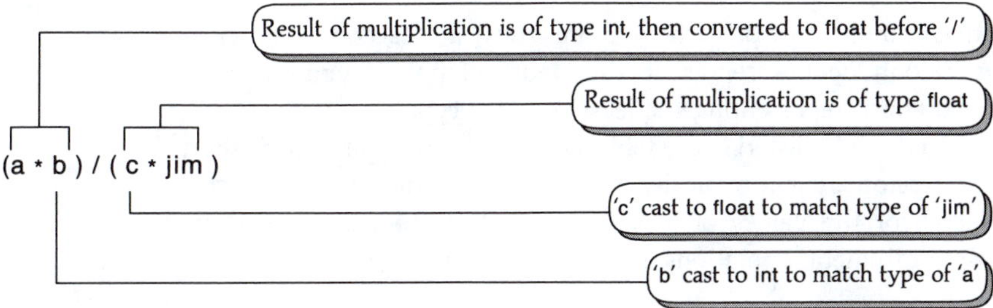

(1) The value of 'b' (a char) is promoted to an int prior to its multiplication by 'a' (an int); the result is also an int, with value 437;

(2) The value of 'c' (a short) is implicitly cast to a float before being multiplied by 'jim' (a float); the result is also a float, with value 141.372;

(3) The int result of the expression 'a * b' is then implicitly cast to a float prior to division by the result of the expression 'c * jim' (a float); thus the resultant type of the whole expression is a float and has the value 3.091 14.

These rules of promotion and implicit casting are summarized in Table 3.5; they are for the most part fairly straightforward, with the compiler ensuring that all operands in an expression are converted to the type of the more complex operand before the expression is evaluated, in an attempt to limit any loss of accuracy or precision. The < symbol in Table 3.5 means smaller or less complex type.

Note that such conversions are only performed at the last possible moment when evaluating the expression, which can sometimes cause some unexpected answers. For example, the expression:

```
a / c * jim
```

produces the answer 0 and not 1.6057 since the expression 'a / c' is evaluated using integer arithmetic to yield the integer result 0, which is only then implicitly cast to the floating point value 0.0 prior to multiplication by 'jim'.

Table 3.5 Rules of implicit casting for mixed arithmetic expressions.

Operand 1	*Operand 2*	*Operand 2 converted to*	*Result of expression*
long double	< long double	long double	long double
double	< double	double	double
float	< float	float	float
unsigned long int	< unsigned long int	unsigned long int	unsigned long int
long int	unsigned int	(See text)	(See text)
long int	< long int	long int	long int
unsigned int	< int	unsigned int	unsigned int
int	< int	int	int

The relative complexities of each type are given in descending order in Table 3.5; thus a long double represents the most complex type, with int (including char and short) representing the least complex types.

In addition to the rules listed in the table, all variables of type char or short that arise in an expression are automatically promoted to a (signed) int, if an int is able to represent all of the values of a char or short, or to an unsigned int otherwise. Thus no arithmetic operations are performed with a precision shorter than an int.

Note that if one operand is a long int and the other is an unsigned int, then the unsigned int will be converted to a long int only if a long int is able to represent all values of an unsigned int; that is, if the long int is a bigger quantity than an unsigned int, as may well be the case on an 8/16 bit system and the result is a long int. If, however, a long int is not able to represent all the values of an unsigned int (as might be the case on a 32 bit system), then *both* are cast to an unsigned long int and the result is an unsigned long int.

As an example, consider a float appearing in the same expression as a long int quantity. Given the above rules, the long int will be implicitly cast to a float, possibly resulting in a loss of precision. For example, the long int value 2 147 483 648L might only be precise to seven digits if converted to a float, that is, 2.147 483 e09.

3.1.6 *The assignment operator: '='*

The assignment operator '=' is used to assign the result of an expression to a variable. The general format for such an assignment is shown below:

Value of *expression* assigned to *variable*

```
variable = expression ;
```

Here, the result of the expression appearing to the right of the '=' operator is assigned to the variable appearing to the left. Therefore, given the following statement:

```
c = a + b ;
```

the result of the expression 'a + b' is assigned to the variable 'c'. The assignment operator '=' has one of the lowest orders of precedence and is generally evaluated last in an expression.

It is worth noting that the '=' operator also yields the result of its own assignment, a fact that may be found useful as an operand in further expressions. For example, consider the statement below:

```
a = (b = 3 + 4) ;
```

Here, because addition takes precedence over assignment, the expression '3 + 4' is evaluated first and consequently '7' is assigned to 'b', and since the '=' operator yields the result of its own assignment – that is, the value assigned to 'b' – this too becomes the value assigned to 'a'. Now, because the assignment operator is evaluated in a right to left manner, the parentheses are not really necessary and the statement could be reduced to:

```
a = b = 3 + 4 ;
```

This form of multiple initialization is often seen when several variables are to be initialized with the same value. For example:

Success of this multiple assignment depends on right–left associativity of '='

```
a = b = c = d = 0 ;
```

As another example, consider the following statement:

Result of this expression is the value assigned to 'c'

```
while((c = getchar()) != EOF)
  statement ;
```

Here, the function getchar() is called and the character it returns is assigned to the variable 'c'. The result of this expression is the value of the operand to the left of the '=' – that is, the value of 'c' – which after comparison with the symbolic constant EOF is used to control the while loop. In other words, while the value of the character read and assigned to 'c' is not equal to EOF, repeat the loop.

Note how an extra pair of parentheses was required around the expression (c = getchar()). This is because the '!=' operator has a higher precedence than '=' (see Table 3.13) and without them, the whole expression would have been interpreted as if it had been written as while(c = (getchar() != NULL)), which has the effect of comparing the character read by getchar() with NULL and yielding the result 0 or 1 depending upon the outcome of the test. This 0 or 1 is then assigned to 'c', the result of which may or may not terminate the loop (see Section 4.2.3).

Note also that assignment is somewhat more sophisticated an operation than it might at first appear. For example, given the statement below, where 'i' has been defined as an int:

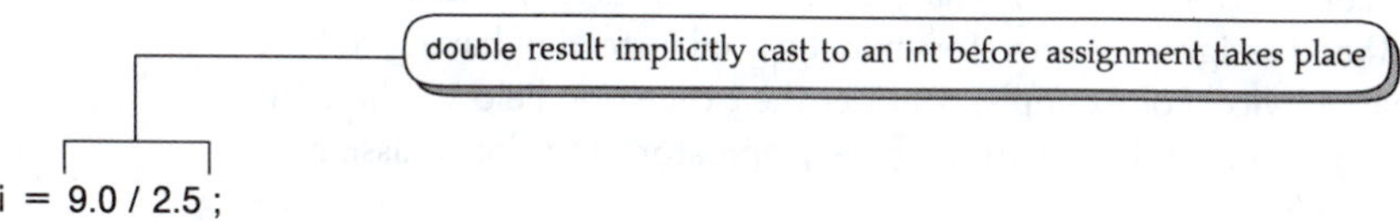
double result implicitly cast to an int before assignment takes place
i = 9.0 / 2.5 ;

the expression '9.0 / 2.5' is evaluated by the rules in Table 3.5 to yield the double precision result '3.6'. However, this value cannot be directly assigned to 'i' since 'i' is an int. To resolve this problem, the compiler implicitly casts the type of any expression, in this case a double, to match the type of the variable to which it is assigned. Thus the compiler ensures that the floating point result 3.6 is implicitly cast to an int prior to its assignment to 'i'. This could – and does in this instance – lead to the result being truncated or even becoming undefined if 'i' cannot represent part or all of the result. You can verify this for yourself by displaying the value of 'i', which you will see to be 3, not 3.6.

One potential pitfall to watch out for is identified below, where both 'a' (a float) and 'b' (an int) are initialized with the same statement:

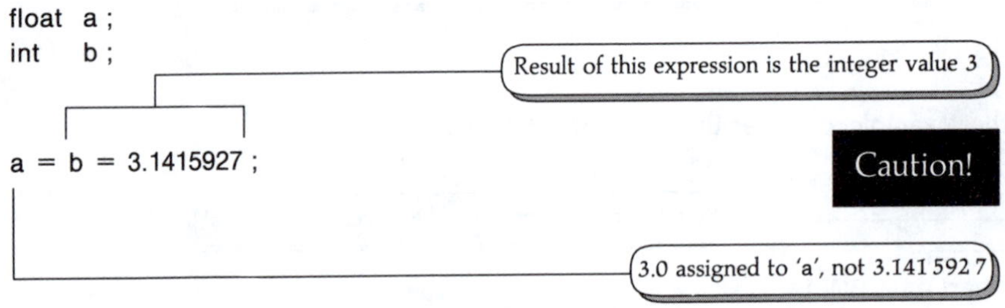

float a ;
int b ;
Result of this expression is the integer value 3
a = b = 3.1415927 ;
Caution!
3.0 assigned to 'a', not 3.141 592 7

Here, it is the value 3.0 which is assigned to 'a' and not the value 3.141 592 7 as you might have expected. This is due to the fact that the expression 'b = 3.141 592 7' yields the integer value 3 (that is, the value of 3.141 592 7 cast to an int), which in turn is assigned to 'a' (after casting back to a float) as the floating point value value 3.0. To prevent this sort of problem arising during the multiple initialization of variables, the most complex variables should be initialized first, for example:

```
b = a = 3.1415927 ;
```

3.1.7 *C's shorthand assignment operators*

When a variable name appears both to the left and right of the assignment operator and in conjunction with any binary operator such as '+', '*' and so on, a number of shorthand assignment operators may be used instead of having to type the variable's name twice. For example, consider the expression below, where the variable 'c' is used in conjunction with the binary operator '+' prior to assigning the result back to 'c':

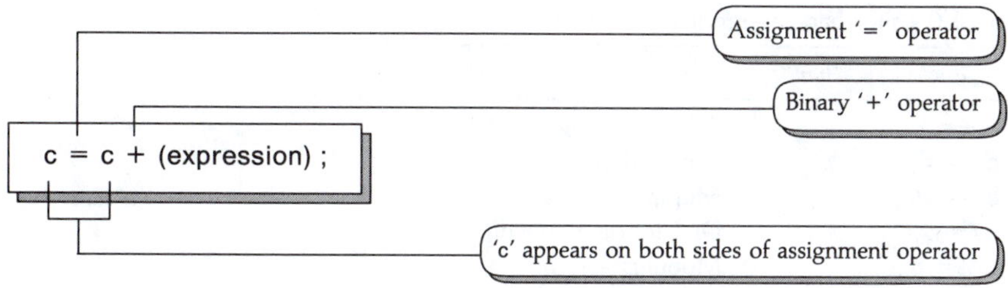

Using a shorthand notation, the above expression could have been reduced to:

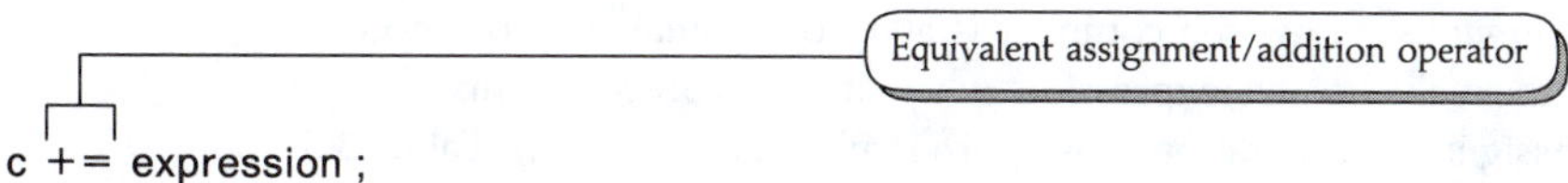

The rule for constructing the new shorthand form of the assignment operator is simple. Remove the common variable name that appears to the right of the '=' operator in the longhand form, and then reposition the binary operator (in this case '+') immediately prior to the '='. The illustrations below demonstrate the principle, where the statement:

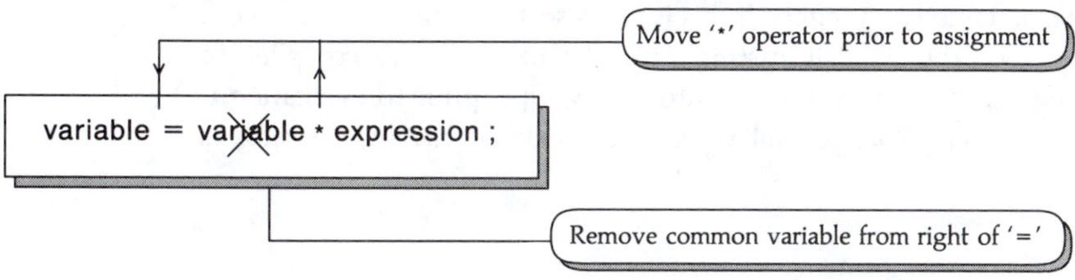

becomes

```
variable *= expression ;
```

The most obvious benefit to the programmer of using this shorthand form is a reduction in the amount of typing involved, particularly when the name of the variable is long. This reduces the chances of misspelling the variable's name, although such an error would obviously be detected at compile time. Table 3.6 summarizes some of the shorthand assignment operators. (A full list can be found in Table 3.13.)

Table 3.6 Some of C's shorthand assignment operators.

Longhand	*Equivalent shorthand*	*Operation*
c = c + 1 ;	c += 1 ;	Addition/assignment
c = c − x ;	c −= x ;	Subtraction/assignment
c = c * 3.0 ;	c *= 3.0 ;	Multiplication/assignment
c = c / a ;	c /= a ;	Division/assignment
c = c % b ;	c %= b ;	Modulus/assignment

3.1.8 *The explicit casting operator:* (type)

We have seen previously how the compiler is able to automatically promote or implicitly cast the value of an expression when it is involved in mixed type arithmetic or assignment operations, using the rules laid down in Table 3.5. We also noted that the compiler only applies such promotions and casts at the last possible moment when evaluating an expression, which can sometimes lead to undesirable side effects. You will recall that the expression 'a / c * jim' from Section 3.1.5 produced the result 0.0 and not 1.6057 as you might have expected.

To overcome this problem, either 'a' or 'c' could have been defined as a double, forcing the division to be performed using real arithmetic, but this may not always be appropriate and there may be good reasons why these variables may have to be maintained as integers. If this is the case, the programmer may call upon the services of the explicit casting operator to force the compiler to explicitly cast the value of an expression into a new type, prior to evaluating it within other expressions. The general form of the explicit casting operator is shown below:

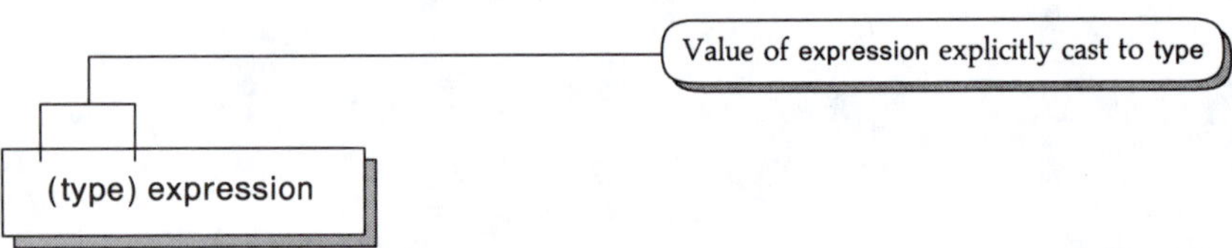

where type is any data type recognized by the compiler (which includes any that the program may have defined for itself; see Chapter 12) such as char, float, double and so on. The explicit cast operator has one of the highest precedence levels in C, certainly higher than any of the arithmetic operators (see Table 3.13), and associates from right to left. Thus we could rewrite the example mixed data type expression from Section 3.1.5 in the form shown below, forcing the division of 'a' by 'c' to be performed using double precision arithmetic:

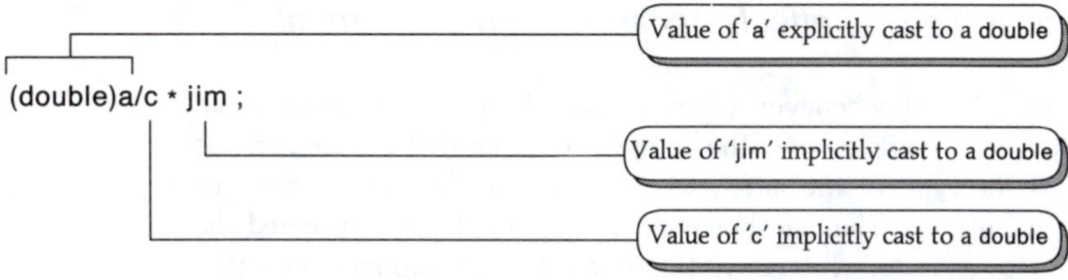
Value of 'a' explicitly cast to a double
(double)a/c * jim ;
Value of 'jim' implicitly cast to a double
Value of 'c' implicitly cast to a double

Here, the value of 'a' is explicitly cast to a double which, by the rules of mixed arithmetic operands presented in Table 3.5, forces the compiler to implicitly cast both 'c' and eventually 'jim' to doubles also. As an alternative, we could have written the statement in the form shown below, where 'c' is explicitly cast to a double, forcing the compiler to implicitly cast 'a' and 'jim' to a double:

Value of 'c' explicitly cast to a double

```
a/(double)c * jim ;
```

Note, however, that the form of the expression below achieves nothing, since 'a' and 'c' are still divided as integers before the integer result 0 is explicitly cast to the double precision value 0.0 (an operation that would have been performed implicitly without the need for the explicit cast):

Value of 'a/c' explicitly cast to a double

```
(double)( a/c ) * jim ;
```

Using the explicit casting operator thoughtfully within a program allows the programmer to force their own conversions of data and intermediate results, thus removing any element of doubt as to the type of an expression or operand and reducing the likelihood of rounding and truncation errors arising.

Important note: When any type of implicit or explicit cast is applied to a variable, constant or expression, the compiler only casts a *copy* of that data, thus you cannot use the cast operator to change the representation of a variable in memory. For example, the statement:

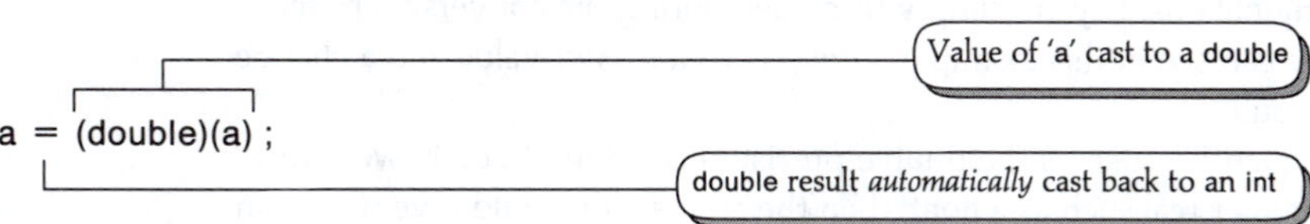
Value of 'a' cast to a double
a = (double)(a) ;
double result *automatically* cast back to an int

where 'a' is an int, although syntactically correct, is meaningless, since a copy of 'a' is made prior to being cast to a double, but as the result is then assigned back to 'a' the effects of this explicit cast are negated by the assignment operator, which implicitly casts the result back to an int.

3.1.9 *The possible side effects of casting and assignment*

We saw in Table 3.5 that whenever a simpler data type was involved in an expression with a more complex one, the compiler ensured that the former was implicitly cast to the type of the latter, to minimize any loss of accuracy or precision in the calculation. Thus far, however, we have not yet considered the possible side effects associated with converting one data type into another, either explicitly through the use of the cast operator or implicitly during, for example, assignment. That is to say, what are the side effects of assigning a double to an int or an int to a float? Table 3.7 summarizes these side effects for each of the four possible conversions.

Table 3.7 Possible side effects of explicit cast or assignment operators.

Initial type	*Cast/assigned to*	*Operation/possible side effect*
Integral type	Simpler integral type	Higher order bits are discarded with possible loss of value and change of sign
Real type	Simpler real type	Value rounded or truncated, leading to possible overflow and undefined result
Real type	Any integral type	Implementation dependent, possible loss of value/precision
Integral type	Any real type	Implementation dependent, possible loss of precision

Let us consider some examples. Firstly, whenever any simpler data type is cast/assigned to a more complex one, such as casting/assigning a char to a long int, or a float to a long double, there should be no loss of accuracy or precision in the result, since the more complex type should always be able to represent all of the values of the simpler one with at least the same precision (see Tables 2.10 and 2.11).

However, if a signed integral quantity such as the 16 bit binary value [10010111 00101000] were cast/assigned to, say, a simpler integral quantity such as an 8 bit signed char, the result (assuming a two's complement representation of integral values) is simply binary [00101000] because the higher order bits (bits 8–15) of the original quantity are simply discarded during the conversion process. This may, as we can see in this example, give rise to a loss of value and a change of sign in the result.

If a real quantity such as the double precision constant 1.2e200 were cast/assigned to a simpler real such as a float, then the conversion could give rise to an overflow, if the float were not able to represent the value of the original double. Similarly, assigning the double constant 1.2456477567e23 to a float would preserve the value (since a float should be able to represent values in the range $1.0e \pm 38$), but not the precision, and thus the result might be rounded to 1.24565e23.

If a real quantity such as the double precision constant 12 354 645.645 64 is cast/assigned to an integral quantity such a long int, the fractional part is simply discarded, leading in this instance to the value 12354645L. However, if the original value was too large to be represented by the integral quantity, such as 2.0e300, then the result will be undefined.

If an integral quantity is cast/assigned to a real quantity, the original value should be retained, but it may give rise to a loss of precision. For example, casting/assigning the long int constant 1234567890L to a float might result in the value being rounded to 1.23457e9.

3.1.10 *Sign extension with two's complement integer values*

Sign extension is an operation that is performed automatically when promoting, assigning or comparing two different sized signed integral values. For example, suppose that a signed char with the value −128 were assigned to a full int. The char would be represented in two's complement binary form as shown below:

Decimal value	Signed 8 bit value	Type
−128	10000000	Signed 8 bit two's complement char

A full integer, on the other hand, may be 16 or 32 bits in size and thus the compiler cannot simply copy the value of the lower 8 bits of the char to the integer (remembering to clear the upper 8 or 24 bits to zero) since the value of the int would alter, becoming +128, as shown below (see Tables 2.8 and 2.9):

Decimal value	Signed 16 bit value	Type
+128	00000000 10000000	Signed 16 bit two's complement int

Instead, the compiler uses the technique of sign extension to alter the representation of the signed char without altering its value. Sign extension involves copying the most significant or 'sign' bit (MSB) of the smaller quantity into the higher order bits of the larger quantity. This operation is illustrated below, where a signed 8 bit char is promoted to a 16 bit int:

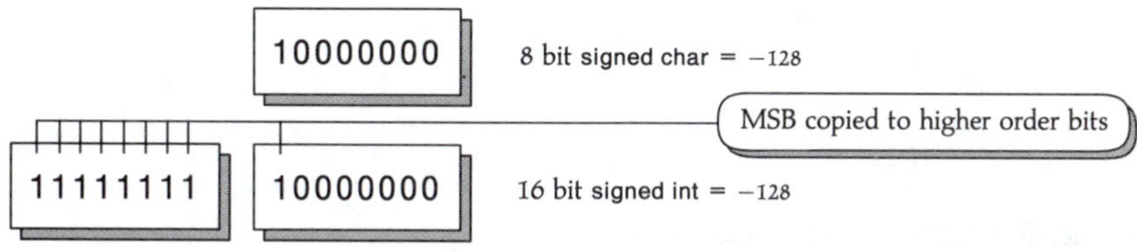

If the quantity is unsigned, then sign extension is not necessary and the higher order bits of the integer variable are simply cleared to zero, as illustrated below:

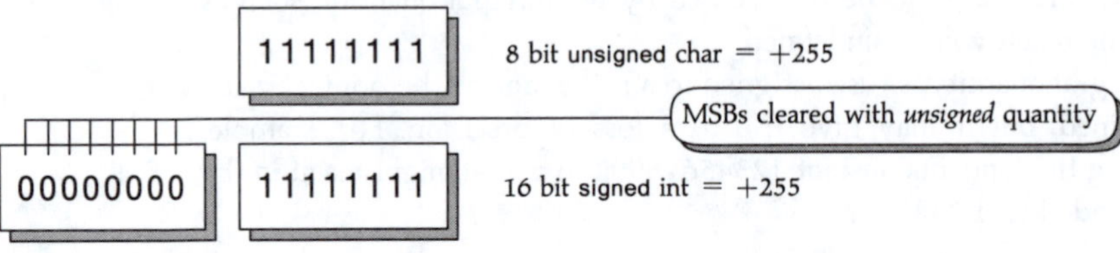

Application 3.1

A projectile fired at an angle θ to the horizontal and velocity V metres per second impacts with a slope inclined at angle φ to the horizontal, as shown in Figure 3.1. Determine the distance AB up the slope that the projectile travels before impact. It can be shown that the distance AB travelled is given by the following equation, where g represents the earth's gravitational constant, equal to 9.81 ms^{-1}:

$$AB = \frac{2V^2 Cos^2\theta(\tan\theta - \tan\phi)}{(g\cos\phi)}$$

The program in Application 3.1a shows a possible implementation of this problem but, because it uses simple integer constants and floats rather than doubles, the compiler is forced to implicitly cast the values of many of the constants, variables and results of expressions appearing in the program into another form prior to their evaluation. These are indicated in the program itself.

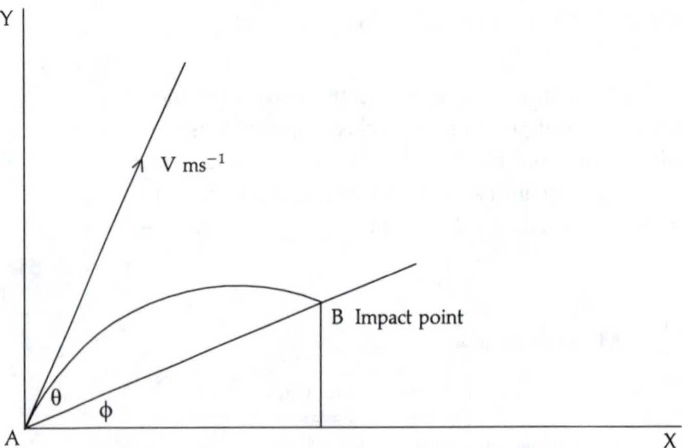

Figure 3.1 A projectile impacting on an inclined plane.

Application 3.1a A poor implementation of the projectile problem.

```
#include   <stdio.h>
#include   <math.h>

int main( void )
{
   float  theta, phi;             /* angle of projectile and place respectively */
   float  v;                      /* velocity of projectile */
   float  distance ;              /* distance AB up slope projectile travels */

   printf("Enter angles theta and phi: ") ;
   scanf("%g %g", &theta, &phi) ;

   printf("Enter Velocity of Projectile V: ") ;
   scanf("%g", &v) ;

   phi = 3.1415927/180 * phi ;        /* convert phi to radians */
   theta = 3.1415927/180 * theta ;    /* convert theta to radians */

   distance = 2 * v * v * cos(theta) * cos(theta) * (tan(theta) - tan(phi))/(9.81 * cos(phi)) ;

   printf("Distance AB = %g\n", distance) ;
   return 0 ;
}
```


Application 3.1b, on the other hand, makes much more appropriate use of doubles rather than floats, and double precision rather than integer constants to make a more efficient and compact program. (Of course the program could be further improved upon in other areas, such as evaluating 3.141 592 7/180.0 and cos(theta) once in the program rather than twice.)

Application 3.1b A better implementation of Application 3.1a.

```
#include   <stdio.h>
#include   <math.h>

int main( void )
{
   double  theta, phi;          /* angle of projectile and place respectively */
   double  v;                   /* velocity of projectile */
   double  distance ;           /* distance AB up slope projectile travels */

   printf("Enter angles theta and phi: ") ;
   scanf("%lg %lg", &theta, &phi) ;

   printf("Enter Velocity of Projectile V: ") ;
   scanf("%lg", &v) ;

   phi = 3.1415927/180.0 * phi ;        /* convert phi to radians */
   theta = 3.1415927/180.0 * theta ;    /* convert theta to radians */

   distance = 2.0 * v * v * cos(theta) * cos(theta) *
              (tan(theta) - tan(phi))/(9.81 * cos(phi)) ;

   printf("Distance AB = %g\n", distance) ;
   return 0 ;
}
```

The improvements proposed in this version of the program also reduce the likelihood of any rounding and/or truncation errors when doubles are assigned to floats. These, among others, are the main reasons why programmers generally prefer to use doubles rather than floats in their programs.

3.1.11 *A closer look at the '++' and '--' operators*

We met the increment and decrement operators '++' and '--' in Chapter 1 and noted how they were particularly effective when used in conjunction with simple loops. What may not have been apparent then is that both operators may be used in a **prefix** or **postfix** notation, where they are placed, respectively, prior or subsequent to the variable's name. The general formats for the increment operator '++' are given below:

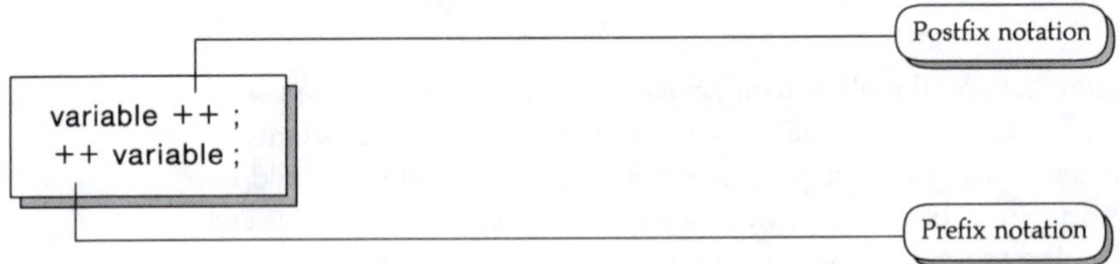

Those for the decrement operator '--' are:

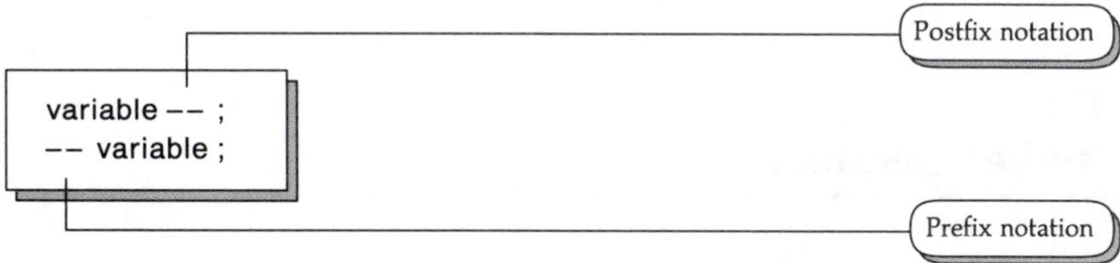

Normally, it makes very little difference whether prefix or postfix notation is used but in some instances it can affect the result of a subsequent expression and particularly assignment. For example, consider the statement shown below:

'a' assigned the value of 'b' *before* 'b' is incremented

```
a = b ++ ;
```

Because the postfix form of the '++' operator was used, the result of the expression 'b++' is the value of 'b' *before* 'b' was incremented. Therefore, had the value of 'b' initially been 10, then 'a' would have been assigned the value 10 before 'b' was incremented to 11. However, had the statement been written using prefix notation, as shown below:

'a' assigned the value of 'b' *after* 'b' is incremented

```
a = ++ b ;
```

then 'b' would have been incremented to 11 before its value was assigned to 'a', thus 'a' is also given the value 11. A word of caution here. Never apply these operators to the same variable more than once within the same expression. For example, the statement:

```
a = b++ / b++ ;
```

Caution!

may not necessarily achieve the same result as the combined effect of the statements:

```
a = b++ ;
a = a / b ++ ;
```

because a clever optimizing compiler may **cache** or **buffer** the original value of 'b' in the first example such that, although 'b' is still incremented twice, 'a' is set to the value of 'b / b'. In the second example, the compiler is forced to use the incremented value of 'b' brought about by the statement 'a = b++' when evaluating the expression 'a = a/b++', thus 'a' is set to the equivalent of 'a/(b + 1)'.

3.2 C's bitwise operators

In addition to the arithmetic operators described previously, C also provides a number of operators for performing bit manipulation. These operators evolved early on in the development of the C language to facilitate the manipulation of individual bits within variables.

Such operations are frequently employed by systems or computer engineers to test and set individual bits, perhaps within the registers of complex input/output chips such as serial and parallel communications ports or analog to digital (ADC) and digital to analog converters (DAC). Examples of this can be found in Chapter 8.

Bitwise operators may also be found in error detection and correction algorithms used in communications. Table 3.8 lists these operators. With the exception of the bitwise one's complement operator '~', all of the operators are binary, requiring two operands.

Table 3.8 C's bitwise operators.

Operator symbol	*Interpretation*	*Example statement*
&	Bitwise AND	c = c & 23 ;
|	Bitwise OR	c = b | 45 ;
^	Bitwise EXCLUSIVE OR	c = 19 ^ joe ;
<<	Bitwise shift left	c = c << 2 ;
>>	Bitwise shift right	c = a >> b ;
~	Bitwise one's complement	x = ~x ;

These operators may only be applied to integral type quantities. The normal integral promotions occur prior to evaluating the expression, that is, char and short type operands are promoted to int, and if one operand is a long int, then with the exception of the operators '<<' and '>>' the other operand is promoted to a long int. Each operator yields the type of its own promoted operands except '<<' and '>>' which yield the type of their promoted left operand.

3.2.1 *The bitwise AND operator: '&'*

The '&' operator performs the bitwise AND of its two operands. Each bit of operand 1 is ANDed with its corresponding bit in operand 2 (often referred to as a mask). The result only contains a 1 for those bit positions where there was a corresponding 1 in *both* operands, otherwise that bit is set to 0. Therefore, given the following statement:

```
c = 0x49e5 & 0x53b6 ;
```

The hexadecimal value 0x41a4 is assigned to 'c', an operation which is illustrated below:

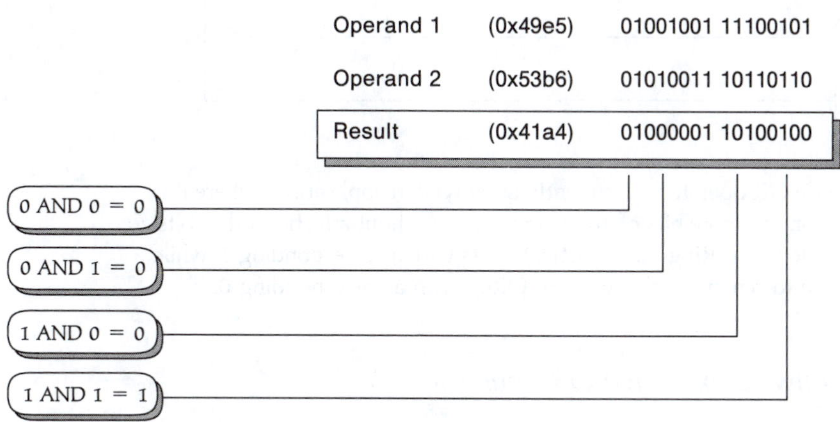

The result thus contains a 1 in bit positions 2, 5, 7, 8 and 14. The bitwise '&' operator is often found in applications where it is necessary to **clear** one or more bits of an operand to 0, without affecting other bits. This can be achieved by ANDing those particular bits with a 0, while those bits that are to remain unchanged could be ANDed with a corresponding 1.

3.2.2 *The bitwise OR operator: '|'*

The '|' operator performs the bitwise OR of its two operands. Each bit of operand 1 is ORed with its corresponding bit in operand 2. The result only contains a 1 in those bit positions where either one OR other OR both of the corresponding bits in each operand contained a 1. In other words, the result contains a 0 only if the corresponding bits in each operand are both 0. Therefore, given the following statement:

```
c = 0x49e5 | 0x53b6 ;
```

the hexadecimal result 0x5bf7 is assigned to 'c', an operation which is illustrated below:

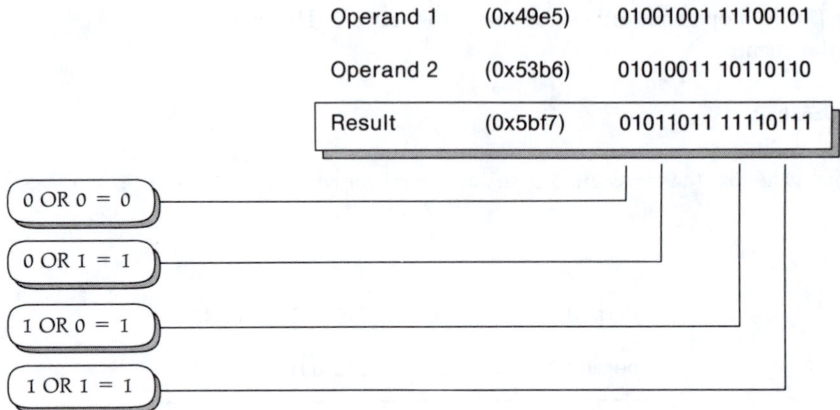

The bitwise OR operator is frequently employed in applications where it is necessary to **set** one or more bits of an operand to 1, without affecting other bits. This can be achieved by ORing those particular bits with a corresponding 1, while those bits that are to remain unchanged are ORed with a corresponding 0.

3.2.3 *The bitwise exclusive OR operator: '^'*

The '^' operator performs the bitwise exclusive OR (EXOR) of its two operands. Each bit of operand 1 is EXORed with its corresponding bit in operand 2. The result only contains a 1 for those bit positions where corresponding bits in both operands are different, and a 0 where they are the same. Therefore, the statement:

```
c = 0x49e5 ^ 0x53b6 ;
```

assigns the result 0x1a53 to 'c', an operation that is illustrated below:

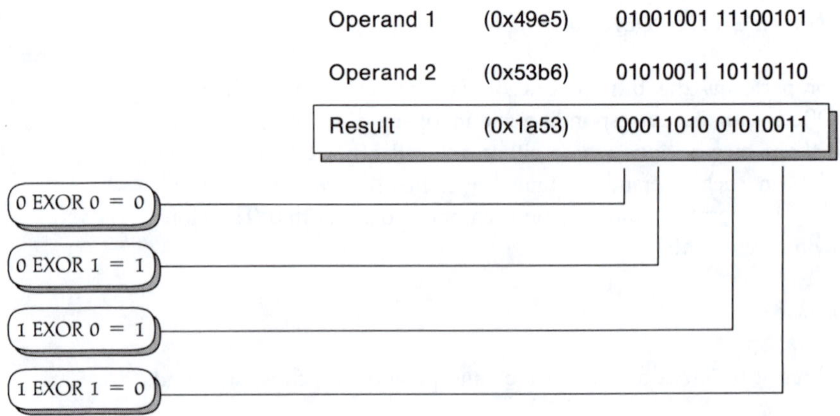

The bitwise EXOR operator '^' is frequently employed in applications where it is necessary to change or **invert** the value of one or more bits in an operand without affecting other bits. For example, EXORing a bit position with 0 leaves the value of that bit unchanged, while EXORing it with 1 inverts it. This technique is often used in graphics applications while moving a cursor over a screen to change and restore the colour of the screen under the cursor.

3.2.4 *The shift left operator: '<< '*

The result of the expression `operand <<n` is a *copy* of the operand with all bits shifted *n* places to the left. The least significant bit (LSB) is always filled with a 0, while the most significant bit (MSB) is lost. Thus, the statements:

```
c = c << 2;
x = x << a;
```

shift all bits in the variable 'c' two places to the left, and shift all bits in 'x' left by the number of bits specified by the variable 'a'. Figure 3.2 illustrates an operation that shifts the value of the 8 bit `char` with the hexadecimal value `0xA5` two places to the left.

The shift left operator is sometimes employed as an alternative to multiplying an integer value by 2. Table 3.9 shows what happens when a 16 bit integer with value 1 is shifted left a number of places. As you can see, with each shift to the left the integer value is doubled.

Other applications include generating integer quantities with a particular bit set to 1. The result is frequently employed as a mask, which can later be used

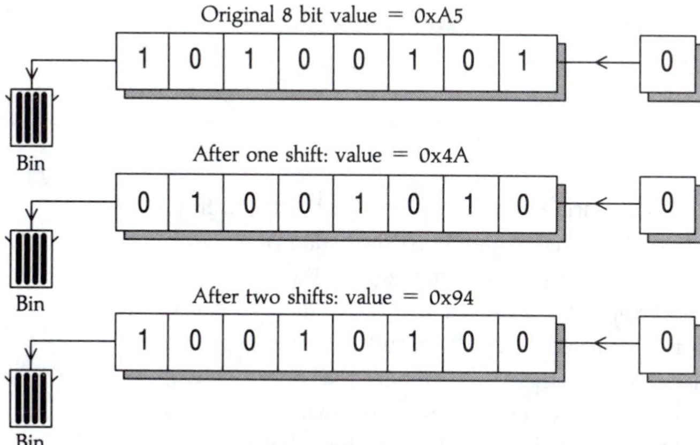

Figure 3.2 Shifting left an operand.

Table 3.9 Doubling an integer with a shift left operation.

Value	*Shifted left by*	*Binary value*	*New value*
1	–	00000000 00000001	1
1	1 place	00000000 00000010	2
1	2 places	00000000 00000100	4
1	3 places	00000000 00001000	8
1	4 places	00000000 00010000	16

with the '&', '|' '^' operators and so on. For example, the following statement assigns 'c' an integral value with bits 4 and 8 set to logic 1:

```
c = ( 1 << 4 ) | ( 1 << 8 ) ;
```

3.2.5 *The shift right operator: '>>'*

The result of the expression 'operand >>*n*' is a *copy* of the original operand with all bits shifted *n* places to the right. The LSB is lost while the MSB may or may not be filled with a zero, depending upon the compiler and generally upon whether the operand is a signed or an unsigned quantity. Thus, the following statement shifts all bits in the variable 'c' two places to the right:

```
c = c >> 2 ;
```

When shifting right a signed quantity, the compiler may or may not attempt to preserve the value of the MSB to ensure that the sign of the variable is not altered. The standard defines this operation to be implementation dependent. If the compiler does not attempt to preserve the sign or MSB, then the MSB will be filled with a zero from the left. This is called a **logical shift right**. Consider, then, the statement:

```
c = c >> 2 ;
```

which attempts to shift the value of the variable 'c' two places to the right. If 'c' were a signed char, Figure 3.3 illustrates what happens to the value of 'c' with each shift if the compiler does *not* attempt to preserve the sign or the MSB.

If, however, the compiler attempts to preserve the sign bit, a so-called **arithmetic shift right**, the MSB is preserved, with the result that if a negative number is shifted too many place to the right, all bits in the operand will eventually become 1. Likewise, if a positive value is shifted too many places, all bits in the operand will eventually become 0. Figure 3.4 illustrates what happens during a shift right *with* sign preservation.

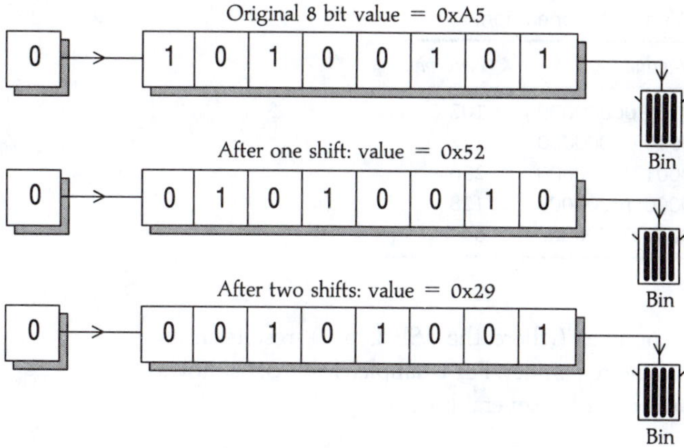

Figure 3.3 Shifting right a signed operand, no sign preservation.

When an unsigned operand is shifted right, the compiler should not attempt to preserve the sign or the MSB. It should thus be filled from the left with 0s during each shift. The operation is thus a **logical shift right**, identical in operation to shifting a signed quantity *without* sign preservation.

The shift right operator '>>' is often used as an alternative to dividing an integer by 2. Table 3.10 shows what happens when the (signed or unsigned) integer value 1024 is shifted right a number of places. At each point, the value of the quantity is halved, until ultimately the operation results in zero.

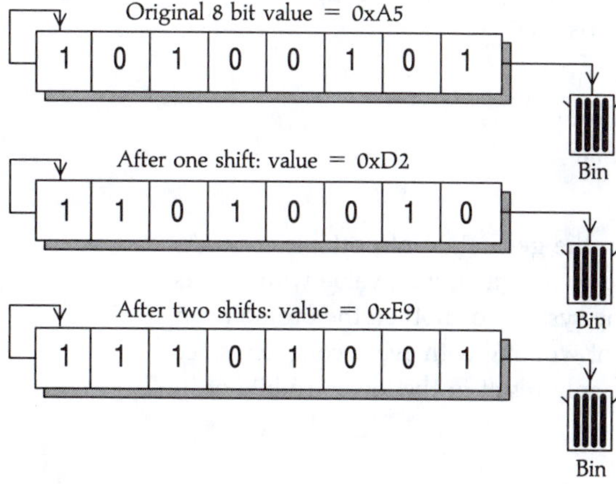

Figure 3.4 Shifting right a signed operand, with sign preservation.

Table 3.10 Halving an integer with a '>>' operation.

Value	*Shifted right by*	*Binary value*	*New value*
1024	–	00000100 00000000	1024
1024	1 place	00000010 00000000	512
1024	2 places	00000001 00000000	256
1024	3 places	00000000 10000000	128
1024	4 places	00000000 01000000	64

Note that shifting an odd number (where the LSB is a 1), results in an inaccurate division, with the loss of the remainder. For example, Table 3.11 shows the effect of shifting the value 1023 right by several bits.

Table 3.11 Effect of shifting right an odd number.

Value	*Shifted right by*	*Binary value*	*New value*	*Remainder*
1023	–	00000011 11111111	1023	–
1023	1 place	00000001 11111111	511	1 (lost)
1023	2 places	00000000 11111111	255	1 (lost)
1023	3 places	00000000 01111111	127	1 (lost)
1023	4 places	00000000 00111111	53	1 (lost)

3.2.6 *The one's complement operator: '~'*

The result of the expression '~operand' is a *copy* of its operand with the value of all bits inverted; thus, where there was previously a 1, there will now be a 0 and vice versa. This is demonstrated below where the '~' operator is applied to the hexadecimal value 0xfa50 to yield the result 0x05af.

```
11111010 01010000     Value before = 0xFA50
00000101 10101111     Value after = 0x05AF
```

The '~' operator finds applications in the generation of portable code. As an example, suppose that a program wished to assign an int a value with all bits set to 1. As the size of an int varies from one system to another, the programmer could not rely upon the following assignment working with every compiler, since if 'i' were a 32 bit integer, then this would only result in the lower 16 bits of 'i' being set to 1:

```
i = 0xffff ;
```

Similarly, the following statement, although achieving the desired goal for a 32 bit int, would more than likely generate warnings from a compiler that used 16 bit integers:

```
i = 0xffffffff ;
```

To overcome these problems, we could take the integer constant 0, which may be 16 or 32 bits in size, depending upon the compiler, and complement it with the statement:

```
i = ~0 ;
```

which gives rise to an integer value for 'i' with all bits set to 1 regardless of compiler and size of int.

3.2.7 *Precedence and associativity of C's bitwise operators*

All of C's bitwise operators are evaluated from left to right with the exception of the unary one's complement operator '~', which is evaluated right to left. Table 3.12 summarizes their precedence and associativity. The higher an operator appears in the table, the earlier in an expression it will be evaluated.

Table 3.12 Precedence and associativity of C's bitwise operators.

Operator	*Operation*	*Type*	*Associativity*
~	One's complement	Unary	Right to left
<< >>	Shift left and right	Binary	Left to right
&	AND	Binary	Left to right
^	EXOR	Binary	Left to right
|	OR	Binary	Left to right

From Table 3.12, we can therefore assume that the following expression:

would be evaluated as if it had been written in the form shown below, which is much clearer:

```
(~0x55) | ((a & b) ^ (~c))
```

A particularly common mistake when using these operators in conjunction with C's relational operators is highlighted below:

'==' has higher precedence than '&'

```
if( a & 0x43 == 0)
```

Caution!

Here, parentheses *are* required around the bitwise AND operator '&' and its operands since the equivalence operator '==' has a higher precedence than bitwise AND (see Table 3.13), and thus the test expression should have been written as:

```
if( (a & 0x43) == 0)
```

Application 3.2

Write a program to read two integral hex operands and display the bitwise AND, OR, EXOR, NAND and NOR of those operands along the values of operand 1 shifted left and right by the number of bits specified by operand 2.

Application 3.2 Simple bitwise operator test program.

```
#include    <stdio.h>

int main( void )
{
    int op1, op2;

    printf("Enter the Values of Operands 1 and 2 in Hexadecimal: ");
    scanf("%x %x", &op1, &op2) ;

    printf("0x%x ANDed with 0x%x = 0x%x\n", op1, op2, op1 & op2);
    printf("0x%x ORed with 0x%x = 0x%x\n", op1, op2, op1 | op2);
    printf("0x%x EXORed with 0x%x = 0x%x\n", op1, op2, op1 ^ op2);
    printf("0x%x Shifted Right by %u bits = 0x%x\n", op1, op2, op1 >> op2 ) ;
    printf("0x%x Shifted Left by %u bits = 0x%x\n", op1, op2, op1 << op2 ) ;

    return 0 ;
}
```

When the program in Application 3.2 was run, the following sample display was produced:

```
Enter the Values of Operands 1 and 2 in Hexadecimal: 0xfa 0x5f
0xfa ANDed with 0x5f = 0x5a
0xfa ORed with 0x5f = 0xff
0xfa EXORed with 0x5f = 0xa5
0xfa Shifted Right by 95 bits = 0x0
0xfa Shifted Left by 95 bits = 0x0
```

```
Enter the Values of Operands 1 and 2 in Hexadecimal: 0xa5  3
0xa5 ANDed with 0x3 = 0x1
0xa5 ORed with 0x3 = 0xa7
0xa5 EXORed with 0x3 = 0xa6
0xa5 Shifted Right by 3 bits = 0x14
0xa5 Shifted Left by 3 bits = 0x528
```

Application 3.3

A random number generator is a useful tool for both hardware and software engineers. Now, although the standard library defines the function rand() for just such a purpose, Figure 3.5 illustrates the design of a digital circuit that may be used to develop random binary numbers in the range 1–32767. It relies upon a 15 bit **shift register**, which is repeatedly shifted left under the control of a digital clock (not shown).

After each shift operation the logic output from bits 14 and 13 of the shift register are EXORed to produce a 0 or 1 result, which is then fed directly into bit 0 of the shift register during the next shift left operation. Provided the shift register is pre-initialized with a value other than all bits set to zero, a new random number is available at the output of bits 0–14 of the shift register after each shift left. Write a program to simulate this circuit and thus produce random numbers.

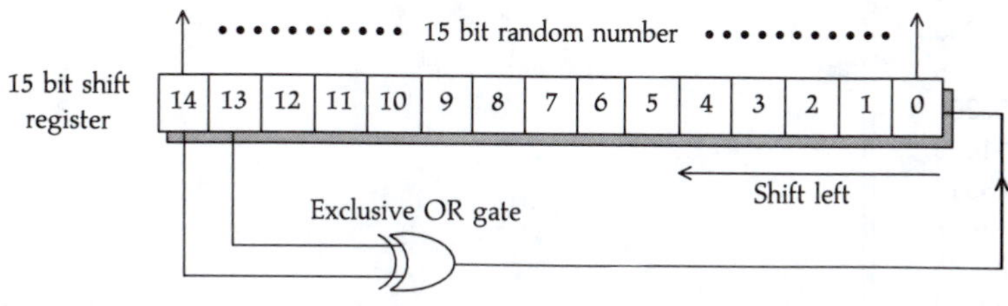

Figure 3.5 A digital pseudo-random binary number generator.

Application 3.3 Generating pseudo-random binary numbers.

```
#include  <stdio.h>

#define   SEED 3254         /* A preset value for shift register, any value other than 0*/

/* A function to produce random numbers in the range 1 – 32767 */

int  random( void )
{
   static  int reg = SEED ;           /* a 16 bit variable to simulate a shift register */
   int     bit13, bit14 ;             /* the value of bits 13 and 14 in shift register */
   int     exor ;                     /* the result of EXOR of bits 13 and 14 */

   bit14 = (reg & 0x4000) >> 14 ;     /* get value of bit 14 from shift register */
   bit13 = (reg & 0x2000) >> 13 ;     /* get value of bit 13 from shift register */
   exor = bit14 ^ bit13 ;             /* EXOR bits 13 and 14 */
   reg = reg << 1 ;                   /* shift all bits in shift register 1 place to left */

/*
** Now set bit 0 to the value of the exclusive OR of bits 14 and 13 and then
** mask or set the most significant bit of reg (bit 15, which is not used) to 0
*/

   reg = (reg | exor) & 0x7fff ;

   return reg ;                       /* return the new random number */
}

int main( void )
{
   int i ;

   for( i = 0; i < 10; i ++ )
      printf("Random Number = %d\n", random() ) ;

   return 0 ;
}
```

If the program in Application 3.3 is run, then the following display is produced:

```
Random Number = 6508
Random Number = 13016
Random Number = 26033
Random Number = 19298
Random Number = 5829
Random Number = 11658
Random Number = 23317
Random Number = 13867
Random Number = 27735
Random Number = 22702
```

Notice how the integer variable reg was used to simulate the shift register and how it was defined as a **static** variable. This latter feature prevents it from being re-initialized to the value of SEED each time the function random( ) is called.

3.3 A summary of C operators

Table 3.13 summarizes the precedence and associativity of all of C's operators. Some of them have been met already, the rest will be met in later chapters. The higher an operator appears in the table, the higher its precedence, while operators with the same precedence appear in the same group.

Table 3.13 The precedence and associativity of all of C's operators.

Operator	*Description*	*Associativity*
( )	Parentheses and function	Left to right
[ ]	Array subscript	
.	Structure access	
->	Structure access with pointer	
+	Unary '+'	Right to left
–	Unary '–'	
++	Increment	
––	Decrement	
~	One's complement	
!	Logical NOT	
*	Pointer indirection	
&	Address	
sizeof	Size of an operand	
(type)	Casting	
*	Multiplication	Left to right
/	Division	
%	Modulus	
+	Addition	Left to right
–	Subtraction	
<<	Bitwise shift left	Left to right
>>	Bitwise shift right	
<	Less than	Left to right
>	Greater than	
<=	Less than or equal	
>=	Greater than or equal	
==	Equal to	Left to right
!=	Not equal to	
&	Bitwise AND	Left to right
^	Bitwise EXOR	Left to right
|	Bitwise OR	Left to right

Table 3.13 *(cont.)* The precedence and associativity of all of C's operators.

&&	Logical AND	Left to right
||	Logical OR	Left to right
? :	Conditional	Right to left
=	Assignment	Right to left
+=	Assignment addition	
−=	Assignment subtraction	
*=	Assignment multiplication	
/=	Assignment division	
%=	Assignment modulus	
<<=	Assignment shift left	
>>=	Assignment shift right	
&=	Assignment bitwise AND	
|=	Assignment bitwise OR	
^=	Assignment bitwise EXOR	
,	Comma	Left to right

Note that C (like many other languages) does not guarantee the order in which the operands of an operator or the arguments to a function are evaluated (the exceptions to this are the '&&', '||', ',' and '?:' operators). This can in some instances lead to unpredictable behaviour if the programmer is not careful. Take, for example, the following statement, where the function scanf() modifies the value of 'b':

```
a =scanf("%d", &b) * (b + c) ;
```

The question here is, does the compiler use the value of 'b' in the expression '(b + c)' before or after it has been acted upon by scanf()? The answer is implementation defined, as is the result assigned to 'a'. Consider also the statement:

```
printf("%d %d", a++, a+b) ;
```

Here the display produced is dependent upon whether the compiler evaluates the expression 'a++' before or after 'a + b'.

3.4 Chapter summary

(1) Simple arithmetic operations may be performed using the operators '+', '–', '*' and '/'. Integer division truncates a result rather than rounding it up or down. The modulus operator '%' may be used to determine the remainder of an integer division. Assignment is achieved with the '=' operator, which yields the result of its own assignment.

(2) The unary operators '–' and ' + ' may be placed prior to an expression and effectively serve to multiply it by −1 and +1, respectively.

(3) The precedence of an operator determines the order in which it is evaluated in an expression. The higher its precedence, the earlier it is evaluated. Associativity describes the order in which two operators with the same precedence will be evaluated.

(4) An implicit or explicit cast is used to change the representation of a value while attempting to maintain as closely as possible its value. The general form of the explicit cast is given as '(type)value', where *type* is any recognizable data type. A cast cannot be used to change the way a variable is represented in memory, only a copy of it.

(5) Mixing different data types within an expression is permitted, but the compiler will cast/promote simpler data types to more complex ones in accordance with a strict set of rules. The explicit cast operator may be used to override these built in rules and force one's own conversions.

(6) The bitwise operators '&', '|', '^', ' << ', ' >> ' and '~' provide for bitwise AND, OR, EXOR, shift left, shift right and one's complement, respectively.

(7) The operators ' ++ ' and '−− ' provide a convenient means of incrementing and decrementing a variable. The position of the operator dictates whether it is used as a pre- or post-increment/decrement operator.

3.5 Exercises

3.1 What is meant by the terms 'precedence' and 'associativity' in relation to operators?

3.2 What is meant by an 'implicit' and 'explicit' cast?

3.3 Write programs to calculate whether a number is odd or even, and whether one integer value is exactly divisible by another.

3.4 What is the 'type' and 'value' of the following expressions? (You can test your ideas by displaying the value using printf( ) along with the appropriate '%' formatter.) Explain also what, if any, conversions, promotions or implicit casts occur when evaluating these expressions and at what point they occur in the evaluation of the expression.

(a) `1/3    3.6/2.5    1/0    1.0 / 3.0`

(b) `2 + 3/6 – 5`

(c) `5%3*2 + 12/5 −− 13.6/9`

(d) `2.0f * 4.5/3 – 12.6*–3.3/45.0 – 10 / 9`

3.5 Rewrite Exercise 3.4(c) and (d) to use parentheses to make the order of evaluation in each sub-expression clear. Check your results using printf() once again.

3.6 Rewrite Exercise 3.4(a)–(d) to include explicit casts using the '(type)' casting operator to show where and what conversions/promotions/casts occur. Check your results using printf() once again.

3.7 Given that 'x1' and 'x2' are floating point variables (doubles or floats), explain why the following test expression controlling the while loop might be unsafe:

```
do{ ... } while( x1 != x2) ;
```

Explain how you might go about correcting the problem.
Why would the problem not occur if 'x1' and 'x2' were integers?

3.8 List three types of numerical/computational errors that can arise as a result of using floating point numbers. Test these ideas using example statements in conjunction with printf().

3.9 What is potentially wrong with the following for loops, given that 'i' has been defined as an int and 'f' as a float.

(a)
```
for( i = 0; i < 45000; i ++ )
    ...
```

(b)
```
for( f = 0.0; f < 1e7; f += 0.1 )
    ...
```

(c)
```
for( f = 2.0; f < 1e20; f = f * f)
    ...
```

3.10 List the various types of side effects that can sometimes arise when the value of an object of one type is assigned/cast to another type. Discuss what side effects can arise as a result of the following variable definitions and expressions. Again, test your knowledge using printf().

```
short s = 250 ;
int i = 32000 ;
long L = 2000000000L ;
float f = 3.14159 ;
double d = 2.3e78 ;

i = 3.141, f = 2.345534564,
s = d, d = s, f = d, i = d, d = f, d = i, i = L, f = L, i = 23L, d = 2.34545L
```

3.11 Determine the value of the following operations for the bitwise operators '&', '|' and '^'.

(a) Operand 1 0111001010010101

(b) Operand 2 1001101000101100

3.12 Given that 'a' and 'b' are unsigned ints initialized with the hexadecimal values 0x32fa and 0xa1bd, respectively, determine the numeric value of the following expression,

```
~(a & b) >> 2 ^ (~0x3124 << 3)
```

3.13 By making use of the '<<' operator in conjunction with a sliding bit 1, that is, an integer with value 1 and a for loop, write a function to display the value of an int in binary. *Hint:* Do not assume the size of an int, but make use of sizeof to determine it portably.

Test your function by re-writing Application 3.2 to display the results in binary rather than hexadecimal.

3.14 Modify your program from Exercise 3.13 to read in two operands and thus perform a very simple hexadecimal calculator function where the operator is prompted for the two operands and the appropriate operator, such as '&', '|' and so on. The program should also choose to have the results displayed in octal, decimal, hexadecimal or binary.

3.15 Write a function to allow an operator to enter an integer value in binary. Incorporate this into the program in Exercise 3.14 to allow either operand to be entered in binary.

3.16 Write a function to extract the value of the bits 'm' through 'n' of an integer, when 'm' and 'n' are in the range 0–15. The result should have the value of these bits in the least significant 'n–m' bits of the result.

3.17 Application 3.3 presented a simple logic circuit and program to produce pseudo-random binary numbers. Modify the numbers produced by this program to implement the following functionality where 'b_n' represents the value of bit 'n'.

$x = b_{10}$ OR b_{11}

$y = b_3$ AND b_5 AND b_9

$Z = b_1$ EXOR b_3 EXOR ($\tilde{}b_{10}$)

3.18 The table below is the transition table for a three bit state machine and the conditions on inputs A, B, C and D required before progressing to the 'next' state. X represents a 'don't care'. If the conditions are not met for the required state, the machine remains in that state.

Inputs: ABCD	*Current state*	*Next state*
0000	000	001
11XX	001	011
1X0X	011	010
0X01	010	110
1111	110	100
1X01	100	101
1100	101	111
100X	111	Program stop

Using integer variables to represent the values of the inputs A, B, C and D and the current state (which is loaded with the value of next state upon successful transition), design the above system using values for A, B, C and D supplied by the program's operator (in binary). The output of the state machine is to be displayed in binary on the operator's screen with every change of state.

4 A Closer Look at Program Selection

There comes a point in even the simplest of programs where decisions must be made about what actions the program will perform next. In Chapter 1 we introduced the basic if and if-else tests, along with their equivalent flowcharts, to demonstrate how a program could selectively choose one or more alternative paths of execution based upon the result of expressions evaluated at run time.

In this chapter we take a more in-depth look at these two mechanisms and, for completeness, introduce and discuss the two other selection mechanisms that C provides in the form of the switch statement and the ternary operator. Let us start, however, with a simple review of the basic if test.

4.1 The conditional if and if-else tests

The simplest form of the if test is shown below, consisting of a single statement that is only executed if the result of the test expression resolves to true:

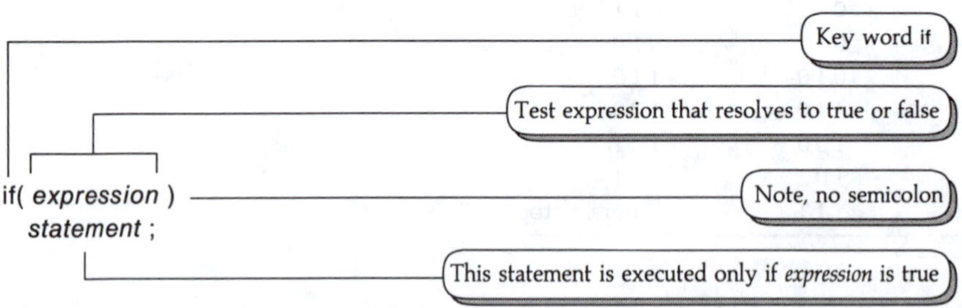
Key word if
Test expression that resolves to true or false
if(expression)
statement ;
Note, no semicolon
This statement is executed only if expression is true

In other words, this form of test can be interpreted as 'if expression evaluates to true, then execute statement, otherwise statement is skipped'. A flowchart illustrating the if test mechanism was given in Figure 1.3, while

Table 4.1 A summary of C's relational operators.

Operator	*Example expression*	*Interpretation*
>	c > b	True, if value of 'c' is greater than that of 'b'
>=	c >= b	True, if value of 'c' is greater than or equal to that of 'b'
<	c < b	True, if value of 'c' is less than that of 'b'
<=	c <= b	True, if value of 'c' is less than or equal to that of 'b'
==	c == b	True, if value of 'c' is equal to that of 'b'
!=	c != b	True, if value of 'c' is not equal to that of 'b'

Table 4.1 summarizes C's relational operators, which are frequently used as part of the test expression.

These operators are, for the most part, common to nearly all programming languages. Take care, however, to note that the equivalence operator '==' consists of two equals signs. A very common mistake here is to use a single sign, '=', which will be interpreted as assignment with possibly dire consequences for the program. We will explore this effect later.

Program 4.1 demonstrates the application of these operators and of the if test when making decisions about the value of a number entered by an operator. Each if test is considered separately within the program, as part of a natural sequence of statements within the function main(). Thus the outcome of one if test does not influence or affect any other test (in this example).

Program 4.1 Example use of an if test.

```
#include  <stdio.h>
#include  <stdlib.h>

int main( void )
{
   char  buff [ BUFSIZ ] ;
   int     b ;

   printf( "Enter a value for b: ") ;

/*
** Read Value for 'b' from keyboard
*/

   b = atoi(gets( buff )) ;

/*
** Test for a range of conditions such as
** negative, positive, zero and non zero
*/
```

```
    if( b < 0 )
      puts( "Number is Negative " ) ;

    if( b >= 0 )
      puts( "Number is Positive " ) ;

    if( b == 0 )
      puts( "Number is equal to 0" ) ;

    if( b != 0 )
      puts( "Number is not equal to 0 " ) ;

    return 0 ;
}
```

If Program 4.1 were run and the program's operator had supplied the values 0 and −5 in response to the program's request for a value for 'b', then the following messages would be observed on the screen:

```
Enter a value for b: 0
Number is Positive
Number is equal to 0
```

```
Enter a value for b: –5
Number is Negative
Number is not equal to 0
```

Try to evaluate what messages would be displayed if other values were entered. The equivalent flow chart for the series of if tests given in Program 4.1 is illustrated in Figure 4.1.

4.1.1 *A common mistake with* if *tests*

A particularly common mistake made by the novice and (sometimes) experienced programmer alike is to accidentally place a semicolon ';' at the end of the if test, as shown below:

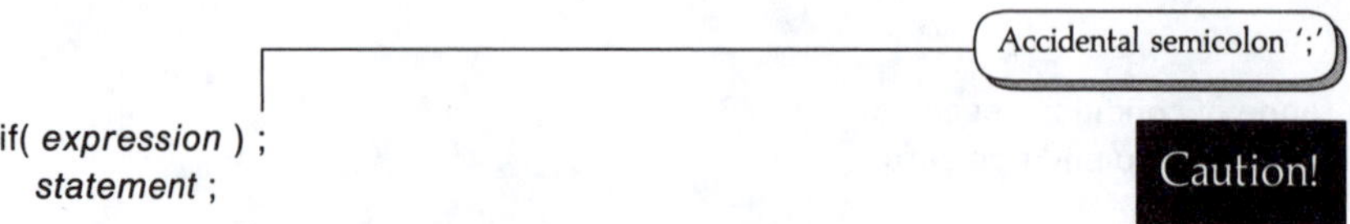
Accidental semicolon ';'
if(expression) ;
statement ;
Caution!

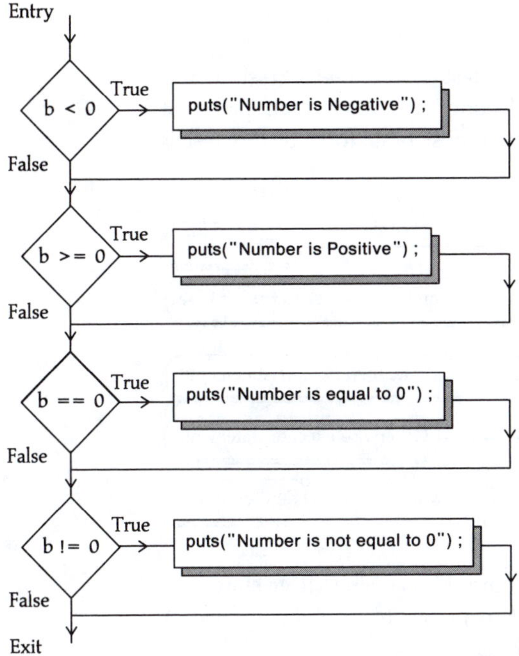

Figure 4.1 Equivalent flowchart for the sequence of if tests in Program 4.1.

Now, although this is not illegal, the compiler interprets the semicolon as a 'do nothing' or NULL statement, which it assumes is the single statement associated with the if test. It therefore appears to the compiler as if the program had been written in the manner below:

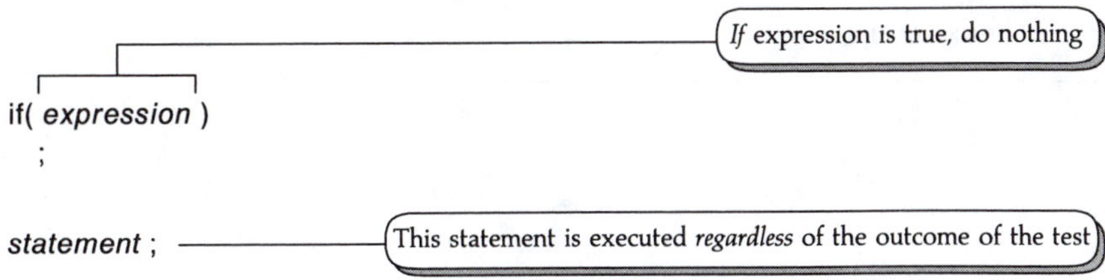

Thus 'statement' is now regarded by the compiler as not being associated with the if test and will be executed regardless, thus negating the reason for the test in the first place! This type of problem can be particularly difficult to track down.

4.1.2 *The* if-else *test*

A simple and useful variation on the basic if test is the if-else test, which provides the program with a means of selecting two alternative paths of execution through the program. The general and most basic form of this test is given below:

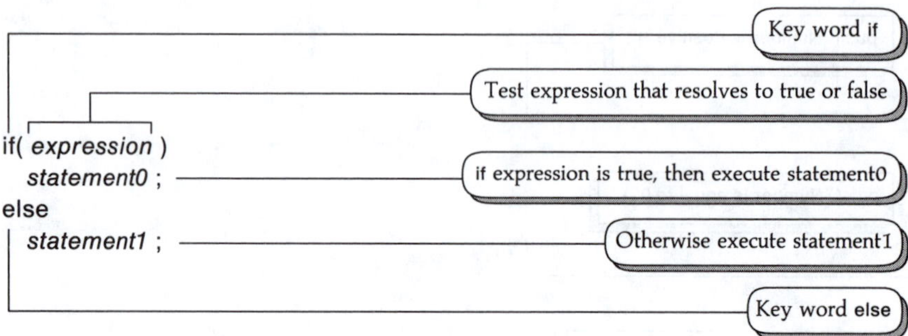
Key word if
Test expression that resolves to true or false
if(*expression*)
statement0 ;
if expression is true, then execute statement0
else
statement1 ;
Otherwise execute statement1
Key word else

As we saw in Chapter 1, the else option provides an alternative statement or sequence of statements that are executed if 'expression' resolves to false. A flowchart for the if-else statement was given in Figure 1.4.

This type of test is particularly useful in combining two **mutually exclusive** or **opposite** tests into one. For example, the current flowing in an electrical circuit of resistance 'r' with applied voltage 'v' is given by the equation 'i = v/r'. To avoid the possibility of a divide by zero occurring the program might well elect to evaluate the expression only if 'r' is non-zero, Such a program could be written to contain two conditional if tests, as shown below:

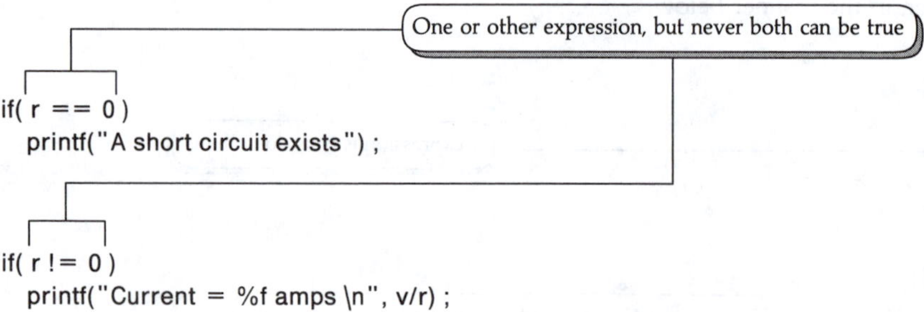
One or other expression, but never both can be true
if(r == 0)
printf("A short circuit exists") ;
if(r != 0)
printf("Current = %f amps \n", v/r) ;

Here, it is guaranteed that at least one, but never both if tests will be true – that is, either the value of 'r' is zero OR it is not. The above two if tests can thus be reduced to a single if-else test of the form shown below, which improves both the efficiency and the size of the compiled program, because only one test expression need now be evaluated:

Two mutually exclusive if tests replaced by one if-else test

```
if( r == 0 )
  printf("A short circuit exists") ;
else
  printf("Current = %f amps \n", v/r) ;
```

4.1.3 *Nested* if *tests*

As far as the compiler is concerned, the evaluation of a single if or if-else test and the execution of the single statement associated with each part are viewed as a single statement (and hence braces '{ }' are not required around a single statement if test). This feature permits us to nest or embed several if tests within one another and thus implement a logical AND function. For example:

Statement executed only if 'r1' > 0 AND 'r2' > 0 AND 'r3' > 0

```
if( r1 > 0 )
  if ( r2 > 0 )
    if( r3 > 0 )
      printf("Resistance = %g\n", 1.0/(1.0/r1 + 1.0/r2 + 1.0/r3 )) ;
```

Here, if the value of 'r1' is *greater* than 0, then the statement associated with that first if test is evaluated. In this instance, that statement just happens to be a second (nested) if test. This is then evaluated and if the value of 'r2' is also found to be greater than 0, a third (nested) if test is evaluated; thus, the call to printf( ) is made only if the values of 'r1' AND 'r2' AND 'r3' are greater than 0. Figure 4.2 illustrates this operation in the form of a flowchart.

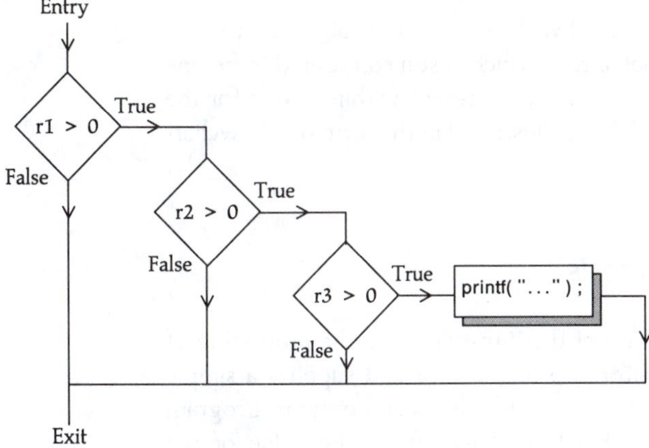

Figure 4.2 Flowchart for a nested if test.

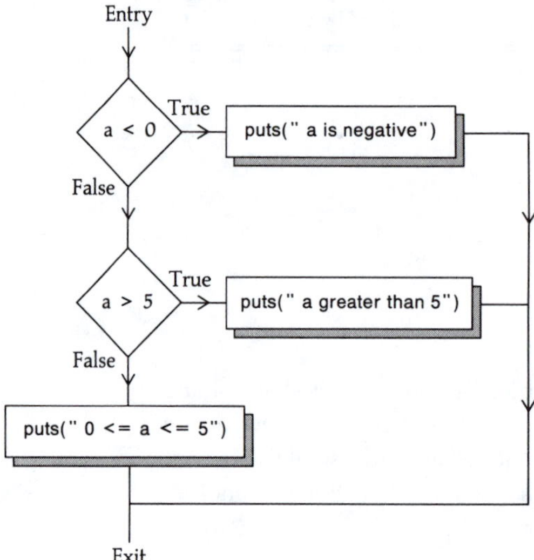

Figure 4.3 Flowchart for a nested if-else test.

Such a technique may be carried to any depth and level of complexity required. For example, we could write:

```
if( a < 0 )
  puts(" a is negative ... ") ;
else
  if( a > 5)
    puts("a greater than 5" ) ;
  else
    puts(" 0 <= a <= 5") ;
```

Nested if-else test evaluated if 'a' >= 0

Here, the single statement associated with the else part of the first if test has itself been replaced by a nested if-else test, which is still considered to be one single statement, even though two statements are present within it (one for the second if and one for the second else). This is illustrated in the form of a flowchart in Figure 4.3.

4.1.4 *Multi-way conditional tests*

Another particularly common application of the if test lies with the processing of menu driven systems, where an operator is prompted for and supplies a simple numeric or character response to select one of perhaps several options. Program 4.2, for example, invokes one of four functions based upon the value of the variable 'a'.

Program 4.2 Example use of multi-way if tests.

```
#include   <stdio.h>
#include   <stdlib.h>

int main( void )
{
  int    a ;
  char  buff[ BUFSIZ ] ;

  printf("Make a choice in the range [0 - 3] ") ;
  a = atoi( gets( buff )) ;

  if( a == 0 )
    puts("Choice 0") ;
  if( a == 1 )
    puts("Choice 1") ;
  if( a == 2 )
    puts("Choice 2") ;
  if( a == 3 )
    puts("Choice 3") ;

  return 0 ;
}
```

When Program 4.2 is run, the following sample display is produced, showing how the correct choice was made in response to the operator's entry:

```
Make a choice in the range [0 - 3] 3
Choice 3
```

Now, although such an approach will be successful – the correct function is invoked to deal with the operator's selection – it is not necessarily the most effective solution. For example, consider what happens, if choice 0 is made. When the correct call to puts() is made and subsequently returns, the program then proceeds to test the value of 'a' against all other possible choices, even though there is no possibility of success since all the above options were mutually exclusive.

A far more effective solution would be to make use of a cascaded set of nested if-else tests, as shown in Program 4.3. A further benefit of this approach is the ability to easily intercept an invalid choice, that is, a choice that has no match, with a trailing else.

Program 4.3 Use of cascaded if-else tests.

```
#include   <stdio.h>
#include   <stdlib.h>

int main( void )
{
  int    a ;
  char  buff[ BUFSIZ ] ;

  printf("Make a choice in the range [0 - 3] ") ;
  a = atoi( gets( buff )) ;

  if( a == 0 )
    puts("Choice 0") ;
  else
    if( a == 1 )
      puts("Choice 1") ;
    else
      if( a == 2 )
        puts("Choice 2") ;
      else
        if( a == 3 )
          puts("Choice 3") ;
        else
          puts("Error: Invalid Choice ... Range is [ 0 - 3 ]") ;
  return 0 ;
}
```

Here, the else part of each if test is itself an if-else test. The program thus begins by comparing the variable 'a' with the value 0. If false, further comparisons are made with the values 1, 2 and 3 and finally, if no match for 'a' is found, the final else part of the test is taken, which displays the error message 'Error: Invalid Choice ... Range is [0 - 3]'.

The efficiency of the program has now been improved, since having acted upon a particular selection, no other comparisons are then made. Unfortunately, however, the use of 'correct' program indentation makes the program rather untidy and difficult to follow, particularly when the number of choices is large. In fact, the programmer may well find that the program disappears off the right-hand edge of the screen.

Under these circumstances, a programmer might well decide to use a different form of indentation, which is altogether more readable, as demonstrated in Program 4.4, which is functionally equivalent to Program 4.3.

It is worth pointing out that C provides a special type of selection mechanism specifically to deal with this type of application, in the form of the switch statement, which we shall meet in Section 4.4.

Program 4.4 Alternative layout for Program 4.3.

```
#include   <stdio.h>
#include   <stdlib.h>

int main( void )
{
  int    a ;
  char  buff[ BUFSIZ ] ;

  printf("Make a choice in the range [0 - 3] ") ;
  a = atoi( gets( buff )) ;

  if( a == 0 )          puts("Choice 0") ;
  else if( a == 1 )  puts("Choice 1") ;
  else if( a == 2 )  puts("Choice 2") ;
  else if( a == 3 )  puts("Choice 3") ;
  else puts("Error: Invalid Choice . . . Range is [ 0 - 3 ]") ;

  return 0 ;
}
```

4.1.5 *Default* if-else *association*

The previous section highlights a particularly nasty trap into which a novice programmer can all too easily fall. Consider for a moment the simple nested if-else test shown below:

```
if( a >= 0 )
  if( a <= 5 )
    puts(" 'a' is in the range 0 <= a <= 5 ") ;
else
  puts(" 'a' must be less than zero " ) ;
```

Caution!

It appears at first sight and from the indentation used as if the programmer had intended to associate the else with the first if test. Unfortunately, this is not the case, since the compiler is unconcerned with any cosmetic indentation the program may contain, and simply associates the else with the last or most recent if. To avoid such confusion, the programmer should take care to lay out the program in the manner shown below:

```
if( a >= 0 )
  if( a <= 5 )
    puts(" 'a' is in the range 0 <= a <= 5 ") ;
  else
    puts(" 'a' must be less than zero ") ;
```

Had the programmer wished to attach it to the first if, then a statement block would have been required to effectively screen or hide the inner if from the else, as shown below:

```
if( a >= 0 )  {
   if( a <= 5 )
      puts(" 'a' is in the range 0 <= a <= 5 ") ;
}
else
   puts(" 'a' must be less than zero ") ;
```

Programs 4.5 and 4.6 demonstrate examples of the use of statement blocks and default if-else associations.

Program 4.5 Use of statement blocks to group statements.

```
#include   <stdio.h>
#include   <stdlib.h>

int main( void )
{
   int    b ;
   char  buff[ BUFSIZ ] ;

   printf("Enter a value for b:") ;
   b = atoi(gets( buff )) ;

   if( b >= 0 )  {
      if( b <= 10 )  {
         if( b == 0 ) puts("Value is 0") ;
         else if ( b == 1 ) puts("Value is 1") ;
         else if ( b == 2 ) puts("Value is 2") ;
         else if ( b == 3 ) puts("Value is 3") ;
         else puts("Value is in range 4 to 10") ;
      }
      else              /* if b > 10 */
         puts("Value greater than 10 ") ;
   }
   else                 /* if b < 0 */
      puts("Value is negative") ;
   return 0 ;
}
```

Program 4.6 Solving the quadratic equation $ax^2 + bx + c = 0$.

```
#include   <stdio.h>
#include   <stdlib.h>
#include   <math.h>

int main( void )
{
   char     buff[ BUFSIZ ] ;
   double   a, b, c, div, descr, r1;

   printf("Enter Value for Coefficient 'a': ") ;
   a = atof( gets( buff )) ;
   printf("Enter Value for Coefficient 'b': ") ;
   b = atof( gets( buff )) ;
   printf("Enter Value for Coefficient 'c': ") ;
   c = atof( gets( buff )) ;

/*
** if a is equivalent to zero, then the equation reduces to bx + c = 0 and thus
** x = -c/b, provided b does not equal zero. If 'c' and 'a' are zero, then x = 0
*/

   if( a == 0 )
      if( c ==0)
         printf("Root is at 0\n") ;
      else
         printf("Only one solution for x = %g\n", -c/b) ;

/*
** If 'a' not equal to zero and b² >= 4ac then there are two possible
** values for x given by the equations
**    x1 = (-b + sqrt(b² - 4ac))/(2a)
**    x2 = (-b - sqrt(b² - 4ac))/(2a)
**
** However, if b² < 4ac, the solution for x is complex and is given by the equations
**    x1 = -b/2a + i sqrt( absolute value of (b² - 4ac))/(2a)
**    x2 = -b/2a - i sqrt( absolute value of (b² - 4ac))/(2a)
*/

   else  {              /* else if a not equal to 0 */
      div = 2.0 * a ;
      descr = b * b - 4.0 * a * c ;
      if( descr >= 0 )  {
         printf("Roots are real\n");
         printf("Root1 = %g\n", (-b + sqrt( descr ))/div) ;
         printf("Root2 = %g\n", (-b - sqrt( descr ))/div) ;
      }
      else {            /* if roots are complex */
         div = 2.0 * a ;
         r1 = sqrt( fabs( descr ))/div ;
```

```
            printf("Roots are complex\n");
            printf("Root1 = (%g) + i(%g)\n", -b/div, r1) ;
            printf("Root2 = (%g) + i(%g)\n", -b/div, r1) ;
        }
    }
    return 0 ;
}
```

Program 4.6 demonstrates an application of the if and if-else tests in solving the roots of the quadratic equation $ax^2 + bx + c = 0$. The two roots are given by the equations:

$$r1 = (-b + sqrt(b^2 - 4ac))/2a$$

$$r2 = (-b - sqrt(b^2 - 4ac))/2a$$

Note also the following points:

if a == 0	there is a single root given by the expression $-c/b$, or 0 if c is also 0
if $b^2 < 4ac$	the roots are complex

Note also that the program makes use of the standard library functions sqrt() and fabs() to obtain the square root and absolute values of a floating point number, hence the header file <math.h> is included because it contains their function prototypes.

If Program 4.6 is run, then the following sample displays are produced:

```
Enter value for Coefficient 'a' : 6
Enter value for Coefficient 'a' : 3
Enter value for Coefficient 'a' : -5
Roots are real
Root1 = 0.696485
Root2 = -1.19648
```

```
Enter value for Coefficient 'a' : 0
Enter value for Coefficient 'a' : 6
Enter value for Coefficient 'a' : 4
Only one solution for x = -0.666667
```

```
Enter value for Coefficient 'a' : 6
Enter value for Coefficient 'a' : 3
Enter value for Coefficient 'a' : 4
Roots are complex
Root1 = (-0.25) + i(0.777282)
Root2 = (-0.25) - i(0.777282)
```

4.2 Logical operators

The logical operators '&&' and '||' permit several individual test expressions to be evaluated as a single expression. A further unary NOT operator '!' is also provided to invert the sense of an expression; in other words, where an expression might yield a true result, applying the NOT operator would invert this and result in the condition false and vice versa. These operators and some example test expressions are shown in Table 4.2.

Table 4.2 C's logical operators.

Operator	*Interpretation*	*Example* if *test*
&&	Logical AND	if(a < b && c > d)
||	Logical OR	if (x >= y || z != 5)
!	Logical NOT	if(!(a < b))

Study them carefully, for they are easy to confuse with their bitwise counterparts '&' and '|', but do not always give the same result. For example, the expression '7 && 3' does not yield the same result as the expression '7 & 3', a fact that may easily be verified by displaying the result of each expression using printf( ) with the %d formatter.

The logical AND operator '&&' yields a result which is true only if both operands are also true, otherwise the result is false. Thus, the combined effect of the two separate if tests below:

```
if( x > y )
  if( s !=23 )
    statement ;
```

Statement executed if x > y AND s != 23

may be reduced to a single if test of the form:

Combined result is true if x > y AND s != 23

```
if( x > y && s != 23 )
  statement ;
```

Of course, by expressing the test in this way, it will not be possible to associate an else option uniquely for the expression 's != 23', only for the test as a whole.

The logical OR operator '||' yields a result which is true if one or other or both operands are true. In other words, the result will be false, only if both operands were false. Thus, the multi-way if-else statement shown below:

```
if( a == 1)
  a++ ;
else if ( a == 2 )
  a++ ;
```

Note identical statements

may be reduced to a single statement of the form:

Combined result is logical true if a == 1 OR a == 2

```
if( a == 1 || a == 2 )
  a++ ;
```

The logical not operator '!' inverts the sense of an expression, such that the two separate if tests shown below:

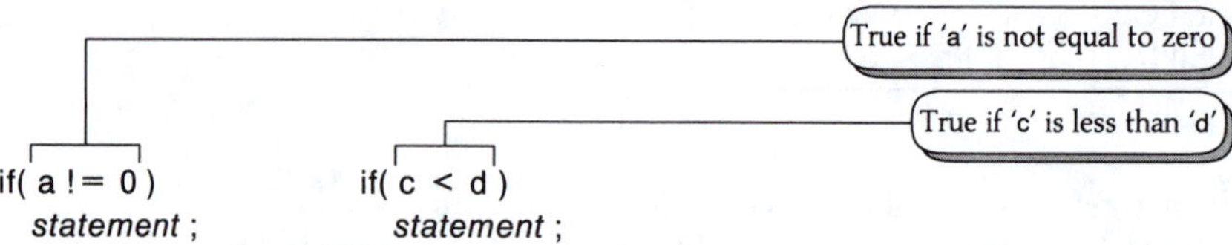
True if 'a' is not equal to zero
True if 'c' is less than 'd'
if(a != 0)
statement ;
if(c < d)
statement ;

may be written using the '!' operator as:

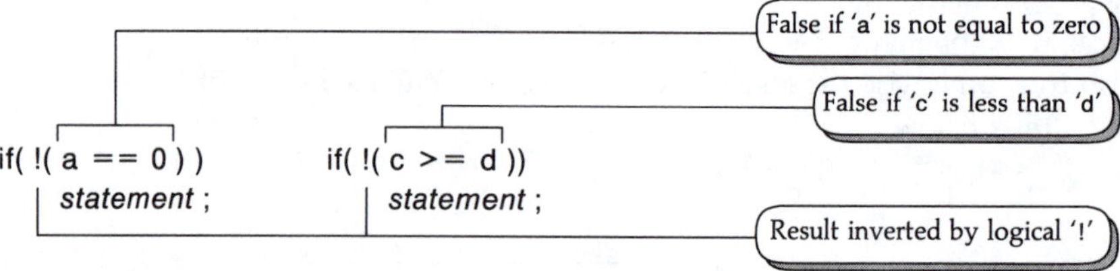
False if 'a' is not equal to zero
False if 'c' is less than 'd'
if(!(a == 0))
statement ;
if(!(c >= d))
statement ;
Result inverted by logical '!'

Application 4.1

An electrical components company offers the discounts shown below on various components ordered in quantity. Write a program to read in the quantity, component number and unit cost and then display the discount offered along with the total discounted price.

Item number	*Description*	*Discount 0–999*	*Discount 1000–1999*	*Discount 2000+*
0	Resistor	5%	5%	10%
1	Capacitor	5%	5%	10%
2	Transistor	2.5%	7.5%	10%
3	IC	2.5%	7.5%	10%

Application 4.1 Calculation of discount on bulk component purchase.

```
#include    <stdio.h>
#include    <stdlib.h>

int main( void )
{
    int       quantity, item ;
    double    discount = 0, cost, total ;
    char      buff[ BUFSIZ ] ;

    printf("Enter Quantity: ") ;
    quantity = atoi( gets( buff )) ;

    printf("Enter Item Code: ") ;
    item = atoi( gets( buff )) ;

    printf("Enter Unit Cost: ") ;
    cost = atof( gets( buff )) ;

    if( quantity >=0 && quantity <= 999 )  {
        discount = 2.5 ;                /* basic discount of 2.5% offered */
        if(item == 0 || item == 1)
            discount += 2.5 ;           /* extra discount on resistors and capacitors */
    }

    else if( quantity >= 1000 && quantity <= 1999 )  {
        discount = 5.0 ;                /* basic discount of 5% offered */
        if( item == 3 || item == 4)
            discount += 2.5 ;           /* extra discount on transistors and ICs */
    }

    else if( quantity >= 2000 )
        discount = 10.0 ;               /* 10.0% discount offered on all components */

    total = quantity * cost ;

    printf("Order for %d items @ £%g each = £%g\n", quantity, cost, total) ;
    printf("Less discount of %g%% = £%.2f\n", discount, total - (total * discount/100.0)) ;

    return 0 ;
}
```

When the program in Application 4.1 is run, the following sample displays are produced:

```
Enter Quantity: 2500
Enter Item Code: 0
Enter Unit Cost: 0.02
Order for 2500 items @ £0.02 each = £50
Less discount of 10% = £45.00
```

```
Enter Quantity: 1500
Enter Item Code: 2
Enter Unit Cost: 0.12
Order for 1500 items @ £0.12 each = £180
Less discount of 5% = £171.00
```

```
Enter Quantity: 50
Enter Item Code: 3
Enter Unit Cost: 1.25
Order for 50 items @ £1.25 each = £62.5
Less discount of 10% = £60.94
```

Application 4.1 demonstrates the use of nested if tests, the use of statement blocks to force the correct association of an else with an if and the use of the logical operators '&&' and '||'.

4.2.1 *Precedence and associativity of relational and logical operators*

The relative precedence and associativity of each relational and logical operator is shown in Table 4.3 (see also Table 3.13). The higher an operator appears in the table, the earlier it will be evaluated in an expression. Operators appearing at the same level have equal precedence and all are evaluated in a left to right manner.

Table 4.3 Precedence and associativity of relational and logical operators.

Operators	*Interpretation*	*Associativity*
!	Logical NOT	Left to right
< <= > >=	Relational	Left to right
== !=	Relational	Left to right
&&	Logical AND	Left to right
||	Logical OR	Left to right

Thus, the following expression:

```
a < b && c > d
```

does not require parentheses around each sub-expression because the relational operators '<' and '>' have higher precedence than '&&' and are thus evaluated first. However, the expression:

```
a ==5 || b < 3 && c > 5
```

will be evaluated as:

```
a == 5 || (b < 3 && c > 5 )
```

since '&&' has higher precedence than '||'.

4.2.2 *Partial evaluation of logical operators*

One interesting and useful feature of the '&&' and '||' operators is that they lead to the production of code which may not bother to evaluate *all* operands in the expression, if the outcome of one of them yields a result that is sufficient to determine the outcome of the test as a whole. For example, consider the following expression:

```
if( a == 5 || c != 3 )
```

This expression is only evaluated if 'a == 5' is false

Logical '||' only requires one operand to be true for a true result

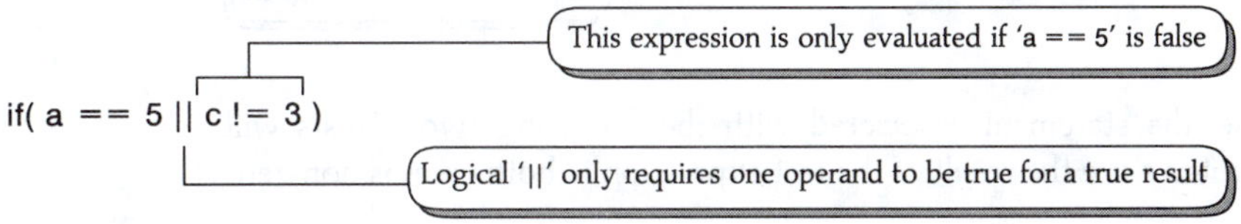

Here, if the result of the expression 'a == 5' were true, then it would make no difference whether the expression 'c != 3' were true or false, since the logical OR operator '||' only requires one of its operands to be true for the result of the whole test to be true. Given this circumstance, the program would not bother to evaluate the expression 'c != 3' at run time. Likewise, given the following expression:

```
if( a != 0 && (c / a > 5 ))
```

This expression is only evaluated if 'a != 0' is true

Logical '&&' requires both operands to be true for a true result

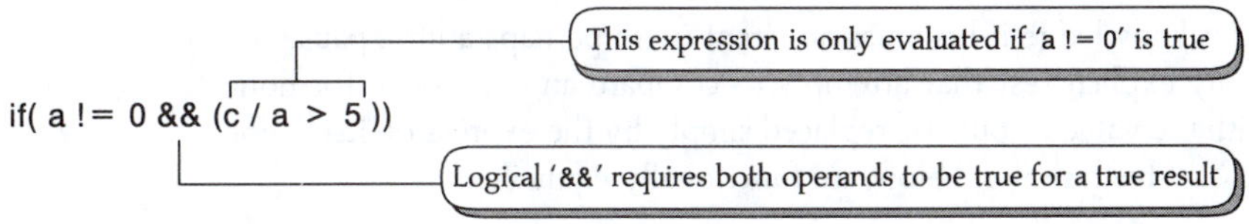

the expression 'c/a > 5' is only evaluated if the expression 'a != 0' is true and thus there is no possibility of the program performing a division by zero.

Using this knowledge, the programmer might wish to improve the speed of execution of programs by arranging for 'simpler' expressions to be placed ahead of more complex ones, particularly if the expressions are evaluated repeatedly within a loop.

4.2.3 *The numerical value of true and false*

So far in this chapter, the terms true and false have been used to describe the outcome of a range of relational and logical operators, but no attempt has been made to put a numerical value to these conditions. This will now be rectified. In C, an expression is said to resolve to false if it resolves to the answer zero. Likewise, an expression that resolves to a non-zero value (positive as well as negative) is deemed to be true.

It follows from this that the statement associated with the if test shown below, where the traditional test expression involving one or more relational or logical operators ('<', '>', '<=', '>=', '==', '!=', '&&', '||', '!'), has been replaced by the value of the integer constant '0'. As such the outcome of the test expression is always going to be 0 – that is, logical false – and thus the statement(s) associated with the test will never be executed:

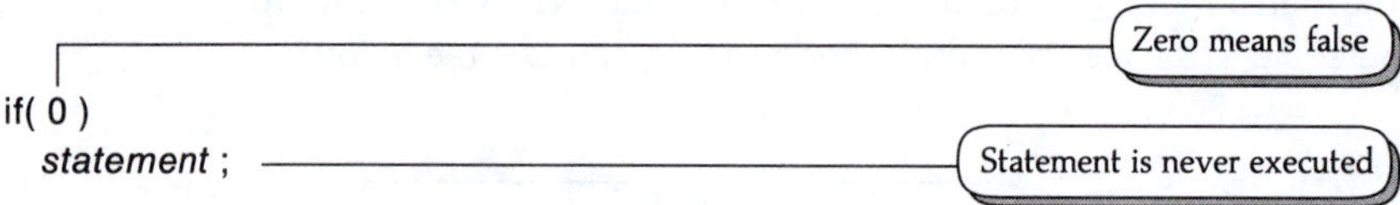

Likewise, the statement associated with the following two if tests will always be executed since the result of the test expression in both cases is non-zero – that is, true:

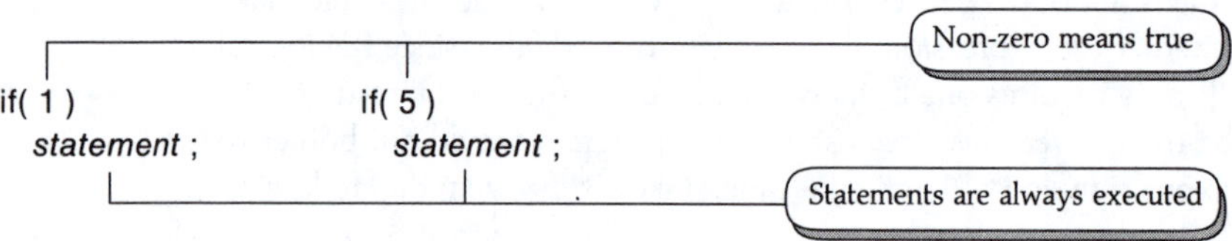

Using this knowledge it becomes apparent (with perhaps a little pause for thought) that any explicit test that attempts to compare an expression for non-equivalence with the value 0 could be replaced simply by the expression itself. For example, the two if tests shown below are functionally equivalent:

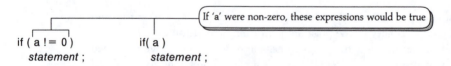

If 'a' were non-zero, these expressions would be true

```
if ( a != 0 )           if( a )
   statement ;             statement ;
```

and it therefore follows that by inverting the sense of each test, the following two if tests are also functionally equivalent:

If 'a' were 0, these expressions would be logical true

```
if ( a == 0 )           if( !a )
   statement ;             statement ;
```

Try substituting values of zero (false) and non-zero (true) for the variable 'a' in the above expressions to satisfy yourself that this is the case. You may well argue (as does the author) that the explicit form of the comparison with zero is far more intuitive and easy to follow than the implicit (assumed) form. However, as your experience of C grows you are likely to encounter the implicit form of the test in other books and programs; thus it is covered here mainly for completeness. Which form of the test you use is of course a personal choice.

What this all boils down to is the simple fact that an if test is only interested in comparing the value of an expression on the basis of zero meaning false or non-zero meaning true. How, then, do the relational and logical operators fit into this scheme? What values do they produce? The answer is simple. All relational and logical operators produce one of two possible integer results, 1 meaning true and 0 meaning false. You can verify this for yourself with the following statement, where the value 1 is displayed if 'b' is in fact greater than 'c', or 0 if not:

'>' operator yields result 1 if 'b' is greater than 'c', or 0 otherwise

```
printf("%d\n", b > c) ;
```

Similarly, the statement:

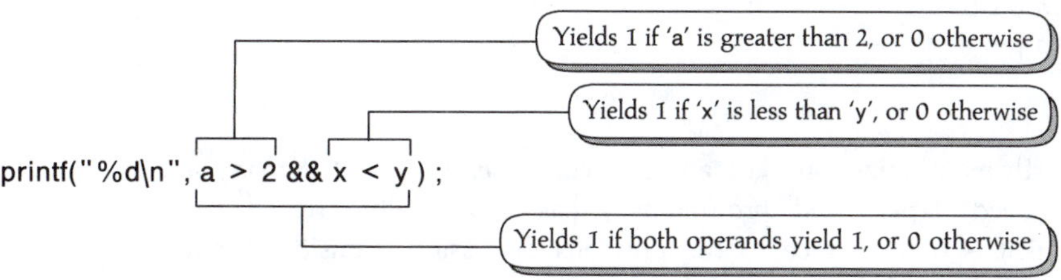
Yields 1 if 'a' is greater than 2, or 0 otherwise
Yields 1 if 'x' is less than 'y', or 0 otherwise
printf("%d\n", a > 2 && x < y) ;
Yields 1 if both operands yield 1, or 0 otherwise

would display the value 1 if 'a' were greater than 2 AND 'x' were less than 'y'. Looked at from another point of view, we could have written the above statement in the following manner:

```
c = a > 2 ;
d = x < y ;
e = c && d ;
printf("%d\n", e ) ;
```

To summarize the discussion so far, Table 4.4 contains some sample expressions involving arithmetic, logical and relational operators. The results of those expressions, in terms of their numeric and logical (or boolean) outcome are also given. All examples assume the following variable initializations, regardless of 'type':

```
a = 5, b = 10, c = 1, d = 2 , e = 0 ;
```

Table 4.4 Sample boolean expressions.

Expression	*Numeric value*	*Boolean result*
a	5	True
!a	0	False
!!a	1	True
a – b	–5	True
a – b + 5	0	False
!(a – b + 5)	1	True
a < b	1	True
!(!a || !b)	1	True
!(a && b)	0	False

Note that the logical NOT operator '!' applied twice to the same expression does not necessarily yield the original value of the expression. The reader is also invited to study the identities shown in Table 4.5.

Table 4.5 Some useful identities.

Expression	*Equivalent expression*
!(!a || !b)	a && b
!(!a && !b)	a || b

It is worth mentioning one last and particularly *nasty* bug that many a novice, and indeed experienced programmer, has accidentally created for themselves, which is of relevance to the previous discussion. Consider for a moment the if test shown below:

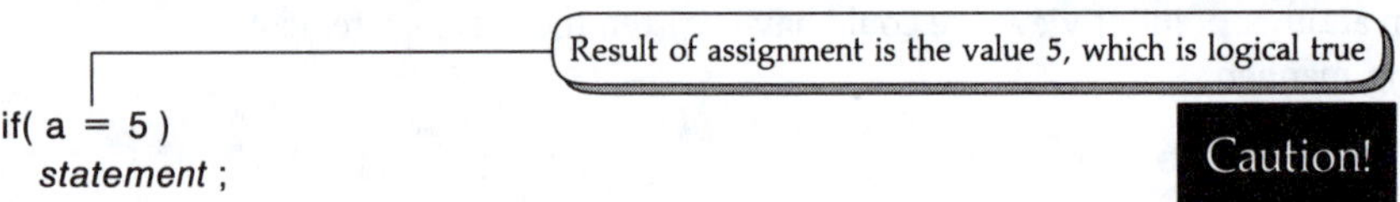
Result of assignment is the value 5, which is logical true
if(a = 5)
statement ;
Caution!

Here, the program *intended* to establish whether the value of 'a' was equal to 5. Unfortunately, the assignment operator '=' was inadvertently used instead of the equivalence operator '=='. What does the compiler make of this? Well, firstly, it is not obliged to report this as an error or a warning, since the statement is syntactically correct and not illegal. So what does the compiler do with it?

Firstly, it interprets the '=' operator to mean assignment (as you expect) and thus the value 5 is assigned to 'a', resulting in the loss of a's original value. Now, you will recall from Chapter 3, that the assignment operator '=' yields the result of its own assignment, that is, the value of 'a', which is 5 in this example.

This value, because it is non-zero, is subsequently interpreted as meaning logical true and thus the single statement associated with the if test is always executed regardless of the original value of 'a'.

4.3 The conditional or ternary operator: '?:'

The conditional or ternary operator '?:' is another useful tool for evaluating conditional expressions. It is an unusual operator in the sense that it is the only operator in the C language to require three operands (hence its name). Its general form is given below and may be interpreted as 'if expression1 is true, then evaluate expression2, otherwise evaluate expression3':

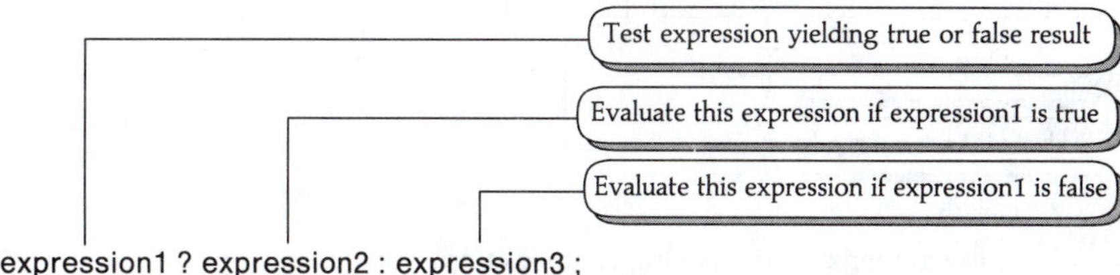

The result of the whole expression – that is, that of the ternary operator itself – is deemed to be the value and type of whichever of expression2 or expression3 (which must both be of the same type, or be cast/promoted to the same type) is chosen for evaluation and is not limited to the boolean values 0 or 1. For example, consider the following expression which assigns 'a' the absolute value of 'b':

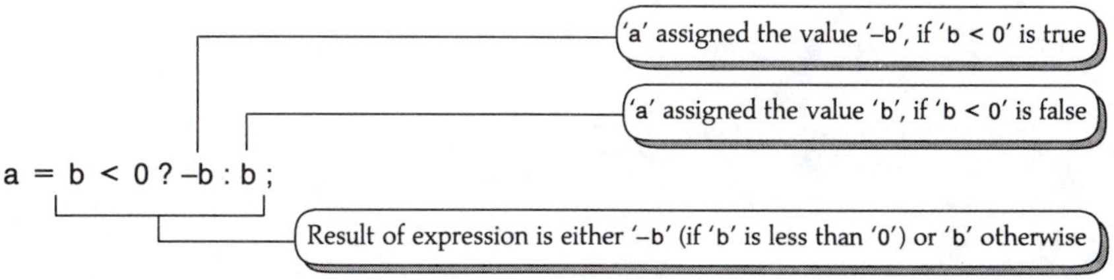

Here, expressions 2 and 3 have been replaced by the expressions '–b' and 'b', respectively, Therefore, if the value of 'b' is less than '0', 'a' is assigned the value of '–b', otherwise it is assigned the value of 'b'. In this way, the above statement is equivalent to the simple if-else test shown below:

```
if( b < 0 )
  a = -b ;
else
  a = b ;
```

4.3.1 *Applications of the ternary operator*

One of the more useful applications of the ternary operator lies with the creation of macros using #define (see Chapter 13) where a complex series of nested if-else tests can be reduced to one single line of code. Another use is returning the value of complex expressions from a function with a single statement. For example, the statement:

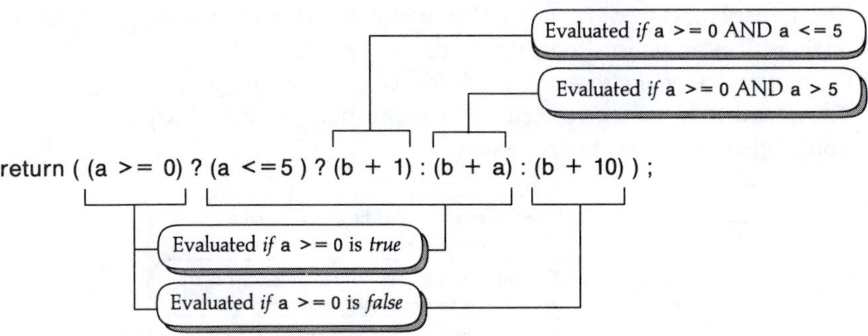

which, although appearing rather cryptic, is simply an example of nesting one ternary operator inside another. Here, if the initial expression 'a >= 0' resolves to false, then the value of the expression 'b + 10' is returned. However, if the expression 'a >= 0' resolves to true, then the inner ternary operator is evaluated where, depending upon the outcome of the expression 'a <= 5', the value of 'b + 1', or 'b + a' is returned. In this way, the above example is functionally equivalent to the section of code shown below:

```
if( a >= 0 )  {
   if( a <= 5 )
      return( b + 1 ) ;
   else
      return( b + a ) ;
}
else
   return( b + 10 ) ;
```

For example, a function to read a character and validate it for upper case, where a response of 'Y' means yes and 'N' means no, is given below. The function returns 1 (true) if a 'Y' character is entered, 0 (false) if a 'N' character or (−1) if an invalid response is given.

```
int get_yes_no_response( void )
{
   char c = toupper(getchar( )) ;
   return ((c == 'Y') ? 1 : (c == 'N') ? 0 : (–1) ) ;
}
```

4.4 The switch statement

You will recall from Section 4.1.4 that a particularly common application of selective execution lay with menu driven systems, where the program would, in response to a choice made by the program's operator, select one of perhaps several possible options. For example, a typical database program might present the options shown below to an operator, who would then be expected to enter a single character response to select the appropriate option:

```
C – Create New Database.
I – Insert Record.
S – Search For Record.
M – Match Record.
N – Display Next Record.
P – Display Previous Record.
D – Delete Current Record.
```

We noted earlier that an efficient way of dealing with this type of problem lay in the use of nested **if-else** statements (Section 4.1.4), an example of which is shown below:

```
if( choice == 'C')          create_database() ;
else if( choice == 'I' )    insert_record() ;
else if( choice == 'S' )    search_for_record() ;
else if( choice == 'M' )    match_record() ;
else if( choice == 'N' )    next_record() ;
else if( choice == 'P' )    previous_record() ;
else if( choice == 'D' )    delete_record() ;
else                        puts("Error: Unrecognized choice ... " ) ;
```

Now although this approach works well, it is possible to achieve the same operation using the **switch** statement instead, which, as we shall later, has a number of benefits over the use of nested **if-else** tests.

The general form of the **switch** statement is given below:

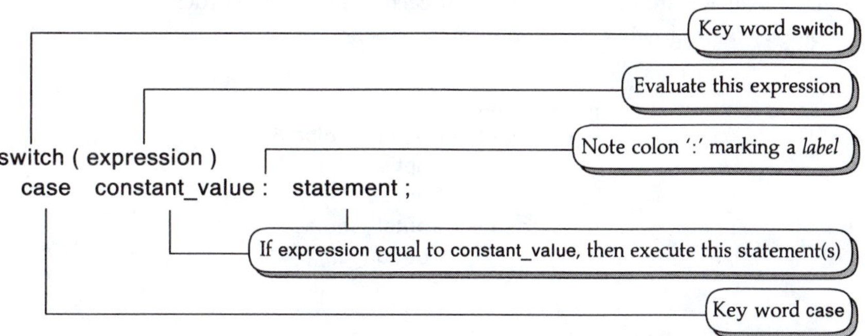

where switch and case are C key words, 'expression' is a test expression that must resolve to an integer value, and 'constant_value' is a constant integer value. Its operation can be explained in the following way.

The program begins by evaluating 'expression' and comparing the result, in turn, with the 'constant_value' associated with each case (there may be more than one case). If a match is found, then the execution of a sequence of statements associated with that case begins. As a simple example, an if test and its equivalent representation using switch are given below:

expression resolves to the value of variable 'a'

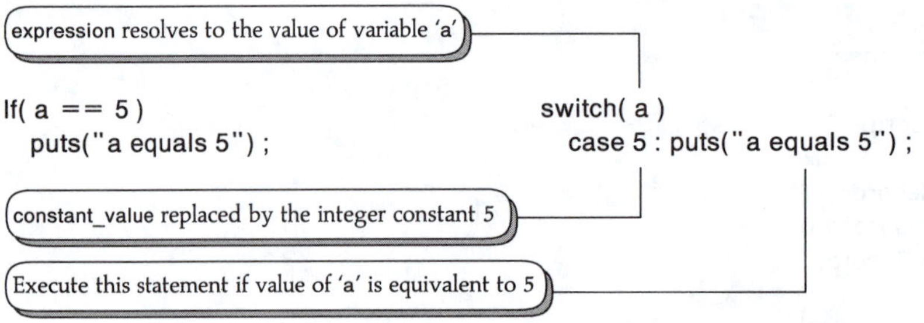

```
If( a == 5 )                          switch( a )
  puts("a equals 5") ;                  case 5 : puts("a equals 5") ;
```

constant_value replaced by the integer constant 5
Execute this statement if value of 'a' is equivalent to 5

In the switch version, the test 'expression' has been replaced by, and therefore resolves to the value of the variable 'a', while 'constant_value' has been replaced by the value of the integer constant 5. In both examples, if 'a' is equivalent to the value 5, the call to puts() is made.

Note that several statements may be attached to a case option simply by providing a sequence of statements, in which case a statement block will be required. For example, the following two conditional tests are also equivalent:

```
if( a == 5 )  {                       switch( a )  {
  puts("choice 5") ;                    case 5 :  puts("choice 5") ;
  option_5() ;                                    option_5() ;
  puts("Finished ... !!!") ;                      puts("Finished ... !!!") ;
}                                     }
```

Where it becomes even more interesting is that multiple case options may be included within the switch statement, provided that each is unique (the order is irrelevant). For example, the following two conditional tests are equivalent:

```
if( a == 5 )  {                       switch( a )  {
  puts("choice 5") ;                    case 5 :  puts("choice 5") ;
  option_5() ;                                    option_5() ;
}                                                 break ;
else if ( a == 6 )  {                   case 6 :  puts("choice 6") ;
  puts("choice 6") ;                              option_6() ;
  option_6() ;                        }
}                                     ...
```

Here, if the value of 'a' is equal to 5, the switch version of the program commences with the execution of a sequence of statements associated with case option 5. When the break statement is encountered that sequence is terminated and the program leaves the switch statement altogether. If the value of 'a' had been equal to 6, then the statements associated with case option 6 would have been chosen instead. (Note that a final break is not obligatory with the last case since the closing '}' serves the same purpose and terminates switch.) If none of the case options matches the value of 'a' then in this example no action is taken.

Note that without the break in the above program for 'case 5:', the program would have continued to execute those statements associated with 'case 6:' (and indeed any other case options that might also have been encountered afterwards) until the closing brace '}' marking the end of the switch or a subsequent break was encountered.

4.4.1 *The* default *case option*

One further useful refinement that may optionally be incorporated into a switch statement is the single instance of a default option. This is useful as a safety net to catch values for 'expression' that have no matching case. This is nothing more sophisticated than a simple else found at the end of a series of nested if-else statements (see Program 4.4 as an example). For example, the following two sections of code are functionally equivalent. Note that the default case does not have to appear at the end of the sequence, but frequently does:

```
if( a == 1 )
  statement1 ;
else if ( a == 2 )
  statement2 ;
else
  statement3 ;
```

```
switch ( a )  {
  case 1 :   statement1 ;
             break ;
  case 2 :   statement2 ;
             break ;
  default :  statement3 :
}
```

Take the default option if 'a' is not equal to 1 or 2

Using the knowledge we have gained so far, we are now in a position to rewrite the database option selection program met earlier, in the form of the switch statement shown below. Note how a character constant has been used for each case option. You will recall from Chapter 2 that characters are represented by full integers and the program is thus comparing the equivalent integer code for the ASCII characters 'C', 'M', 'P' and so on with the code for a character entered by the program's operator at the keyboard:

```
switch( getchar() ) {
   case 'C' :    create_database() ;         break ;
   case 'I' :    insert_record() ;           break ;
   case 'S' :    search_for_record() ;       break ;
   case 'M':     match_record() ;            break ;
   case 'N':     next_record() ;             break ;
   case 'P':     previous_record() ;         break ;
   case 'D':     delete_record() ;           break ;
   default :     puts("Error: Unrecognized choice ..." ) ;
}
```

Application 4.2

The resistance of an electrical resistor is identified by means of three colour bands printed onto the body of the component itself, as shown in Figure 4.4. The first two colour bands represent the values of the first two digits of the resistor's value, while the third band identifies a multiplication factor. A fourth band indicates the precision of the resistor's values expressed as a percentage of stated value, such as 220 ohms ±5%. The colour codes are given in Table 4.6.

Table 4.6 A table of resistor colour codes.

Colour	*First/second bands*	*Third band*
Gold	–	Multiply by 10^{-1} or 0.1
Black	0	Multiply by 10^{0} or 1
Brown	1	Multiply by 10^{1} or 10
Red	2	Multiply by 10^{2} or 100
Orange	3	Multiply by 10^{3} or 1000
Yellow	4	Multiply by 10^{4} or 10 000
Green	5	Multiply by 10^{5} or 100 000
Blue	6	Multiply by 10^{6} or 1 000 000
Violet	7	
Grey	8	
White	9	

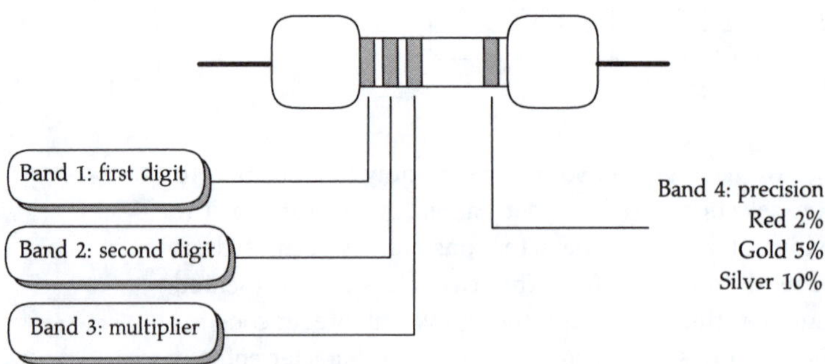

Figure 4.4 Resistor colour code bands.

For example, the colour code 'Brown, Black, Black' indicates a resistor of value 10 (that is, 10×10^0) ohms, 'Red, Red, Brown' indicates a resistor of value 220 (that is, 22×10^1) ohms, 'Green, Blue, Yellow' indicates a resistor of value 560 000 (560 K) ohms and finally, 'Red, Yellow, Gold' indicates a resistor of value 2.4 ohms. Using this knowledge, write a program to accept a resistance value and display the colour codes required to identify it within a mixed bag of resistors.

Application 4.2 Resistor colour code lookup program.

```
#include   <stdio.h>
#include   <stdlib.h>

/*
** Function to accept a digit character in range 0–9
** and display the resistor colour code for that value.
** Note the case option '–1' is there to catch a multiplier value of –1
** e.g. for resistance values such as 1.2 ohms
*/

void colour_lookup( int i )
{
  switch( i )  {
    case –1:  printf("Gold ") ;
              break ;
    case 0:   printf("Black ") ;
              break ;
    case 1:   printf("Brown ") ;
              break ;
    case 2:   printf("Red ") ;
              break ;
    case 3:   printf("Orange ") ;
              break ;
    case 4:   printf("Yellow ") ;
              break ;
    case 5:   printf("Green ") ;
              break ;
    case 6:   printf("Blue ") ;
              break ;
    case 7:   printf("Violet ") ;
              break ;
    case 8:   printf("Grey ") ;
              break ;
    case 9:   printf("White ") ;
  }
}
```

```
int main( void )
{
   char     buff[ BUFSIZ ] ;
   int      i, multiplier ;
   double   value ;

/*
** First read in value of resistor as a string of characters
** and then convert to a numeric value
*/

   printf("Enter Resistor Value: ") ;
   value = atof(gets(buff));

/*
** Determine the multiplication factor for the resistor value
** by keeping a count of how many times the resistor value divides by 10
** e.g. a resistance value of 22000 ohms is divisible by 10, four times, which
** represents an actual multiplication factor of 3, i.e. 22 * (10 to the power 3).
**
** However, if a value of say 1.2 ohms was entered this is represented
** as 12 * (10 to the power -1) hence multiplier value is -1 or "Gold".
*/

   for( multiplier = -1 ; value >= 10.0 ; multiplier ++)
      value = value / 10.0 ;

/*
** Enter a loop which sends two characters from the operator's numeric
** entry to be converted into colours. If a decimal point is entered e.g. 1.2, then
** ignore this character but convert the next (presumed 3rd) character (if valid)
** If no second character is entered e.g. 1, then convert 0 which implies
** black as a second band.
**
** Each character is converted to its equivalent numeric (integral) value
** by subtracting the value of the character '0' (hex value 30. See Figure 2.5).
** Thus the character '9' (hex value 39) becomes integer value 9 prior to lookup.
*/

   for( i = 0; i < 2; i ++ )  {
      if( buff[ i ] >= '0' && buff[ i ] <= '9')
         colour_lookup( buff[ i ] - '0') ;
      else if (buff[ i ] == '.' && ( buff[ i + 1] >= '0' && buff[ i+1 ] <= '9'))
         colour_lookup( buff[ i + 1] - '0') ;
      else
         colour_lookup( 0 ) ;                 /* no second digit */
   }

   colour_lookup( multiplier ) ;          /* convert multiplier to a colour */
   return 0 ;
}
```

A sample of the display produced when the program in Application 4.2 is run is given below:

```
Enter Resistor Value: 33000
Orange Orange Orange
```

```
Enter Resistor Value: 270000
Red Violet Yellow
```

```
Enter Resistor Value: 1.2e5
Brown Red Yellow
```

```
Enter Resistor Value: 3.3
Orange Orange Gold
```

```
Enter Resistor Value: 0.3
Black Orange Gold
```

Application 4.3

A components manufacturer offers the following discounts on quantity for components V, W, X, Y and Z:

	Quantity		
Code	*10–49*	*50–99*	*100+*
V	1%	2%	5%
W	2%	4%	7.5%
X	1%	2.5%	5%
Y	5%	10%	12.5%
Z	10%	12.5%	15%

Write a program to read the quantity, unit cost and component code and thus determine the bill including appropriate discount for that purchase of component.

Application 4.3 Component discount problem.

```
#include <stdio.h>
#include <stdlib.h>         /* for function exit() */
#include <ctype.h>          /* for function toupper() */

int main( void )
{
   int       code, num ;
   double    cost, discount, total ;
```

```
    printf("Enter Component Code: ") ;
    scanf("%c", &code ) ;

    printf("Enter Unit Cost: ") ;
    scanf("%lf", &cost) ;

    printf("Enter Quantity: ") ;
    scanf("%d", &num) ;

    switch( toupper( code ))  {
    case 'V':
      discount = (num > 9) ? (num > 49 ) ? (num > 99) ? 0.05 : 0.02: 0.01: 0 ;
      break ;
    case 'W':
      discount = (num > 9) ? (num > 49 ) ? (num > 99 ) ? 0.075 : 0.04: 0.02: 0 ;
      break ;
    case 'X':
      discount = (num > 9) ? (num > 49 ) ? (num > 99 ) ? 0.05 : 0.025: 0.01: 0 ;
      break ;
    case 'Y':
      discount = (num > 9) ? (num > 49 ) ? (num > 99 ) ? 0.125 : 0.1: 0.05: 0 ;
      break ;
    case 'Z':
      discount = (num > 9) ? (num > 49 ) ? (num > 99) ? 0.15 : 0.125: 0.1: 0 ;
      break ;
    default:
      printf("Unrecognized Component Code ... \n") ;
      exit( 0 ) ;                       /* terminate program */
    }

    total = cost * num ;

    printf("\nTotal Cost = £ %g\n", total) ;
    printf("Less Discount of %g %% = £ %g\n", discount * 100.0, total * discount) ;
    printf("Total = £ %g\n", total - (total * discount)) ;
    return 0 ;
}
```

An example of the display produced by the program in Application 4.3 is given below:

```
Enter Component Code: z
Enter Unit Cost: 2.25
Enter Quantity: 35

Total Cost = £78.75
Less Discount of 10 % = £7.875
Total = £70.875
```

```
Enter Component Code: w
Enter Unit Cost: 0.25
Enter Quantity: 5

Total Cost = £1.25
Less Discount of 0 % = £0
Total = £1.25
```

```
Enter Component Code: x
Enter Unit Cost: 1.25
Enter Quantity: 100

Total Cost = £125
Less Discount of 5 % = £6.25
Total = £118.75
```

4.4.2 *Multiple* case *association with* switch

Finally switch allows several case options to be associated or intercepted by the same statement (or group of statements), simply by tagging those statements with multiple case labels, thus effecting a logical OR function. For example, the following if test:

```
if( a == 0 || a == 1 || a == 2 || a == 3 || a == 4 )
   puts("a is range 0–4" ) ;
```

is functionally equivalent to a switch statement of the form:

```
switch ( a )
   case 0: case 1: case 2: case 3: case 4: puts("a is range 0–4" ) ;
```

As a further example, the following switch statement determines whether the value of the character 'c' is a vowel, that is, any of the characters 'a', 'e', 'i', 'o' or 'u':

```
switch( c )  {
   case 'a': case 'e': case 'i': case 'o': case 'u':
      printf("%c is a Vowel\n", c) ;
      break ;
   default: printf("%c is NOT a Vowel\n", c) ;
}
```

4.5 Chapter summary

(1) The if test provides a means for the program to evaluate a test expression at run time and thus choose whether or not to execute a given statement. If the test expression resolves to true, then the single statement associated with the if is executed, otherwise it is not (that is, it is skipped).

(2) By including an optional **else** with an if test, the program can select one of two possible paths of execution. If the test expression resolves to true, then the single statement associated with the if part of the test is executed, otherwise (if the test expression resolves to false) the single statement associated with the **else** is executed. It is guaranteed that one or other, but never both, statements will be executed.

(3) By using a statement block indicated by the presences of braces '{ }', more than one statement may be associated with an if or **else** part of a test.

(4) In C a test expression is said to resolve to the condition true if it resolves to a non-zero value, or the condition false if it resolves to zero.

(5) The relational operators '<', '>', '<=', '>=', '==' and '!=' may be used to compare two expressions. Each operator yields the result 1 if the outcome of the comparison is true, or 0 if false.

(6) The logical AND operator '**&&**' and the logical OR operator '||' provide a means of combining the result of smaller test expressions into a single expression. The logical NOT operator '!' inverts the result of a test expression. All three operators yield the value 1 or 0 to indicate, respectively, true or false.

(7) The conditional ternary (or three operand) operator '?:' offers an alternative means of expressing an if-**else** test in the form of an expression. The operator yields the type and value of whichever expression is evaluted.

(8) The switch statement provides a more convenient and compact mechanism to evalute a multi-way conditional test, that is, a sequence of nested if-**else** tests based upon the outcome of a simple integer expression.

4.6 Exercises

4.1 Draw a flowchart for the following sequence of if-**else** tests:

```
if( a != 0 )
  statement0 ;
if( a > 5 )
  if( b < 10 )
    statement1 ;
```

```
    else if ( b == 0 )
      statement2 ;
    else
      statement3 ;
else if (a < 0 )
    statement4 ;
else
    statement5 ;
```

4.2 Tidy up the following program section so that 'correct' – that is, conventional – indentation and layout is used. Identify where appropriate which if and else belong together:

```
if( b != 0) if( b + 3 > a ) statement0 ;
else if( a + b < c ) statement1 ; else if ( b < 10 ) statement 2 ;
else { statement3; if( a – b > x) statement 4; } else statement 5 ;
```

4.3 What are the numerical and logical (true or false) values of the following expressions given that 'a' has been initialized with the value 0, 'b' with the value 10 and 'c' with the value −6.

```
a     !a     !!b     a > 0     !(a > b)     b >= a+c     a > b && c < 5
a++      ++a      !(!(a > b) || !( a != b )      (a = b)      !( b = !a)
!(!(a && !b) || !(!c || !b && !a))
```

4.4 Rewrite the following expressions in a different way to remove the logical NOT operators '!' shown:

```
!( a > 5 )     !( b < 3 )     !( b >= a )     !( (c + b) <= z)
!(!(!a && !(c || d )) || !(!b || !( c && d )))
```

4.5 By making use of the conditional operator, write expressions to classify a character based on the following conditions:

(a) True if a character is a decimal digit in the range 0–9, false otherwise.

(b) True if the character is a hex digit in the range 0–9 or a–f, false otherwise.

4.6 Derive equivalent if-else statements for the following tests:

```
( x > y) ? 1 : 0     (x > a && b < c ) ? a : b     (a > b ) ? (b < c ) ? a : b : c
(x > y ) ? (a < b ) ? (c > d ) ? (m < n ) ? (!z) ? a : b : c : d : e : 0
```

4.7 Replace the following series of nested if-else statements with an equivalent expression:

(a) Using the conditional operator.

(b) Using the logical operators '&&' and '||'.

```
if( a > b )                          if( a < d )
  if( b < c )                          return a ;
    return (c – b) ;                 else if( b < c )
  else if( m > p )                     return a ;
    return m ;                       else if ( b < d )
```

```
    else
        return p ;
else
    return b ;
```

```
{
    if( c < d )
        return c ;
    else
        return d ;
} else return (–1) ;
```

4.8 Express the following conditional tests in terms of nested if-else statements with and without the use of the logical operators '&&', '||'.

(a) True if 'a' is greater than 'b', and 'c' is less than 'd' or if 'a' is greater than 'b' and 'd' is less than 1. False otherwise.

(b) False if both 'c' and 'd' are greater than 'b' and if both 'j' and 'k' are less than 'm' and greater than 'z'. True otherwise.

(c) True if 'm' and 'n' and 'p' are true and if both 'c' and 'd' are false. False otherwise.

(d) False if 'm' is false or if 'b' is less than either of 'j' and 'k' and greater than 'm'. True otherwise.

(e) True if 'a' or 'b' is greater than '0' and less than either of 'x' or the sum of 'p' and 'q'. True also if 'm' is less than 'n' and greater than 'r + s' or less than 'r + t'. False otherwise.

Discuss what, if any, ambiguities arise when interpreting the above.

4.9 Write two versions of a program using if-else and the conditional operator to determine whether a year is a leap year or not.
Hint: Any year exactly divisible by 4 is a leap year. However, if that same year is exactly divisible by 100 it is not, unless it is also exactly divisible by 400.

4.10 Write two versions of a function to return:

(a) The maximum value

(b) The minimum value.

of either two, three or four integer values. The first version of each function should be written to make use of if-else statements. The second version should be written to make use of the conditional operator '?:'.

4.11 Rewrite the solutions developed for Exercise 4.5 in the form of functions but making use of the switch statement in place of the conditional operator.

4.12 A salesman is paid wholly on the commission he earns each month, which is calculated as a percentage of the total monthly sales using the commission scales shown below:

Sales < £5,000.00	0%
Sales > £5,000.00 and < £10,000.00	2.5%
Sales > £10,000.00 and < £25,000.00	4%
Sales > £25,000.00 and < £35,000.00	7.5%
Sales > £35,000.00 and < £50,000.00	9%
Sales > £50,000.00	12%

Write a program to read in the monthly sales figures and hence determine the basic commission each saleman earns. In addition to the basic commission scheme offered above, a salesman who has been with the company for three or more years is entitled to the following additional commission using the scales shown below. Modify your program to read in the length of service of each salesman and hence calculate the total commission.

Sales < £10,000.00	an additional 0.5%
Sales > £10,000.00 and < £25,000.00	an additional 1%
Sales > £25,000.00 and < £35,000.00	an additional 2.5%
Sales > £35,000.00	an additional 4%

4.13 A student's final year award is classified on the basis of what overall aggregate mark he or she achieves. The classification is governed using the following equations:

1st class honours	>= 70%
2:1 with honours	>= 60%
2:2 with honours	>= 50%
3rd class honours	>= 40%
Pass	>= 35%
Fail	< 35%

Write a program to read in the aggregate mark for a student and thus award the student the correct degree classification.

In addition to these classifications, the university regulations state that no student shall obtain a 1st class honours degree unless they have obtained at least a 2:1 classification for each of the seven subjects that combine (in equal proportion) to form the aggregate mark.

Additionally, a student is referred (no classification is offered) if he or she is deemed to have failed (< 35%) three subjects. Finally, no student is to be awarded any degree (that is, he or she is referred) unless they achieve at least a 3rd class honours classification for their final year project.

Redesign your program to read the marks for the seven subject areas (one of which is the project) to take into account these restrictions and thus produce an overall classification/referral for the student.

5 A Closer Look at Repetition

An essential requirement for most programs is the ability to create and execute repetitive sections of code; that is, code which is executed while some condition remains true or until some condition becomes false. For example, the simple action of printing the numbers 0 to 10 might involve a section of code that repeatedly displays and then increments a variable, from its initial or starting value of 0, while it is less than or equal to 10.

Most repetition is based around this basic concept of a control variable, initialized at the start of the loop to a preset or starting value and either incremented or decremented by statements within the loop, while some test expression resolves to true or, thought of in another way, until the test expression resolves to false, which then terminates the loop.

C supports three types of looping constructs in the form of the while, the do-while and the for loops, each of which were met briefly in Chapter 1, and all of which are fairly closely related. In this chapter, we are going to expand our knowledge and understanding of loops by considering new features not previously discussed, and in the process, highlight some of the pitfalls into which a novice programmer can all too easily fall.

5.1 The while loop

A flowchart and simple discussion of the while loop were given previously in Figure 1.6 and its general form is summarized below:

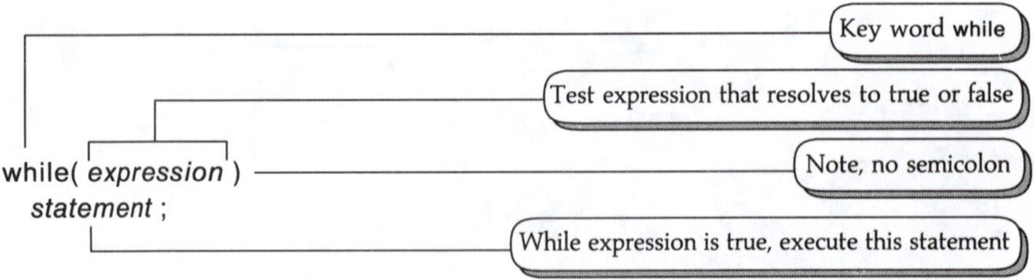

Key word while
Test expression that resolves to true or false
while(expression)
statement ;
Note, no semicolon
While expression is true, execute this statement

Here, a test expression is evaluated at the start of the loop. If that test expression resolves to false, then the loop terminates immediately and the body of the loop, in this instance a single statement, is never executed. However, if the test expression resolves to true, the body of the loop *is* executed once, which is known as an **iteration** of the loop, after which the program loops back to re-evaluate the test expression for a second time. If this is still found to be true, the body of the loop is executed again for a second iteration.

Thus the sequence of evaluate test expression, followed by the execution of the body of the loop, is repeated while the test expression resolves to true, or, looking at it in a different way, until the test expression becomes false.

Generally speaking, most loops are required to control the execution of more than one statement and, as we saw in Chapter 1, a statement block comprising braces '{ }' may be used to associate more than one statement with the body of the loop. An example is given below, where statements '1' to 'n' are executed as a sequence with every iteration of the loop:

```
while( expression ) {
   statement1 ;
   . . .
   statementn
}
```

Execute these statements in sequence, while expression is true

Application 5.1

Write a program to display a table of temperature conversions from Fahrenheit to Celsius or vice versa. The starting, ending and incremental temperatures should be requested at run time, along with the required conversion type (C to F or F to C). Temperature conversion can be performed in accordance with the equation $C = 1.8 \times F + 32.0$, where C and F are temperatures expressed in Celsius and Fahrenheit, respectively.

Application 5.1 Temperature conversion with a while loop.

```
#include   <stdio.h>
#include   <stdlib.h>        /* for atof() */
#include   <ctype.h>         /* for toupper() */
#include   <math.h>          /* for fabs() */

int main( void )
{
   double   start_temp, end_temp, increment ;
   char     buff[BUFSIZ] ;

   printf("Enter Starting Temperature: ");
   start_temp = atof( gets( buff )) ;
```

```
    printf("Enter Ending Temperature: ");
    end_temp = atof( gets( buff )) ;

    printf("Enter Temperature Increment: ");
    increment = fabs(atof( gets( buff ))) ;

    printf("C to F or F to C conversion [C or F]: ") ;

    if( toupper(getchar()) == 'C' )  {         /* Celsius to Fahrenheit conversion */
      printf("\n%10s%15s", "Celsius", "Fahrenheit") ;
      printf("\n%10s%15s\n", "-------", "----------") ;
      while( start_temp <= end_temp )  {
        printf("%10g%15g\n", start_temp, start_temp * 1.8 + 32) ;
        start_temp += increment ;
      }
    }
    else  {                                     /* Fahrenheit to Celsius conversion */
      printf("\n%10s%15s", "Fahrenheit", "Celsius") ;
      printf("\n%10s%15s\n", "----------", "-------") ;
      while( start_temp <= end_temp )  {
        printf("%10g%15g\n", start_temp, (start_temp - 32.0) / 1.8 ) ;
        start_temp += increment ;
      }
    }
    return 0 ;
  }
```

When the program in Application 5.1 was run, the following sample displays were produced:

```
Enter Starting Temperature: 0
Enter Ending Temperature: 10
Enter Temperature Increment: 1
C to F or F to C conversion [ C or F ] : C

   Celsius     Fahrenheit
         0             32
         1           33.8
         2           35.6
         3           37.4
         4           39.2
         5             41
         6           42.8
         7           44.6
         8           46.4
         9           48.2
        10             50
```

```
Enter Starting Temperature: 30
Enter Ending Temperature: 60
Enter Temperature Increment: 5
C to F or F to C conversion [ C or F ] : F

Fahrenheit        Celsius
        30       -1.11111
        35        1.66667
        40        4.44444
        45        7.22222
        50             10
        55        12.7778
        60        15.5556
```

5.1.1 *Manipulating arrays with loops*

Another useful application for loops lies in the processing of arrays. For example, a loop could easily be designed to initialize an array of 10 integers with the values 0 to 9, as shown in Program 5.1, where the control variable whose value is successively incremented with each iteration of the loop serves as the **index** or subscript to the array.

Program 5.1 Initializing an array with a while loop.

```
#include  <stdio.h>
#define   NUM 10                /* the number of elements in the array */

int main( void )
{
   int  array[ NUM ] ;
   int  i = 0 ;

   while( i < NUM )  {

      array[ i ] = i ;
      printf("Element array[ %d ] = %d\n", i, array [ i ] ) ;
      i ++ ;
   }
   return 0 ;
}
```

Control variable 'i' used as the subscript to the array

Application 5.2

Write a program to read characters from the keyboard using the function getchar() and convert all lower case characters to their equivalent upper case and vice versa before storing them in successive elements of an array. The program should stop when an end-of-file condition is received from the keyboard (simulated by pressing <Control-Z> on an MS-DOS machine, <Control-D> on UNIX) and then redisplay the converted string.

Application 5.2 Simple string manipulation using a while loop.

```
#include   <stdio.h>
#include   <ctype.h>          /* required for toupper( ) and tolower( ) */

int main( void )
{
  int    i = 0, c ;
  char  array[ BUFSIZ ] ;

  while((c = getchar( )) != EOF )  {
    if( c >= 'a' && c <= 'z')
      c = toupper( c ) ;
    else if( c >= 'A' && c <= 'Z' )
      c = tolower( c ) ;
    array[ i ++ ] = c ;
  }
  array[ i ] = '\0' ;
  puts( array ) ;
  return 0 ;
}
```

getchar( ) returns EOF upon detection of end of input

Integer variable 'i' used as the subscript to the array

Notice how the while loop began as

```
while( (c = getchar( )) != EOF )
```

Here, the inner set of parentheses around the expression 'c = getchar( )' ensures that the character returned by getchar( ) is assigned to the variable 'c' *before* the comparison is made with the symbolic constant EOF (a value returned by getchar( ) upon detection of the program's end of input). Without these parentheses, the relational operator '!=', having a higher precedence than assignment '=', would have been evaluated first, resulting in 'c' being assigned the value 0 (false) if getchar( ) returned EOF or 1 (true) otherwise.

Notice also how 'c' was also defined as an int (or a signed char) and not just a char. This is to ensure correct comparison with the signed int quantity EOF (remember the signedness of chars is implementation dependent). When the program in Application 5.2 was run, the following sample display was produced:

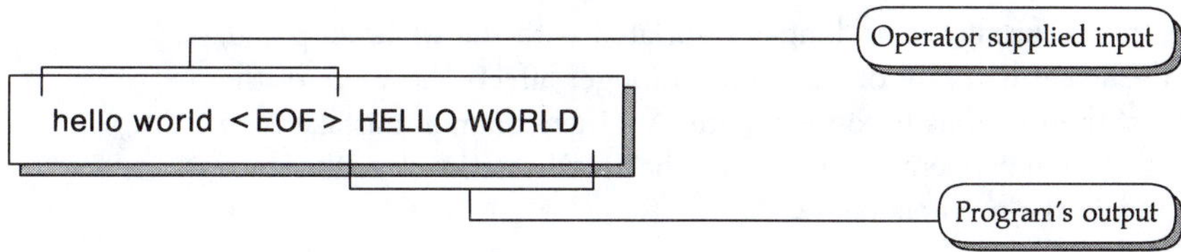

Try running the above program with its input redirected to come from a disk file instead, using an operating system command such as:

```
$ prog <test.txt
```

where '$' is the UNIX operating system prompt (or 'c:' (typically) on an MS-DOS machine), 'prog' is the name of your executable program and 'test.txt' is a text file whose contents serve as the input to your program in place of the operator's data entered at the keyboard.

5.1.2 *Common mistakes with* while *loops*

As with an if test, there are a number of simple errors that are all too easy for the novice programmer to make with a while loop. Consider for a moment the following program section:

```
while( a < 5 ) ;
  printf("%d\n", a++ ) ;
```

Accidental semicolon

Caution!

Here, the programmer has accidentally placed a semicolon at the end of the while, which is similar to the problem that we saw in Chapter 4, where a semicolon was placed at the end of an if test. Since the compiler is unconcerned with program layout, it assumes the ';' to a be a single NULL or do nothing statement associated with the execution of the loop; thus it appears to the compiler as if the loop had been written in the manner shown below:

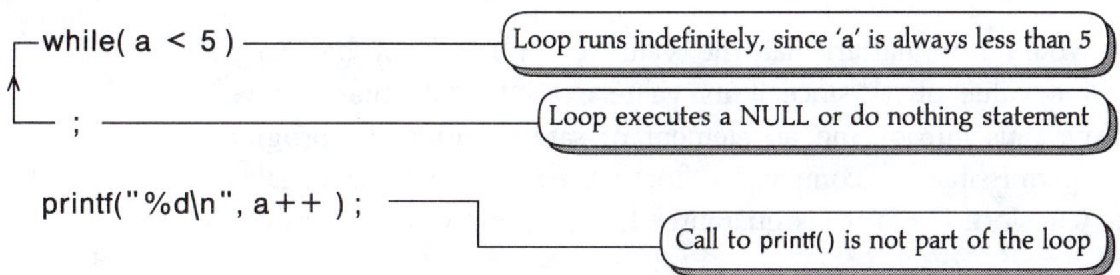

Now the call to printf() is no longer associated with the while loop and, more importantly, since the body of the loop no longer affects the value of the control variable 'a' the loop has become infinite. Another common mistake is to use the '=' or assignment operator instead of the '==' relational equivalence operator, as shown in the example below:

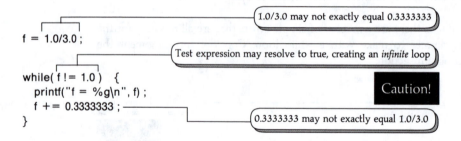

Accidental use of assignment rather than '=='

```
while( i = '\n' )
  i = getchar() ;
```

Caution!

Here, because 'i' is assigned the value of the new line character '\n', which has a non-zero value, the test expression controlling the loop will always resolve to true, thus creating another infinite loop.

Finally, take care when using real or floating point values in expressions that control the termination of a loop, since it may not always be possible to compare exactly two floating point values for equivalence (due to their restricted precision). For example, consider the following section of code, where 'f' has been defined as a double:

1.0/3.0 may not exactly equal 0.3333333

Test expression may resolve to true, creating an *infinite* loop

0.3333333 may not exactly equal 1.0/3.0

```
f = 1.0/3.0 ;

while( f != 1.0 )  {
  printf("f = %g\n", f) ;
  f += 0.3333333 ;
}
```

Caution!

Because the implicit floating point constant '0.3333333' may not exactly match the value of '1.0/3.0', then the test expression 'f != 1.0' might always end up resolving to logical true, creating an infinite loop. A more reliable test expression would rely upon the relational operator '<', for example:

Use of '<' ensures loop terminates even if 'f' never exactly equals '1.0'

```
while( f < 1.0 )
  ...
```

Here, it would not matter that the value of '1.0' cannot be exactly represented by the value of 'f', since if its value exceeds '1.0', the loop will terminate anyway, thus introducing an element of safety within the program. Note that it is permissible to compare a floating point value for equality/inequality with '0.0' since the latter is guaranteed to be exactly representable as zero.

Should it be necessary to compare two floating point expressions for equality, then an expression of the form shown below may be used. Here a loop repeats while the difference between 'x' and 'y' is greater than the specified precision of 0.00001:

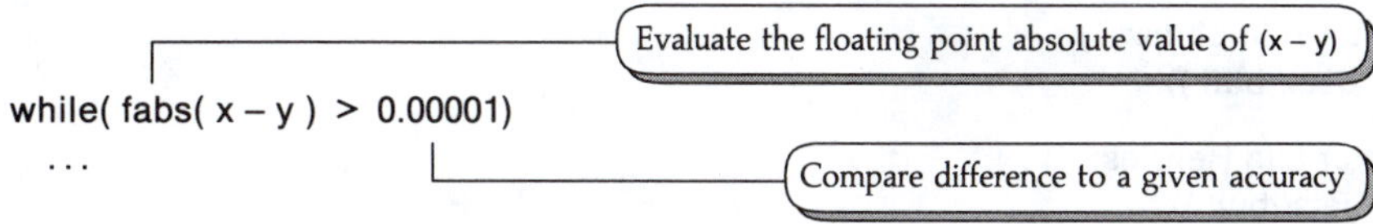

Now that we have considered the while loop in some detail, let us consider some further applications of it.

Application 5.3

The current 'i' in amperes present in the circuit shown in Figure 5.1 at time 't' seconds after voltage 'V' is applied is given by the equation '$i = (V/R)(1 - e^{-Rt/L})$', where 'R' and 'L' represent the resistance and inductance of the circuit, respectively.

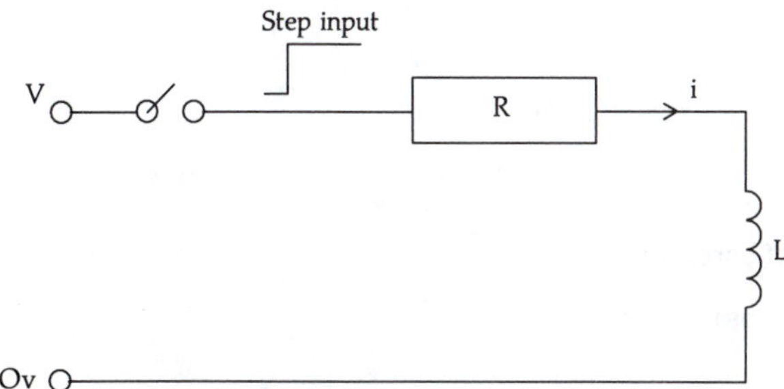

Figure 5.1 An inductive circuit.

Write a program to read values for 'R', 'L' and 'V' and also the final and incremental times for which the circuit will be examined and then display and plot on the operator's screen the values of the current 'i' for these time intervals.

Application 5.3 Growth of current in an inductive circuit.

```
#include   <stdio.h>
#include   <stdlib.h>
#include   <math.h>

#define   Y_SCALE   80        /* width of output screen in columns */
```

```
int main( void )
{
  double  R, L, V ;
  double  t, i, time_increment, final_time ;
  char    buff[BUFSIZ] ;

  printf("Enter R in ohms: ") ;
  R = atof( gets( buff )) ;

  printf("Enter L in Henries: ") ;
  L = atof( gets( buff )) ;

  printf("Enter V in volts: ") ;
  V = atof( gets( buff )) ;

  printf("Enter time increment for t in seconds: ");
  time_increment = atof( gets( buff )) ;

  printf("Enter final time for t in seconds: ");
  final_time = atof( gets( buff )) ;

  printf("%15s%15s\n", "Time (t)", "Current (i)") ;
  printf("%15s%15s\n", "--------", "-----------") ;

/* Now plot table of 'i' against 't' */

  t = 0 ;
  while( t < final_time )  {
    printf("%15g%15g\n", t, (V/R)*(1.0 - exp(-R*t/L))) ;
    t += time_increment ;
  }

/* Now plot the current along x axis of screen */

  printf("\n\n%40s\n", "Current i (Amps)") ;

  i = 0 ;
  while( i < 8 )
    printf("%-10g", V/R * i++ / 8) ;

  printf("\n!----!----!----!----!----!----!----!----") ;
  printf("!----!----!----!----!----!----!----!----\n") ;

/* Now plot value of 'i' across screen against 't' down screen using a scaling factor */

  t = 0 ;
  while( t < final_time )  {

    printf("%*c\n", (int)(Y_SCALE *(1.0 - exp(-R*t/L))) , '*') ;
    t += time_increment ;
  }
  return 0 ;
}
```

See Section 15.2.1 for explanation of '*' in format indicator

With values of R = 5, L = 10 and V = 10 and with a time interval of 1 second and a final time of 15 seconds, the following output was observed on the author's screen:

```
Time (t)     Current (i)
       0               0
       1        0.786939
       2         1.26424
       3         1.55374
       4         1.72933
       5         1.83583
       6         1.80043
       7         1.93961
       8         1.96337
       9         1.97778
      10         1.98652
      11         1.99183
      12         1.99504
      13         1.99699
      14         1.99818

                         Current i (Amps)
0        0.25       0.5      0.75       1       1.25       1.5       1.75
!----!----!----!----!----!----!----!----!----!----!----!----!----!----!----!----
*
                             *
                                                  *
                                                          *
                                                               *
                                                                   *
                                                                      *
                                                                       *
                                                                        *
                                                                         *
                                                                          *
                                                                          *
                                                                          *
                                                                          *
                                                                          *
```

Application 5.4

A bank offers a mortgage to a client, charged at a fixed percentage interest rate per annum, which is calculated monthly. Given that the client repays a fixed amount each month, write a program to read in the initial value of the mortgage, the annual rate of interest and the amount repaid each month and thus determine how long it will take the client to repay the mortgage and the total amount of interest repaid in that time.

Application 5.4 Mortgage repayment.

```
#include   <stdio.h>
#include   <stdlib.h>

int main( void )
{
  char      buff[ BUFSIZ ] ;
  double  loan, repayment, rate, interest, total_interest = 0.0 ;
  int        months=0, years = 0 ;

  printf("Enter the Initial Value of the Loan: £") ;
  loan = atof( gets( buff )) ;

  printf("Enter Interest Rate %% per Annum: ") ;
  rate = atof( gets( buff )) / 12.0 ;                /* calculate monthly interest rate */
  interest = loan * rate / 100.0 ;                   /* calculate initial monthly interest */

  printf("Enter Value of Monthly Repayment. Minimum = £%g: £", interest) ;
  repayment = atof( gets( buff )) ;

  if( interest > repayment )                         /* check repayment > interest */
    printf("Repayment must be at least equal to interest !!!!\n") ;

  else  {
    printf("\n\n%4s%6s%10s%10s%15s%18s\n",
      "Year", "Month", "Interest", "Repaid", "Outstanding", "Total Interest") ;
    printf("%4s%6s%10s%10s%15s%18s\n",
      "----", "-----", "--------", "------", "-----------","--------------" ) ;

    while( loan >= repayment )  {
      interest = loan * (rate / 100.0) ;             /* calculate monthly interest for loan */

      total_interest += interest ;                   /* add it to total interest for loan */
      loan += interest – repayment ;                 /* add interest to outstanding loan */

      if( ++months > 12 )  {                         /* keep track of months and years */
        months = 1 ;
        years ++ ;
      }

      printf("%4d%6d%10.2f%10.2f%15.2f%18.2f\n",
      years, months, interest, repayment, loan, total_interest ) ;
    }

    printf("\nNormal repayments end in %d years and %d months\n",
                years, months) ;
```

```
    if( loan != 0.0 )
        printf("After which one further repayment of £%.2f will be due\n", loan) ;

    printf("Total interest repaid up to that point = £%.2f\n", total_interest) ;
  }
  return 0 ;
}
```

When the program in Application 5.4 was run, the following sample display was produced:

```
Enter the Initial Value of the Loan: £1000
Enter Interest Rate % per Annum: 12.5
Enter Value of Monthly Repayment. Minimum = £10.4167: £150

Year   Month   Interest   Repaid   Outstanding   Total Interest
   0       1      10.42   150.00        860.42            10.42
   0       2       8.96   150.00        719.38            19.38
   0       3       7.49   150.00        576.87            26.87
   0       4       6.01   150.00        432.88            32.88
   0       5       4.51   150.00        287.39            37.39
   0       6       2.99   150.00        140.38            40.38

Normal repayments end in 0 years and 6 months
After which one further repayment of £140.38 will be due
Total interest repaid up to that point = £40.38
```

Application 5.5

Write a program to count the number of lines, spaces, opening and closing comments and braces that appear within a C program. You can use the input redirection operator '<' to allow the contents of a disk file (a C source file is a good example) to be used as the input to the program using a command such as:

```
c: prog_name < file.txt
```

where 'c:' is the typical MS-DOS operating system prompt ('$' for a UNIX machine), 'prog_name' is the name of your compiled, executable program and 'file.txt' is the name of a file whose contents will be redirected as the input to the program. This application also demonstrates the nesting of while loops inside each other, that is, where one type of loop is contained entirely within another one with the inner loop being executed, perhaps many times, for every iteration of the outer loop.

Application 5.5 Character counting from a disk file.

```
#include   <stdio.h>

int main( void )
{
   char  buff[ BUFSIZ ] ;
   int    i, spaces = 0, lines = 0, open_braces = 0 ;
   int    closing_braces = 0, open_comments = 0, closing_comments = 0 ;

/*
** Read lines of text from the file while the end-of-file condition has not been detected.
** Each line of text is placed into the array 'buff' prior to processing
*/
                                                  gets() returns NULL upon end of input/file

   while( gets( buff ) != NULL )   {
      i = 0 ;
      lines ++ ;

   /*
   ** Now process each line as a sequence of characters terminated by a '\0'
   */
                                                  Process one character at a time

      while( buff[ i ] != '\0' )   {
         if( buff[ i ] == ' ' ) spaces ++ ;
         if( buff[ i ] == '{' ) open_braces ++ ;
         if( buff[ i ] == '}' ) closing_braces ++ ;

         if( buff[ i ] == '/' && buff[ i+1 ] == '*')
            open_comments ++ ;
         if( buff[ i ] == '*' && buff[ i+1 ] == '/')
            closing_comments ++ ;

         i++ ;
      }
   }

   printf("\nTotal Number of Lines = [%d] \n", lines) ;
   printf("Total Number of Spaces = [%d] \n", spaces) ;
   printf("Total Number of Opening Comments = [%d] \n", open_comments) ;
   printf("Total Number of Closing Comments = [%d] \n", closing_comments) ;
   printf("Total Number of Opening Braces = [%d] \n", open_braces) ;
   printf("Total number of Closing Braces = [%d]\n", closing_braces ) ;
   return 0 ;
}
```

Using the source file shown below as the input to the program:

```
#include   <stdio.h>

int main( void )    /* start of program */
{
  int i ;
  for( i = 0 ; i < 10 ; i++ )
    printf("Hello World\n") ;
  return 0 ;
}
```

Source file that serves as program input

the following display was produced:

```
Total Number of Lines = [9]
Total Number of Spaces = [39]
Total Number of Opening Comments = [1]
Total Number of Closing Comments = [1]
Total Number of Opening Braces = [1]
Total Number of Closing Braces = [1]
```

5.2 The do-while loop

The do-while loop is in many ways similar to the while loop, but with one important exception. The test expression that controls the termination of the loop is evaluated at the *end* of the loop rather than at the start, which means that the body of a do-while loop is guaranteed to execute at least once, even if the resulting test expression resolves immediately to false when the loop commences. We met the do-while loop, along with its flowchart, in Chapter 1. Its general form is given below:

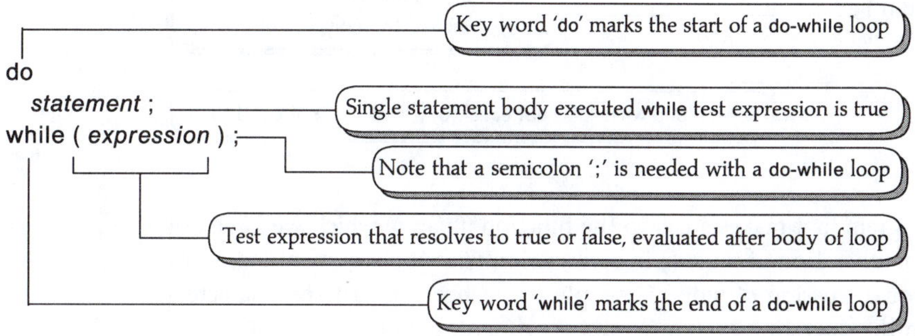
do
statement ;
while (expression) ;
Key word 'do' marks the start of a do-while loop
Single statement body executed while test expression is true
Note that a semicolon ';' is needed with a do-while loop
Test expression that resolves to true or false, evaluated after body of loop
Key word 'while' marks the end of a do-while loop

Unlike a while loop, a semicolon *is* required at the end of a do-while loop, since it marks the end of a statement. Of course, more than one statement can be associated with the execution of the loop if these statements are enclosed with a statement block, an example of which is given below.

The do-while loop is frequently employed in preference to a while loop where it is necessary to perform an action or sequence of actions before deciding whether to repeat them or not. A particularly common example of this is validating an operator's entry made at the keyboard. For example, consider the following section of code which prompts an operator for a choice in the range 1–5. The program reads the operator's choice, and rejects and re-prompts if the choice is invalid:

```
do {
    printf("Enter Option ... 1 - 5: ") ;
    i = atoi( gets( buff )) ;
} while( i < 1 || i > 5 ) ;
```

While 'i' is not in correct range, repeat the execution of the loop

In other words, if the operator's response is invalid – that is, the value of 'i' is less than 1 or greater than 5 – then the test expression resolves to true and the loop repeats, re-prompting for another choice.

The only way for the above loop to terminate is for the operator to supply a valid choice in the range 1 to 5, thus forcing the test expression to resolve to false thus terminating the loop. As another example, consider the program section below, designed to prompt an operator for a single character response of 'y' (for yes) or 'n' (for no):

```
do {
    fflush( stdin ) ;
    printf("\nAre you sure you want to delete the file ... [ y / n ] ? ") ;
    c = tolower( getchar( )) ;
    fflush( stdin ) ;
} while( c != 'y' && c != 'n' ) ;
```

Discard any characters that the operator may have typed ahead

Discard any additional unread characters entered by the operator

Repeat loop while 'c' is not equal to 'y' and 'c' is not equal to 'n'

The program first makes a call to the function fflush( ), which we have not met before. The operation of fflush( ) in conjunction with the argument stdin (see Section 1.11 for discussion of stdin) is simply to flush or discard any characters that may be in the operating system's input (keyboard) buffer.

This has the effect of discarding any characters that the program's operator may have entered ahead of the program's prompt for a 'y' or 'n' response; thus the operator is forced to supply their response at this point rather than earlier. The operator is given the opportunity to reply, with a call to getchar(), and, just for good measure, the function tolower() is called to ensure that the operator's choice is converted to lower case prior to assignment to 'c'.

Next, a second call to fflush() is made. In this instance fflush() discards any superfluous characters that the operator may have entered after the 'y' or 'n' response, thus ensuring that there are no superfluous characters left in the buffer once the loop terminates, which might confuse any other input functions that come later in the program. (Ideally, this section of code would be written in the form of a function that could be called whenever a yes or no response is required from the program's operator.) The loop then repeats if the value of 'c' is not equal to 'y' and not equal to 'n'. Try running the above section of code within a simple program and observe the effect of dispensing with the calls to fflush().

Note that some compilers such as Borland's Turbo C provide the functions getche() and getch() (which are not Standard C functions) to allow a character to be read directly from the keyboard (with and without echoing it back to the screen) without the program's operator having to enter a carriage return. This can sometimes prove more convenient than calling fflush() after a call to getchar().

Another frequent use of the do-while loop lies in repeating the actions of a program once it has come to an end. For example, the program that performed temperature conversions in Application 5.1 is an ideal candidate for incorporating into a loop.

You will recall that the program runs just once and stops. It did not give the operator the opportunity to repeat the operation and prompt for a second, perhaps different, set of temperature values. Program 5.2 rectifies this by placing the whole program inside a do-while loop with an operator verification test at the end to determine whether the program should repeat or stop.

It also demonstrates the use of a do-while loop when verifying input data. In this example, it is used to ensure that the value 'end_temp' is greater than or equal to 'start_temp'.

Program 5.2 Repeated temperature conversions.

```
#include   <stdio.h>
#include   <stdlib.h>      /* for atof() */
#include   <ctype.h>       /* for toupper() */
#include   <math.h>        /* for fabs() */

int main( void )
{
  double   start_temp, end_temp, increment ;
  char     buff[BUFSIZ] ;
```

```
do {
    fflush(stdin) ;

    printf("Enter Starting Temperature: ");
    start_temp = atof( gets( buff )) ;

    do {
        printf("Enter Ending Temperature >= %g: ", start_temp);
        end_temp = atof( gets( buff )) ;
    } while( end_temp < start_temp ) ;          /* ensure end_temp >= start_temp */

    printf("Enter Temperature Increment: ");
    increment = fabs(atof( gets( buff ))) ;

    printf("C to F or F to C conversion [C or F] : ") ;

    if( toupper(getchar()) == 'C' ) {          /* Celsius to Fahrenheit conversion */
        printf("%10s%15s\n", "Celsius", "Fahrenheit") ;
        printf("%10s%15s\n", "-------", "----------") ;

        while( start_temp <= end_temp ) {      /* display table */
            printf("%10g%15g\n", start_temp, start_temp * 1.8 + 32) ;
            start_temp += increment ;
        }
    }
    else {                                      /* Fahrenheit to Celsius conversion */
        printf("%10s%15s\n", "Fahrenheit", "Celsius") ;
        printf("%10s%15s\n", "----------", "-------") ;

        while( start_temp <= end_temp ) {      /* display table */
            printf("%10g%15g\n", start_temp, (start_temp - 32.0) / 1.8 ) ;
            start_temp += increment ;
        }
    }
    printf("Do you wish to try again ? [y/n] : ") ;
    fflush( stdin ) ;          /* remove any characters that may have been typed ahead */
} while( tolower( getchar()) == 'y') ;          /* repeat while operator says so */

return 0 ;
}
```

When Program 5.2 is run it produces the sample display opposite. You can see how, in the first instance, the program rejects an ending temperature less than the starting temperature and re-prompts. Note also how the program repeats if the operator supplies a 'y' response to the prompt 'Do you wish to try again? [y/n]:'.

```
Enter Starting Temperature: 0
Enter Ending Temperature >= 0: -5
Enter Ending Temperature >= 0: 20
Enter Temperature Increment: 2
C to F or F to C conversion [C or F] : C

    Celsius     Fahrenheit
          0             32
          2           35.6
          4           39.2
          6           42.8
          8           46.4
         10             50
         12           53.6
         14           57.2
         16           60.8
         18           64.4
         20             68

Do you wish to try again ? [y/n] : y

Enter Starting Temperature: 50
Enter Ending Temperature >= 50: 100
Enter Temperature Increment: 10
C to F or F to C conversion [C or F] : F
Fahrenheit         Celsius
        50              10
        60         15.5556
        70         21.1111
        80         26.6667
        90         32.2222
       100         37.7778

Do you wish to try again ? [y/n] : n
```

Application 5.6

Given a mathematical function f(x), an approximate root x of that equation is given by Newton's equation as:

$$x = x_0 - f(x)/f'(x)$$

where $f'(x)$ is the first derivative of the equation f(x), that is, df(x)/dx, and x_0 is an initial guess at the root. Using the value of x obtained from each successive evaluation of this equation as the new value for x_0, the approximation can be refined progressively until it converges (hopefully, but not always) on an exact root, at which point x will equal x_0. Using Newton's equation, find the approximate roots of the equation:

$$5x^2 - 6x + 1 = 0$$

The first derivative of this equation is given as:

$$10x - 6$$

The complete program to read in an initial value for x_0 is given below. Notice how the expression 'fabs(x – x0) > 0.00001' is in part used to control the termination of the loop. Because floating point values are not always exactly representable due to their limited precision, it would be unwise to compare two floating values for exact equality. This expression thus determines the absolute – that is, positive – value of the difference between 'x' and 'x0' (using the library function fabs()) and if the difference is greater than 0.000 01 (the required precision to which the calculation of the root of f(x) is to be performed), the loop repeats. This expression, in conjunction with the expression 'guess < NUM_GUESS', ensures that the loop terminates either when the required precision has been reached or when 100 attempts have been made to approximate it.

Application 5.6 An implementation of Newton's solution to root solving.

```
#include   <stdio.h>
#include   <math.h>      math.h contains information about fabs(), which is needed by the compiler

#define  NUM_GUESS  100

int main( void )
{
  int    guess = 0 ;
  float  x, x0, f1, f2 ;

  printf("Enter an initial guess for the root : ") ;
  scanf("%f", &x) ;

  do {
    x0 = x ;
    f1 = 5.0 * x * x - 6.0 * x + 1.0 ;
    f2 = 10.0 * x - 6.0 ;
    x = x0 - f1/f2 ;
    guess ++ ;
  } while( (fabs(x - x0) > 0.00001) && (guess < NUM_GUESS )) ;
```

Execute body of loop while the difference between x and x0 is > 0.000 01 and guess < 100

```
    if( guess == NUM_GUESS )
      printf("Root not found after %d attempts ... ", guess) ;
    else
      printf("Root is (approximately) %f\n", x ) ;
    return 0 ;
}
```

When the program in Application 5.6 was run, the following sample displays were produced:

```
Enter an initial guess for the root : 5
Root is (approximately) 1.000000
```

```
Enter an initial guess for the root : 0
Root is (approximately) 0.200000
```

5.3 The for loop

We met the for loop and its flowchart briefly in Section 1.7.2. This loop is simply a more versatile derivative of the while loop and consists of three expressions, some or all of which may be omitted. These expressions *must* be separated by semicolons, as shown below:

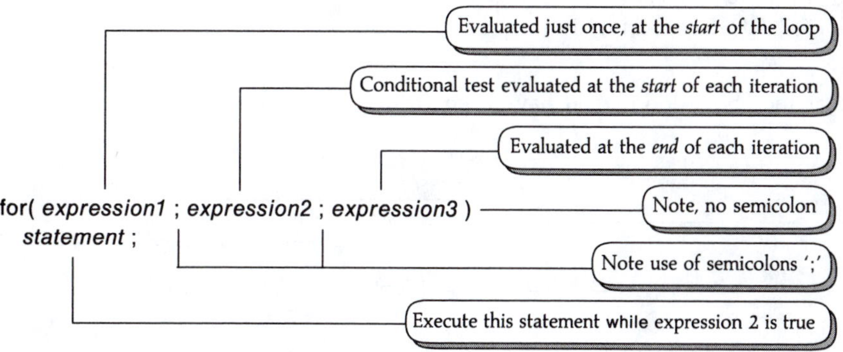

Evaluated just once, at the start of the loop
Conditional test evaluated at the start of each iteration
Evaluated at the end of each iteration
for(expression1 ; expression2 ; expression3)
statement ;
Note, no semicolon
Note use of semicolons ';'
Execute this statement while expression 2 is true

Expression 1 is evaluated once only, at the start of the loop, and often serves to perform some initialization of the loop's control variable or to carry out operations prior to the body of the loop being executed.

Expression 2 is a conditional test expression which is evaluated after expression 1 and is re-evaluated for every iteration of the loop. The statement or body of the loop is repeatedly executed while expression 2 resolves to true.

Expression 3 is evaluated with each iteration of the loop after the body of the loop has been executed and is often used to affect the value of a control variable that will eventually terminate the loop. In general, the for loop looks something like this:

```
for( initialization ; test expression ; post processing )
  statement ;
```

Apart from its use in conjunction with the continue statement (see Section 5.7), a for loop is identical to, and can always be replaced by, a while loop of the form:

```
expression1 ;
while( expression2 ) {
  statement ;
  expression3 ;
}
```

The main attraction of the for loop is that it permits the programmer to view the initial starting condition, the terminating test expression and how the control variable is affected by the loop, all within the same line of code. As an example, a simple program to display the values of all integers in the range 0 to 10 along with their square and cube can be written with one simple statement, as shown below:

```
for ( i = 0 ; i <= 10 ; i ++ )
    printf("%5d%5d%5d\n", i, i*i, i*i*i ) ;
```

Note that the above loop could have been written in the form shown below:

```
i = 0 ;                                      Expression 1 placed outside the loop
for( ; i <= 5 ; ) {                          Semicolons must be preserved
   printf("%5d%5d%5d\n", i, i*i, i*i*i ) ;
   i ++ ;
}                                            Expression 3 placed inside the loop, after the main body
```

where 'expression 1' has been replaced by an equivalent statement *outside* the loop and 'expression 3' by an equivalent statement after the body of the loop. If this approach is chosen (although it would probably make more sense to use a

Program 5.3 Calculation of yearly rainfall figures.

```
#include   <stdio.h>
#include   <stdlib.h>            /* for function atof() */

#define  MONTHS  12

int main( void )
{
    int       i ;
    char      buff[ BUFSIZ ] ;
    double    sum = 0.0 ;

/*
** Start by initializing 'i' to the value 0 and while 'i' is less than MONTHS
** execute the body of the 'for' loop and then increment 'i'.
*/

    for( i = 0 ; i < MONTHS ; i ++ )  {
        printf("Enter Rainfall for month [%d]: ", i) ;
        sum += atof(gets( buff )) ;  /* read in each monthly rainfall figure */
    }
    printf("\nYearly Rainfall Average = %.2f\n", sum / MONTHS ) ;
    return 0 ;
}
```

while loop), then the semicolons that delimit the three expressions in the for loop *must* be preserved. Program 5.3 uses a for loop to calculate the average monthly rainfall figures for a year.

You will often see situations where one for loop is nested inside another, as shown in Program 5.4. This program displays multiplication tables (as taught in

Program 5.4 Generating multiplication tables using nested for loops.

```
#include   <stdio.h>

#define LIMIT 12

int main( void )
{
    int left, right ;

    for( left = 1; left <= LIMIT; left++)  {
        for( right = 1; right <= LIMIT; right ++ )
            printf("%d x %d = %d\n", left, right, left * right) ;
        putchar('\n') ;
    }
    return 0 ;
}
```

school) from 1 × 1 up to 12 × 12. It uses two nested for loops to control the variables 'left' and 'right' used to build the table. The outer loop control variable (left) is set to 1, while the inner loop counts from 1 to 12 (using right).

After the inner loop has terminated, a new line is issued and the outer loop control variable left is incremented to 2 before the inner loop again counts from 1 to 12. This repeats until the outer loop has performed 12 iterations and the inner loop a total of 144 iterations (that is, 12 × 12).

Another example of the use of nested for loops can be seen in Program 5.5, which uses four single bit variables, b0 to b3, to step through a four bit binary sequence and thus exercise a boolean logic function given as:

$$x = (b1 \cdot \overline{b2}) + (b1 \cdot \overline{b2} \cdot b3) + \overline{(b0 + \overline{b3})}$$

Note how the function boolean() which simulates this logic function makes use of the logical operators '&&', '||' and '!' rather than the bitwise '&', '|' and '~' to simulate logical AND, OR and NOT conditions. Can you see why this works? (*Hint:* Think about the numeric value of true and false conditions in C.)

Program 5.5 Boolean algebra problem.

```
#include  <stdio.h>

int  boolean( int b3, int b2, int b1, int b0)
{
   return(( b1 && !b2) || (b1 && !b2 && b3) || !(b0 || !b3 ));
}

int main( void )
{
   int  b0, b1, b2, b3 ;

   printf("b3 b2 b1 b0 Output\n");

   for( b3 = 0; b3 <= 1; b3 ++)
      for( b2 = 0; b2 <= 1; b2 ++)
         for( b1 = 0; b1 <= 1; b1 ++)
            for( b0 = 0; b0 <= 1; b0 ++)
               printf("%2d %2d %2d %2d %2d\n",
                  b3, b2, b1, b0, boolean(b3, b2, b1, b0)) ;
   return 0 ;
}
```

When Program 5.5 is run, it leads to the following display being produced:

```
b3   b2   b1   b0   Output
0    0    0    0    0
0    0    0    1    0
0    0    1    0    1
0    0    1    1    1
0    1    0    0    0
0    1    0    1    0
0    1    1    0    0
0    1    1    1    0
1    0    0    0    1
1    0    0    1    0
1    0    1    0    1
1    0    1    1    1
1    1    0    0    1
1    1    0    1    0
1    1    1    0    1
1    1    1    1    0
```

5.4 Infinite loops

An extremely useful type of repetitive structure is the **infinite** loop. Such loops are easily created with any of the three looping constructs discussed previously by ensuring that the test expression used to control the termination of the loop always resolves to true by substituting a non-zero value for that expression (from Chapter 4 you will recall that any expression that resolves to a non-zero value is deemed to be true). Table 5.1 demonstrates this for each of the three types of loop construct supported by C. Such loops can only be terminated by a suitable return or break statement (see Section 5.6) or by terminating the program itself.

Note that in the special case of the for loop, the compiler is happy to accept an empty test expression, although a non-zero value could be used if required.

Table 5.1 Making an infinite loop.

while *loop*	do-while *loop*	for *loop*
while(1) {	do {	for(; ;) {
statement1 ;	*statement1* ;	*statement1* ;
...	...	...
statementn ;	*statementn* ;	*statementn* ;
}	} while(1)	}

5.5 The comma operator: ','

The comma operator may be used to combine a number of expressions into a single expression. The general form of this operator is given below:

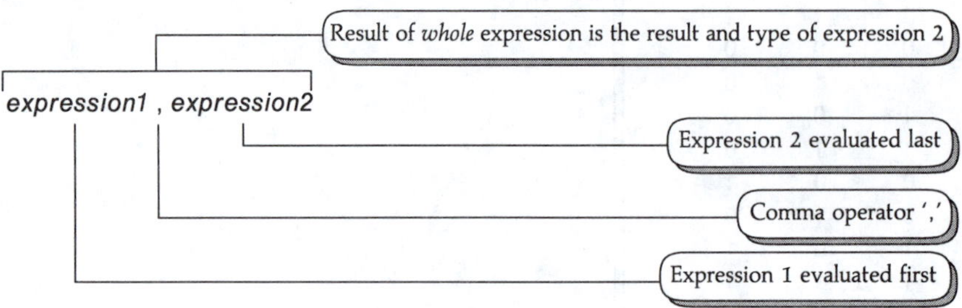

where the result of the whole expression has the type and value given by expression 2. The value generated by 'expression 1' is simply discarded. The comma operator has the lowest precedence of all of C's operators (see Table 3.13) and is evaluated in a left to right manner; thus, 'expression 1' is evaluated prior to expression 2. The following statement therefore assigns the value '3' to 'b' and '7' to both 'a' and 'c':

```
a = ( b = 3, c = b + 4 ) ;
```

Note that parentheses were required around the two inner expressions, since, as we noted above, the comma operator has a lower precedence than '='. What then does the compiler make of the following statement without parentheses?

```
a = b = 3 , c = 4 ;
```

Here, both 'a' and 'b' are assigned the value '3', since assignment has a higher precedence than comma, after which 'c' is assigned the value '4'; the result of the *whole* expression (that is, whatever value was assigned to 'c') is then discarded (leaving 'c' equal to 4).

Probably the single most common application of the comma operator lies in permitting several smaller expressions to be evaluated within each of expressions 1, 2 and 3 of the for loop. As an example, using the comma operator in conjunction with the for loop would allow us to rewrite Program 5.3 to embed the initialization of both 'i' and 'sum' within 'expression 1' of the for loop and to combine the last statement in the body of that loop, 'sum += atoi(gets(buff))' with the 'i++' statement in 'expression 3', as shown below:

Comma operator ','

```
for( sum = 0.0 , i = 0 ; i < MONTHS ; sum += atoi(gets(buff)) , i++ )
   printf("Month %d\n", i ) ;
```

Whether you consider the latter more readable is purely a matter of taste. You are, however, likely to encounter variations on this theme in other programs, particularly in association with the for loop, so watch out for them.

As another, less common, example, the comma operator may be used to associate more than one statement with a conditional test or loop construct without the need for braces. This is particularly useful in the creation of macros (see Chapter 13). For example:

No braces '{ }' required to group these statements with ',' operator

```
printf("Payday ? ") ;
if( getchar() == 'y' )
   printf("Hello Kind World\n"),
   printf("Let's spend, spend, spend !!!\n") ;
else
   printf("Goodbye Cruel World\n"),
   printf("I'm flat bust . . . \n") ;
```

Comma operator ','

Note that the use of a comma appearing in other parts of a program does not necessarily imply the comma operator and may well represent its use as a separator, as in the statement:

```
double   a, b ;
```

Comma here is not an operator, only a separator

5.6 Premature termination of a loop: The break statement

We have already seen how a loop is terminated when the test expression controlling its repetition becomes false. Now, although such an approach is normally quite acceptable, there are many situations where the sequence of statements within the loop are themselves involved in making decisions and these may well conclude that, given the data available at that time, it would be better if the loop could be terminated there and then rather than proceeding on to the end of the current iteration.

You will recall from the previous chapter that we introduced the break statement as a means of terminating the sequence of statements associated with each case in a switch statement. That same break statement can also be put to good use when employed with a loop, to terminate its execution, perhaps prematurely.

For example, we saw earlier how a do-while loop could be used to verify an operator's response for a numeric value in the range 1–5. The example code used is given again below, where the loop naturally terminates as a result of 'i' falling within the range 1–5:

```
do {
    printf("Enter Option ... 1 - 5: ") ;
    i = atoi( gets( buff )) ;
} while( i < 1 || i > 5 ) ;
```

Repeat while operator's response is not in range 1–5

However, we could achieve the same effect with an infinite loop and a break statement, as shown below:

```
do {
    printf("Enter Option ... 1 - 5: ") ;
    i = atoi( gets( buff )) ;
    if( i >= 1 && i <= 5 )
        break ;
} while( 1 ) ;

rest of program
```

If 'i' is in the range 1 to 5 then break out of loop

As a more useful example, we could write a simple section of code to calculate the average of a number of values entered by the program's operator at the keyboard. In this instance, it will be assumed that the operator is allowed to enter as many numbers as they wish and will signal the end of input by simulating the end-of-file condition EOF for the program. (<Control-Z> on MS-DOS, <Control-D> for UNIX).

To enable this to be done, we shall use an infinite for loop which attempts to read numbers forever. Within this loop are statements that read (using scanf()) and sum each number while the EOF condition has not been detected. The code to carry out this operation is given below:

```
for(sum = 0, count = 0 ; ; count ++ ) {

    printf("Enter a number: ") ;
    if( scanf("%d", &num) == EOF)
        break ;
    sum += num ;
}

if( count > 0 )
    printf("Average = %d\n", sum/count) ;
```

Note empty test expression implying infinite loop

Note that if a break statement appears within a nested loop construct, such as that shown below, then it only serves to terminate the innermost loop in which it appears, and not *all* of the loops that surround it:

```
while( i < 5 )  {
  ...
  while( j < 3 )  {
    ...
    if( i == 5 )
      break ;
  }
  ...
}
```

Break from inner while loop to outer while loop

The use of break in a program is considered by some to be 'unstructured'. Personally, the author does not share that view, since a break only serves to transfer program flow in a limited and localized way and is in line with the structured programming philosophy of a 'single entry, single exit point'.

In other words, the program may only resume processing after a break with the statement that would have been executed had the loop been terminated naturally, and is a far cry from the unconditional and unstructured goto statement.

5.7 The continue statement

The continue statement, rather than terminating a loop, forces a *new* iteration of the loop to begin, resulting in any remaining statements within the loop being skipped for that iteration. The operation is illustrated below for each of the three looping constructs:

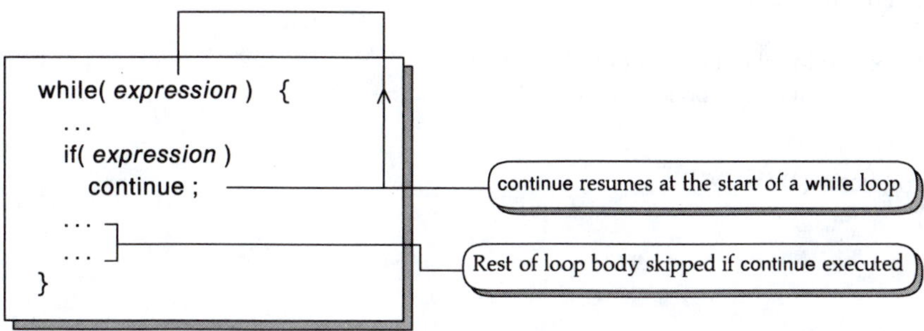

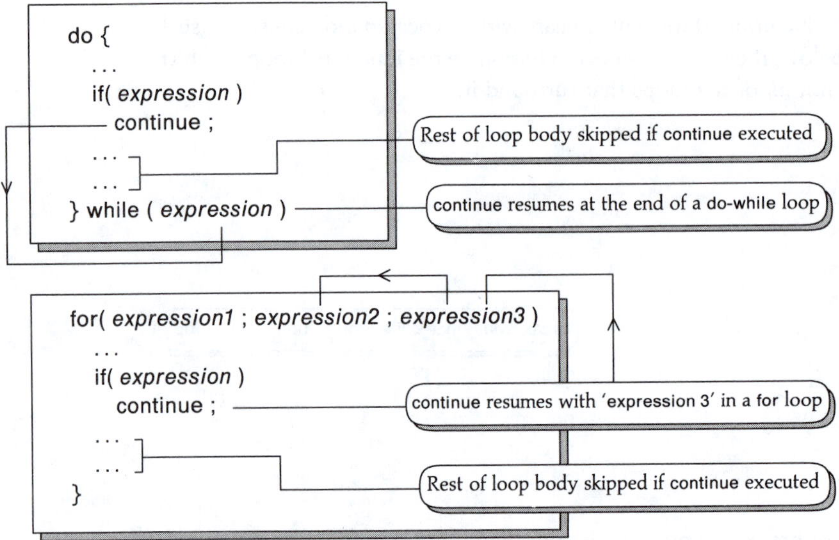

Note how 'expression 3' in a for loop is evaluated *prior* to starting the next iteration, thus ensuring that any post-processing required by the loop is performed first.

It is worth noting that, unlike break, the use of continue within a switch statement has no effect and is illegal except for the case where the switch is nested within a loop. The continue then serves to terminate the switch and start a new iteration. For example:

```
while( 1 )  {
   printf("Enter a choice in the range 0 - 3:");
   if(scanf("%d", &num) == EOF)
      break;
   switch(num)  {
      default : continue ;
      case 0:  option0( ) ; break ;
      case 1:  option1( ) ; break ;
      case 2:  option2( ) ; break ;
      case 3:  option3( ) ; break ;
   }
   printf("Thank you for choosing an option . . . \n") ;
   printf("Would you like to choose another ? ");
   fflush( stdin ) ;
   if( toupper(getchar()) != 'Y')
      break ;
}
...
...
```

It is also worth noting that a continue statement can *always* be replaced by another if or else test, and for this reason many programmers often criticize its use. For example, the program section below:

```
do {
  if( x == y ) {
    statement1 ;
    continue ; ──┐
  }              │
  statement2 ;   ↓
  statement3 ;   │
} while( ... ) ; ┘
```

could always be rewritten without the use of continue using either of the two alternative implementations shown below:

```
do {
  if( x == y )
    statement1 ;
  else {
    statement2 ;
    statement3 ;
  }
} while( ... ) ;
```

```
do {
  if( x != y ) {
    statement2 ;
    statement3 ;
  }
  else
    statement1 ;
} while( ... ) ;
```

There is no gain in efficiency or size of code to be obtained from either implementation (assuming a sensible compiler) so the choice ultimately boils down to what the programmer feels most comfortable with, and whether the use of one or the other increases readability.

5.8 The goto statement

There is an old saying to the effect that if you find yourself using a goto statement within a program, then you have not thought about the problem and its implementation for long enough! It can be shown using this and the previous chapter as examples that an unconditional goto or jump to a specified point in the program is not necessary, and can always be replaced by a selection or repetition mechanism such as if-else or do-while. However, before you write off the goto statement altogether, there are situations where its use can simplify the design of the program code while at the same time making it more readable.

Before looking at examples of this, let us first take a look at the general form of the goto, which consists of a label (identified by a following colon) and a goto statement placed somewhere in the program that references the label. When the goto is encountered during the program, the normal sequence of statement execution is interrupted and an **unconditional jump** to the statement immediately following the specified label is performed, as shown below:

Colon ':' after an identifier indicates a label

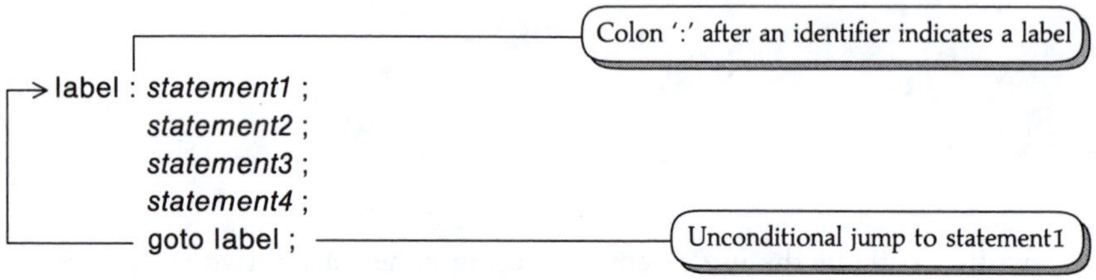

```
label : statement1 ;
        statement2 ;
        statement3 ;
        statement4 ;
        goto label ;
```

Unconditional jump to statement1

As an example, Program 5.6 demonstrates the use of a goto in creating a simple loop to display the values 1–10.

Program 5.6 The use of goto in creating a simple loop.

```
#include   <stdio.h>

int main( void )
{
   int i = 0 ;

loop:
   if( i < 10 )  {
      i++ ;
      printf("%d\n", i ) ;
      goto loop ;
   }
   return 0 ;
}
```

Note that the jump may be forwards or backwards within the program, but may only be used to transfer control of the program to a point within the same function or block: you cannot therefore use goto to jump between functions or blocks. Some examples of the illegal use of goto are shown in Program 5.7.

Program 5.7 Examples of the illegal use of goto.

```
#include   <stdio.h>

int main( void )
{
  int i = 0 ;

  goto   add_i ;
  goto   printi ;
  {
    int i ;
printi: printf("Value of i = %d\n" , i ) ;
  }
  ...
}

void function( void )
{
  int i = 0;

add_i: i = i + 1 ;
}
```

Jump into new function

Illegal!

Jump into new block

5.8.1 *Useful applications of* goto

Perhaps the most (possibly the only) worthwhile use for a goto statement is in prematurely aborting the execution of a set of deeply nested loops, as shown below. Here, the program, upon detecting that 'limit' is greater than 'limit_max', decides to break out of the two while loops altogether:

```
while ( ... )  {
  while ( ... )  {
    if( limit > limit_max )
      goto emergency ;
    else  {
      ...
      ...
    }
  }
  ...
  ...
}
emergency :
  limit = limit_max ;
```

In this situation, a simple goto is easier to implement and follow than the situation where the inner while loop sets a flag (to be tested by the outer loop) prior to executing a break, which is followed immediately by a further break from the outer while loop.

5.9 Chapter summary

(1) The for, while and do-while loops facilitate repetition within a program. Each relies upon a test expression, which terminates the loop if its value resolves to 0 or false.

(2) The test expression controlling the for and while loops is evaluated at the start of each iteration and thus the body of these two loops may not be executed if the test expression is initially false. However, the body of a do-while loop is guaranteed to execute at least once, because its test expression is evaluated at the end of each iteration.

(3) The continue statement forces a new iteration of a loop to begin, while the break statement forces the termination of a loop.

(4) The goto statement provides a means of performing an unconditional jump to a new statement within the program. The jump may be forwards or backwards to a predefined label, but cannot be between functions. Using a goto to create a loop is considered poor programming practice since it leads to programs that are unstructured and difficult to maintain and debug.

5.10 Exercises

5.1 How many times do each of the following for loops iterate and what is the final value of the variable 'i' in each case?

```
for( i = 0; i < 10; i ++ )
  printf("i = %d\n", i );
for( i = 0; i <= 12; i ++ )
  printf("i = %d\n", i );
for( i = 0; i <= 10 ; i += 2 )
  printf("i = %d\n", i );
for( i = 0; i != 10; i ++ )
  printf("i = %d\n", i );
for( i = 0.5; i > 0.0; i -= 0.2 )
  printf("i = %f\n", i );
```

Rewrite the above for loops in the form of while and do-while loops and repeat the exercise. Swap the order of the printf() and the statements that alter the value of 'c' in your versions of the program, and describe what differences this makes to the program and to the final values of 'i'.

5.2 What is the output produced by the following program section?

```
for( i = 1; i < 10; i ++ )
   for( j = 1; j < 10; j++ )
      if( i % j == 0)
         printf("%d / %d = %d\n", i, j, i % j) ;
```

Rewrite the above program section in the form of while and do-while loops.

5.3 Write a program to evalute the sum of all positive integers in the range 0 to 100.

5.4 Write a program to display the words of the famous song 'Ten Green Bottles', down to no green bottles.

5.5 Modify the program in Exercise 5.3 to calculate the sum and average of a number of values entered at the keyboard. Assume that the operator has entered all of the data when an EOF condition is generated at the keyboard.

5.6 Modify the program in Exercise 5.5 to display the smallest and largest values entered at the keyboard.

5.7 Write a program to evaluate the Fibonacci series 1, 1, 2, 3, 5, 8, 13, 21 and so on (that is, each entry is the sum of the previous two numbers in the series).

5.8 Write a program to evaluate factorial n, written mathematically as n!, given that 0! and 1! evaluate to 1 and that $n! = n \times (n - 1)!$.

5.9 In Application 1.3 we presented a program to evaluate the exponential function e^x. Using this program as a basis, write a program to evaluate sin(x) and cos(x) given the following power series:

$$\cos(x) = 1 - x^2/2! + x^4/4! - x^6/6! + x^8/8!$$
$$\sin(x) = x - x^3/3! + x^5/5! - x^7/7! + x^9/9!$$

5.10 The value of a car depeciates at a rate 'd%' of its current value per annum. Write a program to display the depreciation of a car bought for an initial purchase price x for the first five years of its life. Given that its owner wishes to sell the car when it has depreciated by no more than 45% of its purchase price, get the program to tell the purchaser in which year the car should be sold.

5.11 Modify the program from Exercise 5.10 to build in safeguards, that is, to ensure that depreciation and initial purchase prices are positive quantities and to re-prompt with suitable error messages if illegal values are entered. Also, get the program to prompt the operator to decide whether he or she wishes to repeat the program's execution.

5.12 Fred has the opportunity to invest an amount 'm' in a bank savings scheme that pays simple interest at the rate of 'r1%' per annum. Alternatively, Fred could instead invest that same amount 'm' in a different bank that pays compound interest at the rate 'r2%' per annum, where 'r2' is less than 'r1'. Write a program to determine which bank will give

Fred the best return on his investment after 'n' years and also to determine how many years it will take for the investment in the second bank to exceed that offered by the first bank.

5.13 The electrical circuit shown below is that of a high pass filter that attenuates (reduces) low frequency signals. The ratio of the output voltage V_{out} to the input voltage V_{in} can be expressed by the equation:

$V_{out}/V_{in} = (X_L)/(R + X_L)$

where X_L represents the inductive reactance of the inductor L and is given by the equation:

$X_L = 2\pi fL$ ohms

and 'f' represents the frequency of the supply voltage V_{in}. Generate a table of values showing how V_{out}/V_{in} changes with varying supply frequency and satisfy yourself that the output voltage increases as the frequency 'f' rises.

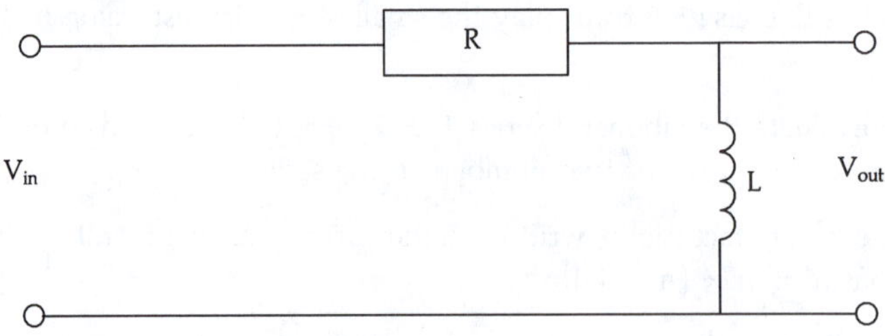

If the inductor in the above circuit were replaced by a capacitor of value C farads, whose capacitive reactance is given by the equation $X_c = 1/(2\pi fC)$, show that the circuit now behaves as a low pass filter, attenuating high frequency signals.

5.14 Rewrite the following program to eliminate the goto statements.

```
#include   <stdio.h>
#include   <stdlib.h>
#include   <ctype.h>

int main( void )
{
  char     buff[BUFSIZ] ;
  double   a, b, count, increment ;

loop1:  fflush( stdin ) ;
        printf("Enter a value for 'a' : ") ;
        a = atof( gets( buff )) ;
```

```
loop2:  printf("Enter a value for b greater than %g ", a ) ;
        b = atof( gets( buff )) ;
        if( b > a )
          goto loop3 ;
        else  {
          printf("Error: ") ;
          goto loop2 ;
        }

loop3:  printf("Enter a positive increment : ");
        increment = atof( gets( buff )) ;
        if( increment >= 0 )
          goto loop4 ;
        else  {
          printf("Error: ") ;
          goto loop3 ;
        }

loop4:  count = a ;
        printf("count = %g\n", count) ;
        count += increment ;
        if( count < b )
          goto loop4 ;
        printf("Run the program again [y/n] ? ") ;
        if( toupper(getchar()) == 'N' )
          goto end ;
        else
          goto loop1 ;
end:    printf("Bye !!!!\n") ;
        return 0 ;
}
```

5.15 Rewrite the following program section to eliminate the break, continue and goto statements.

```
#include   <stdio.h>
#include   <ctype.h>

int main(void)
{
  int  c ;
  int  lines = 0, spaces = 0 ;

  do  {
    do  {
      c = getchar() ;
      if( c == '^' )
        break ;
```

```
        if( c == '%')
            goto end ;
        if( c == ' ' )  {
            spaces ++ ;
            continue ;
        }
        if( c == '\n')  {
            lines ++ ;
            continue ;
        }
    } while( 1 ) ;
    printf("Spaces = %d\n", spaces) ;
    printf("lines = %d\n", lines) ;
    printf("Run again [y/n] ? ") ;
    fflush(stdin) ;
    if( toupper(getchar()) == 'N')
        break ;
  } while ( 1 ) ;

end: printf("Finished !!!!\n") ;
  return 0 ;
}
```

6 A Closer Look at Functions

We saw briefly in Chapter 1 that it was possible for programs to be contructed around a number of separate 'modules' or 'functions', allowing the programmer to replace many occurrences of the same section of code with a single occurrence in the form of a function. Such functions could be called or invoked as often as required by the program and from many separate places within the program code itself. The process of breaking down a program into a number of modules or components is known as **hierarchical decomposition**.

Using a technique known as **top-down** design, the programmer commences with the specification of the problem and attempts to identify at the topmost level the various modules that will be used to construct the program. Each new module is then subject to the same decomposition process, giving rise to a number of smaller modules within the hierarchy of the program as a whole. This process continues until the programmer is satisfied that each module is sufficiently simple to comprehend and can be coded in the form of a function, typically with the function `main()` occupying the topmost level in the hierarchy. This is illustrated in Figure 6.1.

It is important to grasp that a hierarchical decomposition does not imply any algorithm or order of execution for the modules. It is simply a typically graphical illustration of the various component modules in the software and their relationship to each other. By looking at such an illustration, a programmer should be able to identify the modules and hence the functions that he or she will need to write, a technique known as **modular programming**. To put this idea in perspective, Figure 6.2 shows a simple hierarchical decomposition performed on a motor car showing its basic component parts.

From this illustration it is possible to deduce that the gearbox and engine are separate components. The former can be decomposed into cylinder head and block, and further decomposed into valves/camshafts and crank/pistons. The gearbox can be broken down into gears, selection mechanism and drive shafts. It is not possible to deduce from the illustration that the engine and gearbox are, for example, designed to mate, or even what their relationship to each other is, nor that both of them fit inside the bodywork of the car, or even what the capabilities

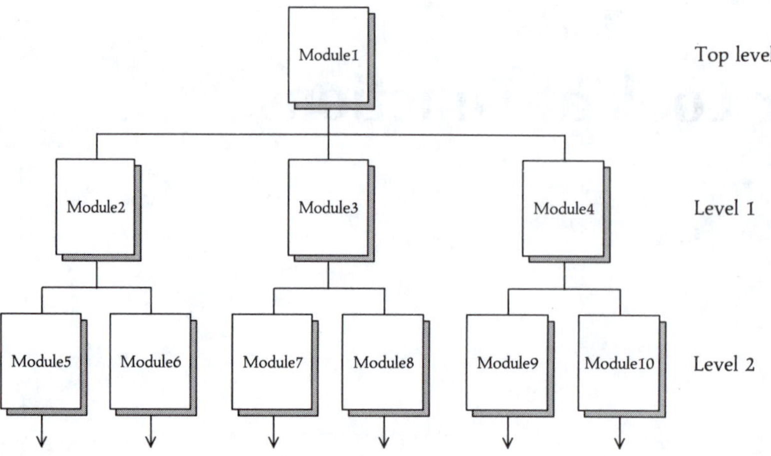

Figure 6.1 An illustration of a hierarchical program decomposition into modules.

of the car are. Only when the modules have been designed, built and tested will this become evident.

Breaking down a program/object in this way not only makes it easier to comprehend but also makes it easier to develop and test. Various components/modules can be developed in parallel and often tested in isolation. It also makes it possible to identify and easily replace one component with another, for example manual or automatic gearbox, V6 or V8 engine and so on. Modules can even be reused in other projects, such as using a range of engines/transmissions across a broad family of cars. A good example of this technique is, of course, the C standard library, with its collection of general purpose, string, maths and input/output functions, which can be reused in a whole variety of programs.

With careful consideration, the designer should be able to separate the design of each component/module into a form that is generally independent of the other components in the system as a whole. By documenting their respective interfaces to the outside world, it should be possible to design a harness for the component to enable it to be integrated into a larger system. In C this interface takes the form of a function and its header and the harness to it is the program responsible for calling or invoking the function. The harness will obviously have to be written to supply the function with all the data (in the form of arguments) that it needs and be prepared to accept back any results it may generate. For example, a function designed specifically to calculate the area of a circle would expect a harness that supplies it with the radius of that circle and accepts back the area as a result. These ideas are illustrated in Figure 6.3.

In this chapter then, we take a closer look at how to design and use functions, along with the mechanisms involved in interfacing them to other parts

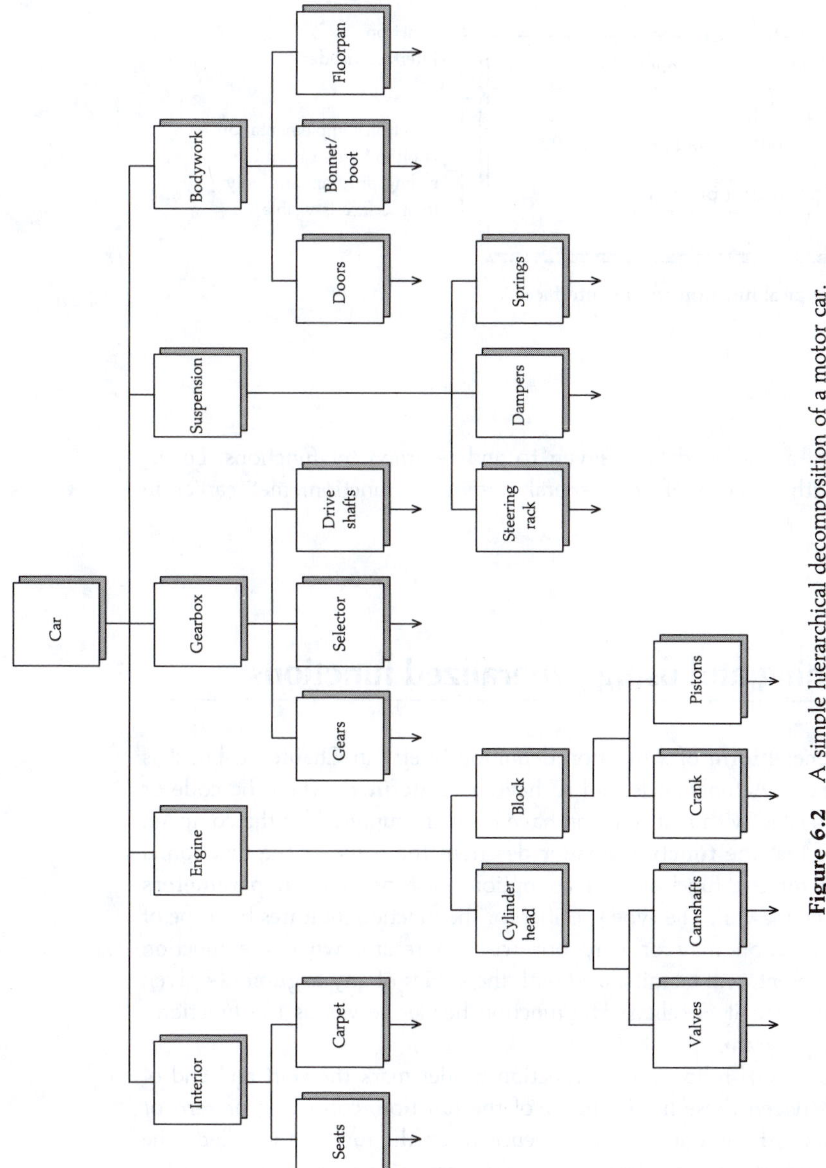

Figure 6.2 A simple hierarchical decomposition of a motor car.

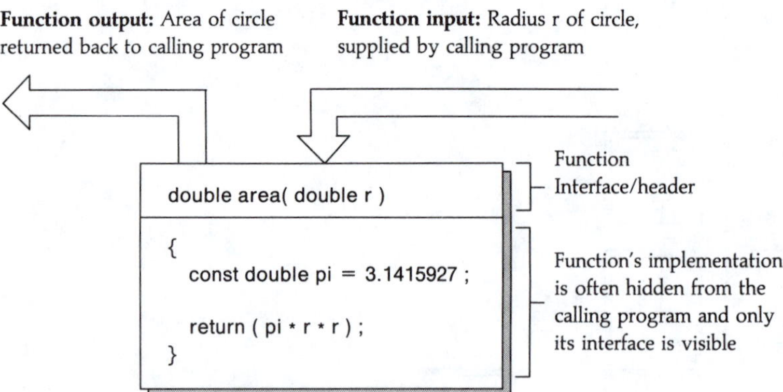
Function output: Area of circle returned back to calling program
Function input: Radius r of circle, supplied by calling program
double area(double r)
{
const double pi = 3.1415927 ;
return (pi * r * r) ;
}
Function Interface/header
Function's implementation is often hidden from the calling program and only its interface is visible

Figure 6.3 A typical function and its interface.

of the program, and how data is given to and returned by functions. Let us begin, then, with a recap of the general form of a function, met earlier in Chapter 1.

6.1 Defining and using generalized functions

We met the general form of a function definition briefly in Chapter 1, but it is given again below. A function is said to have been **defined**, when the code or statements associated with that function have been encountered by the compiler. You will notice that the **function header** describes the name of the function, a **type specifier** for the function and an optional list of function **parameters** declared between the '( )'. The type specifier for the function indicates the type of data that the function may or may not wish to return, while the function parameters, if present, will be initialized with the values of any **arguments** given to the function when it is called. The function header serves as the function's interface to the program.

The braces '{ }' following the function header mark the start and end of the function. Between these lie the **body** of the function, consisting of zero or more statements to be executed as a sequence when the function is called. The function will terminate when either the closing brace '}' marking the end of the function or a return statement is encountered. In the case of the latter, the function is permitted to return a single item of data back to the calling program. In either case, program execution then resumes with that part of the program that called or invoked the function.

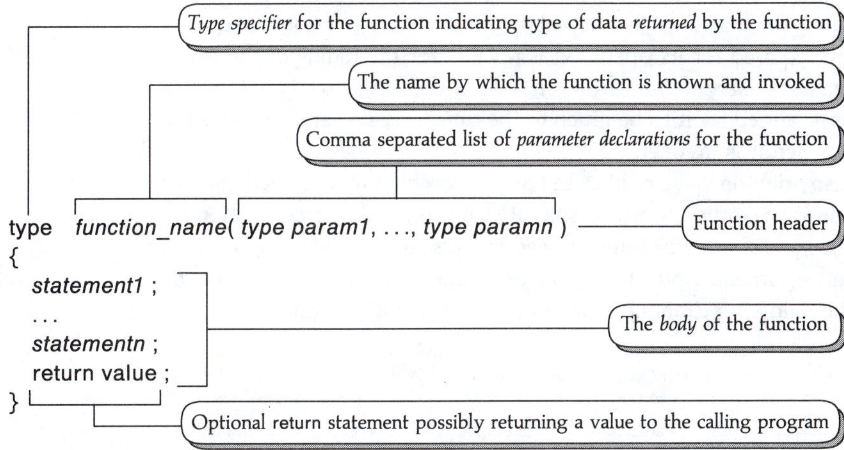

Any function may be called, even if the program does not contain that function's definition (as we have seen when a program makes a call to the standard library printf()) but ultimately, the task of resolving an undefined function call falls to the linker, which must be able to resolve or locate the missing function code or the program will be incomplete.

The order in which the program defines its functions bears no relation to the order in which they will be invoked, so the programmer is generally free to define and invoke them in any order (but read Section 6.1.7 first). Note, however, that it is not permitted, in C at least, to define one function within another, so all functions must be defined separately within a given source file.

As an example, a definition for the function area() is given below, designed to calculate and return the area of a circle whose radius is given to the function by the calling program in the form of an argument. Notice how the function declares the single parameter 'r' to which the argument supplied by the calling program is automatically assigned:

Function returns a double

Function declares a single parameter 'r' of type double

```
double area( double r )
{

  const double pi = 3.1415927 ;
  return ( pi * r * r ) ;
}
```

area() terminates here by returning are of circle, a double, back to the calling program

Notice how the function is completely generic and self-contained. The only information required for its operation is a value for the radius of the circle, and, since this value is likely to vary from one call of the function to another, the programmer has arranged for it to be given to the function as an argument by the calling program when it is invoked.

Notice also how the value of pi (3.141 592 7) was built in or embedded into the program code as an explicit constant, since its value is fixed by the equation for the area of a circle and there was thus no need to pass this value to area() as an additional second argument. Given the above definition of area(), it could now be invoked with the following example statement by the calling program:

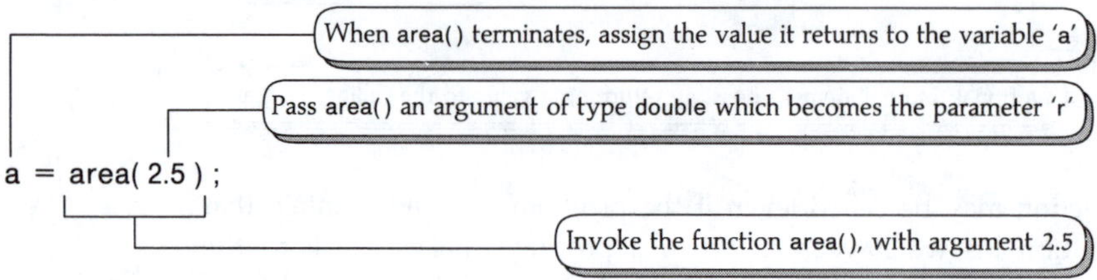

Here, the compiler will generate code to invoke or call the function area() and present it with a single double precision argument equal to the value '2.5'. The compiler ensures that the parameter 'r' declared within area() assumes the value of this argument.

Once the function has completed its calculation it terminates and returns a double precision result, that is, the area of a circle whose radius is '2.5', back to the calling program, whereupon that value is assigned to the variable 'a'. Using this technique, the area of any circle could be calculated by substituting a different argument value.

6.1.1 *Functions with no type specifier*

If the type specifier for a function is omitted, the compiler makes the assumption that the function will return a value of type int. Furthermore, if the type of any parameters declared within the function are omitted, they too are assumed to be int. To illustrate this, consider the function multiply() below, which by default declares two int parameters, 'a' and 'b', and returns an int result:

No type specifier is interpreted to mean that multiply() returns an int

No parameter *types* declared, thus they are int by default

```
multiply( a, b )
{
   return a * b ;
}
```

Return result of expression, an int, since 'a' and 'b' are ints

Such a function could be invoked with a statement of the form:

```
z = multiply( x1, x2 ) ;
```

Call multiply( ) with two arguments 'x1' and 'x2'

Assign returned result to 'z'

where the values of the variables 'x1' and 'x2' are assigned to the parameters 'a' and 'b', respectively, within the function multiply( ) – that is, on a one-to-one correspondence – while the int result returned by multiply( ) is subsequently assigned to the variable 'z' in the calling program.

Interestingly enough, it is quite legitimate to define and invoke a **stub** function; that is to say, a function with an empty body. Such functions serve no useful purpose in a finished program but are often created during early program development to permit other parts of the program to be tested. Obviously, the programmer would return to the function later and fill in the missing code or remove it altogether. An example stub function is shown below:

```
int under_development1( double x, double y )
{
}
```

Stub function

6.1.2 void *functions*

We met the key word 'void' in Chapter 1, where it indicated an absence of data. A 'void' function is one where the key word 'void' appears as the function's type specifier and indicates that the function will not be returning any data back to the calling program.

Similarly, a 'void' (or empty) parameter list indicates that the function does not expect to be given any arguments when it is invoked. The function print_usage( ) below is an example of such a function and might be called to display the program's usage to its operator; as such, it requires no arguments and returns no data:

```
void   print_usage( void )
{
  printf("Error: Incorrect Usage . . . \n") ;
  printf("Usage: Copy [–flags] <source>  <destination>\n") ;
  return ;
}
```

void type specifier means that no data is returned by this function

void parameter list means the function expects no arguments

return is optional, as closing brace '}' serves the same purpose here

return statement must not attempt to return data from a void function

Such a function might be invoked with a statement such as that given below, where no attempt is made to pass any argument data to the function and no attempt is made to save any returned data. Note that it is considered illegal for a void function to attempt to return data although an optional return statement on its own is permitted:

```
print_usage( ) ;
```

No attempt is made to pass any arguments to the function when it is called

No attempt is made to save non-existent *returned* data

Using this, and the knowledge that functions with no type specifier are assumed to return int data by default, we could define the function main() in the manner shown below, which is how you will see it written in many programs and texts:

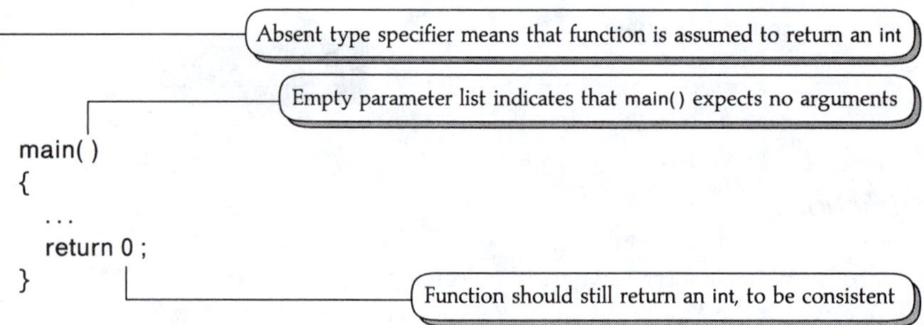

6.1.3 *A closer look at the* return *statement*

It is permissible for a return statement to appear any number of times within the body of a function. If executed, it results in the termination of that function with the subsequent return of any (optional) data back to the calling program. Two forms of return are catered for; the first, shown below, simply terminates the execution of the function with no attempt being made to return any data:

```
return ;
```

return on its own simply terminates the function, with *no* returned data

This form of return statement generally appears only within a void function, for example:

```
void function1( void )
{
  ...
  for ( ... ) {
    while( ... ) {
      ...
      if( scanf( "%d", &i) == EOF )
        return ;
    }
  }
  ...
  return ;
}
```

Terminate function prematurely if *end-of-file* condition met

return here not strictly required, since closing brace '}' serves the same purpose

The second form of the return statement, shown below, not only terminates the execution of the function, but, as we have already seen, permits the result of a single expression – that is, one item of data – to be returned to the calling program. Parentheses are not a requirement around the expression, but are sometimes included for readability when the expression is complex:

```
return expression ;
```

return the result of expression back to calling program

When data is returned by a function in this manner, the compiler ensures that where necessary, that data is *implicitly cast* to match the function's type specifier. The same implicit casting rules that apply during assignment (see Section 3.1.6) also apply here.

For example, the following function returns the product of two integer parameters, 'a' and 'b'. Because these parameters are integers, their product would normally give rise to an int result, but as the type specifier for multiply() states that it returns a double, the compiler casts the result of the expression 'a * b' to a double before returning it:

Type specifier and thus function type are double

```
double multiply( int a, int b )
{
  return a * b ;
}
```

Result of expression, an int, is cast to a double before it is returned

However, it is considered an error for a function to return a result which cannot be cast to match the function's type specifier. For example, both functions shown below generate error messages when compiled:

```
void func1( void )              int func2( void )
{                               {
  ...                             static char x[ 20 ] ;
  ...                             ...
  return 0 ;                      return x ;
}                               }
```

Error!

Cannot cast an array to an int

void functions cannot return a result

Note that it is *not* considered to be an error for a program to ignore any such data that might be returned by a function. For example, the function multiply( ) above could quite legitimately be invoked with the following (rather redundant) section of program code, where no attempt is made to save the returned result, which is consequently lost or discarded:

```
int main( void )
{
  ...
  multiply( 4, 5 ) ;
  ...
}
```

No attempt made to save result returned by multiply( ), which will be thrown away

Integer constant 5 assigned to parameter 'b' in multiply( )

Integer constant 4 assigned to parameter 'a' in multiply( )

The programmer should not worry unduly about what has happened to this lost data, because the compiler will take care of any tidying up operations required when the function returns.

Why, then, should a program bother to call a function and then discard the result it returns? The answer becomes clear when you consider a call to a function such as scanf( ), where the result it returns is more often than not of secondary or sometimes no interest to the programmer, who is far more concerned with the side effects of its operations; that is, in the case of scanf( ), reading, converting and storing data into variables.

Some compilers are equipped to optionally generate warnings (not errors) at compile time if they detect a program attempting to discard the result returned by a function call, but this should not stop the program from being compiled and run.

6.1.4 *A closer look at invoking functions*

We noted in Chapter 1 that when a program invokes a function, either that function's **definition** or its **prototype** must have been encountered by the compiler if the call made to the function at run time is to be performed successfully, otherwise the program's operation may be **undefined**. For programmers wishing to define their own functions, the simplest design approach is to ensure that each function is defined prior to any statements that attempt to invoke it.

As an example, Program 6.1 contains the code for a complete program to calculate the area and circumference of a circle. Here, both functions circumference() and area() are defined ahead of statements in main() that attempt to invoke them.

Apart from defining the code for the function itself, the definition also gives the compiler important information about the function with regard to the type and number of arguments the function is expecting. Furthermore, the function's type specifier informs the compiler about the type of data the function returns.

For example, by the time the compiler encounters the function main() in Program 6.1 it should already have seen the definition of the functions area() and circumference() and would thus have noted from their function headers that both functions expect a single double precision argument and that each returns a

Program 6.1 Calculating the area and circumference of a circle.

```
#include  <stdio.h>
#include  <stdlib.h>

double  circumference( double radius )
{
   return ( 2.0 * 3.1415927 * radius ) ;
}

double  area( double radius )
{
   return (3.1415927 * radius * radius ) ;
}

int main( void )
{
   double  a, c, r ;
   char    buffer[ BUFSIZ ] ;

   printf("Enter Radius of Circle: ") ;
   r = atof( gets( buffer )) ;

   a = area( r ) ;
   c = circumference( r ) ;

   printf("Area of a circle radius %g = %g\n", r, a ) ;
   printf("Circumference of a circle radius %g = %g\n", r, c ) ;
   return 0 ;
}
```

double precision result. Thus when either function is called by main(), the compiler is able to perform the following checks and implicit conversions on the arguments to and data returned by each function.

Firstly, when a function is invoked, the compiler checks that the number of arguments passed to the function by the calling program is in agreement with the number of parameters declared by the function. If they do not agree, an error message is generated.

For example, had Program 6.1 invoked the function area() with the following statement, which incorrectly attempts to pass two arguments to area(), then the compiler, having already seen the function definition, would know that this statement is incorrect, since area() is in fact only expecting a single argument:

Error: incorrect number of arguments, area() declares a *single* parameter

```
a = area( r, r ) ;
```

Error!

Secondly, the compiler also ensures that all argument values given to a function are, where required, implicitly cast to match the type of their corresponding parameter declaration within the function.

For example, had Program 6.1 attempted to call the function area() with the statement shown below, the compiler would have implicitly cast the value of the integer constant 2 to the double precision value 2.0 before it presented this to the function:

Integer value 2 cast to double precision value 2.0 before calling function

```
a = area( 2 ) ;
```

Note that it would also have been considered an error if the compiler could not sensibly cast the argument to match the parameter type.

It is worth noting that function calls (not definitions) may be nested inside one another, to any depth you like. For example, we could calculate and display the area of a circle within main() with a statement such as:

Three nested function calls within printf()

```
printf("Area of circle = %g\n", area( atof( gets( buffer )))) ;
```

Here, the compiler evaluates the inner function calls first, thus gets() is invoked first and the data it returns is used as the argument to atof(), whose returned result is in turn used as the argument to area(), whose returned result is finally used as an argument to printf().

6.1.5 *Passing arguments to functions: By value or copy*

Whenever arguments are passed to a function, it is important to appreciate that except for the case of an array, all arguments are passed to a function by **value** or **copy**. For example, when the function area() was called in Program 6.1, it was a copy of the original variable 'r' defined in main() that was presented to, and eventually became, the parameter radius within area().

This is why function parameters are referred to as **declarations** and not **definitions**, since their storage is allocated during the call to the function, and not by the function itself. Such parameters, like automatic variables, are generally stored on the computer system's **hardware stack**, as illustrated in Figure 6.4.

As you can see, the effects of the modifications that f1() makes to its parameters are **localized** and restricted to the function itself. The function is unable to modify the values of the original variables 'a', 'b' and 'c' in main(). As another example, consider Program 6.2, which attempts to increment the value of 'b' in main(), but is written incorrectly, as it turns out.

In this instance, Program 6.2 fails, since it is only the value of 'x' (a copy of the original variable 'b') that is being incremented, and the value of 'b' is unaffected. The proof of this can be seen when the program is run. The program's operator should see the following displayed on the terminal, demonstrating that it

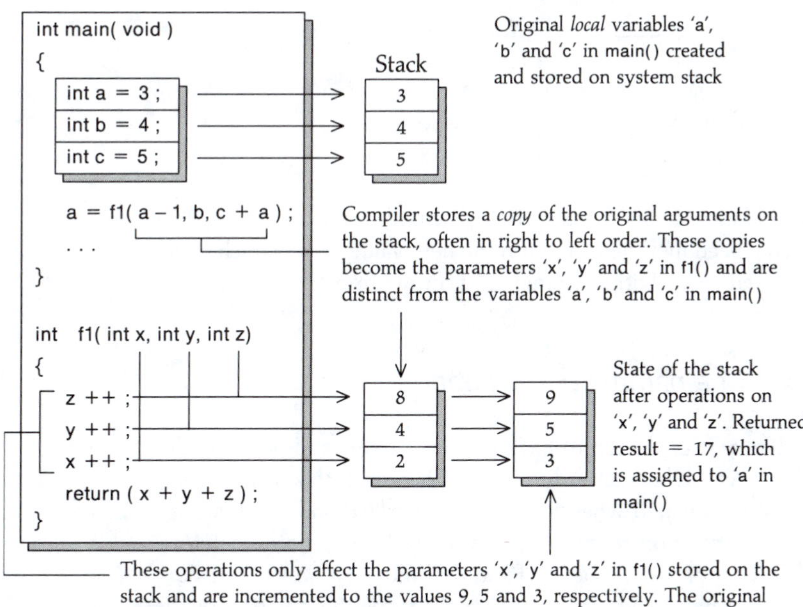

Figure 6.4 Passing arguments by value or copy.

Program 6.2 Passing arguments by value.

```
#include  <stdio.h>

void increment( int x )            Copy of original argument becomes the parameter 'x'
{
   x ++ ;                          Function increments its parameter 'x', not the original argument 'b' in main()

   printf("Within increment(), x = %d\n", x ) ;
}

int main( void )
{
   int b = 5 ;
   printf("b = %d\n", b ) ;
                                   Pass a copy of 'b' to increment(), 'b' is unaffected by call
   increment( b ) ;

   printf("Upon return from increment() b = %d\n", b ) ;

   return 0 ;
}
```

Caution!

was the copy of 'b', given to the function increment(), that was incremented to 6 and not 'b' in main(), which is unaffected by the call:

```
b = 5
Within increment(), x = 6
Upon return from increment() b = 5
```

Had a specific function been required to increment its argument then increment() could have been modified to return the new value of 'x', which could subsequently be assigned to 'b' within main(), as in Program 6.3.

6.1.6 *The scope of a parameter declaration*

All function parameters are considered to have the same scope and privacy rules as automatic variables. As we have already seen in Chapter 2, this means that a function parameter is only created when the function is called and consequently ceases to exist when the function terminates. It is interesting to note, therefore, that a parameter declaration could be prefixed by the key word 'register', suggesting that it should be placed into a CPU register for the duration of the function's execution, which could improve the efficiency and speed of the program.

Program 6.3 Program 6.2 correctly written to increment 'b'.

```
#include  <stdio.h>

int increment( int x )            /* increment() returns an int */
{
   x ++ ;
   printf("Within increment(), x = %d\n", x) ;
   return x ;                     /* Function returns the new value of 'x' */
}

int main( void )
{
   int b = 5 ;
   printf("b = %d\n", b ) ;

   b = increment( b ) ;           /* Pass a copy of 'b' to increment() */
                                  /* Value returned by increment() is saved in 'b' */

   printf("Upon return from increment() b = %d\n", b ) ;
   return 0 ;
}
```

Because of their identical rules of scope, it is not permissible to define a local variable (static or auto) within a function that shares the same name as one of its parameters since the compiler would not be able to distinguish between them. For this reason, the following program section would generate a compile time error:

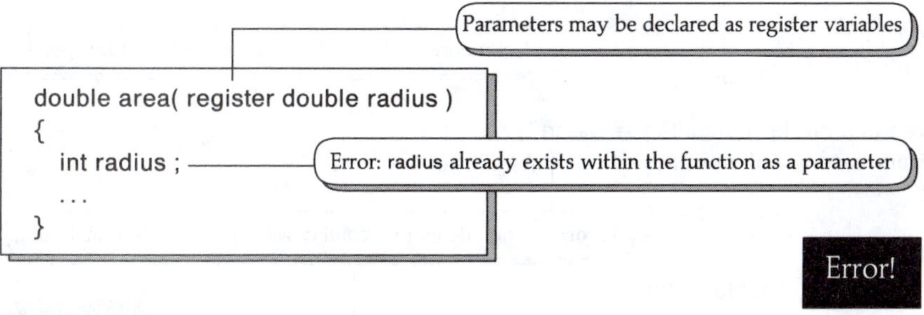

6.1.7 *Function prototyping*

We mentioned in Chapter 1 that a function is only guaranteed to be called successfully at run time if at compile time the compiler has encountered the function's definition prior to any statement that attempts to invoke it. What, then, does the compiler make of any statement that attempts to invoke a function before its definition (or prototype) has been encountered?

This could happen for a number of reasons. Firstly, the function may have been defined within a library or even within another source file (see Chapter 14), in which case the compiler will never encounter its definition. Alternatively, the programmer could have arranged for the function's definition to appear at a point in the program which places it after any statements that attempt to invoke it. In both cases the compiler is being asked to invoke a function that it perhaps knows nothing about.

As an example of the latter, suppose that we had written our area and circumference program in the manner shown in Program 6.4, where the definitions of the functions area() and circumference() will not be encountered by the compiler until *after* statements in main() which attempt to invoke them have been compiled.

Program 6.4 Placing the function definition after its point of invocation.

```
#include   <stdio.h>
#include   <stdlib.h>

int main( void )
{
   double  a, c, r ;
   char    buffer[ BUFSIZ ] ;

   printf("Enter Radius of Circle: ") ;
   r = atof( gets( buffer )) ;

   a = area( r ) ;
   c = circumference( r ) ;

   printf("Area of a circle radius %g = %g\n", r, a ) ;
   printf("Circumference of a circle radius %g = %g\n", r, c ) ;
   return 0 ;
}

double circumference( double radius )
{
   return ( 2.0 * 3.1415927 * radius ) ;
}

double area( double radius )
{
   return (3.1415927 * radius * radius ) ;
}
```

Definitions of these functions not 'visible' at this point

Error: function definitions conflict with compiler's 'assumptions'

Errors!

When the compiler encounters the following statement within main( ):

```
                Compiler assumes that area( ) expects a double argument and returns an int
a = area( r ) ;
```

it will use this first invocation of the function as the basis of a function template. In this instance, because area( ) was invoked with one double precision argument (the value of r), the compiler is forced to assume, correctly as it happens in this instance, that area( ) has been written to receive a single argument of type double. However, as there is nothing in the program at this point to suggest otherwise, the compiler makes the (incorrect) assumption that area( ) returns an int result (see Section 6.1.1).

This is important, because it means that if the definition of a function has *not* been encountered by the compiler (remember that compilation commences from the start of the source file downwards) by the time it encounters any statement within the program that attempts to invoke it, then the responsibility for passing the correct number and type of arguments to the function rests squarely with the programmer. The compiler will be unable to perform any argument number checking and/or casting of actual arguments to match the function's parameters, since it has no idea at that point what those parameter declarations are.

Even assuming, however, that the program attempts to pass the function the correct number and type of arguments that it is expecting (as in the example of the call to the function area( ) above), the compiler will still make the incorrect assumption that the function (and hence area( ) above) will return an int, and thus incorrect code is generated to assign the result returned by the function to any variable, such as 'a' above. The bottom line is that the program will not work in its current form.

In Program 6.4, at least the compiler is in the fortunate position whereby it does eventually encounter the definitions of those functions about which it was forced to make assumptions, namely area( ) and circumference( ), and is thus in a position to check whether or not those assumptions were correct. If any of them were false (as will be the case for the int data type assumed to be returned by both functions), then a compile time error is reported.

Try that program for yourself; you should see two compile time errors relating to these functions. You should also note that if the type specifier for area( ) and circumference( ) were changed to int, then the assumptions made by the compiler would have been correct and thus no errors would have been reported. As another example, let us consider modifying the call to the function area( ) in Program 6.4 in the following way:

```
                Incorrect: function has been written to expect a single argument, not two
a = area( 2, r ) ;
```

Here, the compiler will assume, having not yet encountered the definition of area(), that it is to be given an int and a double argument, thus code is generated by the compiler to invoke area() with two such arguments. It is only when the definition for area() is eventually encountered at the end of the program that the compiler realizes that the above call to area() was incorrect, and compile time errors are generated.

Now, most of this is acceptable provided the definitions for temporarily absent functions are eventually encountered within the program, permitting the compiler to test its earlier assumptions and report any inconsistencies. The programmer can then modify the program to make the necessary corrections. What happens, however, if the definitions of those functions do not appear anywhere within the current source file? For example, what happens when a program invokes a function from the standard library such as the function sin(), or one from another source file (see Chapter 14)?

Unlike some other languages, C has no *intrinsic* knowledge of any of the functions that exist within its standard or other libraries, or indeed any function not yet defined within the current source file. Therefore, the compiler will not know that sin() expects one double argument and returns a double result. This has very important implications for the programmer; if sin() were called by a program, the compiler – because it will never encounter that function's definition – will never be able to check whether the program is invoking it with the correct type and number or arguments. More to the point, the compiler produces code that is simply wrong, since in the absence of the function's definition it will assume that sin() returns an int result.

As an example, compile and run Program 6.5. You will see that although the program compiles without errors, garbage is produced when it is run, even though on the face of it the program appears to be correct.

This failure to execute correctly is due simply to the compiler's assumption that sin() returned an int rather than the double it actually returned. To resolve

Program 6.5 Misuse of standard library functions.

```
#include <stdio.h>

int main( void )
{
  double  angle = 3.1415927 ;
  double  s ;

  s = sin( angle / 2.0 ) ;

  printf("%g\n", s) ;
  return 0 ;
}
```

Compiler gets assignment wrong

Garbage displayed here

Caution!

this problem we need a way of telling the compiler, in advance, that sin() returns a double. Suppose, then, that the following **function prototype** were introduced to the compiler *prior* to that point in the program where the first call to sin() occurs:

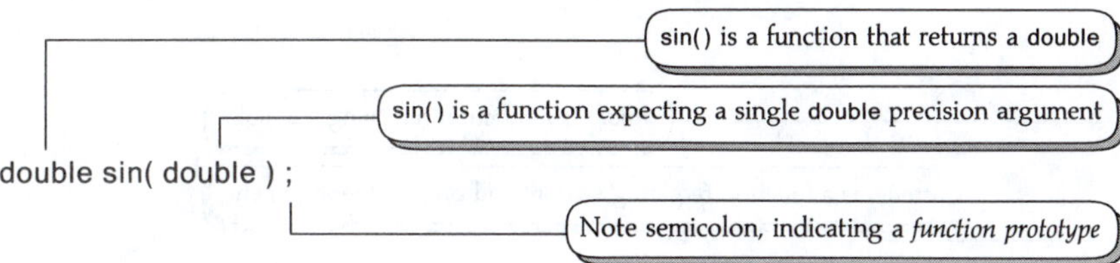

The compiler would interpret this statement to mean that sin() is a function expecting a single argument of type double and returning a result of type double. If Program 6.5 were now rewritten to include this prototype, as shown in Program 6.6, all of the problems discussed above would be resolved. Try it and see.

Program 6.6 Rewriting Program 6.5 to use a function prototype.

```
#include   <stdio.h>

int main( void )
{
   double   angle = 3.1415927 ;
   double   s ;

   double   sin( double ) ;

   s = sin( angle / 2.0 ) ;

   printf("%g\n", s) ;
   return 0 ;
}
```

Function prototype for sin()

Compiler knows sin() returns a double, so assignment is performed *correctly*

Compiler can deduce that argument *number* and *type* are correct

Correct result now displayed here

With the function prototype for sin() now visible, the compiler is able to check the integrity of any calls made to that function and, where appropriate, cast each argument to match its corresponding parameter declaration within the function. More to the point, it is able to assign the returned result correctly to 's' (see Program 6.6).

6.1.8 *Generating a function prototype*

A function prototype is easily derived from the definition of the function, by copying its function header (or re-creating it if that is not available) and placing a semicolon ';' at the end. For example, given the definition of the function fred() below:

fred() is a function returning a double

fred() is a function requiring two int and one double argument

```
double fred( int a, int b, double c )
{
  ...
}
```

its function prototype could be written as:

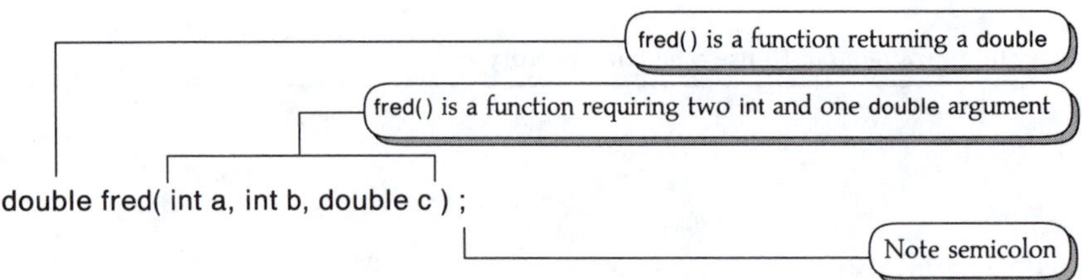

Alternatively, because the names of the parameters in a prototype are irrelevant, the prototype may also be written in either of the two forms shown below:

Parameter names in a prototype need not match actual parameter names

```
double fred( int x, int y, double z ) ;
double fred( int , int , double ) ;
```

In fact parameter names in a prototype are purely optional

To be classed as a full **function prototype** (as opposed to simply a **function declaration**), the prototype must contain explicit information about the function's parameters, even to the point of including the key word void in the parameter list for those functions not expecting any arguments. For example, the following is a declaration of the function fred() rather than a full prototype:

```
double fred( ) ;
```

A declaration of the function fred()

Function declarations contain no information about parameters

When the compiler encounters the above function declaration, the only useful information it is able to gain from it is that fred( ) is a function returning a double. Because the compiler will not know the type or number of any parameters declared within the function fred( ), all argument checking and any implicit argument conversions to match the function's actual parameters are suspended. This means that the function may be invoked with any number and type of arguments the program chooses, which can give rise to programs that do not behave correctly. Function declarations exist mainly to facilitate the compilation of programs written in the days before standard C, where full function prototyping did not exist; consequently they do not have any real use in standard C.

In summary, then, if a function is *called* before its definition is encountered by the compiler, regardless of where that function is defined, it is the programmer's responsibility to ensure that the function's prototype is 'visible' to the compiler (that is, it has been encountered by the compiler), otherwise the integrity of the call cannot be guaranteed, resulting possibly in a faulty program. As an example, Program 6.4 has been correctly rewritten in Program 6.7 to include the function prototypes for area( ) and circumference( ).

Program 6.7 Program 6.4 rewritten to use function prototypes.

```
#include   <stdio.h>
#include   <stdlib.h>

int main( void )
{
   double   a, c, r ;
   char     buffer[ BUFSIZ ] ;

   double area( double radius ) ;
   double circumference( double radius ) ;

   printf("Enter Radius of Circle: ") ;
   r = atof( gets( buffer )) ;

   a = area( r ) ;
   c = circumference( r ) ;
   printf("Area of a circle radius %g = %g\n", r, a ) ;
   printf("Circumference of a circle radius %g = %g\n", r, c ) ;
   return 0 ;
}
```

Function prototypes

```
double circumference( double radius )
{
   return ( 2.0 * 3.1415927 * radius ) ;
}
```

Function definition

```
double area( double radius )
{
   return (3.1415927 * radius * radius ) ;
}
```

Function definition

6.1.9 *The scope of a function prototype*

Function prototypes have the same scope and privacy rules as variables, in that a prototype declared within a function is only 'visible' to the compiler while that function is being compiled. However, a prototype declared outside a function is visible from that point up to the end of the current source file.

Because a function prototype is simply a declaration of a function, in terms of its parameter expectations and returned data type (that is, it does not create any code or allocate any storage) it may occur any number of times within a program, provided that all declarations of the same function are consistent. For example, the program extract below declares both local and global prototypes for the functions area() and circumference() without problem.

'Global' function prototypes

```
double area( double ) ;
double circumference( double ) ;
...
void   print_area( double radius )
{
  double area( double ) ;
  double circumference( double ) ;
  ...
}
```

'Local' function prototypes

The main attraction of using **local** function prototypes is that the function in which they are declared is then self-contained (see print_area() above) and contains all the necessary information to assist in the reuse of that function in other programs.

6.1.10 *The significance of the standard header files*

The subject of function prototyping leads conveniently to a discussion of the standard header files available with every C compiler. We have already seen that the standard library contains a host of useful functions which the programmer is free to call at any time. Considering, then, the previous discussions, programmers would be forced to supply a function prototype for every function in the standard library that they wished to use.

In reality, this is not necessary, since the prototypes for all of the functions in the standard library have already been declared in one or more of the standard header files. For example, if you examine the header file `<math.h>` you might see something like this:

```
double asin( double ) ,  acos( double ) , atan( double ) ;
double sin( double ) ,   cos( double ) , tan( double ) ;
double log( double ) ,   log10( double ) , exp( double ) ;
double sqrt( double ) ,  pow( double, double ) ;
```

which is simply a list of prototypes for some of the maths functions in the standard library. By ensuring that this header file is `#included` right at the start of a program, you can guarantee that the prototypes it contains will be 'globally visible' for the duration of the source file.

The header file `<stdio.h>`, for example, contains prototypes for the functions `printf()`, `scanf()`, `gets()`, `puts()`, `getchar()` and `putchar()`, among others, while `<stdlib.h>` contains the prototypes for `atoi()`, `atol()` and `atof()`. This explains why these files were sometimes `#included` in our programs. Your C compiler library reference manual should state the location of every function prototype.

Try looking up the functions `time()` and `rand()`, for example. In a similar way, programmers can create header files containing the prototypes for those functions that they themselves have developed. These header files could then be `#included` by any source file wishing to call those functions.

Application 6.1

Figure 6.5 shows a parallel inductive/capacitive circuit, where R represents the resistance of the inductor L (and is generally small), and C the capacitance. It can be shown that the current magnification Q and the dynamic impedance Z of the circuit at the resonant frequency F are given by the equations shown below. Write a program to read in values for L, C and R and thus display F, Q and Z.

$F = 1/(2\pi L) \times \mathrm{sqrt}(L/C - R^2) \qquad Q = 2\pi FL/R \qquad Z = L/CR$

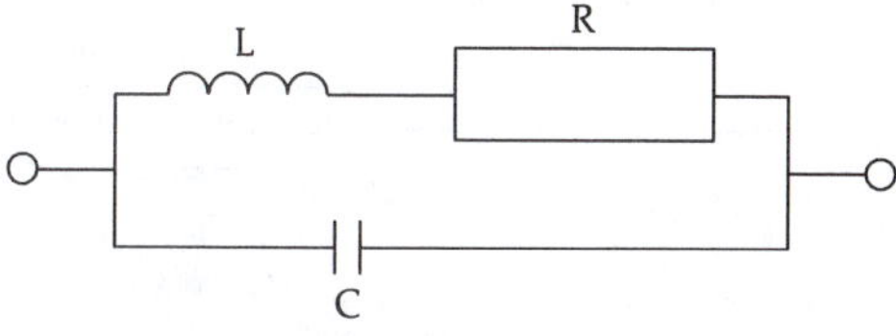

Figure 6.5 A parallel inductive/capacitive circuit.

Application 6.1 A parallel resonant circuit.

```
#include   <stdio.h>
#include   <stdlib.h>
#include   <math.h>

#define  PI  3.141592653

int main( void )
{
   char      buff[ BUFSIZ ];
   double    C, R, L ;
   double    Q, F, Z ;

   double    res_freq( double l, double c, double r ) ;
   double    q_factor( double f, double l, double r) ;
   double    impedance( double l, double c, double r ) ;

   printf("Enter the value of Capacitance C: ");
   C = atof(gets(buff));

   printf("Enter the value of Resistance R: ");
   R = atof(gets(buff));

   printf("Enter the value of Inductance L: ");
   L = atof(gets(buff));

   F = res_freq( L, C, R ) ;
   Q = q_factor( F, L, R ) ;
   Z = impedance( L, C, R ) ;

   printf("\nResonant Frequency = %g Hz\n", F) ;
   printf("Current Magnification factor Q = %g\n", Q) ;
   printf("Dynamic Impedance = %g ohms\n", Z) ;

   return 0 ;
}

double res_freq( double l, double c, double r )
{
   return( 1.0/(2.0*PI*l) * sqrt( l/c - r*r)) ;
}

double q_factor( double f, double l, double r)
{
   return( 2.0*PI*f*l/r ) ;
}

double impedance( double l, double c, double r )
{
   return( l/(c*r)) ;
}
```

'Local' function prototypes

Invoke functions with correct argument number

Function definition

Function definition

Function definition

When the program in Application 6.1 was run, it produced the following sample display:

```
Enter the value of Capacitance C: 1e–6
Enter the value of Resistance R: 100
Enter the value of Inductance L: 0.1

Resonant Frequency = 477.465 Hz
Current Magnification factor Q = 3
Dynamic Impedance = 1000 ohms
```

Application 6.2

If a projectile is fired from the earth at an angle θ degrees to the horizontal at an initial velocity of v metres per second, it will travel, as shown in Figure 6.6, a distance d metres before returning to earth, and will remain in flight for t seconds while reaching a maximum flight height of h metres given by the equations below, where g is the earth's gravitational constant of 9.81 ms^{-2}:

$d = v^2\sin(2\theta)/g \qquad t = 2v\sin(\theta)/g \qquad h = v^2\sin(\theta)/g$

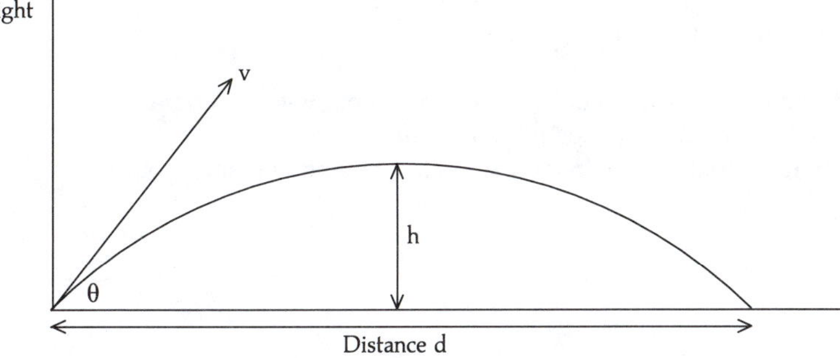

Figure 6.6 Tracing the flight of a projectile.

Write a program to accept values of 'v' and 'θ' from an operator and thus display the values of 'd', 't' and 'h'.

Application 6.2 A projectile calculation.

```
#include  <stdio.h>
#include  <stdlib.h>
#include  <math.h>

#define   GRAVITY   9.81          /* Acceleration due to earth's gravity */
```

```
int main( void )
{
  double  theta, velocity ;
  char    buff[ BUFSIZ ] ;

  double  distance( double velocity, double theta ) ;
  double  time( double velocity, double theta ) ;
  double  height( double velocity, double theta ) ;
  double  degrees_to_radians( double theta ) ;

  printf("Enter the initial projectile velocity in m/sec : ") ;
  velocity = atof(gets(buff)) ;

  printf("Enter the initial projectile angle in Degrees : ") ;
  theta = atof(gets(buff)) ;

/*
** Convert angles from degree to radians as sin( ) expects radians
*/

  theta = degrees_to_radians( theta) ;

  printf("\nProjectile travels a distance of %g m\n", distance( velocity, theta)) ;
  printf("and remains in flight for %g secs\n", time(velocity, theta)) ;
  printf("while reaching a Maximum height of %g m\n", height( velocity, theta)) ;

  return 0 ;
}

/*
** Function to convert an angle expressed in degrees to radians
*/

double degrees_to_radians( double theta )
{
  return (theta * 3.141592653/180.0) ;
}

/* Calculate height travelled by projectile */

double height( double velocity, double theta )
{
  return ( velocity * velocity * sin( theta ) / GRAVITY ) ;
}
```

'Local' function prototypes

Invoke functions

Function definition

Function definition

```
/* Calculate time of flight of projectile */

double time( double velocity, double theta )
{
  return (2.0 * velocity * sin(theta) / GRAVITY ) ;
}
```

Function definition

```
/* Calculate distance attained by projectile */

double distance( double velocity, double theta )
{
  return (velocity * velocity * sin( theta) / GRAVITY ) ;
}
```

Function definition

When the program in Application 6.2 was run, it produced the following sample output:

```
Enter the initial projectile velocity in m/sec : 30
Enter the initial projectile angle in Degrees : 45

Projectile travels a distance of 91.7431 m
and remains in flight for 4.32481 secs
while reaching a maximum height of 64.8722 m
```

Application 6.3

Write a program to calculate the value of an investment whose interest is compounded anually at a percentage rate 'r' for 'n' years. The equation is given by:

$$\text{Total investment} = \text{Initial investment}(1 + r/100)^n$$

Application 6.3 Compound interest rate calculation.

```
#include    <stdio.h>
#include    <stdlib.h>
#include    <math.h>

int main( void )
{
  char      buff[ BUFSIZ ] ;
  int       years ;
  double    initial_investment, final_investment ;
  double    interest_rate ;
```

```
    double growth( double rate, int years ) ;          'Local' function prototype

    printf("Enter the value of the initial investment : ") ;
    initial_investment = atof(gets(buff)) ;

    printf("Enter the annual percentage rate of interest : ") ;
    interest_rate = atof(gets(buff)) ;

    printf("Enter the number of years the investment gains interest : ") ;
    years = atoi(gets(buff)) ;
                                                        Invoke function
    final_investment = initial_investment * growth( interest_rate, years) ;
    printf("\nValue of final investment = %.2f\n", final_investment) ;

    return 0 ;
}

double growth( double rate, int years )                Function definition
{
    return (pow((1.0 + rate/100.0), years)) ;
}
```

When the program in Application 6.3 was run, it produced the following sample display:

```
Enter the value of the initial investment : 1000
Enter the annual percentage rate of interest : 3
Enter the number of years the investment gains interest : 15

Value of final investment = 1557.97
```

6.1.11 *Functions with variable parameters: The ellipsis: '...'*

It is quite feasible that, from time to time, you might wish to write a function whose argument number and/or type are not rigidly fixed, but may in fact change with each call to that function. A example of this concept can be seen in the function printf( ), where the number and type of arguments varies depending largely upon what it is being asked to display.

The obvious question here is how can we define a function and declare its prototype when the number and type of its arguments are not fixed? Furthermore, what effect would this have on the compiler's ability to check any arguments passed to such a function?

The solution to the first question lies with the ellipsis '...' (three successive '.'s) in the function's parameter list. This indicates that the function expects to be given a variable number of arguments of perhaps varying type. For example, the function prototype for printf() *could* be given as:

Ellipsis indicates unknown number and type of arguments

```
int printf( const char [ ] , . . . ) ;
```

stating that printf() expects to be given at least one argument that is an array of constant char, which may or may not be accompanied by other additional arguments of an unspecified type. As you might imagine, given a function definition or prototype containing an ellipsis '...', there is no way that the compiler would be able to check any of the arguments under its control, which is why the following statement displays garbage for the second and third values and even then only displays a sensible value for 'a' if it is an int. Try it for yourself and see:

Incorrect number of arguments for printf(), but compiler cannot check this

```
printf(" %d %d %d \n", a ) ;
```

The explananation of how a function can be written to extract the arguments it has actually been given (from the stack) requires knowledge that has not yet been covered, so discussion of this topic is postponed until Section 18.10.

6.1.12 *Default argument promotions*

Whenever a call is made to a function whose definition or prototype is not 'visible' at the point in the program where the call is made, the compiler will automatically promote any arguments to those functions in accordance with two simple rules described below. Such promotions also apply to any arguments controlled by the ellipsis '...' in the function's parameter list, even if the function's prototype/definition *is* visible.

(1) All arguments of type char and short are promoted to int;

(2) All arguments of type float are promoted to double.

This explains why the '%d' formatter in the call to printf() below correctly displays the value of 'x', if 'x' is defined as either char, short or int since whatever its type, the value of 'x' will be promoted to a full int before it is given to printf():

Argument controlled by ellipsis in prototype, so 'x' is promoted to an int

```
printf( "%d\n", x ) ;
```

Similarly, the '%g' formatter would have correctly displayed the value of 'x' if 'x' had been defined as either a float or a double.

6.2 Recursion

So far in this chapter, the emphasis on program design has concentrated upon the design of **iterative** functions, which may be called on many separate occasions by the main program to perform a simple action, such as calculating the area of a circle for many different radius values.

This, however, is not the only way a program may be written. An alternative approach is to use **recursion**, where a function may actually invoke itself. A function is said to be directly recursive if it contains statements within it that directly call itself. An example of such a function is given below:

```
int r1( void )
{
    ...
    a = r1() ;
}
```

r1() is directly recursive, as it invokes itself with its own statement

However, if a function x() invokes another function y(), which in turn invokes the original function x(), then x() is said to be **indirectly recursive**.

Correctly designed recursive functions are very powerful tools and often provide an elegant solution to a problem that might otherwise be difficult or cumbersome to solve using an iterative approach. A very powerful application of recursion can be found in Section 17.6, but for the moment we will restrict ourselves to some simple problems and consider how we might design recursive (and where appropriate) iterative functions to solve a problem.

Example: Calculating factorials

The value of factorial n, written mathematically as n!, for all positive n is given by the equation:

$n! = 1$ (for $n = 0$)
$n! = n \times (n-1)!$ (for $n > 0$)

That is to say, 5! can be thought of as $5 \times (4!)$, which can be thought of as $5 \times 4 \times (3!)$ and so on, which, fully expanded, is equal to $5 \times 4 \times 3 \times 2 \times 1$. Although an iterative solution to the calculation of n! is fairly straightforward, it is interesting to consider the solution using recursion.

Studying the mathematics again, we see that n! could be expressed by the equation:

$$\text{factorial}(n) = n \times \text{factorial}(n - 1)$$

which means that a function designed to evaluate factorial(n) could proceed to call itself, in a directly recursive manner, with an argument equal to $(n - 1)$, $(n - 2)$ and so on, until, eventually, factorial(1) is calculated, which could be used to stop the recursion. Program 6.8 demonstrates this in the form of a complete working program.

Program 6.8 Calculation of n! using recursion.

```
#include  <stdio.h>
#include  <stdlib.h>

long  factorial( long n )
{
   if( n <= 1L )
      return 1L ;
   else
      return( n * factorial( n - 1 )) ;
}

int main( void )
{
   char  buffer[ BUFSIZ ] ;
   long  n ;

   printf("Enter Value for N: ") ;
   n = atoi(gets( buffer )) ;

   printf("%ld ! = %ld\n", n, factorial( n )) ;
   return 0 ;
}
```

When Program 6.8 is run, the following sample display is produced:

```
Enter Value for N: 8
8 ! = 40320
```

Table 6.1 Representation of Program 6.8.

Function call and argument	*Returned value*
factorial(5)	5 × factorial(4)
factorial(4)	4 × factorial(3)
factorial(3)	3 × factorial(2)
factorial(2)	2 × factorial(1)
factorial(1)	1

To understand the operation of the function factorial(), consider the calculation of 5!. Initially, the function factorial() is given an argument 'n' with value 5 when it is first invoked by main(). This value is then multiplied by the result returned from a further call to factorial() with a value of 'n' equal to 4, which itself is calculated by a third call to factorial() with a value of 'n' equal to 3 and so on, until eventually a final call is made to factorial() with a value of 'n' equal to 1, which stops the directly recursive process. This is summarized in Table 6.1.

Figure 6.7 illustrates the operation graphically for 5!. Note how each call to factorial() uses a value for argument 'n' which is one less each time, and how each call returns a value which is fed back to the function that calls it.

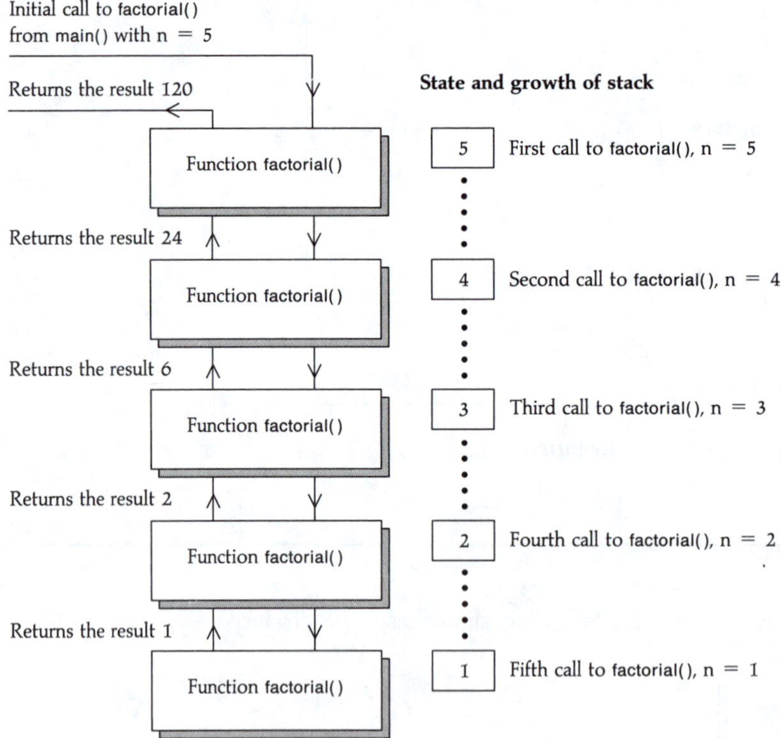

Figure 6.7 Tracing the recursive execution of factorial(5).

It is worth taking some time to study the function factorial() in close detail, as it is actually very representative of the structure of most recursive functions, in that an argument is given to the function, whose value is gradually increased or decreased before the function is called again, and which only stops invoking itself when some predefined argument value is reached.

6.2.1 *Tail end recursive functions*

The function factorial() above is also an example of what is known as **tail end** recursion, where the function contains only one call to itself, at the end of the function. This effectively amounts to, and thus can always be replaced by, an iterative solution using a loop. For example, the function factorial() *could* have been written in the form shown in Program 6.9, where a simple loop replaces the directly recursive call.

Program 6.9 Factorial calculation using iteration.

```
#include   <stdio.h>
#include   <stdlib.h>

long  factorial( long n )
{
   long result = 1L ;                     /* value for 1! */

/*
** While n is greater than 1, calculate n !
*/

   while( n > 1L )
      result *= (n -- ) ;

   return result ;
}

int main( void )
{
   char  buffer[ BUFSIZ ] ;
   long  n ;

   printf("Enter Value for N: ") ;
   n = atoi(gets( buffer )) ;

   printf("%ld ! = %ld\n", n, factorial( n )) ;      /* display result of n! */
   return 0 ;
}
```

Whether you think the recursive approach is more elegant than the iterative approach depends on your point of view. However, it is important to appreciate that with any recursive algorithm the program runs the risk of generating a **stack overflow**.

You can see this for yourself in Figure 6.7, in which each recursive call to `factorial()` increases the storage and thus the length of the stack. If 'n' were sufficiently large, the length of the stack could grow to a point where it exceeds the amount of storage allocated to it at the start of the program's execution, thus generating a run time stack overflow.

This type of run time error can present some difficulty for the programmer, who may not be able to determine at compile time how big the stack is eventually going to become and thus cannot predict whether the program will crash or not. More to the point, the problem may not even show itself until the program has been released for general use.

For example, with the recursive version of the factorial program, the number of times that the function `factorial()` is invoked is dependent upon the value of 'n', which is supplied at run time by the program's operator.

On the author's system, the program aborted with a stack overflow when a value of 'n' greater than 340 was given, although by that time the value of 340! had long since exceeded the point where it could be represented by a 32 bit `long int`. Thus, a recursive function would ideally protect itself by limiting the depth of its own recursion via built in safeguards, for example if (n > 16) return value of 'factorial(16)'.

Example: Calculating the Fibonacci sequence

As another example of recursion, consider the generation of the Fibonacci sequence (a very common sequence occurring in nature) given by the equations:

$fib(n) = 1$	for values of $n = 0$ and 1
$fib(n) = fib(n-1) + fib(n-2)$	for all integer values of $n > 1$

Thus a sequence might be 1, 1, 2, 3, 5, 8, 13, 21 and so on. Program 6.10 demonstrates a recursive function to calculate the value of fib(n).

Here the function `fib()` is directly and recursively called twice. Thus, in calculating the value of fib(4), the function calls itself to calculate the values of fib(3) and fib(2). The call to fib(3) would then in turn call itself to calculate fib(2) and fib(1), while the two calls to fib(2) would calculate the values of fib(1) and fib(0). Follow the program through for yourself; if run, it produces the following display:

```
1, 1, 2, 3, 5, 8, 13, 21, 34, 55, 89, 144, 233, 377, 610
```

Program 6.10 Calculating a Fibonacci number using recursion.

```
#include    <stdio.h>

int fib( int n )
{
  if( n <= 1 )
    return 1 ;
  else
    return( fib( n - 1 ) + fib( n - 2 )) ;
}

int main( void )
{
  int   n ;

  for( n = 0 ; n < 15 ; n++ )
    printf("%d, ", fib( n )) ;
  return 0 ;
}
```

6.2.2 *The Towers of Hanoi problem*

As one final example of recursion, let us consider the famous 'Towers of Hanoi' problem. The game consists of three pegs, a, b and c, and a number of disks of graduated size. Initially, the player of the game chooses the number of disks, which are then stacked on peg a, with the smallest at the top, as shown in Figure 6.8.

The object of the game is to move all of the disks from peg a to peg c, subject to the following two simple rules:

(1) Only one disk may be moved at a time;

(2) A larger disk can never be placed on top of a smaller one.

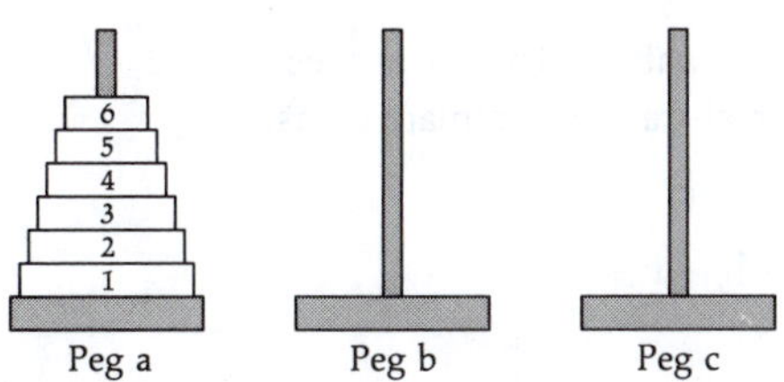

Figure 6.8 The Towers of Hanoi problem.

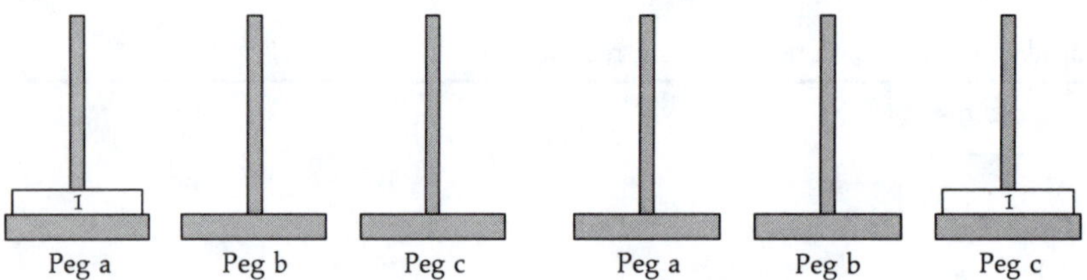

Figure 6.9 The solution with only one disk.

Obviously for the case of a single disk, the problem is trivial and the solution is simply to move the single disk on peg a to peg c, as shown in Figure 6.9.

With two disks, the problem becomes more complex, but is still trivial and involves moving a disk from a to b, then a disk from a to c, and then from b to c, as shown in Figure 6.10.

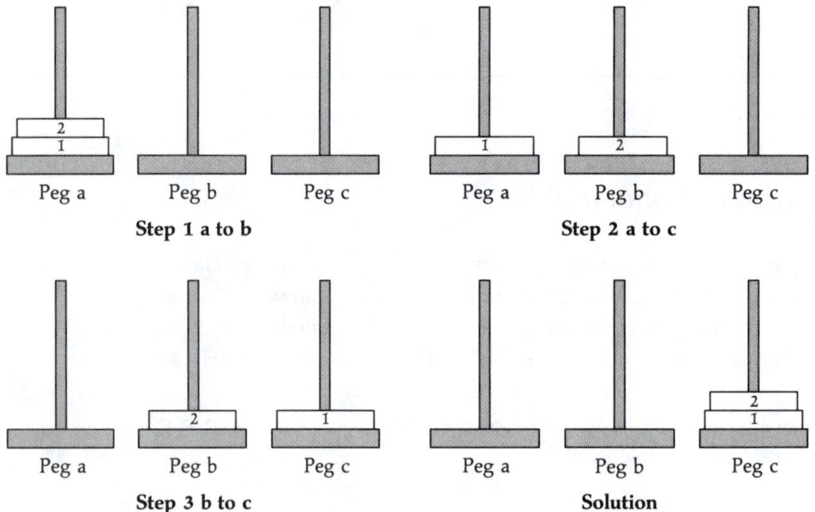

Figure 6.10 The solution with two disks.

With three disks, the problem becomes more difficult. The moves are shown in Figure 6.11.

At first glance, there appears to be no obvious pattern to the moves. However, closer study reveals an emerging pattern, which can be summarized as follows:

(1) Move the first (n – 1) disks from peg a to peg b;

(2) Move the nth disk from peg a to peg c;

(3) Move the remaining (n – 1) disks from peg b to peg c.

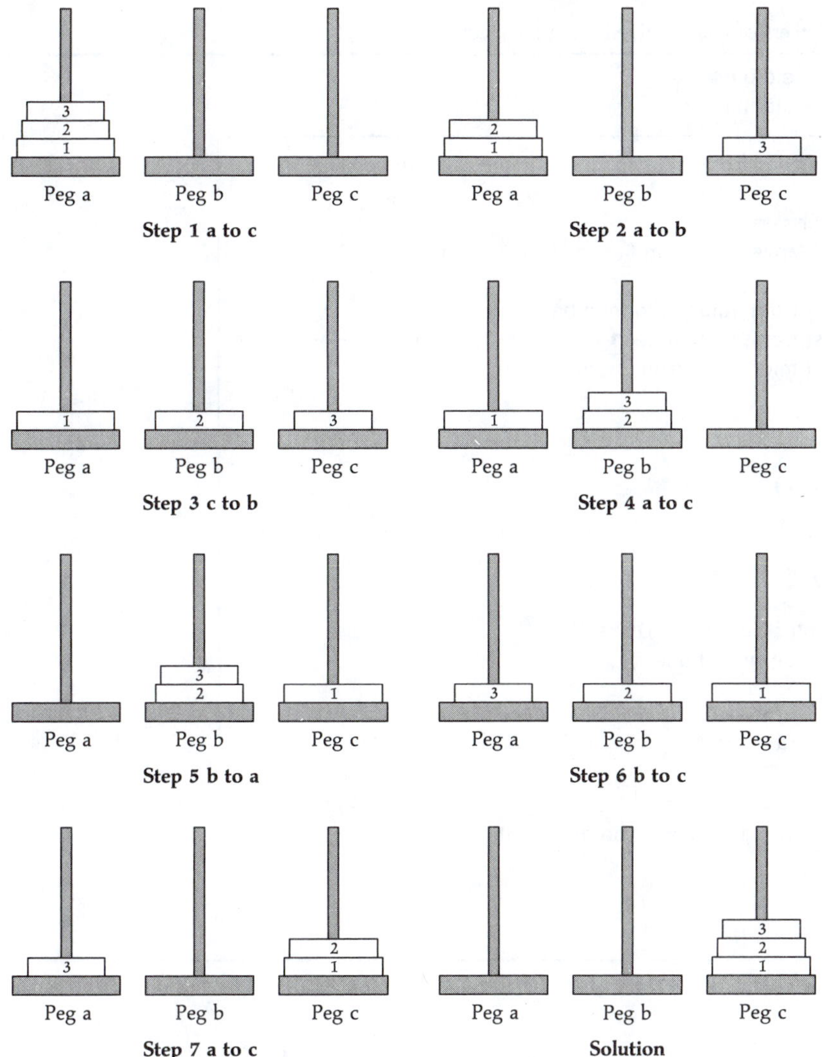

Figure 6.11 The solution with three disks.

Note that steps 1 and 3 both lend themselves to recursion, since if a function can be written to move one disk, it can be recursively called n times to move n disks. The complete program is incredibly short and is presented in Program 6.11. Try to follow it. It is sure to generate a few headaches! You will see that the function **towers()** directly calls itself no less than three times, making the transition to an iterative approach extremely difficult.

Program 6.11 Towers of Hanoi solved using recursion.

```
#include  <stdio.h>
#include  <stdlib.h>

void towers(char from, char to, char middle, int number )
{
  if( number == 1 )
    printf("Move Disk from %c to %c\n", from, to ) ;
  else  {
    towers( from, middle, to, number–1 ) ;
    towers( from, to, middle, 1 ) ;
    towers( middle, to, from, number–1 ) ;
  }
}

int main( void )
{
  int    disks ;
  char  buffer[ BUFSIZ ] ;

  printf("Enter Number of Disks: ") ;
  disks = atoi( gets( buffer )) ;

  if( disks > 0 )
    towers( 'A', 'C', 'B', disks ) ;

  else
    printf("Error Disks must be greater than 0 . . .\n");

  return 0 ;
}
```

When Program 6.11 is run the following sample display is produced:

```
Enter Number of Disks: 3
Move Disk from A to C
Move Disk from A to B
Move Disk from C to B
Move Disk from A to C
Move Disk from B to A
Move Disk from B to C
Move Disk from A to C
```

6.3 Chapter summary

(1) Programs may be decomposed into modules, which may be implemented as functions and used in many different programs. The general form of a function definition is given as:

```
type_specifier function_name( type param1, ..., type paramn )
{
  ...
  return value ;
}
```

where param1 ... paramn represent a comma ',' separated list of parameters, which are matched one-to-one with the actual arguments supplied to the function by the calling program. The function's type_specifier declares the type of any optional data returned by that function. If type_specifier or the type of any parameters are absent, they are assumed to be int.

(2) A function returning no data is said to be a void function. If it declares no parameters then it is said to have a void parameter list. The definition of such a function is shown below. It is illegal for a void function to return a value:

```
void   func1( void )
{
  ...
}
```

(3) A return statement terminates the execution of a function and permits an optional value to be passed back to the calling program (but not with a void function). This value will, where necessary, be implicitly cast to match the function's type specifier.

(4) A function with a variable number of parameters, such as printf(), has additional parameters defined by the ellipsis '...'. The ellipsis cannot be the first (only) parameter for the function but must, where present, be the last.

(5) A function may be invoked by referencing its name, in conjunction with the function invocation operator '()'. At this point a number of arguments may be presented to the function, which are implicitly cast (where necessary) to match the parameters declared for the function. The parameters then assume the value of the actual arguments on a one-to-one correspondence. If the function returns a result, this can be saved by the calling program using the assignment '=' operator but it is not illegal to ignore a returned value.

(6) All arguments, with the exception of arrays, which we shall meet in the next chapter, are passed to a function by value or copy. Thus, the called function cannot alter the original argument that was passed to it (except for an array).

(7) A function prototype informs the compiler about the type and number of arguments that a function expects to be given, and also the type of data it may return. A function prototype can be generated by making a direct copy of the function's header and placing a semicolon ';' at the end. Parameter names in a prototype are optional. For example, the following is a function prototype for the function sin( ), which expects a single argument of type double and returns a double result:

```
double sin( double ) ;
```

(8) A function is only guaranteed to be called correctly at run time, if its function definition or prototype have been encountered by the compiler at that point in the program where the function is first called. It is therefore possible for a program to compile without error but still not run correctly.

(9) All arguments to a function are cast/promoted to match the type of the declared parameters in the function. If no function definition or prototype is visible, or if the parameter(s) are controlled by an ellipsis '...', then the default argument promotions occur; that is, all chars and short ints are promoted to ints, while floats are promoted to doubles.

(10) Recursion is a design technique whereby a function is written to call itself, either directly or indirectly. Tail end recursion occurs when a function directly calls itself at the end of that function and can always be replaced by a simple iterative version using a loop.

6.4 Exercises

6.1 What is meant by 'modular programming'? What benefits does it bring to program development?

6.2 What is meant by the following terms?

- **(a)** Function definition.
- **(b)** Function header.
- **(c)** Function parameters and parameter list.
- **(d)** A function's 'type specifier'.
- **(e)** Function body.

6.3 What is meant by a function argument? What is the difference between this and a function parameter?

6.4 What circumstances lead to a function's execution being terminated?

6.5 How is a function invoked? Explain the mechanisms involved in passing arguments to a function, assigning these to the function's parameters and saving any returned data.

6.6 What is the purpose of a function's type specifier? Why is it necessary at all?

6.7 What implicit casting or promotion may take place when arguments are presented to functions and results are returned by functions? What, if any, are the possible side effects of this?

6.8 What is meant by the following terms?

(a) void function.

(b) Stub function.

(c) void parameter list.

6.9 In the absence of a type specifier for a function, what type of data does the compiler assume to be returned by the function?

6.10 What are the two permissible forms of the return statement? Explain where each can be used.

6.11 What is meant by the terms 'nested function call' and 'nested function definition'? Which are legal/illegal in C?

6.12 What is a 'function prototype'? Explain how one can be constructed. What is the scope of a function prototype? Explain the role that the standard header files play in relation to the functions in the standard library. Why are header files generally #included at the start of the program?

6.13 Explain what happens and what assumptions are made if the compiler encounters a statement that invokes a function whose definition and prototype have not yet been encountered. What happens if the function's definition/prototype is eventually encountered during compilation? What happens if the information in the definition/prototype conflicts/agrees with the assumptions made by the compiler? What happens if the definition/prototype is never encountered by the compiler?

6.14 A compiler encounters the following call to the function f1() before it encounters the function's definition or prototype. Explain the assumptions the compiler makes about this call:

```
a = f1( 3, 2 ) ;
```

6.15 What happens if the function's definition from Exercise 6.14 is eventually encountered and found to be any of the following?

```
double f1( int r )
{
  return (2.0 * PI * r) ;
}
```

```
double f1( double a, double b )
{
  return ((a * a) + (b * b)) ;
}
```

```
int f1( int a, int b )
{
  return ((a * a) + (b * b)) ;
}
```

```
void f1( void )
{
  printf("A Call to f1()\n") ;
}
```

6.16 What would have happened if the definition of any of the four versions of `f1()` from Exercise 6.15 had been encountered prior to the previous statement that attempted to invoke them?

6.17 What is meant by the ellipsis '...' in a parameter list and why is this sometimes useful? If a parameter is controlled by an ellipsis, what default argument promotions might occur for the following data types?

`char` `short` `int` `long` `float` `double` `long double`

6.18 Write functions to:

(a) Convert temperatures expressed in Celsius to Fahrenheit.

(b) Convert temperatures expressed in Fahrenheit to Celsius.

(c) Perform temperature conversion from C to F or F to C based on the value of some choice argument. You should develop two versions of this function, one that is self-contained and one that calls either of the two functions developed in parts (a) and (b).

(d) Prompt the operator for a 'y' or 'n' character response and return the upper case version of that response.

(e) Display the usage of a program.

(f) Determine the absolute value of an integer.

(g) Determine the minimum or maximum value of a floating point number.

(h) Evaluate sinh(x), cosh(x), tanh(x) given the following equations:

$$\sinh(x) = 0.5(e^{x} - e^{-x})$$
$$\cosh(x) = 0.5(e^{x} + e^{-x})$$
$$\tanh(x) = \sinh(x)/\cosh(x)$$

6.19 Explain what is meant by a recursive function and explain the difference between direct and indirect recursion. Explain also what is meant by tail end recursion.

6.20 Rewrite the following programs/applications to be as modular as possible/feasible:

(a) Application 1.3: Evaluating the function e^{x}.

(b) Application 5.6: Implementation of Newton's solutions to root solving.

(c) Application 1.5: Calculation of mean and standard deviation.

(d) Application 5.4: Mortgage repayment.

(e) Program 4.6: Solving the quadratic equation $ax^2 + bx + c = 0$.

6.21 Using the recursive factorial function, write a program to calculate the number of possible ways of selecting 'r' items from a group of 'n' items given by the equation:

$$C(n, r) = n!/(r!(n - r)!)$$

and thus determine the number of possible ways of selecting 3 eggs from a pack of 12.

6.22 Write recursive functions to:

(a) Evaluate the sum of the first n positive integers.

(b) Display the characters from a line of text entered at the keyboard in reverse order.

(c) Evaluate the Chebyshev polynomial, given by the equations:

$C_n(x) = 1$ for $n = 0$
$C_n(x) = 2$ for $n = 1$
$C_n(x) = 2xC_{n-1}(x) - C_{n-2}(x)$ for $n > 1$.

7 A Closer Look at Arrays

In Chapter 1 we introduced the concept of an array as a collection of items of data sharing a common name and type. Access to individual array elements was achieved through the use of the array operator '[ ]' in conjunction with an integer subscript 'n', where the subscript '0' referred to the first element in the array.

In this chapter, we take a closer look at arrays, in particular at how we can initialize arrays and introduce and manipulate arrays with two or more dimensions. We also take a closer look at how the compiler arranges for the elements of an array to be stored in memory, and investigate some simple sorting and searching algorithms to process tables of data stored within arrays.

7.1 Single dimensional arrays

We saw briefly in Chapter 1 that a single dimensional array may be introduced using a definition of the form shown below, where 'n' and 'type' represent the number and type of those elements within the array:

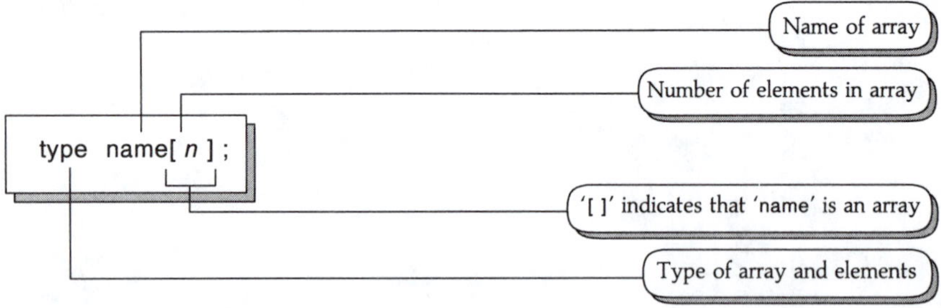

As an example, we could define two separate single dimensional arrays of `int` and `double` to record the ages and heights of 10 pupils in a class with the definitions shown below:

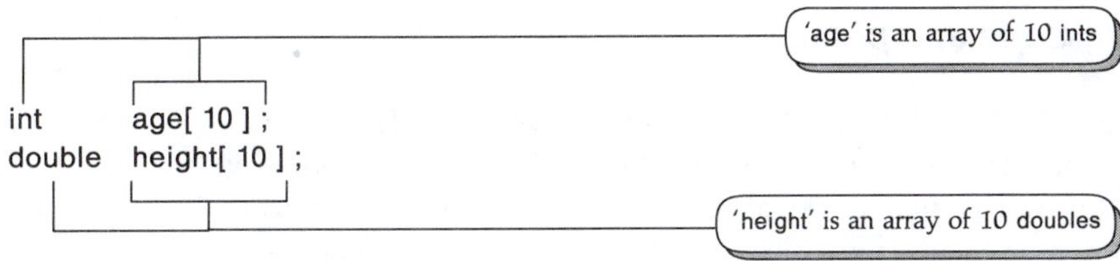

With all array definitions the number of elements within the array must be explicitly stated (either using an implicit constant value such as 10, as above, or via a symbolic constant value created with #define) to enable the compiler to determine the array's total storage requirements. The compiler then arranges for those elements to be stored successively in memory, with element [0] at the lowest address and all other elements placed at successively higher addresses, as illustrated in Figure 7.1 (assuming 2 byte integers).

Whenever an array definition is encountered by the compiler a calculation is performed to determine the storage requirements for the array. This is simply a product of the number of elements in the array and the storage requirements of each element. Thus the compiler is able to determine that the array 'age' in Figure 7.1 requires 20 bytes of storage (10 elements, each of which is assumed to be 2 bytes in size), while the array 'height' would probably require 80 bytes (assuming a double to be 8 bytes).

If need be, this calculation can be performed by the program using the sizeof operator, as in the examples below, which is more portable than a simple 'hand' calculation:

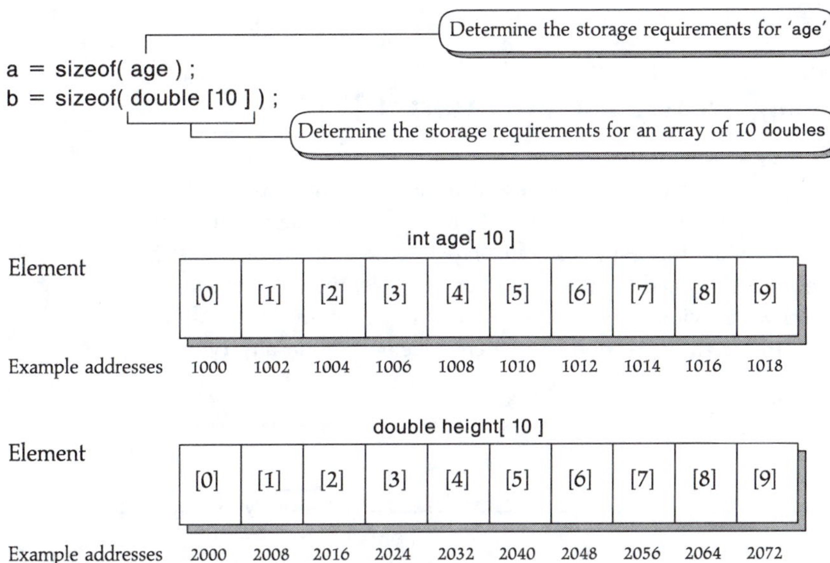

Figure 7.1 The internal representation of two separate single dimensional arrays, each of 10 elements.

7.1.1 *Array scope and privacy*

The scope, privacy and initialization rules relating to arrays are similar to those of any other type variable. For example, the program section below defines two arrays, the first of which, 'age', is global, since it is defined outside a function. Because no attempt was made to initialize 'age' (see later), all of its elements will be implicitly cleared to zero at the start of the program. The second array, 'result', is automatic since it is defined within the bounds of the function main( ) and as such its elements are not implicitly initialized.

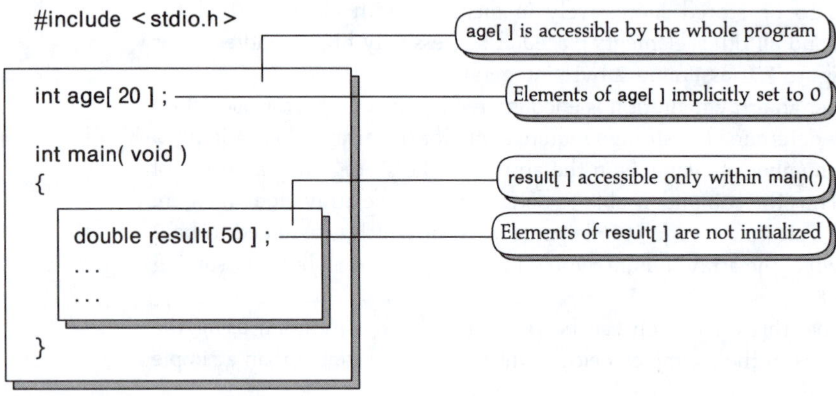

7.2 Accessing arrays: The operator: '[ ]'

Individual elements in an array may be accessed using an integer subscript or index in conjunction with the array operator '[ ]'. In C, the first element in any array is element zero, while the last is element 'n – 1', where 'n' represents the total number of elements defined for the array. For example, the last element in the array 'result' shown previously may be accessed with a subscript value of 49. Thus the general form of an expression to reference element 'y' in any type of array 'x' is given as:

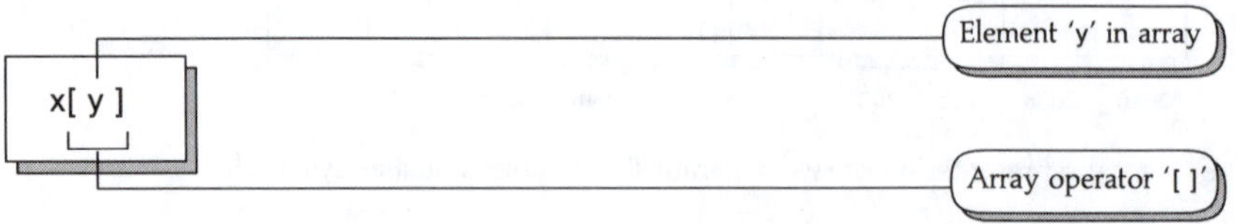

Note: Do not confuse the symbols '[ ]' used during the definition of an array with the same symbols used as the array operator when accessing elements in the array. In the definition of an array, the symbols '[ ]' serve only to inform the compiler that an array is being defined. When used in an expression, however, the array operator '[ ]' is used to fetch or store data from/to a specific element in the array.

As an example, the program section below demonstrates the use of the array operator syntax to access element 0 (the first element) in the array 'result' and element 6 (the seventh element) in the array 'age', which are assigned the values 1.234 and 23, respectively:

```
#include <stdio.h>

int   age[ 10 ] ;

int main( void )
{
   double result[ 50 ] ;

   result[ 0 ] = 1.234 ;
   age[ 6 ] = 23 ;

   printf("result[ 0 ] = %f\n", result[ 0 ] );
   printf("age[ 6 ] = %d\n", age[ 6 ] ) ;

   return 0 ;
}
```

Assign 1.234 to element 0 in 'result'

Assign 23 to element 6 in 'age'

Fetch and display element 6 in 'age'

7.2.1 *Array bounds checking*

It is a fact of life that C, unlike some other languages, performs *no* checking of the validity of an array subscript's value, either at compile or run time, which means that it is perfectly permissible to write, compile and run a program that attempts to access a non-existent array element. In fact, no errors or warnings will be generated either at compile or run time although the program will in all probability crash.

Many new programmers are often caught out by this, particularly when attempting to access one more element than actually exists in an array. For example, given the previous definition of 'age' as an array of 20 integers, the following statement is incorrect (though not illegal), since it attempts to access the 21st element in the array, when in fact only the elements 'age[0]–age[19]' actually exist; in other words, storage has not been allocated for element 'age[20]'.

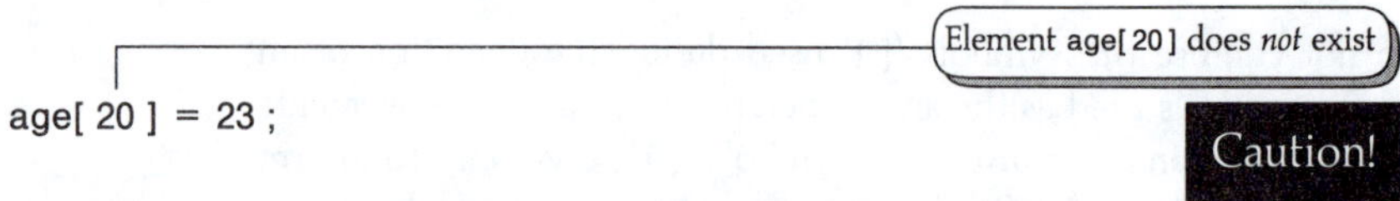
Element age[20] does not exist
age[20] = 23 ;
Caution!

If such a statement were encountered, the compiler would actually generate code to access the location in memory where it believed such an element would exist, had storage been allocated for it. This can, and often does, lead to the corruption of other program variables and the failure of the program as a whole.

Why, then, does C not bother to check array bounds? The answer boils down simply to efficiency. If the compiler were to generate code to check the validity of each array access at run time, then not only would the program become larger, it would also execute more slowly.

We shall also see in Chapter 10 that C permits storage for arrays to be dynamically allocated at run time, using the standard library memory allocation functions malloc(), calloc() and realloc(), and thus it would be very difficult under these circumstances for the compiler to generate code to check the bounds of an array whose size will be determined by run time considerations and data.

On a more positive note, the lack of array bounds checking permits the creation of functions able to accept array arguments with any number of elements, making them more generic and reusable in other applications. This is particularly useful in sorting and searching algorithms, as we shall see shortly.

7.3 Initializing arrays

The elements of any array can obviously be initialized or assigned values during the execution of the program, typically as part of a for loop in conjunction with some integer subscript and the array operator '[ ]'. However, there are many occasions when it is more convenient for the array to be pre-initialized prior to the execution of some section of code. Such pre-initialization is possible only at the time when the array is defined. The general form is given below, where $Val_{[0]}$ ... $Val_{[n-1]}$ represents the initializing data for array elements '0' to 'n-1' and whose values must be implicit constants:

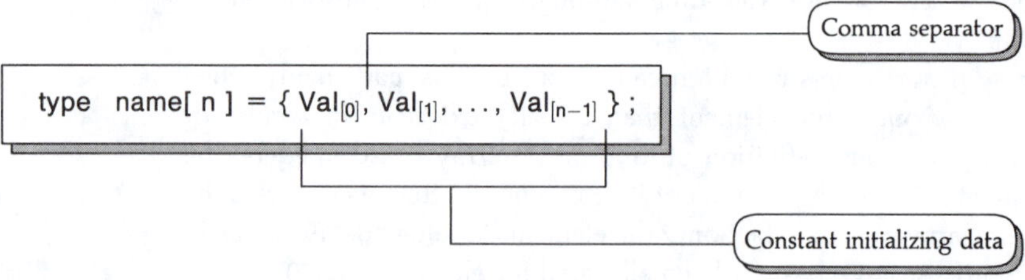
Comma separator
type name[n] = { Val[0], Val[1], . . . , Val[n−1] } ;
Constant initializing data

For example, we could pre-initialize an array of rainfall figures for a given twelve month period, using the definition:

```
float   rainfall[ 12 ] = { 10.1, 12.6, 12.3, 10.0, 4.2, 2.3, 2.1, 3.9, 3.8, 5.4, 5.6, 9.8 } ;
```

Note that it is not necessary to initialize all of the elements of an array. For example, we could have pre-initialized just the first three elements with a definition of the form:

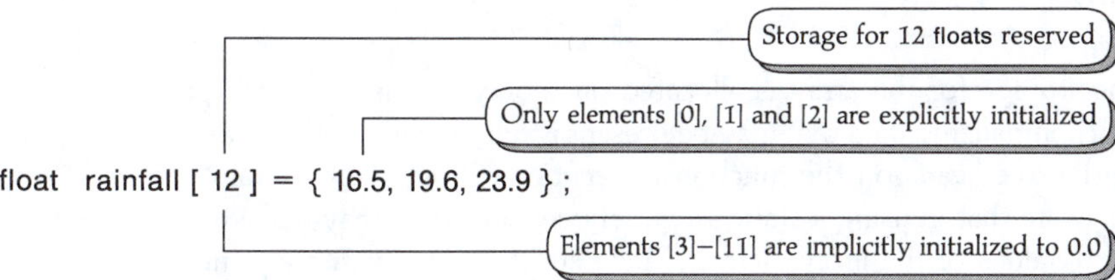

in which case only elements [0], [1] and [2] would be initialized, even though storage for 12 elements is actually reserved for the array. Furthermore, any remaining uninitialized elements ([3]–[11]) are implicitly initialized to zero, even for an array with automatic scope.

This means that all elements of an array may be pre-initialized to zero with a definition of the form shown below, which explicitly initializes rainfall[0] to 0 and relies on the implicit initialization of all the other elements to zero:

```
float   rainfall [ 12 ] = { 0.0 } ;
```

Note, however, that if the initializing list contains more items of initializing data than there are elements defined for the array, then this is regarded as an error. For example;

Initializing list contains too many items

```
int   y[ 2 ] = { 1, 2, 3, 4, 5 } ;
```

Illegal

Usefully, in the presence of an initializing list, the programmer may optionally choose to omit the size specifier for the array. In this instance the compiler determines the number of elements in the array simply by counting the number of items of initializing data, for example:

Size set to 5 by default

```
int   y[ ] = { 1, 2, 3, 4, 5 } ;
```

Initializing list of 5 elements

Whenever an automatic array, such as 'y' above, is initialized, the compiler generates code to allocate storage for the array 'y' at run time on the stack, then commences to copy the initializing data to it one element at a time. As you might image, such initialization can impose sometimes severe overheads on the program in terms of its execution speed because the array has to be allocated and pre-initialized each time the function is called. For this reason, it makes sense to consider the use of a static array such as that shown below:

```
static  int y[ ] = { 1, 2, 3, 4, 5} ;
```

Here, the storage for the array is allocated once only, at the start of the program, and such initializing data that may be present is only copied to the array once, reducing the overheads on the function's execution. Of course, programmers should be aware that in using a static array, any changes they may make to the pre-initialized values of the array elements take effect for every subsequent call to the function.

7.4 Copying arrays

Unlike any other data type in C, the assignment operator '=' cannot be used to copy the contents of one array to another, even if the arrays are of the same type and size. Neither can two arrays be compared with operators such as '<', '>', '<=', '>=', '==', '!='.

If an array must be copied to or compared with another array, then the operation must be performed manually on an element by element basis, as demonstrated in Program 7.1. Here, a for loop is used to copy the elements from the array 'x' into a second array 'y'.

Program 7.1 Copying and displaying array elements.

```
#include   <stdio.h>

#define    SIZE  10

/*
** Now define a global array of 10 integers but pre-initialize the first
** 5 elements. The last 5 will be set to zero
*/

int   x[ SIZE ] = { 0, 1, 2, 3, 4 } ;

int main( void )
{
    int   y[ SIZE ], a ;
```

```
    for( a = 0; a < SIZE; a ++ )
      y [ a ] = x [ a ];

/*
** Now display the corresponding elements in both arrays
** to show that they have been copied
*/

    for( a = 0; a < SIZE; a ++ )
      printf("x[%d] = %d, y[%d] = %d\n", a, x[a], a, y[a]) ;

    return 0 ;
}
```

If Program 7.1 is run, the following display is produced:

```
x[0] = 0, y[0] = 0
x[1] = 1, y[1] = 1
x[2] = 2, y[2] = 2
x[3] = 3, y[3] = 3
x[4] = 4, y[4] = 4
x[5] = 0, y[5] = 0
x[6] = 0, y[6] = 0
x[7] = 0, y[7] = 0
x[8] = 0, y[8] = 0
x[9] = 0, y[9] = 0
```

7.5 Arrays as function arguments

In contrast to other variable types in C, when an array is passed to a function, the compiler does not make a copy of the data it holds and present the copy to the function; rather, it arranges for the address of the first element in the array to be passed to the function. In other words, arrays are passed to functions using a technique known as 'call by reference'.

This is very important, since any function written to receive an array argument is actually given the address of the first element in the array passed to it. If the function then attempts to modify the contents of the array it has been given, it will actually be modifying the original array argument, not a copy of it as we have seen with other data types.

You may be interested to know that we have already made use of this knowledge, probably without realizing it at the time, whenever we called the function **gets( )**. For example, study Program 7.2. Here the functions **gets( )** and

Program 7.2 Passing an array to a function by reference.

```
#include    <stdio.h>

int main( void )
{
   char buffer[ BUFSIZ ] ;

   gets( buffer ) ;
   puts( buffer ) ;

   return 0 ;
}
```

Pass the address of buffer[0] to gets()

puts() finds that gets() has stored characters directly in array

puts() are called with an array argument. The function gets(), as we know, reads characters from the keyboard and stores them in the array whose name was given to it.

In other words, because gets() has been given the address of array element buffer[0], it knows where that array is stored in memory and can thus copy the characters entered at the keyboard directly into the array; thus, there is no need for gets() to return the array.

7.5.1 *Sorting and searching techniques*

The need to sort and search tables of data arises routinely in many programming applications. Everyday examples include word processing and database design. In this section we investigate some fairly straightforward approaches to sorting and searching tables in the form of single dimensional arrays.

The 'bubble sort' algorithm presented here is probably the most well known (and, unfortunately, least efficient) of all sorting techniques. Its main (and some would say only) attraction is the simplicity of its algorithm and the ease with which it can be implemented. Thus, it is an ideal vehicle for introducing sorting techniques to first time programmers.

In Chapter 8, a more sophisticated sort technique will be presented in the form of C.A.R. Hoare's quicksort algorithm, which is generally acknowledged to be one of the best sort algorithms available. However, that approach relies on recursion, and the implementation requires knowledge about C that has not yet been covered.

It is also worth noting that the standard C library defines the sort and search functions qsort() (based around an implementation of the quicksort algorithm) and bsearch(), specifically to ease the burden of performing these operations. However, their main drawbacks lie with their genericity – that is, they do not represent the optimum solution for sorting and searching tables of known data type – and with the fact that they cannot be used to sort and search data resident on disk.

Simple sorting: The bubble sort

Assuming that 'x' is an array of 'n' elements to be sorted, the bubble sort algorithm works by initially comparing element 0 in turn with each successive element in that array. If the comparison shows that two elements are out of order, then they are swapped. The process is then repeated for elements 1, 2, 3, ..., n − 1 and so on until all elements have been compared (and possibly swapped) with all their successive elements.

In the worst case, where the elements are arranged in the opposite order to that required, for example, ascending rather than descending, the algorithm becomes very inefficient, degenerating into a sort time proportional to n^2. Nevertheless, the function **sort( )** shown in Program 7.3 uses this approach to sort an array of integers into ascending order.

Notice how the array parameter is declared simply as an array of integers and that the number of elements in the array does not have to be declared explicitly. This lack of an array size declaration in a function parameter may be explained by recalling that C performs no array bounds checking anyway, and since the array is only declared by the parameter (not defined), a declaration of the array's size serves no practical value. The function will, of course, need to know the actual number of elements that it is required to sort, thus the argument 'n' is included for this purpose.

When the calling program invokes the function **sort( )** it will find that the sorting is performed directly on the array that was given to it; that is to say, upon returning from **sort( )**, the calling program should find that the array is now in the correct ascending order and as such there is no need for **sort( )** to attempt to return an array.

Note that if the array were required to be sorted into descending order, then **sort( )** could be modified to replace the greater than operator ' > ' in the if test

Program 7.3 Function to sort an array of 'n' integers.

Integer parameter declaration

Number of elements to sort

Size is optional in an array declaration so any size array can be sorted

```
void sort( int array[ ] , int n )
{

  int   this, next, temp;

  for( this = 0; this < n ; this ++ )                 /* outer for loop */
    for( next = this + 1; next < n ; next ++ )        /* inner for loop */
      if( array[ this ] > array[ next ] )   {         /* if out of order */
        temp = array[ this ] ;
        array[ this ] = array[ next ] ;               /* swap elements */
        array[ next ] = temp ;
    }
}
```

Program 7.4 Calling the sort routine.

```
#include    <stdio.h>

void sort( int x[ ] , int n ) ;                                    Prototype for sort()

int main( void )
{
   int   i ;
   int   num[ ] = { 9, 8, 7, 6, 5, 4, 3, 2, 1, 0 } ;     /* array to be sorted */
   int   n = sizeof(num)/sizeof( int) ;                  /* calculate number of elements */
                                                          Number of elements in the array

   sort( num, n ) ;                                      /* sort the array */
                                                          Pass array to function sort()

   for( i = 0; i < n; i ++ )
      printf("%d ", num[ i ]) ;                          /* display the sorted array */

   putchar('\n') ;
   return 0 ;
}
```

with the less than operator '<'. If sort() were now called to sort an array of 10 integers, as in Program 7.4 the following display is produced, showing that the data originally in descending order has been sorted into ascending order:

```
0 1 2 3 4 5 6 7 8 9
```

The progress of the sort algorithm can be followed by displaying the array elements after each iteration of the outer for loop, as shown below.

Iteration number	*x[0]*	*x[1]*	*x[2]*	*x[3]*	*x[4]*	*x[5]*	*x[6]*	*x[7]*	*x[8]*	*x[9]*
Unsorted	9	8	7	6	5	4	3	2	1	0
1st	0	9	8	7	6	5	4	3	2	1
2nd	0	1	9	8	7	6	5	4	3	2
3rd	0	1	2	9	8	7	6	5	4	3
4th	0	1	2	3	9	8	7	6	5	4
5th	0	1	2	3	4	9	8	7	6	5
6th	0	1	2	3	4	5	9	8	7	6
7th	0	1	2	3	4	5	6	9	8	7
8th	0	1	2	3	4	5	6	7	9	8
9th	0	1	2	3	4	5	6	7	8	9

Search and find algorithms: The linear search

The most straightforward search algorithm, known as the 'linear' or 'sequential' search, is based upon a comparison of each successive element in the array, generally commencing with element 0, with some predefined 'key' or search value. If a match is found, the index or subscript in the array required to access that data is generally returned to the calling program, or perhaps '–1' in the event that no match is found. The main attraction of this simple algorithm over other more efficient algorithms is that the data is not required to have been sorted prior to initiating a search.

It can be shown (almost intuitively) that searching a table/array of 'n' elements in this manner requires on average 'n/2' comparisons and, in the worst case, where the element to be located is the last element in the array, or perhaps does not exist at all, 'n' comparisons will be required. An implementation of this search algorithm can be found in Program 7.5.

Program 7.5 Implementing a linear search.

```
#include <stdio.h>
#include <stdlib.h>

/*
** An implementation of the linear or sequential search algorithm
*/

int l_search( int array[ ], int n, int key )
{
    int i ;

    for(i = 0; i < n; i ++ )
        if( array[i] == key )                    /* if data matches key */
            return i ;                           /* return subscript into array */
    return (–1) ;                                /* data does not exist */
}

int main( void )
{
    int  data[ ] = { 1, 4, 9, 11, 13, 19, 23, 26, 29} ;   /* data table to be searched */

    int  subscript, key ;
    int  num_elements = sizeof(data) / sizeof(data[0]) ;
    char buff[ BUFSIZ ] ;

    printf("Enter key value . . . ") ;
    key = atoi(gets(buff)) ;                     /* read in key value */

    if((subscript = l_search( data, num_elements, key)) != –1)
        printf("Key exists at element [%d]\n", subscript) ;
    else
        printf("Data does not exist\n");
    return 0 ;
}
```

If Program 7.5 is run, the following sample display is produced:

```
Enter key value ...  16
Data does not exist

Enter key value ... 11
Key exists at element [3]
```

Binary searching

A more powerful and efficient algorithm for searching larger tables of data is to use a **binary** search. Unlike the linear search, this algorithm requires the table/array of data to have been sorted (generally into ascending order) prior to initiating the search.

The algorithm represents a 'divide and conquer' approach, where the array to be searched is divided repeatedly into two smaller arrays, about some midpoint element 'x'. The value of element 'x' is at each stage compared with the 'key' value. If the key value is less than the value of element 'x', then the search resumes in the lower half of the (previously sorted) array, otherwise it resumes in the upper half.

This process is repeated until either the value of element 'x' matches the key, in which case the search is successful, or the division of the array gives rise to an array with 0 elements, indicating that the array does not contain an element matching the key. It can be shown using this algorithm that for the worst case, the number of comparisons required is proportional to $\log_2 n$. Program 7.6 implements this algorithm.

Program 7.6 Implementing a binary search.

```
int  b_search( int data[ ], int num, int key )
{
  int  lower = 0, upper = num – 1, x ;

  while( lower <= upper )  {        /* while there is an array of at least one element */
    x = (lower + upper) / 2 ;       /* choose midpoint element */

    if( key < data[x])              /* if data is in lower half of array */
      upper = x – 1 ;               /* set upper limit to just below midpoint x */
    else if( key > data[x])         /* if data is in upper half of array */
      lower = x + 1 ;               /* set lower limit to just above midpoint x */
    else                            /* otherwise match is found */
      return x ;                    /* return subscript to element */
  }
  return –1 ;                       /* data not found */
}
```

As an example, consider searching the following array for an item of data with value 19:

1, 3, 4, 5, 7, 8, 12, 13, 19, 23

Initially, the array is divided into two halves about element [4], the value of which is 7. As the value of the key (in this instance 19) is greater than the value of this midpoint element, the search resumes in the upper half of the array, consisting of elements [5]–[9].

A midpoint element is again chosen from this array, element [7], the value of which is 13, which once again is less than the value of the key (19), so the search again resumes in the upper half of an even smaller array consisting of just elements [8]–[9].

The midpoint element of this array, element [8], has a value *matching* the key, and thus the integer subscript 8 is returned by the function. The operation is illustrated below:

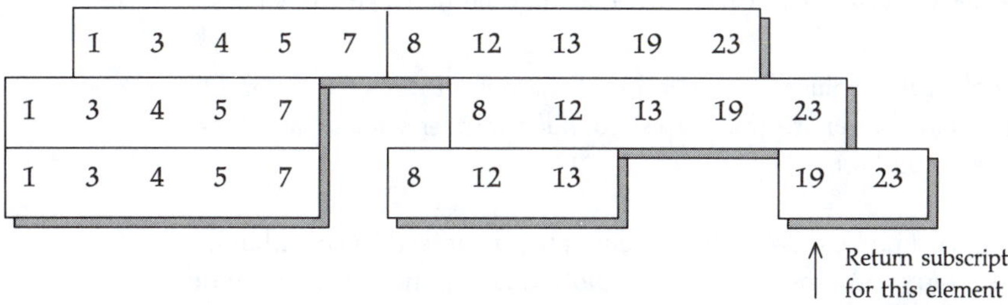

A linear search would have required eight comparisons, whereas the binary search required only three comparisons, a difference that becomes more prominent with larger arrays.

7.5.2 *Simple graph plotting application*

Another useful application of arrays lies with the plotting of graphs for mathematical functions and statistical data. One might, for example, wish to examine the nature of the function $e^{-x}\sin(6x)$ for a specified range of 'x'. Of course, it is relatively straightforward to display a table of mathematical values for the function over a given range, but this often gives little insight into the shape or nature of the function. However, if those values are plotted as a graph, the visual representation is much more informative.

In this section we present a simple program that will permit mathematical functions (and with minor modifications, any table of data) to be plotted on either a terminal/screen or a printer, or, with the help of output redirection, sent to a disk file for later analysis or incorporating into other documents.

Because both terminals and printers are essentially character based devices, this particular program plots its data using the character '*' suitably positioned to represent each value. Since control over a printer or terminal is often limited (paper cannot be re-wound, for example), the program plots its data horizontally with the y-axis running across the paper/screen. This has the advantage that many values of 'x' can be plotted, while the function f(x) is scaled to fit in the 80/132 character columns offered by most terminals and printers. Control over column width and the left and right margins is also offered. The plot algorithm itself is simple and can be summarized as:

(1) Enter a lower, upper and incremental range for 'x' for the function to be evaluated, for example 0 to 10 in increments of 0.1;

(2) Using a loop, evaluate the function f(x) for every value of 'x' and save each result within an element of a suitably defined array;

(3) Find the minimum and maximum value of f(x) over the specified range;

(4) Scale all calculated values of f(x) such that they lie between the values 0 and 1;

(5) Multiply all scaled values by the width of the output device – 80 or 132 columns – and convert to the nearest rounded integer values; save these values in a second array.

We now have a table of data whose values are guaranteed to lie within the range from 0 to 80 (or 132), thus a '*' can be plotted at that horizontal position which represents the value of the function. Program 7.7 presents an implementation of this algorithm, and is heavily reliant upon the use of arrays.

Program 7.7 A simple graph plotting program.

```
#include   <stdio.h>
#include   <stdlib.h>
#include   <math.h>

#define  COLUMNS         80           /* Width of screen/printer in characters */
#define  LEFT_MARGIN     8            /* Number of characters for left margin */
#define  RIGHT_MARGIN    1            /* Ditto right margin */
#define  L_MARGIN        (LEFT_MARGIN - 1)
#define  MARGINS         (LEFT_MARGIN + RIGHT_MARGIN)

#define  NUM 100                      /* maximum number of points to calculate */

/* Function prototypes */

int function( double func[ ], int num, double xmin, double xmax, double xinc ) ;
void scale( double func[ ], int graph[ ], int num, double max, double min) ;
void plot( int graph[ ], int num, double max, double min,
                    double xmin, double xmax, double xinc, char title[ ] ) ;
```

```
double func_min( double func[ ], int num ) ;
double func_max( double func[ ], int num ) ;

int main( void )
{
  double  min,              /* The Minimum calculated value of f(x) */
          max,              /* The Maximum calculated value of f(x) */
          xmin,             /* The Minimum value of x for which f(x) is calculated */
          xmax,             /* The Maximum value of x for which f(x) is calculated */
          xinc,             /* The increment for x */
          func[NUM] ;       /* An array for storing the values of f(x) */

  int     num_points,       /* The number of values of f(x) actually calculated */
          graph[NUM] ;      /* An array to store the rounded integer values of f(x) */

  char    buff[ BUFSIZ ] ;  /* A buffer for the function gets( ) */
  char    title[ BUFSIZ ] ; /* A title for the plot */

/*
** Now prompt operator for the range of values for x over which f(x)
** will be calculated
*/

  printf("Enter Minimum Value for x: ") ;
  xmin = atof(gets(buff)) ;

  printf("Enter Maximum Value for x: ") ;
  xmax = atof(gets(buff)) ;

  printf("Enter Increment for x: ") ;
  xinc = atof(gets(buff)) ;

  printf("Enter a Title for the Plot: ");
  gets( title ) ;

/*
** Go and evaluate f(x) from xmin to xmax in increments of xinc
** and store results in the array func[ ]. Return the actual number
** of values calculated
*/

  num_points = function( func, NUM, xmin, xmax, xinc ) ;

/*
** Now inspect the calculated array looking for the
** Minimum and Maximum values within it prior to scaling
*/

  min = func_min(func, num_points) ;
  max = func_max(func, num_points) ;
```

```
/*
** Now scale all points so that all data can be plotted on a screen
** of width 'COLUMNS' characters (less margins)
*/

   scale( func, graph, num_points, max, min ) ;

/* Now plot the scaled data */

   plot( graph, num_points, max, min, xmin, xmax, xinc, title ) ;
   return 0 ;
}

/*
** This function calculates f(x) in range xmin to xmax and stores
** results directly in array 'func[ ]'. It returns the number
** of points calculated
*/

int   function( double func[ ], int num, double xmin, double xmax, double xinc )
{
   int       i = 0 ;
   double  x ;

   for( x = xmin; x <= xmax; x+=xinc )  {
      if( i == num )
         break ;                    /* make sure bounds of array are not exceeded */

      func[i++] = (sin(x)) ;     /* the function f(x) goes here */
   }
   return i ;                       /* number of points calculated */
}

/*
** This function scales the calculated results so that they all
** fit within the range 0 – 1. The scaled values are multipled by the
** width of the available screen in columns and rounded up prior to
** being stored as integer values/coordinates within the array 'graph[ ]'
*/

void   scale( double func[ ], int graph[ ], int num, double max, double min)
{
   int       i ;
   double  scaled_value ;

   for( i = 0; i < num; i++ )  {
      scaled_value = (COLUMNS – MARGINS) * (func[i] – min) / (max – min) ;
      graph[i] = scaled_value + 0.5 ;
   }
}
```

```
/* This function returns the minimum value of f(x) over the calculated range */

double   func_min( double func[ ], int num )
{
   int        i ;
   double  min = func[0] ;

   for (i = 0; i < num; i ++ )
      if(func[i] < min )
         min = func[i] ;

   return min ;
}

/* This function returns the maximum value of f(x) over the calculated range */

double   func_max( double func[ ], int num )
{
   int        i ;
   double  max = func[0] ;

   for (i = 0; i < num; i ++ )
      if(func[i] > max )
         max = func[i] ;

   return max ;
}

/* This function plots the calculated values and displays margins, title etc. */

void   plot( int graph[ ], int num, double max, double min,
                  double xmin, double xmax, double xinc, char title[ ] )
{
   int        i ;

   printf("%*cTitle: %s\n", L_MARGIN, ' ', title) ;
   printf("%*cRange of x = (%g - %g) in Increments of %g\n",
               L_MARGIN, ' ', xmin, xmax, xinc) ;

   printf("%*cMax f(x) = %g", L_MARGIN, ' ', max) ;   /* display min and max values */
   printf("%*cMin f(x) = %g\n", L_MARGIN, ' ', min) ; /* display min and max values */
   printf("\n\n") ;
   printf("%*c", L_MARGIN, ' ' ) ;

/* Now plot Y-axis across paper/screen */

   for( i = LEFT_MARGIN ; i < (COLUMNS - RIGHT_MARGIN + 1) ; i ++ )   {
      if(((i - LEFT_MARGIN) % 5) == 0)
         printf( "+" ) ;
      else
         printf( "-" ) ;
   }
   printf("\n") ;
```

```
/* Now plot f(x) across the paper, for each value of x */

   for( i = 0; i < num; i++ )  {
      printf("% - *g", L_MARGIN, xmin + (i * xinc)) ;
      printf("|");
      printf("%*c\n", graph[i], '*') ;              /* print a '*' for the point */
   }
}
```

Figure 7.2 illustrates the graph produced by the program for the function $e^{-x}\sin(6x)$.

7.6 Multi-dimensional arrays

So far in this chapter our discussion has centred on the uses and applications of single dimensional arrays, where a single array operator '[ ]' and a single integer subscript were required to access an element within it. However, in many instances it is more natural to consider the concept of a multi-dimensional array.

Take, for example, the game of chess. Here the board on which the game is played is itself two-dimensional, consisting of 8 rows and 8 columns, and it is natural for any player of that game to consider each board position in terms of an (X, Y) coordinate. Thus, the bottom left-hand corner of the board *might* be represented by the coordinates (0, 0), with the top right position represented by the coordinates (7, 7). However, this is not the only way in which each board position could be specified. An alternative approach might simply choose to label all 64 squares on the board using numbers in the range 0–63, which ideally lends itself to implementation using a single dimensional array of 64 elements.

However, if a computer program were written to play chess, the person playing against the computer would naturally feel more comfortable about expressing their movements to the computer using (X, Y) coordinates rather than as a single coordinate in the range 0–63; thus if the program had used a single dimensional array to represent each position in the board, any (X, Y) coordinates expressed in this way would then have to be translated by the program into a single array subscript given by the expression $(X + 8Y)$.

If, however, a *two*-dimensional array consisting of 8 by 8 elements could be introduced, as shown below, then the X and Y coordinates could serve as the subscripts in each separate dimension:

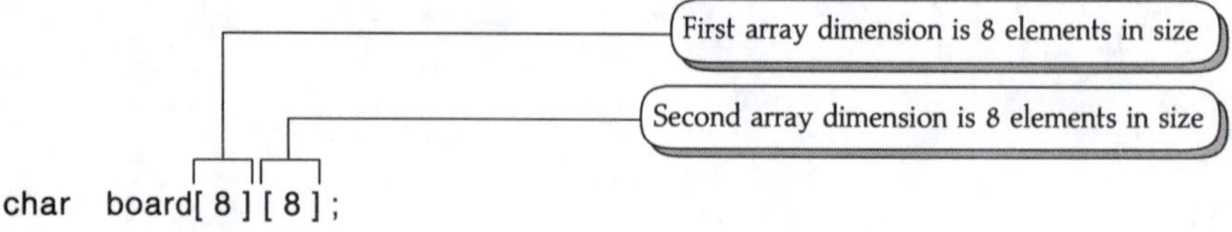
First array dimension is 8 elements in size
Second array dimension is 8 elements in size
char board[8] [8] ;

```
    Title: e(-x)sin(6x)
    Range of x = (0 - 5) in Increments of 0.1
    Max f(x) = 0.763089   Min f(x) = -0.447606
    +----+----+----+----+----+----+----+----+----+----+----+----+----+----+----+-
0   |                           *
0.1 |                                                        *
0.2 |                                                                       *
0.3 |                                                                     *
0.4 |                                                     *
0.5 |                               *
0.6 |           *
0.7 | *
0.8 | *
0.9 |       *
1   |                    *
1.1 |                                *
1.2 |                                        *
1.3 |                                          *
1.4 |                                       *
1.5 |                                *
1.6 |                       *
1.7 |                  *
1.8 |                *
1.9 |                 *
2   |                     *
2.1 |                         *
2.2 |                             *
2.3 |                               *
2.4 |                              *
2.5 |                            *
2.6 |                          *
2.7 |                        *
2.8 |                       *
2.9 |                       *
3   |                        *
3.1 |                         *
3.2 |                           *
3.3 |                           *
3.4 |                           *
3.5 |                           *
3.6 |                           *
3.7 |                          *
3.8 |                         *
3.9 |                        *
4   |                        *
4.1 |                        *
4.2 |                         *
4.3 |                          *
4.4 |                          *
4.5 |                         *
4.6 |                         *
4.7 |                         *
4.8 |                         *
4.9 |                         *
```

Figure 7.2 Plot of the function $f(x) = e^{-x}\sin(6x)$.

For example, moving a chess piece from coordinate (x1, y1) to (x2, y2) could be accomplished using an expression such as 'board[x2][y2] = board[x1][y1]' as opposed to an expression such 'board[x2 + 8 * y2] = board[x1 + 8 * y1]', which would be required if 'board' had been defined as a single dimensional array.

How you choose to *visualize* such arrays, in terms of the storage, depends upon the reason for introducing them in the first place. The most common approach for two-dimensional arrays is to visualize them in terms of rows and columns. For example, consider the two-dimensional array 'x' defined below:

```
int  x[ 3 ][ 4 ] ;
```

This could be visualized as a grid of 3 rows by 4 columns, as shown in Figure 7.3.

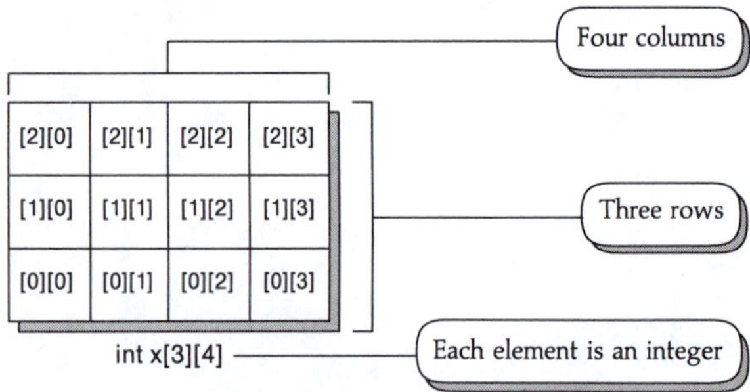

Figure 7.3 Visualizing a two-dimensional array.

However you choose to visualize the arrangement of elements in terms of rows and columns, the compiler actually ensures that all array elements are stored successively in memory as a single dimensional array, regardless of how many dimensions were defined. Thus, given the definition of the two-dimensional array 'x[3][4]', the compiler would represent the array as three successive single dimensional arrays of four elements, as shown in Figure 7.4.

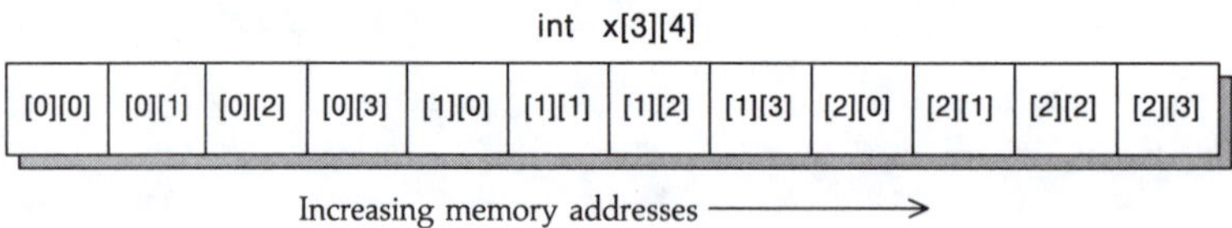

Figure 7.4 Representation of a two-dimensional array in memory.

With a three-dimensional array such as:

```
char  y[ 2 ][ 2 ][ 3 ] ;
```

you might choose to visualize 'y' as an array of elements, each of which is actually a two-dimensional array, that is, 'y' is an array of two individual two-dimensional arrays consisting of two rows by three columns, or 12 elements in total, as illustrated in Figure 7.5.

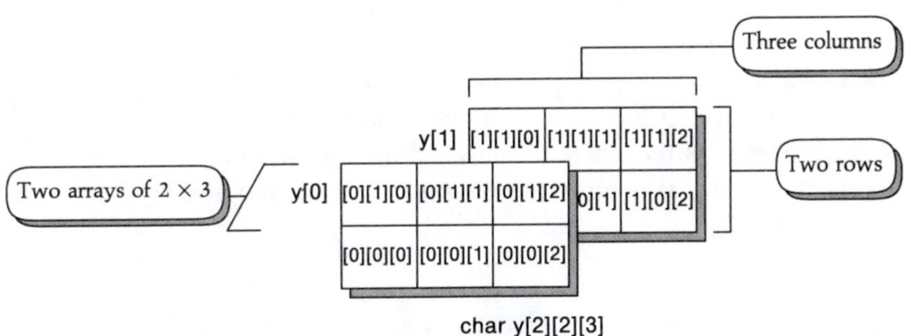

Figure 7.5 Visualizing a three-dimensional array.

Likewise, the compiler would represent this array as two successive two-dimensional arrays, each of which is stored as two successive single dimensional arrays of 3 chars, as shown in Figure 7.6.

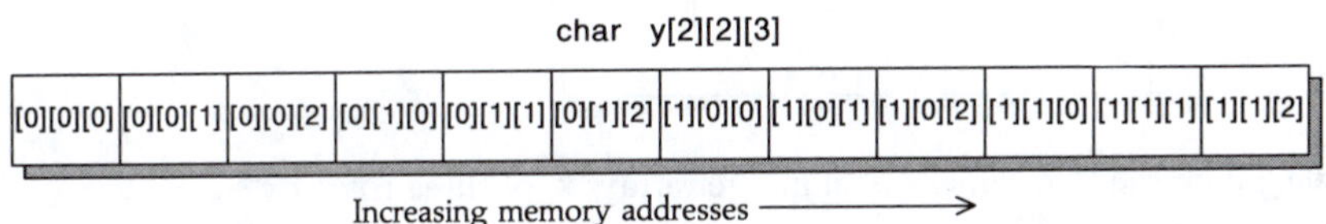

Figure 7.6 Representation of a three-dimensional array in memory.

7.6.1 *Accessing multi-dimensional arrays*

Multi-dimensional arrays are accessed in much the same way as single dimensional arrays, but require several array operators '[ ]' and subscripts to completely reference a unique element. Therefore, given the definition of the two-dimensional array 'z' as:

```
int  z[ x ] [ y ] ;
```

we could access the element at the intersection of the 'nth' row and 'mth' column using two array operators '[ ]' with the following expression, which is translated by the compiler into a single dimensional array access of element 'n + y * m'.

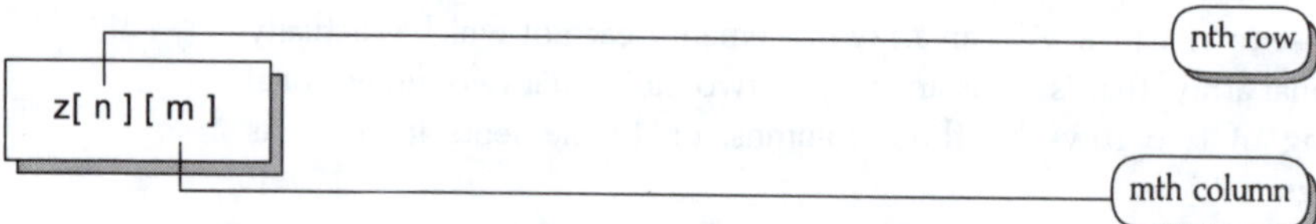

Cautionary Note: Some programmers reading this book may have programmed in other languages where the notation 'z[n, m]' or 'z(n, m)' is used to access a two-dimensional array. In C, the expression 'n, m' represents an example of the comma operator (see Chapter 5), thus the whole expression is equivalent to 'z[m]', which references the single dimensional row 'm' within the array. Whether the compiler flags this as an error depends upon what the program does with the result, so take care.

7.6.2 *Initializing a multi-dimensional array*

Multi-dimensional arrays may be pre-initialized in a similar manner to single dimensional arrays. The general format for initializing a two-dimensional array of 'n' rows by 'm' columns is shown below:

$$\texttt{type name[n][m]} = \{ \{ i_{[0][0]} , i_{[0][1]} , \ldots , i_{[0][m-1]} \}, \{ i_{[1][0]} , i_{[1][1]} , \ldots , i_{[1][m-1]} \}, \ldots \{ i_{[n-1][0]} , i_{[n-1][1]} , \ldots , i_{[n-1][m-1]} \} \};$$

For example, given the two-dimensional integer array 'x' of three rows by four columns, we could define and initialize each element with a statement of the form shown below, where the size of the first dimension is (optionally) omitted and will thus be calculated by the compiler:

Size of first dimension is always optional when an array is being initialized

```
int x[ ] [ 4 ] = { { 0, 1, 2, 3 } , { 4, 5, 6, 7 } , { 8, 9, 10, 11 } } ;
```

Table 7.1 Summary of initialization of array x.

Element	*Initialization*	*Element*	*Initialization*
x[0][0]	0	x[1][2]	6
x[0][1]	1	x[1][3]	7
x[0][2]	2	x[2][0]	8
x[0][3]	3	x[2][1]	9
x[1][0]	4	x[2][2]	10
x[1][1]	5	x[2][3]	11

Table 7.1 shows how this initializing data is assigned to individual elements in the array.

Likewise, the general form for the initialization of a three-dimensional array of 'n' by 'm' by 'p' elements is:

```
type  name[ n ] [ m ] [ p ] = {
   { { i[0][0][0] , i[0][0][1] , . . . , i[0][0][p-1] } ,
     { i[0][1][0] , i[0][1][1] , . . . , i[0][1][p-1] } ,
      . . .
     { i[0][m-1][0] , i[0][m-1][1] , . . . , i[0][m-1][p-1] }
   } ,
   . . .
   . . .
   { { i[n-1][0][0] , i[n-1][0][1] , . . . , i[n-1][0][p-1] } ,
     { i[n-1][1][0] , i[n-1][1][1] , . . . , i[n-1][1][p-1] } ,
      . . .
     { i[n-1][m-1][0] , i[n-1][m-1][1] , . . . , i[n-1][m-1][p-1] }
   }
} ;
```

You can see from both of these initializations that it is the elements of the *last* or rightmost dimension of an array that are initialized first, gradually moving towards the first or leftmost dimension. The three-dimensional integer array 'z[2][3][4]' below could, for example, be defined and initialized with the following statement:

Size of first dimension is always optional when an array is being initialized

```
int  z[ ][ 3 ] [ 4 ] = {
   { { 0, 1, 2, 3 } , { 4, 5, 6, 7 } , { 8, 9, 10, 11 } } ,
   { { -1, -2, -3, -4 } , { -5, -6, -7, -8 } , { -9, -10, -11, -12 } }
} ;
```

where once again the size of the first dimension is optional, since the compiler counts the items of initializing data to determine it for itself. Such a definition would lead to 'z' being initialized in the manner shown in Table 7.2.

Table 7.2 Values assigned to z[2][3][4].

Element number	*Initializing value*	*Element number*	*Initializing value*
z[0][0][0]	0	z[1][0][0]	−1
z[0][0][1]	1	z[1][0][1]	−2
z[0][0][2]	2	z[1][0][2]	−3
z[0][0][3]	3	z[1][0][3]	−4
z[0][1][0]	4	z[1][1][0]	−5
z[0][1][1]	5	z[1][1][1]	−6
z[0][1][2]	6	z[1][1][2]	−7
z[0][1][3]	7	z[1][1][3]	−8
z[0][2][0]	8	z[1][2][0]	−9
z[0][2][1]	9	z[1][2][1]	−10
z[0][2][2]	10	z[1][2][2]	−11
z[0][2][3]	11	z[1][2][3]	−12

7.6.3 *Multi-dimensional arrays as arguments to functions*

As with single dimensional arrays, multi-dimensional arrays may also be passed to functions as arguments. Such a function should declare the array parameter with the same number of dimensions as the array being passed to it. The size of the first dimension, as we saw in the special case of a single dimensional array, need not be explicitly stated in the parameter, but the sizes of all other dimensions must, as this information will be needed by the compiler to determine the address of each element in memory.

As an example, consider Program 7.8, which defines and initializes a two-dimensional array of three by five elements with random integer values. Each row is sorted (as a single dimensional array) by the bubble sort algorithm developed earlier before the whole array is redisplayed.

Program 7.8 Sorting rows of integers in a two-dimensional array.

```
#include    <stdio.h>

#define    COLUMNS    5

void   sort( int array[ ] , int n ) ;                    /* Fn prototypes */
void   display_data( int data[ ][COLUMNS], int num_rows) ;

int   main( void )
{
   int   rows;

/*
** Now define and initialize a two-dimensional array of
** 3 by 5 integers into random order, before attempting to sort
** each row individually.
*/
```

```
    int data[ ][COLUMNS] = {{15,2,9,4,0}, {-1,4,2,3,7}, {2,3,6,1,0}} ;

/*
** Now determine the number of rows in data[ ] in a portable manner
** by dividing the storage required for the whole array by the storage
** required for each row
*/

    int num_rows = sizeof( data ) / sizeof( data[0] ) ;

/*
** As the expression 'data[x]' references the xth row in the two-
** dimensional array data, we can pass this as a single dimensional
** array of 5 integers to the bubble sort algorithm
*/

    for( rows = 0; rows < num_rows; rows ++ )
        sort( data[rows], COLUMNS) ;              /* pass a row from data to sort() */

    display_data( data, num_rows ) ;              /* display each row in array */

    return 0 ;
}

/*
** The bubble sort function to sort a single dimensional array of
** 'n' integers. Passing a row from a two-dimensional array such as
** data above permits the function to sort individual rows from that array
*/

void    sort( int array[ ] , int n )
{
    int    this, next, temp;

    for( this = 0; this < n ; this ++ )               /* outer for loop */
        for( next = this + 1; next < n ; next ++ )    /* inner for loop */
            if( array[ this ] > array[ next ] )  {    /* if out of order */
                temp = array[ this ] ;
                array[ this ] = array[ next ] ;       /* swap elements */
                array[ next ] = temp ;
        }
}

/*
** Function to display rows and columns from a two-dimensional
** array of at least 5 columns
*/
```

```
void display_data( int data[ ][COLUMNS], int num_rows)
{
   int rows, columns ;

   for( rows = 0; rows < num_rows; rows ++ ) {
      for( columns = 0; columns < COLUMNS; columns ++)
         printf(" %d ", data[rows][columns]) ;
      putchar('\n') ;
   }
}
```

If Program 7.8 is run, the following display is produced, illustrating how each of the rows in the two-dimensional array 'data' has been sorted as single dimensional arrays:

```
 0  2  4  9  15
-1  2  3  4  7
 0  1  2  3  6
```

Application 7.1

The game of life is supposed to model the birth, life and death of cells placed in proximity to one another. A cell in this context can mean any living thing able to reproduce. In its simplest form it is played on a two-dimensional grid of 'n' rows by 'm' columns, as shown in Figure 7.7 for an 8 by 8 board, where the symbol '*' represents a living cell. The rules of the game are quite simple and are summarized below:

(1) A cell survives to the next generation if it has two or three neighbours;

(2) A cell dies from overcrowding if it has four or more neighbours and from loneliness if it has less than two neighbours;

(3) A cell is born into an *empty* position if it has exactly three neighbours.

The eight cell positions immediately surrounding each cell on the grid are shown below; some of these, however, may not be valid, if the cell lies on the edge of the board:

1	2	3
4	*	5
6	7	8

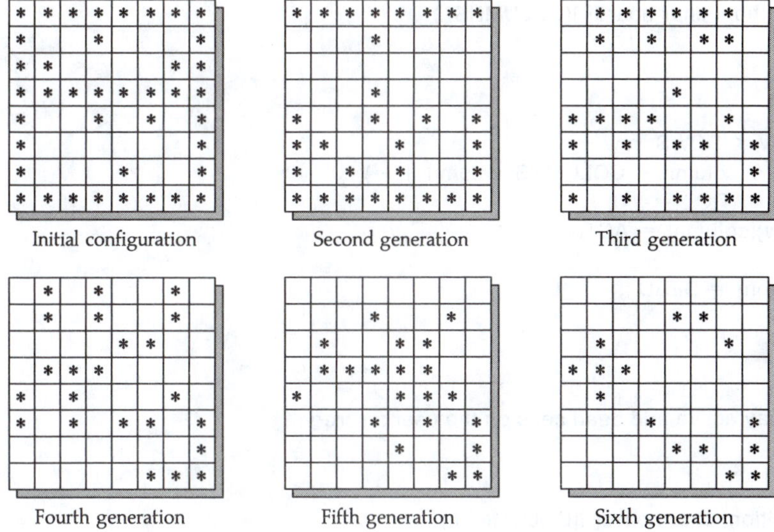

Figure 7.7 Initial configuration and second, third, fourth, fifth and sixth generations of cells.

For example, an initial configuration of cells and the corresponding second, third, fourth, fifth and sixth generations are shown in Figure 7.7.

With this knowledge, write a program to play the game of life, using either a configuration of cells entered at the keyboard by the operator, or a configuration of random cell placements.

Application 7.1 A two-dimensional game of life.

```
#include  <stdio.h>
#include  <ctype.h>          /* for toupper( ) function */
#include  <stdlib.h>         /* for function rand( ) */

#define   ROWS      8        /* Number of rows on board */
#define   COLUMNS   8        /* Number of columns on board */
#define   DEAD      ' '      /* Symbol for dead cell (a space character) */
#define   ACTIVE    '*'      /* Symbol for ACTIVE cell */
#define   RATIO     3        /* Controls ratio of ACTIVE to DEAD cells for random
                                positioning option */

/*
** This function fills the board game with random ACTIVE
** positions. By adjusting the value of RATIO, more or less
** active cells are created by this process.
*/
```

```
void   random_position( char board[ ][COLUMNS] )
{
  int   row, column ;


  for( row = 0; row < ROWS; row ++ )
    for( column = 0; column < COLUMNS; column ++ )
      if((rand( ) % RATIO ) == 0)
        board[row][column] = ACTIVE ;
      else
  board[row][column] = DEAD ;
}


/*
** Function to display active and dead cells on the user's screen
*/


void   display_position( char board[ ][COLUMNS] )
{
  int   row, column ;


  for( row = 0; row < ROWS; row ++ )   {
    for( column = 0; column < COLUMNS; column ++ )
      putchar( board[row][column] ) ;

    putchar('\n') ;
  }
  putchar('\n') ;
}


/*
** Function to allow the user to enter their own positions on the board
** This could of course be achieved by initializing the array 'current_position'
** defined within main( ), during its definition, but that would require
** recompilation each time a modification was performed
*/


void   enter_position( char board[ ][COLUMNS] )
{
  int   row, column ;


  printf("\nEnter the position of your cells ") ;
  printf("on a %d by %d grid\n", ROWS, COLUMNS) ;
  printf("\Use a '%c' character to mark an empty position and '%c' for an active cell\n",
                                                 DEAD, ACTIVE) ;
  printf("Assume that top left cell is position [0,0] and bottom\n") ;
  printf("right is [%d,%d]\n", ROWS-1, COLUMNS-1) ;
```

```
  for( row = 0; row < ROWS; row ++ )  {
    fflush( stdin ) ;                    /* remove any excess characters like C Returns */
    printf("Enter Row %d: ", row) ;
    for( column = 0; column < COLUMNS; column ++ )
      board[row][column] = toupper(getchar());
  }
  printf("\n\n") ;
}

/*
** Function to examine each position on the board
** and determine if a cell dies, survives or is new born
*/

void   calculate_next_position( char current[ ][COLUMNS], char next[ ][COLUMNS])
{
  int   row, column, cell_count ;

  for( row = 0; row < ROWS; row ++ )  {
    for( column = 0; column < COLUMNS; column ++ )  {
      cell_count = 0 ;

/* Is position 1 within board game and if so, is it active? */

      if(( row > 0 ) && (column > 0))
        if( current[row-1][column-1] == ACTIVE)
          cell_count ++ ;

/* Is position 2 within board game and if so, is it active? */

      if(( row > 0 ) && (current[row-1][column] == ACTIVE))
          cell_count ++ ;

/* Is position 3 within board game and if so, is it active? */

      if((row > 0) && (column < (COLUMNS-1)))
        if(current[row-1][column+1] == ACTIVE)
          cell_count ++ ;

/* Is position 4 within board game and if so, is it active? */

      if(column > 0 )
        if(current[row][column-1] == ACTIVE)
          cell_count ++ ;

/* Is position 5 within board game and if so is it active? */

      if(column < (COLUMNS-1))
        if(current[row][column+1] == ACTIVE)
          cell_count ++;
```

```
/* Is position 6 within board game and if so, is it active? */

        if((row < (ROWS-1)) && (column > 0 ))
          if(current[row+1][column-1] == ACTIVE)
            cell_count ++ ;

/* Is position 7 within board game and if so, is it active? */

        if(row < (ROWS-1))
          if(current[row+1][column] == ACTIVE)
            cell_count++ ;

/* Is position 8 within board game and if so, is it active? */

        if(row < (ROWS-1))
          if(column < (COLUMNS-1))
            if( current[row+1][column+1] == ACTIVE)
              cell_count++ ;

/*
** Now calculate survival, birth or death for current cell.
** If the current cell is empty and it has three neighbours
** then a new cell is born here, otherwise it remains dead
*/

        if((current[row][column] == DEAD) && (cell_count == 3))
          next[row][column] = ACTIVE ;
        else
          next[row][column] = DEAD ;

/*
** If an active cell has four or more neighbours, it dies from overcrowding
** or, if it has less than two neighbours, it dies from loneliness
*/

        if(current[row][column] == ACTIVE)   {
          if(( cell_count == 2 ) || (cell_count == 3 ))
            next[row][column] = ACTIVE ;

/*
** If an active cell has two or three neighbours it survives
*/

          else
            next[row][column] = DEAD ;

        }
      }
    }
}
```

```
/*
** Function to copy the next generation of cell positions
** onto the existing board game
*/

void   update_current_position( char old[ ][COLUMNS], char new[ ][COLUMNS])
{
  int   row, column ;

  for( row = 0; row < ROWS; row ++ )
    for( column = 0; column < COLUMNS; column ++ )
      old[row][column] = new[row][column] ;
}

/*
** The game itself
*/

int   main( void )
{
  char   current_position[ROWS][COLUMNS] ;
  char   next_position[ROWS][COLUMNS] ;

  printf("Random or user supplied positions ? [R/U]: ") ;

  if(toupper(getchar()) == 'R')
    random_position( current_position ) ;
  else
    enter_position( current_position ) ;

  fflush( stdin ) ;                          /* remove any spare characters such as C Returns*/

  do  {
    display_position( current_position ) ;
    calculate_next_position( current_position, next_position) ;
    update_current_position( current_position, next_position) ;
    printf("Hit return to see next generation . . . \n") ;

    while(getchar() != '\n')
      ;                                      /* wait for <return> */

  } while( 1 ) ;
  return 0 ;
}
```

7.7 Chapter summary

(1) An array is a collection of data items with a common type, accessible under one name. Arrays may have one or more dimensions, while individual elements in an array may be accessed using the array operator '[n]', where 'n' is an integer subscript.

(2) A single dimensional array of 10 integers may be defined and initialized with a statement of the form:

```
int  a[ 10 ] = { 0, 1, 2, 3, 4, 5, 6, 7, 8, 9 } ;
```

where 'a' is the name of the array, and each element in 'a' is an int. Note that the number of elements in the array, in this case 10, need not be explicitly stated when the array is initialized.

A two-dimensional array 'x' of five by six chars and a three-dimensional array 'y' of two by three by four floats may be defined with statements such as:

```
char  x[ 5 ][ 6 ] ;
float  y[ 2 ][ 3 ][ 4 ] ;
```

The expression 'x[n]' references the nth row of six characters in 'x', while the expression 'x[n][m]' references the mth element of row 'n' in the array 'x'. The expression 'y[n]' references the nth two-dimensional array of three by four integers within 'y' while the expression 'y[n][m]' references the mth row within the nth two-dimensional array in 'y'.

(3) When an array is part-initialized, all uninitialized elements are implicitly initialized to zero, regardless of the scope of the array. This is true even for multi-dimensional arrays whose rows are only part-initialized.

(4) C provides no array bounds checking, so if the program attempts to access an element which has not been allocated storage then it is the programmer's problem.

(5) Unlike other data types in C, arrays are passed to functions by reference – that is, it is the address of the first element in the array that is actually given to the function, which means that the called function has direct access to the original array and not a copy of it. This means that the function may modify the array directly without the need to return a copy of it back to the calling program.

An array parameter may be declared for a function in exactly the same way as the original array that was passed to it; that is, with the same number of dimensions. Explicitly stating the size or number of elements of the first dimension is optional; the sizes of other dimensions must, however, be stated.

7.8 Exercises

7.1 Define suitable arrays to represent the following data:

(a) An array of 20 floats.

(b) An array of 256 characters.

(c) An array of 4 by 5 integers.

(d) An array of 4 by 3 by 6 doubles.

For each array, determine how many elements it contains and what its storage requirements are.

7.2 For each of the arrays in Exercise 7.1 write a simple program to:

(a) Clear all elements to zero.

(b) Assign successive elements with increasing values.

(c) Assign successive elements with decreasing values.

(d) Calculate the average of all elements in the array.

7.3 Write a simple program that makes use of scanf( ) to read in an array of 20 floating point numbers and average them.

7.4 How could the sizeof operator be used to calculate:

(a) The storage requirements for an array?

(b) The number of elements in an array of known type?

7.5 What does the following program display?

```
include    <stdio.h>

int main( void )
{
   int  x[ ] = { 5, 9, 12, 3, 6, –6, 22, 18 } ;
   int  y[ ][4] = { {2, 1, 4, 5}, {12, 14, 16, 18}, {9, 3, 2, 1} } ;

   printf("%d %d %d %d \n", x[ 0 ], x[ 3 ], x[ 5 ], x[ 7 ]) ;
   printf("%d %d %d %d \n", y[ 0 ][ 0 ], y[ 0 ][ 3 ], y[ 1 ][ 1 ], y[ 2 ][ 3 ]) ;
   return 0 ;
}
```

7.6 What is wrong with the following program section?

```
int  i, j, x[ 12 ][ 10 ] ;

for( i = 0; i < 13; i++ )
   for( j = 0; j <= 10; j++)
      x[ i ][ j ] = i+j ;
```

7.7 Why does the number of elements of a single dimensional array not need to be stated when the array is written as a function parameter? Why, then, do the sizes of any subsequent dimensions of a multi-dimensional array parameter need to be stated?

7.8 Write a program to record exam marks, expressed as a percentage, for a class of 40 students, where the students are numbered 0–39, and produce a frequency distribution table for the class marks. Enhance the program to plot the frequency distribution using the graph plotting program presented in Program 7.7.

7.9 Using the bubble sort function presented in Program 7.3 modify the program in Exercise 7.8 to allow the program's operator to sort and display the overall averaged marks for the class in ascending or descending order.

7.10 Modify the previous program so that up to 6 exam marks can be recorded for each student. The program's operator can then elect to plot the class distribution of marks for a single exam, or for the average of all exam marks.

7.11 In Application 5.3 a program was presented to calculate, display and plot the growth of current in an inductive circuit. Modify the program to make use of the graph plotting routines presented in Program 7.7.

7.12 Arrays are often used as look-up tables when an item of data is used as the subscript to the array to produce a new translated value. Using this technique, write a program to encrypt a string of characters into a new string using a look-up table to translate each character.

7.13 Write a program to display a number entered in digit form in word form – for example, the operator entry '1324' is subsequently displayed as 'one three two four'. Remember that a string of the form `"1324"` is represented by an array of `char` terminated by the character '\0'.

7.14 Modify your solution to Exercise 7.10 so that the name of each student can be displayed when the marks have been sorted.

7.15 The UNIX utility 'banner' can be used to create large text messages and is often put to good use when displaying file names on spooled printer listings. An example of the type of output it produces is given below, where the message 'HELLO' is displayed as:

```
H    H EEEEEE L      L      OOOOOO
H    H E      L      L      O    O
HHHHHH EEEEEE L      L      O    O
H    H E      L      L      O    O
H    H EEEEEE LLLLLL LLLLLL OOOOOO
```

By defining a suitable array to allow a 'character set' to be constructed in the form of a 6×7 wide matrix, write a simple program to emulate 'banner', where a string of up to 10 characters can be prompted for and displayed in the form shown above.

7.16 Write a function to perform the following actions on two-dimensional matrices:

(a) Addition

(b) Subtraction

(c) Multiplication

Hint: Think about the size of the array needed to hold the result and ensure that it is big enough.

7.17 Write a recursive version of the binary search function presented in Program 7.6.

8 An Introduction to Pointers

The subject of pointers is perhaps the most interesting and challenging aspect of C, and one that unfortunately causes new students the most headaches, particularly those who have never programmed before or have previously studied other languages such as Pascal or BASIC and have perhaps never experienced the need for a pointer. So what exactly is a pointer and why are they so important in C?

A pointer differs from the other fundamental data types that we have met thus far in this book, by virtue of the fact that the data held by a pointer is the **address** of a location in memory, typically that of another variable, and as such a pointer may be thought of as **pointing** to that address or variable.

This concept is important, since it directly facilitates the creation and manipulation of dynamically sizeable data structures such as arrays, lists and trees. In particular, their use in manipulating arrays and text strings frequently leads to the production of code which is both more efficient and more compact than might otherwise be achieved by more conventional means.

For the systems programmer involved in designing small embedded controllers, the pointer is a particularly useful tool that facilitates direct access to both memory and memory mapped peripherals, allowing the program to control and communicate with its external environment.

In this introductory chapter the reader will learn how to define and initialize pointers to different types of objects and how such objects may be indirectly manipulated via a pointer. The important and intimate relationship that exists between an array and a pointer is presented, as well as a discussion of how dynamically sizeable arrays may be created. For the embedded applications engineer/programmer, some simple example programs demonstrating how pointers may be used to access memory mapped peripherals are presented.

As with previous chapters, the reader is encouraged to study each section carefully and methodically, and experiment with the sample programs contained within them, as a complete and full understanding of these topics is essential for the chapters that follow.

8.1 Defining and using pointers

As with any type of variable, a pointer must have been defined before it can be used. An example of a pointer definition is given below:

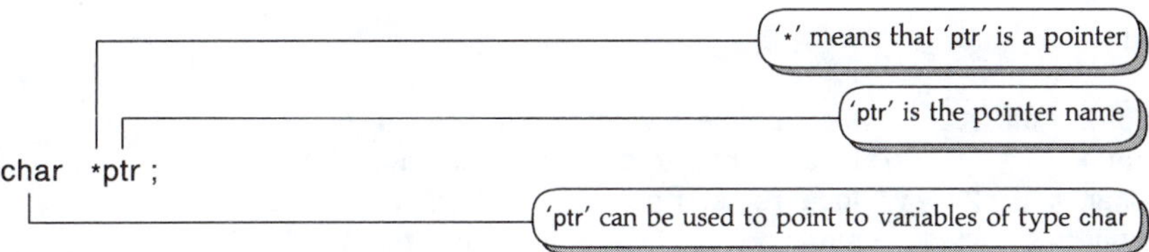
'*' means that 'ptr' is a pointer
'ptr' is the pointer name
char *ptr ;
'ptr' can be used to point to variables of type char

There are two important points to note here. Firstly, it is only through the inclusion of the asterisk '*' placed in front of a variable's name that the compiler knows that a pointer variable is being defined. This is important, since without the '*' the compiler would assume that 'ptr' is simply a char.

Secondly, whenever a pointer is defined, it must be defined as pointing to a specific type of object, for example, a char, int or double. In the above example, 'ptr' has been defined as a pointer to a char type variable and thus 'ptr' is a char pointer. As a further example we could also define a pointer 'p1' able to point to int type variables, as shown below; thus, 'p1' is an int pointer:

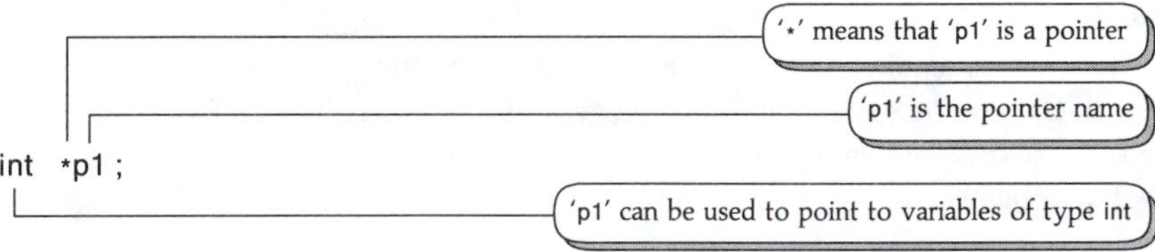
'*' means that 'p1' is a pointer
'p1' is the pointer name
int *p1 ;
'p1' can be used to point to variables of type int

It is important to grasp at this stage that all pointers, because they simply hold an address, require exactly the same amount of storage given a particular CPU/compiler implementation. That is to say, an int pointer is no bigger and requires no more storage than a char or double pointer. Depending upon the compiler and the CPU architecture it produces code for, a pointer is generally either a 2 or a 4 byte variable.

Note that some compilers, such as Borland's Turbo C and several others that produce code to run on the Intel 80x86 family of CPUs with its support for different memory models, support the concept of **near** and **far** pointers, which are able to represent a 16 or 32 bit address and are respectively 2 and 4 bytes in size.

Whenever a pointer is defined, it is important to appreciate that the pointer itself is not by default initialized with the address of any sensible object/variable and as such may be left pointing to unpredictable addresses in memory. This is particularly true for pointers with automatic scope (see Section 2.2.2), which are not even initialized to 0. It is the programmer's responsibility, then, to ensure that

Program 8.1 Some example pointer definitions.

```
#include  <stdio.h>

char  *ptr1 ;                        /* global pointer to char implicitly initialized to 0 */
long  *jim ;                         /* global pointer to long ints implicitly initialized to 0 */

int main( void )
{
   int        *ptr2 , *ptr3 ;        /* local pointers to int, not initialized */
   double     *ptr4 ;                /* local pointer to double, not initialized */
   register   char *p1, *p2 ;        /* local register pointers to char, not initialized */
   static     float *p3 ;            /* static pointer to float implicitly initialized to 0 */
   ...
   ...
   return 0 ;
}
```

a pointer is always properly initialized with the address of a variable or memory location before it is used. Failure to appreciate this is one of the most common errors in C and often results in programs that crash.

Program 8.1 demonstrates how several different types of pointer may be defined with varying degrees of scope, privacy and initialization.

Note how the pointers 'ptr2' and 'ptr3' were both defined with the same statement, and that a '*' was required in front of each. This is important, since the '*' is associated with the pointer's **name** and not the **type** of the object it points to. For example some texts on C have been known to place the '*' next to the pointer type, as shown below:

```
char*  p1 ;
```

Now, although the compiler is happy to accept this, since it is not interested where the '*' is positioned between the char and 'p1' in the definition, such presentation might be misinterpreted by a casual reader. For example, the following definitions for 'p1' and 'p2' appear to suggest that both are char pointers, but in fact only 'p1' is a pointer, 'p2' is just a char.

'p1' is a char pointer

'p2' is simply a char

```
char*  p1, p2 ;
```

Having now seen how a pointer may be defined, let us take a look at how it may be initialized to point to an object or variable.

8.1.1 *An introduction to lvalues and rvalues*

In any programming language, whenever a variable (except a register variable) is introduced, certain locations in memory are reserved to store and represent that variable. In C, we often talk about a variable's **lvalue** and **rvalue**. In fact you may already have seen error messages produced by the compiler expressed in these terms. So, what are 'l' and 'r' values?

- The lvalue of a variable is the address in memory where that variable is stored;
- The rvalue of a variable is the data that the variable holds; in other words, it is the value of the variable.

Consider, then, the following simple definition of the integer 'count' initialized to five:

```
int  count = 5 ;
```

rvalue of 'count' is 5

Here, the rvalue for 'count' is 5, since that is its value – that is, if we incremented 'count' we would actually increment its rvalue. The lvalue for 'count' is the address in memory where the variable is stored and is usually a factor determined at run and/or compile time.

Once a variable has been defined however, its lvalue or address in memory is guaranteed to remain fixed for the duration of that variable's scope. In other words a variable cannot be moved to a different address or memory location once it has been defined. However, there is no guarantee that any given variable will always be stored in the same memory location(s) each time the program is run.

8.1.2 *Initializing a pointer with an address or lvalue*

Having seen how a pointer may be defined, we are now in a position to initialize a given pointer with the address or lvalue of another variable using the '&' address operator. For example, consider the following statement:

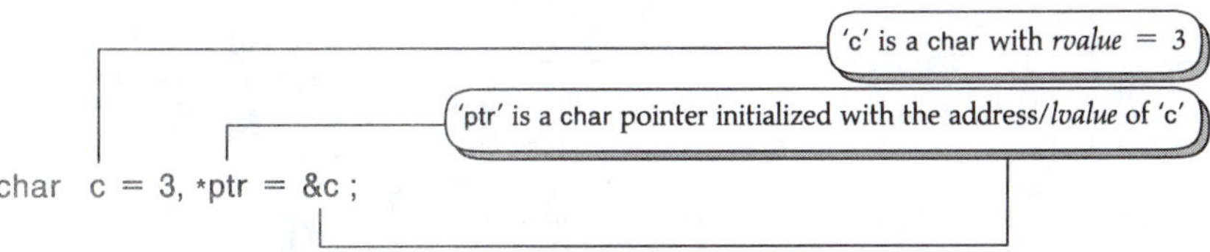
'c' is a char with *rvalue* = 3
'ptr' is a char pointer initialized with the address/*lvalue* of 'c'
char c = 3, *ptr = &c ;

Here 'c' is defined as a char, and 'ptr' as a char pointer that has subsequently been initialized with the address or lvalue of 'c'. In other words,

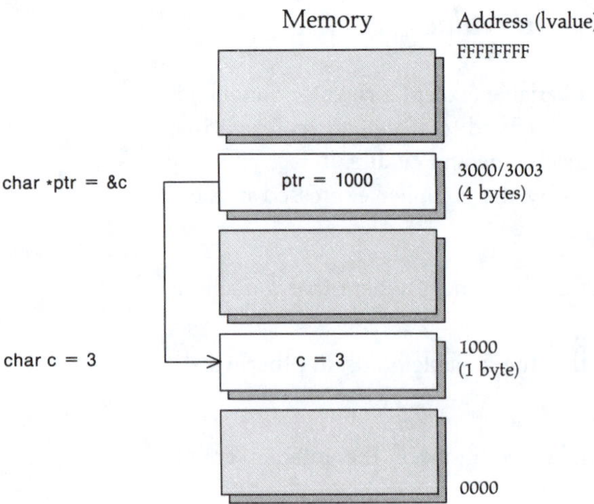

Figure 8.1 Memory map image of a char pointer 'ptr' initialized with the address of the char variable 'c'.

'ptr' can now be thought of as pointing to the location in memory where the variable 'c' is stored.

It may help to visualize the initialization of the above pointer by considering the memory map shown in Figure 8.1, which shows the char variable 'c' (with rvalue equal to 3) residing in memory at address hex 1000, an arbitrary location for this example, since the programmer rarely has any control over where a variable is actually stored, and a (typically) four byte pointer 'ptr' residing at address hex 3000, again arbitrary. Here, the compiler has generated code to take the address or lvalue of the variable 'c' (hex 1000) and assign this to 'ptr' at run time; thus, the (r)value of 'ptr' is now hex 1000.

Looking at it in a slightly different way, you can think of the rvalue of 'ptr' being equivalent to the lvalue of 'c', as shown in Figure 8.2.

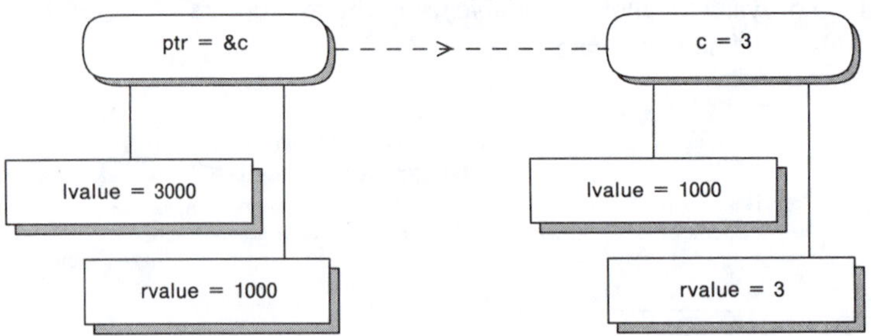

Figure 8.2 Demonstrating that a pointer's rvalue is equivalent to another variable's lvalue.

You will notice from the above initialization of 'ptr' that the type of the pointer (char) is compatible with the type of the variable (char) whose address was assigned to it. This is important, since the compiler is unhappy for a pointer to be initialized with the address of an incompatible object type, although it will not prevent you from doing it.

This means, for example, that a char pointer may only be initialized with the address of a char type variable, and likewise an int pointer may only be initialized with the address of an int type variable. Any attempt to mix different pointer and variable combinations will be flagged as warnings by the compiler. Program 8.2, which you might like to try, demonstrates these ideas with some legal and illegal pointer initializations.

Program 8.2 Some legal and illegal example pointer initializations.

```
#include  <stdio.h>

int  main( void )
{
   register  int  a ;          /* register int */
   register  int  *ptr1 ;      /* register int pointer */

   char       c ;              /* a char */
   char       *ptr2 ;          /* a char pointer */

   int fred ;                  /* an int */

   ptr2 = &c ;                 /* ✔ char pointer initialized with the address of a char */
   ptr1 = &fred ;              /* ✔ int pointer initialized with the address of an int */

   ptr1 = &a ;                 /* ✘ Cannot take the address of a register variable */

   ptr2 = &fred ;              /* ✘ Cannot assign the address of an int to a char pointer */

   ptr2 = &'#' ;               /* ✘ Cannot take the address of an implicit constant */
   ptr1 = &25 ;                /* ✘ Cannot take the address of an implicit constant */
   ptr1 = &(a + 3) ;           /* ✘ Cannot take the address of an expression */

   return 0 ;
}
```

8.1.3 *The indirection operator: '*'*

Having now seen how it is possible to obtain the address of a variable and assign this to a pointer, we are now in a position to use the pointer to manipulate that variable.

The indirection or dereferencing operator '*' (not to be confused with the multiplication operator or even the '*' symbol used in the definition of a pointer) allows us to reference the object whose address is held within a pointer. For example, given the definition and initialization of the pointer 'ptr' below:

```
char  c=3, *ptr = &c ;
```

then the following statement:

'*' here means fetch the value of the *object* pointed to by 'ptr'

```
a = *ptr ;
```

fetches, **extracts** or **retrieves** the value of the object pointed to by 'ptr' (in this example the value of the variable 'c'), and assigns that value to the variable 'a'. Thus, the above statement is equivalent to the expression 'a = c'. By swapping both expressions on either side of the '=' operator, as shown below, we could take the value of the variable 'a' and assign or store this in the object pointed to by 'ptr'. Thus, the following statement is equivalent to the expression 'c = a':

'*' here means save a value in the *object* pointed to by 'ptr'

```
*ptr = a ;
```

This leads to another important observation. When the indirection operator '*' appears in an expression to the right-hand side of an assignment operation, it is interpreted as a 'fetch' or 'extract' operation. However, when it appears to the left of an assignment it means 'store', 'save' or 'replace' an object. Thus the following statement:

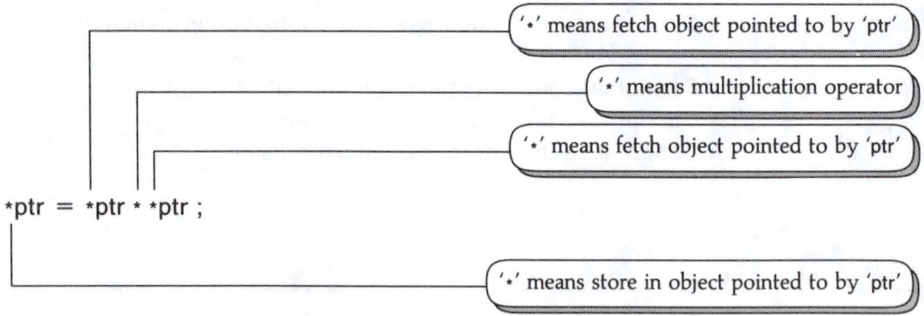

is interpreted as 'multiply the value of the object pointed to by ptr by itself, and store the result back in the object pointed to by ptr'. In effect, if 'ptr' had been pointing to the variable 'c', then the above statement is functionally equivalent to the expression 'c = c * c'.

Note that the operators '*' and '&' have equal precedence in an expression and are evaluated from right to left; thus, the following statement:

```
c = *&a ;
```

Treat address as the value of a char pointer to 'a'

Fetch value from the address of 'a'; that is, the value of 'a'

is interpreted as 'take the address of the char variable a, and treat that address as if it were the value of a pointer to that variable a, that is, a char pointer. (This is an important point since the address operator applied to some object T, that is, if T yields an object of type "pointer to T".) Then, using the indirection operator "*", fetch the value of the object it points to; that is, the value of a'. Thus the combined effects of the '*' and '&' operators in the above expression cancel each other out, and the whole statement is equivalent to the expression 'c = a'.

On the face of it, it would seem thus far that the use of pointers to achieve operations such as 'a = c' and 'c = a', when both 'a' and 'c' are easily accessible by simply referring to their names, introduces an unnecessary level of complexity into the program, and rightly so. However, we shall continue to pursue this approach a little further until other aspects of pointers and their operation have been uncovered.

8.1.4 *The meaning of '*' when using pointers*

Many new C programmers are often confused by the use of '*' when dealing with pointers and find it difficult to figure out where and when it should be used in an expression. You will recall that the '*' appears in both the definition of a pointer and as the indirection operator (and also as the multiplication operator, just to confuse the issue further).

In summary, the use of '*' in the definition of a variable simply informs the compiler that the variable being defined is a pointer, as shown in the definition of 'ptr' below. Without the '*' in the definition, the compiler would assume that 'ptr' is simply a char:

```
char  c, *ptr = & c ;
```

Once the compiler has been informed that 'ptr' is a pointer, it does not forget that fact and should not need reminding of it again, thus the '*' is never again used in conjunction with that pointer in the same context.

When the '*' appears later, such as in the expression 'a = *ptr', the '*' refers to the object pointed to by 'ptr'. Without the '*', no indirection is applied in the expression, and thus it would result in an attempt to assign the value of 'ptr' (not the value of the object it points to) which represents the address of 'c' to the variable 'a', an operation which is obviously illegal since 'a' is not a pointer and

Program 8.3 Example use of pointer indirection.

```
#include   <stdio.h>

int  main( void )
{
   char  c, a = 10 ;
   char  *p1 = &a ;

   c = *p1 ;                 /* equivalent to the expression 'c = a' */
   *p1 = *p1 * *p1 ;         /* equivalent to the expression 'a = a * a' */
   (*p1) ++ ;                /* equivalent to the expression 'a++' */
   c = *&a ;                 /* equivalent to the expression 'c = a' */
   return 0 ;
}
```

thus cannot hold an address. Program 8.3 demonstrates further examples of the use of pointer indirection.

As another example, you will recall from a previous discussion of the function scanf() that it requires each of its arguments to be an address. For example, a simple program to read an integer value from the keyboard is shown in Program 8.4.

Program 8.4 Reading an integer using scanf().

```
#include   <stdio.h>

int  main( void )
{
   int  i ;
                                        Pass the address of 'i' to scanf()
   scanf( "%d" , &i ) ;
   printf("The value of i is %d\n", i ) ;
   return 0 ;
}
```

Realizing, however, that the (r)value of a pointer is equivalent to the address or lvalue of the object it points to, we could rewrite Program 8.4 to make use of a pointer, as shown in Program 8.5, which demonstrates that the address of an object and the value of a pointer to that object are always interchangeable within a program. Similarly, the (r)value of an object – the value of the variable 'i' in Program 8.4 – and the expression '*ptr' where 'ptr' points to 'i' are also interchangeable.

Program 8.5 Using a pointer with scanf().

```
#include <stdio.h>

int main( void )
{
   int i ;
   int *ptr = &i ;

   scanf( "%d" , ptr ) ;
   printf("The value of i is %d\n", *ptr ) ;
   return 0 ;
}
```

'ptr' initialized with the address of 'i'

Pass the (r)value of 'ptr' (the address of 'i') to scanf()

Pass the (r)value of 'i' to printf()

8.1.5 *The scalar value of a pointer*

Whenever a pointer is defined, the compiler automatically associates with it a **scalar value**. This value is important, since it directly affects the code produced by the compiler whenever that pointer is referenced by the program. The scalar value itself is not a variable and thus cannot be accessed or displayed but its effects can be observed. So, what is a scalar value?

> The scalar value of a pointer is simply the size of the object the pointer is defined as pointing to.

For example, on a typical 32 bit system, the size of an int type variable will generally be 4 bytes, thus an int pointer will have a scalar value of 4. This scalar value is *very* important to the compiler, because it determines the size of any data or object that may subsequently be manipulated by the pointer and, as we shall see shortly, affects simple arithmetic operations performed on pointers. Table 8.1 lists the scalar values for several different types of pointers and assumes typical 8, 16 and 32 bit systems.

Table 8.1 Typical scalar values for various different systems.

Pointer definition		*Scalar value for 32 bit system*	*Scalar value for 8/16 bit system*
char	*p1	1	1
short	*p1	2	1
int	*p1	4	2
long	*p1	4	4
float	*p1	4	4
double	*p1	8	8
long double	*p1	10	8

The type of a pointer, and thus its scalar value, plays a very important role when used in conjunction with the indirection operator '*', since the scalar value directly determines the size of the data that is manipulated by the pointer. For example, the following statement:

Pointer 'ptr' has a scalar value of one

```
char   c, *ptr = &c ;
```

defines a char pointer 'ptr', initialized with the address of 'c'. As characters are only one byte in size, the scalar value of 'ptr' is therefore also 1, thus the statement:

Store 1 byte of data into the object pointed to by 'ptr'

```
*ptr = 0x4f ;
```

'0x4f' is a 2/4 byte integer constant

stores one byte of data – the byte sized value hex 4f – into the variable 'c', even though 0x4f itself is actually an implicit integer constant, and may be 2 or 4 bytes in size. In other words, the compiler used the scalar value of 'ptr' to determine that just 1 byte of data should be stored in the object it points to – that is, 'c' which is, after all, a 1 byte variable. From this it follows that the statement:

Store lower byte hex 55 in object pointed to by 'ptr'

```
*ptr = 0xff00aa55L ;
```

results in the lower byte of the four byte long int constant 0xff00aa55L being assigned to 'c'; that is, the single byte hex 55. By analogy, the following statement, where 'p1' has been defined as an int pointer assuming a typical scalar value of 2, would result in the lower two bytes – that is, the 16 bit value 0xaa55 – being stored in the object pointed to by 'p1':

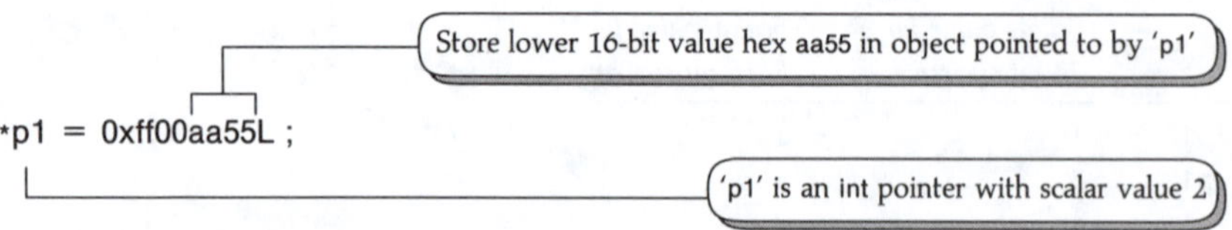
Store lower 16-bit value hex aa55 in object pointed to by 'p1'
*p1 = 0xff00aa55L ;
'p1' is an int pointer with scalar value 2

Lastly, given that 'p2' has been defined as a long int pointer with a (typical) scalar value of 4, then the following statement stores the whole long int value 0xff00aa55 in the object pointed to by 'p2':

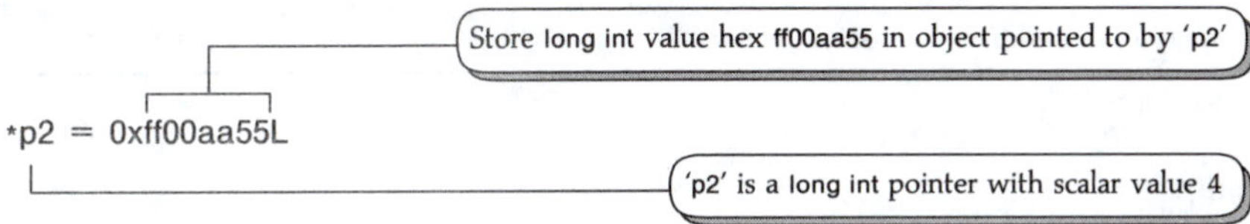

Looking at it from a different angle, the following statement, where 'p2' has been defined as a long int pointer and 'c' a char:

Value of 'c' implicitly cast to the value of a signed long int during assignment

```
*p2 = c ;
```

'p2' is a long int pointer with scalar value 4

forces the compiler into casting/promoting the value of 'c' into a full signed long int before storing its value (now 4 bytes in size) into the object pointed to by 'p2'.

These are important concepts, since they demonstrate that the compiler does *not* keep a track of the objects that every pointer in the program points to, but instead relies upon the pointer's scalar value, obtained from its definition, to determine how big those objects are. This is why the compiler, for example, is unhappy to assign the address of an int to a char pointer, since the char pointer would then not have the correct scalar value required to access and manipulate the int that it would now point to.

8.1.6 *Displaying pointer values and addresses*

It is often useful, particularly for the novice programmer, and when debugging programs that make use of pointers, to be able to display the value of a pointer and/or the address of another variable. Both of these requirements are met by printf() used in conjunction with the '%p' format indicator.

Program 8.6 demonstrates this by displaying the address of the variable 'c' using two different approaches. In the first example, printf() is given the address of 'c' using the expression '&c' while in the second, printf() is given the value of the pointer 'ptr', which has been initialized with the address of 'c'.

The format for the display produced by printf()'s '%p' format indicator is implementation dependent but is often expressed in hexadecimal. However, as a pointer value is often stored and represented in the same way as an unsigned int or unsigned long int, format indicators such as '%u', '%x', '%o' and so on often work just as well.

Program 8.6 Displaying an address or pointer value.

```
#include  <stdio.h>

int  main( void )
{
   char  c ;
   char  *ptr = &c ;

   printf(" 'c' is stored at memory location %p \n", &c) ;
   printf(" ptr points to memory location %p \n", ptr) ;
   return 0 ;
}
```

Use %p to display pointer values or addresses

Pass (r)value of 'ptr' to printf( ); that is, &c

On the author's MS-DOS computer running Borland's Turbo C, Program 8.6 produced the following display:

```
'c' is stored at memory location 359F:1A9D
ptr points to memory location 359F:1A9D
```

8.2 Pointer arithmetic and manipulation of arrays

Simple arithmetic operations, such as the addition and subtraction of integral values as well as determining the difference between two pointer values, are permitted, but the operations are not quite as obvious as they might first appear, because once again, the scalar value of the pointer is taken into consideration during the calculation. As an example, consider the following definition of 'ptr' as a long int pointer with an associated scalar value of 4:

```
long  *ptr ;
```

'ptr' has scalar value of 4

Incrementing the pointer, or simply adding 1 to its value using the statement below, does not increase its value by 1 as you might expect, but results in the addition of the pointer's scalar value – that is, 4 – a fact that is easily verified by displaying the value of 'ptr' before and after the operation:

```
ptr ++ ;
```

'++' operator increments 'ptr' by its scalar value

Similarly, the addition of 3 to 'ptr', as demonstrated in the following statement, results in the value of 'ptr' being increased by 12, or 3 times its scalar value:

Add 3 times scalar value to 'ptr'

```
ptr = ptr + 3 ;
```

In other words, the above statement is equivalent to the *mathematical* (but not C) expression:

```
ptr = ptr + ( 3 * scalar value)
```

You may not think that this makes much sense, until you visualize what is happening. Let us suppose that our pointer 'ptr' has been initialized to point to the *first* element in an array of long integers, where each element is typically 4 bytes in size, with the following statement:

```
long  x[ 5 ], *ptr = &x[ 0 ] ;
```

By incrementing the pointer 'ptr' by its scalar value and not simply by '1', we ensure that 'ptr' is incremented to point to the *next* long integer in the array, and not simply to the next byte of the same element. This is illustrated in Figure 8.3 and is a very important point, since it forms the basis of array manipulation using pointers.

Given, then, that the expression 'ptr + n' resolves to the address of an array element 'n' objects away from the one currently pointed to by 'ptr', this allows us to use the value of a pointer in conjunction with an integer offset or **index** to manipulate any element within that array in much the same way that we might use the array operator '[n]' to reference the 'nth' element. For example, given the previous definition of 'ptr' as a long pointer, initialized to point to the first element in the array 'x', the third element in the array could now be accessed by one of three means. The first and perhaps most obvious method would be to reference the array element directly, with an expression such as 'i = x[2]'.

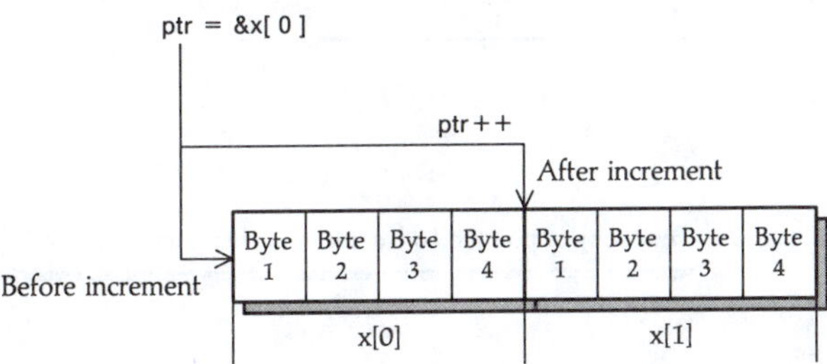

Figure 8.3 Incrementing a pointer by its scalar value.

Alternatively, we could increment 'ptr' twice (or add 2 times its scalar value to its value), to make it point to element 'x[2]' and then use the indirection operator '*' to fetch the value of that element with an expression such as 'i = *p2'. However, the third element in the array could also be accessed using the original value of 'ptr' (that is, the address of element 'x[0]') combined with a temporary offset of 2, as shown by the statement:

```
i = *( ptr + 2 ) ;
```

Temporarily add 2 times scalar value to 'ptr'

These concepts are demonstrated in Program 8.7, which exemplifies three approaches to displaying the contents of an array of long integers.

Program 8.7 Using a pointer to access elements of an array.

```
#include   <stdio.h>

#define  SIZE 10

int  main( void )
{
   int i ;

   long array [SIZE ] = { 0, 1, 2, 3, 4, 5, 6, 7, 8, 9 } ;  /* create and initialize an array */
   long *ptr  =  &array[ 0 ] ;                              /* point ptr to element 0 */

   for( i = 0; i < SIZE; i ++ )
      printf(" %ld ", *(ptr + i) ) ;

   putchar('\n') ;

   for( i = 0; i < SIZE; i ++ )
      printf(" %ld ", array[i] ) ;

   putchar('\n') ;

   for( i = 0; i < SIZE; i ++ )
      printf(" %ld ", *ptr ++ ) ;

   putchar('\n') ;

   return 0 ;
}
```

Equivalent operations

Fetch object pointed to by 'ptr' and then increment 'ptr'

Program 8.7 produces the following display:

```
0 1 2 3 4 5 6 7 8 9
0 1 2 3 4 5 6 7 8 9
0 1 2 3 4 5 6 7 8 9
```

Notice how parentheses were used in the expression '*(ptr + i)'. This is important, since the indirection operator '*' has a higher level of precedence than addition; without the parentheses, the compiler would have interpreted the expression as if it had been written as:

```
(*ptr) + i
```

which fetches the value of the object pointed to by 'ptr' (a long int) and then adds 'i' to that value, which is not the same thing at all.

The difference between two pointer values is defined as the integral number of elements in an array that would fit between the two pointers. Therefore, referring to Figure 8.4, where we see two pointers 'p1' and 'p2' pointing to the first and last elements of an array of 3 long integers, the expression 'p2 – p1' yields the value 2, since there is 'space' for two long integer elements to exist between the locations pointed to by 'p1' and 'p2'. In other words the expressions 'p1 + 2' or 'p1 + (p2 – p1)' both yield the value of 'p2', while the expressions '(p2 – p1) + 1' and '(&x[2] – &x[0]) + 1' both yield the number of elements in the array.

Given the different ways in which a pointer could be represented by a particular compiler, the difference between two pointers could result in a 2 or 4 byte integral value, which then raises portability issues when such a value needs to be saved. To overcome this, the header file <stddef.h> defines the special integral data type ptrdiff_t to represent the difference between any two pointer values.

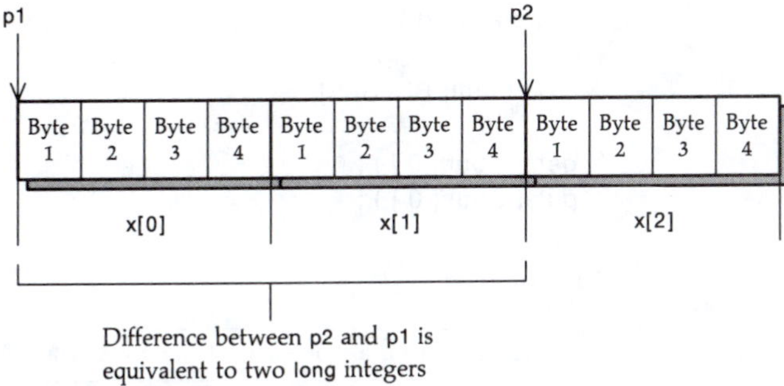

Figure 8.4 The difference between two pointer values.

8.2.1 *Pointers and single dimensional arrays*

We have already seen how a pointer can be initialized with the address of a particular element in an array, using a statement such as:

Take the address of element 'n' within joe

```
ptr = &joe[ n ] ;
```

A particularly common operation in C involves assigning a pointer the address of the first element of an array. This is in fact such a common operation that C provides a shorthand notation for it. That is to say, the address of the first element in an array may be abbreviated simply to the *name* of the array. Thus the following two statements are equivalent:

```
ptr = &joe[ 0 ] ;
ptr = joe ;
```

The name of an array is a shorthand notation for the address of element 0

This too is important, since it implies that wherever the name of any array appears in an expression, it is simply a shorthand notation for the address of the first element of that array. You may not have realized it at the time, but we have already made use of this shorthand notation when we called upon the function gets( ) to read a string from the keyboard into an array.

You may have wondered at the time how gets( ) knew where to store those characters. The answer is simple: you gave it the address when you told it the name of the array. This is demonstrated in the two programs in Program 8.8, which are functionally equivalent.

Program 8.8 Demonstrating the shorthand notation for an array.

```
#include  <stdio.h>

int  main( void )
{
   char  buff[ BUFSIZ ] ;

   gets( buff ) ;
   puts( buff ) ;
   ...
}
```

```
#include  <stdio.h>

int  main( void )
{
   char  buff[ BUFSIZ ] ;

   gets( &buff[ 0 ] ) ;
   puts( &buff[ 0 ] ) ;
   ...
}
```

buff is a shorthand notation for &buff[0]

In other words, whenever an array name is passed as an argument to a function, it is simply a shorthand notation for passing the function the address of the first element in that array.

8.2.2 *The interchangeability of pointer and array notation*

We have already seen that the pointer indirection operator '*' used in conjunction with a temporary 'index' or 'offset' allows the programmer to use a pointer to access any element within a single dimensional array. To illustrate this, imagine a single dimensional char array 'x' of 12 elements, and the pointer 'ptr' initialized with the address of the first element in 'x', as shown in Figure 8.5. Here the element 'x[0]' is assumed to exist at memory location 1000. The nth element in the array could obviously be accessed using straightforward array notation with the expression 'x[n]' but it could also be accessed as we saw in Section 8.2, using pointer notation, with an expression of the form '*(ptr + n)'.

However, given that the expression 'x' (that is, the name of the array) resolves to the address of its first element and is thus equivalent to the value of 'ptr' (which was initialized with that address), it follows that the name of an array and the value of a pointer to its first element are interchangeable and thus the nth element in the array 'x' could also be referenced using the notation 'ptr[n]', which demonstrates two important points: firstly, that the name of an array and a pointer to that array are interchangeable, and, secondly, that the array operator '[n]' is actually translated at compile time into a pointer indirection operation coupled with an offset 'n', thus any expression of the form 'm[n]' is *always* interchangeable with an expression of the form '*(m + n)' where 'm' is either the name of an array or a pointer to the first element in the array.

The above notations are valid for any type of array – char, int, double and so on – since the offset 'n' is multiplied, as we have seen, by the scalar value of 'ptr' to yield the address of the nth element in the array, regardless of the size of each individual array element. This is important, since it means that array and pointer notation may be used interchangeably to access elements within any array.

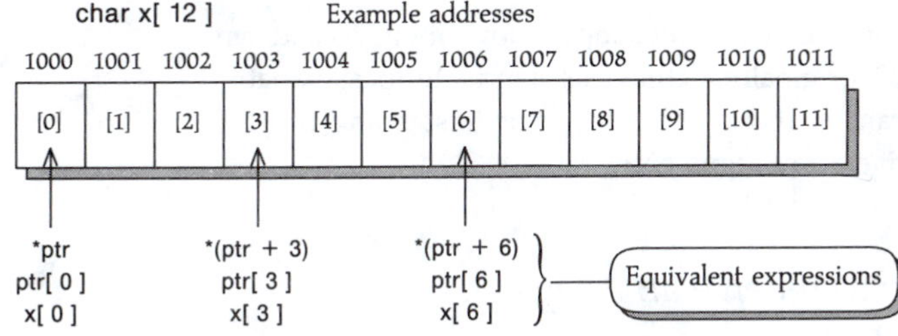

Figure 8.5 Pointer initialized with the address of the first element of a single dimensional char array.

8.2.3 *Passing pointers to functions: By value or copy*

As with any type of simple variable, pointers are passed to and returned from functions by value or copy, which means that whenever a pointer is passed to a function such as printf( ), for example, then that function is given – and is thus written to receive – a copy of the pointer's value and should thus declare its parameter as a pointer. This is demonstrated in Program 8.9. Note how the parameter 'x' in function1( ) has been declared as a char pointer. When this function is invoked by main( ), a copy of the pointer 'ptr' is made and becomes the parameter 'x' within function1( ).

Program 8.9 Passing a pointer to a function by value or copy.

```
#include  <stdio.h>

void  function1( char *x )
{
   printf("function 1( ): Value of Pointer 'x' is %p \n" , x ) ;
}

int  main( void )
{
   char  c, *ptr  =  &c ;

   printf("main( ): Value of Pointer 'ptr' is %p\n" , ptr ) ;

   function1( ptr ) ;
   return 0 ;
}
```

Parameter declared as a char pointer

Pass (r)value of 'x' to printf( )

Pass (r)value of 'ptr' to printf( )

Pass (r)value of 'ptr' as an argument to function1( )

On the author's system, Program 8.9 produced the following display:

```
main( ): Value of Pointer 'ptr' is 413F:1ACB
function1( ): Value of Pointer 'x' is 413F:1ACB
```

which demonstrates that the pointer 'x' within function1( ) now points to and can thus manipulate the variable 'c', originally defined as a private/local variable within main( ). It is also significant in that it leads to an understanding of how functions can be written to receive array arguments.

8.2.4 *Writing a function to receive an array*

We have already seen how the name of an array is simply a shorthand notation for the address of its first element. This means that whenever a whole array is passed to a function, unlike other data types, the compiler does not make a copy of the array. Rather, it passes to the function the address of the first element in the array. (Note, however, that any *individual* array element is still passed to a function by copy.)

In other words, the function is given an address and could thus declare its parameter as a suitable type of pointer, into which the address of that first element could be saved. For example, consider the standard library function puts( ), written to display a text string stored within a char array. The function could well have been written along the lines shown below:

Function declares a char pointer to save address of the first char in the array

```
int puts( char *array )
{
  int i ;

  for( i = 0; *(array + i ) != '\0' ; i ++ )
    putchar( *(array + i )) ;
  ...
}
```

Expression could also have been written as array[i]

Interestingly enough, the compiler will also let you declare the parameter as an actual array, but this really disguises the mechanism involved and makes it appear as though the function is being given a copy of the array, which it most certainly is not. For example, the above function could also have been written as:

Function declares its parameter as an array

```
int puts( char array[ ] )
{
  int i ;

  for( i = 0; array[i] != '\0' ; i ++ )
    putchar( array[i] ) ;
  ...
}
```

Expression could also have been written as *(array + i)

A useful side effect of passing arrays by reference or address is that once passed to a function the original array loses all of the privacy that it might previously have been afforded. This means that the function is able to modify the *original* array directly, and not simply a copy of it, thus negating the need for the function to return a copy of the modified array.

This, for example, is how the function gets( ) in the standard library works. You supply it with the name of an array, and it places successive characters read from the keyboard directly into the array for you; it does not need to return the array it has modified.

8.2.5 *Functions returning arrays*

Because arrays are passed to functions by reference or address, the function itself has automatic access to the original array that was passed to it and can consequently modify it directly. As a consequence of this, a function does not have to return the modified version of an array that was given to it unless, perhaps, the returned value, which will be the address of the first element, is of use as the argument in a further, perhaps nested, function call.

However, there are occasions when it is useful to be able to write a function that allocates storage for its own array and then returns the address of that array to the calling program. The example function read_string() below demonstrates the idea. Notice how the type specifier for the function is declared as returning a char pointer which points to the first element in 'array'.

A rather more important point to note is that the function defines its private array with **static** storage scope. Without this, the array would only have **automatic** scope, resulting in its storage being deallocated when the function returns and the function returning the address of a **non-existent** array. Note, however, that the use of any static variable precludes the successful use of recursion:

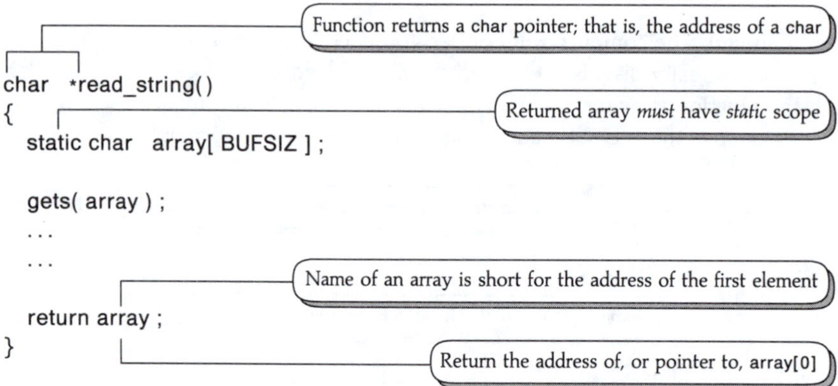

8.2.6 *Passing arguments to functions: By reference*

Although passing arguments to a function by value or copy has many distinct advantages, there are occasions when it is more appropriate and/or efficient to pass the address of the object instead, that is, pass the object by reference. Such an approach would enable the called function to directly modify one or more of the original variables passed to it, as we have seen when arrays are passed by reference, and in the process overcome the two main limitations of passing arguments by value, namely that the function can only return one value, and that the function cannot modify the original argument passed to it.

Program 8.10 Program to swap and sort: incorrect version.

```
#include  <stdio.h>

void  swap( int, int ) ;     /* function prototype for swap() */

int  main( void )
{
  int  i1, i2 ;

  printf("Enter two Integer values: ") ;
  scanf("%d%d", &i1, &i2 ) ;

  if( i1 > i2 )
    swap ( i1 , i2 ) ;

  printf( "After Swapping: i1 = %d, i2 = %d\n", i1, i2 ) ;
  return 0 ;
}

void swap ( int x , int y )
{
  int  temp ;

  temp = x ;
  x = y ;
  y = temp ;
}
```

If numbers are out of order then attempt to swap them

Pass 'i1' and 'i2' to swap() by *value* or *copy*

swap() receives a copy of 'i1' and 'i2', which become 'x' and 'y'

Caution!

FAIL: swapping does not alter 'i1' and 'i2', only 'x' and 'y'

As an example, consider the *incorrect* version of the function swap() shown in Program 8.10, which attempts to swap the values of two arguments passed to it.

Program 8.10 fails to swap 'i1' and 'i2' (if they are deemed to be out of order) because it is only the values of a copy of the local variables 'x' and 'y' within swap() that are exchanged, and not the original variables 'i1' and 'i2' in main(). A sample display typical of that produced when two out of order integer values are entered is given below:

```
Enter two Integer values: 10 5
After Swapping: i1 = 10, i2 = 5
```

Swapping has failed

If, however, we modified the program to pass references to the variables 'i1' and 'i2' to the function swap(), then the function swap() would now be able

Program 8.11 Program to swap and sort: correct version.

```
#include  <stdio.h>

void  swap( int *, int * ) ;          Prototype declares parameters as two int pointers

int  main( void )
{
   int  i1, i2 ;

   printf("Enter two Integer values: ") ;
   scanf("%d%d", &i1, &i2 ) ;
                                      Pass addresses of 'i1' and 'i2' to swap()
   if( i1 > i2 )
        swap ( &i1 , &i2 ) ;

   printf( "After Swapping: i1 = %d, i2 = %d\n", i1, i2 ) ;
   return 0 ;
}                                     Addresses saved in two int pointers, 'x' points to 'i1', 'y' points to 'i2'

void  swap ( int *x , int *y )
{
   int  temp ;

   temp = *x ;
   *x = *y ;                          Swapping performing correctly
   *y = temp ;
}
```

to modify the values of 'i1' and 'i2' directly. The necessary modifications are presented in Program 8.11.

When Program 8.11 is run with the same data that was supplied to Program 8.10, it correctly swaps the values of 'i1' and 'i2' in main() and the following display is produced:

```
Enter two Integer values: 10 5
After Swapping: i1 = 5, i2 = 10       Swapping is successful
```

8.2.7 *Pointer comparison and assignment*

Two pointers may be compared with or assigned to one another only if both pointers are of the same type, or if one of the pointers is a void pointer (see Section 8.4.1). Comparing a pointer with, or assigning it, an integer value is not strictly legal unless an appropriate cast is performed. The only exception to this is for the integer value 0 (NULL), which may be freely compared with or assigned to any pointer type. As an example, the following statement initializes 'ptr' to point to memory location 1000:

Integer value '1000' cast to the value of an 'int pointer'

```
int *ptr = (int *)(1000) ;
```

Notice how the initializing value for 'ptr', the decimal integer 1000, was first cast to be equivalent to the value of an int pointer before the assignment. This keeps the compiler happy since it is now only being asked to assign the value of one int pointer to another.

Care must also be observed during such an assignment to ensure that the address assigned to the pointer is compatible with the storage alignment requirements of the type of object it now points to. For example, an int on most compilers is represented by a 16 or 32 bit quantity. Many CPUs, such as Motorola's 68000, insist that 16 and 32 bit sized objects be accessed at an even value address, otherwise a run time exception is generated.

As far as pointer comparison is concerned, provided the two pointers are of the same type, then they are compared as if they were unsigned integral quantities. Notionally, for the purposes of comparison, a pointer can be thought of as pointing to an array element, where successive elements are stored at increasing addresses. Therefore, a pointer with a greater value points to a higher element in the array. Program 8.12 demonstrates further examples of both legal and illegal pointer comparisons and assignments.

Program 8.12 Some legal and illegal pointer assignments/comparisons.

```
#include <stdio.h>

int main( void )
{
  float x[10] ;

  char *p1 ;
  int  *p2 ;

  float *p3 = x, *p4 = &x[9] ;

  if( p4 > p3 )
    puts("p4 is pointing to a higher element in 'x' than p3") ;

  if( p3 == x )
    puts("p3 points to the first element in 'x' ") ;
```

```
    if( p4 == &x[9] )
      puts("p4 points to last element in 'x' ") ;

    if( p4 > &x[9] )
      puts("p4 points beyond the last element in 'x' ") ;

    if( (p3 < &x[9]) && ( p3 >= x))
      puts("p3 points to an element within the 'x' ") ;

    p2 = 0 ;                  /* ✔ Integer value of zero can be assigned to any pointer */
    p2 = 0xC000 ;             /* ✘ Cannot assign a non-zero integer value to a pointer */
    p2 = (int *)0xC000 ;      /* ✔ Integer value 0xC000 cast to an int pointer */
    p1 = p2 ;                 /* ✘ Cannot assign incompatible pointer types */
    p1 = (char *)p2 ;         /* ✔ Value of p2 cast to a char pointer before assignment */

    if( p1 == p2 )            /* ✘ Cannot compare incompatible pointer types */
      . . .
    if( p1 == (char *)p2 )    /* ✔ Value of p2 cast to a char pointer before comparison */
      . . .
    if( p2 == (int *)1000 )   /* ✔ Integer 1000 cast to an int pointer before comparison */
      . . .
    if( p2 == 0 )             /* ✔ Comparison with the integer value 0 or NULL is legal */
      . . .
}
```

8.3 The 'quicksort' algorithm: An implementation using pointers

In this section, we take a close look at one of the best sorting algorithms available, C.A.R. Hoare's famous **quicksort**. The main attraction of this algorithm over the 'bubble' and most other sort algorithms is its speed, coupled with the fact that the sorting is performed using the original storage allocated to the array – no other additional storage is required. This algorithm is introduced here because the best implementations of it rely heavily on the use of pointers; the example presented here demonstrates many of the features discussed so far in this chapter.

Although it is beyond the scope of this book, it can be shown that the average execution time of quicksort is of the order $n\log_2(n)$, where 'n' represents the number of elements in the array to be sorted. For large arrays it is considerably quicker than the n^2 execution time associated with a bubble sort. A comparison of the two algorithms is presented at the end of this section in Table 8.2. Before that, however, let us take a close look at the essentially recursive algorithm described below:

```
Select a 'pivot' value from the array

Partition the array into two smaller left and right arrays/partitions, such that
    All elements in the left partition have a value less than or equal to the
        pivot value
    All elements in the right partition have a value greater than or equal to
        the pivot value

Sort left partition
Sort right partition
```

In a perfect world, a pivot value would be chosen such that the partitioning process gave rise to two smaller, equal sized partitions, but given the random nature of the data to be sorted, such a choice is rarely possible without prior analysis of the data to be sorted. However, acceptable results are obtained using one of the two approaches discussed below.

The first – and often best – approach is to select a pivot value equal to the average value of a number of elements from within the array, typically the first, last and middle elements, an approach which is often known as the 'median of three'.

The second approach, and the one adopted by Program 8.13, is to a select a pivot value equal to the value of some randomly chosen element in the array. In the example below, the pivot value is chosen to be the value of the middle element, but in fact *any* pivot value will do, provided it lies somewhere between the smallest and largest values in the array/partition. In fact, it does not even have to coincide with the value of any element in the array.

Program 8.13 A pointer implementation of the quicksort algorithm.

```
#include <stdio.h>
#include <stddef.h>          /* included for the definition of the data type 'ptrdiff_t' */

/*
** A function to swap two integer elements. Note that this function
** expects to be passed the addresses of, or references to, the elements
** to be swapped. This function is similar to that presented in Program 8.11
*/

void swap( int *p1, int *p2)
{
  int  temp ;

  temp = *p1 ;
  *p1 = *p2 ;
  *p2 = temp ;
}
```

```
/*
** This implementation of quicksort expects to be given the
** addresses of the first and last elements in the array/partition to be sorted
*/

void quick_sort( int *first, int *last )
{
   int *left = first ;                /* left set to point to first element in partition */
   int *right = last ;                /* right set to point to last element in partition */
   int pivot_value ;

   ptrdiff_t   p_diff ;               /* a variable to hold the difference between two pointers */

/*
** Choose a pivot value equal to the value of the
** middle element in the array/partition to be sorted
*/

   p_diff = (right - left) / 2 ;          /* number of elements in partition / 2 */
   pivot_value = *(left + p_diff ) ;      /* value of middle element */

/*
** Now partition the current array into two smaller
** arrays/partitions which may then be sorted in turn
*/

   while( left <= right )   {          . /* while pointers have not crossed */

/*
** By moving forwards, find the next element in the partition
** whose value is greater than or equal to the pivot value
*/

      while( *left < pivot_value )
         left ++ ;

/*
** By moving backwards, find the next element in the partition
** whose value is less than or equal to the pivot value
*/

      while( *right > pivot_value )
         right -- ;

/*
** If the left pointer has overtaken the right pointer then the array must
** have been partitioned, otherwise the two values pointed to by 'left' and 'right'
** must be out of order, so swap them and move the pointers on
*/
```

```
        if( left <= right )  {
          swap( left, right ) ;
          left ++ ;
          right -- ;
        }
      }

   /* provided there are at least two elements then sort each partition (recursively) */

      if( first < right )
        quick_sort( first, right ) ;                  /* sort left partition */

      if( left < last )
        quick_sort( left, last ) ;                    /* sort right partition */
   }

   int main( void )
   {

   /* the array of integers to be sorted */

      int  array[ ] = { 3, 6, 5, -1, 0, 7, 2, -9, -3, -7, -12 } ;
      int  i, num ;

   /* Determine how many elements are in the array in a portable manner */

      num = sizeof( array ) / sizeof(array[0]) ;

      quick_sort( &array[0], &array[num - 1] ) ;  /* sort initial array */

      for( i = 0; i < num; i ++ )
        printf("%d ", array[i]) ;                     /* display sorted array */

      putchar('\n') ;
      return 0 ;
   }
```

The partitioning of the array into two smaller, though not necessarily equal sized, partitions is achieved within the outer while loop. Within this lie two further while loops, the first of which searches from the start of the current array/ partition attempting to locate the first occurrence of an element whose value is greater than or equal to that of the pivot value.

The second inner while loop searches backwards from the end of the array, attempting to locate the first occurrence of an element whose value is less than or equal to that of the pivot value. Once two (out of order) elements have been located, they are swapped and a further search resumes. Note that one or other (or even both) inner while loops may converge on the pivot element itself, in which case, the pivot element is swapped, possibly with itself.

Once the array has been partitioned the program is left with two smaller arrays/partitions such that all elements in the left partition are less than or equal to all elements in the right partition; as such, the partitions themselves are in order but the elements within those partitions are not. However, by repeating the process recursively for each partition (provided there are at least two elements in that partition), the whole array can be sorted.

As an example, consider sorting the following array of integers:

3, 6, 5, –1, 0, 7, 2, –9, –3, –7, –12

The process of partitioning the array and swapping out of order elements is shown in Figure 8.6, where small shaded boxes identify those elements that are swapped during the partitioning process.

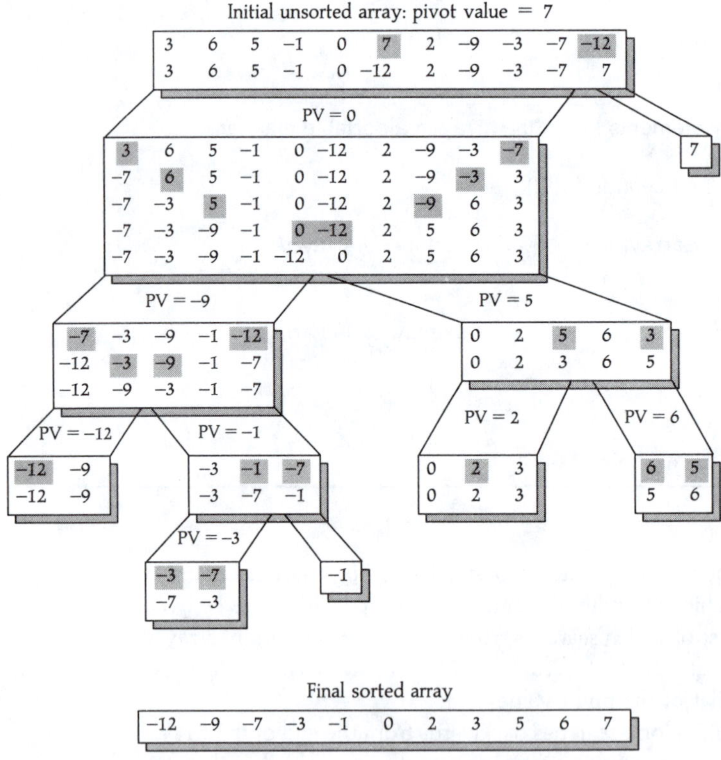

Figure 8.6 An illustration of the partitioning and sorting of the integer data presented in Program 8.13.

You will notice from Figure 8.6 that the process of partitioning the initial array gave rise to two smaller arrays, one of which contained just a single integer element. This arises if the chosen pivot value happens to coincide with the value of the largest element in the array/partition. If this happens for every partition (which is rare, given a random distribution of unsorted data) then the speed of quicksort degenerates to that of a bubble sort; that is, of the order of n^2.

Table 8.2 shows the number of swaps required for both the quicksort and bubble sort algorithms for varying numbers of array elements 'n'. The initial array data was generated via repeated calls to the standard library function rand( ).

Table 8.2 A comparison of quicksort and bubble sort for random data.

n	*Quicksort (swaps required)*	*Bubble sort (swaps required)*	*Relative performance*
256	533	16 042	×30
512	1 214	63 134	×52
1024	2 658	262 912	×99
2048	5 852	1 036 649	×177
4096	12 469	3 999 652	×320
8192	26 814	15 510 616	×578

8.4 NULL, void, const and volatile pointers

A NULL pointer is a term used to describe any type of pointer with a value equal to 0; in other words, any pointer that points to memory location 0. A NULL pointer is universally used within the C language to indicate an **invalid** or **illegal** pointer value (−1 cannot be used because pointers are unsigned quantities).

We shall see in later chapters that many of the functions in the standard library are written to return the address of, or a pointer to, some object. These include string, memory and file manipulation functions, among others. As you might well imagine, calls to these functions sometimes encounter problems that have to be reported back to the calling program. In this instance, the function returns a NULL pointer, the value of which can be tested by the calling program to check for the error.

Program 8.14 demonstrates this in conjunction with the file manipulation function fopen( ), which, as we saw in Chapter 1, attempts to open a disk file. If successful, fopen( ) returns a valid FILE pointer; if unsuccessful, it returns a FILE

Program 8.14 Example application for a NULL pointer.

```
#include <stdio.h>

int main( void )
{
  FILE *fp ;                    Check for NULL pointer returned by fopen() indicating an error

  if(( fp = fopen( "file.txt", "r")) == NULL ) {
    printf("Unable to open file 'file.txt' for reading ... \n") ;
    return 0 ;
  }
  ...
  ...
}
```

pointer with the value NULL. The calling program can then carry out a test to check the validity of the returned pointer.

8.4.1 void *pointers*

Because of the restrictions C imposes upon the assignment and comparison of different types of pointers (see Section 8.2.7) and because such comparisons and assignments frequently arise when functions return or accept pointer arguments to abstract or generic data types, a special type of void pointer has been introduced with no associated scalar value. What makes these void pointers interesting is that they may be freely assigned to and compared with any type of pointer without an explicit cast being required (although one can be – and often is – used).

Being scalarless also means that operations such as pointer indirection, incrementing/decrementing, addition/subtraction, indexing and so on – in other words those operations that would require and are dependent upon a pointer's scalar value – cannot be performed unless the value of the void pointer is first cast to that of another pointer with a known scalar value.

It is important to grasp that assigning a void pointer the value of, say, an int pointer does not give the void pointer the scalar value of an int pointer: it is, and always will be, scalarless. Functions that declare their parameters and/or type specifier as 'void *' may in fact receive/return any type of pointer but the compiler still regards the pointer as scalarless. Program 8.15 illustrates these concepts with various legal and illegal pointer assignments.

In Section 8.4.2 we shall see how void pointers are put to good use when dynamically requesting memory from the operating system.

Program 8.15 Example usage of void pointers.

```
void  *joe( void ) ;          /* function 'joe()' returns a pointer to void data */
int   *fred( void * ) ;       /* function 'fred()' returns a pointer to integers */
                              /* and expects a void pointer argument */

int main( void )
{
  int     a, c ;
  int     *p1 ;               /* p1 is an int pointer */
  char    *p2 ;               /* p2 is a char pointer */
  void    *p3 ;               /* p3 is a scalarless void pointer */

  p3 = p2 ;                   /* ✔, but p3 is still a scalarless void pointer */
  p1 = p3 ;                   /* ✔ p1 is still an int pointer, p3 is a void pointer */

  p3 = &c ;                   /* ✔, but p3 is still a scalarless void pointer */
  a = *p3 ;                   /* ✘ p3 is still scalarless */
  a = *(int *)(p3) ;          /* ✔ p3 cast to an int pointer, p3 is still a void pointer */
  p3 ++ ;                     /* ✘ p3 is still scalarless */
  c = *(p3 + 2) ;             /* ✘ p3 is still scalarless */

  p1 = joe( ) ;               /* ✔ joe() returns a void pointer, p1 is still an int pointer */
  p1 = fred(p1) ;             /* ✔ fred() returns an int pointer */
  p3 = joe( ) ;               /* ✔ joe() returns a void pointer, p3 is still a void pointer */
  p3 = fred(p3) ;             /* ✔ fred() returns an int pointer, p3 is still a void pointer */

  return 0 ;
}

void  *joe( void )            /* joe() returns a void pointer */
{
  int *p1 ;
  ...
  ...
  return (p1) ;               /* p1 is returned as a void pointer, no cast needed */
}

int  *fred( void *ptr )
{
  int  *p1 = ptr ;            /* p1 is still an int pointer */
  ...
  ...
  return (p1) ;               /* return p1 as an int pointer */
}
```

8.4.2 *The memory allocation functions*

C provides four memory allocation functions in the form of malloc(), calloc(), realloc() and free() to facilitate the dynamic allocation, resizing and possible release of additional memory when it is needed by the program. Such memory is allocated from what is known as the program's 'heap', which is simply a large block of additional memory given to the program when it is run. The programmer can usually specify the size of the heap at compile time and, in a small embedded application with no host operating system, where it is located.

Some sophisticated examples of the use of these four functions can be seen in Chapter 17, but to illustrate why they might be of use to us here, consider the case of a programmer faced with the task of writing a program to read an unknown quantity of data from the program's operator, which must be stored pending later analysis. If the programmer uses an array to store this data, how big does the array need to be? If it is too small there is the possibility that its end may be overwritten, leading to subsequent loss of data and possibly a program crash. On the other hand, if the array is too large, then memory is wasted as it may not be used by the program.

To solve these problems, the programmer could allocate storage for the array dynamically and if the need arose, it could be resized and eventually released to suit the varying demands of the program. Let us take a look at each of these functions in turn and consider a simple example program.

The function malloc( ) requests a specified amount of **contiguous** memory (that is, memory allocated in a single continuous block) and if successful (there is sufficient memory left in the heap to satisfy the request), a pointer to the start of that memory is returned to the calling program. The function prototype for malloc( ) (as with each of these four functions) can be found in the header file <stdlib.h> and is given below:

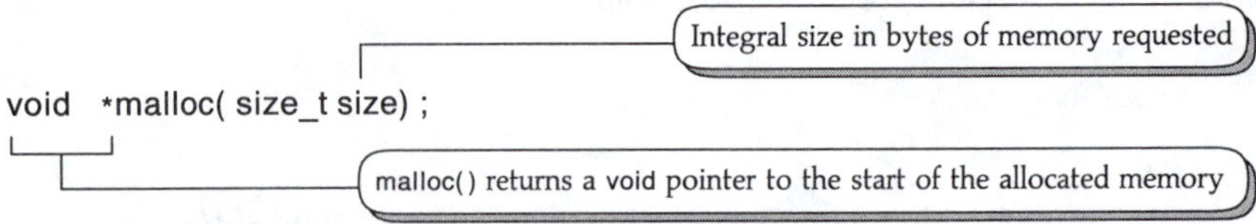
Integral size in bytes of memory requested
void *malloc(size_t size) ;
malloc( ) returns a void pointer to the start of the allocated memory

where 'size' is the size of memory being requested in bytes and is usually obtained via the sizeof operator, and is an unsigned integral quantity of type size_t (defined in <stdlib.h>). Upon success, a pointer to the start of the allocated block is returned, or if there is insufficient memory, a NULL pointer (a pointer with the value 0) is returned.

Because malloc( ) has no idea of the use to which the requested memory will be put and thus will not know the type of the data to which it is returning a pointer, it elects to return a void pointer, thus enabling the calling program to assign this pointer freely to any other pointer within the program without a cast being required (although a cast is invariably employed to improve program readability and to serve as an additional level of defence against programmers who do not know what they are doing).

The function calloc( ) is similar to malloc( ) except that a number of contiguous blocks of memory are requested from the heap, making it ideal for allocating storage for an array. Also calloc(), unlike malloc(), ensures that the requested blocks of memory are initialized to zero. The prototype for calloc() is given below:

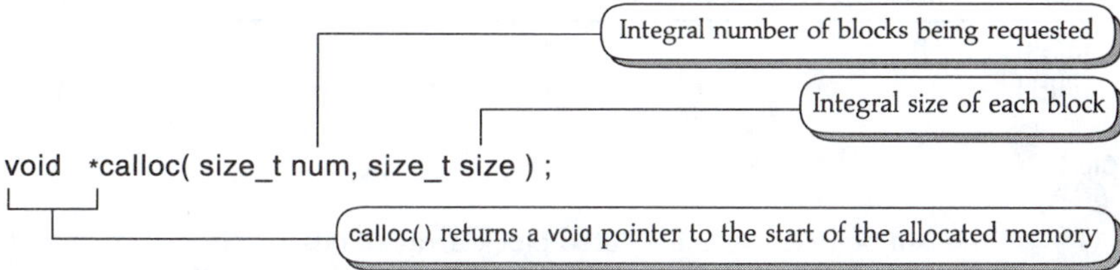

where 'num' is the integral number of contiguous blocks to allocate, each of which is 'size' bytes in size. Again, a void pointer to the start of the requested memory is returned to the calling program, or NULL if insufficient memory exists to satisfy the request.

The function realloc() permits the program to readjust or resize a block of memory previously requested via malloc(), calloc() or realloc(). The function prototype is given below:

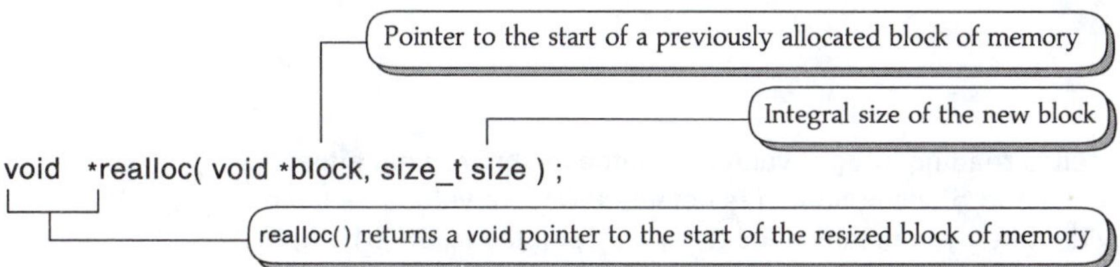

where 'block' is a void pointer to an area of memory that must have been granted previously by a successful call to malloc(), calloc() or realloc() and 'size' is the new size of the block of memory. The new block may be larger or smaller in size than the previously allocated block. Any attempt to enlarge a block results in realloc() attempting to allocate more memory to it. If, however, the block cannot be enlarged in a contiguous manner, a new block is allocated and the contents of the old block are copied to it. Finally, a pointer to the (possibly new) block is returned to the calling program (and must therefore be saved by the program) or a NULL pointer if insufficient memory exists to satisfy the request.

Lastly, the function free() releases a block of memory previously obtained by a successful call to one of the three functions described above. The function prototype is given as:

Pointer to the block of memory to be released

```
void  free( void *block ) ;
```

where block is a pointer to a previously granted block of memory. Program 8.16 demonstrates the use of these functions in allowing a program to read unlimited integer data into a program (up to the limits of memory given to the heap) and then display that data back to the user.

Program 8.16 Example memory allocation program.

```
#include  <stdio.h>
#include  <stdlib.h>

int  main( void )
{
   int  *p1 ;                  /* a pointer to the allocated block/array of ints */
   int  i = 0, j, data ;

/*
** Start off by allocating storage for an array of one integer using malloc( ) and
** saving the returning address in 'p1'. Check that this has been done correctly
** with an 'if' test and a comparison with the value NULL
*/

   if((p1 = malloc( sizeof( int ))) == NULL )  {
      printf("No Memory ... \n") ;
      exit( 0 ) ;
   }

/*
** Now commence reading integer values from the keyboard until either
** an error or the end-of-file condition is detected. Once a value has been
** read, copy it to the dynamically allocated array pointed to by 'p1'. Note
** that 'p1' is not changed, since its value (an address) will be needed later
** when the storage allocated to the array is released. Once this has been done
** resize the array using realloc( ) to include storage for one more integer and repeat.
*/

   while(scanf("%d", &data) == 1)  {
      p1[ i++ ] = data ;
      p1 = realloc( p1, (i+1) * sizeof( int )) ;
   }

/*
** Now display the data in the dynamically allocated array before
** releasing it back to the heap using free( )
*/

   for( j = 0; j < i ; j ++ )
      printf("%d \n", p1[ j ]) ;

   free( p1 ) ;                /* release block back to heap */
   return 0 ;
}
```

8.4.3 *Constant pointers and pointers to constant data*

A constant pointer is one whose value cannot be altered by the program, other than to initialize it during its definition. Any subsequent attempt to alter the value of such a pointer is illegal. In other words, a constant pointer always points to the same object in memory and it cannot be modifed to point to any other object/ variable. An example of such a pointer definition is given below, in which 'ptr' is defined to be a **constant char pointer** initialized with the address of the first element within the char array 'c':

```
char *const ptr = &c[0] ;
```

'ptr' is a constant pointer

'ptr' can only ever point to 'c[0]'

'ptr' points to char type variables

Given the above definition, the following two statements are thus illegal:

```
ptr ++ ;
ptr = ptr + 1 ;
ptr = &c[3] ;
```

Illegal!

However, the two statements below are legal, because the value of 'ptr' is unaffected:

```
i = *(ptr + 1) ;
j = ptr[5] ;
```

Legal!

Interestingly enough, a pointer could also be defined as pointing to constant data, for example a pointer to constant int, which implies that although the pointer is *not* constant, the object it points to is, thus any attempt to use the pointer to change the object is illegal. For example, given the following definitions:

```
const int i[ ] = { 1, 2, 3, 4 } ;
const int *p1 = &i[ 0 ] ;
```

'p1' points to constant int

the following statements are legal (since 'p1' is not constant):

```
p1 ++ ;
p1 = p1 + 3 ;
p1 = &i[2] ;
```

Legal!

but the statements shown below are illegal, since the pointer points to constant data which cannot be modified:

```
*(p1 + 2) = -1 ;
p1[5] = 10 ;
```

Illegal!

A pointer to constant data may be initialized with the address of either a constant or a non-constant object. Pointers to constant data may also be assigned the values of pointers to either constant or non-constant data, but pointers to non-constant data may only be assigned the address of a non-constant object or the value of another pointer to non-constant data. Some examples of these assignments are shown in Program 8.17.

It is possible to combine both const qualifiers for a pointer definition/declaration to create a constant pointer to constant data, where both the pointer and the data it points to are constant and neither may be changed, except to initialize them during their definition.

Program 8.17 Examples of constant pointers and pointers to constant data.

```
#include <stdio.h>

int main( void )
{
  char   a ;                 /* a is not constant */
  const  char b = '#' ;      /* b is constant */
  const  char *p1 ;          /* p1 is a pointer to constant char */
  char   *p2 ;               /* p2 is a pointer to non-constant char */

  p1 = &b ;     /* ✔ p1 assigned the address of a constant char */
  p1 = &a ;     /* ✔ p1 assigned the address of a char */
  p2 = &a ;     /* ✔ p2 assigned the address of a char */
  p2 = &b ;     /* ✘ cannot assign p2 the address of a constant char */

  *p1 = 5 ;     /* ✘ p1 points to constant char */
  *p2 = 5 ;     /* ✔ p2 points to non-constant char */
  p1 = p2 ;     /* ✔ p1 assigned address of a pointer to char */
  p2 = p1 ;     /* ✘ cannot assign address of a pointer to constant char to p2 */

/*
** The above operation may be performed if a cast is used, as shown below, but
** this could leave p2 pointing to a constant char. If p2 were then used to
** modify that object, it could result in a possible run time error
*/

  p2 = (char *)(p1) ;
  ...
}
```

For example, the following statements define 'c' as a constant char and 'ptr' as a constant pointer to constant char initialized with the address of 'c', which means that neither the pointer nor the data it points to may be changed:

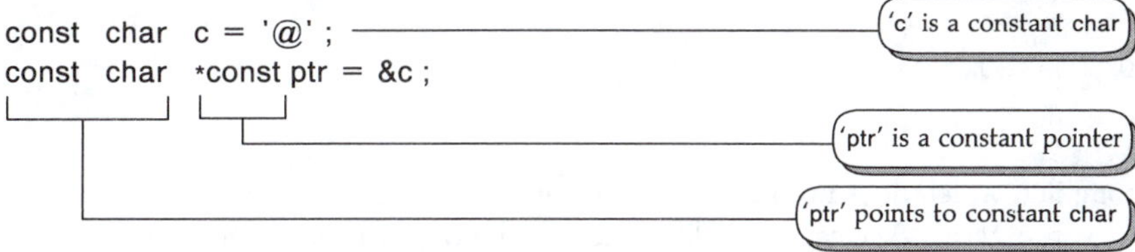
const char c = '@' ;
const char *const ptr = &c ;
'c' is a constant char
'ptr' is a constant pointer
'ptr' points to constant char

If all this is beginning to sound rather complicated and unnecessary, then it is worth remembering that the main reason why the type qualifier const appears at all in a definition/declaration is to make compile time checking more robust. Provided *you* know what you are doing with a pointer, and which objects you intend to modify with it, a simple (non-constant) pointer (to non-constant data) will suffice, but do not expect the compiler to point out potential inconsistencies for you.

8.4.4 volatile *objects and pointers*

The concept of a volatile object is a recent addition to the language, introduced to remove any ambiguity that might exist about whether a compiler is permitted to optimize accesses to certain variables or memory locations.

By defining an object to be volatile, you are telling the compiler that the value of that object may change in an unpredictable way, and under no circumstances is the compiler to generate code that would enable the program to **cache** that value within a CPU register. This forces the compiler to generate code that will always fetch the value of the variable from memory each time it is referenced. This is particularly important in many small embedded controller applications and concurrent systems.

As an example, imagine that a program is designed to access a small hardware communications chip whose address is known to exist at, say, 0x1000 in the memory map. Within this chip (see Figure 8.7) lies an 8 bit status register, bit 7 of which indicates, via a logic 1, that data has been received from an external device such as a keyboard or a serial port and can now be read by the program.

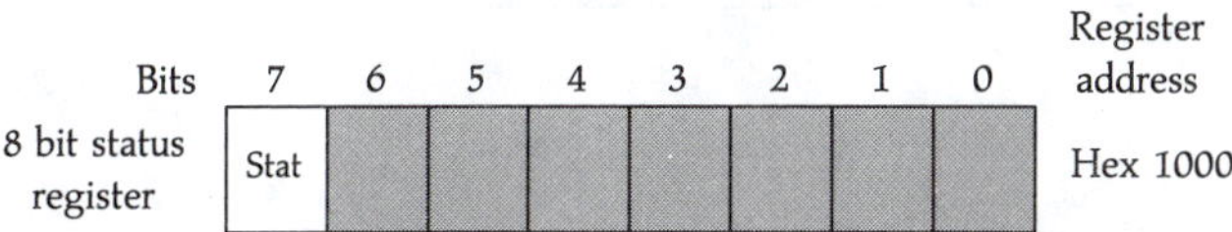
Bits
7 6 5 4 3 2 1 0
Register address
8 bit status register
Stat
Hex 1000

Figure 8.7 Hardware communications chip.

To detect the arrival of this data, the program would probably be written to **poll** the status of bit 7 in this register, waiting for it to become logic 1. This is demonstrated by the section of program code shown below, where 'stat' represents an unsigned char pointer initialized to point to the address 0x1000.

```
while(( *stat & 0x80 ) != 0x80 )
  ;
```

To the compiler, which does not have the necessary insight to realize that stat is pointing to an external **device**, it would seem that the object it points to could not possibly change within the domain of the while loop, since it is not modified or assigned a new value by the program.

Given this, the compiler could, in the interests of efficiency, size of code and speed of execution, arrange for the data pointed to by stat – that is, the device's status register – to be read *once* only, at the start of the loop, and its value assigned to an internal CPU register. For the programmer, such an assignment is fatal, since from then on the program is testing the value of a CPU register each time around the loop and not the actual status register and, consequently, the program is no longer in a position to recognize any change that occurs to bit 7 within the device and results in a loop that never terminates; that is, it fails to recognize the changed status of the device.

The solution to this lies with volatile objects and data. Had stat been defined as a pointer to volatile data, the compiler would know that the data it pointed to is subject to change without the knowledge of the compiler, and thus the compiler should under no circumstances attempt to cache the value of that data. In other words, it should generate genuine accesses to the object every time it is referenced by the program. Such a pointer could be defined with the statement shown below:

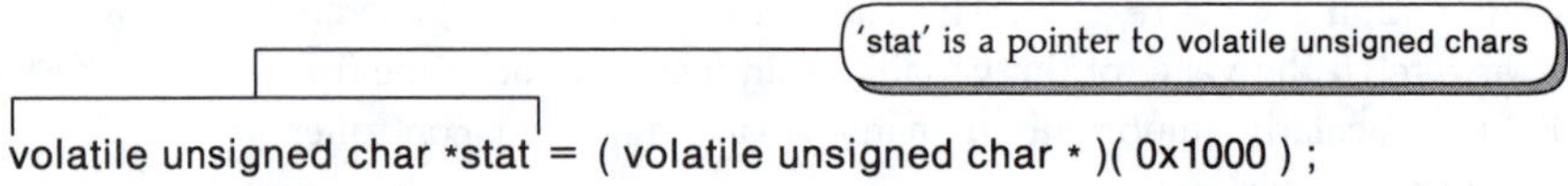

'stat' is a pointer to volatile unsigned chars
volatile unsigned char *stat = (volatile unsigned char *)(0x1000) ;

As a further example, consider the simple integer variable 'a' defined within the program. Suppose that upon receipt of an interrupt from an external device, the device's interrupt handler program is called, which subsequently modifies the value of 'a' in a way that cannot be predicted by the compiler. If the compiler had arranged for the value of 'a' to be cached, as in the example loop shown below:

Wait for interrupt handler to set 'a' to the value 1

```
while( a != 1 )
  ;
```

this change would go unnoticed by the program since the compiler has not generated code to read the value of 'a' each time around the loop. Again, this results in an infinite loop. The solution to this is once again to define 'a' as a volatile int in the manner shown below:

```
volatile int a ;
```

'a' is a volatile int

Similarly, if an array, structure or union is qualified as volatile, then all of its member elements are deemed to be volatile also.

Interestingly enough, a pointer could also be defined as a volatile variable, in much the same way as a pointer may be defined as constant with a statement such as that shown below, which means that the value of 'ptr' is likely to change in ways unknown to the compiler and thus references to 'ptr' may not be optimized.

```
int *volatile ptr ;
```

'ptr' is a volatile int pointer

8.4.5 *Mixing* const *and* volatile *qualifiers*

One great misconception among new programmers is that the type qualifiers const and volatile are somehow opposites and must therefore exclude each other. They are not, since an object can in fact be declared as both, as demonstrated in the examples below:

```
volatile const  int a = 5 ;
volatile const  int *volatile const ptr = &a ;
```

Here, 'a' has been defined as a volatile constant integer. This means that because of the const in the definition, the program code is not allowed to modify the value of 'a' (except to initialize it during its definition), but, because of the volatile part of the definition, its value may change unpredictably as a result of external events.

Likewise, the pointer 'ptr' is itself a volatile constant pointer, which means that its value may change unpredictably, but the program is *not* allowed to alter 'ptr's' value. Furthermore, 'ptr' points to volatile constant objects which may themselves change unpredictably, but whose values cannot be altered by using the pointer.

The rules for mixed assignment of volatile and non-volatile data to a pointer to volatile and non-volatile data are similar to those relating to const objects and data, and are summarized below:

(1) A pointer to a volatile object may be assigned the address of or the value of a pointer to a volatile or a non-volatile object, since access to the object will not be optimized, but a specific cast is required if a pointer to a non-volatile object is assigned the address of a volatile object or the value of a pointer to volatile data;

(2) The address of a volatile object may only be assigned to a pointer to a volatile object. A specific cast is required, if the address of a volatile object is assigned to a pointer to a non-volatile object, in which case the object may, due to compiler optimizing, lose its volatile status when accessed by such a pointer.

Program 8.18 demonstrates these rules in action.

Program 8.18 volatile pointers and objects.

```
#include  <stdio.h>

int  main( void )
{
   int         a = 3 ;             /* a is a non-volatile integer */
   volatile   int b = 4 ;          /* b is a volatile integer */

   volatile   int *p1 ;            /* p1 points to volatile integers */
   int          *p2 ;              /* p2 points to non-volatile integers */

   p1 = &a ;                       /* ✔ p1 points to volatile objects, a is volatile */
   p1 = &b ;                       /* ✔ p1 points to volatile objects */

   p2 = &a ;                       /* ✔ a is non-volatile */
   p2 = &b ;                       /* ✘ b is volatile, p2 points to non-volatile objects */

   p2 = (int *)(&b) ;              /* ✔ address of volatile object cast to be non-volatile */

   p1 = p2 ;                       /* ✔ object accessed by p1 will be volatile */
   p2 = p1 ;                       /* ✘ p2 is pointer to non-volatile object */
   p2 = (int *)(p1) ;              /* ✔ but b is non-volatile if accessed with p2 */

   return 0 ;
}
```

8.5 Direct access of memory mapped peripherals

One of the most useful and interesting applications of pointers, particularly for the author, lies with their ability to support direct access to memory mapped peripherals. In a traditional computing environment, it is the host operating system that is responsible for intercepting and dealing with the program's I/O requests. However, with an increasing number of small ROM based systems, such as video games and engine management controllers, now being written in C, the use of a host operating system to handle the I/O frequently adds an unnecessary level of complexity and cost to the system, and many designers are looking at alternative ways of accessing I/O directly from within their programs.

Although the need to access 'standard' peripherals such as disk drives, printers and terminals is rare on these types of systems, they nevertheless frequently need to communicate with more specialist devices such as parallel and serial I/O ports, analog to digital converters (ADCs), digital to analog converters (DACs) and, more frequently, liquid crystal displays.

Provided that the programmer has a complete understanding of how the peripheral device works (manufacturers' data sheets are a mine of information in this respect) and where it is located in the memory map of the system, a pointer to that device can be initialized and its internal registers accessed via the indirection operator. Let us take a look at a simple example.

Figure 8.8 illustrates a particularly common parallel I/O chip, Motorola's M6821 device. This device is intended to interface a host computer to a multitude

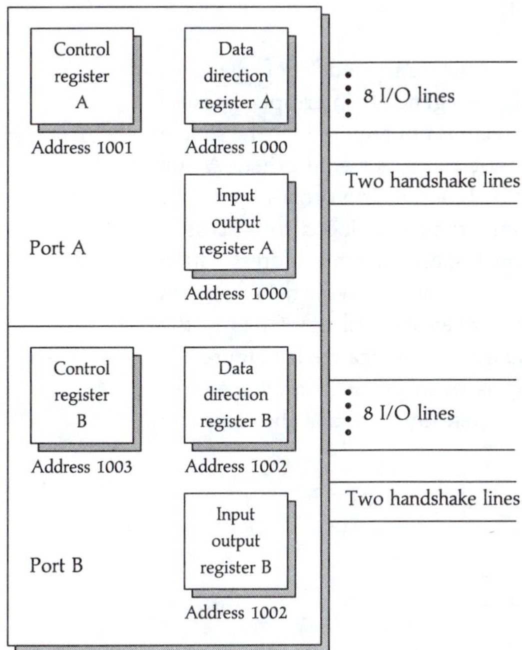

Figure 8.8 Motorola M6821 PIA programming model.

of bit and byte wide peripherals such as push button switches, light emitting diodes (LEDs), relays, parallel printer ports and so on.

The device is logically split into two halves, A and B, with each half controlling up to eight individual I/O lines and two programmable handshake lines. A total of 6 byte wide registers reside within the chip, 3 for each half, some of which share common addresses. As a result, the device occupies just 4 bytes in the memory map of the computer.

Assuming that the base address of the device has been fixed at hex 1000, and that the system's designer has arranged for the registers in the device to occupy successive memory locations (which may not be always the case particularly with a 16 or 32 bit host CPU), these six registers may be accessed at the addresses shown in Table 8.3.

The data direction registers are used to control the direction of the 8 input/output lines associated with each I/O port. By programming each bit of this register with a 0 or 1, each corresponding I/O line for that port is programmed to operate as an input or output line, respectively. For example, if bit 0 of data direction register A were programmed with 0, then input/output line 0 of port A could be used to read data connected to that line. Similarly, setting bit 5 to 1 programs input/output line 5 for output operation, enabling any output device connected to that line to be controlled via the PIA.

Once the individual input/output lines for a port have been programmed for the respective input or output modes, data may be read from or written to an I/O line by reading from or writing to the corresponding bits within the input/output register.

The byte wide control registers mainly determine the modes of operation of the two handshake lines and the device's ability to generate interrupts. Because the facilities are complex and understanding of them is not required for the simple example presented here, these facilities will not be discussed further. A full discussion of the operation of this register can be found in Motorola's literature.

However, bit 2 of the control register is important since it controls access to the data direction and input/output registers which share the same address within each respective port (see Table 8.3). If this bit is set to 0 or 1, then the data direction register or input/output register, respectively, is available. All other bits in the control register can safely be set to 0. These features are summarized in Figure 8.9.

Now that the introduction to this chip is over, let us present a simple problem and see how we could solve it using pointers. Imagine that the computer

Table 8.3 Typical register addresses for the M6821 PIA device.

Address	*Register*
0x1000	Data direction and input/output register A
0x1001	Control register A
0x1002	Data direction and input/output register B
0x1003	Control register B

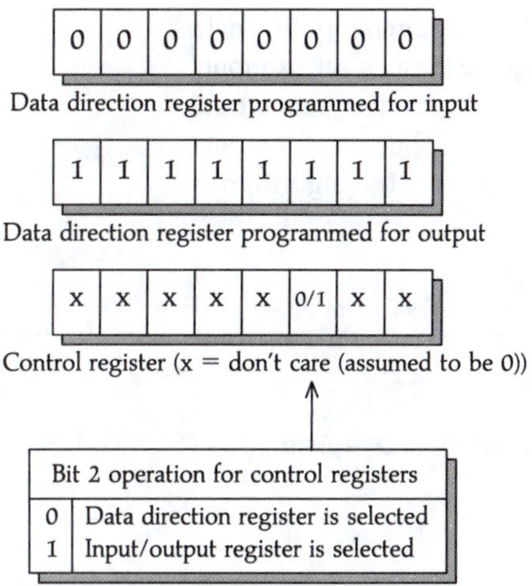

Figure 8.9 Data direction and control register operation.

you are using has to be interfaced to eight push button or toggle switches and eight LEDs. The intention is that a program will be written to monitor these switches and reflect their status (on or off) on their corresponding LED. The arrangement is illustrated in Figure 8.10, where the eight switches and eight LEDs are assumed to be connected to ports A and B, respectively.

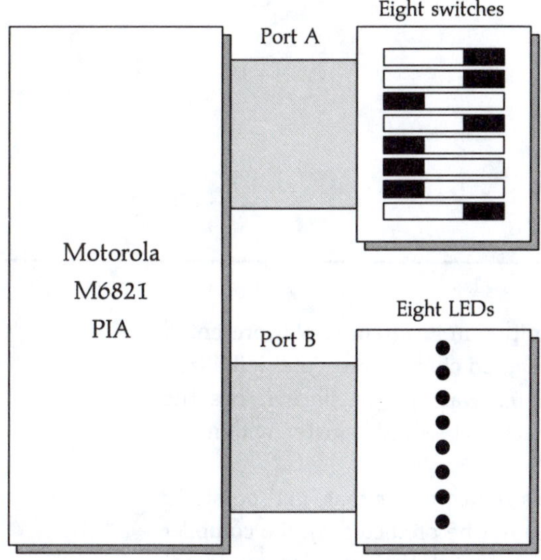

Figure 8.10 Interfacing switches and LEDs to a PIA.

From a software aspect, the problem involves programming the data direction registers of ports A and B such that their eight I/O lines act as inputs and outputs, respectively. Then, as part of a continuous loop, the program would copy the eight switch settings to the eight LEDs by copying the value of input/output register A to input/output register B. A description of the algorithm is presented in Program 8.19.

Program 8.19 Programming a PIA to read eight switches and reflect them on eight LEDs.

```
Begin
/*
** Ensure data direction register can be selected rather the I/O register
*/

   Program bit 2 of control register A to 0
   Program bit 2 of control register B to 0

/*
** Program all lines of port A to be inputs and all lines of port B to be outputs
*/

   Program data direction register A to 0000 0000
   Program data direction register B to 1111 1111

/*
** Ensure that I/O register can be selected
*/

   Program bit 2 of control register A to 1
   Program bit 2 of control register B to 1

   while ( true )  {
      read input/output register A
      store value at input/output register B
   }
End
```

The C code implementation of the algorithm in Program 8.19 is presented in Program 8.20. It makes use of a volatile unsigned char pointer 'pia' initialized with the address 0x1000. This type of pointer was chosen since it has the correct scalar value of 1 required to access each byte sized register within the PIA.

The volatile part of the declaration tells the compiler that 'pia' points to data that is likely to change in ways that could not be predicted by the compiler (that is, as a result of a switch being pressed) and as such the compiler should not arrange for the data read from input/output port A to be cached within the while

Program 8.20 A C code program to drive a PIA.

```
/*
** This program manipulates the registers in a
** Motorola 6821 PIA chip using char pointers.
** The chip is assumed to reside at address 0x1000
** and occupy successive addresses.
*/

int main( void )
{

/*
** Define a pointer pia initialized with the base address of the PIA
*/

    volatile unsigned char  *pia = (unsigned char * )( 0x1000 ) ;

/*
** Now set bit 2 of both control registers to 0 to select the data direction registers
*/

    *(pia + 1 ) = 0 ;
    *(pia + 3 ) = 0 ;

/*
** Now program port A for input and port B for output modes
*/

    *pia = 0 ;                  /* set all bits of DDR A to 0 */
    *( pia + 2 ) = 0xff ;       /* set all bits of DDR B to 1 */

/*
** Now set bit 2 of both control registers to 1 to select the I/O registers
** at addresses 0x1000 and 0x1002.
*/

    *( pia + 1 ) = 0x04 ;
    *( pia + 3 ) = 0x04 ;

/*
** Now a continuous loop that reads port A and writes the data to port B
*/

    while( 1 )
      *( pia + 2 ) = *pia ;

    return 0 ;
}
```

loop. The unsigned part of the declaration informs the compiler that 'pia' points to unsigned 8 bit data and as such the most significant bit of this data is not to be treated as a sign bit (that is, sign extension is never to be performed).

8.5.1 *An analog to digital converter example*

The following example introduces a pseudo 8 bit analog to digital converter (ADC) assumed to reside in the memory map of the computer at a base address of 0xC000. This device is designed to convert an analog voltage, typically in the range 0 to +10 volts, present on input into an unsigned 8 bit digital quantity in the range 0 to 255 representative of that voltage. In this particular example, the device can be programmed to sample from one of eight different analog sources with the aid of a multiplexer.

The block diagram and programming model for the device are shown in Figure 8.11, and consist of three byte wide registers labelled 'Control/status', 'Convert' and 'Result'. Bits 3–5 of the control/status register (CSR) are programmed to select which of the eight possible analog channels is to be sampled.

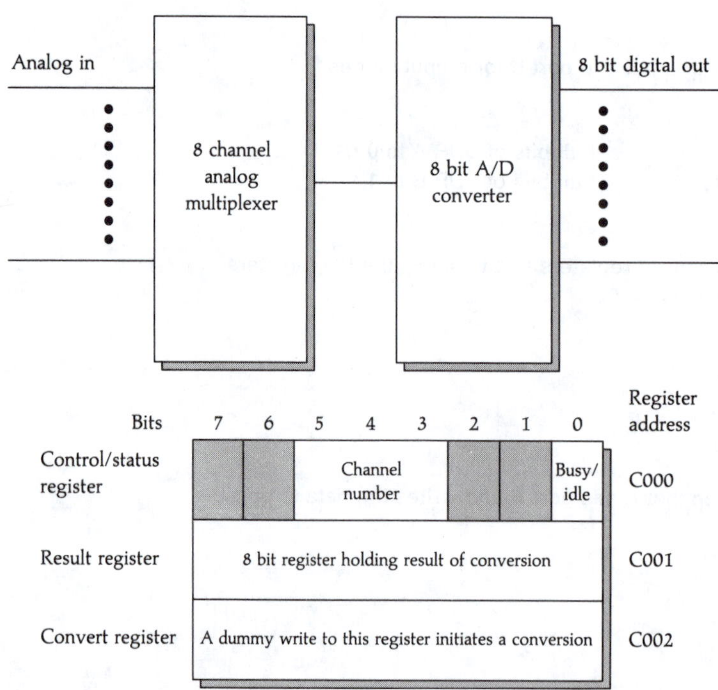

Figure 8.11 Hardware and programmer's model of the ADC.

A conversion is initiated by the simple act of writing to the convert register (any value will do), while the progress of the conversion, which can take several microseconds, can be followed by monitoring bit 0 of the CSR. If the device is busy – that is, still converting – then bit 0 will be set to 1. After a conversion, the result register contains the 8 bit unsigned result of the conversion, which may then be read by the program.

Program 8.21 defines a simple function that expects to be passed a 3 bit channel argument and returns the 8 bit unsigned result of a conversion performed on that channel. The function programs the channel number into the correct bits

Program 8.21 The analog to digital converter program.

```
#include  <stdio.h>

unsigned char convert( unsigned char chan )
{
/*
** First define a pointer to the ADC device at address hex c000
*/

   static volatile unsigned char *adc = (unsigned char *)( 0xc000) ;

   chan = chan & 07 ;              /* Mask off bits 3–7 in chan number argument */
   chan = chan << 3 ;              /* Shift channel number into bits 3–5 */

   *adc = chan ;                   /* Select channel number */
   *(adc + 2) = 0 ;                /* Initiate a conversion */

   while( (*adc & 0x01) == 0x01 )  /* test device status in Bit '0' */
      ;                            /* Wait for end of conversion */

   return (*(adc +1) ) ;           /* Return data in result register */
}

/*
** Now a simple program to drive the above function
*/

int main( void )
{
   unsigned char  channel = 5 ;    /* select channel 5 */
   unsigned char  c ;              /* to hold result of conversion */

   c = convert( channel ) ;
   printf("Signal on channel %u is %u \n" , channel, c ) ;

   return 0 ;
}
```

of the CSR and then initiates a conversion. A loop is then entered, which tests the status of the ADC (reflected in bit 0 of the CSR) and waits for the end of a conversion, after which the value held in the result register is returned.

8.5.2 *Driving a liquid crystal display*

In this last example, we take a look at a program designed to display text on a liquid crystal display (LCD). This is interesting in as much as it demonstrates the use of the standard library function sprintf( ) (for which there is a corresponding function sscanf( ) for input), which provides all of the formatting abilities of printf( ) but stores its output as an array of char, rather than writing it to a physical device. Given the output in this form, a function could easily be written to take successive characters from the array and send them to a specific device, such as the LCD display.

Figure 8.12 illustrates the arrangement along with a typical programmer's model. This device consists of three registers, occupying two addresses in the memory map. The 1 bit read only status register located at address 0xE000 indicates the status of the device, either busy (1) or idle (0). The read and write data registers located at 0xE001 allow the character currently under the LCD's cursor to be read and/or a new character/command to be written to the display.

Program 8.22, in conjunction with the ADC function developed in Section 8.5.1, demonstrates a complete program, to gather and display data obtained from an analog source onto an LCD display.

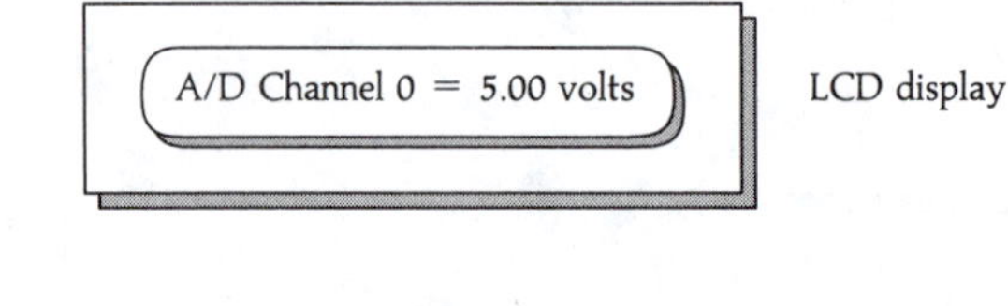

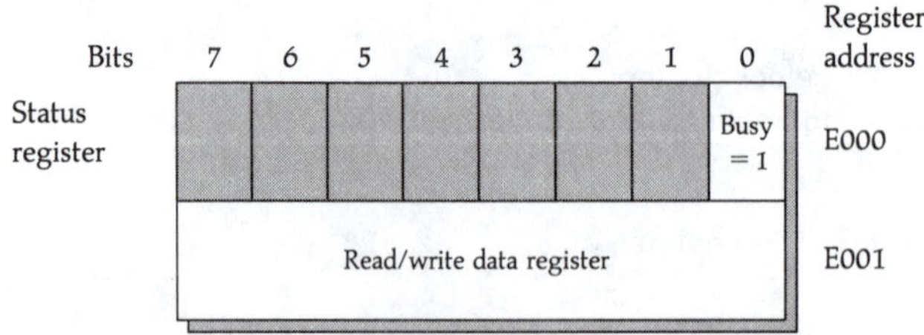

Figure 8.12 Hardware and programmer's model of the LCD display.

Program 8.22 An LCD driver program.

```
#include   <stdio.h>                    /* for sprintf( ) */

unsigned char convert( unsigned char chan ) ;     /* function prototype */

/*
** A function to display a single character to the LCD display
*/

void lcd_putchar( char c )
{

/*
** Define a pointer to the base address of the LCD display
*/

  static volatile unsigned char *lcd = (unsigned char * )( 0xe000 ) ;

/*
** Wait until the device becomes idle
*/

  while((*lcd & 0x01) == 0x01 )
    ;

/*
** Now write a single character to the display
*/

  *(lcd + 1) = c ;                      /* Write char to display */
}

/*
** This function accepts a text string argument represented by an array of char
** and presents each character from that array, in turn, to the function
** lcd_putchar( ) where it is displayed.
*/

void lcd_puts( char text[ ] )           /* function to display a string of char */
{
  int count = 0 ;

  while( text[ count ] != '\0' )  {
    lcd_putchar( text [ count ] ) ;
    count ++ ;
  }
}
```

```
/*
** This part of the program gathers one sample from channel 0 of the ADC
** developed earlier and, using sprintf(), writes a formatted string into a char
** array before passing that array to lcd_puts() for display.
*/

int  main( void )
{
   double   volts ;
   char      lcd_text[ 256 ] ;                         /* Message array for LCD */

   volts = convert( 0 ) * 10.0 / 255.0 ;     /* Gather and scale result from channel 0 */

   sprintf( lcd_text , "A/D Channel 0 = %4.2g Volts" , volts ) ;
   lcd_puts( lcd_text ) ;                               /* display message */

   return 0 ;
}
```

8.6 Chapter summary

(1) A pointer is defined by placing a '*' prior to the pointer's name in its definition, as shown in the example below where 'p1' is a pointer to double:

```
double * p1 ;
```

All uninitialized global and static pointers are implicitly cleared to 0 (NULL). An uninitialized automatic/register pointer is not implicitly initialized and consequently points to an unpredictable address.

(2) The scalar value of a pointer is the size of the object it points to, thus 'p1' above has a scalar value of (typically) 8.

(3) The lvalue of a variable is the address of the memory location where that variable is stored. Its rvalue is the data that it holds.

(4) A pointer may be initialized with the address or lvalue of another variable with the '&' operator, as shown below:

```
p1 = &x ;
```

(5) It not permitted to assign the address of one type of variable to a pointer of an incompatible type, for example, assigning the address of a double to a char pointer.

(6) A pointer's (r)value or an address may be displayed using printf() in conjunction with the '%p' format indicator.

(7) The object pointed to by a pointer may be accessed using the indirection operator '*', for example:

```
a = *p1 ;        /* fetch object pointed to by p1 and assign to a */
*p1 = a ;        /* assign value of a to the object pointed to by p1 */
```

(8) All arithmetic operations performed with a pointer take into account the pointer's scalar value. For example, incrementing a double pointer increments its value by (typically) 8.

(9) A pointer plus offset 'n' may be used to access the nth element in an array. Either pointer offset plus indirection or array notation may be used. For example, the following two expressions are equivalent and the scalar value of 'ptr' is again considered in determining the location of the nth object.

```
*( ptr + n )     and     ptr[ n ]
```

(10) A function written to receive an array could declare its parameter either as a pointer or as an array of a suitable type. Elements from the array could be accessed using either of the above notations.

(11) A NULL pointer is any type of pointer that points to address 0 in memory and is used to represent an invalid or illegal pointer value. NULL pointers are often returned by functions to indicate an error.

(12) A void pointer is a generic scalarless pointer able to point to any object. It may be freely assigned and compared with any other type of pointer without a cast being required. It is illegal to apply any operators to this pointer that require knowledge of a scalar value, such as '*', '++', '[ ]' and so on.

(13) Two incompatible pointers (with different scalar values) cannot be assigned to or compared with each other, unless one of them is a void pointer. However, any pointer may be assigned or compared with the integer value 0 (NULL). Comparison with and assignment of any other integer value is illegal, unless a cast is used.

(14) The memory allocation functions malloc(), calloc(), realloc() and free() offer a way of dynamically requesting, resizing and releasing memory for the program at run time.

(15) A pointer to a constant object such as an int may be defined as shown below. It is illegal to subsequently alter the object that 'ptr' points to, but the pointer itself may be modified:

```
const int *ptr ;
```

(16) A constant pointer may be defined as shown below, where 'ptr' may be used to modify the variable 'i', but it is illegal to modify 'ptr' later.

```
int *const ptr = &i ;
```

(17) Both types of const qualifier may be combined to create a constant pointer to constant data, as shown below:

```
const int      *const ptr = &i ;
```

Here, neither the pointer nor the object it points to may be modified.

(18) A volatile object is one whose value may change in ways that are not predictable by the compiler, usually as a result of external influences, such as interrupts or a change in status within a memory mapped peripheral. References to volatile objects are never optimized or cached by the compiler and always result in true accesses to the object.

8.7 Exercises

8.1 What is the effect of applying the '&' operator to a variable? What is the type of the expression '&i'? To what class of variables can this operator *not* be applied?

8.2 What is the effect of applying the indirection operator '*' to a pointer? What is the result of the following expression: '*ptr = *ptr **ptr', where 'ptr' is a pointer?

8.3 What is meant by the scalar value (SV) of a pointer? How does a pointer's SV affect operations such as incrementing and decrementing a pointer, applying an offset to a pointer and manipulating a variable indirectly via a pointer? Write a simple program to determine and display the scalar value of a given pointer.

8.4 Why is the '&' operator not required when passing or assigning the address of an array to a function or pointer, for example in the expressions 'scanf("%s", array)' and 'ptr = array'?

8.5 Given that 'ptr' is a pointer to an element within an array, what is the result of the following four expressions?

```
*ptr      *( ptr + n )      ptr[ n ]      ( ptr + n ) – ptr
```

8.6 Write a program to show that successive elements of an array are stored at successively higher addresses in memory.

8.7 Given the variable definitions below:

```
char  c, *cptr ;
int   n = 2, i[ 100 ], *iptr ;
```

explain whether the following expressions are legal or illegal. What, if any, is their effect?

```
cptr = c               cptr = &c                    *cptr = &c
cptr = &i              &cptr = c                    &cptr = &c
iptr = &i              iptr = i                     iptr = &i[0]
((iptr = i) + n)       *((iptr = i) + n) = 5
```

8.8 Given the following variable definitions:

```
char  c ;
int   i ;
float f[10] ;
```

what is the resultant type, value and, where appropriate, scalar value of the following expressions?

```
&c            &i              &f[0]        f
*&c           &*&i            *&*&i        *f
(f + i)       *(f + i)        &f[0] + i    f[0] + i
&f[9] - f     *f * *&f[5]
```

8.9 Given the following variable definitions:

```
int  x[10], *xptr = x ;
int  y[10], *yptr = y ;
```

what, if any, is the effect of the following expressions and statements?

```
x = y      xptr = yptr      *xptr = *yptr      sizeof(xptr)      sizeof(*xptr)      sizeof(x)
for(i = 0 ; i != 10 ; xptr[i++] = *yptr++) ;
```

8.10 What is the effect of the following program section, where 'ptr' is assumed to point to a '\0' terminated text string:

```
while( *ptr++ != '\0' )
   puts(ptr) ;
```

8.11 Using the bubble sort function presented in Chapter 7, suggest how the function could be rewritten to use a pointer declaration in place of the array declaration in the parameter list. Explain why the function continues to operate correctly even though the function body still uses array notation. Rewrite the function in as many ways as you can think of to use varying combinations of array and pointer operations and parameter declarations.

8.12 Apply Exercise 8.11 to the function that performs a binary search of an array (see Chapter 7).

8.13 Write a function to read an array of floating point numbers and return that array to the calling function.

8.14 Write a single function to calculate (not display) the square, cube and square root of its floating point argument and make those results available to the calling program.

8.15 Write a function to convert between polar and rectangular coördinates.

8.16 Modify the quicksort algorithm presented in Program 8.13 to sort a text string represented by an array of characters into ascending order.

8.17 Modify the dynamic memory allocation problem presented in Program 8.16 to resize an array of doubles.

8.18 What is meant by the terms NULL pointer, void pointer, constant pointer and a pointer to constant data? Why is it only permissible to assign a pointer to constant data to another such pointer? Given the following definitions:

```
char   c1, *cptr1 ;
const  char   c2 = '@' , *cptr2 ;
char   *const cptr3 = &c1 ;
const  char *const cptr4 = &c2 ;
```

which of the following statements are legal and which illegal? Explain why.

```
c1 = c2 ;               c2 = c1 ;               cptr1 = &c1 ;
cptr1 = &c2 ;           cptr2 = &c1 ;           cptr2 = &c2 ;
cptr1 = cptr2 ;         cptr2 = cptr1 ;         cptr3 = &c2 ;
cptr3 = cptr1 ;         cptr3 = cptr2 ;         cptr4 = &c1 ;
cptr4 = &c2 ;           cptr4 = cptr3 ;         cptr1++ ;
(*cptr1)++ ;            cptr2++ ;               (*cptr2)++ ;
cptr3++ ;               (*cptr3)++ ;            cptr4++ ;
(*cptr4)++ ;
```

8.19 What is meant by a volatile object and why are such objects, particularly pointers to those objects, important in small embedded controller applications? Explain what might happen if the pointer 'pia' in Program 8.20 were not a pointer to volatile data. Why is it safe to allow a pointer to non-volatile data to be assigned to a pointer to volatile data but not the other way around?

8.20 Modify the variable definitions in Exercise 8.18 such that:

(a) All occurrences of the key word const are replaced by volatile.

(b) All occurrences of the key word const are combined with the key word volatile.

Discuss for each case which of the assignments in Exercise 8.18 are now valid.

8.21 Using the PIA programming example from Section 8.5, write a program to:

(a) Count in binary on the eight LEDs.

(b) Move an illuminated LED backwards and forwards across the row of eight LEDs.

(c) Produce display (a) or (b) depending upon the condition of switch 5.

8.22 Using the PIA programming example from Section 8.5, write a program to illuminate the following LEDs when their corresponding 'true' conditions are met:

LED	*True when*
0	Switch 0 is on
1	Switch 0 or switch 1 is on
2	Switches 0, 1 and 2 are on and switch 7 is off
3	Switch 3 is not the same as switch 7
4	(Switch 1 and 2 are on) or (switch 4 or 7 is off)
5	Any switch is on
6	Switch 6 or 7 is on but switch 0 is off
7	As LED 6 and provided switch 1 and 2 but not 3 and 4 are on

8.23 Assuming that the PIA hardware is now modified such that both port A and port B are acting as output ports connected to eight LEDs each, write a program to display random numbers in the range 0–32 767 using the random number generator presented in Chapter 3.

8.24 Modify the analog to digital converter program (Program 8.21) presented in Section 8.5.1 to assume a 16 bit device with 16 bit registers and generating a 16 bit result. Explain any assumptions you make in the program.

9 String and Character Manipulation

The manipulation of characters and text strings is one of the most frequent operations performed in any programming language. Because of this, some languages, such as BASIC, permit the use of arithmetic operators such as '=' and '+' to be applied to strings. This enables string comparison, copying and appending to be performed in a relatively straightforward manner.

Unfortunately (depending upon how you look at it), C does not permit the use of these operators in the context of string manipulation. This means that programmers may have to define their own functions to perform these operations 'manually'. In this chapter we take a closer look at strings, in particular at how a string may be created and manipulated and how it is represented within memory.

We shall also be taking a look at some of the string manipulation functions defined by the standard library which, among other more complex operations, provide facilities for the copying, comparing and appending of two strings. However, before we delve too deeply, let us first begin with a recap of what a string is and how it is represented in memory.

9.1 Creating and manipulating text strings

You will recall from Chapter 2, that a **literal** or **implicit** text string is created whenever text is placed within double quotation marks, as shown below:

```
"Greetings"
```

To the compiler, such a string is represented by a hidden (in the sense that it does not possess a name) array of char, terminated with the NULL character, '\0'. The length or number of characters in the above string is 9, but the size of the hidden array required to represent it is 10, as shown in Figure 9.1.

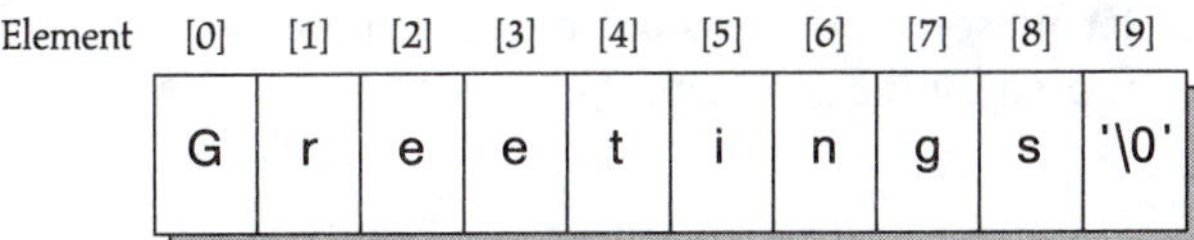

Figure 9.1 The internal representation of a character string.

To further demonstrate that strings really are represented by an array, you can try executing the following simple (and rather pointless) loop:

```
for( i = 0; i < 9; i ++ )
  putchar("Greetings"[i]) ;
```

Here, the message "Greetings" is displayed, one character at a time, via repeated calls to putchar( ). How does this work? Recalling that a literal string is represented by an array and that when an array is passed to a function, it is the address of the first element that is passed, the literal text string "Greetings", resolves to the address of character 'G'. Thus the expression "Greetings"[i] is simply array notation using the array subscript 'i' to access the ith character in the string, which is then given to putchar( ).

Although the above example is unusual, it illustrates an important concept for the reader to grasp for the sections that follow, namely that whenever a literal text string such as "Greetings" appears in an expression, it resolves to the address of the first character in that string. Thus, the following statement is translated by the compiler into a call to the function puts( ), with the address of the letter 'G' as its argument:

Pass the address of 'G' to puts( )

```
puts("Greetings") ;
```

Now apart from its obvious use in a program as a source of text that could be displayed on the operator's terminal, the above string in its present form serves little other useful purpose, mainly because it is represented by an array of implicitly constant characters and should not be modified by the program, even though it may be possible to do so on some computers.

Furthermore, the program has no control over the storage allocated to the (hidden) array used to represent it and it would therefore be *unwise* to attempt to append further text onto the end of the string (an action which if permitted could corrupt the program's code itself). In other words there are only two useful operations that may be performed with a literal text string such as this:

(1) It may be displayed using printf( ), puts( ) and so on.

(2) It may be copied/appended/compared with other arrays, thus forming part of a possibly enlarged string that the program may choose to construct from several sources.

With these limitations in mind let us see how we could create a more versatile text string that could be manipulated by the program.

9.1.1 *Creating a variable text string*

Perhaps the most obvious way of introducing a variable text string is for the program to define a suitably sized char array into which a string of characters could later be copied. As an example, the array text[ ] below would be capable of representing a string of up to 99 characters in length. Once defined as a variable, functions such as gets( ) or scanf( ) could be called to read a line of text from the operator's keyboard and store it in the array.

Size of array is defined as 100 characters

```
char text[ 100 ] ;
```

Although the use of the '=' operator to copy one array to another is illegal, its use during the definition of an array is permitted and allows an array to be pre-initialized with text. There are two ways in which this could be achieved, the first of which is shown below:

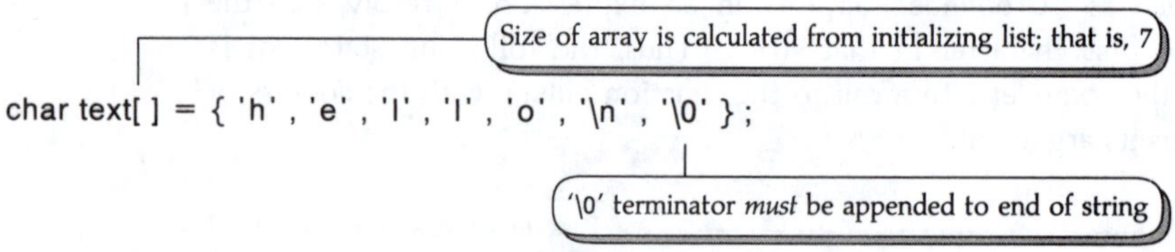
Size of array is calculated from initializing list; that is, 7
char text[ ] = { 'h' , 'e' , 'l' , 'l' , 'o' , '\n' , '\0' } ;
'\0' terminator *must* be appended to end of string

Here, the array 'text' has been initialized with individual characters from an initializing list. You will notice that such initialization does not automatically place a '\0' onto the end of the string and so this was performed explicitly.

As you can see, the above approach is not only tedious, but is also prone to programmer error when entering the program. Thus, a second, more readable, method exists, which initializes the array with the characters from an implicit text string as shown below:

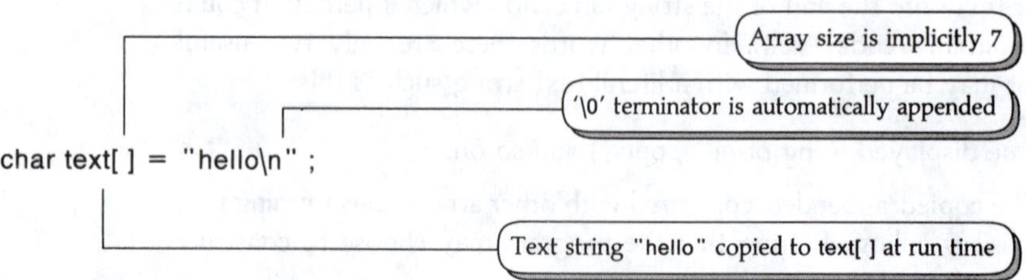
Array size is implicitly 7
'\0' terminator is automatically appended
char text[ ] = "hello\n" ;
Text string "hello" copied to text[ ] at run time

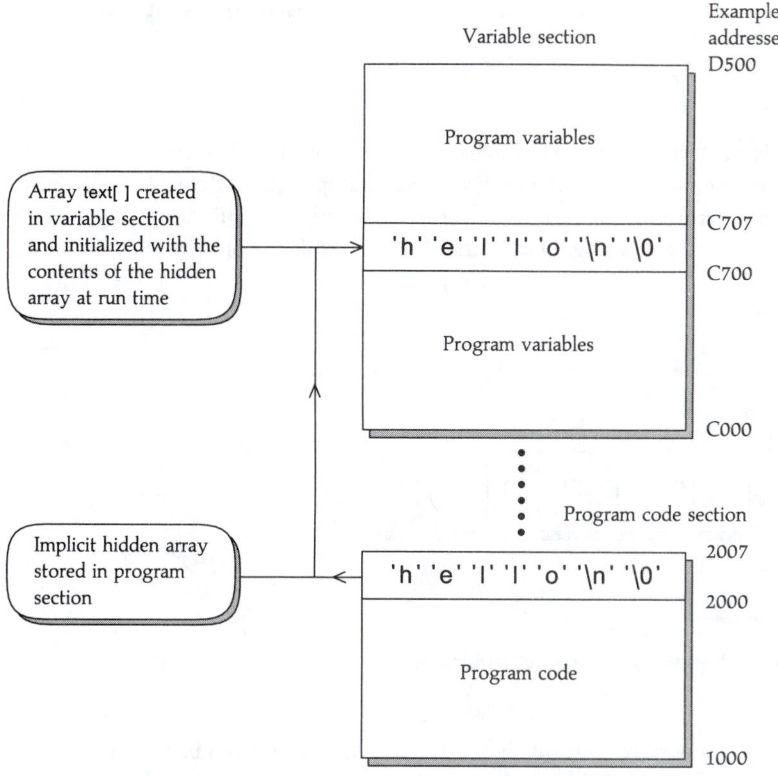

Figure 9.2 Initializing a variable array with an implicit text string.

In both cases, the initializing characters are copied to the array text[ ] at run time. Thus, in the example immediately above, two identical arrays physically exist within the program at run time. The first is the implicit hidden array containing the text string "hello\n", which is constant and is part of the program code produced by the compiler. The second is the variable array text[ ], which is initialized with a copy of the string "hello\n" at run time. This is illustrated in Figure 9.2.

Note that with both types of initialization, the size or number of elements defined for the array need not be explicitly stated, in which case the compiler simply counts the number of characters in the initializing list to determine its size. Thus the array text[ ] above is 7 characters in size. However, if the size of the array were explicitly stated, then its size must be at least sufficient to accommodate all of the characters in the initializing list, otherwise a compile time error is produced.

Because the name of an array resolves to the address of its first element, the string contained in the array text[ ] could be displayed using a simple call to the functions puts( ) or printf( ), as shown below:

```
puts( text ) ;
printf("%s", text) ;
```

Pass the address of text[0] to puts()

but of more interest is the fact that as the array text[ ] is a variable, the characters contained within it may be modified by the program. For example, the statement below places a '\0' terminator into the fifth character in the array, thus truncating the contents of the array to the string "hell", the effect of which is shown in Figure 9.3.

```
text[ 4 ] = '\0' ;
```

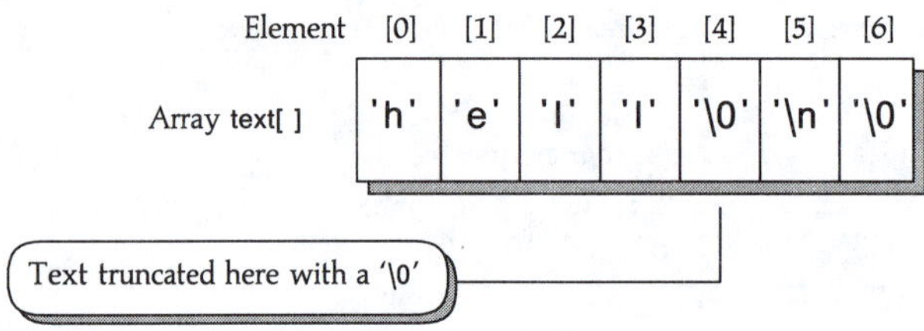

Figure 9.3 Truncating a text string using a '\0' terminator.

Should the program wish to prevent the contents of the array from being altered by the program, then it could of course define text[ ] as an array of constant char in the manner shown below, in which case the array should be initialized at its point of definition if it is to be of any use:

const qualifier prevents the array contents being changed later

```
const char text[ ] = "hello\n" ;
```

9.1.2 *Alternative string creation using pointers*

Even more interesting is the third method of creating a text string, using a pointer. Consider for a moment the following statement:

Create an implicit text string using a hidden array

```
char *p1 = "hello\n" ;
```

Create a char pointer and initialize it with the address of the hidden array

Here, a hidden char array is created at compile time, containing the literal text string "hello\n". At run time, a char pointer 'p1' is introduced and initialized with the address of the first character in that array; that is, the address of the letter 'h' in the string "hello\n". Thus 'p1' is said to point to the text string "hello\n". This is illustrated in Figure 9.4, where arbitrary memory addresses have again been assumed.

It is essential to appreciate that with this type of string creation, the only *variable* that has been introduced is the pointer 'p1', which is now pointing to the first character of a literal or implicitly constant text string. In other words, 'p1' is pointing to a constant text string. The programmer has no control over the size of the (hidden) array where the string is stored, and furthermore should not attempt to alter its contents using the pointer.

Many programmers often elect to impose their own restrictions on such pointers by declaring them as pointers to const char, as shown below. The compiler would thus alert the programmer of any attempt made by the program to alter the string using 'p1':

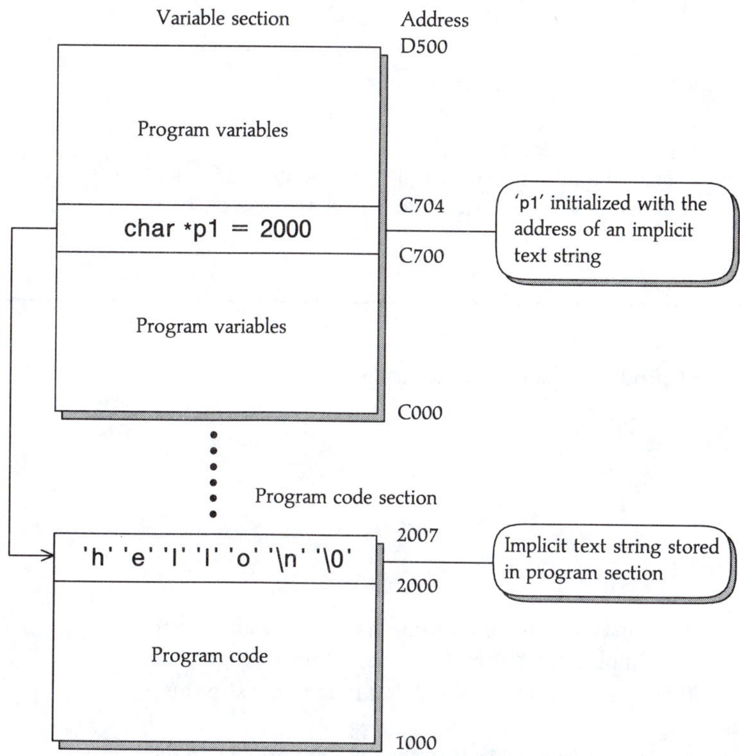

Figure 9.4 Initializing a pointer to point to an implicit text string.

```
const char *p1 = "hello\n" ;
```

(Callout: const qualifier prevents the hidden array from being changed using the pointer)

Since the only variable that we now have access to is the pointer, how could the string it points to be displayed? You will recall that puts( ) (or printf( ) in association with the format indicator '%s') expects to be given the array containing the text to be displayed.

Now we know that when an array is passed to a function it resolves to the address of its first element. From this we can deduce that what puts( ) and printf( ) really expect is the address of the first element in the array. Given that 'p1' was previously initialized to point to the first character 'h' in the hidden array – that is, 'p1' contains the address of the letter 'h' – then passing puts( ) or printf( ) the (r)value of 'p1' would effectively pass it the address of the hidden array. Program 9.1 demonstrates this idea.

Program 9.1 Displaying a string using a pointer or an array.

```
#include <stdio.h>

int main( void )
{
   char *p1 = "hello\n" ;
   char text[ ] = "hello\n" ;

   puts( "hello\n" ) ;        /* pass the address of 'h' */
   puts( text ) ;             /* pass the address of 'text[0]'; that is, the address of 'h' */
   puts( p1 ) ;               /* pass the value of 'p1'; that is, the address of 'h' */
   return 0 ;
}
```

Executing Program 9.1 produces the following display:

The fact that a text string may be displayed using a pointer is important, since it means that wherever an implicit text string appears within a program, it can always be replaced by either an explicit array containing the same text or by a pointer to the same text.

For example, Program 9.2 makes several calls to the function printf( ). In the first case, the format string is an implicit text string, which we are already familiar

Program 9.2 The interchangeability of strings, pointers and arrays.

```
#include  <stdio.h>

const  char s1[ ] = "a = %d, b = %d \n " ;
const  char *s2  = "a = %d, b = %d \n " ;

int  main( void )
{
   int a = 2 , b = 3 ;
                                          Pass the address of 'a' to printf()
   printf( "a = %d, b = %d \n " , a , b ) ;
                                          Pass the address of 's1[0]' to printf()
   printf( s1 , a , b ) ;
                                          Pass the value of 's2' to printf()
   printf( s2 , a , b ) ;
   return 0 ;
}
```

with; in the second and third cases, the format string has been replaced by an array and a pointer, respectively. All three produce exactly the same display.

Executing Program 9.2 produces the following display:

```
a = 2, b = 3
a = 2, b = 3
a = 2, b = 3
```

Perhaps the main benefit of using a pointer rather than an array to create a string is that the pointer may be freely assigned any value and thus may be initialized to point to any string within the program using a simple assignment. Program 9.3 demonstrates this.

Program 9.3 Assigning a string to a pointer.

```
#include  <stdio.h>

int  main( void )
{
   const  char message[ ] = "Hello" ;
   const  char *p1 = "Goodbye" ;
   const  char *p2 ;

   puts( message ) ;        /* display the contents of message[ ]; that is, "Hello" */
   puts( p1 ) ;             /* display the string pointed to by 'p1'; that is, "Goodbye" */
   p2 = message ;           /* p2 now points to the array message[ ]; that is, "Hello" */
   puts( p2 ) ;             /* display the string pointed to by p2; that is, "Hello" */
```

```
    p2 = p1 ;                /* p2 points to the same string as p1; that is, "Goodbye" */
    puts( p2 ) ;             /* display the string pointed to by p2 */

    return 0 ;
}
```

Executing Program 9.3 leads to the following display:

```
Hello
Goodbye
Hello
Goodbye
```

What you must always remember, and this is a pitfall into which many a good programmer has fallen, is that a *variable* text string – that is, one which the program wishes to modify – can only be created by allocating storage for an explicit array. In other words if you wish to copy or append to or otherwise manipulate a text string, then the string must exist within a variable array first. Attempting to modify an implicit string causes unpredictable behaviour. Given the definitions below:

```
char  name[100 ] ;
char  message[ ] = "Hello" ;
char  *p1 = "Goodbye" ;
```

the statements shown below are all either illegal or may lead to unpredictable behaviour on some systems, particularly if the program is blown into read only memory (ROM):

```
*(p1 + 4) = '\0' ;        /* string pointed to by p1 is implicitly constant */
gets( p1 ) ;              /* string pointed to by p1 is implicitly constant */
name = "Hello" ;          /* an array may only be initialized during its definition */
name = p1 ;               /* cannot re-initialize an array */
message = message + "All" ;   /* cannot append strings with ' + ' and ' = ' */
```

9.2 Writing a function to receive a text string

We have already seen that an implicit text string is represented by a hidden char array and as such is passed to a function as the address of its first character. If we wished to generate our own string manipulation functions, then they would have to be written in such a way as to receive an array. We could do this in one of two ways, as we saw briefly in Chapter 8. Firstly, we could declare the parameter to that function as a char pointer into which the address of the first element in the array argument could be assigned. Alternatively, we could declare the parameter as an array of char, a declaration which, as we have seen, only serves to disguise the fact that such a parameter is really represented as a pointer.

Either version of the function could then use either pointer notation – for example, '*(s + n)' where 's' is an array argument (parameter) – or array notation 's[n]' to access the nth character within the string given to it. For example, a function to determine the length of or number of characters in a string could be written in one of the following ways, and, indeed, in a number of other ways:

```
int string_length( const char *s)
{
  int count = 0 ;
  while( *s++ != '\0')
    count ++ ;
  return count ;
}
```

```
int string_length( const char *s)
{
  int count = 0 ;
  while( *(s + count) != '\0')
    count ++ ;
  return count ;
}
```

```
int string_length( const char s[ ])
{
  int count = 0 ;
  while( *s++ != '\0')
    count ++ ;
  return count ;
}
```

```
int string_length( const char s[ ])
{
  int count = 0 ;
  while( s[count] != '\0')
    count ++ ;
  return count ;
}
```

Notice how the parameter 's' in all four versions of string_length() was declared as a pointer to, or an array of, const char. Can you think why this was done? The reason lies with how the original string passed to the function as an argument was defined.

If the programmer had created the original string using either of the two definitions below (indicating that both strings are constant and should not be changed by any part of the program), then passing them to a function whose parameter was simply declared as an array of, or pointer to, (*non*) constant char would have permitted that function to illegally modify the original string:

```
const char text [ ] = "This is a Constant char Array" ;
const char *text = "This is a Constant char Array" ;
```

Recalling from Section 8.4.3 that the compiler is happy to permit the address of either a constant or non-constant char to be assigned to a pointer to constant char, and that the function string_length( ) does not intend to modify the array argument it is given, its parameter was declared with the const qualifier.

This is an important point, since many of the string manipulation functions in the standard library declare their string parameters as pointers to constant char,

Program 9.4 Passing constant and non-constant strings to a function.

```
#include <stdio.h>

const char *s1 = "Hello " ;              /* Pointer to constant char */
const char s2[ ] = "Great " ;            /* Array of constant char */
char *s3 = "World\n" ;                   /* Pointer to non-constant char */
char s4[ ] = "Goodbye\n" ;               /* Array of non-constant char */

/*
** Now a simple function to display the string passed to it, one character at a time
*/

void display_string( const char *ptr )
{
    char c ;

    while( ( c = *ptr++ ) != '\0')       /* see Section 9.2.1 for explanation */
        putchar( c ) ;
}

int main( void )
{
    display_string( s1 ) ;               /* display constant char array */
    display_string( s2 ) ;               /* display constant char array */
    display_string( s3 ) ;               /* display non-constant char array */
    display_string( s4 ) ;               /* display non-constant char array */
    display_string( " Cruel World ") ;   /* pass constant char array */
    return 0 ;
}
```

where they do *not* intend to modify the string argument(s) they have been given. Program 9.4 demonstrates this in action.

9.2.1 *Traversing a string*

Notice how in Program 9.4 a simple while loop was used to step or increment the pointer 'ptr' (not the character it points to) through each character in the string, thus traversing the string from start to end. This is shown below:

Increment 'ptr' through string

Stop when 'ptr points to '\0'

```
while( (c = *ptr++) != '\0')
    putchar( c ) ;
```

This is an important technique, since it forms the basis of many string manipulation routines and is a much more efficient and faster technique than using

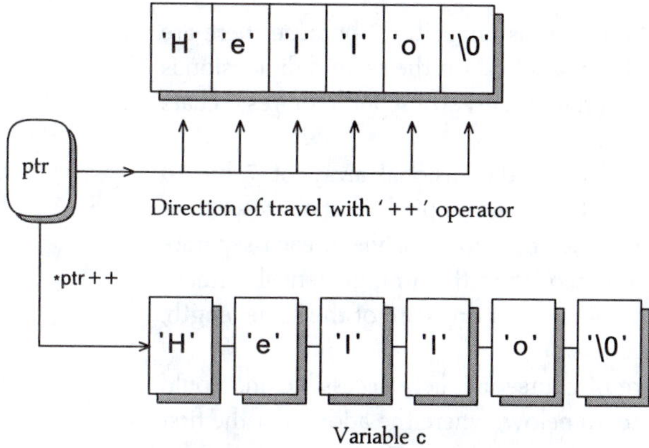

Figure 9.5 Traversing a string with a pointer.

array notation coupled with an index/subscript, for example, '[n]' to access each successive character in the string. Figure 9.5 illustrates the operation for the string "Hello".

As an example, a section of code written to skip over leading space characters in a string is given below, where 'p1' is assumed to point to the start of a '\0' terminated string:

while character is a space and not a '\0'

```
while( *p1 == ' ' && *p1 != '\0')
  p1++ ;
```

9.3 Arrays of text strings

Many applications call for the creation of arrays of text strings. Now as a string is simply an array in the first instance, an array of strings would require a two-dimensional array of char. For example, to record the days in the week, we could create the two-dimensional array of 7 by 10 chars shown below:

Size is implicitly '7' due to there being 7 strings in initializing list

```
const char days[ ] [ 10 ] = { "Monday" ,
                              "Tuesday" ,
                              "Wednesday" ,
                              "Thursday" ,
                              "Friday" ,
                              "Saturday" ,
                              "Sunday"
                            } ;
```

Note how the size of the first dimension is implicitly 7 because there are seven text strings in the initializing list. The size of 10 for the second dimension is derived from the fact that "Wednesday" is the longest string and requires 9 chars to represent it, plus 1 for the '\0' terminator.

When this statement is compiled, a two-dimensional array of 7 by 10 chars is created, and the individual text strings are copied to their respective elements in the array at run time. From a memory point of view, each separate string may be thought of as being represented using the arrangement illustrated in Figure 9.6. You can see from this that not all the strings are of the same length, resulting in some wastage of memory.

Each of the text strings above are of course uniquely accessible and could be displayed with the section of code shown below, where the address of the first character in each single dimensional array is passed to puts() in turn; that is, '&days[0][0] ... &days[6][0]':

```
for( i = 0; i < 7; i++ )
   puts( days[ i ] ) ;
```

Alternatively, each string could be displayed on a character by character basis using the code:

```
for( i = 0; i < 7; i++ )  {
   for( j = 0; (( c = days[ i ][ j ] ) != '\0' ) ; j++ )
      putchar( c ) ;
   putchar( '\n') ;
}
```

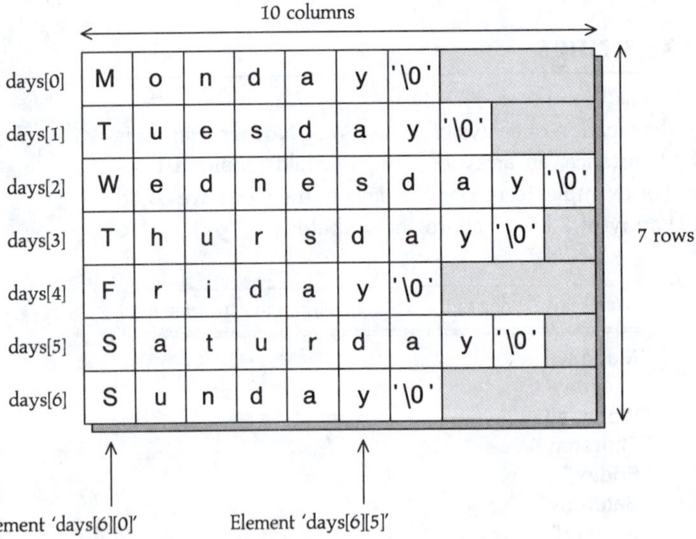

Figure 9.6 An array of seven text strings.

However, an alternative solution exists in the form of an array of pointers to (constant) char, as shown below:

Size is implicitly '7'

```
const char *days[ ] = { "Monday" ,
                        "Tuesday" ,
                        "Wednesday" ,
                        "Thursday" ,
                        "Friday",
                        "Saturday" ,
                        "Sunday"
                      };
```

Here, seven pointers have been created, 'days[0] – days[6]', each of which has been initialized to point to the first character of the corresponding implicit text string defined in the initializing list, as illustrated in Figure 9.7.

The main attraction of this approach is that apart from the storage required by the pointers themselves, there is no wastage associated with the text strings. A further benefit is that sorting an array of strings becomes much easier and more efficient because only the pointers themselves have to be swapped, rather than the text they point to. Again, each string could be displayed using code of the form shown below, which passes the value of each pointer in turn to puts( ):

```
for( i = 0; i < 7; i++ )
  puts( days[ i ] ) ;
```

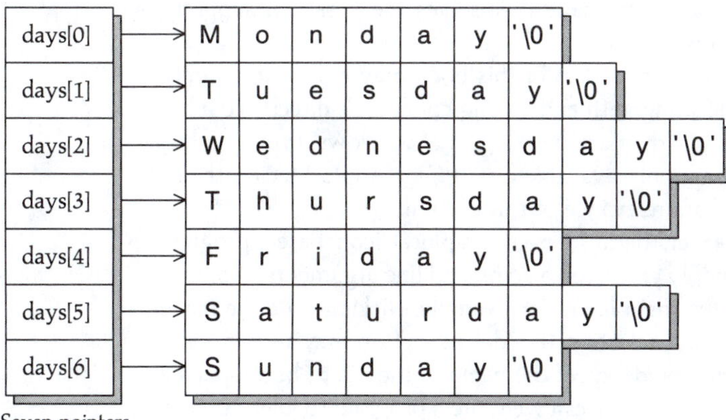

Figure 9.7 An array of seven pointers to implicit char strings.

or alternatively on a character by character basis using code of the form:

```
for( i = 0; i < 7; i ++ )  {
    ptr = days[ i ] ;              /* point to first character in ith string */
    while( *ptr != '\0' )
        putchar( *ptr++ ) ;
        putchar( '\n' ) ;          /* issue new line */
}
```

9.4 Command line arguments and program environments

As an example of many of the concepts introduced so far in this chapter, let us introduce the concept of command line arguments and see how a program could be written to access them. A command line is a list of arguments that may have been supplied by an operator when the program was set running from the operating system shell. For example, a typical MS-DOS operating system command line to copy a disk file might look something like this:

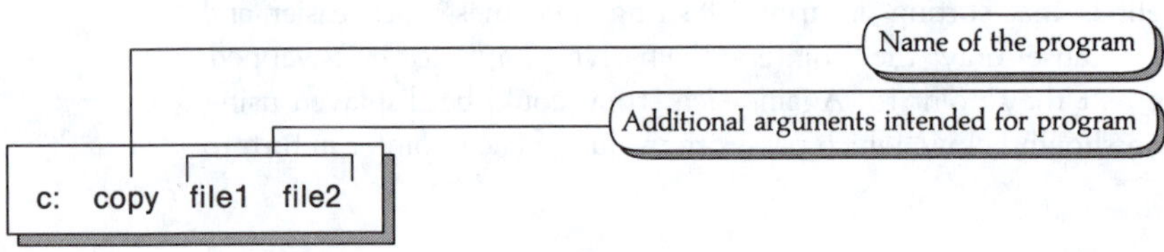

Here copy represents the name of the program invoked to copy the file, while file1 and file2 are additional **source** and **destination** file names that the copy program will eventually need to know to complete its operation. By supplying these names on the command line, that is, the same line that was used to invoke the program, operators can save themselves the hassle of supplying them later once the program is running.

It is quite feasible that some readers of this book may not be too familiar with the concept of communicating with and issuing commands directly to a host operating system, particularly if they are working in a 'windows' type graphical environment such as that commonly available on a PC or Apple Macintosh, and thus may not see the immediate relevance of this section.

It is important, however, because even graphical/icon based programs sometimes have a need to supply and receive command line arguments to prevent the program having to ask for them later. For example, clicking on a file name/icon from a directory listing and selecting the 'delete' option may well invoke a specific 'delete' utility, which would expect the name of the file to be supplied as an argument. The question, then, is how can we write a program to 'pick up' these command line arguments? The answer lies with the parameter list declared for the function main().

9.4.1 *Arguments to the function* main( )*:* argc *and* argv

So far in this book, the function main( ) has always been defined as having a void or empty parameter list, since there was no obvious way that main( ) could receive any arguments. However, since it is the operating system that deals with the processing of the operator's command line and invokes the program itself, it would seem to be in the ideal position to supply these command line arguments to main( ) when the program is run.

In order for main( ) to receive these arguments, its parameter list will have to be modified to include two parameter declarations, namely, the integer argc and the array of char pointers argv, as shown below (note that these parameters have traditionally been known as argc and argv, but there is no reason why they should not assume any other valid variable names):

Integer command line argument count

An array of pointers to the command line arguments

```
int main( int argc, char *argv[ ] )
{
   ...
}
```

Consider, then, what happens when the following command line is supplied to invoke the copy program under MS-DOS:

```
c:  copy  file1  file2
```

Here, the operating system processes the command line and determines that it contains three arguments, separated by white space, the first being the name of the program itself – that is, copy – while the other two arguments are the source and destination file names for use by copy.

When the operating system calls the copy utility it presents its function main( ) with a copy of all three command line arguments. Thus, the copy program should in this instance find that argc and argv have been set to the following values:

```
argc = 3
argv[ 0 ] = "copy"
argv[ 1 ] = "file1"
argv[ 2 ] = "file2"
```

Program 9.5 demonstrates this by displaying the command line arguments supplied to the program on the operator's terminal.

Program 9.5 Displaying command line arguments.

```
#include   <stdio.h>

int  main( int argc, char *argv[ ] )
{
   int i ;

   printf("Argument count : argc = %d\n", argc ) ;

   for( i = 0; i < argc; i ++ )
      printf("argv[ %d ] = %s\n", i , argv[ i ] ) ;

   return 0 ;
}
```

9.4.2 *Accessing environment parameters:* envp

Many operating systems, such as UNIX and MS-DOS, also support the concept of an operating environment, which is often customized by users when they log in or may be set when the system is booted up. For example, MS-DOS supports several environment parameters which are set within the autoexec.bat file, the most useful of these being the 'path' environment, which describes a list of directories to be searched when attempting to locate a program.

For those operating systems that support such environments, C permits an additional argument to the function main( ), commonly referred to as envp. Like argv, envp is an array of pointers to the user's environment strings. However, unlike argv, you are not told how many strings are contained within it. The only thing you know is that the last pointer in envp is a NULL pointer.

Program 9.6 demonstrates how these environment parameters could be displayed. Note that argc and argv must still be included in the parameter list, to gain access to envp, even if they are not used by the program.

Program 9.6 Accessing the program's environment parameters.

```
#include   <stdio.h>

int  main( int argc, char *argv[ ], char *envp[ ] )
{
   int i = 0 ;

   while( envp[ i ] != NULL )
      puts( envp[ i++ ] );

   return 0 ;
}
```

An array of pointers to the command line arguments

An array of pointers to the environment

On the author's MS-DOS machine Program 9.6 produced the following display:

```
COMSPEC=C:\COMMAND.COM
PROMPT=$p$g
PATH = C:\DOS;C:\BATCH; C:\WINDOWS
TEMP = C:
windir = C:\WINDOWS
```

9.5 Standard library string manipulation functions

The remainder of this chapter is set aside for a discussion of string and character manipulation. In particular, some of the more commonly used functions from the standard library are described, along with their simple dissection. A complete list of string and character manipulation functions can be found in Chapter 18, Sections 18.2 and 18.14.

The header file <string.h> contains the function prototypes for all string manipulation functions in the library, while <ctype.h> contains a number of macros/prototypes relevant to character manipulation.

9.5.1 *Finding the length of a string: The function* strlen( )

Let us begin with the simplest of the string manipulation functions, strlen( ), which determines the length or number of characters in a string (excluding the '\0' terminator). This function performs an identical operation to the function string_length( ) developed earlier, and its prototype is given as:

```
size_t  strlen(const char *s) ;
```

strlen( ) expects to be given the address of a char array

Length of string returned as an unsigned integer

Note that the data type size_t returned by strlen() can, in effect, be considered as an unsigned integral quantity containing the number of characters in the array (which is not necessarily the number of elements in the array itself). As an example, consider the array x[ ] consisting of 10 chars, as shown below. The expression strlen(x) yields the integral value 4; that is, the number of characters in the array up to, but *not* including, the '\0' terminator.

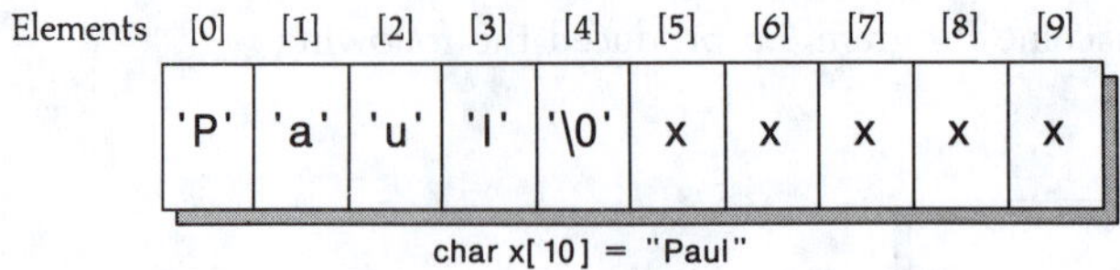

Program 9.7 shows an example of how strlen( ) may have been written. If you wish to try this function for yourself, then rename it something like strlen1( ) so that it does not clash with the function strlen( ) defined in the standard library.

Program 9.7 Calculating the length of a string: the function strlen( ).

```
/*
** Function to calculate the length of a string pointed to by 's'
*/

size_t  strlen( const char *s )        /* function expects a pointer to a string */
{
  size_t count = 0 ;

  while( *s ++ != '\0' )               /* count each character up to the '\0' */
    count ++ ;

  return( count ) ;                    /* return the count */
}
```

Again, we see that the pointer indirection operator '*' is used in conjunction with the post-increment operator '++' to step the pointer 's' through the array argument until the '\0' terminator marking the end of the string is encountered.

The length of the string which is recorded in the variable count is then returned. Program 9.8 demonstrates several examples of how strlen( ) could be used in a program.

Program 9.8 Example use of strlen( ).

```
#include  <stdio.h>
#include  <string.h>             /* for strlen( ) function prototype and 'size_t' data type */

int  main( void)
{
  size_t  len1, len2, len3 ;     /* three unsigned integer variables */
  char    name[ ] = "Paul" ;
  char    *ptr = "Hello World" ;
  char    buffer[ BUFSIZ ] ;
```

```
    len1 = strlen( "a simple string") ;  /* pass address of 'a' in string */
    len2 = strlen( name ) ;               /* pass address of 'P' in "Paul" */
    len3 = strlen( ptr ) ;                /* pass value of pointer; that is, address of 'H' */

    printf( "Length of 'a simple string' = %u\n" , len1 ) ;
    printf( "Length of '%s' = %u\n" , name , len2 ) ;
    printf( "Length of '%s' = %u\n" , ptr , len3 ) ;

    printf("Enter a string : ") ;
    gets( buffer ) ;                      /* read a string */

    printf("Length of your string = %u\n", strlen( buffer )) ;
    return 0 ;
}
```

When Program 9.8 was run, the following sample display was produced:

```
Length of 'a simple string' = 15
Length of 'Paul' = 4
Length of 'Hello World' = 11
Enter a string : Testing 123
Length of your string = 11
```

9.5.2 *String copying: The function* strcpy()

Because a string cannot be copied directly from one array to another with the '=' operator, the function strcpy() exists to perform this operation on our behalf. It copies all of the characters from a specified source array, including the '\0' terminator, into a destination array.

Obviously, it is the programmer's responsibility to ensure that there is sufficient storage allocated for the destination array to accommodate the new string, otherwise the operation may be undefined. Should it be of any interest or use to the program, strcpy() returns a pointer to the first element in the destination array. The function prototype for strcpy() is given below:

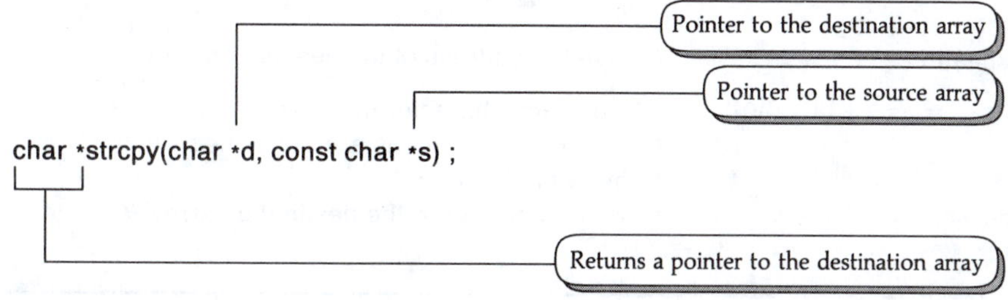

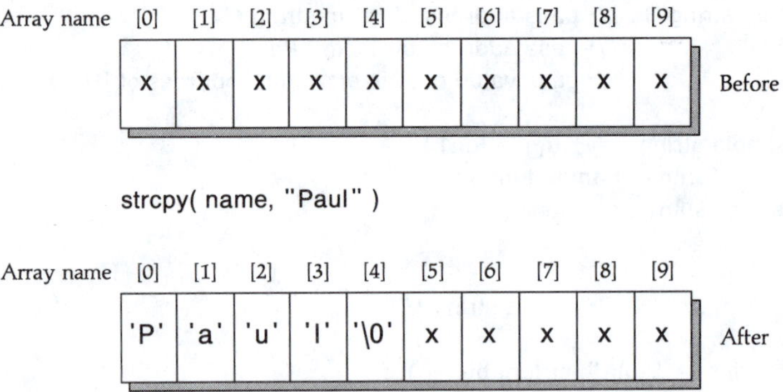

Figure 9.8 The literal text string "Paul" is copied into the array "name" using strcpy( ).

where 'd' is a pointer to the destination array and 's' is a pointer to the source array containing the text to be copied. Note that it is the destination array that is the first argument. It is a very common and easy mistake to get these the wrong way around, with potentially disastrous results.

Note how parameter 'd' is declared as a pointer to non-constant char, since the function modifies the array that 'd' points to. As an example, consider the following statements:

```
char name[10 ] ;
strcpy( name, "Paul") ;
```

Here, strcpy() copies the literal text string "Paul" into the array "name". This is shown in Figure 9.8, where 'x' indicates an unknown value or uninitialized array element.

Program 9.9 shows an example of how strcpy() may have been written. If you wish to try this function for yourself, then rename it something like strcpy1() so that it does not clash with the function strcpy() defined in the standard library.

Program 9.9 Copying a string: the function strcpy().

```
/*
** Function strcpy() to copy a string from a source array to a destination array
*/

char *strcpy ( char *d , const char *s )
{
    char *destination = d ;              /* save the address of the destination array */

    while((*d++ = *s++) != '\0')         /* copy each character from array 's' to 'd' */
        ;                                /* do nothing as actions are performed within */
                                         /* the 'while' itself */
    return ( destination ) ;             /* return a pointer to the destination array */
}
```

Program 9.10 Example usage of strcpy().

```
#include  <stdio.h>
#include  <string.h>                  /* for strcpy() function prototype */

int  main( void )
{
   const  char *s1 = "Goodbye" ;
   char   destination[ BUFSIZ ];       /* space to hold copy of string */

/* copy string "Hello" to destination array */

   strcpy ( destination , "Hello") ;
   printf("Array now contains the string : %s\n", destination) ;

/* copy string "Goodbye " to destination array */

   strcpy ( destination , s1) ;
   printf("Array now contains the string : %s\n" , destination );

/*
** Now copy "Farewell" to the destination array and use the address
** it returns (the address of the destination array) as the argument to printf()
*/

   printf("Array now contains the string : %s\n" , strcpy ( destination , "Farewell" )) ;
   return 0 ;
}
```

Here, two pointers, 'd' and 's', were used to step through successive elements of both the source and destination arrays, copying each character one at a time. Program 9.10 demonstrates how strcpy() might be used in a program.

When Program 9.10 was run, the following display was produced:

```
Array now contains the string : Hello
Array now contains the string : Goodbye
Array now contains the string : Farewell
```

9.5.3 *Comparing two strings: The function* strcmp()

The function strcmp() compares two strings for equality. The comparison is performed by comparing successive and respective characters in each of its two string arguments until either a difference is found or the end of both strings is

Table 9.1 Value of integer result returned by strcmp().

Comparison	*Returned result*
s1 greater than s2	An integer value greater than 0
s1 less than s2	An integer value less than 0
s1 equivalent to s2	An integer value equal to 0

reached. Based upon this comparison, an integer result is returned, the value of which is summarized in Table 9.1.

A string 's1' is said to be greater than a string 's2' if, at the first occurrence of a differing character in the two strings, the encoded (usually ASCII) value of that differing character in 's1' is greater than the encoded value of the corresponding character in 's2'. Likewise, the string 's1' is said to be less than the string 's2' if the encoded value of that differing character in 's1' is less than the encoded value of the corresponding character in 's2'. The string 's1' is only deemed to be equivalent to 's2' if both strings are of identical length and content.

Note that if one string is a subset of the other a non-zero value is returned. Can you see why this works from the function shown in Program 9.9? (*Hint:* Think about what comparison takes place when the end of the shorter string is reached.) The function prototype for strcmp() is given below:

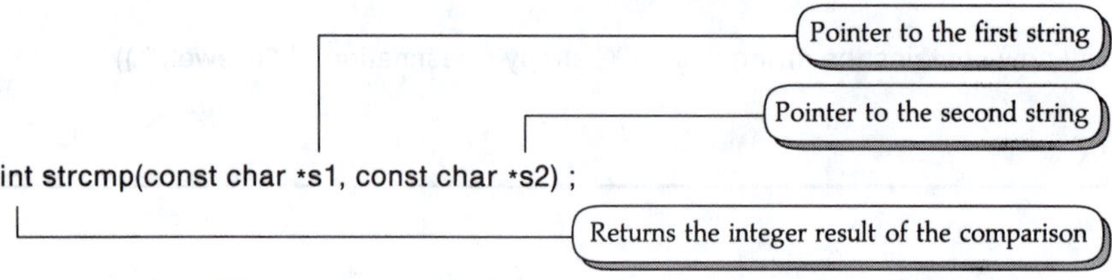

where 's1' and 's2' are pointers to the strings to be compared. Table 9.2 details the results of using strcmp() to compare several strings.

Program 9.11 shows an example of how strcmp() may have been written. If you wish to try this function for yourself, then rename it something like strcmp1() so that it does not clash with the function strcmp() defined in the standard library.

Table 9.2 Example string comparisons.

Example strcmp() call	*Result*	*Interpretation*
strcmp("Hello", "Hello") ;	0	Strings are equivalent
strcmp("Hello", "Hell") ;	> 0	"Hello" is longer than "Hell"
strcmp("Hell", "Hello") ;	> 0	"Hell" is shorter than "Hello"
strcmp("Helm", "Help") ;	< 0	'm' in "Helm" is less than 'p' in "Help"
strcmp("Sat", "Cat") ;	>0	'S' in "Sat" is greater than 'C' in "Cat"

Program 9.11 Comparing two strings: the function strcmp().

```
/*
** Function to compare two strings for equivalence
*/

int strcmp( const char *s1 , const char *s2 )
{
  int a , b ;

/*
** Start by reading two corresponding characters from each string
** and then increment the pointers s1 and s2. If the end of either string
** is encountered (that is, a '\0' is found), then break from the loop and compare
** the two characters. If both s1 and s2 are pointing to '\0's then strings
** must be identical, otherwise return difference (in codings) between the two
** characters, otherwise repeat until a difference is found
*/

  do  {
    a = *s1++ ;
    b = *s2++ ;

    if((a == '\0') || (b == '\0'))   /* a or b are pointing to end of string */
      break ;                          /* stop loop */

  }while( a == b ) ;

  return ( a - b ) ;             /* return the difference between two character codings */
}
```

In the implementation of strcmp() in Program 9.11, the difference between the encoded values of two differing characters was returned, which equates to 0 if the strings were identical. Program 9.12 demonstrates the use of strcmp() to compare several different strings. You might like to run this for yourself to verify your understanding of how this function operates.

Program 9.12 Example usage of strcmp().

```
#include   <stdio.h>
#include   <string.h>

int  main( void )
{
  char a[ BUFSIZ ], b[ BUFSIZ ] ;

  printf("Enter two text strings:\n") ;
```

```
    gets( a ) ;
    gets( b ) ;

    if( strcmp( a, b ) == 0)
      printf("\"%s\" is equivalent to \"%s\" \n", a, b ) ;

    else if( strcmp( a, b ) < 0 )
      printf("\"%s\" is less than \"%s\" \n", a, b) ;

    else
      printf("\"%s\" is greater than \"%s\"\n", a, b ) ;

    return 0 ;
}
```

One of the most common applications for string comparison lies with sorting an array of text strings into order. An example of this is given later in the chapter.

9.5.4 *String concatenation: The function* strcat()

The function **strcat()** appends or concatenates one string onto the end of another. The '\0' at the end of the destination array is overwritten by the first character of the appended string. A pointer to the first character in the destination string is then returned, should it be of any use. Note that it is the programmer's responsibility to ensure that there is sufficient storage allocated at the destination array to represent the enlarged string. The function prototype for **strcat()** is given below:

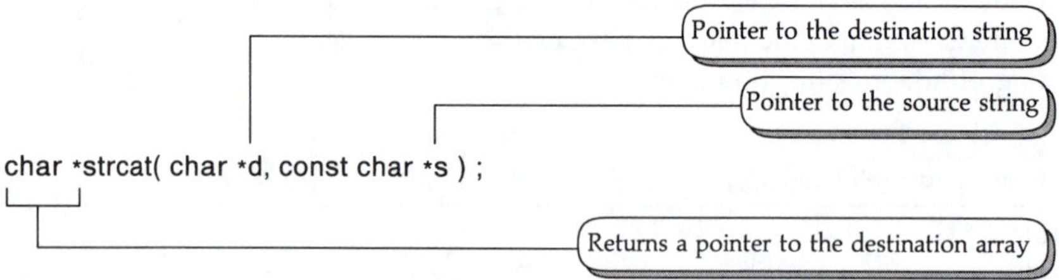

where 's' points to the string to be appended to the end of the string pointed to by 'd'. Note that as with the function **strcpy()**, it is a pointer to the start of the destination array that is given as the first argument. Figure 9.9 illustrates the effects of using **strcat()** on an array.

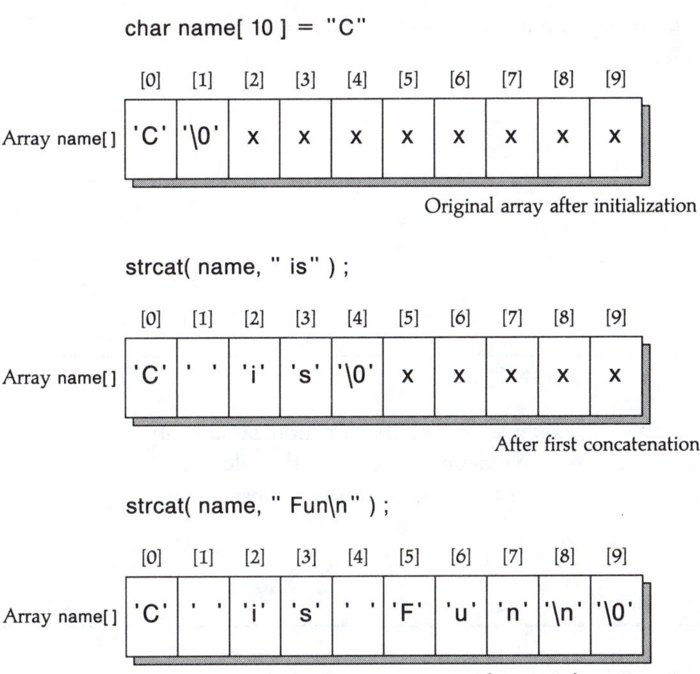

Figure 9.9 The effects of using strcat( ) on an array.

Program 9.13 shows how the function strcat() might have been implemented. If you wish to try this for yourself, then rename the function to something different such as strcat1() to avoid a name clash with the function strcat() in the standard library.

Program 9.13 Concatenating two strings: the function strcat().

```
/*
** An implementation of the function strcat() to concatenate two strings
*/

char *strcat( char *d , const char *s )
{
   char c;
   char *ptr = d ;             /* make a copy of the address of the destination array */

/* First find the end of the source string, ptr will be left pointing to the '\0' at the end */

   while (*ptr != '\0')
      ptr++ ;
```

```
/* Now copy successive characters from the source to the destination array */

    do {
      c = *s++ ;
      *ptr++ = c ;
    } while (c != '\0' ) ;

/* Return the pointer to the destination array */

    return ( d ) ;
}
```

Program 9.14 demonstrates an example use of the function strcat() in conjunction with strcpy(). Note the program's dependence upon the address of the destination arrays returned by these two functions, as they are subsequently used as the arguments in later calls.

Program 9.14 Example usage of strcat().

```
#include   <stdio.h>
#include   <string.h>

int  main( void )
{
    const  char *p1 =  "And I Think" ;
    const  char *ptr1 =  " to Myself." ;
    char   name[ BUFSIZ ] ;              /* array to hold concatenated string */

    puts( strcat( strcat( strcpy( name, p1 ), ptr1), " What a Wonderful World. " )) ;
    return 0 ;
}
```

When Program 9.14 was run, the following display was produced:

```
And I Think to Myself. What a Wonderful World.
```

9.5.5 *Character searching: The function* strchr()

The function strchr() searches a string, attempting to locate the first occurrence of a specified character. If found, a pointer to that character within the string is returned, otherwise if the string does not contain that character, a NULL pointer is returned. Note that if the specified character is '\0', then a pointer to the '\0' at the end of the string is returned. The function prototype for strchr() is given below:

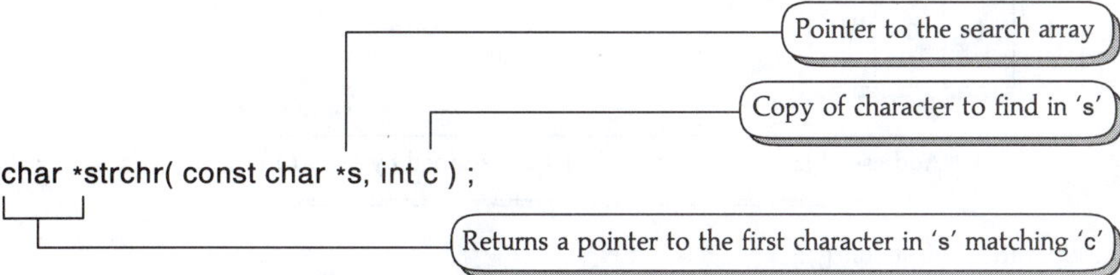

where 'c' contains the character to be located within the string pointed to by 's'. Figure 9.10 illustrates the operation of strchr() in searching for the first occurrence of the character 'l' in the string "Hello".

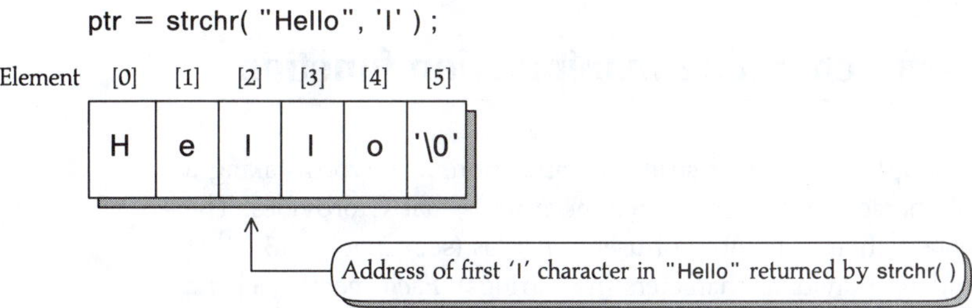

Figure 9.10 The operation of strchr( ).

9.5.6 *Reverse character searching: The function* strrchr()

The function strrchr() performs a similar operation to the function strchr(), except that it locates and returns a pointer to, or the address of, the *last* occurrence of a specified character in a string, by searching backwards for that character from the end of the string. If the string does not contain the character, a NULL pointer is returned. The function prototype for strrchr() is given below:

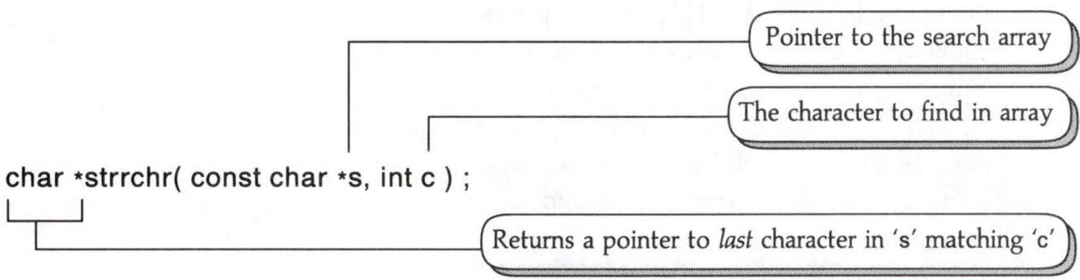

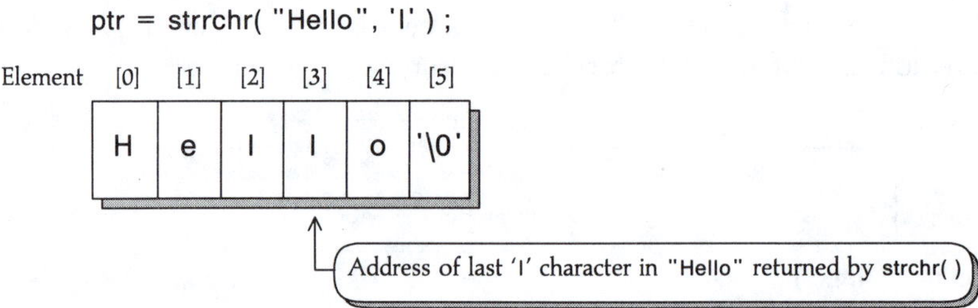

Figure 9.11 The operation of strrchr( ).

where 'c' contains the character to be located within the string pointed to by 's'. Figure 9.11 illustrates the operation of strrchr() in searching for the *last* occurrence of the character 'l' in the string "Hello".

9.6 Some useful character manipulation functions

While we are discussing the subject of string manipulation, it is worth taking a look at the range of character validation functions/macros that C provides. The header file <ctype.h> defines a number of useful macros (see Chapter 13) that may be used to validate individual characters (not strings). Each macro yields a non-zero value if the parameter 'c' passes the specified test. Table 9.3 summarizes these macros and tests.

Program 9.15 uses the macro ispunct( ) to determine and display which ASCII characters (in the range 0–7f) are considered to be punctuation characters.

Table 9.3 Commonly used character macros.

Character test	*Macro name*	*True if 'c' in range*
Alphanumeric	isalnum(c)	a–z, A–Z, 0–9
Alphabetic	isalpha(c)	a–z, A–Z
ASCII	isascii(c)	0–127
Control code	iscntrl(c)	0–31 and 127
Numeric digit	isdigit(c)	0–9
Printable character	isgraph(c)	33–126, excluding space
Lower case	islower(c)	Lower case characters
Upper case	isupper(c)	Upper case characters
Printable character	isprint(c)	32–126, including space
Punctuation	ispunct(c)	Not control or alphanumeric
White space	isspace(c)	Space, LF, tab and so on
Hex digit	isxdigit(c)	0–9, a–f, A–F

Program 9.15 A simple character test program.

```
#include   < stdio.h >
#include   < ctype.h >

int  main( void )
{
   int i;

   for ( i = 0; i <= 0x7f ; i++ )
      if( ispunct( i ) != 0)             /* if character passes ispunct( ) test */
         printf( "%c", i) ;

   putchar('\n') ;
   return 0 ;
}
```

Program 9.15 produced the following display on the author's system:

```
! " # $ % & ' ( ) * + , - . / : ; < = > ? @ [ \ ] ^ ` { | } ~
```

9.7 Case conversion functions

The standard library also includes two functions for case conversion of a character. Their prototypes are given below and can be found in the header file <ctype.h>:

```
int toupper( int c ) ;
int tolower( int c ) ;
```

Both functions convert their character parameter 'c' into its upper or lower case version, respectively, before returning the converted character back to the calling program. If the character is unsuitable for such conversion, for example the character '@', then the character is returned unaltered.

Application 9.1

Write a function to convert the text in the array pointed to by 's' into upper or lower case, depending on the parameter format, which if equivalent to 0 forces the function to convert the string to upper case. A pointer to the converted string should then be returned.

Application 9.1 A string conversion function.

```
/*
** Upper to lower or lower to upper case conversion function
*/

char *string_convert( char *s, int format )
{
   char *ptr = s ;                    /* save pointer to string */

   if( format != 0 )                  /* if format != 0, convert to lower case */
      while( *s != '\0' )
         *s++ = tolower( *s ) ;       /* function prototype in <ctype.h> */
   else
      while( *s != '\0' )
         *s++ = toupper( *s ) ;

   return (ptr) ;                     /* return pointer to converted string */
}
```

Application 9.2

Write a function to sort an array of strings, each of which may be up to 'BUFSIZ' characters in length, into ascending order.

Application 9.2 Sorting an array of strings into ascending order.

```
/*
** This function uses the bubble sort algorithm to sort an array of strings of up to
** 'BUFSIZ' elements in length by swapping the strings themselves. The
** parameter 'count' contains the number of strings in parameter 's'.
*/

void sort_array( char s[ ][ BUFSIZ ], int count)
{
   int this, next ;
   char temp[ BUFSIZ ] ;

   for( this = 0; this < count ; this ++ )
      for( next = this + 1; next < count ; next ++ )
         if( strcmp(s[this], s[next] ) > 0)  {   /* if out of order */
            strcpy(temp, s[ this ]) ;            /* copy one string to temp */
            strcpy(s[this], s[next] ) ;          /* now swap the strings over */
            strcpy(s[next], temp ) ;
         }
}
```

Application 9.3

Write a function to sort an array of pointers to strings, such that displaying the array of pointers in linear order displays the strings in ascending order.

Application 9.3 Sorting an array of pointers to strings.

```
/*
** This function uses the bubble sort algorithm to sort an array of strings by sorting
** the pointers that point to them. The parameter 'count' contains the number of
** pointers in the argument 's'.
*/

void sort_pointers( char *s[ ], int count )
{
   int this, next ;
   char *temp ;

   for( this = 0; this < count ; this ++ )
      for( next = this + 1; next < count ; next ++ )
         if( strcmp(s[this], s[next] ) > 0)  {    /* if out of order */
            temp = s[ this ] ;
            s[ this ] = s[ next ] ;               /* swap pointers */
            s[ next ] = temp ;
         }
}
```

Application 9.4

Write a function to validate a string, which should contain a name in the form 'surname.initial'. The surname may consist of several characters, but there must be at least one. The '.' and at most one 'initial' character must be present.

Application 9.4 Validating a name string.

```
/*
** Function to validate a name of the following format 'surname.initial' where
** 'surname' may consist of several characters and 'initial' is a single character.
** Both 'surname' and the 'initial' must consist of alphabetic characters in the
** range [a-z] and [A-Z].
*/

int validate_name( char *s)
{
   int length, i ;
```

```
/* Check that name contains at least three characters and save length of string */

    if((length = strlen( s )) < 3)
        return (-1) ;

/*
** Now check that the last character is alphabetic in the range
** [a-z] or [A-Z], and that penultimate character is a '.'
*/

    if(s[length - 2] != '.' || ( ! isalpha( s[length - 1] )))
        return (-1) ;

/* Check that all characters up to the penultimate character are also alphabetic */

    for( i = 0; i < length - 2; i ++)
        if(!isalpha( s[i] ))
            return (-1);

/* If we get this far, string must be in correct format */

    return 0 ;
}
```

Application 9.5

Write a function to convert a name of the form 'surname.initial' such that 'initial' and the first character of 'surname' are upper case. All other characters in 'surname' are to be converted to lower case.

Application 9.5 Name conversion.

```
/*
** Function to convert a string of the form 'surname.initial'
** into the form 'Surname.Initial'
*/

void convert (char *s)
{
    *s++ = toupper( *s ) ;          /* convert first character to upper case */

/* Convert the rest of the surname, up to the '.', to lower case */

    while ( *s != '.' )
        *s++ = tolower( *s ) ;

    s++;                            /* skip over the '.' */

    *s = toupper( *s ) ;            /* convert initial to upper case */
}
```

9.8 Chapter summary

(1) An implicit constant string is introduced by enclosing text within quotation marks, such as:

```
"Hello One and All"
```

All strings are represented internally by hidden single dimensional arrays of characters terminated by the NULL character '\0'.

(2) A variable (non-constant) string can be created using a char array. It may be initialized with text in the manner shown below, where the size of message is implicitly assumed by the compiler:

```
char message[ ] = "A Simple String" ;
```

Although such a string is variable and may be altered, there is insufficient storage allocated within an implicitly sized array to permit any additional characters to be appended to the string. To overcome this, the size of the array could be explicitly stated, for example:

```
char message[100] = "A Simple String" ;
```

(3) A constant string could also be created using a pointer, as shown below. Here, the only variable is the pointer 's1'; everything else is constant:

```
const char *s1 = "Hello One and All" ;
```

(4) A char pointer may also be used to access a non-constant string, as shown below. Here 's1' points to the first character in the text string message:

```
char *s1 = "message" ;
```

(5) Any implicit text string can always be replaced by an array initialized with the same text, or a pointer to an equivalent text string.

(6) An array of strings may be created using either a two-dimensional array of char or an array of pointers to char, as shown below:

```
const char months[ ][ 4 ] = { "Jan", "Feb", "Mar", . . . , "Dec" } ;
const char *months[ ] = { "Jan", "Feb", "Mar", . . . , "Dec" } ;
```

(7) It does not make sense to use the C operators '=', '<', '>', '+' and so on to assign, compare or append two text strings since the program will in effect be attempting to assign, compare or add two addresses, not the text strings themselves. These operations must be dealt with by the program code or by functions in the standard library.

(8) A string may be traversed by stepping a pointer along each character until the '\0' is encountered, for example:

```
while(*ptr++ != '\0')
   . . .
```

(9) The functions strcpy(), strcat() and strcmp() permit, respectively, the copying, appending and comparison of two text strings. The function strlen() determines the length of a string, while strchr() and strrchr() permit the first and last occurrence of a character to be located within a string.

Other string functions are also provided, and are discussed in Chapter 18. All function prototypes for string manipulation functions may be found in the header file <string.h>.

(10) Command line arguments and program environment settings are available to the program if the function header for main() is defined as:

```
int main( int argc, char *argv[ ], char *envp[ ])
```

argc contains the integer number of command line arguments present as strings within argv, while envp contains pointers to the program environment parameters. The last pointer in envp is a NULL pointer.

(11) The header file <ctype.h> contains many simple macros to determine the type of a character, such as isupper() and islower(), as well as function prototypes for the case conversion functions toupper() and tolower().

9.9 Exercises

9.1 What are the differences between the following three representations of the text string "Paul" shown below in terms of:

- **(a)** What variables and constants are created?
- **(b)** Where the text strings reside at run time, in the program or variable section?
- **(c)** The program's ability to alter the string, in other words whether the various strings are constant or variable and how and when they are initialized/created?

```
"Paul"
char  name[ ] = "Paul" ;
char  *name = "Paul" ;
```

9.2 Compile and run the following program and explain what you see.

```
#include   stdio.h >

void  display( void )
{
   char text[ ] = "Hello" ;
   puts( text ) ;                  /* display the text string */
   text[4] = '\0';                 /* change the last letter of string */
   puts( text ) ;                  /* display the text string */
}
```

```
int main( void )
{
  display( ) ;
  display( ) ;
  return 0 ;
}
```

Now change the definition of the array text in display( ) above so that it is now a char pointer, that is:

```
char *text = "Hello" ;
```

Does the program behave in the same way? Explain this. On some machines the latter version of the program may not run at all. Explain why not and identify what is fundamentally wrong with the new program.

9.3 Discuss the benefits of using an array of pointers to text strings rather than a two-dimensional char array to record and sort up to 'n' strings of varying length.

9.4 The standard library defines many string manipulation functions over and above those discussed in this chapter. A description of these can be found in Chapter 18. Write your own functions to emulate the following standard library functions:

strchr( ), strrchr( ), strncmp( ), strstrpbrk( ), strcspn( ), strcspn( ), strstr( )

9.5 A simple word processor is designed to be invoked from the operating system shell with a command of the form:

```
wp [options] filename
```

where [options] may be any of the following:

-p=pagelength	where pagelength specifies the integer number of lines per page
-t=title	where title is an optional text string to be printed at the top of each page
-w=width	where width specifies the width of the paper in characters
-m=margin	where margin specifies the left and right margins in characters

Write a program to recognize those options specified and to extract the various parameters associated with them.

9.6 Using the character validation macros defined in the header file <ctype.h>, write a program to verify that a filename consists entirely of characters in the range:

A-Z, _, +, –, 0-9

9.7 In Section 9.2 two pairs of functions called string_length( ) were presented. Taking either pair, compare their operation in terms of their relative speed and size of compiled code.

9.8 Write a program to convert a string of characters into Morse code. The following table of Morse codes should prove useful:

A ._	J .___	S ...	1 .____
B _...	K _._	T _	2 ..___
C _._.	L ._..	U .._	3 ...__
D _..	M __	V ..._	4 ...._
E .	N _.	W .__	5 .....
F .._.	O ___	X _.._	6 _....
G __.	P .__.	Y _.__	7 __...
H	Q __._	Z __._	8 ___..
I ..	R ._.	0 _____	9 ____.

9.9 Write a simple program to encrypt a text string using a look-up table or simple algorithm; for example, the text string "Hello World" could be encrpyted into the string "Ifmmp Xpqme" simply by translating each character into its next character in the alphabet – a becomes b, x becomes y and so on.

9.10 Write a program to translate simple words written in, say, English to another language such as French or German.

9.11 Write a function to emulate the standard library function atoi( ).

10 Advanced Pointer Concepts

In this chapter, we take a look at some of the more advanced aspects of pointers and their declarations, in particular, the use of pointers to access multi-dimensional arrays and the concept of a pointer to a pointer and a pointer to a function. The reader is encouraged to study this chapter only after the 'basics' of Chapter 8 have been fully absorbed and understood. Alternatively, readers may choose to defer the study of this material until a later time when they have gained more experience and feel more at ease with the concept of pointers, for it is not until Chapter 17 that some of the material presented here will be required again.

10.1 Accessing multi-dimensional arrays with pointers

We have already seen in Chapter 7 that the introduction of a multi-dimensional array allows the programmer to emulate more closely the physical characteristics of the object being modelled, for example a two-dimensional array to represent a chess board, and that such a representation ultimately improves the readability and understanding of the code, with a corresponding reduction in programming errors. Now, as you will recall, the compiler ultimately arranges for all multi-dimensional arrays to be stored successively in memory, one row after another, as if they were one large single dimensional array. Consider, then, for a moment the definition of the two-dimensional array 'y' shown below:

```
int y[ 4 ][ 5 ] ;
```

Assuming that this array is stored in memory commencing at address 1000, then each of the 20 elements within it will be stored at the (decimal) addresses shown in Figure 10.1, assuming 2 byte integers.

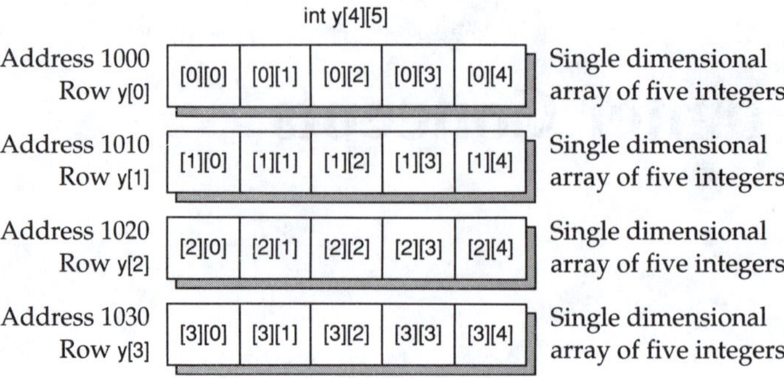

Figure 10.1 A two-dimensional array of four by five integers.

We have already seen how the application of two consecutive array operators as in the expression 'y[2][3]' may be used to access the integer element at the intersection of row 2 and column 3, but have not perhaps fully understood or appreciated the mechanism by which the compiler applies these operators to determine the actual address of that element. Furthermore, you may not have previously considered the effect of using a single array operator to partially reference a multi-dimensional array. For example, what is the effect of an expression such as 'y[2]' and what is the type and value of its result?

These and other questions will now be answered, since they are important for an understanding of how multi-dimensional arrays may be allocated dynamically (using malloc(), calloc() and so on) and how they may be passed as arguments to functions and accessed via pointers.

From Chapters 8 and 9, you will recall that elements of a single dimensional int array 'y' could be accessed using a simple int pointer 'p1', which has been previously initialized with the address of the first element in 'y' with an expression such as 'p1 = y' or 'p1 = &y[0]'. Thus, 'p1' can be thought of as pointing to the first element in 'y'. After this a variety of methods exist to access any element within 'y'. For example, the indirection operator '*', coupled with an offset 'n', as in the expression '*(p1 + n)', could be applied, to reference the nth element within 'y'.

Alternatively we could apply the array operator '[]' to the pointer to achieve the same effect with an expression such as 'p1[n]', demonstrating once again that the array operator '[]' in conjunction with an integer subscript 'n' is nothing more than a convenient shorthand way of expressing pointer indirection plus offset; in other words, the expressions 'p1[n]' and '*(p1 + n)' are equivalent. Finally, the pointer 'p1' could of course be stepped through the array and made to point to successive elements with a statement such as 'a = *p1++;' all of which rely upon 'p1' having a scalar value equal to the size of each element in the array, 2 in this example.

We also know that accessing an 'm' dimensional array requires the use of 'm' array operators '[]' to fully reference the array and allow access to an individual element within it. Given our previous knowledge that each '[n]' operator is translated by the compiler into an equivalent expression of the form '*(p1 + n)' (provided 'p1' points to the first element in 'y'), and that the array operator is evaluated left to right, it follows that the two expressions below, where 'p1' has been initialized to point to the array 'y', are equivalent:

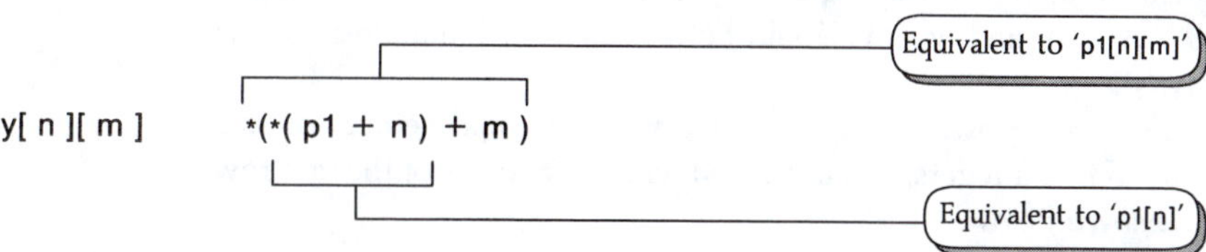

In other words, two successive array operators are translated by the compiler into two pointer indirection operations with corresponding offsets. Given that the expressions 'p1[z]' and '*(p1 + z)' are interchangeable, we note that any of the expressions in Table 10.1 are also equivalent when it comes to accessing elements within 'y'.

The first and last notations in the table are both interesting and important since they imply that once a pointer has been initialized to point to an array, then the array operator '[]' may be applied either to the array name itself or to a pointer to that array with the same net effect.

The expression '*(*(y + n) + m)' is also interesting, as it once again demonstrates that the name of an array is simply a shorthand notation for the address of the first element in the array. Thus, the expression 'y' – the name of the array – can be thought of as resolving to a pointer, initialized with the base address of the array 'y', and thus pointer notation can be applied equally to 'y'. Of course we have not yet discussed how the pointer 'p1' should be defined. To understand this, we shall, once again, have to think carefully about the scalar value associated with a pointer.

Table 10.1 Equivalent expressions for accessing the array 'y'.

Expression	*Interpretation*
y[n][m]	Pure array notation used with the array 'y'
((p1+n) + m)	Pointer offset plus indirection used with 'p1'
*(p1[n] + m)	Mixture of pointer offset plus indirection and array notation used with 'p1'
(*(p1 + n))[m]	Different mixture of pointer offset plus indirection and array notation used with 'p1'
((y+n) + m)	Pointer offset plus indirection used with array 'y'
*(y[n] + m)	Mixture of pointer offset plus indirection and array notation used with array 'y'
(*(y + n))[m]	Different mixture of pointer offset plus indirection and array notation used with array 'y'
p1[n][m]	Pure array notation used with the pointer 'p1'

You will recall that the scalar value of any pointer is simply the size of the object that it points to. If 'p1' could be given a scalar value equal to the size of a row within array 'y' – that is, if it possessed a scalar value given by the expression 'sizeof(int) * 5' (remember 'y' is an array of four rows, where each row is a single dimensional array of five integers, as shown in Figure 10.1) – then incrementing 'p1' would allow us to step it through the array, one row at a time. Furthermore, the expressions '(p1 + n)' and 'y + n' would both resolve to the address of the nth row of array 'y'.

To ensure that 'p1' possesses such a scalar value, it could be defined as a pointer to an array of five integers, and initialized with the address of the first row in 'y' (row 0), as shown below:

```
int (*p1)[ 5 ] = y ;
```

where of course the expression 'y' is equivalent to the expression '&y[0]', that is, the address of the first row in 'y', a single dimensional array of 5 integers. Notice how parentheses were required around 'p1' during its definition. Without these, 'p1' would have been defined as an array of 5 pointers to int, which is not the same thing at all. Alternatively, 'p1' could have been initialized to point to the nth row in 'y' with a statement such as 'p1 = y + n', which is illustrated in Figure 10.2.

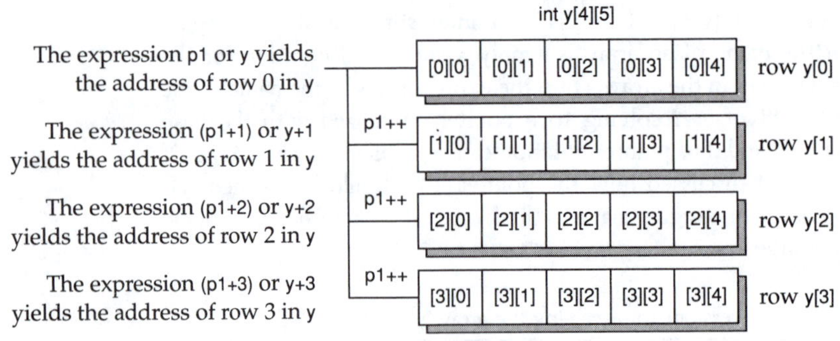

Figure 10.2 Accessing rows within a two-dimensional array.

Now, given that 'p1' points to the first row within 'y' – that is, a single dimensional array of five integers – applying the indirection operator '*' to 'p1' yields the address of the first element in that row. Looking at it in another way, it yields a pointer to the first element (although no separate pointer variable exists as such) with a scalar value equal to the size of an int.

Therefore the expression *(p1 + 3)' (which could also have been written as 'p1[3]' or 'y[3]') yields the address of, or an int pointer to, the first element in row 3 of 'y' – that is, the address of element 'y[3][0]'. If required, this address could be assigned to an actual int pointer, 'p2', with any of the four statements given opposite:

```
p2 = *( p1 + 3 ) ;
p2 = p1[ 3 ] ;
p2 = *( y + 3 ) ;
p2 = y[ 3 ] ;
```

Because 'p2' now points to the first integer element within row 3 of 'y' (as shown in Figure 10.3) the expression '(p2 + n)' resolves to the address of the nth integer element within that row, and thus the expression '*(p2 + n)' or 'p2[n]' fully references the array 'y' and yields the value of the integer element 'y[2][n]'.

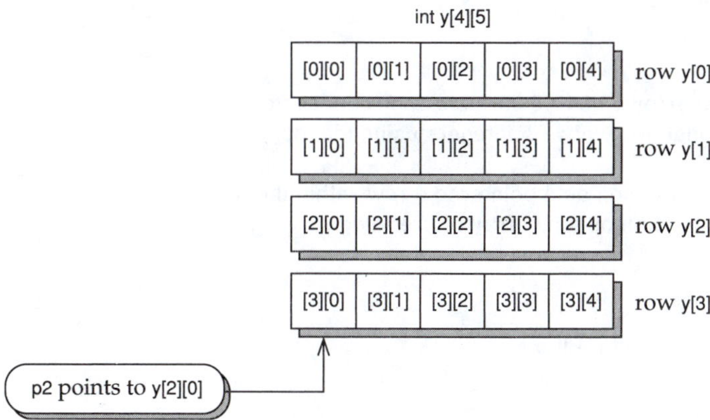

Figure 10.3 Pointer 'p2' pointing to the first element in row 2 of 'y'.

We can see the application of these ideas put into practice in Program 10.1, which defines a two-dimensional array 'y' of four rows of five integers. Storage for a second array of identically sized dimensions (four rows of five integers) is then requested using the memory allocation function malloc( ). The address of this dynamically allocated array is assigned to the pointer 'ptr', which has been suitably defined to give it the correct scalar value to allow it to point to a row within that requested array. Elements from both arrays are then initialized with incremental values, prior to being displayed via a call to the function display_array( ).

Notice how the parameter within display_array( ) has been declared to enable it to point to a row within the array 'y' or the array pointed to by 'ptr'; it could also have been declared using pure array notation as 'int p1[ ][5]', which, as we have seen before, simply disguises the fact that the parameter is really a pointer.

Program 10.1 Accessing two-dimensional arrays using pointers.

```
#include  <stdio.h>
#include  <stdlib.h>

void  display_array( int (*p1)[ 5 ] )
{
   int i, j ;
```

```
    for( i = 0; i < 4; i ++ )  {
        for( j = 0; j < 5 ; j ++ )
            printf(" %2d ", p1[ i ][ j ]) ;
        putchar( '\n' ) ;
    }
    putchar( '\n' ) ;
}

int main( void )
{
    int i, j, k = 0 ;

/*
** Define a two-dimensional array y of 4 * 5 integers and request storage
** for another two-dimensional array of 4 * 5 integers using malloc( )
**
** Note how the pointer ptr is defined as a pointer to a row within the array;
** that is, a pointer to a single dimensional array of five integers
*/

    int y[ 4 ][ 5 ] ;
    int (*ptr)[ 5 ] = malloc( sizeof( int [ 4 ][ 5 ] )) ;

    for( i = 0; i < 4; i++ )
        for( j = 0; j < 5; j ++ )
            ptr[ i ][ j ] = y[ i ][ j ] = k++ ;

    display_array( ptr ) ;
    display_array( y ) ;

    return 0 ;
}
```

On the author's system, Program 10.1 produced the following display:

```
 0   1   2   3   4
 5   6   7   8   9
10  11  12  13  14
15  16  17  18  19

 0   1   2   3   4
 5   6   7   8   9
10  11  12  13  14
15  16  17  18  19
```

As an exercise, you might like to modify Program 10.1 to verify that the expressions 'ptr[i][j]' and 'p1[i][j]' can in fact be replaced by the expressions '*(*(ptr + i) + j)' and '*(*(p1 + i) + j)', respectively, or indeed by any suitable combination of the expressions given in Table 10.1. You might also like to change the declaration of 'p1' in display_array() to 'int p1[ ][5]', that is, a two-dimensional array of integers, and observe that it makes no difference to the compiler or program.

Program 10.2 demonstrates an alternative way in which the function display_array() could have been written and relies upon incrementing the pointer 'p1' to point to each successive row (a single dimensional array of five integers) within its array argument. At each stage the address of the first element in that row is assigned to a second pointer 'p2', which is itself incremented along the row until the last integer element in that row is displayed. It might help to refer to Figures 10.2 and 10.3 when following this.

Program 10.2 An alternative function to display an array of 4 × 5 integers.

```
void  display_array( int (*p1)[ 5 ] )
{
    int  i, j , *p2 ;                    /* a simple pointer to an integer */

    for( i = 0 ; i < 4; i ++ )  {

/*
** Now assign the address of the first integer element in the row pointed to by
** p1 to the int pointer p2, and then increment p1 to point to the next row
*/

        p2 = *p1++ ;
        for( j = 0; j < 5 ; j ++ )
            printf(" %2d ", *p2++) ;

        putchar('\n') ;
    }
}
```

Taking this discussion further, we could apply the same principles to an array with any number of dimensions. For example, Program 10.3 initializes and displays a four-dimensional array of 2 * 3 * 4 * 5 doubles. The parameter 'p1' within display_array() is suitably declared to allow it to point to a row within a four-dimensional array, where each row is of course a three-dimensional array of 3 * 4 * 5 doubles and thus possesses a scalar value given by the expression 'sizeof(double) * 3 * 4 * 5'.

Once again, the reader might like to verify that the expression 'ptr[i][j][k][l]' could have been written as '*(*(*(*(ptr + i) + j) + k) + l)' and

Program 10.3 Manipulating a four-dimensional array.

```
#include  <stdio.h>
#include  <stdlib.h>

void  display_array( double (*p1)[ 3 ][ 4 ][ 5 ] )
{
   int  i, j, k, l ;

   for( i = 0; i < 2; i++ )
      for( j = 0; j < 3; j++ )
         for( k = 0; k < 4; k++ )
            for( l = 0; l < 5 ; l++ )
               printf("%g ", p1[ i ][ j ][ k ][ l ] ) ;
   putchar( '\n' ) ;
}

int  main( void )
{
   int       i, j, k, l ;
   double  num = 0.0 ;

/*
** Define a four-dimensional array z and a pointer to a row within
** a four-dimensional array. Then allocate storage for a second four-
** dimensional array and assign the address to ptr, which will then point
** to the first row in that array.
*/

   double  z[ 2 ][ 3 ][ 4 ][ 5 ] ;
   double  (*ptr)[ 3 ][ 4 ][ 5 ] = malloc( sizeof( double [ 2 ][ 3 ][ 4 ][ 5 ] )) ;

/* Initialize each element in both arrays with an incremental number */

   for( i = 0; i < 2; i++ )
      for( j = 0; j < 3; j++ )
         for( k = 0; k < 4; k++ )
            for( l = 0; l < 5 ; l++ ) {
               z[ i ][ j ][ k ][ l ] = ptr[ i ][ j ][ k ][ l ] = num++ ;
            }

   display_array( z ) ;             /* display the elements in z */
   display_array( ptr ) ;           /* display the elements in dynamic requested array */
   return 0 ;
}
```

that likewise the expression 'z[i][j][k][l]' could have been written as '*(*(*(*(z + i) + j) + k) + l)'. Also, the declaration of 'p1' in display_array() could have been declared as 'double p1[ ][3][4][5]'.

Program 10.4 shows how the function display_array() from Program 10.3 could have been written along similar lines to that of Program 10.2, where several pointers have been incremented along their respective rows. The pointer parameter 'ptr' is still a pointer to a three-dimensional array and thus points to a row within the original four-dimensional array passed to it.

The expression 'p1 = ptr[i]' (or the expression 'p1 = *(ptr + i)') assigns 'p1' the address of the first element within the ith row of the original array. This element is of course a two-dimensional array of four by five doubles. The expression 'p2 = p1[j]' (or the expression 'p2 = *(p1 + j)') assigns 'p2' the address of the first element in the jth row of the row pointed to by 'p1'. This element is a single dimensional array of five doubles.

The expression 'p3 = p2[k]' (or the expression 'p3 = *(p2 + k)') assigns 'p3' the address of the first element (a double) within a single dimensional array of doubles within the row pointed to by 'p2', while the expression 'p3[l]' (or '*(p3 + l)') fully references the array and accesses a unique double within the array; that is, array element '[i][j][k][l]'.

These pointer declarations and the expressions that relate to them in Program 10.4 are summarized in Table 10.2.

Program 10.4 Displaying a four-dimensional array using multiple pointers.

```
void display_array( double (*ptr)[ 3 ][ 4 ][ 5 ] )
{
  int i, j, k, l ;

  double (*p1)[ 4 ][ 5 ] ;       /* pointer to two-dimensional array of 4 * 5 doubles */
  double (*p2)[ 5 ] ;            /* pointer to an array of 5 doubles */
  double *p3 ;                   /* pointer to a double */

  for( i = 0; i < 2; i++)  {
    p1 = ptr[ i ] ;
    for( j = 0; j < 3; j++ )  {
      p2 = p1[ j ] ;
      for( k = 0; k < 4; k++ )  {
        p3 = p2[ k ] ;
        for( l = 0; l < 5 ; l++ )  {
          printf("%g ", p3[ l ]) ;
        }
      }
    }
  }
}
```

Table 10.2 Explanation of pointer declarations used in Program 10.4.

Pointer declaration	*Interpretation*
double (*ptr)[j][k][l]	ptr is a pointer to a three-dimensional array of double, with a scalar value equal to (sizeof(double) * j * k * l). The expressions ptr[a] or *(ptr + a) reference the ath row within the array pointed to by ptr and yield the address of the first two-dimensional array of double within it.
double (*p1)[k][l]	p1 is a pointer to a two-dimensional array of double, with a scalar value equal to (sizeof(double) * k * l). The expressions p1[b] or *(p1 + b) reference the bth row within the array pointed to by p1 and yield the address of the first single dimensional array of double within it.
double (*p2)[l]	p2 is a pointer to a single dimensional array of double, with a scalar value equal to (sizeof(double) * l). The expressions p2[c] or *(p2 + c) reference the cth row within the array pointed to by p2 and yield the address of the first element within it, a double.
double *p3	p3 is a pointer to a double, with a scalar value equal to sizeof(double). The expressions p3[d] or *(p3 + d) reference the dth element (a double) and yield its value.

10.2 Pointers to pointers

A particularly interesting type of pointer is the pointer to pointer – that is, a pointer that can be initialized with the address of another pointer. For example, 'p2' below has been defined as a pointer to an int pointer, and as such has a scalar value equal to the size of, or storage requirements of, an int pointer on that system:

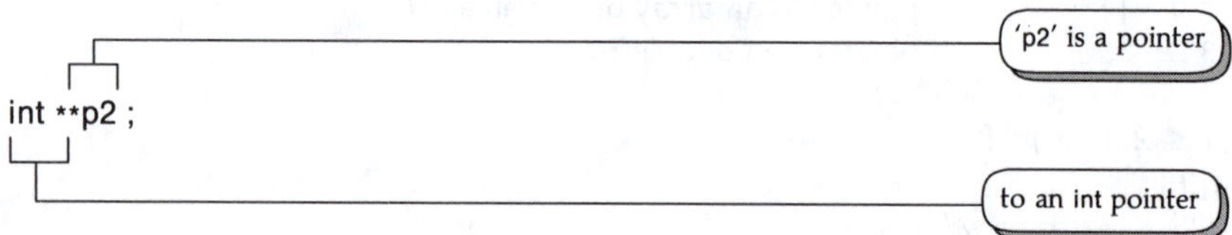

Given that an int pointer 'p1' already exists, initialized with the address of the int variable 'i', the address of 'p1' could be assigned to 'p2' with the following statement:

```
p2 = &p1 ;
```

Now 'p2' can be thought of as pointing to the int pointer 'p1', which in turn points to the int variable 'i', an arrangement which is illustrated in Figure 10.4, where, again, arbitrary addresses have been assumed.

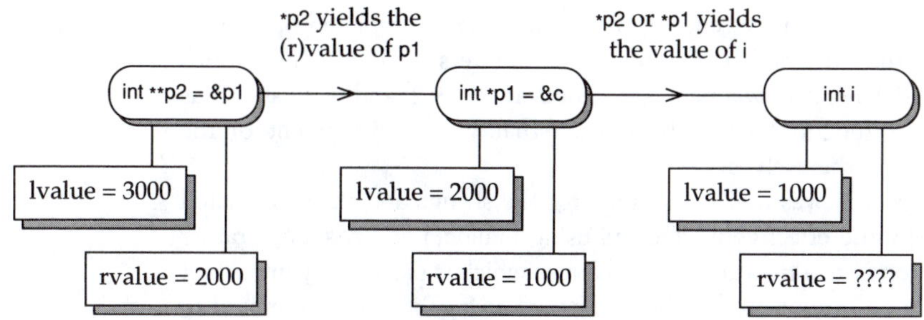

Figure 10.4 Memory model illustrating a pointer 'p2' to an int pointer 'p1'.

The variable 'i' could now be accessed in one of three ways, directly with an expression of the form 'i = 5', indirectly using the pointer 'p1' with an expression such as '*p1 = 5' or alternatively via *two* levels of indirection using an expression of the form '**p2 = 5'.

We can extend this idea of multi-level indirection to virtually any depth required, limited only by the programmer's ability to make sense of it all. For example, we could define a third pointer 'p3', defined as a pointer to a pointer to an int pointer, and initialize it with the address of the previous pointer 'p2' with the statement below:

```
int  ***p3 = &p2 ;
```

which would then allow the variable 'i' to be accessed via three levels of indirection using an expression such as '***p3 = 5'. Table 10.3 summarizes the effect of applying a varying number of indirection operators to each of the previous pointers.

Table 10.3 Multi-level indirection.

Expression	*References*	*Expression*	*References*
*p3	p2	*p2	p1
**p3	p1	**p2	i
***p3	i	*p1	i

10.2.1 *Applications for pointers to pointers*

One of the most common applications for pointers to pointers lies with the creation of dynamically sizeable arrays. For example, we saw in Chapter 9 that a number of strings could be represented either by a two-dimensional array of char, or by a single dimensional array of char pointers, initialized to point to each string.

The latter approach was generally favoured since it simplified operations such as sorting the strings because only the pointers and not the strings themselves would have to swapped (see Applications 9.2 and 9.3) and thus generic string sort functions could be written that were independent of the lengths of the strings themselves.

A further benefit was that the storage for the strings and their associated pointers could be more effectively allocated using malloc() and realloc(), rather than attempting to resize a two-dimensional array, which is particularly important when the application cannot predict the number of strings it will be required to work with at the outset.

As an example of this, and to demonstrate the use of pointers to pointers, let us write a program to read in an unknown number of text strings, such as the names on a mailing list, then redisplay them back to the operator. The end of the data is to be signified by the operator simulating the end-of-file status from their keyboard (<control-D> under UNIX, <control-Z> under MS-DOS). This will allow the program to have its input redirected from a disk file later. The complete program is given in Program 10.5.

Program 10.5 Dynamically sizing an array of pointers to char.

```
#include  <stdio.h>
#include  <stdlib.h>
#include  <string.h>

int  main( void )
{
  int    i, n ;
  char  buff[ BUFSIZ ] ;
                                                    Define 's', a pointer to a char pointer

  char **s  =  malloc( sizeof( char * )) ;
                                                    Request storage for one char pointer

/*
** Read strings into the array 'buff' until EOF detected
** then resize the array of pointers pointed to by 's' to increase its size
** to 'n + 1' pointers
*/

  for( n = 0; gets( buff ) != NULL; n++ )  {
    s = realloc( s, ((n + 1) * sizeof(char *))) ;
                                                    Resize the array of pointers pointed to by 's'
/*
** Now allocate sufficient storage for the new string plus one byte for the '\0',
** then copy the string from the array 'buff' to the new storage area.
*/
```

```
        s[n] = malloc( strlen( buff) + 1 ) ;
        strcpy( s[ n ], buff ) ;
    }                   Access the value of the nth pointer in the array

/*
** Now display each string in turn
*/

    for( i = 0; i < n; i ++ )
        puts( s[ i ]) ;
                        Access the value of the ith pointer in the array
    return 0 ;
}
```

Notice how the pointer 's' was defined as a pointer to a char pointer. Storage for a single char pointer, that is, an array of 1 char pointer is initially allocated using malloc() at the start of the program and is used to point to the first text string read by the program.

The heart of the program is based around a for loop, which reads, allocates storage for and copies one string at a time from the input device (assumed to be the operator's keyboard unless input has been redirected) to an area of memory allocated by malloc(). As each new text string is read, the array of pointers (pointed to by 's') is resized using realloc() to add one further pointer, an arrangement which is shown in Figure 10.5.

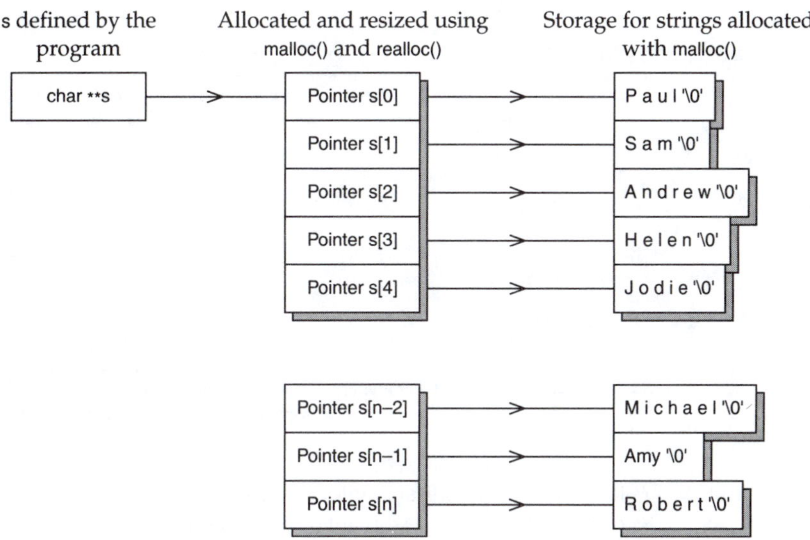

Figure 10.5 Dynamically allocating an array of pointers and strings.

Notice how the notation 's[i]' was used in the program. You will recall from Section 10.1 that this is simply a shorthand notation for, and is thus equivalent to, the expression '*(s + i)', and as 's' has a scalar value equal to the size of a char pointer, the expression yields the value of the ith char pointer in the array pointed to by 's'. Thus the expression 'puts(s[i])' presents puts() with the *value* of the ith pointer in the array of pointers pointed to by 's', and the value of this pointer is the address of the ith string read by the program, which is consequently displayed.

Having now written a program able to accept a virtually unlimited number of text strings, let us now modify the quicksort algorithm developed in Chapter 8 to sort the strings before redisplaying them. In the interests of efficiency, especially as all strings are not guaranteed to be of the same length, the algorithm swaps the pointers to the strings, rather than the strings themselves.

An implementation of this algorithm as a function is given in Program 10.6, which could be called by Program 10.5 with a statement of the form 'string_sort(&s[0], &s[n−1]);'.

Program 10.6 Sorting an array of pointers to strings.

```
/*
** This implementation of quicksort expects to be passed the addresses
** of the first and last pointers in the array of pointers to strings to be sorted
*/

#include   <stddef.h>          /* for data type ptrdiff_t */

/* Function to swap two pointers to char */

                                  Parameters declared as pointers to char pointers

void  swap_ptr( char **left, char **right )
{
    char       *temp ;

    temp = *left ;
    *left = *right ;
    *right = temp ;
}

                                  Parameters declared as pointers to char pointers

void  string_sort( char **first, char **last )
{
    char       **left = first ;      /* left set to point to first pointer in partition */
    char       **right = last ;      /* right set to point to last pointer in partition */
    char       *pivot_ptr ;
    ptrdiff_t  p_diff ;
```

```
/*
** choose a pivot pointer value equal to the value of the
** middle pointer in the array/partition to be sorted
*/

   p_diff = (right – left) / 2 ;        /* the number of elements in the array / 2 */
   pivot_ptr = *( left + p_diff ) ;
```

Extract the value of the middle pointer from the array

```
/*
** Now partition the current array of pointers into two smaller
** partitions each of which can be sorted in turn
*/

   while( left <= right )  {         /* while pointers have not crossed */

/*
** By moving forwards, find the first/next pointer in the partition
** which points to a string which is considered to be greater than or equal
** to the string pointed to by the pivot pointer
*/
```

Compare the strings pointed to by left and pivot_ptr

```
      while( strcmp(*left, pivot_ptr ) < 0)
         left++ ;
```

Increment left to next pointer in array

```
/*
** By moving backwards, find the first/next pointer in the partition
** which points to a string which is considered to be less than or equal
** to the string pointed to by the pivot pointer
*/
```

Compare the strings pointed to by right and pivot_ptr

```
      while( strcmp(*right, pivot_ptr ) > 0 )
         right-- ;
```

Decrement right to previous pointer in array

```
/*
** If the left pointer has overtaken the right pointer then the array must
** have been partitioned, otherwise the two strings pointed to by 'left' and 'right'
** must be out of order, so swap them and move the pointers on by one pointer
*/

      if( left <= right )  {
         swap_ptr( left, right ) ;
         left ++ ;
         right -- ;
      }
   }
```

Swap the pointers pointed to by left and right

```
/* Provided there are at least two pointers in each partition sort each (recursively ) */

    if( first < right )
        string_sort( first, right ) ;      /* sort left partition */

    if( left < last )
        string_sort( left, last ) ;        /* sort right partition */
}
```

One last application of pointers to pointers worth mentioning is their use in relation to the declaration of the parameters argv and envp to the function main( ) (see Chapter 9). You will recall that both of these parameters have until now been declared as arrays of pointers to char, which were given to main( ) by the operating system when the program was run. The example function header below illustrates this:

```
int   main( int argc, char *argv[ ], char *envp[ ])
```

Realizing, of course, that all arrays in C, which includes the parameters argv and envp, are passed to a function by reference (that is, it is the address of their first element that is given to the function, which in the case of argv and envp is the address of their first char pointer), allows us to declare the parameters to main( ) in the manner shown below:

```
int   main( int argc, char **argv, char **envp)
```

Of course this alternative declaration does not affect the way the rest of the program is written, and simply demonstrates once again that an array declaration as a parameter to a function is simply an alias for a pointer, a fact that can be verified easily by incrementing argv, an operation which occurs frequently in many applications written by more experienced programmers.

10.3 Pointers to functions

One final and particularly useful type of pointer is the function pointer. What you may not have appreciated thus far is that a function's name is (once again!) simply a shorthand notation, or alias, for the address of that function. Such an address may be thought of notionally as the address of the first statement in that function; thus, given the statement:

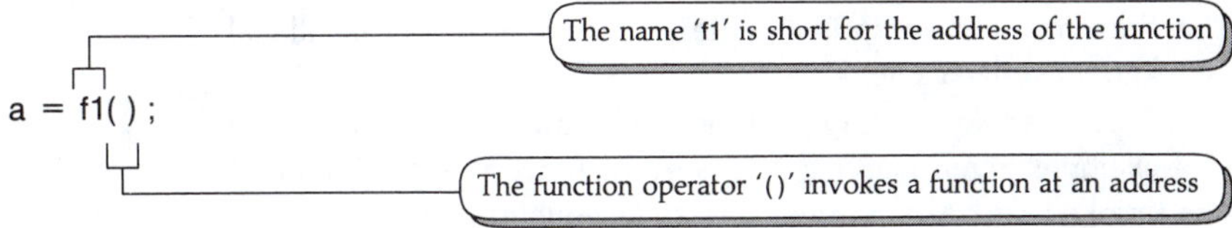
The name 'f1' is short for the address of the function
a = f1( ) ;
The function operator '()' invokes a function at an address

the expression 'f1' resolves to the address of the function 'f1', while the function invocation operator '()' is simply a convenient means of invoking a function based upon its address. It follows from this that we should be able to assign the address of a function to a pointer, and via the application of the '()' operator, invoke that function via the pointer. This is indeed the case. For example, given the function prototype for the function sin() as:

```
double sin( double ) ;
```

we could define and initialize a pointer to function 'p1' to point to sin() with the statement shown below, where 'p1' is defined as a 'pointer to a function expecting a single argument of type double and returning a double', which is consistent with the definition of the function that it now points to:

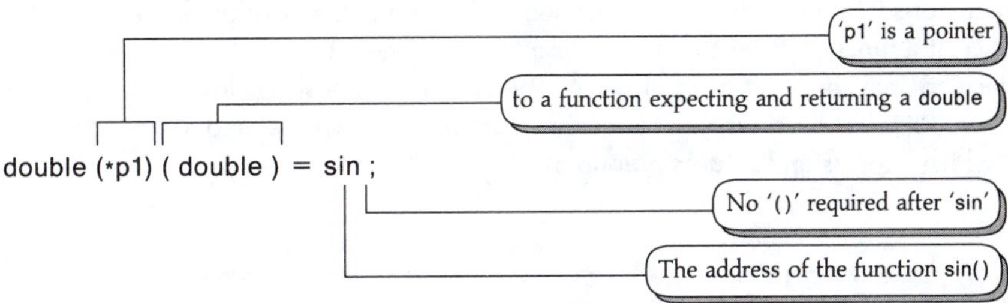
'p1' is a pointer
to a function expecting and returning a double
double (*p1) (double) = sin ;
No '()' required after 'sin'
The address of the function sin()

Notice how 'p1' was assigned the address of the function sin(). Parentheses or the address operator '&' were *not* required and must not be used after the name of the function whose address we are taking, since the expression sin is the address of that function – that is, it is a shorthand notation. If parentheses *were* placed after the function name, such as 'p1 = sin()', then this would attempt to invoke the function sin() and attempt to assign the result it returns (a double) to 'p1', which would of course be illegal.

Observe also how parentheses were required around the pointer variable name itself, for example '(*p1)'. Without these, for example 'double *p1()', 'p1' would have been defined as a function returning a pointer to double, which is not the same thing at all.

Given that the sizes of all functions are likely to vary depending upon what operation they were written to perform, the compiler does not associate a scalar value with a function pointer (in much the same way as a scalar value is not associated with a void pointer). Consequently, there are only a limited number of useful operations/operators that can be performed/applied to it. Any arithmetic operations such as incrementing or applying the array operator '[]' are illegal since they imply a known scalar value.

However, it is permissible to apply the function invocation operator '()' to such a pointer. For example, given that 'p1' points to the function sin(), then that function could be invoked with the argument '1.2', (a double) and the result it returns assigned to the variable 'a' with either of the following two statements:

Invoke sin() directly with the argument '1.2'

```
a = sin( 1.2 ) ;
a = p1( 1.2 ) ;
```

Invoke sin() indirectly via the pointer 'p1' with the argument '1.2'

10.3.1 *Passing a function to a function*

Since the name of a function resolves to its address, this provides us with a convenient mechanism for passing a function as an argument to another function. There are many reasons why this might be useful, some of which will be explored shortly. In essence, if a function is written to *receive* a function, then its prototype (and function header) may be written in either of the two ways shown below, where the function 'f2()' has been written to receive a double argument 'a' and a function math (which expects and returns a double):

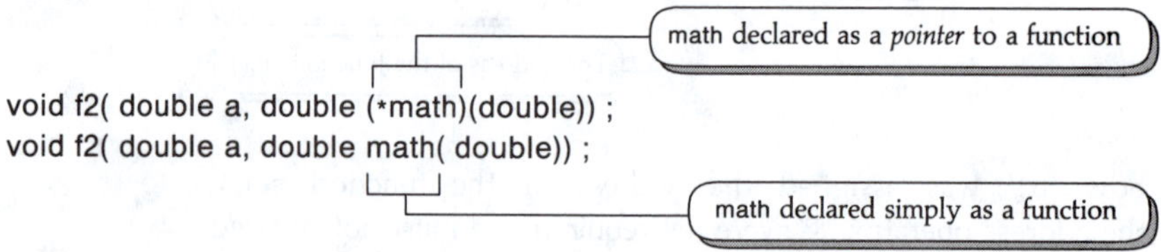
math declared as a pointer to a function
void f2(double a, double (*math)(double)) ;
void f2(double a, double math(double)) ;
math declared simply as a function

In the first example, the parameter math was declared simply as a pointer to a function, while in the second it has been declared as a function, which provides a more readable alternative, but disguises the fact that 'f2()' will ultimately be given a pointer. This is analogous in many ways to the declaration of an array as a function parameter, which can be declared either as an array or as a pointer. The function 'f2()' could now be invoked with a statement such as:

'f2()' passed the address of or a pointer to the function sin()

```
f2( 3.141, sin ) ;
```

As an example, Program 10.7 displays sine, cosine and tangent tables for all angles 'x' in the range 0 < x < PI in increments of 0.2 radians. The function that

Program 10.7 A simple program to demonstrate pointers to functions.

```
#include  <stdio.h>
#include  <math.h>

#define  PI  3.141592653

void  display( double start, double end, double inc, double math( double ))
{
   double i ;

   printf("%15s%15s\n", "x", "f(x)") ;

   for( i = start; i <= end; i += fabs(inc))
      printf("%15g%15g\n", i, math( i )) ;

   putchar( '\n' ) ;
}

int  main( void )
{
   printf("Displaying Sine Values\n\n") ;
   display( 0.0, PI, 0.2, sin ) ;

   printf("Displaying Cosine Values\n\n") ;
   display( 0.0, PI, 0.2, cos ) ;

   printf("Displaying Tangent Values\n\n") ;
   display( 0.0, PI, 0.2, tan ) ;

   return 0 ;
}
```

math declared as a function

Invoke the function math( )

Notionally pass the function sin( ) to display( )

Notionally pass the function cos( ) to display( )

Notionally pass the function tan( ) to display( )

carries out all of the work is the function display(), which is given either the function sin(), cos() or tan() as an argument by main().

10.3.2 *The standard library functions* bsearch() *and* qsort()

The two standard library functions bsearch() and qsort(), which provide a convenient means of searching and sorting an array of any data, are also heavily dependent upon the use of functions as arguments. The function qsort() uses an implementation of the quicksort algorithm to sort an array into ascending order, while the function bsearch() performs a binary search on a previously sorted array, looking for and returning a pointer to the first element found in the array that matches the specified key, or NULL if no such data exists.

Both functions are capable of working with arrays of any type and size of data provided that the calling program presents them with a suitable function that can be invoked by either to compare two items of data within the array. Their function prototypes are given below and can be found in the header file <stdlib.h>:

```
void *bsearch( const void *key, const void *base, size_t num,
                         size_t size, int compare(const void *, const void *) ) ;
void qsort( void *base, size_t num, size_t size,
                         int compare(const void *, const void *) ) ;
```

where 'key' is a pointer to an item of data to be located within the array, 'base' is a pointer to the first element in the array, 'num' specifies the number of elements in the array and 'size' specifies the size of each array element.

The parameter 'compare' is declared as expecting two const void pointers to any two items of data to be compared from the array. This function should be written to return a value of less than zero, zero, or greater than zero, depending upon whether the first pointer in that function points to data that is considered to be less than, equivalent to or greater than the data pointed to by the second pointer. Program 10.8 demonstrates the use of these two functions in relation to the sorting and searching of an array of integers.

Program 10.8 Sorting and searching an array of integers.

```
#include  <stdio.h>
#include  <stdlib.h>

/* The array to be sorted and searched */

int array[ ] = { 5, 8, 3, 4, 23, 17, 19, 12, 4 };

/*
** The user-supplied comparison function to compare, in this instance, two integer
** values at the address held by the two pointers p1 and p2. Note how the cast (int *)
** was required to cast a 'void' pointer argument to an 'int' pointer before
** applying the indirection operator '*'. This was required to give 'p1' and 'p2' the
** correct scalar values to access an int.
*/

int compare_int( const void *p1, const void *p2 )
{
   return( *(int *)(p1) - *(int *)(p2)) ;
}
```

```
int  main( void )
{
  int      i ;
  int      key ;
  size_t element_size ;
  size_t num_elements ;

  char buff[ BUFSIZ ] ;

/* Calculate the size of each element and the number of elements in the array */

  element_size = sizeof( int ) ;
  num_elements = sizeof( array ) / element_size ;

/* First display the unsorted array elements */

  printf("In UNSORTED order\n") ;
  for( i = 0; i < num_elements; i ++ )
    printf("%d ", array[ i ]) ;

/* Now sort the array using qsort( ) and user-supplied comparison function */

  qsort( array, num_elements, element_size, compare_int) ;

/* Now display the sorted array elements */

  printf("\n\nIn SORTED order\n") ;
  for( i = 0; i < num_elements; i ++ )
    printf("%d ", array[ i ]) ;

/* Now search for a specified key value in the array */

  do{
    printf("\n\nEnter a Key value to search for ... ") ;
    key = atoi( gets( buff )) ;

    if(bsearch( &key, array, num_elements, element_size, compare_int) != NULL )
      printf("YES Value %d is in array", key) ;
    else
      printf("NO Value %d is NOT in array", key ) ;
  } while( 1 ) ;

  return 0 ;
}
```

Notice how the function compare_int() was given to, and subsequently invoked by, bsearch() and qsort() as part of their operation. This comparison function is in turn given two void pointers to two objects in the array, which are subsequently cast (in this example, at least) to two int pointers before using the '*' operator to fetch two integer values, which are then compared by simple subtraction.

If the program were modified later to sort and search an array of doubles, then it would only need minor alterations to define a new function compare_double(), whose void pointer parameters would now be cast to pointers to double.

10.3.3 *Arrays of pointers to functions*

Another useful application of pointers to functions lies with the design of state machines. Here, the sequence of operations and actions performed by the program are not rigidly defined by statements within the program itself, but are instead encoded into data tables, generally implemented as an array of functions. The heart of such a machine often consists of a simple loop in conjunction with an integer variable identifying the current **state** of the machine, which is used to invoke a function from the table.

To support these ideas in C we can deploy an array of pointers to functions, whose pointers may be initialized with the addresses of several functions designed to perform actions on behalf of the machine. Such an array could be defined in the manner shown below, which defines 'actions' to be an array of five pointers to functions expecting no arguments and returning no data:

```
void ( *actions[ 5 ] )( void ) ;
```

As an example, let us design a simple state machine to simulate a washing machine. This example was chosen mainly for its simplicity because it allows us to demonstrate the use of pointers to functions without becoming too wrapped up in the intricacies of more general purpose state machines.

As a washing machine is essentially sequential in nature, the progression through a number of states, such as water on, water off, wash, rinse, spin and so on, can be performed automatically after a suitable time delay, which allows us to simplify the design of our state transition table considerably. The complete simulation is written in Program 10.9.

The array state_table[] defines a number of pointers to functions, which are invoked in turn as the machine progresses through states 0 to 5, while the array state_delays[] defines a software 'slug' designed to pause the program before a new state begins.

The state of the machine is maintained by the integer variable state, which is incremented as part of a loop and is used as the subscript in the two previous arrays. By changing the size, or the order of entries in state_table, the machine

Program 10.9 A washing machine simulation using pointers to functions.

```
#include <stdio.h>

#define NUM 6                          /* number of states in simulation */

/*
** Now define the code for each of the functions
** that simulate an action within the washing machine
*/

void water_on(void) { puts("Water ON ... ") ; }
void water_off(void) { puts("Water OFF ... ") ; }
void wash(void)      { puts("Washing ... ") ; }
void spin(void)      { puts("Spinning ... ") ; }
void drain(void)     { puts("Draining ... ") ; }
void stop(void)      { puts("Finished ... ") ; }

int main( void )
{
  void delay( int delay_time ) ;        /* function prototype */

/*
** Now define an array of pointers to void functions
** initialized with the addresses of the functions above
*/

  void (*state_table[ NUM ] )(void) = { water_on, water_off, wash, spin, drain, stop } ;

  int state, state_delays[ NUM ] = { 20, 5, 40, 20, 30, 0 } ;

  for( state = 0; state < NUM; state ++ )  {
    state_table[ state ] () ;           /* invoke function from table */
    delay( state_delays[ state ] ) ;    /* pause between states */
  }

  return 0 ;
}

void delay( int delay_time )
{
  long del = delay_time * 100000L ;     /* time constant, adjust to suit */

  while( del != 0 )
    del -- ;
}
```

can be made to behave in a completely different way. When Program 10.9 was run, the following display was produced, where there was a suitable delay between each line of output:

```
Water ON ...
Water OFF ...
Washing ...
Spinning ...
Draining ...
Finished ...
```

10.4 Interpreting declarations: The right–left rule

In the course of this chapter, some rather complicated variable declarations have been presented, which has probably caused much confusion in the minds of many readers. It is worth noting that C does have a very simple rule that permits any variable declaration, including pointers and functions, to be interpreted easily. It is called the 'right–left' rule, and is the same rule that is used by the compiler to interpret any simple or complex declaration. It works like this.

You begin with the name of the variable/constant/function in the declaration, and work outwards in a right–left manner until all terms in the declaration have been used. For example, the rather complex declaration of 'ptr' below:

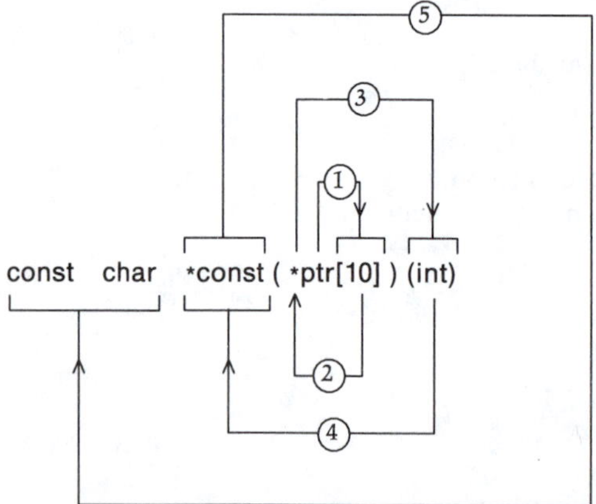

declares 'ptr' to be an array of 10 pointers to functions requiring a single integer argument and returning constant pointers to constant chars. More examples are given in Table 10.4. See if you can apply the above rule to achieve the same interpretation as the author.

Table 10.4 Some example variable declarations and their meaning.

Declaration	*Interpretation*
char a	'a' is a char
char a[10]	'a' is an array of 10 chars
const char a[10]	'a' is an array of 10 constant chars
const char *a	'a' is a pointer to constant char
const char *const a	'a' is a constant pointer to constant char
char *a[10]	'a' is an array of 10 pointers to char
const int *a[10]	'a' is an array of 10 pointers to constant integer
char (*a)[15]	'a' is a pointer to a single dimensional array of 15 chars
int (*a)[10][15]	'a' is a pointer to a two-dimensional array of 10 by 15 ints
char **a	'a' is a pointer to a pointer to char
const char **a	'a' is a pointer to a pointer to constant char
const char *const *a	'a' is a pointer to a constant pointer to constant char
const char *const *const a	'a' is a constant pointer to a constant pointer to constant char
char **a[10]	'a' is an array of 10 pointers to pointers to char
const char **a[10]	'a' is an array of 10 pointers to pointers to constant char
const char *const *const a[10]	'a' is an array of 10 constant pointers to constant pointers to constant char
char a(int[10])	'a' is a function returning a char and expecting a single dimensional array of 10 integers
double *a(double)	'a' is a function returning a pointer to a double and expecting a double as an argument
int (*a)(int, int)	'a' is pointer to a function expecting two integer arguments and returning an integer result
char (*a[20])(void)	'a' is an array of 20 pointers to functions expecting no arguments and returning a char

10.5 Complex pointer application: Dealing with interrupts

In Chapter 8 we took a brief look at how memory mapped peripherals could be accessed directly using a simple pointer, initialized with the address of a specific I/O device or chip within the system. In those examples, communication took place between program and device using a 'polled' approach, whereby the program would test the status of the device and wait for it to become idle before reading or transmitting further data.

Although such an approach is simple, there are many situations that would benefit from an interrupt driven scheme. Here the device would, via an interrupt request, inform the CPU when some 'event' had occurred rather than have the program poll the device waiting for it to happen. This would free up the CPU's time to deal with other aspects of the system.

Dealing with exceptions (a generic term for an asynchronous event, which includes an interrupt) is mostly a straightforward affair on a hosted system like the IBM PC running MS-DOS, since many compiler vendors will have figured out how exceptions are dealt with by the operating system and will have included suitable library functions that will enable your program to intercept these exceptions as they arise. An example is the function **setvect( )**, available with Borland's Turbo C, and the function **vector( )**, available with Introl's 68000 UNIX Cross Compiler.

In this more specialized section, we shall be taking a look at how interrupts and exceptions can be dealt with in a non-hosted or stand-alone environment. Although many of the underlying principles discussed here are common to a great many CPUs, the author has chosen Motorola's 68000 as the specific example. This CPU is able to recognize and deal with up to 255 different types of 'exceptions'. Seven of these are reserved specifically for handling seven different levels of prioritized interrupts. Other exceptions arise as a result of division by zero, an address error, an illegal instruction and, most fundamental of all, a reset.

Table 10.5 shows the exception vector table for the 68000, consisting of 256 entries/vectors. Each of these vectors (except vector 0 which contains an initial value for the CPU's stack pointer after a hardware reset) will have been programmed with the four byte address (think of this as a pointer in C) of a function designed to handle that type of exception. For example, vectors 1 and 2, located in memory at addresses 00000004 and 00000008 respectively, contain the addresses of functions designed to handle hardware resets and bus errors, while vectors 25–31, located at addresses 00000064 to 0000007C, are designed to handle the seven autovectored interrupt requests.

When an exception arises, the 68000 temporarily suspends the execution of the current program and, via the appropriate vector in Table 10.5, invokes a function to deal with it. Upon completion, the CPU may return to its original state prior to the exception and continue to execute the original program.

Because the exception table *must* be resident in read only memory (ROM) at power-on time and consequently cannot be changed at run time, many designers of small stand-alone systems often design their boot or reset code to build an intermediate RAM based exception table. This allows the application to change or install its own exception handler/function at run time. We shall see this shortly.

Figure 10.6 illustrates the concept of a RAM based vector table for the seven autovectored interrupt requests. It works as follows. When an exception is recognized, say an autovectored level 2 interrupt using vector number 26, the CPU extracts, from address 00000068, the 4 byte address of the function, which has been designed to deal with that particular exception. In Figure 10.6, vector 26 contains the address hex 00001006.

Table 10.5 The 68000 exception vector table.

Vector number	*Hex address*	*Assignment*
0	00000000	Reset: initial stack pointer
1	00000004	Reset: initial program counter
2	00000008	Bus error
3	0000000C	Address error
4	00000010	Illegal instruction
5	00000014	Divide by zero
6	00000018	CHK instruction
7	0000001C	TRAPV instruction
8	00000020	Privilege violation
9	00000024	Trace
10	00000028	Line 1010 emulation
11	0000002C	Line 1111 emulation
12–14	00000030	(Unassigned reserved)
	00000038	–
15	0000003C	(Uninitialized interrupt vector)
16–23	00000040	(Unassigned reserved)
	0000005F	–
24	00000060	Spurious interrupt
25	00000064	Level 1 interrupt autovector
26	00000068	Level 2 interrupt autovector
27	0000006C	Level 3 interrupt autovector
28	00000070	Level 4 interrupt autovector
29	00000074	Level 5 interrupt autovector
30	00000078	Level 6 interrupt autovector
31	0000007C	Level 7 interrupt autovector
32–47	00000080	Trap 0–16 instruction vectors
	000000BF	–
48–63	000000C0	(Unassigned reserved)
	000000FF	–
64–255	00000100	User interrupt vectors
	000003FF	–

The CPU then performs an unconditional jump to that location in RAM (00001006), whereupon it immediately finds a 'jmp' or jump instruction directing it to the address of the *real* interrupt handler, assumed in this example to exist at location hex 00040040. By substituting the address of the program's own exception handler function in place of the 4 byte address 00040040 in the RAM-based exception table, the program can install and change its own exception handler routine at run time.

Take care, however, since the design of an exception handler function is a little different to that of a conventional function, in as much as it is generally

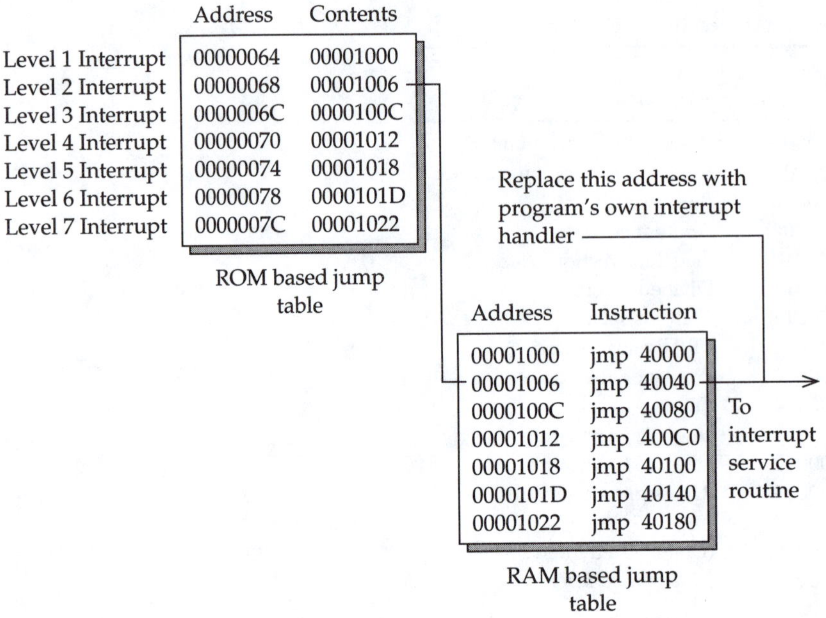

Figure 10.6 Creating a RAM-based vector table for the 68000 CPU.

written to preserve and restore most, if not all, of the entire state of the CPU, including its internal registers (and those of other devices affected by the execution of the exception handler such as a floating point co-processor) upon entry and exit to the function. Furthermore, such functions are written to terminate with an RTE (assuming a 68000 CPU) rather than the conventional RTS instruction.

To facilitate this, many compilers support an additional function modifier/ qualifier to indicate their exception handler status. For example, Borland's Turbo C uses the qualifier `interrupt`, while Introl's 68000 compiler uses '`_mod2_`'. You will have to look up the relevant qualifier for your compiler. When such a function is compiled, code is automatically generated to save and restore the CPU's state and to ensure that the function returns with an RTE instruction.

Program 10.10 uses these ideas to install a level 2 interrupt request handler for a stand-alone 68000 system. The example assumes the existence of the RAM-based vector table shown in Figure 10.6. Notice how the definition of the function `level2()` has been qualified with `interrupt` to indicate that it is an exception handler function.

The function `setvect()` has been designed to install an exception handler function to deal with any exception type. It must be invoked with the vector number of the relevant exception and a pointer to the `interrupt` qualified function designed to handle that exception.

Program 10.10 Installing exception handlers using a RAM based vector table.

```
/*
** This function installs an exception handler function for a specified exception
** The function expects the integer exception number and a pointer to a function
** with exception handling capabilities; that is, one which expects and returns no
** arguments/data and which saves and restores the CPU state on entry and exit
** and returns with an RTE rather than an RTS instruction
*/

void setvect( int vector, void interrupt (*except)(void))
{

/*
** Assuming the ROM based vector table commencing at address 0
** can be thought of as an array/table of pointers to function pointers, then define
** 'rom_table' as a pointer to the first pointer in that table
** at address 0
*/

    void interrupt (***rom_table)( void ) = 0 ;
    void interrupt (**ram_table)(void) ;

/*
** Now obtain the address of the function designed to handle that
** exception, for example address 0x00000068 for vector 26
*/

    ram_table = rom_table[ vector ] ;

/*
** Now cast the value of the pointer to that of a char pointer with
** scalar value 1, so that we can add the absolute value of 2 to enable
** the pointer to skip over the 'jmp' instruction to point to the address
** (of a function) that we wish to change in the RAM-based jump table
*/

    ram_table = (void interrupt (**)(void)) ((char *)(ram_table) + 2) ;
    *ram_table = except ;              /* install new Interrupt service routine */
}

void interrupt level2( void )
{
    ...                                /* deal with level 2 interrupts here */
    ...
}
```

```
int main( void )
{
   setvect( 26, level2 ) ;            /* install level2( ) to handle level 2 interrupts */
   ...                                /* rest of program here */
   return 0 ;
}
```

10.6 Chapter summary

(1) An array of 'n' dimensions may be accessed one row at a time using a pointer to an array of 'n – 1' dimensions. For example, given the array 'x' below as a three-dimensional array:

```
int x[ 2 ][ 3 ][ 4 ] ;
```

a pointer 'p1' could be defined and initialized with the address of the first row in 'x' with a statement such as:

```
int (*p1)[ 3 ][ 4 ] = x ;
```

'p1' now has a scalar value of 'sizeof(int) * 3 * 4'. The nth row in 'x' (a two-dimensional array of 3 by 4 integers) could be referenced using either of the expressions:

```
p1[n]   or   *(p1 + n)
```

Both yield the address of the first element in the two-dimensional array, which could be assigned to another pointer declared as:

```
int (*p2)[ 4 ] ;
```

'p2' has a scalar value of 'sizeof(int) * 4'. The mth row in 'x' (a single dimensional array of 4 doubles) could be referenced using either of the expressions:

```
p2[ m ]   or   *(p1 + m)
```

Both yield the address of the first element in a single dimensional array, which could be assigned to another pointer declared as:

```
int *p3 ;
```

Finally, the xth element in that array could be accessed with an expression such as:

```
p3[ x ]   or   *(p3 + x)
```

(2) A pointer to a pointer is declared in the manner shown below, where 'p1' is a pointer to an int pointer and thus has the scalar value given by the expression 'sizeof(int *)':

```
int **p1 ;
```

Pointers to pointers are commonly used to access elements from an array of pointers or to swap/exchange pointers.

(3) The name of a function is simply a shorthand notation for the address of that function. Such an address may be assigned to a suitably declared function pointer in the manner shown below:

```
int (*p1)(const char *, ...) = printf ;
```

Such a pointer has no scalar value and thus may not be used with any operator that implies knowledge of such a scalar value, for example '++', '[]', 'sizeof' and so on, but the function 'f1' may be invoked via the pointer 'p1' with a statement such as:

```
a = p1( "%d * %d = %d\n", a, b, a * b ) ;
```

(4) When a function is given as an argument to another function, the receiving function may declare its parameter either as a function or as a pointer to a function, but in reality that parameter is represented by a pointer, regardless of how it is declared.

10.7 Exercises

10.1 Given the definition of an array 'x' as 'int x[4][3][2]', what is the type and value of the following expressions?

```
x          x[0]         x[0][0]           x[0][0][0]
x[2]       x[2][2]      x[3][2][1]
*x         *(x + i )    *(*(x + i) + j)   *(*(*(x + i) + j) + k)
&x[0]      &x[0][0]     &x[0][0][0]
```

10.2 Given that the expressions '&x[0]', '&x[0][0]' and '&x[0][0][0]' all resolve to the same address, why do the following expressions not give the same result?

```
*(&x[0] + 2*i + 3*j + k)
*(&x[0][0] + 2*i + 3*j + k)
*(&x[0][0][0] + 2*i + 3*j + k)
```

10.3 Given the definition of the pointer 'p1' as 'int (*p1)[3][2]' and the array 'x' from Exercise 10.1, what is the type and value of the following expressions?

```
p1[i]           p1[i][j]          p1[i][j][k]
*p1             *(p1 + i)         *(*(p1 + i) + j)   *(*(*(p1 + i) + j) + k)
*(p1[i] + j)    *(*(p1 + i)[j])
```

10.4 Describe two methods in which the parameter of a function could be declared to receive an array of 4 × 3 × 2 integer elements. Write a function to display the contents of a three-dimensional array of 4 × 3 × 2 integers given as an argument to the function:

(a) By using pure array notation using only the array operator '[]'.

(b) By using pure pointer notation using only the indirection operator '*' plus an optional offset.

(c) By introducing several pointers and stepping them through sub-elements/rows of the array.

(d) By stepping a simple int pointer through the entire array.

10.5 Given the following definitions, complete the table below:

```
int i, *p1=&i, **p2=&p1, ***p3 = &p2, ****p4 = &p3 ;
```

Value of	*Using p1*	*Using p2*	*Using p3*	*Using p4*
i				
p1				
p2				
p3				
p4				

10.6 In Application 7.1, an example implementation of the game of life was presented using a two-dimensional array. Modify this game such that the size of the two array dimensions is prompted for and storage allocated at run time.

10.7 In Application 5.6, we presented a program to find the roots of a function f(x) using Newton's approximation equation, given below:

$$x = x_0 - f(x)/f'(x)$$

Modify the program to include a function called newton() that expects to be given pointers to the functions f(x) and $f'(x)$ and use it to find the roots of the equation $5x^2 - 6x + 1 = 0$.

10.8 Write a program to convert temperatures expressed in Celsius to Fahrenheit and vice versa. Your implementation should be based around an array of two pointers to the two temperature conversion functions which are invoked via an integer subject (0 or 1) supplied by the program's operator.

Based on your experience of answering this question, modify the program developed for Exercise 10.7 so that an array of pointers to the two functions f(x) and $f'(x)$ is given as an argument to the function newton().

10.9 Write a function to:

(a) Compare

(b) Swap

any two items of generic data.

Hint: Use void pointers to the two objects to be compared/swapped and try to make use of some of the memory manipulation functions described in Section 18.14.

10.10 Rewrite the specific implementations of the binary search function given in Chapter 7 and the quicksort functions given in Chapter 8 and in Program 10.6 as generic functions able to search for and sort any type of data; in other words, write your own version of the standard library functions bsearch( ) and qsort( ).

Hint: Take a look at how both bsearch( ) and qsort( ) expect to be given a function argument able to compare two generic objects for correct order. This requires the use of generic or void pointers. You can also make use of the standard library functions memcpy( ), memcmp( ) and so on (see Section 18.14).

10.11 Expand upon the state machine design of the washing machine controller presented in Program 10.9 so that instead of moving to the next state after a set time period, the transition to a new state is dictated by external inputs such as switches.

You may assume the existence of a PIA, as illustrated in Chapter 8, connected to eight switch inputs, which may be used to signal important data such as door closed, temperature and water level reached and so on. The eight LEDs may be used to indicate the state of the machine; that is, fill, wash, rinse, spin and so on.

Hint: It may be useful to define a table describing the conditions required to move from one state to the next. This table could in fact consist of an array of pointers to functions, which return true or false if the condition is met or not. A similar table of pointers to functions can be used to change the status of the LEDs during a transition to a new state.

11 Structures and Unions

The need for 'structures' grew directly from a desire to group and manipulate many related but perhaps different types of data as a single object or variable, which is in contrast to an array where all elements must be of the same type. To understand why this need arose, consider how you might develop a program to enter, record and manipulate the following information about an individual:

Name
Address
Age
Height
Weight

An analysis of this data reveals much of it to be of differing type. For example, recording the individual's height and weight would probably require floating point type variables, while age might be more effectively represented using an int. The individual's name and address, on the other hand, would probably require char arrays to record them as strings. Program 11.1 demonstrates this and identifies some of the problems associated with manipulating the individual's details.

Program 11.1 Recording an individual's details without a structure.

```
#include  <stdio.h>
#include  <stdlib.h>

void  get_data( char name[ ], char address[ ], int *age, float *height, float *weight )
{
   char  buff[ BUFSIZ ] ;
   gets( name ) ;
   gets( address ) ;
   *age = atoi(gets(buff)) ;
   . . .
}
```

Complex parameter list

Complex parameter list

```
void  display_data( char name[ ], char address[ ], int age, float height, float weight )
{
  printf( "%s\n%s\nAge = %d\nHeight = %g\nWeight = %g\n",
      name, address, age, height, weight ) ;
}

int  main( void )
{
  char  name[ BUFSIZ ] ;
  char  address[ BUFSIZ ] ;
  int   age ;
  float height ;
  float weight ;
   ...

  get_data( name, address, &age, &height, &weight ) ;       /* read individual's data */
  display_data( name, address, age, height, weight ) ;      /* display individual's data */

  return 0 ;
}
```

Data stored within main() as local variables

Pass complex list of arguments to function

You can see from Program 11.1 that the manipulation of an individual's details is quite complex, since they are all stored in separate variables, each of which has to be passed as an argument to any function that manipulates it. This is a problem that can only grow bigger, as more and more details are recorded about an individual, such as eye and hair colour, requiring major modifications to the program and functions that manipulate them.

Furthermore, given the way the data is structured at the moment, the task of saving and recovering an individual's details to and from, say, a disk file is not particularly efficient, since it requires that a number of separate and distinct variables be written/read to/from a file. Let us now see how the introduction of a **structure** to record the data would solve these problems.

11.1 Defining and using structures

The introduction of a structure variable is unusual in the sense that it requires two stages. Firstly, the compiler is given details of a structure **template** describing the names and types of the data objects or **member elements** that will eventually be stored within such a structure variable. The structure template is generally given a name or **tag** by which it can be referenced later when introducing the structure variable itself. As an example, the structure template person given below could be used to describe the information we previously stored as separate variables in Program 11.1:

Key word struct to introduce structure template

Template name is person

```
struct person  {
   char  name[ BUFSIZ ] ;
   char  address[ BUFSIZ ] ;
   int   age ;
   float height ;
   float weight ;
} ;
```

Member elements of the structure

Note use of semicolons ';'

When a template such as this is declared, it is important to appreciate that the compiler generates *no code*, and *no variables* are introduced into the program. A very common mistake among new programmers is to assume that person is somehow the name of a variable that can be manipulated by the program. It is not; it is simply a name that has been used to describe a blueprint or plan for a structure variable that we might introduce later.

Secondly, having declared such a template, the program could introduce a structure variable based upon it, as shown in the example statement below, where the structure variable 'p1' has been introduced or **defined** based upon the structure template person:

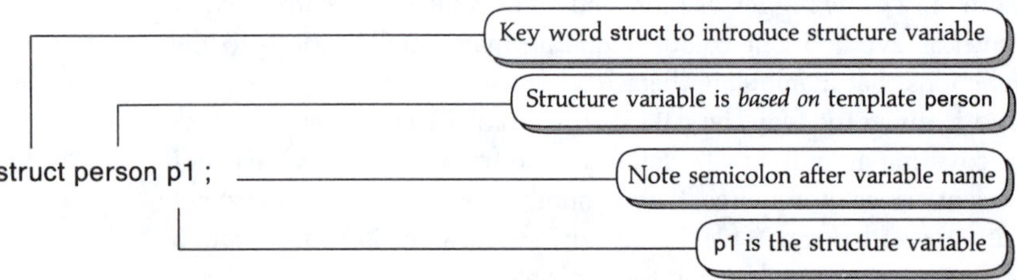

It is important to appreciate that it is 'p1' that is the variable (not person), and that it is sufficiently large to be able to simultaneously hold or represent the member elements name, address, age, height and weight within it.

It is worth considering at this point an analogy between the design and construction of a house and declaring and defining a structure template and variable, because this will help to clarify much of the confusion that often surrounds structures.

When someone wishes to build a house, the first stage is to commission an architect to draw up the blueprint or plans, which can then be submitted to the planning authorities for approval. If the plans are approved, a builder can be employed to construct the house based on them.

With a structure, you are the architect and the template represents the plans of an object you wish to build. The compiler plays the dual role of the planning authority and builder, checking your plans before approval and building objects based upon them. In other words, a set of plans or a template is no substitute for a finished house or variable.

In the above example, the template person and the variable 'p1' were declared and defined using two separate statements. If necessary, these can be combined into one, where the inclusion of the template name or tag is optional. An example of this is shown below, where 'p1', 'p2' and 'p3' are all structure variables based upon an unnamed template:

Key word struct to introduce structure template

Template name is optional

```
struct  {
  char  name[ BUFSIZ ] ;
  char  address[ BUFSIZ ] ;
  int   age ;
  float height ;
  float weight ;
} p1, p2, p3 ;
```

Note semicolon after variable name

Comma ',' separated list of structure variables 'p1', 'p2' and 'p3'

Note, however, that if such an approach is adopted, and the program chooses *not* to name the template, then it follows that all structure variables based upon that template *must* be defined at the same time as the template is declared, as there will be no way to introduce further structure variables without a template name to refer to.

Interestingly enough, the compiler permits the introduction of a structure *template* and a structure *variable* with a common name. In fact, one of the member elements of that structure can also share this name without problem. For example:

Structure template called temp

```
struct temp  {
  int  temp ;
  int  x ;
} temp ;
```

Member element called temp

Structure variable called temp

11.1.1 *Accessing structure elements: The dot operator: '.'*

Once a structure variable has been defined, its member elements – that is, those declared within its template – may be individually accessed using the dot '.' (a decimal point) operator, the general form of which is given as:

Dot '.' operator used to access a member element within a structure

```
structure_variable . member_element
```

For example, Program 11.2 introduces the structure template 'car' and a structure variable 'c1' and demonstrates how the member elements of 'c1' may be accessed using this notation.

Program 11.2 Accessing member elements: the dot operator '.'.

```
#include   <stdio.h>

/*
** Describe the structure template 'car' and define the structure variable 'c1'
*/

struct  car  {                          /* Structure template 'car' */
  int    capacity ;
  short  doors ;
} c1 ;                                  /* Structure variable 'c1' */

int  main( void )
{
  c1.capacity = 2495 ;                  /* Dot '.' operator */
  c1.doors = 4 ;

  printf("Engine Capacity = %d\n", c1.capacity ) ;   /* Dot '.' operator */
  printf("Number of doors = %d\n", c1.doors ) ;

  return 0 ;
}
```

11.1.2 *The storage requirements of a structure*

We have already seen that when a structure variable is defined, the compiler ensures that sufficient storage is allocated to the structure to enable it to represent all of its member elements *simultaneously*. However, it would be quite unsafe for the programmer to assume that the storage requirements for the structure could be determined simply as the sum of the storage required by each member element. For example, given the structure variable 'x' as:

```
struct temp {
  char c;
  int  i ;
} x ;
```

it would be unsafe for the programmer to assume that the storage required by 'x' is given by the expression 'sizeof(char) + sizeof(int)'. The only guaranteed way of determining the size of a structure is to use the sizeof operator, as demonstrated by either of the expressions shown below:

```
sizeof( struct temp ) ;
sizeof( x ) ;
```

The justification for this is simply that the compiler *may* introduce spare or 'unused' bytes of data into a structure to 'pad out' member elements to ensure that, where appropriate, they can be accessed on a 'word' (16 bit) or 'long word' (32 bit) memory boundary (depending on CPU architecture and system).

For example, assuming that integers are represented by 16 bit quantities, the compiler might, on a 16 or 32 bit CPU, introduce an additional byte of padding after the element 'c' in structure 'x' above, to ensure that the integer 'i' will be accessed on a word boundary. Thus the size of the structure 'x' might be four bytes, as illustrated in Figure 11.1.

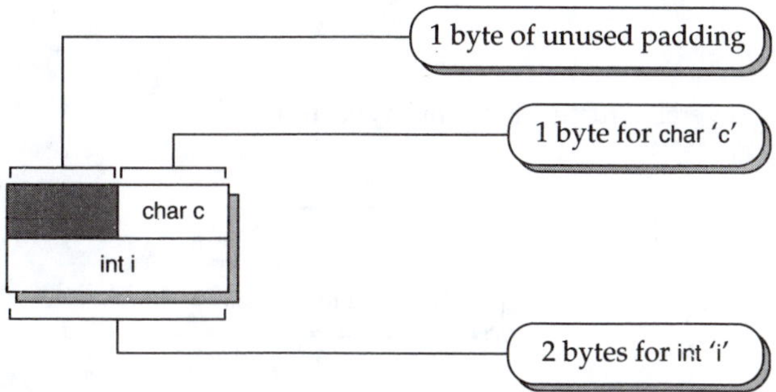

Figure 11.1 Typical representation for the structure 'x' in memory for a 16 or 32 bit CPU.

11.1.3 *Initialization of a structure's member elements*

As with other data types, the programmer can assume that unless explicitly initialized by the program, the member elements of a global or static structure variable will be cleared to zero when the program is run and that the member elements of an automatic structure are not initialized in any way and therefore have undefined values.

However, as with arrays, it is often desirable to be able to initialize the member elements of a structure during the definition of the structure itself. This can be achieved using the general format shown below:

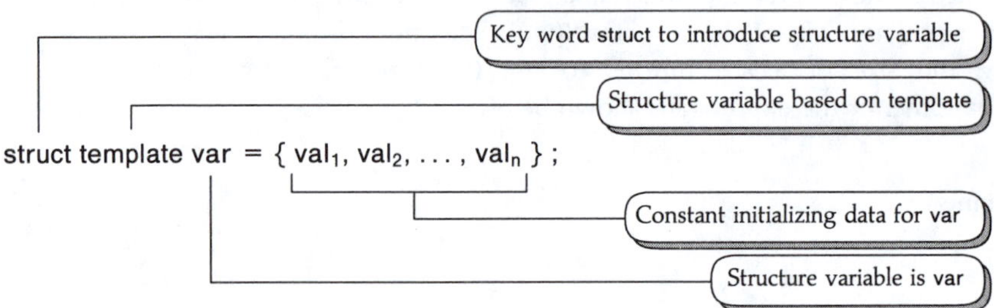

where the initializing values '$val_1 \ldots val_n$' must be constant data and where 'val_1' is assigned to the first member element and the value 'val_n' is assigned to the nth member element in the structure variable var. If 'n' initializing values are present, then there *must* be at least 'n' member elements declared in the structure template. If the template contains more than 'n' elements, then only the first 'n' are initialized.

The compiler checks that the initializing data is compatible with the type of the member element to which it is assigned and where necessary will perform the required implicit casting/promotion to ensure compatibility. Therefore, given the structure template complex below, designed to represent a complex number:

```
struct  complex  {
  double  real , imag ;
} ;
```

we could now define and initialize several structures of this type using the following statements and definitions:

'1.0' assigned to 'x1.real'

'2.0' assigned to 'x1.imag'

```
int  main( void )
{
  struct  complex  x1 = { 1.0, 2.0 } ;
  struct  complex  x2 = { 2.33, -12.0 } , x3 = { -56.3, -21.0 } ;
  . . .
}
```

11.1.4 *Structure copying and assignment*

It is permissible (unlike arrays) for the contents of one structure to be assigned to another, using the assignment operator '=', provided that both structures have been derived from the same template (see Section 11.1.6), although operations such as structure comparison and addition are not permitted. In assigning one structure to another, the compiler copies or assigns every member element from the 'source' structure to its corresponding member element in the 'destination' structure.

Program 11.3 demonstrates structure assignment where the structure variable 'p1' is assigned to 'p2'. This feature is important, since it allows a function to return a *copy* of a structure and assign that copy to another structure variable.

Program 11.3 Demonstrating structure assignment.

```
#include <stdio.h>

struct person {
  char  name[ BUFSIZ ] ;
  char  address[ BUFSIZ ] ;
  int   age ;
  float height ;
  float weight ;
} ;

struct person p1 ;      // 'p1' and 'p2' are based on the same template person

int main( void )
{
  struct person p2 ;
  ...
  ...
  p2 = p1 ;             // Copy all member elements in 'p1' to their corresponding elements in 'p2'
  ...
  return 0 ;
}
```

11.1.5 *The scope and privacy of a structure variable*

Structure variables adhere to the same scope and privacy rules as any other type of variable, in that a structure defined within a function or statement block is local and private to that block, while a structure variable defined outside a function is accessible, along with its member elements, by any statement that appears *after* the structure definition. Examples of various structure scopes are demonstrated below:

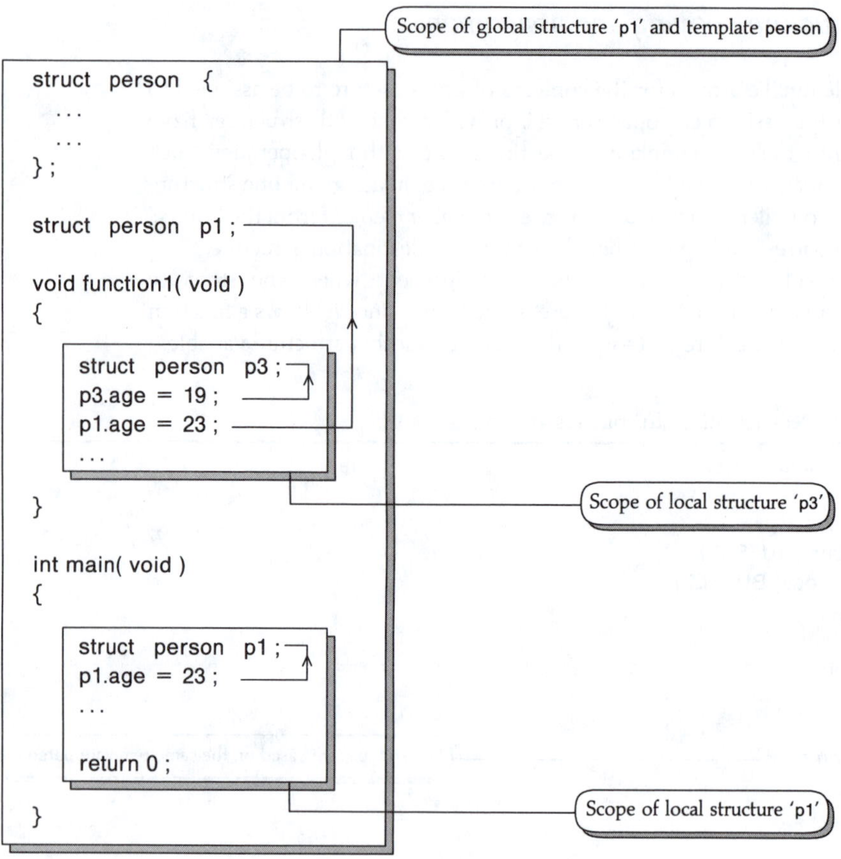

11.1.6 *The scope and privacy of a structure template*

The same scope and privacy rules that apply to structure variables also apply to their templates. Thus it is possible to have both local (private) and global templates sharing a common template or tag name, but with differing levels of scope. Given this possibility, the compiler will always base a structure variable's definition upon the template that is 'most in scope' at the time; in other words, a local template takes precedence over a global one with the same tag name.

This is important, because two structure variables are only considered to be of the same structure 'type' if they have been based around *exactly* the same template. As far as the compiler is concerned, declaring two templates with a common tag name, one with global scope, the other with local or private scope, introduces two *different* templates, even if they declare identical member elements. Thus, two structure variables derived from these two separate templates are not considered to be compatible and *cannot* be assigned to each other.

Program 11.4 Demonstrating the scope of a structure template.

```
#include   <stdio.h>

/*
** Global structure template and variable 'x'
*/

struct  complex  {
   double  real ;
   double  imag ;
} x ;

int main( void )
{

/*
** Local structure template and variable 'y'
*/

   struct  complex  {
      double  real ;
      double  imag ;
   } y ;

   x = y ;

   return 0 ;

}
```

Scope of 'x' and template complex

Scope of 'y' and template complex

Illegal!

'x' and 'y' are considered different, thus their assignment is illegal

This is demonstrated in Program 11.4, where two structure templates are declared, with the same tag name `complex`. One is global, since it is declared outside a function, the other is local and private to the function `main()`. Two structure variables 'x' and 'y' have also been introduced, which, because of the scope rules relating to templates, are in fact treated by the compiler as different types of structure variables; as such, the assignment of 'x' to 'y' is illegal.

To demonstrate the point, the declaration of the structure template `complex` in `main()` *could* be removed and the compiler would then no longer object to the assignment, since 'y' would then have been derived from the same global template as 'x'. In general, then, unless there are very good reasons, it is recommended that structure templates should be declared globally, since this will remove the possibility of any mismatch between structure variables.

11.2 Structures as function arguments

For reasons of program modularity, it is often desirable to be able to pass a structure as an argument to a function. Unlike an array, however, the compiler makes a copy of such a structure – that is, a copy of all its member elements – and presents the copy to the function. Thus structures by default are passed to function by value or copy.

This is important, since the function will then not have access to and will thus not be able to modify the original structure variable presented to it, only the copy. As an example of this pass by value technique we could rewrite the function display_data() from Program 11.1 to work with a structure variable as its argument. This is shown below:

Parameter 'x' is a copy of a structure based on template person

```
void display_data( struct person x )
{
  printf("Name = %s\n", x . name ) ;
  printf("Address = %s\n", x . address ) ;
  ...
  ...
```

Dot operator '.' used to access member element

Note how the function has declared its parameter 'x' as a structure based upon the template person. We could now rewrite part of the function main() from Program 11.1 to make use of this and pass a copy of a local structure to the function display_data(), as shown below:

```
int main( void )
{
  struct  person  p1 ;
  ...
  ...
  display_data( p1 ) ;
  return 0 ;
}
```

Local structure 'p1' based on template person

Pass a *copy* of 'p1' to display_data()

11.2.1 *Functions returning structures*

Structures are also returned from functions by copy. For example, the function get_data() that we met earlier in Program 11.1 could be modified to read data from an operator, store it in a temporary structure, then return a copy of that structure back to the calling program, as shown below:

```
struct  person  get_data( void )      /* Function returns a copy of a structure based on template person */
{
  struct  person  temp ;              /* Local structure temp based on template person */

  printf("Name ... ") ;
  gets( temp.name ) ;                 /* Read a name and store in structure temp, element name */
  ...

  return( temp ) ;                    /* Return a copy of structure variable temp */
}
```

We can now rewrite all of Program 11.1 to make use of a structure rather than a number of separate variables, as shown below in Program 11.5, and compare both approaches.

Program 11.5 Program 11.1 rewritten to use structure copying.

```
#include  <stdio.h>
#include  <stdlib.h>

/*
** Global structure template 'person' describing an individual's details
*/

struct  person  {
  char  name[ BUFSIZ ] ;
  char  address[ BUFSIZ ] ;
  int   age ;
  float  height ;
  float  weight ;
} ;

void display_data( struct person x )      /* Parameter 'x' is a structure based on template person */
{
  printf("Name = %s\n", x.name ) ;
  printf("Address = %s\n", x.address ) ;
  printf("Age = %d\n", x.age ) ;
  printf("Height = %g\n", x.height ) ;
  printf("Weight = %g\n", x.weight ) ;
}

struct  person  get_data( void )          /* Function returns a copy of a structure based on template person */
{
  char   buff[ BUFSIZ ] ;
  struct  person temp ;
```

```
/*
** Prompt and read data from operator
*/

   printf("Name ... ") ;
   gets( temp.name ) ;
   printf("Address ... ") ;
   gets( temp.address ) ;
   printf("Age ... ") ;
   temp.age = atoi( gets( buff )) ;
   printf("Height ... ") ;
   temp.height = atof( gets( buff )) ;
   printf("Weight ... ") ;
   temp.weight = atof( gets( buff )) ;

   return( temp ) ;
}

int main( void )
{
   struct  person  p1 ;

   p1 = get_data( ) ;          /* Save structure returned by get_data() in 'p1' */
   display_data( p1 ) ;        /* Display structure returned by get_data() in 'p1' */

   return 0 ;
}
```

If Program 11.5 is compared with Program 11.1, a number of obvious improvements are immediately apparent:

(1) The parameter list passed to a function such as display_data( ) is now in the form of a single structure variable and is thus independent of the complexity of the data that exists within that structure. This makes the manipulation of an individual's details much simpler because they can all be passed to a function within a single variable. Should the program be enhanced later to record more characteristics about an individual, the function definition and prototypes for get_data( ) and display_data( ) need not be altered.

(2) Copying an individual's details is now considerably simplified, since the assignment operator '=' can be used to copy them.

(3) Saving and recovering an individual's details to/from a disk file have also been simplified since only one variable need be saved/recovered (see Chapter 16).

11.3 Pointers to structures: The operator: '−>'

An alternative method of accessing a structure is via a pointer. For example, given the structure template **person** and the structure variable 'x' based upon that template, a pointer 'ptr' could be defined and initialized to point to 'x' with a statement of the form:

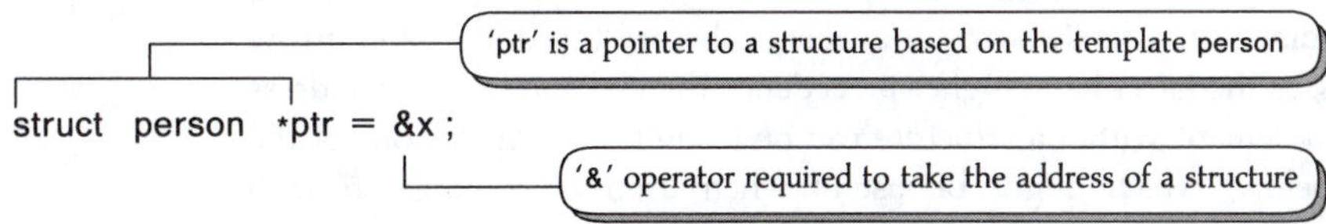

Notice how 'ptr' has been declared as a pointer to a structure based on the template **person** prior to initializing it with the address of 'x'. This is to ensure that 'ptr' is compatible with the object it points to; that is, the structure variable 'x'. The following statement, for example, would not be permitted, as 'x' and the pointer 'p1' are incompatible ('p1' is a pointer to a structure based upon the template **data**).

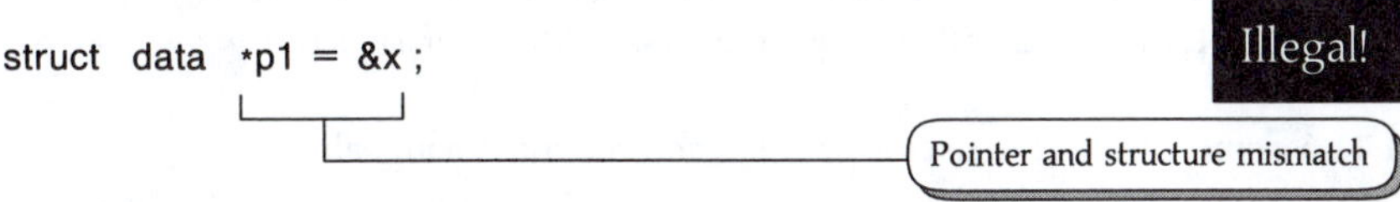

Note also that, unlike an array, the name of a structure does *not* constitute a shorthand notation for the address of its first member element, thus the address operator '&' must be used to take the address of a structure.

Having correctly defined and initialized 'ptr' to point to 'x', the member elements of 'x' could now be accessed using the pointer in conjunction with the arrow operator '−>', (a minus sign '−' followed by a greater than sign '>'). For example, the following statement uses 'ptr' to reference the member element **age** within the structure it points to:

```
ptr -> age = 45 ;
```

From this we can conclude that the following two expressions are equivalent:

```
x.name
ptr -> name
```

Furthermore, realizing that the (r)value of 'ptr' is the address of the structure 'x' – that is, 'ptr' and (&x) are equivalent when used in an expression –

and also remembering that the indirection and address operators, '*' and '&', applied to the same variable cancel each other out – that is, the expression '*&var' is equivalent to 'var' – then the expressions:

```
(*ptr) . member
(&x) -> member
```

are also interchangeable. Note that the parentheses *are* required to force the address and indirection operators to be evaluated before the dot '.' and arrow '->' operators, as the latter have higher precedence than '*' and '&'. The address of any member element within a structure can be taken using expressions of the form shown below, which might be useful when used in conjunction with functions such as scanf( ):

```
&x . age                &ptr -> age
&x. weight              &ptr -> weight
x.name                  ptr -> name
&x.name[0]              &ptr -> name[0]
```

Note that the standard header file <stddef.h> (see Chapter 18) also defines the macro offsetof( ) to enable a program to determine the address of a member element in terms of an offset from the base address of structure itself.

Program 11.6 demonstrates the use of pointers and the interchangeability of the dot and arrow operators.

Program 11.6 The arrow and dot operators in action.

```
#include  <stdio.h>

struct  complex {
   double  real ;
   double  imag ;
} x ;

int main( void )
{
   struct  complex  *ptr = &x ;

/*
** Access structure 'x' using dot '.' operator in conjunction with structure variable
** and arrow operator '->' in conjunction with pointer
*/

   x.real = 23.0 ;
   x.imag = 45.12 ;
   printf("real = %g, imag = %g\n", ptr -> real, ptr -> imag ) ;
```

```
/*
** Access structure 'x' indirectly with arrow '->' operator
** and dot operator '.' in conjunction with pointer
*/

    (&x) -> real = 23.0 ;
    (&x) -> imag = 45.12 ;
    printf("real = %g, imag = %g\n", (*ptr).real, (*ptr).imag ) ;

    return 0 ;
}
```

A particularly common mistake when using pointers to access a structure is forgetting to allocate the storage for the structure variable itself. For example, consider Program 11.7.

Program 11.7 A common mistake with pointers to structures.

```
#include <stdio.h>

struct complex {
    double real ;
    double imag ;
} ;

int main( void )                    'ptr' has not been initialized
{
    struct complex *ptr ;

    ptr -> real = 23.533 ;                                Caution!
    ptr -> imag = 345.342 ;
    ...
    ...
    return 0 ;
}
```

Here, the programmer has correctly defined the pointer based upon the structure template complex, but because the pointer was not initialized in any way, has proceeded to access the member elements of a structure whose location in memory is unknown.

To overcome this, the program could either pre-initialize 'ptr' with the address of an existing structure, or, more commonly, dynamically request memory from the operating system using malloc( ) (see Section 11.3.1).

11.3.1 *Dynamically allocating storage for a structure*

As an alternative to explicitly defining a structure variable, the program may allocate storage for a structure dynamically using the memory allocation functions malloc( ), calloc( ) or realloc( ). An example statement is shown below. This type of structure allocation forms the basis of many implementations of linked lists, which are demonstrated in Chapter 17.

Request this many bytes of storage

```
ptr = (struct person *) malloc( sizeof( struct person )) ;
```

Cast pointer returned by malloc( ) to a pointer to structure person

You will recall that malloc( ) returns the address of the start of a block of memory that has been granted by the operating system for use by the program. The use of a correctly defined structure pointer means that the program can save the address returned by malloc( ) and then access the member elements within it, using the arrow operator '->'. An example of this is given in Program 11.8.

Program 11.8 Dynamic allocation of storage for a structure.

```
#include <stdio.h>
#include <stdlib.h>

struct complex {
    double real ;
    double imag ;
} ;

int main( void )
{
    struct complex *ptr ;

/*
** Allocate storage for the structure using malloc( ) and save returned address.
** then access structure indirectly with arrow '->' operator
*/

    if(( ptr = (struct complex *)malloc( sizeof( struct complex))) == NULL ) {
        printf("Insufficient Memory for allocating Structure ... \n") ;
        exit( EXIT_FAILURE ) ;
    }

    ptr -> real = 12.65 ;
    ptr -> imag = 19.23 ;

    printf("real = %g, imag = %g\n", ptr -> real, ptr -> imag ) ;
    return 0 ;
}
```

11.3.2 *Passing and returning structures by reference*

The fact that we can pass structures to functions by value or copy is all well and good if the structure variable is quite small, but the overheads involved when copying larger structures sometimes force the programmer to consider passing the structure by reference or address.

To achieve this, a function designed to receive a structure by reference *must* declare its parameter as a pointer to that type of structure. It will, however, mean that the '->' operator will be required to access the structure's member elements. For example, the function display_data() that we saw earlier could be rewritten to receive a structure reference in the manner shown below:

Parameter is a *pointer* to structure based on person

```
void display_data( struct person *ptr )
{
   printf("Name = %s\n", ptr -> name ) ;
   printf("Address = %s\n", ptr -> address ) ;
   ...
}
```

Similarly, the function get_data() could be rewritten to work with a structure reference into which it could directly store the operator's data, thus dispensing with the need to return a structure:

Parameter is a *pointer* to structure based on person

```
void get_data( struct person *ptr )
{
   char   buff[ BUFSIZ ] ;

   printf("Name ... ") ;
   gets( ptr -> name ) ;
   ...
}
```

Store program operator's entry directly in original structure argument

If these modifications are employed, the calling function main() would need to be modified to pass the address of a structure to both functions, as shown below:

```
int main( void )
{
   struct   person   p1 ;

   get_data( &p1 ) ;
   display_data( &p1 ) ;
   ...
}
```

Pass *address* of structure 'p1' to get_data()

Pass *address* of structure 'p1' to display_data()

Alternatively, we could have rewritten the function get_data( ) to allocate its own static structure (to ensure that it is not deallocated when the function returns) and let it return the address of a pointer to this structure back to the calling function, as demonstrated below:

Function returns a *pointer* to a structure of type person

```
struct person *get_data( void )
{
  char  buff[ BUFSIZ ] ;
  static struct person p1 ;

  printf("Name ... ") ;
  gets( p1.name ) ;
  ...
  return ( &p1 ) ;
}
```

static structure 'p1'

Return address of static structure 'p1'

The function main( ) could now be rewritten as shown below:

```
int main( void )
{
  struct person *ptr ;

  ptr = get_data( ) ;
  display_data( ptr ) ;
}
```

Pointer 'ptr' to a structure of type person

Save *address* of structure returned by get_data( )

Pass *address* of structure returned by get_data( ) to display_data( )

11.4 Arrays of structures

Arrays of structures are also possible and may be accessed in a similar manner to any other type of array. For example, given a structure template complex, we could define a single dimensional array 'x' of 10 structure elements based on that template with the statements shown below:

```
struct complex {
  double real ;
  double imag ;
} ;

struct complex x[ 10 ] ;
```

Each element is a structure based on template complex

Array name is 'x'

Single dimensional array of 10 elements

Similarly, a three-dimensional array 'y' of 10 by 12 by 4 structure elements could be defined with the statement:

```
struct  complex  y [ 10 ] [ 12 ] [ 4 ] ;
```

Individual structures within such arrays may be accessed using the array operator '[ ]', after which the dot operator may be applied to reference a specific member element. For example:

```
x[ I0 ] . real = 2.5 ;
a = y[ I0 ][ I1 ][ I2 ] . imag ;
```

Likewise, the address of a unique structure within either of the arrays 'x' or 'y' could be obtained with statements of the form:

```
struct  complex  *p1 = &x[ I0 ] ;
struct  complex  *p2 = &y[ I0 ][ I1 ][ I2 ] ;
```

while the addresses of their member elements could be obtained with statements such as:

```
double  *p3 = &x[ I0 ] . real ;
double  *p4 = &y[ I0 ][ I1 ][ I2 ] . real ;
```

11.4.1 *Passing arrays of structures to functions*

As with all arrays in C, the compiler arranges for them to be passed to functions by reference; that is, it is the address of the first element in any array that is given to the function. This means that a function designed to receive an array of structures could declare its parameter either as a pointer to that type of structure or as an array of structures (a declaration which simply disguises the fact that it is a pointer).

Given, then, the single dimensional array 'x' of 10 complex structures discussed previously, we could pass 'x' (the whole array) to the functions get_complex( ) and display_complex( ) developed earlier, as shown in Program 11.9.

You will notice that both forms of parameter declaration are demonstrated, a pointer in the case of get_complex( ) and an array in the case of display_complex( ). Notice also how the pointer 'ptr' in get_complex( ) is part of a for loop. Such an operation increments the pointer by its scalar value, which is the size of the structure it is pointing to. Thus the pointer is incremented to point to the next structure element in the original array 'x'.

Program 11.9 Passing an array of structures to a function.

```
#include  <stdio.h>
#include  <stdlib.h>

#define  NUM  10

struct  complex  {
  double  real ;
  double  imag ;
} ;
                                        Parameter declared as a pointer to a structure
void get_complex( struct complex *ptr, int num )
{
  int    i ;
  char  buff[ BUFSIZ ] ;

  for ( i = 0; i < num ; i ++ )  {
    printf("Element %d\n", i ) ;

    printf("Enter Real part ... ") ;
    ptr -> real = atof(gets(buff)) ;

    printf("Enter Imaginary part ... ") ;
    ptr -> imag = atof(gets(buff)) ;
    ptr ++ ;
  }                                     Increment pointer to next structure in array
}
                                        Parameter declared as an array of structure
void display_complex( struct complex c[ ], int num )
{
  int i ;

  for ( i = 0; i < num ; i ++ )  {
    printf("Element %d\n", i ) ;
    printf("Real part = %g ", c[i].real ) ;
    printf("Imaginary part = %g\n", c[i].imag) ;
  }
}

int main( void )          'x' is equivalent to '&x[0]'; that is, the address of the first structure in 'x'
{
  struct  complex  x[ NUM ] ;

  printf("Reading Complex Numbers\n") ;
  get_complex( x, NUM ) ;

  printf("\n\nDisplaying Complex Numbers\n") ;
  display_complex( x, NUM ) ;
  return 0 ;
}
```

Notice how we have used the shorthand notation 'x' in the function main( ) as the argument to get_complex( ) in place of the notation '&x[0]' since the name of an array is shorthand for the address of the first element.

11.5 Nested and self-referential structures

In the real world, complex objects are often based upon and constructed around a number of other smaller objects. Take, for example, the motor car. This could be thought of in terms of several smaller components or objects such as the gearbox, engine, chassis, bodywork and so on. In modelling these more complex types of objects within our software, it is often desirable to be able to declare a template in terms of a number of other smaller templates.

For example, consider the various structure templates shown below, which describe four major components used in the construction of a motor car:

```
struct  engine_type  {
   int     capacity ;
   char   num_cylinders ;
   char   num_valves ;
   char   carbs_or_EFI ;
} ;

struct  gearbox_type  {
   char   auto_man ;
   char   num_gears ;
} ;

struct  chassis_type  {
   float  wheelbase ;
   char   num_wheels ;
   char   suspension_type ;
} ;

struct  body_type  {
   char   colour ;
   char   num_doors ;
   char   hatch_or_boot ;
} ;
```

We could now describe a structure template for a complete motor car in terms of the four templates above, and define a structure variable 'car' based on it, as shown below:

```
struct car_type {
  struct engine_type    engine ;
  struct gearbox_type   gearbox ;
  struct chassis_type   chassis ;
  struct body_type      body ;
} car ;
```

Member elements are all structures

Structure variable 'car'

Such an approach is useful, since it allows any complex objects to inherit the more useful features of simpler ones, and perhaps add new features of their own along the way.

Note that the previous separate templates could even have been combined into one single template, as shown below, where the embedded template names have in this instance been omitted. The reader is left to decide which approach is more readable.

```
struct car_type {

  struct {
    int   capacity ;
    char  num_cylinders ;
    char  num_valves ;
    char  carbs_or_EFI ;
  } engine ;

  struct {
    char  auto_man ;
    char  num_gears ;
  } gearbox ;

  struct {
    float wheelbase ;
    char  num_wheels ;
    char  suspension_type ;
  } chassis ;

  struct {
    char  colour ;
    char  num_doors ;
    char  hatch_or_boot ;
  } body ;

} car ;
```

Template name optional for a nested sub-structure

Sub-structure variable 'engine'

Sub-structure variable 'gearbox'

Sub-structure variable 'chassis'

Sub-structure variable 'body'

Sub-structure variable 'car'

Provided the nested templates are not required later in the program, it is purely optional whether the program chooses to name them or not.

The member elements of the structure variable 'car' could now be accessed using **multiple** dot '.' operators in the following way, where the symbolic constants AUTO, RED and HATCH are assumed to have been defined elsewhere:

```
car.engine.capacity = 1997 ;
car.engine.num_cylinders = 4 ;
car.engine.num_valves = 16 ;
car.gearbox.auto_man = AUTO ;
car.chassis.wheelbase = 167.5 ;
car.body.colour = RED ;
car.body.num_doors = 4 ;
car.body.hatch_or_boot = HATCH ;
```

In fact, the member elements of 'car' – that is, the gearbox, engine and so on – and their member elements – capacity, cylinders and so on – could even be pre-initialized with constant data during their definition. For example:

```
struct car_type car = {
  {1994, 4, 16, CARBURETTOR} ,   /* Engine data */
  {MANUAL, 5 } ,                 /* Gearbox data */
  { 167.5, 4, 1 } ,              /* Chassis data */
  { BLUE, 4, HATCH }             /* Body data */
};
```

11.5.1 *Self-referential structures*

Although it is perfectly feasible for a structure to contain member elements that are themselves structures, the compiler will not allow you to define a recursive structure where a member element is of the same type as the structure template being described, since this would make the structure's storage requirements indeterminate at compile time. For example, the following structure template is *illegal*, since the member element 'z' is a structure based upon the template currently being declared:

```
struct temp {
  float  x ;
  float  y ;
  struct temp z ;
};
```

Illegal!

Member elements cannot be based upon current template

However, having a pointer to a structure as a member element is permitted, as shown below. Such an approach is commonly used in the creation of linked lists (see Chapter 17):

```
struct  temp  {
  float    x ;
  float    y ;
  struct  temp *p1 ;
} ;
```

Pointer to this type of structure is permitted

11.6 Some further structure applications

Application 11.1

Write functions to convert numbers stored in polar form to rectangular and vice versa. Rectangular coordinates for a point 'p' are expressed in terms of the distance 'x' along the horizontal axis and distance 'y' along the vertical axis. Polar coordinates for a point 'p' are expressed in terms of angle 'θ' moving anticlockwise from a line along the horizontal axis and a radius stretching from the origin (rectangular coordinates (0, 0)) to the point 'p'. The equations relating to the two forms are given below:

$$\text{radius} = (x^2 + y^2)^{1/2} \qquad \text{and} \qquad \tan(\theta) = y/x \qquad \text{in range } -\text{PI} < \theta < \text{PI}$$

Application 11.1 Polar to rectangular conversion.

```
#include   <stdio.h>
#include   <math.h>              /* For sqrt(), sin() and cos() */

/*
** Structure templates for the two data formats
*/

struct  rectangular  {
  double   x, y ;
} ;

struct  polar  {
  double   radius, theta ;
} ;

/*
** Functions to perform the conversion. Each function expects an argument of one
** type of structure and returns a structure of the other type.
*/
```

```
struct  polar  rectangular_to_polar( struct rectangular coord )
{
  struct  polar  p ;

/*
** Check to see if the origin (0,0) has been given
** If so set theta and radius to zero
*/

  if((coord.x == 0) && ( coord.y == 0))
    p.radius = p.theta = 0 ;

  else  {
    p.radius = sqrt( coord.x * coord.x + coord.y * coord.y ) ;
    p.theta = atan2( coord.y, coord.x ) ;
  }

  return ( p ) ;
}
```

Function returns a copy of structure type polar

Parameter is a copy of structure rectangular

```
struct  rectangular  polar_to_rectangular( struct polar coord )
{
  struct  rectangular  c1 ;

  c1.x = coord.radius * cos( coord.theta ) ;
  c1.y = coord.radius * sin( coord. theta ) ;

  return ( c1 ) ;
}

int main( void )
{
  struct rectangular c1, c2 = { 1.0, 1.0 } ;
  struct polar p1, p2 = {1.414213562373095, 0.78539816339} ;

  p1 = rectangular_to_polar( c2 ) ;
  c1 = polar_to_rectangular( p2 ) ;

  printf("Radius = %f\nTheta = %f Radians\n", p1.radius, p1.theta ) ;
  printf("x = %f\ny = %f\n", c1.x, c1.y ) ;

  return 0 ;
}
```

Function returns a copy of structure type rectangular

Parameter is a copy of structure polar

Application 11.2

Write a suite of functions to perform addition, subtraction, multiplication and division of complex numbers and also to permit the entry and display of numbers in complex notation.

Application 11.2 Arithmetic functions for complex numbers.

```
#include  <stdio.h>
#include  <stdlib.h>        /* for atof() */
#include  <string.h>        /* for string manipulation functions */

/* First declare a template for the complex structure */

struct  complex {
   double  real ;
   double  imag ;
} ;

/* Now write the functions that perform the input and displays in complex notation */

struct  complex  in( void )
{
   char    buff[ BUFSIZ ] ;
   struct  complex temp ;

   printf("Enter Real Part ... ") ;
   temp.real = atof( gets( buff )) ;
   printf("Enter Imaginary Part ... ") ;
   temp.imag = atof( gets( buff )) ;
   return( temp ) ;
}

void display( struct complex x )
{
   printf("(%g ", x.real ) ;
   if( x.imag < 0.0 )
      printf("- i%g)\n", x.imag ) ;
   else
      printf(" + i%g)\n", x.imag ) ;
}

/*
** This function writes the complex number into the array
** parameter buffer and returns a pointer to the generated
** string. If buffer is NULL, then the string is saved internally.
** This is useful for use with printf().
*/
```

```
char  *display1( struct complex x , char *buffer)
{
  static  char buff[ BUFSIZ ] ;
  char    buff1[ BUFSIZ ] ;
  char    *p1 ;

  if( buffer == NULL )
    p1 = buff ;                /* save string internally */
  else
    p1 = buffer ;              /* save string in buffer array */

  sprintf( p1, "(%g ", x.real ) ;

  if( x.imag < 0.0 )
    sprintf(buff1, "– i%g)", x.imag ) ;
  else
    sprintf(buff1, " + i%g)", x.imag ) ;

  strcat( p1, buff1 ) ;
  return( p1 ) ;
}

/* Now the functions that perform simple arithmetic on complex numbers */
/* Add two complex numbers */

struct  complex  add( struct complex a, struct complex b )
{
  struct  complex z ;

  z.real = a.real + b.real ;
  z.imag = a.imag + b.imag ;
  return ( z ) ;
}

/* Subtract two complex numbers */

struct  complex  sub( struct complex a, struct complex b )
{
  struct complex z;

  z.real = a.real – b.real ;
  z.imag = a.imag – b.imag ;
  return ( z ) ;
}

/* Multiply two complex numbers */

struct  complex  mult( struct complex a, struct complex b )
{
  struct complex z ;
```

```
    z.real = a.real * b.real - a.imag * b.imag ;
    z.imag = a.real * b.real + a.imag * b.imag ;
    return ( z ) ;
}

/* Divide two complex numbers */

struct  complex  divide( struct complex a, struct complex b )
{
    struct   complex z ;
    double  denom ;

    denom = (b.real * b.real) + (b.imag * b.imag) ;
    z.real = ((a.real * b.real) + (a.imag * b.imag))/denom ;
    z.imag = ((a.imag * b.real) - (a.real * b.imag))/denom ;
    return z ;
}

/* Find the magnitude of a complex number */

double  mag( struct complex a )
{
    double  sqrt( double );      /* function prototype */

    return( sqrt( (a.real * a.real) + (a.imag * a.imag))) ;
}

int main( void )
{
    struct  complex x ;
    struct  complex y ;
    char    x_buff[ BUFSIZ ], y_buff[ BUFSIZ ] ;

/* The following structures are used in another example below */

    struct  complex z1, z2, z3, two = { 2.0 , 0 } ;

/* Read in two complex numbers */

    x = in( ) ;
    printf("Magnitude of %s is %g\n", display1( x, NULL ), mag( x ) ) ;
    y = in( ) ;
    printf("Magnitude of %s is %g\n", display1( y, NULL ), mag( y ) ) ;

    display1( x, x_buff ) ;
    display1( y, y_buff ) ;
    printf(" %s + %s = %s\n", x_buff, y_buff, display1( add(x, y ), NULL )) ;
    printf(" %s - %s = %s\n", x_buff, y_buff, display1( sub(x, y ), NULL )) ;
    printf(" %s * %s = %s\n", x_buff, y_buff, display1( mult(x, y ), NULL )) ;
    printf(" %s / %s = %s\n", x_buff, y_buff, display1( divide(x, y ), NULL )) ;
```

```
/* Now print (2 * z1 * z2)/ z3 where z1, z2 and z3 are complex */

  printf("\n\nEnter value for z1 ... \n") ;
  z1 = in( ) ;
  printf("Enter value for z2 ... \n") ;
  z2 = in( ) ;
  printf("Enter value for z3 ... \n") ;
  z3 = in( ) ;

  printf("Result of 2 * z1 * z2 / z3 is %s\n",
       display1( divide( mult( mult( two, z1) , z2 ), z3) , NULL )) ;
  return 0 ;
}
```

Application 11.3

The complex impedance 'Z' and power factor 'p.f' of the series electrical network shown in Figure 11.2 are given by the equations:

$$Z = R + j(2\pi fL - 1/2\pi fC)$$
$$p.f = R/Z$$

where R is the resistance expressed in ohms, L is the inductance in henries and C is the capacitance in farads. Write a program using the complex number functions developed in Application 11.2 to read values for f, R, L and C and thus determine Z and p.f.

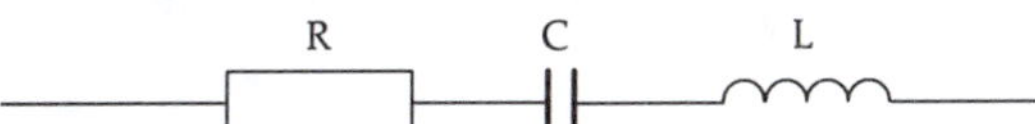

Figure 11.2 A series resistive, inductive and capacitive electrical network.

Application 11.3 Complex impedance of an electrical network.

```
#include  <stdio.h>

#define  PI  3.141592653

int main( void )
{
  char  buff[ BUFSIZ ] ;

  struct    complex Z, R = {0.0, 0.0}, C = {0.0, 0.0}, L = {0.0, 0.0} ;
  double   pf, f ;
```

```
    printf("Enter Frequency F: ") ;
    f = atof(gets(buff)) ;

    printf("Enter Resistance R: ") ;
    R.real = atof(gets(buff)) ;

    printf("Enter Capacitance C: ") ;
    C.imag = atof(gets(buff)) ;
    C.imag = 1.0 / (2.0 * PI * f * C.imag);

    printf("Enter Inductance L: ") ;
    L.imag = atof(gets(buff)) ;
    L.imag = 2.0 * PI * f * L.imag ;

    Z = add(R, sub(C, L)) ;
    printf("Impedance = %g ohms\n", mag(Z)) ;

    pf = mag(divide(R,Z)) ;
    printf("Power factor = %g\n", pf) ;
    return 0 ;
}
```

On the author's system, the program in Application 11.3 produced the following sample display:

```
Enter Frequency F: 1000
Enter Resistance R: 100
Enter Capacitance C: 0.1e-6
Enter Inductance L: 1e-4
Impedance = 1594.06 ohms
Power factor = 0.0627329
```

11.7 Unions

A union is in many ways similar to a structure. They are even defined in a similar manner, as both are based around a template and their member elements may be accessed using the '.' or '->' operators. However, where a union principally differs from a structure is that the compiler only allocates sufficient memory to a union to hold or represent a *single* member element at any one time. In other words, all member elements of a union *share* the same common storage.

A more traditional application of the union, and one that still finds use in small embedded microprocessor applications, is in allowing a program to reuse storage for different variable types, which can in some instances lead to useful reductions in the amount of memory required by applications. However, other applications do exist, as we shall see.

To introduce a union, the program must first declare a union template describing the name and type of its member elements, an operation which is similar to declaring a structure template except that the key word struct is replaced by union, as shown below:

Key word union to introduce union template

Template name is temp

```
union  temp  {
  char     name[ 20 ] ;
  double  x, y ;
  int       i ;
} ;
```

Member elements of union

A union variable and a pointer to that union could then be introduced using statements such as those shown below:

Key word union to introduce union variable

union variable is *based on* template temp

```
union  temp  u1 ;
union  temp  *ptr = &u1 ;
```

'u1' is the union variable

union pointer initialized with address of 'u1'

'ptr' is a pointer to a union

The member elements of 'u1' may then be accessed with the dot '.' or arrow '->' operators. For example:

```
u1 . x = 23.245 ;
ptr -> i = 19 ;
```

An array of unions and an (uninitialized) array of pointers to such unions can be defined with statements such as:

'u1' is an array of 100 unions based on temp

```
union  temp  u1[ 100 ] ;
union  temp  *ptr[ 100 ] ;
```

'ptr' is an array of 100 *pointers* to unions based on temp

11.7.1 *Storage requirements of a union*

Unlike a structure, when a union template is declared, the compiler examines the declaration of its template to determine the size of the largest member element. This then becomes the size of any union variable based upon that template. For example, when the union template temp was declared previously, each member element would typically require the storage shown in Table 11.1.

Table 11.1 Storage requirements for union 'u1'.

Typical member	*Type*	*Storage requirements (bytes)*
name	Array of char	20
x	double	8
y	double	8
i	int	2

However, in examining the template, the compiler concludes that the largest element in the union is the array name, requiring 20 bytes, and thus the union variable 'u1' would be allocated 20 bytes of storage, a fact that can be determined using the sizeof operator with the statement below. This is in contrast to a structure, which would have required at least 38 bytes of storage.

Calculate size of 'u1'

```
printf("Union is %u bytes\n", sizeof( u1 ) ) ;
```

11.7.2 *Accessing union members*

Since a union is allocated only sufficient storage to represent its largest member, it follows that each member element must in fact share the same storage with all other member elements. For example, the addresses of each of the member elements name, 'x', 'y' and 'i' are all the *same*.

This is an important concept, because assigning a value to any member element of a union will automatically overwrite the value of any other member element, since they all share the same storage. It is, therefore, the programmer's responsibility to keep a record of which element is in use within the union at any one time.

Program 11.10 demonstrates this shared storage principle by defining a union variable 'u' containing the integer and double member elements 'x' and 'y'. The program begins by introducing and displaying the addresses of both the union and its member elements, thus demonstrating that they share common

Program 11.10 Accessing member elements of a union.

```
#include  <stdio.h>

/* Describe a union template */

union  temp  {
  int       x ;
  double  y ;
} ;

int main( void )
{

  union   temp u ;

/* Display the storage requirements for the union 'u' */

  printf("Sizeof union temp = %d\n\n", sizeof( u )) ;

/* Now show that each member element shares the same address as the union */

  printf("Address of u.x= %p\n", &u.x ) ;
  printf("Address of u.y = %p\n", &u.y ) ;
  printf("Address of u = %p\n\n", &u ) ;

/* Now place a value into union member 'x' and then display it */

  u.x = 23 ;
  printf("u.x = %d\n", u.x ) ;

/* Now place a value into 'u.y' and this should overwrite 'u.x' */

  u.y = -1055.0 ;
  printf("u.y = %g\n", u.y ) ;

/* Display 'u.x' to show that it has altered after writing to 'u.y' */

  printf("After changing y, u.x now = %d\n", u.x ) ;
  return 0 ;
}
```

storage. A value is then assigned to 'x', which is displayed prior to a value being assigned to 'y'. You will observe that this last assignment overwrites the value of 'x'.

When Program 11.10 was run on the author's computer, the following display was observed:

```
Sizeof union temp = 8

Address of u.x = 7157:1CC4
Address of u.y = 7157:1CC4
Address of u = 7157:1CC4

u.x = 23
u.y = -1055
After changing y, u.x = 0
```

11.7.3 *Initializing a union*

Initialization of a union is possible and is performed in a similar manner to the initialization of a structure. The only exception, of course, is that the initializing list may only contain a single item of data, which is then assigned to the first member element declared in the template. For example, given the union template temp below:

```
union temp {
   char     name[ 20 ] ;
   double x, y ;
   int        i ;
} ;
```

the following statement would initialize the first member element name within the union 'u' with characters from the string "Hello World".

Initializing data is assigned to element u1.name

```
union temp u = { "Hello World" } ;
```

11.7.4 *Further applications of unions*

Imagine that you are designing a graphics based CAD system where an operator draws objects on the screen with a mouse or some other input device, and these objects are to be stored and redisplayed later. A subset of these objects might include points, lines, triangles, circles and so on.

To record each object a structure could be declared containing a number of other nested structures that describe each type of object. A collection of objects could then be stored within an array of such structures. However, this would be very wasteful in memory and disk space if ever the collection of objects were saved to a file, since each structure would only be called upon to record one single object at a time; that is, a point, a line, a circle and so on.

By introducing a union as an element of the structure, the program could reduce the amount of storage it requires to record the details of each separate object. A further variable could describe which union member is in use within that structure. For example, the template for such a structure is shown below:

```
struct object {
  int object_type ;          — This describes which element in union data is in use
  union {
    struct point p ;    ┐
    struct line l ;     ├—— These member elements share common storage
    struct circle c ;   │
    struct triangle t ; ┘
  } data ;                   — Structure template describes a union member
} ;
```

An extract from a simple program designed to read and record these four different types of objects is shown in Program 11.11. In this simple example, the data is assumed to come from an operator via the keyboard, but that should not detract from the principles involved.

Program 11.11 Using structures to store different types of objects.

```
#include <stdio.h>
#include <stdlib.h>
#include <ctype.h>

/* Structure templates for each type of object */

struct point     { int x, y ; } ;
struct line      { int x1, y1, x2, y2 ; } ;
struct circle    { int x, y, radius ; } ;
struct triangle  { int x1,y1, x2, y2, x3, y3 ; } ;

struct object {
  int object_type ;
  union {
    struct point     p ;
    struct line      l ;
    struct circle    c ;
    struct triangle  t ;
  } data ;
} ;

/* Function prototypes */

void get_point( struct object *ptr );
void get_line( struct object *ptr ) ;
void get_triangle( struct object *ptr ) ;
void get_circle( struct object *ptr ) ;
```

```
/* Constants used to identify each object */

const  int  POINT = 0 ;
const  int  LINE = 1 ;
const  int  TRIANGLE = 2 ;
const  int  CIRCLE = 3 ;

int main( void )
{
  int    i ;
  char  c ;

/* Restrict ourselves to 100 objects */

  struct  object  object[ 100 ] ;

  for( i = 0; i < 100 ; i ++ )  {
    printf("\n\nEnter object Type ... P(oint), L(ine), C(ircle), T(riangle) ") ;
    c = toupper( getchar( )) ;
    fflush(stdin) ;                     /* get rid of '\n' left behind by getchar( ) */

    switch ( c )  {
      case 'P':   get_point( &object[ i ] ) ;
                  break ;
      case 'L':   get_line( &object[ i ] ) ;
                  break ;
      case 'C':   get_circle( &object[ i ] ) ;
                  break ;
      case 'T':   get_triangle( &object[ i ] ) ;
                  break ;
    }
  }

  return 0 ;
}

void get_point( struct object *ptr )
{
  char buff[ BUFSIZ ] ;

/* Example section of code to read coords for a point from operator */

  ptr -> object_type = POINT ;
  printf(" \nEnter 'X' Coord for Point ... " ) ;
  ptr -> data.p.x = atoi( gets( buff )) ;
  printf("Enter 'Y' Coord for Point ... " ) ;
  ptr -> data.p.y = atoi( gets( buff )) ;
}
```

```
void get_line( struct object *ptr )
{
   ptr -> object_type = LINE ;
/* Read data on LINE from operator */
   ...
}

void get_triangle( struct object *ptr )
{
   ptr -> object_type = TRIANGLE ;
/* Read data on TRIANGLE from operator */
   ...
}

void get_circle( struct object *ptr )
{
   ptr -> object_type = CIRCLE ;
/* Read data on CIRCLE from operator */
   ...
}
```

The use of structures and unions also facilitates the creation of generic functions able to receive data of differing type. For example, if a collection of functions such as display_point(), display_line() and so on were included in Program 11.11 to display each different type of object, then rather than have the program call these individual functions itself depending upon the object – triangle, point, circle and so on – it could instead be written to call a generic function display() and present that with a structure of type object. The function could then examine the contents of the member element object_type and call the corresponding display function for that type of object. For example:

```
void   display( struct object x )
{
  if( x.object_type == TRIANGLE)
     display_triangle( &x ) ;
  if( x.object_type == LINE )
     display_line( &x ) ;
  ...
}
```

Now the main program could display all objects with a simple loop such as:

```
for( i = 0; i < 100 ; i ++ )
  display( object[ i ] ) ;
```

11.8 Chapter summary

(1) A structure is a convenient way of grouping together several items of related data under one variable name. Unlike an array, the member elements of a structure need not be of the same type.

(2) A structure is defined in two parts. The first part involves the declaration of a template describing the names and types of the structure's member elements, for example:

```
struct  t1  {
   int a ;
   int b ;
} ;
```

where 't1' is the template or tag name. The second part introduces a structure variable based upon a previously declared template, for example:

```
struct t1 x ;
```

where 'x' is the structure variable based around the template 't1'. Both parts may be combined into a single definition if required, in which case a template name is optional.

(3) A structure variable may be initialized with constant data when it is defined in a manner similar to that of initializing array elements, for example:

```
struct t1 x = { 1, 2 } ;
```

(4) Member elements of a structure (or union) may be accessed using the dot '.' operator in conjunction with the structure variable and a member element, for example:

```
x.a = x.b = 32 ;
```

(5) A pointer to a structure may be defined and initialized with the address of a structure, as shown below:

```
struct t1 *ptr = &x ;
```

The arrow '->' operator may then be used to access the structure indirectly via the pointer, for example:

```
ptr -> a = ptr -> b = 64 ;
```

(6) Unlike arrays, two compatible structures may be assigned to each other using the assignment operator '='. However, other operations such as comparison, addition and so on, are not legal and must be performed on an element by element basis.

(7) All structures are passed to and returned from a function by copy; that is, the compiler makes a copy of the whole structure and passes or returns the copy to/from the function. Passing and returning structures by reference is achieved by passing/returning a pointer to the address of a structure.

(8) A structure template may not be recursive; that is, it cannot contain a member element which is a structure of the same type as that which is being declared. However, a pointer to a structure of the same type is permitted as a member element.

(9) A union is similar to a structure, but differs principally in respect of the storage allocated to it, which is sufficient to represent only the largest member element. As all members of a union share the same storage, only one member element can physically exist at any one time; thus, it is the programmer's responsibility to remember which member is in use at any one time.

11.9 Exercises

11.1 What is the principal advantage of a structure over an array? What key word is used to describe a structure?

11.2 How does the use of a structure simplify the coding of a program when large amounts of data of varying type are passed between functions?

11.3 What is meant by the terms 'structure template' and 'structure template or tag name'? Why is the latter generally required? Under what circumstances may the template name be omitted? What are the implications for the programmer if it is omitted?

11.4 Why would it be unsafe for a programmer to 'hand calculate' the size or storage requirements of a structure by summing the storage requirements for each member element? From this, explain why structure comparison does not make sense.

11.5 How are structures passed to functions, by value/copy or by reference? What do the dot '.' and arrow '->' operators do and when can they be used? Write two versions of a function to compare two complex numbers (see Application 11.2) for equality using 'pass by value' and 'pass by reference' techniques.

11.6 What is wrong with the following structure template?

```
struct data {
  int      data ;
  double   data1 ;
  struct   data data2 ;
} data, data1, data2 ;
```

11.7 Declare a single structure template to record a given date and time, for example 11/04/92 12:21:15. Given this, write:

(a) A function to allow an operator to enter date and time information expressed in the above format.

(b) A function to display date and time in the above format.

(c) A function to convert a given date and time into the number of seconds that have elapsed since 00:00:00 1st January 1995.

(d) A function to perform the reverse operation to that in part (c).

(e) A function to determine the time in seconds that have elapsed between two dates/times.

(f) A function to update a given date/time by 't' seconds.

11.8 Break down your time structure template from Exercise 11.7 such that date and time are now recorded within two smaller structure templates. Now describe a structure template that contains these two smaller templates as its member elements. Rewrite the six functions from Exercise 11.7 to make use of this new data structure.

11.9 Declare a structure template to describe the arrangement of registers within:

(a) The PIA chip

(b) The analog to digital converter (ADC)

(c) The liquid crystal display (LCD)

examples of which were discussed in Chapter 8. Rewrite the example programs given there to make use of structures and templates.

11.10 Rewrite Exercises 8.21, 8.22, 8.23 and 10.11, relating to the PIA, to make use of structures.

11.11 A given computer system has 4 PIA chips within it located at hex addresses 8000, 8004, 8008 and 800C. Using the example structure template developed for this chip in Exercise 11.9, create an array of pointers to these four chips and modify the functions developed in Exercises 11.9 and 11.10 to allow them to work with a particular PIA.

11.12 What is the principal difference between a union and a structure? How much storage is allocated to a union?

11.13 Expand the partially implemented graphics progam under development in Program 11.11 into a complete working program such that up to 100 objects – points, lines, triangles and so on – can be recorded and displayed back to the operator (in text form rather than graphically).

11.14 Further enhance the program developed in Exercise 11.13 to cater for a wider variety of objects, for example rectangles, and perhaps including outline and fill colours, and to allow objects to be edited/modified and deleted.

11.15 Further enhance the program developed in Exercises 11.13 and 11.14 so that the restriction to 100 objects is removed.

Hint: Use the dynamic memory allocation functions, `malloc()`, `calloc()` and `realloc()`. There are two ways in which this could be achieved; see Programs 8.16 and 10.5 for ideas.

12 Type Defined, Enumerated and Bit Field Data

In this relatively short chapter we conclude our discussion of C's data types by taking a look at the subject of **type defined**, **enumerated** and **bit field** data. Although each topic is ultimately important for a fuller understanding of the language, none in itself provides the reader with any new or essential knowledge that will enable him or her to solve otherwise unsolvable problems. Instead, they simply provide a means of repackaging and reusing existing ideas in a more convenient manner and perhaps in a more readily understood form. With this in mind, the reader may like to defer the study of these topics until later.

12.1 Creating new data types

A `typedef` statement allows the programmer to extend or add to the range of data types within the language by defining new ones. There is nothing very clever or particularly significant about this since any new data types are in essence nothing more than an *existing* data type masquerading under a new type name; thus there are no operations that can be performed on variables of the new type that could not be performed on variables of the old or existing type upon which they are based.

Whether defining new data types is considered useful of not depends upon your own point of view and your reasons for introducing them in the first place. Their major attraction seems to be that they increase readability and understanding of the program by allowing variables to be defined using a data type that more readily indicates their role in the program. For example, the programmer might define the new data type `colour` with the following statement:

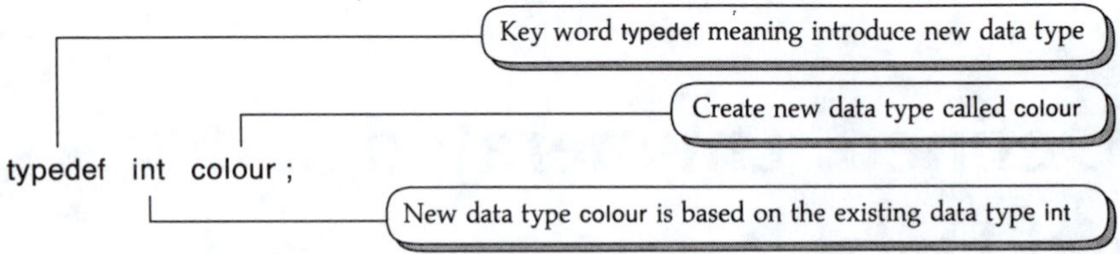
Key word typedef meaning introduce new data type
Create new data type called colour
typedef int colour ;
New data type colour is based on the existing data type int

which simply means that the new data type colour is a **synonym** or **alias** for the data type int and can thus be used wherever an int type declaration could be used. For example, the following statement introduces three variables 'a', 'b' and 'c' of type colour. The compiler will thus treat these variables exactly as if they had been defined as type int:

```
colour  a = 0, b = 1, c = 2 ;
```

('a', 'b' and 'c' are variables of type colour, which means they are ints)

Program 12.1 demonstrates this.

Program 12.1 Example use of typedef.

```
#include <stdio.h>
#include <stdlib.h>

#define  RED      0
#define  BLUE     1
#define  YELLOW   2
#define  WHITE    3

typedef  int  colour ;          Create new data type colour

                                Parameter 'c1' is of type colour
void set_colour( colour c1 ) ;
colour get_colour( void ) ;
                                Function returns data of type colour

int main( void )
{
  colour  background = YELLOW ;
  colour  foreground = WHITE ;  Variables of type colour
  colour  text = RED ;
  colour  col1;

  set_colour( text ) ;
  printf("Colour is %d\n", text ) ;

  col1= get_colour( ) ;
  set_colour( BLUE ) ;
```

```
    return 0 ;
}

void set_colour( colour c1 )
{
    ...
}

colour get_colour( void )
{
    colour x ;
    ...

    return x ;
}
```

As another example, consider the following definition of the new data type string, absent from the C language:

```
typedef  char  *string ;
```

Create new data type called string

string is really a char pointer

Using this new data type, it would now be possible to define variables of type string within the program, resulting in the compiler representing them as 'char pointers'. Therefore, the following statement defines the literal text string "Paul Davies" and a char pointer name which is subsequently initialized with the address of the first character in the string:

```
string  name = "Paul Davies" ;
```

Variable name is really a char pointer

The new type string may now be used in place of any char pointer declaration with the same effect, such as in function arguments, definitions and prototypes. For example:

```
int     strlen( string s ) ;
string  strcpy( string dest, string source ) ;
```

Parameter 's' is of type string; that is, a char pointer

Function returns a string; that is, a char pointer

In reality, then, the compiler is simply treating type defined variables in exactly the same manner as if they had been defined as variables of the original type on which they were based.

The syntax for defining new data types often causes some confusion for new programmers, so it is worth noting that the same right–left rule that we met in Section 10.4 also applies when defining a new type. For example, taking a typical typedef statement and commencing with what *appears* to be the variable name (but is in fact the new type name), we work outwards in a right–left manner until all terms in the expression have been used. Therefore, the following typedef statement:

```
typedef  int  chess_board[ 8 ][ 8 ] ;
```

defines the new data type chess_board to be a two-dimensional int array of 8 by 8 elements, and thus the variable 'x' below is an array of 8 by 8 integers:

```
chess_board  x ;
```

'x' is of type chess_board; that is, an array of 8 by 8 int

More importantly (and more commonly), new data types can be based upon existing structure templates. For example, given the structure for a complex number shown below:

```
struct  c  {
  double  real ;
  double  imag ;
} ;
```

we could type define the structure template 'c' to create the new data type complex, as shown below:

```
typedef  struct c  complex ;
```

Create new data type complex

Data type complex is really a structure based on template 'c'

Note that this could, if required, have been combined into a single statement of the form:

```
typedef  struct  {
  double  real ;
  double  imag ;
} complex ;
```

Create new data type complex

where the template name is optional (since we have created a type by which to refer to it) and has thus been omitted. This would now allow us to rewrite some of the complex number manipulation functions we encountered in Chapter 11 to make use of the new data type complex. An extract from the complete program is shown in Program 12.2. The reader is left to rewrite the remaining functions as a simple exercise.

Program 12.2 Rewriting functions to use the new data type complex.

```
/*
** First introduce the new data type complex
*/

typedef struct {
    double real ;
    double imag ;
} complex ;

/*
** Now a function to display a complex number
*/

void display( complex x )
{
    printf("(%g ", x.real ) ;

    if( x.imag < 0 )
        printf("- i%g)\n", x.imag ) ;
    else
        printf(" + i%g)\n", x.imag ) ;
}

/*
** Now the functions that perform simple arithmetic on complex numbers, for example
** add two complex numbers
*/

complex add( complex a, complex b )
{
    complex z ;

    z.real = a.real + b.real ;
    z.imag = a.imag + b.imag ;

    return ( z ) ;
}
```

```
/*
** Subtract two complex numbers
*/

complex   sub( complex a, complex b )
{
    complex z ;

    z.real = a.real - b.real ;
    z.imag = a.imag - b.imag ;

    return ( z ) ;
}
```

12.1.1 *Useful applications of* typedef

Another useful application for user defined data types lies in the generation of portable code. Place yourself in the position of a programmer faced with the problem of writing one version of a program that could be compiled under a variety of different compilers that may each choose to represent the int data type in different ways, for example 16/32 bit.

By defining a new data type INT based around a suitable *existing* data type, such as short or long, and then basing all integer variable definitions around the new defined type INT, it is easy to write programs that are portable. For example, let us assume that all integers in a program are required to be 16 bit quantities and that all characters are required to be signed 8 bit quantities. Assuming that the compiler uses 16 bit ints we could create the new type INT using the statement:

```
typedef   int   INT ;     // Create new data type INT as an int
```

For a compiler using 32 bit ints we would probably define INT as:

```
typedef   short   INT ;     // Create new data type INT as a short
```

On both systems, the data type CHAR could unambiguously be defined as a signed quantity with the statement:

```
typedef   signed char   CHAR ;     // Type CHAR is a signed char
```

When porting the program from one machine to another, the only modifications required to ensure that chars are signed, and that ints are 16 bits, would be simple modifications to the typedef statements above. This is demonstrated in Program 12.3, written in this instance to assume a 32 bit sized integer, thus the data type INT has been defined as a short int (presumed to be 16 bit) quantity.

Program 12.3 Writing portable code on a 32 bit system with typedef.

```
#include  <stdio.h>

typedef  short int  INT ;

INT mult( INT a, INT b )
{
   INT result ;
   result = a * b ;

   return( result ) ;
}

INT main( void )
{
   INT a = 3, b = 4 ;
   printf(" %d * %d = %d\n", a, b, mult( a, b )) ;

   return (INT)(0) ;
}
```

To recompile the above program for use on an 8 or 16 bit system, only the following simple change to the definition of data type INT would be required:

```
typedef  int  INT ;
```

Another application for user defined data types lies with embedded systems, where a programmer frequently has to deal with and manipulate byte (8 bit), word (16 bit) and long word (32 bit) sized data, often represented as values within the registers of I/O chips. To aid readability, the new data types BYTE, WORD and LONG could be introduced, as shown below, assuming that short and long ints are represented by 16 and 32 bit quantities, respectively:

```
typedef volatile unsigned char BYTE ;
typedef volatile unsigned short int WORD ;
typedef volatile unsigned long int LONG ;
```

Data type LONG is a volatile unsigned long int

A pointer to each of these data types could then be defined and initialized with an absolute address in the manner shown below, where the integer constants 0xc000, 0xe10000 and 0xffc00 that represent the addresses to be assigned to 'p1', 'p2' and 'p3' are first cast to the value of BYTE, WORD and LONG pointers, to keep the compiler happy:

```
BYTE   *p1 = (BYTE *)(0xc000) ;
WORD   *p2 = (WORD *)(0xe10000) ;
LONG   *p3 = (LONG *)(0xffc00) ;
```

12.2 Enumerated data types

The enumerated data type has generally evolved in other languages from a desire to provide closer type checking of variables, usually with the aim of restricting their values to a specific range. For example, a programmer might wish to introduce a variable of type 'boolean' which would only be permitted to assume the values 'true' or 'false'. Any operation attempting to assign such a variable a value other than this would be flagged as an error at compile or run time.

Unfortunately, the C language, probably for reasons of efficiency, has chosen not to include this last and probably only useful attribute in its implementation of enumerated data, with the result that a C compiler performs absolutely no checking of an enumerated variable's value at compile time, nor does it generate code to check its value at run time.

After reading these sections you may well conclude that enumerated data is not particularly useful in C, but as it is part of the language, it will be discussed briefly here. Its only practical application in C is to reduce the amount of effort required when creating a large number of symbolic integer constants. Let us start by taking a look at how enumerated data is declared.

12.2.1 *Declaring an enumerated data type*

An enumerated data type, like a structure, is introduced in two parts. Firstly, a template is declared describing a list of symbolic names/constants, all of which are assumed to be of type int. The general format for describing such a template is given below:

enum name { sym_0, sym_1 ... sym_n } ;

Key word enum

Enumerated type/template name

Comma ',' separated list of symbolic names

where enum is a reserved word used to indicate an enumerated data type and name is the name of the enumerated template. The symbolic constants sym_0, sym_1 ... sym_n are user supplied names and by default (unless overidden) assume successive integer values, commencing with 0 upwards to 'n'. As an example, we could introduce the new enumerated data type colour using the following statement:

```
enum  colour  {
  RED, GREEN, BLUE, YELLOW, MAGENTA, CYAN, WHITE, BLACK
} ;
```

Here, the symbolic constants RED, GREEN, BLUE ... BLACK assume the integer values 0, 1, 2 ... 7, respectively. An enumerated variable based on that template could then be defined using a statement such as that shown below, which creates an enumerated (for which read integer) variable 'c1' initialized with the value 7:

'c1' is an enumerated variable assigned the value 7

```
enum  colour  c1  =  BLACK ;
```

Defining enumerated variables in this manner can become a bit of a handful and many programmers often elect to type define enumerated templates in a similar manner to structures and unions. This improves the readability of the program and more readily suggests the role of any variable based upon that type. As an example, we could type define the above template to create the new data type colour using a statement such as that below, where the enumerated template name is optional and in this instance has been omitted:

```
typedef  enum  {
  RED, GREEN, BLUE, YELLOW, MAGENTA, CYAN, WHITE, BLACK
} colour ;
```

Create new data type called colour as an enumerated data type

The variable 'c1' could now be defined in the manner shown below, which is easier both to read and to type in:

```
colour  c1  =  BLACK ;
```

It is important to realize that in C, at least, all enumerated variables are treated by the compiler exactly as if they had been defined as integers, thus their use should be indistinguishable from an int within the program. This means that any operations that are valid for integers are equally valid for an enumerated variable, and thus the following statement is perfectly legitimate, even though it may result in 'c1' being assigned a value that was 'not defined' for its type. Other language compilers may well report this as an error, but not C.

```
c1 ++ ;        'c1' is incremented to the value '8', undefined for its type
```

As another example, we could define the new data type BOOLEAN as shown below, which allows a BOOLEAN type variable to assume the value 0 meaning FALSE and 1 meaning TRUE:

```
typedef  enum { FALSE, TRUE } BOOLEAN ;
```

Thus, a function could return a BOOLEAN (that is, integer) value in the following manner:

```
BOOLEAN   confirm( void )
{
  printf("Are you sure ... ? [y/n]") ;
  if( getchar() == 'y' )
    return TRUE ;
  else
    return FALSE ;
}
```

If this looks a little confusing, just think of the type specifier BOOLEAN as meaning int while TRUE and FALSE are simply integer constants with values 1 and 0, respectively.

From time to time, it may be necessary to assign explicit integer values to some or all of the symbolic names of an enumerated type. This can be achieved using the assignment operator '=' for each individual symbol name in the enumerated type. Any symbols not explicitly initialized simply assume incremental values 1 greater than the previous symbol's value. This can in some circumstances lead to several symbols assuming the same value. For example, in the statement below, both the symbols ROVER and BMW assume the value 0, while FORD and RENAULT assume the value 1:

```
enum  car  {
  ROVER, FORD, JAGUAR = -1, BMW, RENAULT
} ;
```

12.2.2 *The scope of enumerated variables*

Enumerated variables adhere to the same rules of scope and privacy as integers, while the scope of their templates follows similar rules to those of structures and unions. It is therefore possible to introduce enumerated variables with auto, register, static and global scope. Of more importance, however, is the fact that the symbolic names defined within an enumerated template also have their own scope and privacy, which means that other enumerated symbol names or any explicit constants and variables cannot be introduced with the same name and scope as an existing enumerated symbol since this would lead to the multiple declaration of the same identifier. The following program section therefore produces an error at compile time, since the symbolic constant BLACK is multiply defined:

```
int main( void )
{
  typedef  enum  { BLACK, WHITE } colour ;
  const  int  BLACK = 23 ;

  int  WHITE = 32 ;

  ...
}
```

Illegal!

Multiple definition of BLACK

Multiple definition of WHITE

It follows from this that two enumerated templates with the same level of scope cannot both describe the same symbolic constant(s). Thus the following program section also produces an error, since WHITE is multiply defined:

```
int main( void )
{
  typedef  enum  { RED, WHITE, BLUE } palette1 ;
  typedef  enum  { BLACK, WHITE } palette2 ;
  ...
}
```

Illegal!

Multiple definitions of constant WHITE

12.3 Bit fields

Bit fields provide a convenient means of specifying the size of a variable in terms of the number of bits of storage required to represent it. This can in some instances lead to considerable savings in storage for a program, particularly in small embedded microprocessor applications. As an example, consider a program required to record the following information about an individual:

Sex	0 = Male, 1 = Female
Height	0 = Tall, 1 = Average, 2 = Short
Weight	0 = Overweight, 1 = Average, 2 = Underweight
Eye colour	0 = Blue, 1 = Brown, 2 = Green, 3 = Grey

Hair colour	0 = Blond, 1 = Brown, 2 = Ginger, 3 = Black
Marital status	0 = Married, 1 = Single, 2 = Divorced, 3 = Widowed
Number of children	0–6 children, 7 = more than 6 children
Home ownership	0 = Owner, 1 = Rented
Car owner	0 = Yes, 1 = No

Perhaps the most obvious way to record this data would be to declare a structure template, describing nine member elements of type char. An array of such structures could then be introduced to record information relating to perhaps 100 or more individuals. Such an arrangement would lead to a storage requirement of at least 900 bytes for the program.

However, a closer analysis of the data reveals that each piece of information requires between 1 and 3 bits of storage to represent all possible values that could be associated with it, thus the information about any individual could in fact be **packed** into a single two byte (unsigned) integer, as illustrated in Figure 12.1 for the variable 'i'.

An array of 100 such 16 bit integers might then only require 200 bytes of storage. Of course if the programmer chooses to represent the data in this way, then he or she will have to take responsibility for the **packing** (storing) and **unpacking** (retrieving) of each item of data using C's range of bitwise AND, OR and SHIFT operators. For example, data could be stored/packed into the individual fields within 'i' using statements such as:

Packing

```
i = i | ( (height << 1) & 0x06 ) ;
i = i | ( (weight << 3) & 0x18 ) ;
i = i | ( (car_owner << 15 ) & 0x8000 ) ;
```

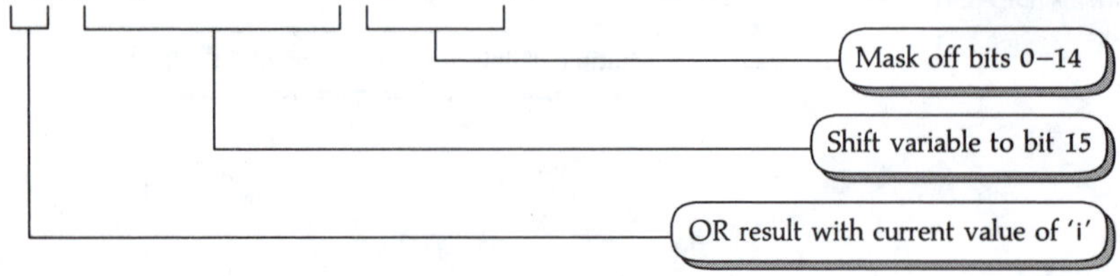

Mask off bits 0–14

Shift variable to bit 15

OR result with current value of 'i'

and unpacked/retrieved with statements such as those shown below, a technique which – for the programmer at least – is both tedious and prone to error:

16 bit Unsigned Integer i

Car	Home	Number of children	Marital status	Hair colour	Eye colour	Weight	Height	Sex
15	14	13–11	10–9	8–7	6–5	4–3	2–1	0

BitNum

Figure 12.1 Packing an individual's details into a 2 byte integer.

```
printf("Height = %u\n", ( i & 0x06 ) >> 1 ) ;
printf("Weight = %u\n", ( i & 0x18 ) >> 3 ) ;
printf("Car = %u\n", ( i & 0x8000 ) >> 15 ) ;
```

Unpacking

Shift to bit position 1

Extract bit 15 from 'i'

Fortunately, these complex operations can be automated through the use of C's 'bit fields', which leave the tedious and complex operations of creating a 'mask' for the '&' operator and appropriate values for the '<<' and '>>' operators to the compiler. Let's take a look at how this is done.

12.3.1 *Introducing a bit field*

A bit field can only be introduced as a member element of a structure or union. The general form of a bit field declaration is given below:

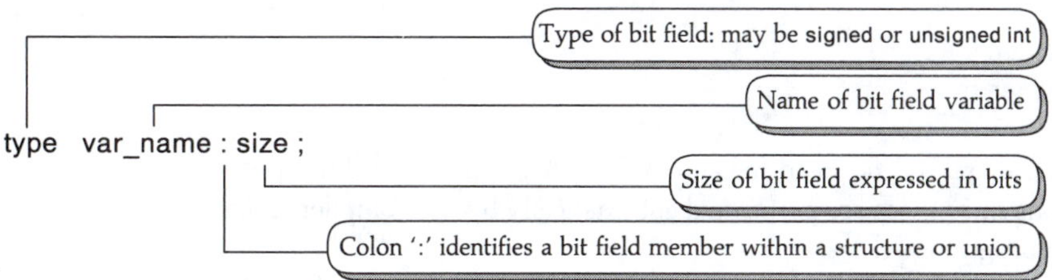

where type may be either signed or unsigned (the use of int is implied) and size defines the number of bits needed to represent that variable. For example, given the need to represent the information about an individual discussed earlier, we could declare the following structure template with nine bit fields as member elements ranging in size from 1 to 3 bits:

```
struct individual {
  unsigned  sex : 1 ;
  unsigned  height : 2 ;
  unsigned  weight : 2 ;
  unsigned  eye_colour : 2 ;
  unsigned  hair_colour : 2 ;
  unsigned  marital_status : 2 ;
  unsigned  children : 3 ;
  unsigned  home_ownership : 1 ;
  unsigned  car_owner : 1 ;
} ;
```

Member requires 1 bit of storage

Member requires 3 bits of storage

Now, the compiler can determine that any variable derived from this template requires at least 16 bits of storage to represent it. Therefore, given the definition of person below:

```
struct individual person ;
```

the compiler would probably allocate two bytes of storage to it, a fact that can easily be verified with the sizeof( ) operator, for example:

```
printf("size of person is: %u bytes\n", sizeof( person ) ) ;
```

12.3.2 *Accessing a bit field*

Because bit fields are member elements of a structure or union, they can be accessed using the standard dot '.' or arrow '->' operator notation in conjunction with the structure/union variable name or pointer as appropriate. For example, given the structure variable person defined previously, its member elements could be accessed in the following simple manner:

```
person . height = 0 ;
person . car_owner = 1 ;
```

Note that there was no need for any AND ('&'), OR ('|') or Shift ('<<' '>>') operations since these are performed automatically by the compiler and are invisible to the programmer.

It is also worth noting that the compiler is not obliged to point out any inconsistencies in your assignments to bit field members. For example, even though a 3 bit unsigned field may have been defined, there is nothing to prevent the programmer from attempting to assign it values such as −234 or +1024. Such operations, although obviously leading to unpredictable results for that variable, should not adversely affect other bit fields.

12.3.3 *The storage and alignment of bit field members*

The compiler will arrange for bit field members to be packed into what are known as 'storage units'. These are generally related to the size of a 'machine word' and are typically representative of the size of an int on that compiler. The programmer should make no assumptions about the order in which individual bit fields will be stored within a given storage unit because this aspect of storage is deemed to be implementation dependent.

For example, some compilers may store the bit fields in a left to right manner, while others may store them right to left, as illustrated in Figure 12.2. However, where appropriate, the compiler should arrange for successive bit field

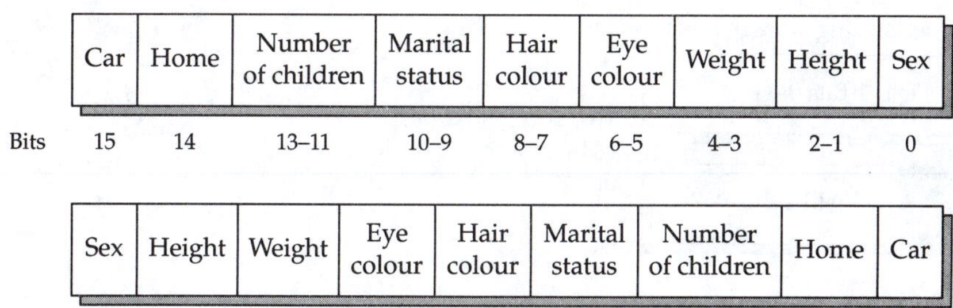

Figure 12.2 Two possible representations of structure variable person within a 16 bit storage unit.

members to co-exist within the *same* storage unit provided they can be completely accommodated.

If, however, two successive bit fields cannot be completely accommodated, then whether the compiler permits them to straddle two separate storage units, or separates them into completely different storage units, is also deemed to be implementation dependent. For example, given the structure template **test** shown below, declaring two bit field members of 12 and 8 bits and the structure variable 'x' based upon it:

```
struct test {
  unsigned field1 : 12 ;
  unsigned field2 : 8 ;
} x ;
```

the compiler could arrange for the bit fields to be stored in either of the two ways shown in Figure 12.3. Here some spare (unused) bits of padding may be introduced between storage units. Note that these illustrations assume a two byte (16 bit) storage unit.

Where required a program may introduce its own padding by declaring **dummy** bit fields, with or without a name, while alignment to the next storage unit can be forced using a bit field of size 0. An example of this can be seen in the template 'cs' below:

```
struct cs {
  unsigned a0   : 1 ;
  unsigned      : 2 ;    /* 2 bits of unused padding */
  unsigned chan : 3 ;
  unsigned      : 0 ;    /* align to next storage unit */
  unsigned a1   : 2 ;
  signed   a2   : 4 ;
} ;
```

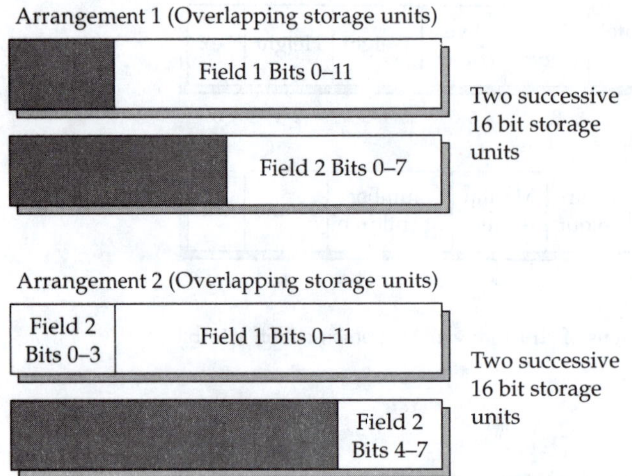

Figure 12.3 Separate or overlapping storage units.

These techniques are particularly useful when emulating the layout of bits within the registers of an I/O chip, but make sure you understand how your compiler stores its bit fields, left to right, or right to left. Your C compiler reference manual should state this information along with the size of a storage unit.

12.3.4 *Practical applications of bit fields*

Because the manipulation of bit fields gives rise to quite complex code, it is possible that any storage saved through the introduction of a number of bit field variables could be negated by the increased size of the program code required to manipulate them. The programmer should therefore consider their introduction and use very carefully. One possible application lies in the manipulation of arrays of structures that contain bit field members. For example:

```
struct individual person[ 1000 ] ;
```

Here, the array person would probably be accessed as part of a loop, and thus the increased size of code required to manipulate it is probably negligible compared with the savings in storage gained through the use of bit fields.

Another common application lies in emulating a particular arrangement of bits within the register of an I/O chip in a small embedded microcontroller. A template might be used to describe the arrangement of bits within the registers of a device, such as the analog to digital converter we met in Chapter 8. An example is shown in Figure 12.4.

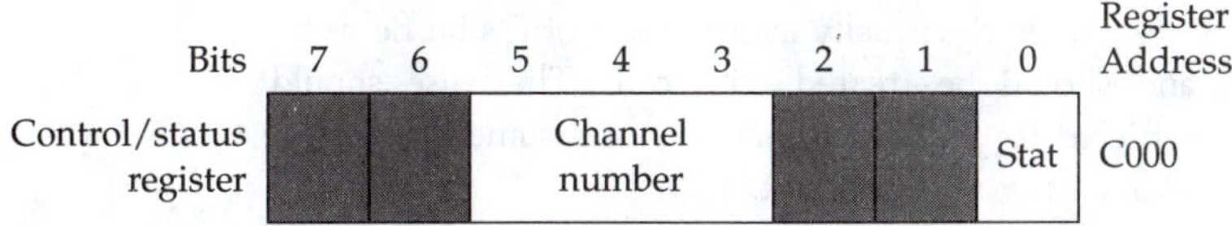

Figure 12.4 Arrangement of bits within an I/O device.

Here, the programmer could describe a structure template using bit fields to describe the layout and position of 'Channel number' and 'Stat' as shown below (but check the order in which your compiler stores its bit fields first):

```
volatile struct adc  {
   unsigned stat      : 1 ;
   unsigned           : 2 ;                /* 2 bit dummy field for padding */
   unsigned channel : 3 ;
   unsigned           : 2 ;                /* 2 bit dummy field for padding */
} *ptr = (volatile struct adc * )(0xc000) ; /* pointer ptr to chip at address 0xc000 */
```

12.3.5 *Limitations of bit fields*

(1) Arrays of bit fields are not permitted, therefore the following structure template, which attempts to create an array of 40 bit fields, each of which is 6 bits in size, is illegal:

```
struct  Bit_Array  {
   unsigned  x[ 40 ] : 6 ;
} ;
```

Illegal!

Arrays of bit fields are not permitted

(2) There is often a restriction placed upon the maximum size of a bit field, generally limited to the bit size of an int on that compiler – usually 16 or 32 bits. Therefore, the following statement would almost certainly be illegal:

```
struct  Big_Field  {
   unsigned  x : 256 ;
}
```

Illegal!

Size of bit field exceeds bit size of a storage unit

(3) It is not permitted to take the address of or declare a pointer to a bit field member, since several bit fields may in fact share the same address and it would not be possible for the compiler to determine the bit position or size of the field that was being accessed from the pointer definition itself.

As you have probably gathered, virtually every aspect of C's bit fields are implementation specific and should be treated with care. Their use should, however, be portable if restricted to operations that do not assume the storage order or position of the fields within a storage unit.

12.4 Chapter summary

(1) New data types may be defined using typedef. The compiler treats such new types in exactly the same way as the data types upon which they are based, thus the new and donor data types are indistinguishable.

(2) Enumerated data types were intended to provide closer type checking of values assigned to variables. This feature is absent in C, thus enumerated data serves no practical purpose other than as a convenient method of introducing integer constants.

(3) A bit field permits the program to save storage by packing small integral values into consecutive bits in a storage unit. Be careful, however, as the code produced by the compiler to pack and unpack a bit field could easily exceed the storage saved through their use.

(4) A bit field may only be introduced as a member element of a structure or union. The general format for defining a bit field member is given as:

```
type var_name : size ;
```

where 'size' is the size of the bit field, and is generally limited by the bit size of a storage unit, typically the size of an int. A size of 0 forces the next bit field to align to the next storage unit, while an absent bit field name reserves the specified number of bits.

(5) Bit fields may be accessed using the '.' or '->' operators in conjunction with the structure/union variable name or pointer.

(6) Bit fields are only of limited use, such as attempting to emulate the storage alignment of some external device. Not all compilers follow the same alignment and storage rules, so watch out for portability issues here.

12.5 Exercises

12.1 What is the primary attraction of introducing type defined variables?

12.2 What new operations are permissible with type defined variables?

12.3 It is often said that defining a new data type using typedef is not really necessary since the same thing can easily be achieved using the pre-processor directive #define. Discuss whether this is true or not. Your answer should also consider the scope and privacy of both approaches.

12.4 Introduce the following new data types:

(a) PIA: a pointer to unsigned volatile chars.

(b) ADC: a pointer to a structure defining the registers with the ADC chip discussed in Chapter 8.

(c) F_ARRAY: an array of pointers to functions expecting a single integer argument and returning an integer result.

12.5 What are the major motivating factors that have led to the introduction of enumerated data types in other languages? Why is C a disappointment in this respect?

12.6 What are the only attractions of using enumerated variables in C?

12.7 What values do the uninitialized symbolic names of an enumerated data type assume?

12.8 Introduce enumerated data types to describe the following information and write functions that are designed to accept and return arguments/data of that type:

(a) The acceptance conditions 'yes' and 'no'.

(b) The sex status 'male' and 'female'.

(c) The married status 'single', 'married', 'cohabiting', 'divorced', 'separated' and 'widowed'.

12.9 A company pays a salary to its employees based upon whether they are classed as part-time or full-time, temporary or permanent. Write a suitable program to record the salary status of all employees and to list those that fall into each group. Your solution should make use of enumerated and type defined data types wherever possible.

12.10 What is meant by the term 'bit field'? What distinguishes them from other integer variables?

12.11 Where is it permissible to introduce a bit field?

12.12 What are the principal benefits of using bit fields? Why is it not beneficial to introduce a bit field for just one or two small integer variables?

12.13 What is meant by the term 'storage unit'? What is the size of a storage unit on your compiler? What is the maximum size of a bit field permitted by your compiler?

12.14 In what order are bit fields stored within a storage unit using your compiler?

12.15 Does your compiler permit bit fields to straddle storage units?

12.16 Under what conditions is the use of bit fields portable?

12.17 What are the effects of the following bit fields?

```
signed    status  : 4 ;
unsigned  control : 2 ;
unsigned          : 2 ;
unsigned          : 0 ;
```

12.18 What is the permissible range of values of each of the following bit fields?

```
signed    stat1 : 1 ;
signed    stat2 : 2 ;
unsigned  stat3 : 1 ;
unsigned  stat4 : 4 ;
```

12.19 With the help of several bit fields, describe structure templates for the complete PIA, ADC and LCD chips given in Chapter 8 and rewrite the example programs/functions given there.

13 The C Pre-processor

In this chapter, we will be taking a closer look at the facilities provided by the C pre-processor, particularly in relation to the creation of user defined **macros** and the pre-processor's ability to selectively or **conditionally compile** a source file depending upon conditions that exist at compile time (as opposed to run time). Now, although the facilities discussed in this chapter are important, less experienced C programmers reading this book may wish to defer their study until they are more familiar with the C language itself.

It is not that the topics discussed here are particularly difficult, it is simply that many of them have been introduced into the language to allow the programmer to generate program code that cannot be expressed, or expressed as easily, using the C language itself, and unless the programmer is aware of those limitations, they are unlikely to appreciate the need for many of these facilities.

Do not make the assumption that the whole chapter can be dismissed, however, as there are topics here that are of considerable importance, even for the novice programmer. These can be found in Sections 13.1–13.3 relating to file inclusion and macro creation, and also in Section 13.8, on conditional compilation.

Traditionally, the pre-processor has always been thought of as a separate program, run as part of the overall compilation process, responsible for the pre-processing of a source file prior to its actual compilation. However, with the growing sophistication of many modern compilers, much of its functionality has been integrated into the compiler itself, making it all but transparent to the operator. However, it is (arguably) easier to consider the operation of the pre-processor from the point of view of a separate program divorced from the compiler itself, which can be invoked (as was the case with many traditional/non-standard conforming compilers) separately. Thus, this chapter presents its material and discussions in that way. So, just how does the pre-processor work?

In the majority of cases the pre-processor is automatically invoked at compile time to read and process the original source file; that is, the one entered by the programmer using the editor. Unless specifically directed by code encountered

Table 13.1 Pre-processor directives.

Directive	*Interpretation*
#include	File inclusion
#define	Define a macro
#undef	Undefine a macro
#	NULL or do nothing directive
#line	Control current line number and file name
#error	Abort compilation with error message
#pragma	Implementation specific directive
#if	Conditional if test
#elif	Conditional else-if test
#else	Conditional else
#ifdef	Conditional if macro defined
#ifndef	Conditional if macro *not* defined
#endif	Conditional end directive

within the source file or by option flags specified on the compiler command line, the pre-processor takes few actions of its own, other than to save the processed file to disk in preparation for compilation. However, specific **directives** may be placed virtually anywhere within the source file to direct the pre-processor to perform some specified action. This might include, along with other facilities, the creation of macros and the inclusion of other source or header files.

A pre-processor directive always begins on a fresh line and commences with the character '#'. Tabulation or white space may be used to indent directives if that aids readability, but, unlike the C language itself, each 'directive' is terminated at the end of the current line. Thus, the conventional statement terminator ';' means nothing to the pre-processor. However, the line continuation character '\' *is* recognized, permitting pre-processor directives to transcend line end boundaries if required. A summary of the pre-processor directives can be found in Table 13.1.

13.1 Including header files: The #include directive

The #include directive, as we saw briefly in Chapter 1, requests the pre-processor to locate and 'merge' the contents of the named header file with the program source file prior to compilation. If successful the pre-processor *replaces* the directive by substituting the contents of the header file in its place, an action which does *not* affect the original source file. It thus appears subsequently to the compiler as if the programmer had entered the contents of the header file as part of his or her original source file. There are two forms of this directive, as shown below:

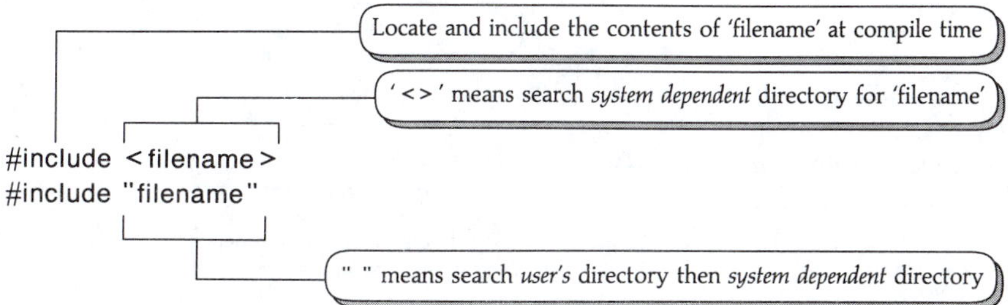

Angle brackets '< >' around the file name requests the pre-processor to search for the header file in a system dependent or default directory. If the compiler has been correctly installed, the pre-processor should know where this is, but facilities exist on many compilers to allow the programmer to specify the location of this directory. For example, on Borland's Turbo C this is achieved via the Directories option in the Options menu. Under UNIX, the default directory is generally /usr/include.

If quotation marks '" "' are used in place of the angle brackets, then the search for the header file takes place firstly in the user's default (often working) directory. This is useful, as it facilitates the creation and inclusion of the programmer's own header files. If the file cannot be found here, a search of the system dependent directory then begins, exactly as if angle brackets '< >' had been used. In both cases, failure to locate the named header file results in a compile time error.

Note that most compilers permit a pathlist to be used with the header file name, to enable the programmer to specify the exact location of the header file, for example:

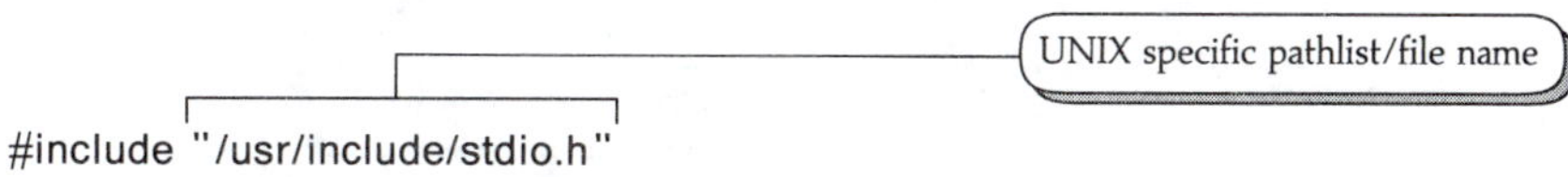

13.2 Creating macros with #define

The #define directive is useful for the creation of macros, of which there are two forms: with and without parameters. The basic form of a non-parameterized macro is shown below, where macro_name is the name of the macro (which must conform to the same identifier naming conventions (see Chapter 1) as the compiler) and token_sequence represents the macro's (optional) expansion and may consist of virtually any character sequence, including white space:

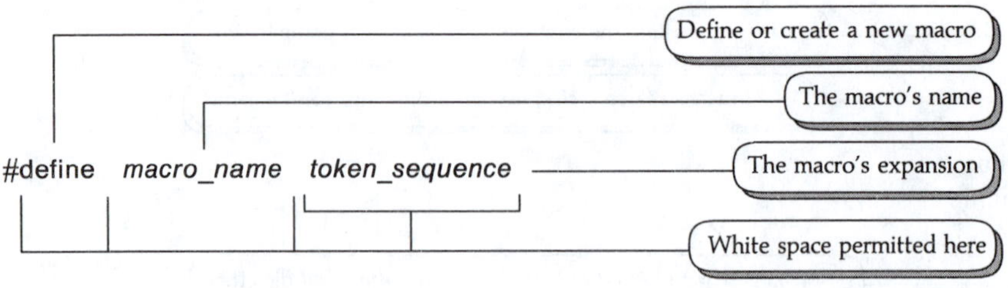

At compile time, the C pre-processor arranges for all occurrences of macro_name, wherever they appear in the program (except as part of a literal text string), to be replaced by the macro's expansion or token_sequence.

Any amount of white space is permitted before and between the three fields in a macro definition and between the '#' and its 'define'. Furthermore, any amount of white space may be included within token_sequence to aid readability, but not within macro_name. Some examples of non-parameterized macros are given below:

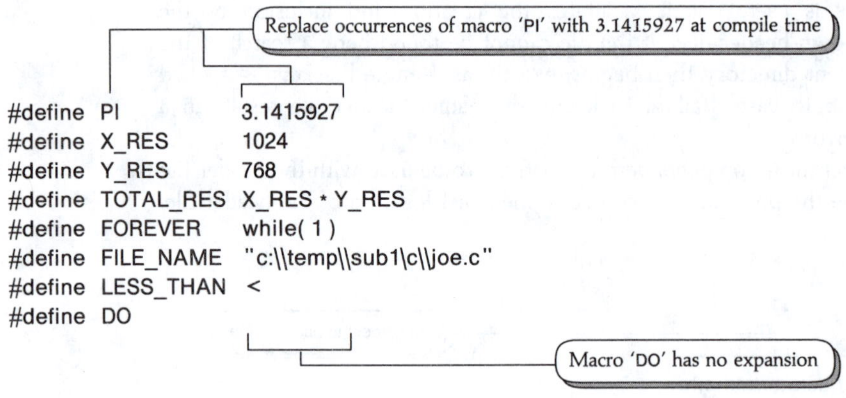

You will note that these macros have all been defined with upper case names, which although not obligatory, has become something of a tradition among many programmers because it enables a macro reference to be easily identified within the source file.

Upon encountering the definition of a macro, the pre-processor records the sequence of tokens associated with the macro name, then as references to the macro are encountered later within the source file, they are replaced by their corresponding expansion, or token_sequence. The programmer must obviously take care to ensure that the result of such an expansion ultimately makes sense to the compiler. Note, however, the following exceptions and important points relating to macro expansion:

(1) Macro references are *not* recognized if they appear within the confines of a literal text string. This prevents the accidental recognition and replacement of any literal text that may form an essential part of the program's output;

(2) Macro references are *not* recognized prior to their definition; thus macro expansion is not performed retrospectively;

(3) A macro reference within the program will *not* be recognized unless it can be distinguished as a separate identifier, for example surrounded by white space or separated by an operator;

(4) A macro expansion may be defined in terms of other previously defined macros, resulting in a macro expansion with several levels of nested expansion, as is the case with the example macro TOTAL_RES above.

Referring to points (1) and (3), the pre-processor would thus not recognize the following two statements as containing a reference to any of the example macros defined previously:

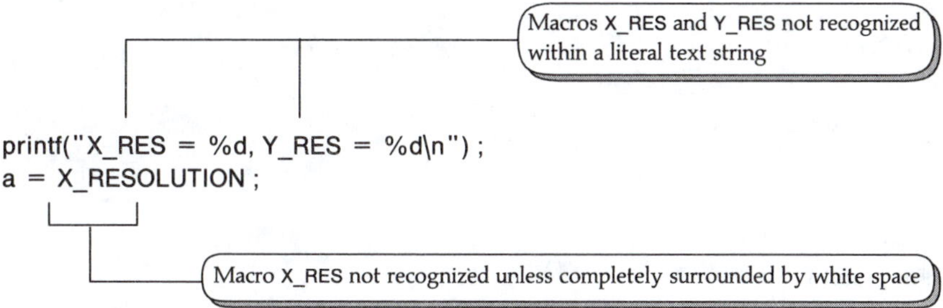
Macros X_RES and Y_RES not recognized within a literal text string
printf("X_RES = %d, Y_RES = %d\n") ;
a = X_RESOLUTION ;
Macro X_RES not recognized unless completely surrounded by white space

Note also that multiple definitions of the same macro may appear any number of times within a file, provided that each definition is consistent. This is particularly useful when a macro might have to be defined within many separate header files, some or all of which may eventually end up being #included into a program.

A good example of this is the macro NULL, which is defined as 0 by several standard header files. It is, however, considered to be an error for a program to redefine a macro with a *different* expansion, unless the macro is first 'undefined' (see Section 13.6).

Program 13.1 demonstrates the use of several macro definitions within a simple program. As you can see, a judicious approach to macro definition can sometimes lead to a program that bears little resemblance to C.

Note that many compilers permit a macro to be defined on the command line, frequently using the '–D' option, which is useful when conditionally compiling a program (see Section 13.8). Check out your compiler's reference manual for details of how this is achieved.

Program 13.1 Example use of non-parameterized macros.

```
#include  <stdio.h>

#define  SIZE                10
#define  FOREVER             while( 1 )
#define  MESSAGE             "Enter a number :"
#define  ARRAY_ELEMENT       x[ i ]
#define  GET_INT             scanf("%d", &temp) ;
#define  CONDITION           ( i == SIZE )
#define  SUM_ARRAY           for( i = 0, total = 0 ;\
                               i < SIZE ;\
                                 total += ARRAY_ELEMENT, i ++ )

int main( void )
{
  int  temp = 0, i = 0, total = 0 ;
  int  x[ SIZE ] ;

  FOREVER  {
    printf( MESSAGE ) ;
    GET_INT ;

    if( CONDITION )
      break ;

    ARRAY_ELEMENT = temp ;
    i ++ ;
  }

  SUM_ARRAY ;
  printf("%d\n", total ) ;
  return 0 ;
}
```

13.2.1 *Predefined non-parameterized macros*

All standard C compilers have the following predefined macros that are assumed to exist at the time of compilation. In other words, the program does not have to define them for itself.

`__STDC__` An integral constant equal to the integer value '1' if the compiler conforms to the C standard.

This macro is mainly used by the conditional compilation directives to prevent the compilation of a program by a non-standard compiler.

`__TIME__` A string constant of the form "hh:mm:ss" set to the time of compilation.

__DATE__ A literal string constant set to the current date of compilation.

__FILE__ A literal string constant set to the name of the source file being compiled.

__LINE__ An integral constant whose value is always set to the current line number of the statement being compiled (blank lines are included in the total).

References to these macros may appear anywhere in the program where it would be appropriate to use their expansion. Program 13.2 demonstrates this.

Program 13.2 Example use of predefined standard macros.

```
#include   <stdio.h>

int main( void )
{
   printf("Compiling File '%s' ", __FILE__ ) ;
   printf("at Time %s on %s\n", __TIME__, __DATE__ ) ;
   printf("Current Line Number is %d\n", __LINE__ ) ;
   return 0 ;
}
```

On the author's system, Program 13.2 produced the following output:

```
Compiling File 'macro.c' at Time 06:44:30 on May 18 1993
Current Line Number is 7
```

The most common application of these predefined macros lies with the generation of error messages when the operator might wish to be informed of the name and line number of the file where an error has occurred. In fact the assert macro (see Section 13.9) defined in the header file <assert.h> has been written specifically for this purpose and makes use of these predefined macros.

Note that the pre-processor directive #line (see later) may be used to control the value of the macros __FILE__ and __LINE__. Also, for future reference, none of these macros may be undefined with an #undef directive.

13.3 Parameterized macros

The second form of a macro definition is shown below; it may include a number of optional parameters. The format of such a macro is intended to resemble that of a function, particularly in its usage:

#define *macro_name*($param_1$, ..., $param_n$) *token_sequence*

Here, macro_name is immediately followed, without any intervening white space, by a parenthesized list of comma separated parameters, after which the macro's expansion is expressed as a sequence of tokens, usually in terms of its parameters.

Should the pre-processor later encounter a reference to a parameterized macro, it will identify the arguments used in the macro reference and expand the macro, replacing the parameters in that expansion with the corresponding macro arguments.

Rescanning of the macro expansion then occurs, whereby the pre-processor attempts to identify other macro references within the newly expanded macro (but see Sections 13.4 and 13.5, on the '#' and '##' operators). This rescanning and subsequent expansion continues until no further expansion takes place. As an example, consider the definitions of the parameterized macros SQR( ), CUBE( ) and SUM( ) shown below:

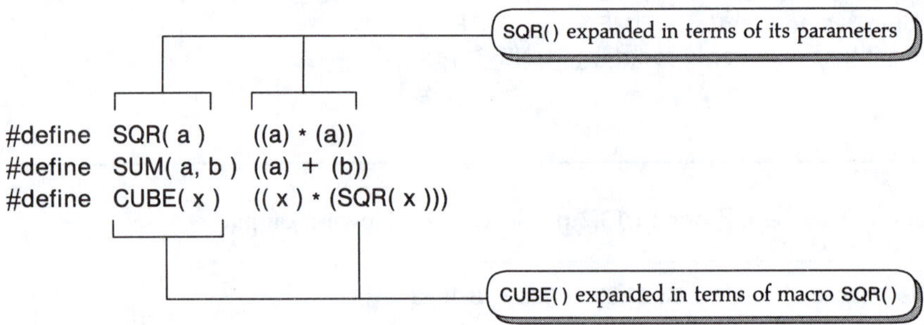
SQR( ) expanded in terms of its parameters
#define SQR(a) ((a) * (a))
#define SUM(a, b) ((a) + (b))
#define CUBE(x) ((x) * (SQR(x)))
CUBE( ) expanded in terms of macro SQR( )

Note how CUBE( ) was expressed in terms of the previously defined macro SQR( ); thus a reference to the macro CUBE( ) of the form:

```
a = CUBE( 2.5 ) ;
```

is initially expanded as:

```
a = ((2.5) * (SQR( 2.5 ))) ;
```

after which the pre-processor rescans the expansion and identifies a reference to the macro SQR( ), which it then expands as:

```
a = ((2.5) * ((2.5) * (2.5))) ;
```

Likewise, a reference to the macro SUM( ) with a statement such as:

```
b = SUM( CUBE( 3 ), SQR( 2) ) ;
```

is expanded initially as:

```
b = ((( 3 ) * (SQR( 3 ))) + ((2) * (2))) ;
```

and eventually as:

```
b = ((( 3 ) * (((3) * (3)))) + ((2) * (2))) ;
```

To prevent the possibility of infinite recursion during the rescanning and re-expansion of a macro reference, the pre-processor does not re-expand a macro whose definition references itself, either directly or indirectly via another macro expansion.

As a further example, the macro PRINT( ) could be defined to display the sine, cosine and tangent of its argument, and the macro ABS( ) could be defined to yield the absolute value of its argument, as shown below:

```
#define  PRINT(a)  printf("%10g%10g%10g\n", sin( a ), cos( a ), tan( a ))
#define  ABS(x)    ((x) >= 0 ? (x) : -(x))
```

13.3.1 *Differences between function and macro definitions*

Where the definition of a macro differs from that of a function is that the code for a function is only generated once by the compiler. The program may then call or invoke the code for that function any number of times. However, referencing a macro generates a unique 'in-line' copy of its expansion each time it occurs in the program; thus the use of macros can and frequently does give rise to programs that are physically larger than if an equivalent function had been used.

However, if the use of macros is restricted, as it often is, to critical sections of code, such as those that execute within fast loops, referencing a macro has two distinct advantages over invoking an equivalent function. Firstly, a macro reference does not generate the same overheads applicable to calling a function, thus a macro generally executes faster. Secondly, a macro is able to work with any type of argument whereas a function is often restricted to an argument matching the type of its corresponding parameter (or one that can be implicitly cast to match its parameter, but this may lead to loss of accuracy, result or precision). It should also be noted that in using macros, the compiler will be unable to perform any type checking between program argument and macro parameter, thus it is possible that a macro may behave differently to its equivalent function.

For example, the macro SQR( ) defined previously could have been referenced with an integer or a floating point argument and would have produced, respectively, an integer or floating point result, something that could not have been achieved with a single function.

13.3.2 *Problems associated with parameterized macro expansions*

You will have noticed in the previous examples that the expansion of each macro, and those parameters within them, were enclosed within parentheses. This is not merely cosmetic, but is actually very important if the macros are to be expanded correctly for all types of argument. Let us see why. Consider for a moment the macro SQR( ) defined without these parentheses in its expansion, as shown below:

```
#define  SQR(a) a * a
```

If this macro were referenced with an argument that is an expression rather than a constant value, for example:

```
a = SQR( 6 + 4 ) / 2 ;
```

then the pre-processor would simply expand this as:

```
a = 6 + 4 * 6 + 4 / 2 ;
```

which, because of the compiler's rules of precedence and associativity relating to the '+', '*' and '/' operators, would result in the statement being evaluated as:

```
a = 6 + (4 * 6 ) + ( 4 / 2 ) ;
```

Thus 'a' is assigned the value 32, rather than the intended value of 50. A further problem also exists with macro arguments that produce side effects. For example, referencing the original parenthesized macro SQR(a) defined as '((a) * (a))' with the statement:

```
b = SQR ( a++ ) ;
```

produces, upon expansion, the statement:

```
b = ((a++) * (a++)) ;
```

which may result in 'a' being incremented twice, which may not have been what the programmer intended.

Some useful examples of parameterized macros for testing characters are shown in Program 13.3. They are often found in the header file <ctype.h>. Each macro yields a non-zero value, in this case 1, if the character passes that particular test. Note that the examples below were written for clarity; those in <ctype.h> are often more elaborate but result in more efficient macro expansions with less code and reduced execution times.

Program 13.3 Character test macros.

```
#include <stdio.h>

#define  isdigit( c )    ((c) <= '9' && (c) >= '0' ? 1 : 0 )
#define  isascii( c )    ((c) < 128 ? 1 : 0 )
#define  islower( c )    ((c) <= 'z' && (c) >= 'a' ? 1 : 0 )
#define  isupper( c )    ((c) <= 'Z' && (c) >= 'A' ? 1 : 0 )
#define  isalpha( c )    ((islower( c )) || isupper( c ))
#define  isalnum( c )    ((isdigit( c )) || isalpha( c ))

int  main( void )
{
  int  c ;

  while( ( c = getchar()) != EOF )  {
    if( isdigit( c ) )
      printf("Digit ...\n") ;
    if( isupper( c ) )
      printf("UPPER ... \n") ;
    if( islower( c ) )
      printf("LOWER ... \n") ;
    if( isalpha( c ) )
      printf("ALPHA ... \n") ;
    if( isalnum( c ) )
      printf("ALNUM ... \n") ;
  }
  return 0 ;
}
```

13.4 Further macro expansions: The stringizing operator: '#'

If the '#' or 'stringizing' operator appears prior to a parameter in the expansion of a macro, the pre-processor will automatically place quotation marks '" "' around the expansion of the argument. The argument thus takes on the form of a literal text string in the expansion. For example, consider the macro PRINT( ) defined below:

'#' in expansion forces parameter 's' to be converted to a string

```
#define  PRINT( s )  printf( "%s\n", #s )
```

Now because an argument to this macro will automatically be expanded into the form of a string, we could display the message "Hello World" with a macro reference such as that shown below:

```
PRINT( Hello World ) ;
```

Notice how quotations marks around the message were *not* necessary, since these are inserted when the above macro reference is expanded into:

```
printf("%s\n", "Hello World" ) ;
```

To appreciate the use of this operator, consider the problems associated with the macro shown below:

```
#define PRINT_SQR( NUM, FORMAT) \
                    printf("NUM * NUM = FORMAT\n", NUM*NUM)
```

You will recall from point (1) of the list in Section 13.2 that the pre-processor does not recognize a macro reference that occurs within the confines of a literal text string. For example, referencing the above macro with a statement such as:

```
PRINT_SQR( 3, %d) ;
```

results only in the expansion to:

```
printf("NUM * NUM = FORMAT\n", 3 * 3 ) ;
```

since NUM in the format string to printf() was not regarded as a macro reference. However, by making use of automatic string concatenation (see Chapter 1), and the stringizing operator '#' we could write the macro as:

```
#define PRINT_SQR( NUM, FORMAT) \
                printf(#NUM " * " #NUM " = "#FORMAT "\n", NUM*NUM) ;
```

which will now be expanded using the previous reference to the statement:

```
printf("3" " * " "3" " = " "%d" "\n", 3 * 3 ) ;
```

which contains a number of strings that the compiler subsequently concatenates into a single string equivalent to:

```
printf("3 * 3 = %d\n", 3 * 3 ) ;
```

thus achieving the desired expansion. Lastly, note that because the '#' operator always gives rise to a string literal in the corresponding expansion, the preprocessor will not (because of Section 13.2, rule (2)) recognize any further macros when rescanning that particular expansion. For example, if the following program were compiled:

```
#define JOE    1
#define X( a )  ( #a )

int main( void )
{
  puts( X( JOE )) ;
  return 0 ;
}
```

the reference to the macro X() within the call to puts() would be replaced by "JOE" and not by the string "1".

13.5 The token pasting operator: '##'

When the '##' token pasting operator appears in the expansion of a macro, it causes the text on either side of it in the expansion to be joined together. This is most commonly used to paste or insert a macro argument somewhere into a text expansion. For example, the macro definition:

'##' in expansion forces parameter 's' to be joined to 'ptr'

```
#define PTR( s )  ptr##s
```

when referenced with the statement:

Argument to PTR() is constant '1'

```
puts( PTR( 1 ) ) ;
```

expands to the statement:

Result of expansion is '1' pasted to 'ptr'

```
puts( ptr1 ) ;
```

Note that the pasted tokens may themselves result in macro references, which will be further expanded. For example, given the following macro definitions:

```
#define  F1( a )   ((a) * (a))
#define  F2( a )   ((a) * (a) * (a))
#define  F3(x, y)  F##x( y )
```

a statement of the form:

```
printf("%d\n", F3(2, 3) ) ;
```

is expanded into:

```
printf("%d\n", F2(3) ) ;
```

producing the answer 27. As an example of the use of the '##' operator, try to figure out what Program 13.4 displays when it is run.

Program 13.4 Example use of the '##' token pasting operator.

```
#include  <stdio.h>
#define   P_STRING( s )  while( *ptr##s != NULL) putchar ( *ptr##s++)

int main( void )
{
   char  *ptr1  =  "Hello\n" ;
   char  *ptr2  =  "Goodbye\n" ;

   P_STRING( 1 ) ;
   P_STRING( 2 ) ;
   return 0 ;
}
```

Lastly, because of rule (3) in Section 13.2, any macro argument whose corresponding expansion involves the '##' operator and which itself contains a macro reference, may not be recognized during rescanning as a further macro and thus may not be re-expanded. For example:

```
#define  JOE   1
#define  Y( a )  ptr##a

int main( void )
{
   char  *ptr1 ;
   Y(JOE)  =  NULL ;
   return 0 ;
}
```

Here, the reference to Y( ) with the argument JOE (which is itself a macro) is expanded to ptrJOE and not ptr1.

13.6 Undefining a macro

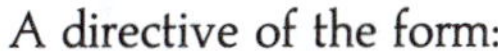

A directive of the form:

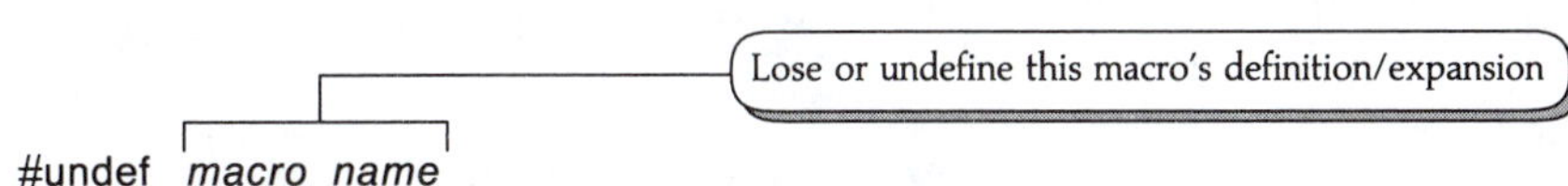

simply undefines a macro, resulting in its definition being lost. Any subsequent references to the macro result in an error or non-recognition of that macro. This may be found useful when a program wishes to change the definition of a macro that has previously been defined.

A particularly useful application of this is in 'losing' the definition of a parameterized macro. In this way, subsequent references to the undefined macro will no longer be expanded and are left for the compiler to interpret as a function call.

For example, consider the use of the macro isupper() described earlier. You will recall that this macro is #defined in the header file <ctype.h>, but interestingly enough it also exists in the form of a function in the standard library, leaving the choice of function call or macro expansion to the programmer.

If the header file <ctype.h> were not #included into a program at compile time, then the pre-processor would not recognize the reference to isupper() as a macro and would thus leave it to be dealt with by the compiler as a function call. Unfortunately, this approach results in all of the macros defined in <ctype.h> not being recognized, thus references to them are also treated as functions. A more practical solution would be to include the header file <ctype.h> in the program but undefine the macro isupper() with the directive:

```
#undef  isupper
```

leaving all references to isupper() within the program to be recognized as function calls but other references to, for example, islower(), to be expanded as macros. Lastly, note that you cannot undefine any of the predefined macros __STDC__, __TIME__, __DATE__, __FILE__ and __LINE__.

13.7 Other pre-processor directives

The NULL directive:

——— A NULL or do nothing directive to the pre-processor

represents a 'do nothing' directive and consequently has no effect. It is analogous to the NULL statement ';' in C code and serves little useful purpose.

13.7.1 *Controlling the macros* __LINE__ *and* __FILE__

A directive of the form:

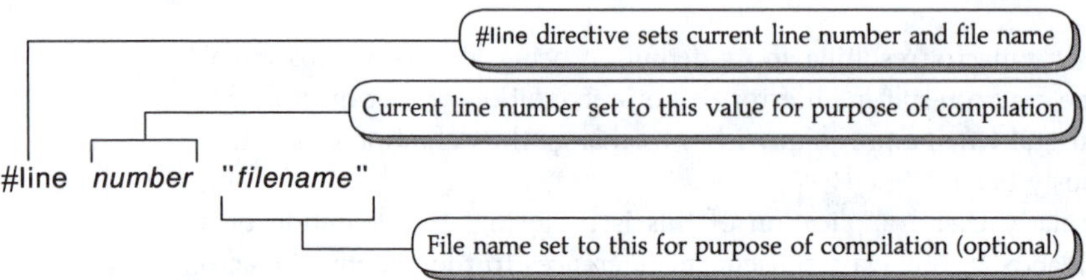

sets the predefined macro __LINE__ to the value of number, which must be a decimal integer constant, and the predefined macro __FILE__ to the value of "filename", a literal string constant.

This directive is of little interest to most programmers but may be found useful when used in conjunction with the assert( ) macro (see Section 13.9), or as a directive issued by other compilers that generate C source code as their output, such as a number of AI packages; in the latter case, the directive allows the compilers to direct the pre-processor and hence the C compiler to the original (perhaps non-C) source file that gave rise to the C file currently being compiled.

Note that "filename" is an optional part of this directive; if it is omitted, __FILE__ remains set to the name of the source file being compiled. If necessary, both parameters may themselves be macros, provided they expand to the correct type and format.

13.7.2 *Unconditionally terminating a compilation*

A directive of the form:

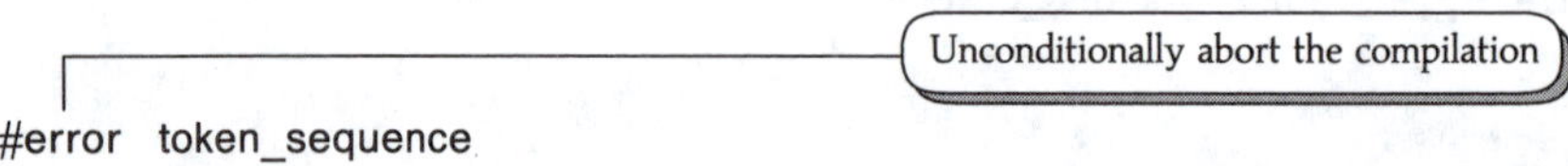

if encountered forces the unconditional termination of the compilation and leads to the generation of an implementation specific error message, incorporating token_sequence as part of its output. As an example, the following directive placed in a sample source file compiled under Borland's Turbo C:

```
#error "Macro 'NUM' not defined"
```

aborted the compilation and displayed the error message:

```
Fatal test.c 12: Error directive: "Macro 'NUM' not defined"
```

where test.c represents the name of the current source file and '12' was the line number where the directive #error was encountered. Note that this directive is generally employed by conditional compilation directives (see Section 13.8) to abort compilation if certain compile time prerequisites have not been met, such as macros not having been defined.

13.7.3 *Implementation specific directives:* #pragma

In the days before standard C, many compilers were written that recognized a number of non-standard, implementation specific directives placed within the source file. These were often used to control the actions of the compiler from within the source file itself, rather than through flags set on the compiler command line. For example, a compiler could have been written to recognize non-standard directives such as those shown below, indicating that 68000 machine code should be generated and that integers should be 16 bits in size:

```
#CPU 68000
#INT   16
```

A particularly common pair of directives provided by many compilers were #asm and #endasm, permitting assembly language code to be embedded directly within the C source file. All statements lying between these two directives were not compiled in any way but were simply passed straight through to the assembler phase of compilation, where they were dealt with. For example:

```
void f1( void )
{
#asm
     move.b   #$32, d0
     move.b   d0, $ffe00
#endasm
}
```

As you might imagine with all of these implementation specific directives, the issue of source code portability reared its ugly head, particularly if the source file were ever re-compiled by a compiler not recognizing these directives, and, quite rightly, threw them out as errors.

Rather than trying to accommodate and anticipate the current and future needs of each compiler vendor, the standard instead caters for all implementation specific directives with a #pragma directive, whose general form is shown below:

```
#pragma  implementation_specific_directive  token_sequence
```

The important point about any #pragma directive is that any unrecognized directive will be ignored and will not lead to the generation of an error, thus ensuring portability of source code. The two previous examples of non-standard directives could now be catered for in the form shown below:

```
#pragma  CPU  68000
#pragma  INT    16
```

It is important to appreciate that a #pragma directive could mean anything or nothing to any individual compiler so you will have to look up each specific directive in your compiler's reference manual. However, some examples of #pragma directives specific to Borland's Turbo C are listed below:

```
#pragma  argsused
```

This controls the generation of certain warnings issued by the compiler relating to argument usage within a function.

```
#pragma  hdrfile  "filename"
```

This forces the compiler to store pre-compiled header files in "filename".

```
#pragma  option  [ options ... ]
```

This permits the source file to override any command line options that may have been specified.

```
#pragma  warn  [ options ... ]
```

This permits the source file to control whether certain compile time warnings will be displayed.

13.8 Conditional compilation

One of the most useful features of the pre-processor is its ability to selectively include or exclude various sections of program code from the compilation process, based upon conditions that exist at compile time. This is achieved

Table 13.2 Conditional compilation directives.

Directive		Interpretation
#if	expression	Conditional if expression true
#elif	expression	Conditional else if expression true
#else		Conditional else
#ifdef	macro	Conditional if macro has been defined
#ifndef	macro	Conditional if macro has not been defined
#endif		End of conditional section directive

through the use of several conditional compilation directives placed within the source file. The important point about this is that it enables several different executable versions of a program to be generated from a single source file. The directives associated with conditional compilation are listed in Table 13.2.

The directives #if and #elif are analogous to the if and else-if tests that we met in Chapter 4. However, the use of braces '{ }' to group statements affected by the outcome of a test expression is not required since all subsequent statements up to a #endif directive are assumed to be associated with that test.

13.8.1 *The* #endif *directive*

Each of the directives #if, #elif, #ifdef and #ifndef may be terminated by a #endif directive. Because the pre-processor allows nesting of conditional directives, several #endif directives may be required to terminate the nesting correctly. For example:

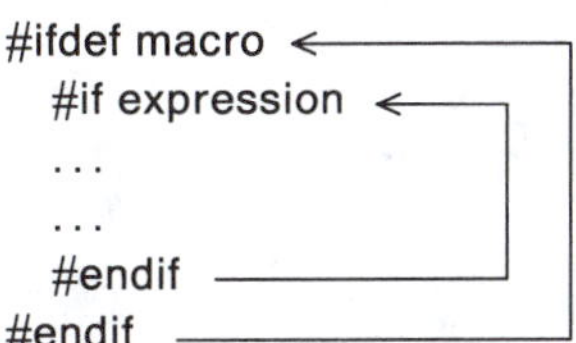

13.8.2 *The* #if *directive*

A directive of the form:

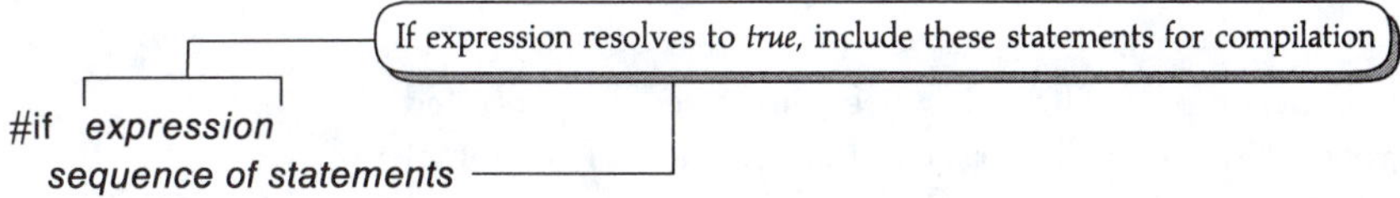

requests the pre-processor to evaluate 'expression' (which must be constructed of macro and implicit constant values, but not any variable names) at compile time. The expression itself may be constructed using any of the standard C operators such as '<<', '>>', '&', '|', '^', '~' and so on, as well as the logical operators '!', '&&' and '||' to determine if the result is true (non-zero) or false.

If 'expression' resolves to false, then the sequence of program statements that follows (up to a #endif, #elif or #else directive) are *excluded* from the process of compilation, otherwise they are left in for subsequent compilation. For example:

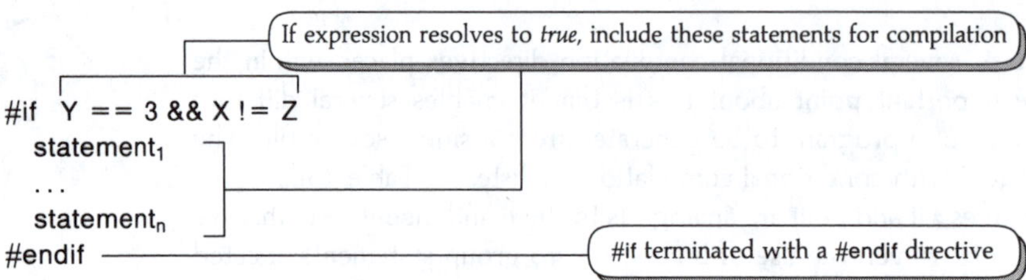

Here statements 1 to n are only included for later compilation if the macro Y expands to '3' and the expansion of X is not equivalent to that of Z.

13.8.3 *The #else directive*

A directive of the form:

```
#else
```

provides an alternative sequence of program code that may be included/excluded from compilation if a previous #if, #elif, #ifdef or #ifndef directive was logical false. For example:

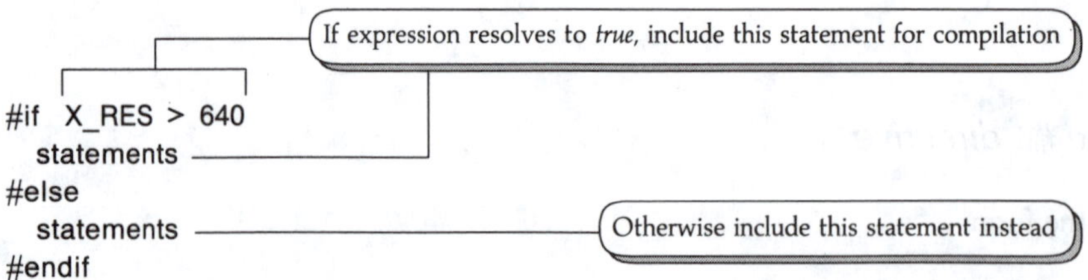

If required, nesting of #if and #else directives is permitted, but a corresponding #endif directive will be required at each level. For example:

```
#if X_RES < 640
    statements1
#else
    #if X_RES >= 640 && X_RES <= 1024
        statements2
    #else
        #if X_RES > 1024 && X_RES < 1600
            statements3
        #else
            statements4
        #endif
    #endif
#endif
```

13.8.4 *The* #elif *directive*

As one further refinement, a directive of the form:

#elif *expression*

which is analogous to an else-if construct in the C language provides for the multi-way conditional evaluation of a test expression. For example, the previous combination of nested #if-#else directives could be rewritten using #elif as:

```
#if X_RES < 640
    statements1
#elif X_RES >= 640 && X_RES <= 1024
    statements2
#elif X_RES > 1024 && X_RES < 1600
    statements3
#else
    statements4
#endif
```

13.8.5 *The* #ifdef *directive*

A directive of the form:

#ifdef *macro*

If this macro has been defined, result of directive is logical *true*

simply asks the pre-processor if 'macro' has been defined prior to this point in the source file. If the macro has been defined, then that macro, for the purposes of this test, is deemed to resolve to the value '1' or logical true, regardless of the value of its expansion. This results in subsequent lines of program code being left in or included for later compilation.

If, however, 'macro' has not been defined at this point in the source file, then the result of the test is deemed to be 0 or logical false, resulting in the exclusion of subsequent lines of code from further compilation. Note that this directive is also equivalent to a directive of the form:

```
#if defined(macro)
```

which is sometimes more useful since it may then be possible to determine if a number of macros have been defined with one directive. For example:

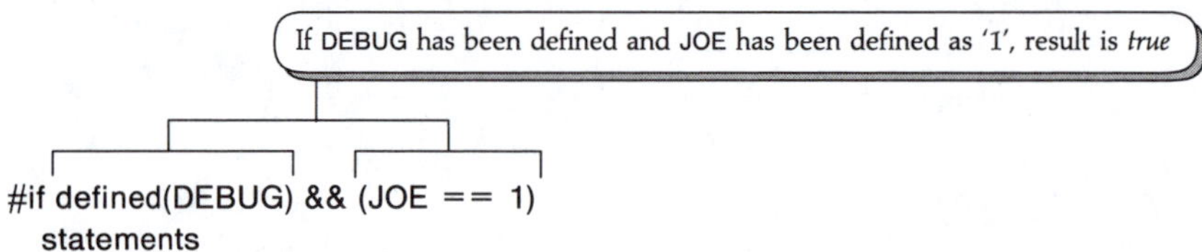

If DEBUG has been defined and JOE has been defined as '1', result is *true*


```
#if defined(DEBUG) && (JOE == 1)
   statements
```

13.8.6 *The #ifndef directive*

A directive of the form:

If this macro has *not* been defined, result of directive is logical *true*

```
#ifndef   macro
```

is complementary to the directive #ifdef, in the sense that if the specified macro has *not* been defined, then for the purposes of this test, 'macro' is deemed to resolve to the value '1' or logical true, and results in subsequent lines of program code being left in or included for later compilation.

If however 'macro' *has* been defined, then the outcome of the test is deemed to be 0 or logical false and subsequent lines of program code are excluded from further compilation. Note that this directive is also equivalent to the directive:

```
#if   !defined(macro)
```

It is worth noting that many compilers permit you to define a macro on the command line at compile time, often using the '–D' option (see your compiler documentation for details), thus providing the programmer with an effective means of controlling conditional compilation without the need to modify the source file.

Remember, conditional compilation is *not* the same as conditional execution. With conditional execution (see Chapter 4), choices are made and statements are executed based upon conditions that are determined at run time. All possible outcomes have been catered for within the program and are there to be executed when the condition arises. With conditional compilation, however, a section of code is included or excluded from compilation based upon the outcome of conditions that are determined at compile time; thus some of the original program source code may never find its way into the executable version of the program.

A particularly useful application of conditional compilation arises during program development, where a programmer may frequently insert lines of 'debug code' into the program to permit the program to be tested and debugged. Ultimately, of course, these statements should be removed before the final version of the program is compiled. However, rather than remove them by re-editing the source code, the programmer could instead arrange for them to be placed within a conditional compilation directive that permits them to be excluded at compile time.

As an example, consider Program 13.5, where a call to printf() has been inserted for debugging purposes. Notice how it has been placed within a conditional #ifdef directive.

Now, if the program is compiled with the macro DEBUG having been defined, either within the program source code or on the compiler command line (see example below, which assumes a UNIX based compiler), then the call to printf() will be compiled and will appear in the final program. However, if DEBUG has not been defined, then the call to printf() is not compiled and is excluded.

Program 13.5 Example use of conditional compilation for debugging.

```
#include   <stdio.h>

int  main( void)
{
   int  array [ 1024 ], count ;

   for( count = 0 ; count < 1024 ; count++ )  {
      array[ count ] = count ;

#ifdef  DEBUG
   printf("Count = %d , array[ count] = %d\n", count, array[ count ] ) ;
#endif
   ...
   ...

   }
   return 0 ;
}
```

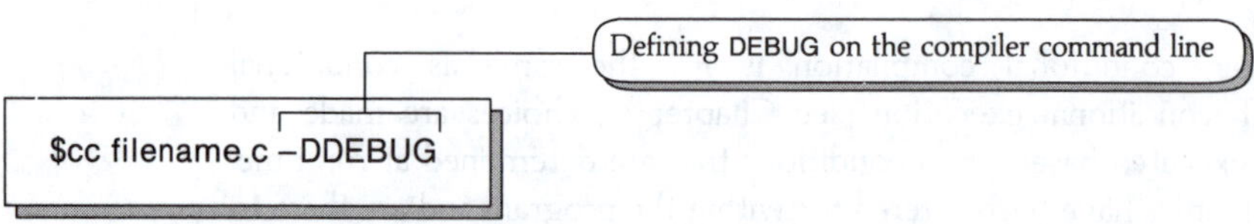

As another example, suppose that a programmer is developing a graphics application for a range of different graphics cards, each with the differing resolutions and colours summarized below:

	Machine A	Machine B	Machine C
Resolution	640 × 480	1024 × 1024	1280 × 1024
Number of colours	16	256	4096
Palette	256	4096	32768

Ideally, the programmer would like to maintain just one source file and produce three different versions of the program from that file. Program 13.6 demonstrates how this could be achieved with conditional compilation directives, revolving around the definition of the macro MACHINE.

Program 13.6 Example conditional compilation problem.

```
#include  <stdio.h>

#ifndef  MACHINE
  #error  "Macro 'MACHINE' Not Defined ... "
#endif

#if  (MACHINE == 1)
  #define  X_RES     640
  #define  Y_RES     480
  #define  COLS      16
  #define  PALETTE   256
#elif  (MACHINE == 2)
  #define  X_RES     1024
  #define  Y_RES     1024
  #define  COLS      256
  #define  PALETTE   4096
#elif  (MACHINE == 3)
  #define  X_RES     1280
  #define  Y_RES     1024
  #define  COLS      4096
  #define  PALETTE   32768
```

```
#else
  #error  "Illegal Definition of MACHINE ... "
#endif

int main( void )
{
  printf("Screen Resolution = %d by %d pixels\n", X_RES, Y_RES) ;
  printf("Number of Colours = %d from a palette of %d", COLS, PALETTE) ;
  return 0 ;
}
```

If MACHINE has not been defined, either within the program or on the compiler command line, then compilation is aborted by the #error directive. If, however, MACHINE has been defined, then the non-parameterized macros X_RES, Y_RES, COLS and PALETTE are defined with different values, based on the value of MACHINE. For example, if MACHINE were defined as the constant '2', then X_RES and Y_RES would both be defined as 1024.

Now, provided the program makes no assumptions about its resolution, colours and so on, and expresses all such calculations in terms of X_RES, Y_RES and so on, then it should be possible to generate three different versions of the program from a single source file. Thus the program could be compiled as shown below, where MACHINE is actually defined on the command line, rather than in the program:

```
$ cc prog.c -DMACHINE=2
```

As one final example, consider the development of a program with a range of run time options depending upon how much the customer is prepared to pay. Rather than generate several versions of the program, conditional compilation could be used to remove specific options from the final program, as shown in Program 13.7.

Here, everything relating to choice 3 is excluded from compilation if the macro EXPENSIVE has *not* been defined. Follow it through for yourself.

Program 13.7 Further example of conditional compilation.

```
#include  <stdio.h>
#include  <stdlib.h>

const char  *menu[ ] = {
  "1  -  Choice 1" ,
  "2  -  Choice 2" ,
```

```
#ifdef  EXPENSIVE
   "3  -  Choice 3" ,
#endif
   NULL
} ;

void choice1( void ) { puts("Choice 1") ; }     /* function definition for choice 1*/
void choice2( void ) { puts("Choice 2") ; }     /* function definition for choice 2 */

#ifdef  EXPENSIVE
void choice3( void ) { puts("Choice 3") ; }     /* function definition for choice 3 */
#endif

int main( void )
{
   int     choice, i = 0 ;
   char  buff[ BUFSIZ ] ;

   while( menu[ i ] != NULL )
      puts( menu[ i++ ]) ;

   while( 1 )  {
      choice  =  atoi(gets( buff )) ;

      switch( choice )  {
         case 1  :  choice1( ) ;  break ;
         case 2  :  choice2( ) ;  break ;
#ifdef  EXPENSIVE
         case 3  :  choice3( ) ;  break ;
#endif
         default : puts("Unrecognized choice . . . \n") ;
      }
   }
}
```

13.9 The assert( ) macro

A particularly interesting example of a parameterized macro can be found in the header file <assert.h>. The assert( ) macro provides the programmer with a simple means of testing an expression at run time. If the expression is found to be false, then assert( ) displays the failing expression, along with the name and line number of the file where the assertion failed, and an error message is displayed on the operator's screen before the program is aborted.

An example of how assert() might be defined is shown below. You will see that it makes use of many of the features described in this chapter, such as the stringizing operator '#' and conditional compilation:

```
#ifdef NDEBUG
  #define assert(p)
#else
  #define assert(p) \
    if( !(p) ) { \
      fprintf(stderr, "Assertion failed: %s, File %s, Line %d\n", \
        #p, __FILE__, __LINE__ ) ; \
      abort( ) ; \
    }
#endif
```

assert() has no expansion if NDEBUG has been defined

Note how the assert() macro is effectively turned off if the macro NDEBUG (meaning no debugging) has been defined at compile time. Otherwise, assert() is defined in terms of an if test, a call to fprintf() and a call to abort() to terminate the execution (not compilation) of the program.

As an example of the use of this as a debugging tool, consider its use in relation to array bounds checking, as shown in Program 13.8. Here the programmer has included a reference to the assert() macro to check that the value of 'x' is within the correct range to act as the subscript to the array 'a'; that is, 0–99. If not, the program will abort.

Program 13.8 Example use of assert() as a debugging aid.

```
#include <stdio.h>
#include <assert.h>

int main( void )
{
  int a[ 100 ] ;
  int x ;

  for( x = 0 ; x < 100 ; x ++ ) {
    assert( x >= 0 && x < 100 ) ;
    a[ x ] = x ;
  }
  ...
  ...
  return 0 ;
}
```

On the author's system, if the conditional test within the for loop was changed to 'x < 101', then the assert 'failed' when 'x' reached 100 and the program aborted with the following message:

```
Assertion failed: x >= 0 && x < 100, file test.c, line 10
```

A compiler command line of the form shown below, where NDEBUG has been defined, would disable all run time assertions at compile time:

```
$cc test.c -DNDEBUG
```

13.10 Chapter summary

(1) The creation of macros using #define is probably the most powerful and widely used feature provided by the pre-processor since it facilitates the creation of 'in-line' functions, but beware of side effects in the expansion. Always place parameterized macro expansions inside parentheses to reduce the likelihood of these occurring.

(2) Header files provide a convenient place to store commonly used macro definitions and function prototypes, particularly when these are included in several related source files, and ensure consistency of declarations at compile time.

(3) Conditional compilation is particularly powerful because it offers the ability to selectively include/exclude statements within the source file at compile time, thus permitting several different versions of the program to be generated from one common source file.

(4) The other facilities provided by the pre-processor are more specialist and are less commonly used, but sometimes provide the only solution to an otherwise tricky or impossible problem. The #error directive provides a convenient means to abort a compilation if certain compile time prerequisites have not been met, while the assert( ) macro similarly provides a means to abort the execution of a program if certain run time prerequisites are not met.

13.11 Exercises

13.1 What is meant by the terms parameterized macro and non-parameterized macro? What is meant by the term side effect? Identify some of the side effects associated with macro expansion and explain how they can be reduced.

13.2 How does the code for a macro call differ from that of a function call? Can a macro be called recursively? Explain why or why not.

13.3 Define macros to evaluate the following:

(a) The area and circumference of a circle.

(b) To convert temperatures between Celsius and Fahrenheit.

(c) To yield the minimum or maximum of two values.

(d) To swap two values.

(e) To swap two values if they are out of (ascending) order.

13.4 Define a macro to set the first 'n' elements of an array to the value 'x'.

13.5 Define a macro STRCOPY( ) to copy a string from one location to another.

13.6 Assuming that matrices may be represented by suitable sized and dimensioned arrays, define macros to:

(a) Multiply the elements of a matrix by a scalar value (not to be confused with the scalar value of a pointer).

(b) Add two matrices together.

(c) Subtract one matrix from another.

13.7 Define two macros, isvowel( ) and isoctal( ) to extend the range of the character test macros aleady defined in <ctype.h> to include checking for a vowel (the letters 'a', 'e', 'i', 'o' and 'u') and an octal character in the range 0–7.

13.8 A PIA chip (see Chapter 8) is known to exist in memory at base address hex 8000. Write four macros that will allow access to the six registers (occupying four successive locations) within this chip. Now combine these four macros in a single macro that uses an offset argument to specify the address of the required register relative to the PIA base address.

13.9 Define two macros to set or clear the nth bit of an integer variable.

13.10 Define two macros to set or clear a range m–n of bits within an integer variable.

13.11 Define a macro BIT( ) to yield the value, 0 or 1, of the nth bit of an integer variable. Now define a further macro P_BINARY( ) in terms of BIT( ) to display the value of an integer in binary. Your answer should not assume the size of an int; use sizeof( ) instead.

13.12 In Chapter 8 we presented an implementation of the quicksort algorithm (Program 8.13). Try to rewrite this function to use as many macros as possible/feasible in an attempt to aid readability.

13.13 getchar( ) and putchar( ) are often implemented as macros within <stdio.h> and are often expressed in terms of two other macros, getc( ) and putc( ). Examine the <stdio.h> header file that comes with your compiler to confirm this. What happens if either of these macros is undefined by a program using #undef that later makes use of getchar( ) and putchar( )?

13.14 One of the nice features of macros is that their arguments are permitted to be data types such as int, double and so on, whereas arguments to functions must always be the *values* of such types. Using this useful feature define a macro NEW(x) in terms of the function malloc( ) to allocate storage for and yield a pointer suitably cast to match the object of type 'x', for example you should be able to say int *p1 = NEW(int) ;.

13.15 In Section 18.10 we shall learn how to write functions that expect to receive and are able to extract a variable number of arguments from the calling function. The operations are heavily reliant upon three macros, va_start( ), va_end( ) and va_arg( ). Try to figure out how these macros work and follow Program 18.5. Also, try to figure out how the macro offsetof( ) (defined in <stddef.h>, see Section 18.11) works.

13.16 Consult your compiler documentation and determine what, if any, compiler specific directives are supported by the #pragma directive.

13.17 What is the principal difference between conditional compilation and conditional execution? How can conditional compilation help to maintain a single piece of software intended for use on a variety of different computer systems?

13.18 A program is being written that will eventually run on two different (although not necessarily unrelated) computer systems, based respectively around a 16 and a 32 bit CPU. Because of the differences in size of CPU registers, their respective compilers choose to implement the data type int as a 16 and 32 bit quantity, respectively, which can give rise to some portability issues. To overcome this, the program will be written to use the data type INT, which must be guaranteed to be a 16 bit quantity. How can this be done without creating two separate versions of the program source file?

13.19 In an 8 bit computer system, the registers of a PIA chip are mapped into memory such that they occupy successive addresses. However, because the PIA is only an 8 bit peripheral device, if it is interfaced to a 16 bit system, the registers will occupy alternate bytes commencing with either an even or an odd address. Using conditional compilation techniques, write a single source code version of a program that defines the four macros developed in Exercise 13.8, in different ways depending upon whether the target CPU is 8 or 16 bits in size and, in the case of the latter, if odd or even addressing is selected. These options are to be controlled by defining macros on the compiler command line. Compilation is to be aborted if the relevant macros are not defined.

14 Separate Compilation and Embedded Assembly Language

In this chapter we are going to take a look at a particularly useful and powerful feature of the C language in the form of **separate compilation**, a technique that permits any reasonably sized program to be divided or split into a number of distinct and quite separate source files, each of which may be compiled separately. The resultant **relocatable object files** (ROFs) that arise as a result of such compilations can then be linked to produce the final executable program, a process that is illustrated in Figure 14.1.

This technique is particularly powerful when a team of programmers are employed to develop the software jointly. Each team member might be given the task of writing some aspect of the program that he or she could develop within his or her own source file(s), independently of other programmers, and could rely on the power of separate compilation to compile and ultimately link the various sections of the program together.

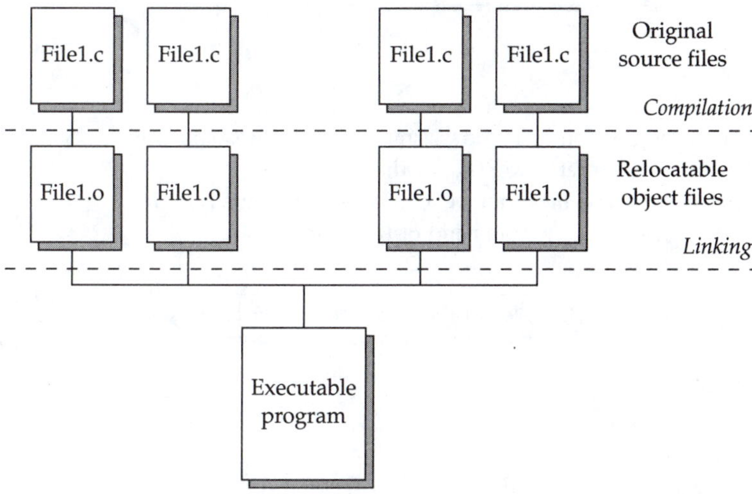

Figure 14.1 Typical compile and link procedure for a multiple source file program.

From the point of view of an individual programmer involved in the development of a medium to large-scale program, the same techniques could prove useful in improving productivity. For example, rather than placing the code for the whole program into one large source file which might take more than 10 minutes to compile, the programmer could arrange for the program to be composed of, say, five separate source files, each of which might take only 2 minutes to compile, thus a modification to one source file would only require 2 minutes of compilation time rather than 10.

14.1 The process of separate compilation

Because separate compilation implies that the complete source code for a program is broken down or expressed as a number of separate source files, care must be taken during compilation to ensure that the compiler does not assume that each source file constitutes a complete program in its own right.

In other words, we only want the compiler to generate the intermediate ROF and not to proceed to link in the standard library and attempt to make the final executable program. The mechanisms involved in achieving this vary somewhat from one compiler to another, thus readers are referred to their own compiler documentation for exact details. The operation is, however, very similar to a full compilation except that **flags** are generally set on the compiler command line to halt the compilation after the generation of the ROF. For example, under UNIX the compiler flag '–c' achieves this, as shown in the example below:

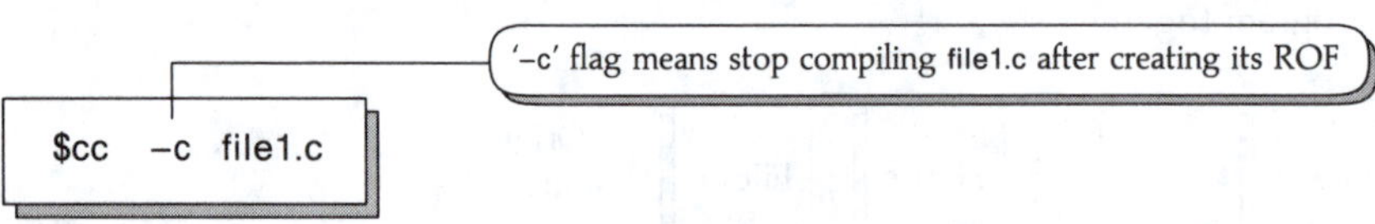

Note that if you are running Borland's Turbo C, simply choose the Compile option from the Compile menu to generate the ROF for that source file.

Where required, several source files can be compiled (sequentially) to produce several distinct ROFs with a UNIX command of the form:

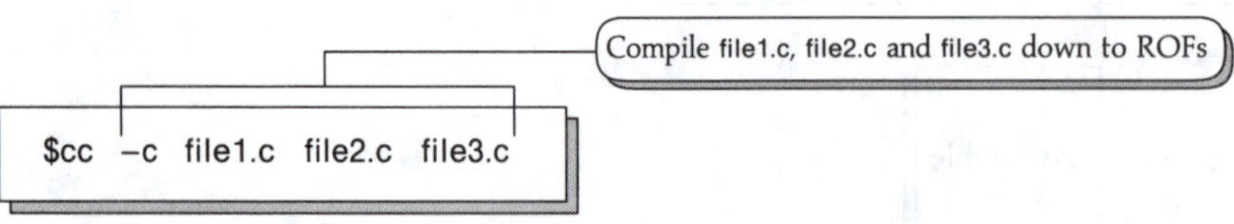

The name given to each ROF is usually derived in some way from the name of the original source file, for example file1.o under UNIX and file1.obj using Borland's Turbo C, but consult your compiler documentation for exact details.

Once the source files that constitute the complete program have been compiled to their respective ROFs, these can then be linked together, along with the C standard library, to produce the final executable version of the program with a UNIX command similar to the one shown below, where the executable version of the program is saved to disk using the name prog:

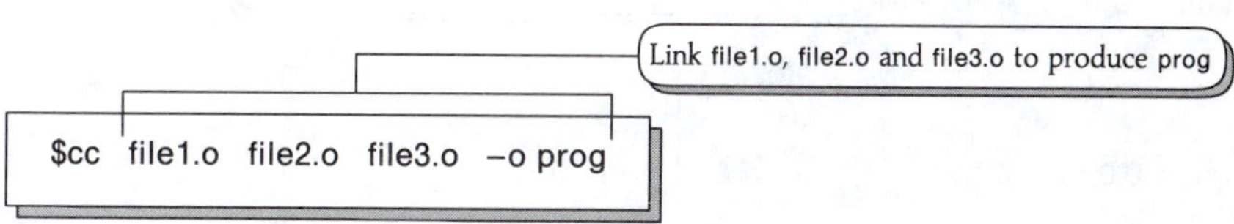

Note that it is usually possible to compile a file and link several ROFs with a command of the form shown below, where file1.c is compiled to its ROF form and then linked with the ROFs file2.o and file3.o to produce the executable file prog:

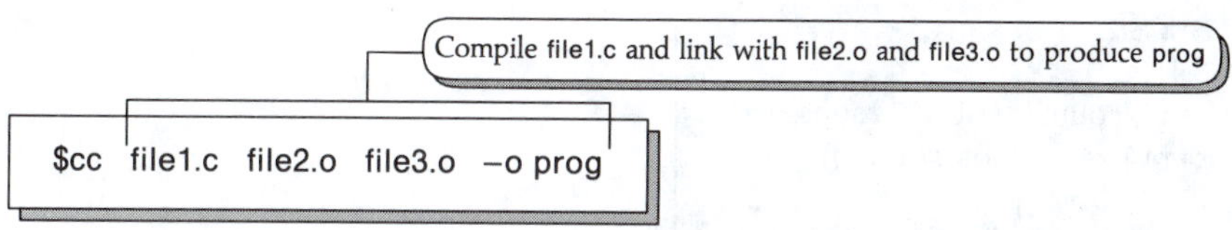

Although the above operations can be achieved with Borland's Turbo C through the use of appropriate Compile and Link options, the use of the Projects menu can automate the process. Here, the programmer specifies, via the Open project and Add item options in the Project menu, a list of source files that constitute a project (that is, a complete program). When either of these source files is modified, the compiler can be made to automatically compile those files that have changed and link their ROFs to generate the executable program. A similar type of automation is often accomplished under UNIX using the make utility (see Section 14.4) and is also available with most other good compilers.

In the remainder of this chapter, we will be taking a look at the problems and associated techniques of separate compilation. To illustrate these, an example source file has been chosen, which will be split into two smaller source files. These files will each be compiled separately and, finally, their ROFs linked together to produce a program that should be indistinguishable from the original in the sense that it will be no bigger and run no less efficiently than if the program had been generated from a single source file. Let us first consider the original source file, shown below:

The original source file: original.c

```
#include <stdio.h>
#include <stdlib.h>

#define NUM 10

int     count ;
double  result[ NUM ] ;

double average( void )
{
  double sum = 0.0 ;

  for( count = 0 ; count < NUM ; count ++)
    sum += result[ count ] ;

  return ( sum / NUM ) ;
}

int main( void )
{
  char buff[ BUFSIZ ] ;

  for( count = 0 ; count < NUM ; count ++ )
    result[ count ] = atof( gets( buff )) ;

  printf("Average = %f\n", average( )) ;
  return 0 ;
}
```


Let us now imagine that our programmer, using the block 'cut and paste' facilities of most editors, divides the source file in half to generate the two separate source files opposite, which are subsequently saved to disk.

What happens when we attempt to compile each source file to its ROF form? Well, firstly it is important to consider the two files in isolation, as that is how the compiler will see them. So, referring to the original source file, we note that it #included the header files <stdio.h> and <stdlib.h> into the program, because these contain the function prototypes for gets( ), printf( ) and atof( ) as well as the definition of the symbolic constant BUFSIZ.

Due to the way that the source file has been split, file2.c no longer #includes these header files, so the prototypes they contain are no longer visible to the compiler when file2.c is compiled, which is important for atof( ), which returns a double.

Similarly, the definition of the function average( ), which was placed ahead of the function main( ) in the original file, is no longer visible to the compiler

File1.c: After splitting, compiles without errors

```
#include <stdio.h>
#include <stdlib.h>

#define NUM 10

int      count ;
double   result[ NUM ] ;

double average( void )
{
   double sum = 0.0 ;
   for( count = 0 ; count < NUM ; count ++)
      sum += result[ count ] ;

   return ( sum / NUM ) ;
}
```

File2.c: After splitting, compiles with errors

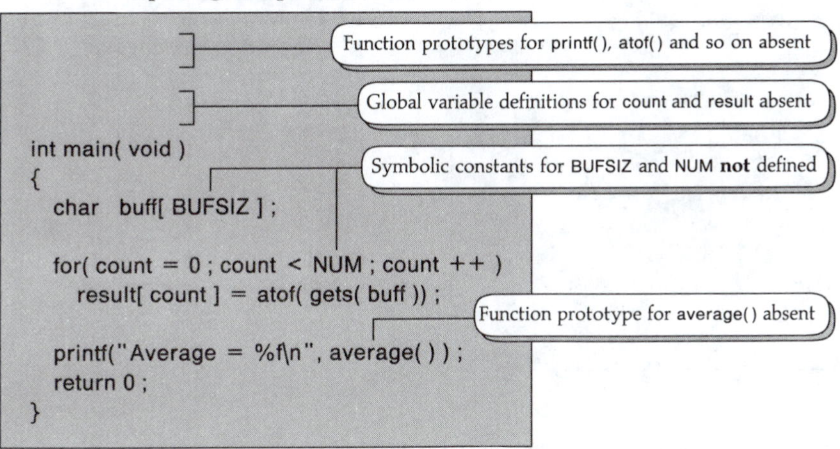
Function prototypes for printf(), atof() and so on absent
Global variable definitions for count and result absent
int main(void)
{
char buff[BUFSIZ] ;
Symbolic constants for BUFSIZ and NUM **not** defined
for(count = 0 ; count < NUM ; count ++)
result[count] = atof(gets(buff)) ;
Function prototype for average() absent
printf("Average = %f\n", average( )) ;
return 0 ;
}

when file2.c is compiled, thus the compiler will assume, incorrectly, that average( ) and atof( ) return an int rather than a double.

A further problem also exists in the definition of the symbolic constants NUM and BUFSIZ (the latter is defined in <stdio.h>) and those of the global variables count and result, which are also not 'visible' to the compiler when file2.c is compiled and thus lead to compile time errors, resulting in the ROF for file2.c not being generated.

On the other hand, file1.c is completely self-contained, since it makes no references to any variables or functions (other than those in the standard library whose prototypes are visible through the inclusion of the appropriate header files) outside of its own source file, and will thus compile to a ROF without problem.

Overcoming the problems associated with file2.c requires some subtle understanding. Let us tackle the problem of the missing prototypes, symbolic constants and header files first, because these are relatively easy to overcome. Because the introduction of a symbolic constant or function prototype only provides the compiler with information – that is, it does not lead to the generation of any additional program code or increase the storage requirements for the program – we could overcome the aforementioned problems by duplicating many of the missing parts of the program that now reside only within file1.c. This is shown below in file2a.c:

File2a.c: First modification, but still compiles with errors

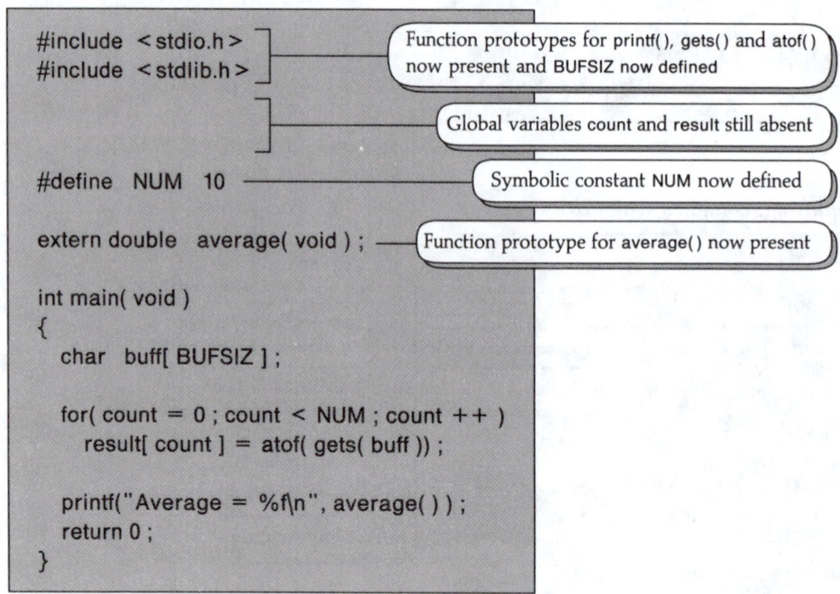

Of course, file2a.c will not yet compile, since the variables count and result are still unknown to the compiler, but we have significantly reduced the problems associated with compiling that file.

14.1.1 *External functions*

You will notice from the above modifications to file2a.c that the key word extern was used when the function prototype for average( ) was introduced. This informs the compiler that average( ) is a function defined elsewhere, or externally, typically within another source file.

The use of extern here is not strictly speaking necessary, since the compiler always assumes that a function is externally defined even if it does eventually encounter the function's definition later within the source file. Ultimately, of course, the task of locating and resolving the calls that a program makes to an external function fall to the linker.

Therefore, the only information that the compiler extracts from the prototype for average( ), is that it returns a double and expects no arguments, thus the key word extern could be omitted without problem, although it aids clarity and readability to include it.

14.1.2 *External variables*

Solving the problems associated with the global variables missing from file2a.c requires a slightly more complex analysis and solution. In the original source file (original.c), you will recall that the global variables count and result were defined and were both referenced by the functions main( ) and average( ). Now, given the way the original file was split, the definition for these two variables now lies within file1.c. Thus, when file2a.c is compiled, count and result are unknown to the compiler and the compilation of that file will ultimately be aborted.

The obvious temptation here is to define count and result again, within file2a.c, thus overcoming the immediate problem of generating a ROF from that file. However, this only serves to create problems further down the line for the linker, as the program has now effectively defined (that is, allocated global storage for) the variables count and result twice, once in file1.c and once in file2a.c. Because the linker cannot resolve the difference between the two variables count and result contained within both ROFs, the link is aborted with a multiple definition error along the lines of:

```
Link error: 'count' is multiply defined within 'file1.o' and 'file2a.o'
Link error: 'result' is multiply defined within 'file1.o' and 'file2a.o'
```

What we really require within file2a.c is a **declaration** of the variables count and result. The declaration of a variable provides the compiler with all the information it needs to know about the variable, such as its name and type, but does not force the compiler to allocate any storage for it. Such a declaration is easily formed by prefixing a copy of its definition with the key word extern, as shown below:

extern declaration means storage is *not* allocated for the variable

```
extern int      count ;
extern double   result[ NUM ] ;
```

Now let us introduce the extern variable declarations into file2b.c and take a look at the two completed source files, which can now be compiled and linked to produce a final executable program.

File1.c: First and final version

```
#include <stdio.h>
#include <stdlib.h>

#define NUM 10

int       count ;
double    result[ NUM ] ;

double average( void )
{
  double sum = 0.0 ;

  for( count = 0 ; count < NUM ; count ++)
    sum += result[ count ] ;

  return ( sum / NUM ) ;
}
```

File2b.c: Final version

```
#include <stdio.h>
#include <stdlib.h>

extern  int      count ;
extern  double   result[ NUM ] ;

#define  NUM 10

extern  double  average( void ) ;

int main( void )
{
  char  buff[ BUFSIZ ] ;

  for( count = 0 ; count < NUM ; count ++)
    result[ count ] = atof( gets( buff )) ;

  printf("Average = %f\n", average( )) ;
  return 0 ;
}
```

Contains function prototypes for printf( ), atof( ) and so on and BUFSIZ

Declaration of count and result

Symbolic constant NUM

Function prototype for average( )

14.1.3 *A word of caution concerning* extern *declarations*

You will recall from Chapter 2 that a standard C compiler should be able to distinguish between two identifiers (that is, the names of functions, variables, structures and so on) that are unique within the first 31 characters of their names. Unfortunately, this may not necessarily be true in relation to external indentifiers.

The reason for this lies with the fact that all references made by your program to an external identifier (which includes, by the way, all references to functions/variables defined externally to the current source, including the standard library) have to be resolved by the linker. Now, some C compilers are, unfortunately, forced to work in environments where the linker is not an integral part of the compiler package itself, but is supplied with the operating system as part of a suite of tools comprising editor, assembler, linker and so on. Consequently, such linkers are not forced to comply with the letter of the C standard itself.

What this means is that such linkers may only be able to distinguish between two external identifiers that are unique within the first *six characters* of their names! Worse still is the fact that some of them are also incapable of distinguishing between upper and lower case, so take care. In the author's experience, this has never proved to be a problem, probably because most linkers have the common sense not to be so restrictive, but for maximum portability of code, the programmer should be aware of this.

14.2 Restricting variable access and information hiding

Whenever a team of programmers are involved in the joint development of a program through the use of separate source files, there inevitably comes a time when one or more programmers accidentally define two global variables that happen to share the same name. For example, consider an extract from two source files shown below:

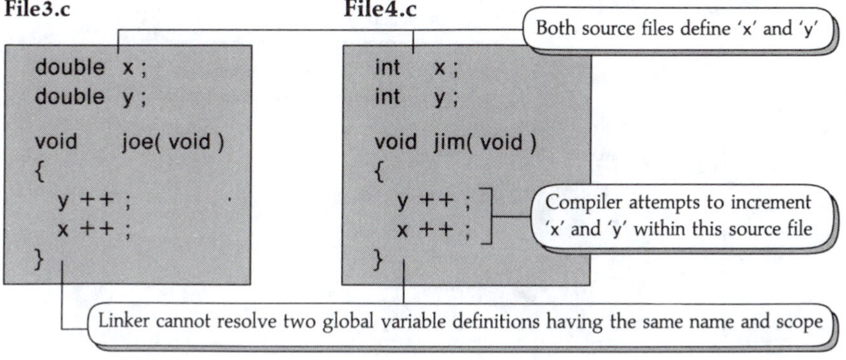
File3.c
double x ;
double y ;
void joe(void)
{
y ++ ;
x ++ ;
}
File4.c
int x ;
int y ;
void jim(void)
{
y ++ ;
x ++ ;
}
Both source files define 'x' and 'y'
Compiler attempts to increment 'x' and 'y' within this source file
Linker cannot resolve two global variable definitions having the same name and scope

Here, both file3.c and file4.c define the variables 'x' and 'y' for their own purposes, unaware that another file has also defined them. The linker is now left in an impossible position, where it cannot distinguish between the two variables 'x' and 'y' defined by both files. For example, is jim() attempting to increment the variable 'x' defined within file3.c or the variable 'x' defined within file4.c? The original programmers know, since they wrote the code, but the linker does not.

Obviously, the programmers' attention would be drawn to this type of problem by the linker, because it issues appropriate error messages as we saw in Section 14.1.2, and these problems *could* be overcome by modifying one or other source file to make the variable names unique. However, this may not always be the most appropriate solution.

Consider the problem from a different angle. We already know that if a file introduces an extern declaration of a variable (as we saw in file2b.c for the variables count and result), then there is nothing to prevent global variables defined in one source file being accessed by code residing in another.

What happens, then, if a source file wishes to ensure that a global variable that *it* defines *cannot* be accessed by any other part of the program defined outside that source file, perhaps because the program wishes to hide the implementation and representation of a particular data structure from other parts of the program?

Both of these problems can be overcome if the definition of a global variable is prefixed with the key word static. You will recall that we introduced the concept of a static variable in Chapter 2 – that is, a static variable defined within a function (and thus said to be a local static variable) – but the use of the word static applied to a global variable has a somewhat different interpretation, since it serves to restrict or limit the scope of that variable to the source file in which it is defined.

In other words, a global static variable is only accessible by functions that are defined within the *same* source file as the variable itself, since outside that file the variable is considered not to exist. Imagine, then, the situation we discussed earlier, where a team of programmers accidentally defined variables with the same name. Provided those variables were not intended to be shared by other source files, each programmer could modify their variable definitions to give them global static storage, thus restricting their scope to that source file. For example:

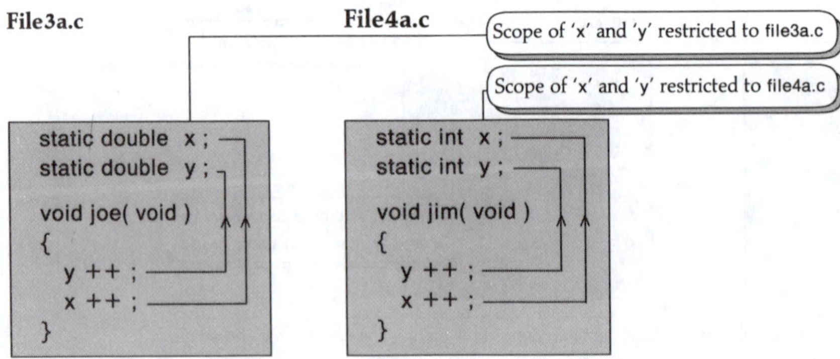
File3a.c
File4a.c
Scope of 'x' and 'y' restricted to file3a.c
Scope of 'x' and 'y' restricted to file4a.c
static double x ;
static double y ;
void joe(void)
{
y ++ ;
x ++ ;
}
static int x ;
static int y ;
void jim(void)
{
y ++ ;
x ++ ;
}

Here, because, both 'x' and 'y' in each source have well-defined scope, the linker can resolve their multiple definitions and determine that the statement 'x++' in file3a.c references the variable 'x' defined in that file and not the variable 'x' defined in file4a.c and vice versa. Even if another source file attempts to access this restricted variable with an extern declaration, the linker would not permit it.

Of course, given this simplistic approach, there is no way to *selectively* permit or exclude individual source files, on a file by file basis, from accessing global variables defined elsewhere. In other words, a global variable is either static and thus private to its own source file, or it is completely accessible by any source file that cares to reference it with an extern declaration.

14.2.1 *Function hiding*

The same technique of information hiding may also be applied to functions to restrict their scope. Remember that all functions are implicitly assumed to have been defined externally and are thus accessible by any source file that cares to reference them. The only way to restrict access to them is, once again, via the static prefix in their definition.

This technique is again useful where several source files accidentally define two or more functions with the same name. For example, the following two source files define the functions add(), which – although possessing identical names – perform quite different operations.

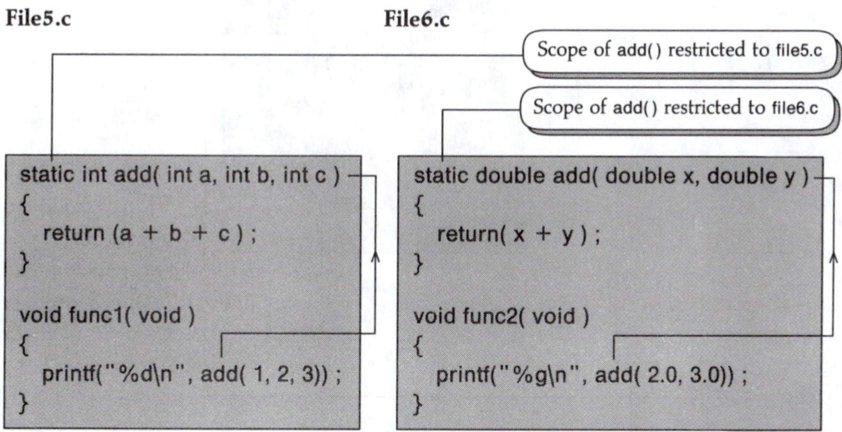
File5.c
File6.c
Scope of add() restricted to file5.c
Scope of add() restricted to file6.c
static int add(int a, int b, int c)
{
return (a + b + c) ;
}
void func1(void)
{
printf("%d\n", add(1, 2, 3)) ;
}
static double add(double x, double y)
{
return(x + y) ;
}
void func2(void)
{
printf("%g\n", add(2.0, 3.0)) ;
}

By making add() in each source file a static function, the linker is able to resolve the calls made by each file to its respective function, since their scope is now well defined. It does, of course, mean that there is no way for add() in file5.c to be called by code within file6.c and vice versa.

14.3 The use of header files in separate compilation

All of this hiding and sharing of data and functions can sometimes get a little out of hand for the poor old programmer who always has to ensure that the declarations of all external variables and functions within many different source file are consistent with the variable's/function's actual definition.

It is all too easy, for example, for the programmer to *declare* a variable as an external int in one file, only to find that it is defined as a float in another file, particularly during program development, where variable types (and array sizes) may change. This sort of potential problem cannot, unfortunately, be detected by the compiler because it is only able to 'see' one source file at a time.

The use of header files can help enormously here. Given that a number of functions and variables are shared by several source files, the programmer could

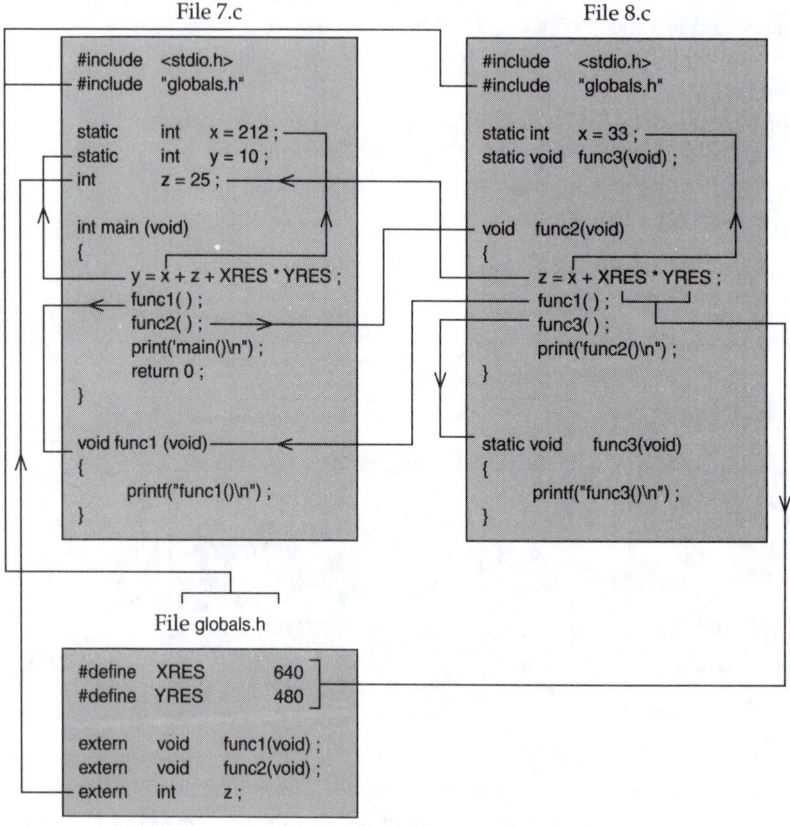

Figure 14.2 Using a header file to ensure consistent function/variable definitions and external declarations across several source files.

arrange for their declarations/prototypes to be placed into a common header file, which is #included by each source file that wishes to access them.

The definitions for those functions/variables/constants could then be placed in any of those source files, or, as sometimes happens, placed into their own source file and compiled to a ROF. Those functions/variables that are private to a source file could be defined as static within their respective source files. Figure 14.2 illustrates this for the simple case of two source files.

Now, if the definition of a shared variable or function changes, the programmer need only alter its declaration in the header file and then recompile the files that include that header file. The changes will then take immediate effect within the ROFs.

14.4 The UNIX utility: make

Although the compilation and subsequent linkage of a *small* number of source and object files can easily be achieved via simple compiler command lines such as cc file7.c file8.c -o prog, there comes a point in the development of very large-scale applications where an individual programmer, perhaps working as part of a team, has great difficulty in keeping track of all of the compiler command lines required to create the final executable version of a program from a large number of separate source files.

More to the point, that same programmer has even greater difficulty remembering the list of source files required to build the executable program and the effect an alteration to one or more of them might have on the remaining files.

For example, referring to Figure 14.2 and studying the three source files file7.c, file8.c and globals.h, we immediately see that both file7.c and file8.c are *dependent* upon the symbolic constants XRES and YRES defined within the header file globals.h. If globals.h were modified, perhaps to define different values for XRES or YRES, then care must be taken to ensure that both file7.c and file8.c are re-compiled to take account of these modifications.

Of course, the simplest solution to this kind of problem would involve re-compiling *every* source file that is required to generate the final executable program – that is, file7.c and file8.c – regardless of whether those source files are affected by the change or not. Now although such an approach can be relied upon, it rather negates the prime reason for introducing separate source files in the first place, namely that it leads to a reduction in the compilation time required to make simple modifications to a single source file, and is not really practical when the program might be composed of perhaps 1000+ source files.

A better solution would be to make use of the make utility available under UNIX (although Borland and many other compiler vendors provide an equivalent utility as part of their compiler package for non-UNIX environments). The primary use of make (although other applications do exist) is to automate the compilation and linkage of multiple source file programs with the aim of reducing the amount of re-compilation required to a minimum and thus ensuring that all ROFs are up to date and a true reflection of the current source code.

It does this through the use of a **makefile**, which is simply a text file generated by the programmer. The general format for an entry within a makefile is shown below:

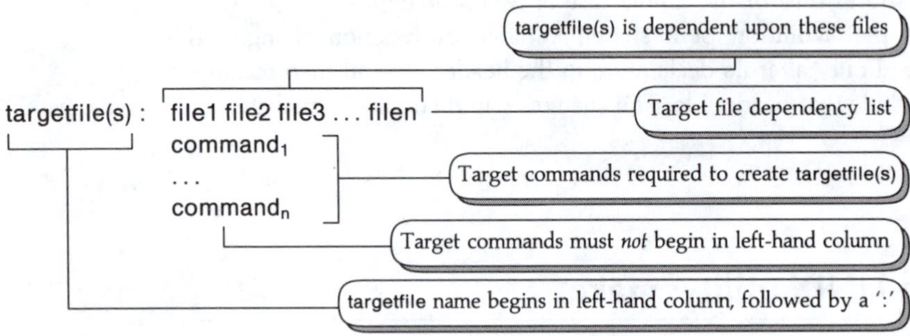

which means that targetfile is dependent upon those files given in the dependency list and that in order to build an up-to-date version of targetfile, target commands 1 to n must be executed. For example, a suitable UNIX makefile to create the executable version of the program, prog, using the source files given in Figure 14.2 is given below:

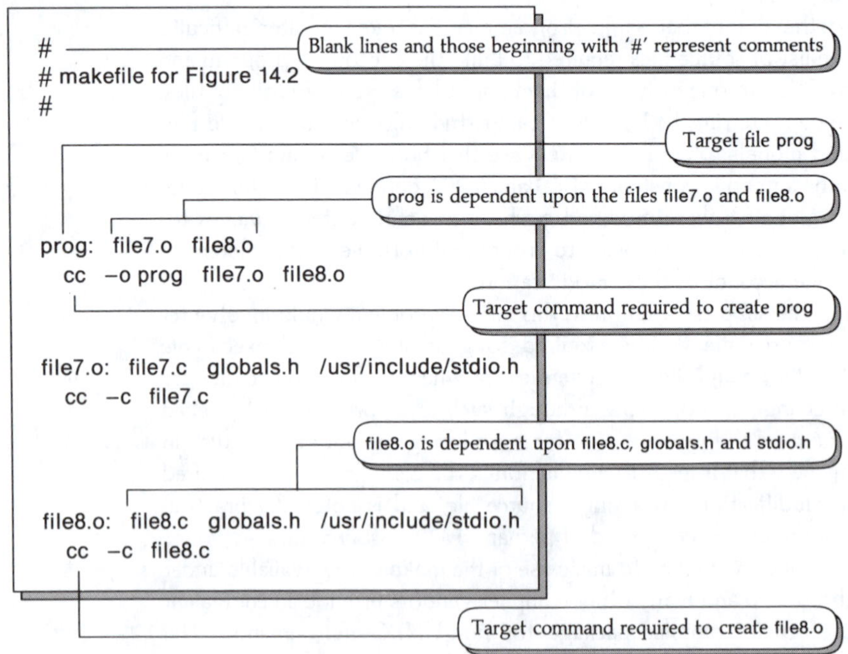

In order to create the target file prog we could invoke make with an operating system shell command of the form:

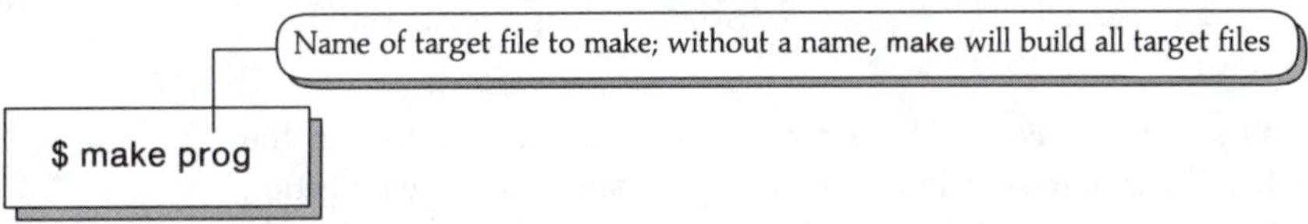
Name of target file to make; without a name, make will build all target files

```
$ make prog
```

When make is invoked, it reads, by default, the makefile from the current directory. From this it determines the name of each of the target files listed within it. In the above example the target files are prog, file7.o and file8.o.

make then builds a table of source file dependencies associated with each target file. For example, make determines that prog is directly dependent upon the object files file7.o and file8.o. It also determines that file7.o (and hence prog) is directly dependent upon the source file file7.c and the header files globals.h and /usr/include/stdio.h; likewise, file8.o (and hence prog) is directly dependent upon the source file file8.c and the same header files globals.h and /usr/include/stdio.h.

Now in order to make the specified target file prog, with the *minimum* of compilation, make examines the *last modified dates and times* of all of its dependent files – that is, file7.o, file8.o and all of their dependent files, file7.c, file8.c, globals.h and /usr/include/stdio.h.

If make discovers that any target file is out of date – that is, has a last modified date/time older than any one or more of its dependent source files – then that target file is brought up to date by executing the associated target command.

For example, suppose that both object files file7.o and file8.o are out of date (perhaps because the programmer has modified the dependent files file7.c and file8.c), or perhaps because they do not even exist yet. When make is invoked to build prog, it automatically invokes the following sequence of target commands to ensure that both file7.o and file8.o, and thus prog, are brought up to date:

```
$cc –c file7.c
$cc –c file8.c
$cc –o prog file7.o file8.o
```

Likewise, the same sequence of target commands would have been invoked had either globals.h or stdio.h been modified more recently than file7.o or file8.o.

However, if only the object file file7.o was out of date, perhaps because file7.c (but not file8.c) had been modified (or the UNIX utility touch had been used to bring up to date the last modified date and time of file7.c), then make would only execute the target commands shown below, since file8.c does not need to be re-compiled to build prog:

```
$cc –c file7.c
$cc –o prog file7.o file8.o
```

As you can see, the make utility is a powerful and effective tool in the battle to ensure that object and executable files are up to date and a true reflection of the source files upon which they depend. However, its effectiveness is entirely dependent upon an accurate representation of source file dependencies within the makefile. Get these wrong, and you can introduce more problems than you solve.

For a fuller, more in-depth discussion of the facilities provided by make, the reader is referred to the relevant operating system/compiler manual, because many of these facilities vary in subtle ways from one operating system/compiler to another.

14.5 Mixing C with assembly language

Although modern compilers are quite capable of generating fast and efficient code, programmers may occasionally be faced with the need to write some assembly language for themselves. The rationale behind this is summarized below:

(1) To achieve an action or operation over which the compiler offers little or no control, such as directly accessing CPU registers or peripherals that are not memory mapped (as is the case with many 80x86 CPUs).

(2) To hand-optimize a section of code so that it runs faster or more efficiently.

(3) To access specific CPU instructions such as enabling or disabling the recognition of interrupts.

(4) To design a section of code to run at a certain time-critical speed.

(5) To interface the compiler to functions or libraries that use a different calling convention and different techniques for passing and returning arguments and results.

Essentially, there are two methods of integrating assembly language into a C program. The first approach, popular for reasons (4) and (5) above, relies on programmers generating their own assembly language functions as part of a separate source file. The assembled version of this file, now in the form of a ROF, may subsequently be linked, as we have seen already in this chapter, with the relevant ROFs produced by the compiler, using an example assembler and compiler command line of the form shown below:

```
asm68 my_assembly.a -o=my_assembly.o
c68 prog1.c -l=my_assembly.o -o=prog1.exe
```

The second approach, often popular when only a small amount of assembly language is required, is to embed the lines of assembly code directly into the C source file using a (non-standard) compiler directive such as '_asm' and let the compiler deal with them, as shown in Program 14.1, where Motorola 68000 assembly language has been used.

Program 14.1 Embedding assembly language directly into a C program.

```
#include <stdio.h>

int main( void )
{
  ...
  ...
_asm  move.b  #0,$FFE00
_asm  move.w  d0, d1
_asm  add.w   totol(a6),d1
  ...
  ...
  return 0 ;
}
```

With both approaches, it is essential that the programmer has a clear understanding not only of the host CPU's assembly language, but also of the workings of the compiler. In mixing assembly language with a C based application, the programmer may have to address the following issues:

(1) How are the fundamental and basic data types represented? For example, is an int 2 or 4 bytes in size?

(2) How and in what order are arguments passed to functions, and how are those arguments accessed?

(3) How is data returned by a function?

(4) What CPU registers are free for the programmer to change and which registers must be preserved upon entry and exit to/from a function?

(5) How are global variables/constants accessed; that is, what addressing modes are used to access them?

The answers to these questions can, it is hoped, be found in your C compiler's reference manual along with a few examples of how to write a sample function in assembly language. By careful study, it should be possible to use these as the basis for the design of your own functions.

If your only requirement is to optimize a particular section of the code produced by the compiler, then it is helpful to have a listing of the assembly language output produced by the compiler saved to a file. Many compilers are capable of producing such an output if the relevant options are specified on the compiler command line.

For example, the following compiler command line on the author's system saves the compiler's assembly language output, complete with original source code as comments, into the file program1.a:

```
cc  -ca  program1.c
```

The file can now be studied/edited and various optimizations effected before the modified file is assembled and linked with the compiler command line:

```
cc  program1.a  -o=program1.exe
```

14.6 Chapter summary

(1) Separate compilation permits a large source file to be broken down into several smaller ones, each of which may then be compiled to a relocatable object file (ROF). The resultant ROFs may then be linked together to produce the final executable program.

(2) A source file may access a global variable or function defined in another source file by introducing an extern declaration of that variable or function.

(3) All global variables/functions defined as static have their scope restricted to the current source file in which they are defined. They cannot be accessed by code from other source files even if those files contain an extern declaration of the variable or function.

(4) A header file provides a convenient place to store extern declarations, constants and function prototypes. The inclusion of that file into each source file provides consistency of type declarations.

(5) The make utility is a powerful and effective tool in the battle to ensure that object and executable files are a true reflection of the source files upon which they depend.

14.7 Exercises

14.1 Under what circumstances is it beneficial to consider separate compilation techniques during program development?

14.2 What is the difference between a variable definition and a variable declaration?

14.3 How many times can a global variable be defined and declared within a program?

14.4 What is the principal difference between a 'local static' and a 'global static' variable?

14.5 What is the principal difference between a 'global static' and a 'global (external)' variable?

14.6 What is information hiding and how is it achieved?

14.7 What are meant by the terms 'scope' and 'privacy'? Explain why they do not always imply the same thing.

14.8 Does a variable declaration prefixed by the key word extern also ensure that the variable is defined elsewhere – that is, that its definition will come later? Take a look at the following program and analyse why it will not run:

```
#include  <stdio.h>
#define   LIMIT 12

extern    int i, j ;

int main( void )
{
  for( i = 0 ; i <= LIMIT ; i ++ )
    for( j = 0 ; j <= LIMIT ; j ++ )
      printf("%d * %d = %d\n", i, j, i*j ) ;

  return 0 ;
}
```

If the declaration of the variables 'i' and 'j' above were changed such that the key word extern were replaced by the key word static what effect would this have on the program? What is achieved if the declaration of those same variables is replaced by the following:

```
extern int i = 0, j = 0 ;
```

What conclusions can you draw about the introduction of initialized external variables?

14.9 In Application 11.2 we developed several functions to manipulate complex numbers. Enter and save these functions within a source file complex.c and generate a header file complex.h containing any information in support of these functions, such as function prototypes, structure declarations, the inclusion of additional header files such as <math.h> and so on.

Making sure that the header file is #included by complex.c, compile the latter to its ROF form using appropriate compiler options and flags. Now enter the remaining function main() from this application (or that from Application 11.2) into a separate source file and compile and link this with the ROF generated above to produce the executable version of the program.

14.10 Split the following program into two separate source files and make whatever modifications are necessary to ensure that it works in the same way. Your first solution should attempt to split the file such that everything up to and including the function main() is placed in one file, while the function display() resides in another.

Your second solution should place the function main() in one source file and the function display() in another, while all global variables are defined within a third source file, globals.c. A header file data.h should then be created, which contains all of the information required by each source file.

```
#include <stdio.h>
#include <stdlib.h>

#define NUM 10

typedef struct object {
    int         age ;
    double      height ;
    char        name[ BUFSIZ ] ;
} DATA ;

DATA a[NUM] ;

void display( void )
{
    int i ;

    for( i = 0 ; i < NUM ; i ++ ) {
        printf("Name = %s\n", a[NUM].name ) ;
        printf("Age = %d\n", a[NUM].age ) ;
        printf("Height = %g\n", a[NUM].height ) ;
    }
}

int main( void )
{
    int   i ;
    char  buff[ BUFSIZ ] ;
```

```
    for( i = 0; i < NUM; i ++ )  {
        printf("Enter your name : ") ;
        gets( a[NUM].name) ;
        printf("Enter your age : ") ;
        a[NUM].age = atoi( gets( buff )) ;
        printf("Enter your height : ") ;
        a[NUM].height = atof( gets( buff )) ;
    }
    display() ;
    return 0 ;
}
```

14.11 Generate a makefile for use with the make utility to automate the compilation of both versions of the split source file program presented in Exercise 14.10, and experiment with it by modifying a source file to check that make compiles only those files that need compiling.

15 A Closer Look at printf() and scanf()

In this chapter we take a much closer look at the formatting abilities of printf(), in particular how the programmer may control the field width, precision and text justification for a particular display type and the effects of these on each of the '%' format indicators recognized by printf(). The second half of the chapter is set aside for a closer study of the corresponding input function scanf(), where the reader will learn how to write programs to accept or reject input of a certain format and how these facilities are of use when a program's input has been redirected to come from a text file rather than from the operator's keyboard.

It is important for the reader to appreciate that both printf() and scanf() are complex functions, providing the programmer with a great deal of flexibility when formatting data; thus this chapter should be viewed more as reference material that can be looked up on a 'need to know' basis, rather than as information to be committed to memory.

For the embedded applications programmer, neither function is of much use because of the frequent absence of a host operating system in these types of application. However, provided the programmer is able to supply primitive, low level I/O functions to communicate with a raw device on a character by character basis (as we saw in Chapter 8), then the closely related library functions sprintf() and sscanf() (and others) should provide all the flexibility and formatting required to emulate printf() and scanf() but with the important exception that data is written to and/or read from a char array rather than an actual device. Table 15.1 lists the functions that may be of interest for these applications.

Table 15.1 Operating system independent I/O functions.

Function name	*Description*
atoi(), atol(), atof()	Text to numeric conversion
sprintf(), sscanf()	Formatted conversion to and from an array

15.1 Formatted text and numeric output: printf()

We have already seen how printf() caters for the mixed display of data to the operator's terminal using a format string containing a number of '%' format indicators. These mark the position and format where other data, in the form of additional arguments, will be displayed. In summary, the general form of a call to printf() is given below:

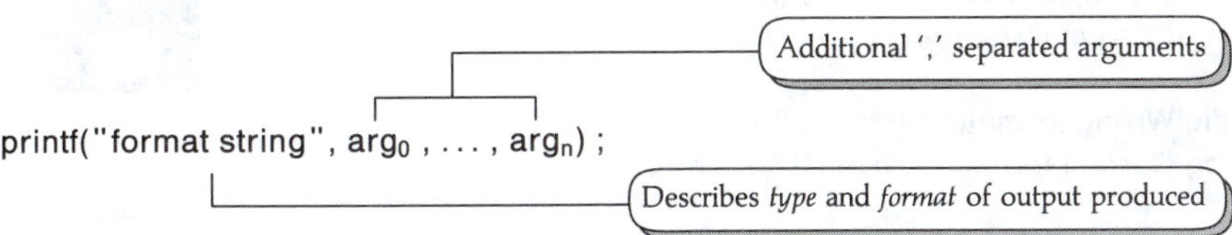
Additional ',' separated arguments
printf("format string", arg0 , . . . , argn) ;
Describes *type* and *format* of output produced

where 'format string' contains any literal text to be displayed by printf(), along with an optional number of '%' formatters, which control the type, position and format of any additional data to be displayed. The relationship between the '%' formatter and each additional argument is shown below:

New line character '\n'

```
printf( "tot=%d, av=%d\n" , x , y ) ;
```

Arguments and formatters matched on on-to-one basis

Notice how each additional argument is matched with its corresponding '%' formatter on a one-to-one basis. Therefore, in place of the two '%d' formatters in the example above, the values of the variables 'x' and 'y' would be displayed. Assuming, then, that 'x' and 'y' have the values '23' and '45', respectively, the operator would see the following output displayed on his or her screen:

```
tot = 23 , av = 45
```

Note that printf() does not *automatically* begin a new line at the end of its output, and the programmer may well have to insert the new line character '\n' into the format string if one is required. This is an important consideration when running programs under the UNIX operating system, which does not display any output until a new line is issued by the program.

Frequent mistakes when using printf()

Undoubtedly, the single most frequent mistake relating to the use of printf() is to specify the wrong '%' formatter for the type of argument to be displayed, for example using '%d' to display a real quantity, or using '%f' to display an integer.

Program 15.1 Example incorrect usage of '%' formatter.

```
#include  <stdio.h>

int main( void )
{
   int     a = 5 ;
   double  b = 3.141592 ;

   printf("Using Wrong formatter, a = %f\n", a ) ;
   printf("Using Correct formatter, a = %d\n", a ) ;

   printf("Using Wrong formatter, b = %d\n", b ) ;
   printf("Using Correct formatter, b = %f\n", b ) ;

   return 0 ;
}
```

Floating point formatter

Integer variable

Caution!

This can lead to all sorts of garbage being displayed because printf() simply misinterprets the argument it has been given. Try Program 15.1, which contains some obvious errors, and observe the effect on your terminal.

Another frequent mistake is to supply printf() with the wrong number of '%' formatters for the number of arguments to be displayed. An example of this can be seen in the statement below:

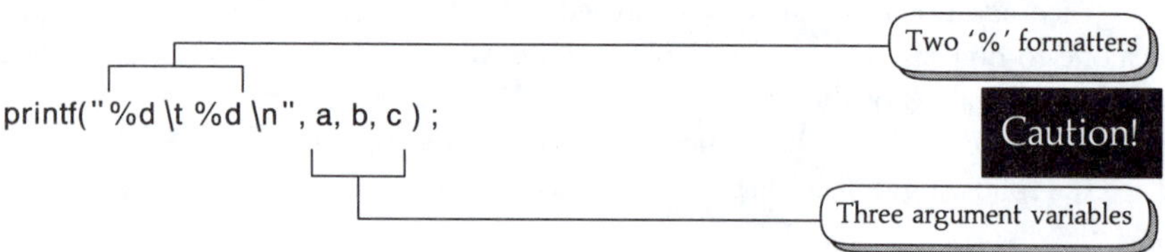

Here printf() has been asked to display two integer variables, since only two '%' formatters were present in the format string. The fact that the variables 'a', 'b' *and* 'c' have been passed to printf() is irrelevant; printf() will only display 'a' and 'b'. A more serious version of this problem is shown below:

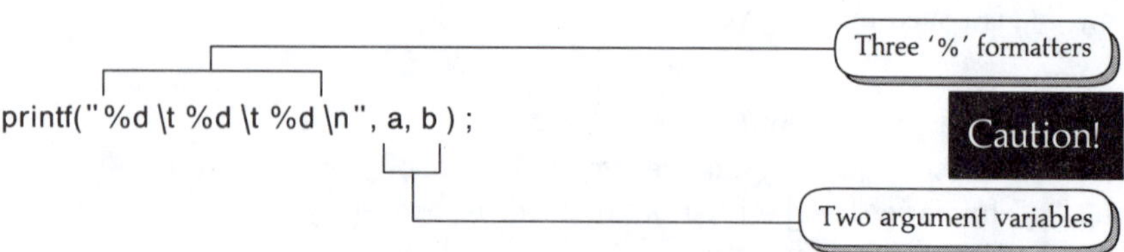

Here printf() has been asked to display three integer values, but the programmer has only supplied it with two additional arguments. When the program is run, the values of 'a' and 'b' are correctly displayed, but printf() invents a third value (by pulling garbage off the stack) to go with the third '%' formatter. Try it and see. The full set of '%' formatters recognized by printf() is summarized in Table 15.2 and we shall be considering each of these in detail shortly.

Table 15.2 Format indicators recognized by printf().

'%' formatter	*Type of display*	*Type of argument*
%d or %i	Signed decimal integral	char, short, int
%u	Unsigned decimal integral	char, short, int
%x or %X	Unsigned hexadecimal integral Displays lower case 'abcdef' using %x and upper case 'ABCDEF' using %X	char, short, int
%o	Unsigned octal integral	char, short, int
%e or %E	Scientific notation Format: [−]m.dddddd e ± xx with %e or [−]m.dddddd E ± xx with %E Default precision dddddd is 6 digits	float or double
%f	Floating point notation Format: [−]mmm.dddddd Default precision dddddd is 6 digits	float or double
%g or %G	Shortest of %e (%E) or %f with %g (%G) If exponent is less than −4, %e (%E) is used Default precision dddddd is *at most* 6 digits	float or double
%c	Text character	char, short, int
%s	'\0' terminated text string	char array
%p	Address/pointer value Format: system dependent	Address/pointer (see Section 8.1.6)
%n	Number of characters displayed printf() stores the number of characters it has displayed so far into the argument supplied, which must be the address of or pointer to an integer	Pointer to int
%%	'%' sign	None

15.1.1 *Displaying integral values:* '%d', '%u', '%i', '%x', '%X', '%o'

printf() is able to display any integral quantity such as a char, short or int in a variety of numeric bases including decimal, hexadecimal and octal (but not

Table 15.3 Integer display formatters: printf( ).

Formatter	*Interpretation*	*Typical 16 bit int*	*Displayed as*
%d, %i	Signed decimal	0000 0000 1111 1111	255
		1000 1111 0000 0000	–28928
%u	Unsigned decimal	0100 0111 0100 1110	18254
		1000 1111 0000 0000	36608
%x	Unsigned hexadecimal	1000 1111 0000 1010	8f0a
%X	Unsigned hexadecimal	1000 1111 0000 1010	8F0A
%o	Unsigned octal	1000 1111 0000 1010	107412
		1111 1111 1111 1111	177777

binary), using the format indicators shown in Table 15.3. Note that both chars *and* shorts are promoted to full ints before they are displayed.

None of these formatters by default issues any leading zeros in the output (except for the actual value zero, of course), thus the hex value 0x00fa is displayed as 'fa', and not as 00fa or 0x00fa.

The width of the display field issued by printf( ) will thus vary depending upon the actual value being displayed, which in turn is heavily influenced by the range of values for that quantity. With a 32 bit integer, perhaps 10 or more displayable characters might be issued with a '%d' formatter. Try Program 15.2 on your computer to see what type of display is produced. See if you can explain the unusual displays that arise in some instances.

Program 15.2 Displaying an integral quantity.

```
#include   <stdio.h>

int main( void )
{
    char  a1 = 23, a2 = –19 ;
    short b1 = 53, b2 = –12 ;
    int   i1 = 32000, i2 = –32000 ;

    printf("a1 = %d, a2 = %d\n", a1, a2 ) ;
    printf("a1 = %x, a2 = %X\n", a1, a2 ) ;
    printf("b1 = %o, b2 = %o\n", b1, b2 ) ;
    printf("i1 = %u, i2 = %u\n", i1, i2 ) ;

    return 0 ;
}
```

15.1.2 *Displaying real values: '%f', '%e', '%E', '%g' and '%G'*

printf() can display a real quantity, such as a float or double, using the format indicators '%f', '%e', '%E', '%g' and '%G'. The general format of the display produced by the '%f' formatter is given below:

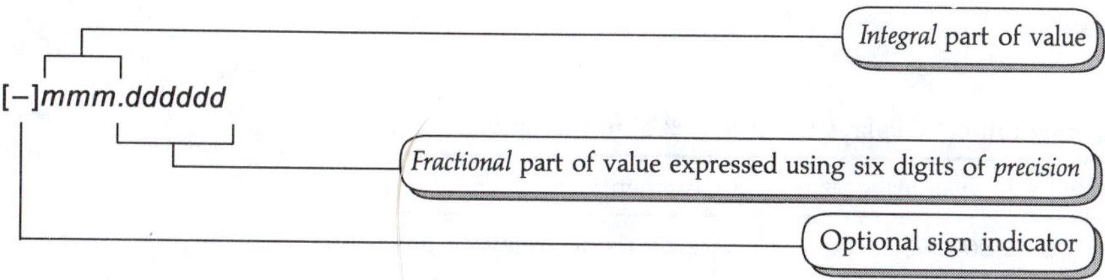

where 'mmm' represents the integral part of the floating point value and 'dddddd' represents the fractional part. Any number of digits may be issued for the real 'mmm' part to ensure that its value is accurately displayed, but six digits of precision are *always* issued for the fractional part 'dddddd'. Trailing zeros will be appended if necessary, but this can be overridden by specifying a precision (see Section 15.2.2). Table 15.4 demonstrates how various real values would be displayed using the '%f' formatter.

Table 15.4 Example printf() displays using the '%f' format indicator.

Real value	*Output using '%f'*	*Comments*
0.0	0.000000	Six digits of precision
2.3e10	23000000000.000000	Large real part to ensure accuracy
2312.545 343 42	2312.545343	Truncated fractional part to six digits
0.001	0.001000	Trailing zeros in display
1e−23	0.000000	Unable to display with six digit precision

The scientific formatters: '%e' and '%E'

printf() can be asked to display a real quantity in scientific form using the formatters '%e' or '%E'. The general form of the display produced is given below:

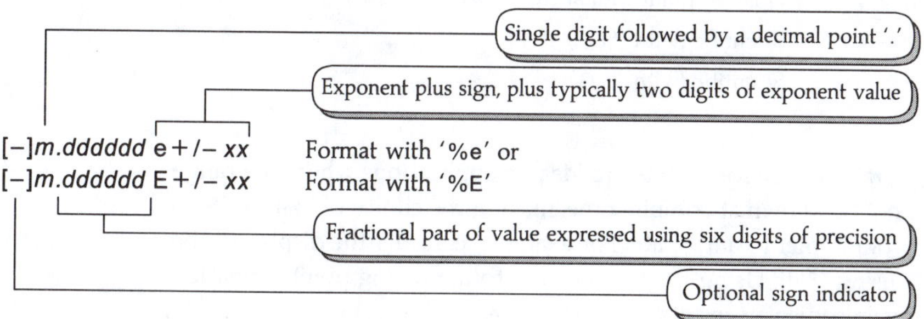

Note how the decimal point always follows the first digit, and that six digits of precision are, by default, always displayed. Following this, the letter 'e' or 'E', depending upon choice of '%e' or '%E' formatter, is used to mark the start of the exponent. This is followed by the sign of the exponent ('+' or '–') followed lastly by *typically* two digits of exponent value, but more than two may be issued if the exponent is large. Table 15.5 demonstrates the display produced by the '%e' formatter for a range of typical real values.

Table 15.5 Example printf() displays using the '%e' format indicator.

Floating point value	*Display using '%e'*	Comments
0.0	0.000000e+00	Six digits of irrelevant precision
23000.0	2.300000e+04	
2312.545343	2.312545e+03	Truncated fraction part to six digits
0.00100	1.000000e–03	Trailing zeros in display

Here, the value 1.000000e–03 is scientific notation for 1.0×10^{-3} and is thus equal to 1.0×0.001 or the value 0.001; that is, the exponent value 'e–03' indicates that the decimal point should be moved three places to the left. Likewise, the value 2.312545e+03 is scientific notation for 2.312545×10^3, which is equal to 2.312545×1000 or 2312.545, thus the exponent value 'e+03' indicates that the decimal point should be moved three places to the right.

The general purpose real format indicators: '%g' and '%G'

The general purpose format indicators '%g' and '%G' may also be used to display a real quantity, but the exact choice of display format is left to printf(). There are two basic formats, which closely resemble those of '%f' or '%e' and are summarized below. Which of these formats will be chosen by printf() depends largely upon the value being displayed.

[–]*mmm.dddddd*	Floating point format (with '%g' or '%G')
[–]*m.dddddd* e+/– *xx*	Scientific (with '%g')
[–]*m.dddddd* E+/– *xx*	Scientific (with '%G')

These general purpose formatters are ideal in applications where the range of a value might not be known at compile time, making the choice of '%f' or '%e' difficult for the programmer to anticipate. For example, consider the display of the real value $2.3e^{20}$ using '%f'. Using the format rules for a floating point formatter, the following ungainly display results:

```
23000000000000000000.000000
```

Similarly, had the programmer chosen '%e' to display a value '3.0' then the following unnecessarily complicated display would have been produced:

```
3.000000e+00
```

In both examples, if the programmer had specified '%g', printf() would have used scientific notation (similar to specifying '%e') if the value of the exponent was less than −4; that is, if the value was smaller than 0.0001 or if the integral part of the quantity was larger than six digits, for example 123 456 789.0. Otherwise, printf() would choose a floating point format similar to '%f'.

Where these formatters differ from '%f' and '%e' is that a decimal point and trailing zeros are only displayed when there is a fractional part, in which case *up to* six digits of precision may result. Table 15.6 demonstrates how several real values would be displayed using '%g'.

Table 15.6 Example printf() displays using the '%g' format indicator.

Real value	*Output using '%g'*	*Comments*
3.0	3	Zero digits of precision, no decimal point
23 000.0	23000	Floating point format, no decimal point
2 300 000.0	2.3e+06	Scientific format, one digit of precision
0.000 123 456 7	0.000123	Similar output to '%f'
0.000 012 345 67	1.23457e−05	Similar output to '%e'

15.1.3 *Displaying characters: The '%c' format indicator*

'%c' asks printf() to interpret the lower byte of an integral argument (which includes chars, shorts and ints) as a text character and display it as such. For example, the printf() statement below displays the letter 'K' (assuming an ASCII encoded system) on the operator's screen:

```
printf("%c\n", 0x4B ) ;
```

This operation/conversion is illustrated in Figure 15.1. A table of ASCII codes for each character was given previously in Chapter 2.

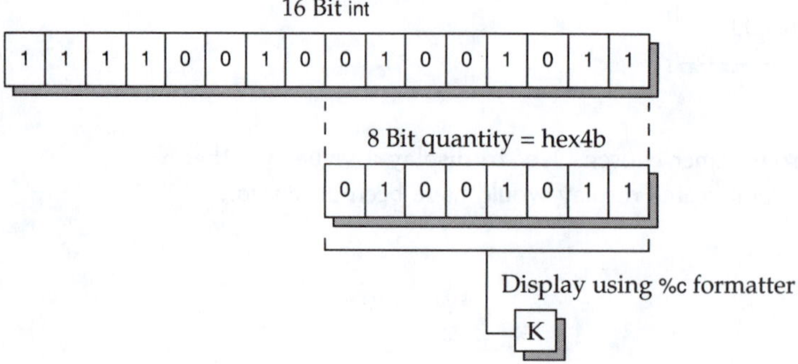

Figure 15.1 Displaying an integral quantity as a text character.

Program 15.3 uses the '%c' format indicator to display the whole (displayable) ASCII character set and its equivalent value in hex.

Program 15.3 Displaying the ASCII character set.

```
#include   <stdio.h>

int main( void )
{
  int i ;

/*   display characters '!' though to '~' */

  for( i = 0x21; i <= 0x7e; i++ )
    printf("Character %c = Hex %x \n", i, i ) ;

  return 0 ;
}
```

15.1.4 *Displaying text strings: The '%s' format indicator*

The '%s' formatter requests printf() to interpret its corresponding argument as the address of an array of characters. Each successive character in that array is then displayed as a character (equivalent to the format of the display produced by '%c') until a NULL character '\0' is encountered in the array, which may not necessarily be the last array element.

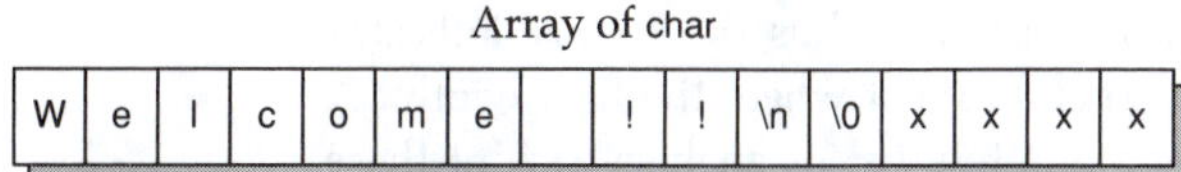

Figure 15.2 A text string represented by a char array.

For example, if the array containing the text shown in Figure 15.2 were displayed using '%s', then the message 'Welcome !!' would be displayed.

Note that as a literal text string is also represented by an array of characters terminated with a '\0' character we could display the text string "Hello World\n" in either of the two ways shown below:

```
printf("Hello World\n") ;
printf("%s\n", "Hello World" ) ;
```

15.1.5 *Recording the number of characters displayed: '%n'*

The '%n' formatter requests printf() to record/store the total number of characters displayed so far, into the integer argument whose address is given in the corresponding argument. For example, the statement:

```
printf("Saving the number of Characters Displayed\n%n", &i) ;
```

would set the value of 'i' to 42.

15.2 Advanced format control using printf()

In this section, we consider ways in which we can control text justification, field width and field precision using printf(). To enable us to do this, we shall have to consider printf()'s format indicators from a more general point of view, as shown below:

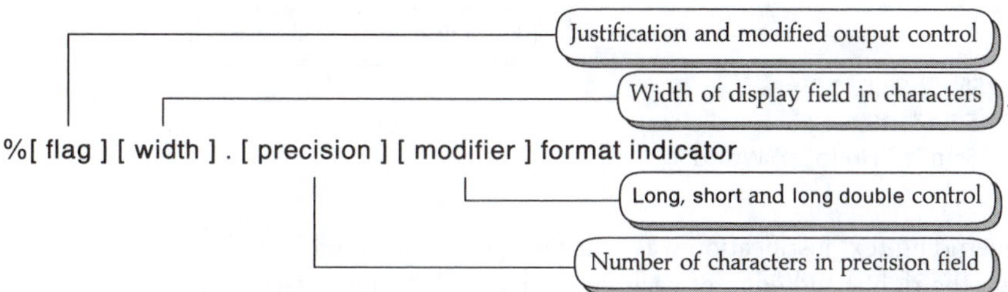

Here, the fields denoted by '[ ]' are optional, thus the format indicator '%x' is a specific example of the above general format where the flag, width, '.', precision and modifier fields have all been omitted. Let us analyse each of these fields in turn and discuss their effect, if any, on the type of format indicator used, starting with the width field.

15.2.1 *Specifying a field width*

We noted earlier that printf() would, by default, issue just sufficient characters (including any default precision) to accurately display a text or numeric value. However, by making use of printf()'s width field we can control the minimum width of a field (in terms of the number of characters) that printf() uses to display the value.

If necessary, additional space characters will be automatically inserted (or appended, depending upon text justification) to the display field to pad out the field to the specified width. This is most useful when aligning columns and tables of floating point values. For example, consider the following three printf() statements written *without* any width control:

```
printf("%f %f\n", 23.0, 1.0) ;
printf("%d %d\n", 19, -1 ) ;
printf("%s %s\n", "Hello", "World") ;
```

These produce the following ragged displays, where the fields do not align in any obvious columns.

```
23.000000 1.000000
19   -1
Hello World
```

However, if a field width of 15 is specified with each format indicator, as in the following three statements, then printf() ensures that *at least* 15 characters are issued for each field:

Width field of fifteen characters

```
printf("%15f %15f\n", 23.0, 1.0 ) ;
printf("%15d %15d\n", 19, -1 ) ;
printf("%15s %15s\n", "Hello", "World") ;
```

As no overriding text justification was specified, printf() uses right justified output to line up the right-hand edge of each field. This leads to the insertion of additional space characters at the start of each field, as shown below, which produces a much more acceptable display:

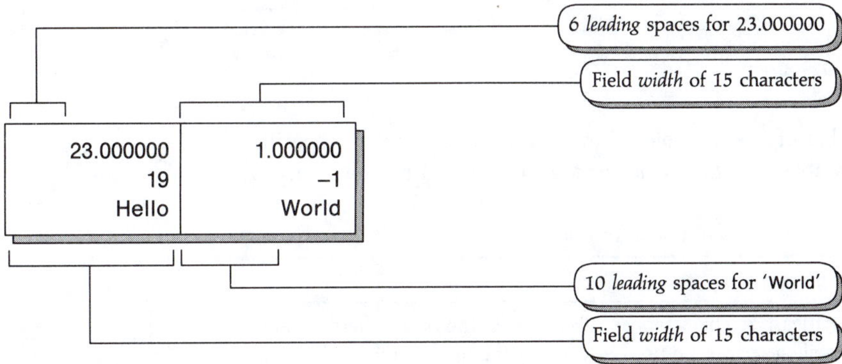

Note that leading spaces may be replaced by leading zeros if a flag field of zero '0' is specified. For example, the following statement:

'0' *flag* field: *spaces* replaced by leading *zeros*

```
printf("%012f %012f\n", 23.0, 1.0) ;
```

produces a display of the form:

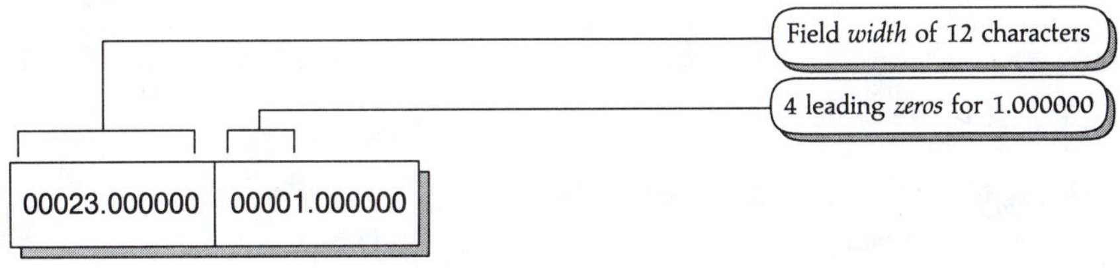

Variable field width control with printf()

If required, one of the arguments itself may be used to control the field width. This argument must be an integral value and must precede the actual argument to be displayed in the argument list. The presence of a field width argument is indicated by a '*' in the width field. For example, the following statement:

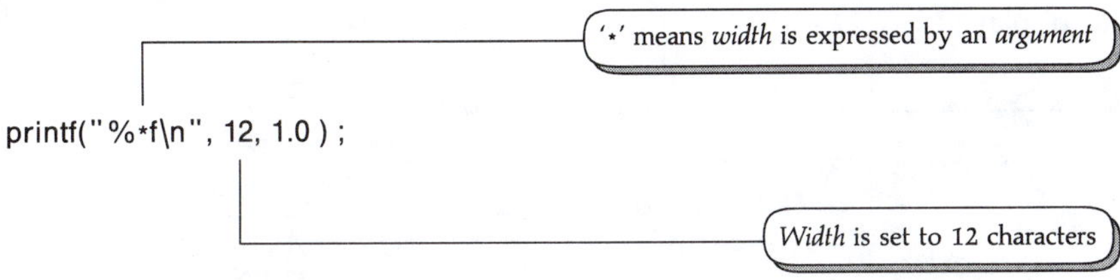

tells printf() to display the value 1.000 000 in a field of 12 characters. Likewise, the statement:

Width is specified by the value of 'x'

```
printf("%*f\n", x, y ) ;
```

displays the value of the variable 'y' in a field whose width is specified by the value of the variable 'x'. These features are summarized in Table 15.7.

Table 15.7 Specifiying a width field for printf().

Width value	*Effect on output*
n	At least 'n' characters are displayed in the output field. Leading or trailing spaces are used to pad out the field if right or left justified output is specified, respectively.
0n	As above, but if right justified text is used (the default), then leading spaces are replaced by leading zeros '0'.
* or 0*	The integer argument immediately prior to the argument to be displayed contains the width specifier. Leading spaces may be replaced with leading zeros using '0*'.

Note that a width field is always overridden if printf() is unable to accurately display the value within that field.

15.2.2 *Specifying a precision*

The precision field is separated from the (optional) width field by a period '.' and defines the precision of printf()'s display. The effect of a precision field varies with the '%' formatter used; these effects are summarized below.

The effect of a precision field on '%f', '%e' ('%E') and '%g' ('%G')

The precision field may be used in conjunction with the real formatters '%f' and '%e' (and '%E') to restrict the number of digits that will be displayed after a decimal point. For example, the display of the mathematical constants 'PI' and 'e' could be restricted to two decimal places with the following statement. Note that printf() may well round up the result to the nearest decimal place, for example 2.718 28 might be displayed as 2.72 using '%f' or 2.72e+00 using '%e'.

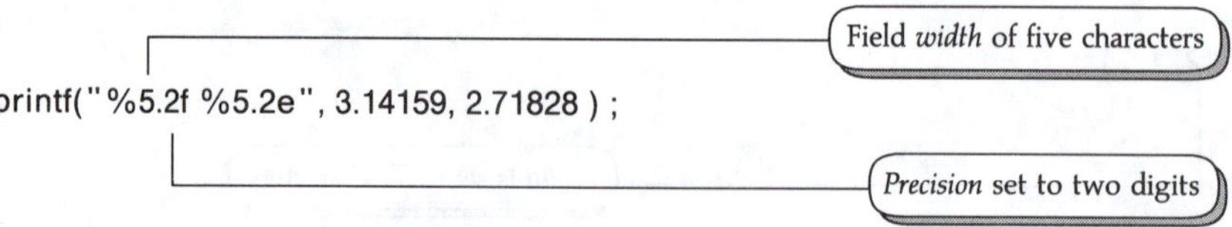
Field *width* of five characters
printf("%5.2f %5.2e", 3.14159, 2.71828) ;
Precision set to two digits

However, when a precision field is specified for '%g' (or '%G'), then it defines the total number of digits to be displayed. Thus the following statement:

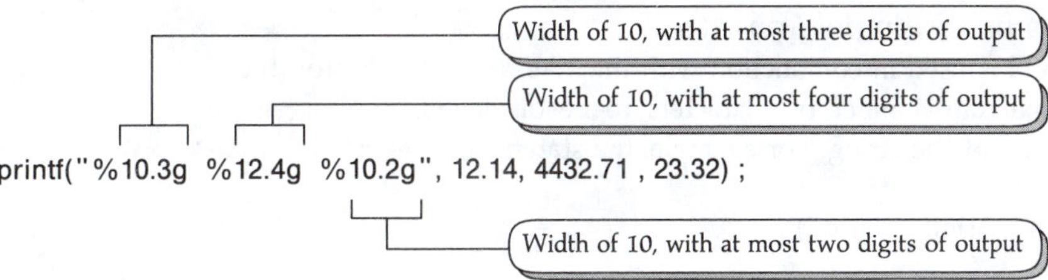

might produce the following display:

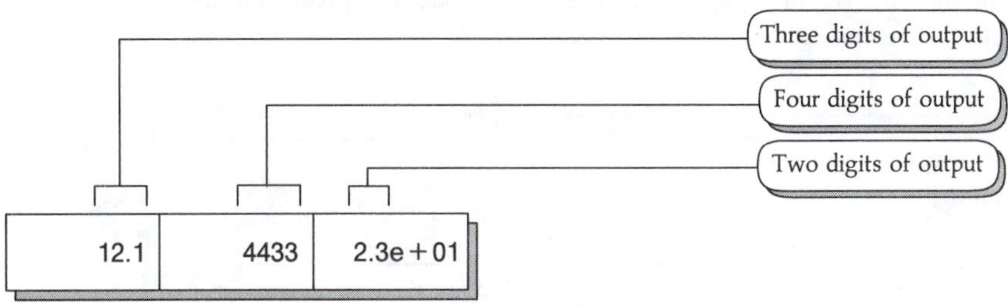

The effect of a precision field on '%d', '%u', '%i', '%x', '%X' and '%o'

A precision field may be used in conjunction with an integer formatter to specify the *minimum* number of digits to be displayed. For example, the statement:

```
printf("%10.5d\n", 1) ;
```

would display the integer value '1' in a field of 10 characters with at least 5 digits of output being displayed. Therefore, printf() displays the output in the following manner, where five leading spaces, followed by four leading zeros and finally the digit 1 are displayed.

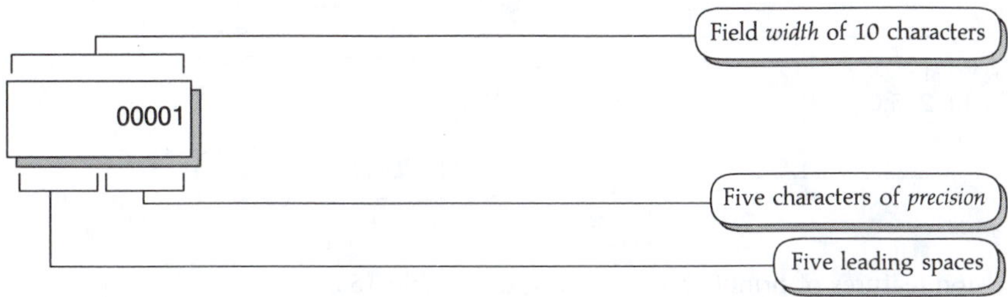

Note that if the value of an integer is zero and '%d' is specified with a precision of zero, printf() will not display any value.

The effect of a precision field on '%s'

If a precision field is used in conjunction with the '%s' format indicator, then it restricts the maximum number of characters to be displayed, resulting in the possible truncation of the string. For example, the statement:

```
printf("%20.5s\n", "Hello World") ;
```

would display the string in a field 20 characters wide, but truncate the string to just 5 characters. This is of most use when the function sprintf() is being used to write its output to an array and serves as a useful guard against a long string output exceeding the size of the array. Thus, the above example produces the following output:

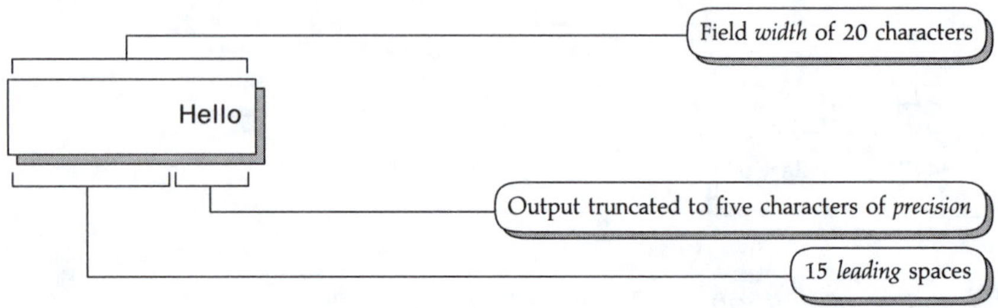

The effect of a precision field on '%c' and '%p'

A precision field has no effect on the '%c' and '%p' format indicators.

Variable precision control with printf()

Finally, just as we were able to specify a variable width field, using an additional argument, and an '*' in the format indicator, we may also specify a variable precision field in the same way. The following statement uses both variable width and precision fields to display the floating point value '5.0' in a field of 10 characters with a precision of 2 digits after the decimal place:

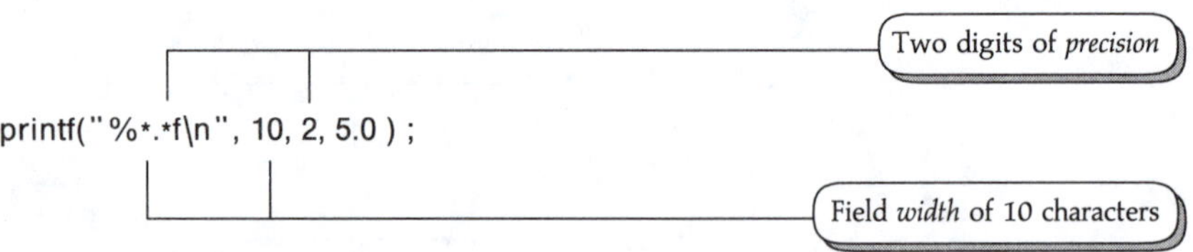

The precision features of printf() are summarized in Table 15.8.

Table 15.8 The precision field for printf().

Precision value	Effect on output
Absent	printf() uses the following default number of precision digits: One for '%d', '%i', '%o', '%u', '%x' and '%X' Six for '%e', '%E' and '%f' format indicators All digits for '%g' and '%G' format indicators No effect on '%s', '%p' or '%c' format indicators
0	Zero digits of precision; that is, truncate to an integer value when used in conjunction with either '%f', '%e' or '%E' format indicators. Assumed to mean 1 when used with '%g' or '%G'.
n	At least 'n' characters are printed for the output field. If this conflicts with the width field, then the width field is overridden.
*	The printf() integer argument immediately prior to the variable being displayed contains the precision specifier.

15.2.3 *Format flags:* printf()

The permitted format flags are all single characters that precede the width field (if present), and several may be combined to achieve the required effect. Each flag is described in Table 15.9.

Table 15.9 Format flags: printf().

Flag	Operation
–	Output is left justified. Spaces may be appended to the display to pad out the field to the required width (if a width field is specified).
+	The sign of a decimal result is always displayed. Normally, printf() would only display the sign of a negative value.
<space>	If the result is positive, printf() inserts a space prior to the result. If the result is negative, a minus '–' sign is displayed instead. Note that '+' overrides <space> if both are given. This feature is useful when aligning digits in columns, since a minus sign would offset the output if a field width was not specified.
#	This character is used to modify the way in which the default formatters display their output.

Note that the flags '+' and '<space>' are only relevant when displaying decimal values and generally have no effect when used, for example, with '%c', '%s', '%o', '%x' and '%p'. Let us take a look at each of the format flags in turn and observe their effect on the display produced by printf().

Left justified display: The '–' flag

Left justification of printf()'s display may be controlled (in conjunction with a width field) by specifying the '–' flag. printf() will then append space characters to the output to fill the display to the specified field width. For example, the following three statements:

Left justified output in a field of 15 characters

```
printf("%-15f %-15f\n", 23.0, 1.0 ) ;
printf("%-15d %-15d\n", 19, -1 ) ;
printf("%-15s %-15s\n", "Hello", "World") ;
```

produce the following left justified display:

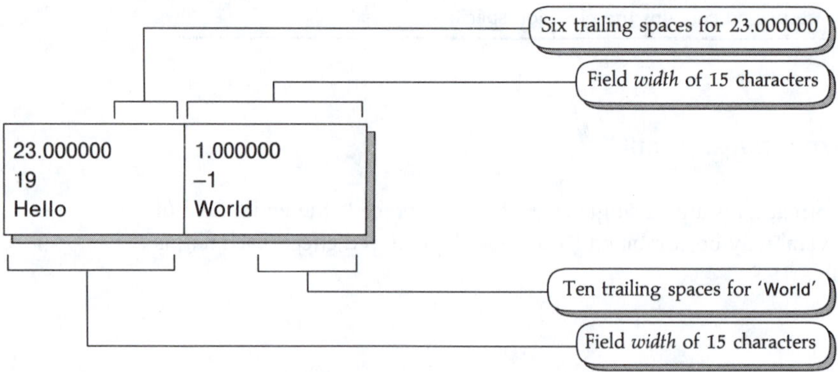

Sign control: The '+' flag

By default, printf() will not display a plus '+' sign for positive quantities. This may be overridden if a '+' flag is specified. For example, the statement:

Always display *sign* of quantity

```
printf("%+f\n", 3.1415927) ;
```

would force printf() to display the value 3.141 5927 as:

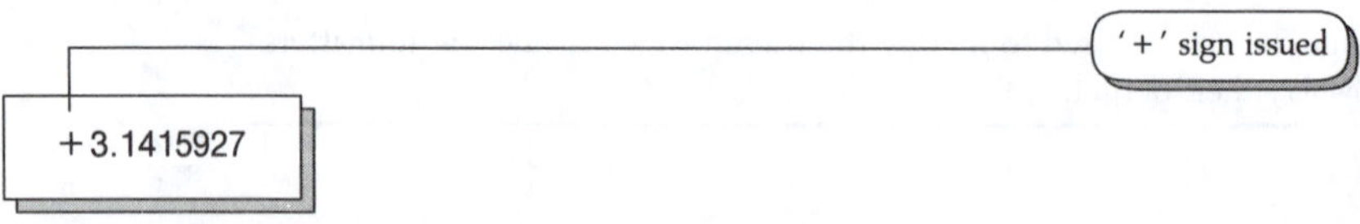

Leading space control: The <space> flag

If a <space> flag is specified, printf() will issue a leading space character prior to the display of a positive quantity. This may be found useful when aligning columns of positive and negative quantities using left justification, where a negative value would be offset by the '–' sign. For example, the following statements:

'*Space*' flag inserts a space for positive quantities in display

```
printf("%- f\n", 23.0 ) ;
printf("%- f\n", -1024.0 ) ;
printf("%- f\n", 3.1415927 ) ;
```

produce the following display:

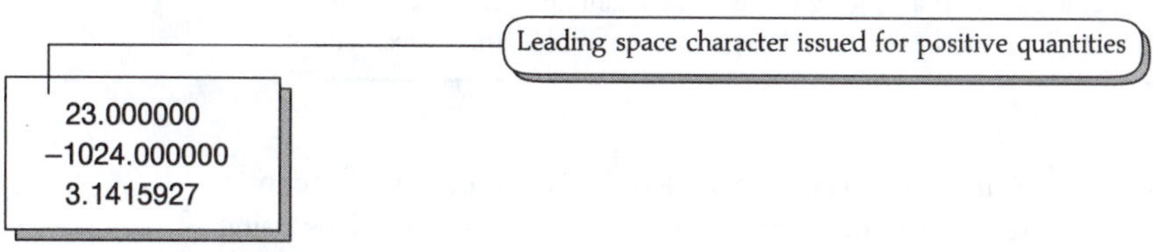
Leading space character issued for positive quantities
 23.000000
-1024.000000
 3.1415927

Note that the '+' flag overides the <space> flag if both are specified.

The display modifier flag: '#'

When the modifier flag '#' is specified, printf()'s display is altered in a number of subtle but useful ways. These effects are summarized in Table 15.10.

Table 15.10 Display modifier flag: '#'.

Format indicator	*How '#' affects display*
%d, %i, %u, %s, %c, %p	No effect
%o	Adds a leading '0' (zero) to the output to indicate that the result is an octal quantity, for example, 0177
%x, %X	Adds a leading '0x' (or '0X') to the output to indicate that the result is a hex quantity, for example, 0xffca
%e, %E or %f	Forces a decimal point '.' to be displayed in the output, even if no digits follow it. This may be useful if the precision is 0, which would produce no digits after the decimal point
%g, %G	As above but trailing zeros may be added to the fractional part so that the output fills the field width (if specified)

15.2.4 *Displaying* long *and* short *data: The type modifier field*

Table 15.11 summarizes the various type modifiers recognized by printf() for displaying long int, short int and long double values. The modifier character should be placed immediately prior to the format character, for example %10.2Lf or %10.2ld, to display a long double or long int respectively.

Table 15.11 Type modifier fields for printf().

Modifier	*Effect on argument*
l	Argument is treated as a long integer, for example %ld, %lx
L	Argument is treated as a long double, for example %Lf, %Lg, %Le
h	Argument is treated as a short integer, for example %hd, %hx, %hu

Note that the 'h' modifier has been added for symmetry with scanf(), which we shall meet later, and is not required to display short int values using printf() since these values are automatically promoted to a full int when passed to printf() (see Chapter 6).

15.2.5 *Error detection and returned data:* printf()

printf() returns the integer number of characters displayed, should this be of any use to the programmer. If an error is detected while writing to the output device (remember that program output may have been redirected to a disk file or other such device) then printf() returns the value of the symbolic constant EOF (usually the value −1) which is defined in <stdio.h>.

Other functions related to printf()

The functions sprintf(), fprintf(), vprintf(), vsprintf() and vfprintf() are related to printf().

15.3 Formatted input of data: The function scanf()

The function scanf() performs the converse operation to that of printf(), converting formatted text input into values that are subsequently stored directly to variables. The operation of scanf() closely resembles that of printf() and is based around the similar concept of a format string containing a number of '%' format indicators. The general form of a call to scanf() is given below. Note the important use of the '&' address operator for each additional argument:

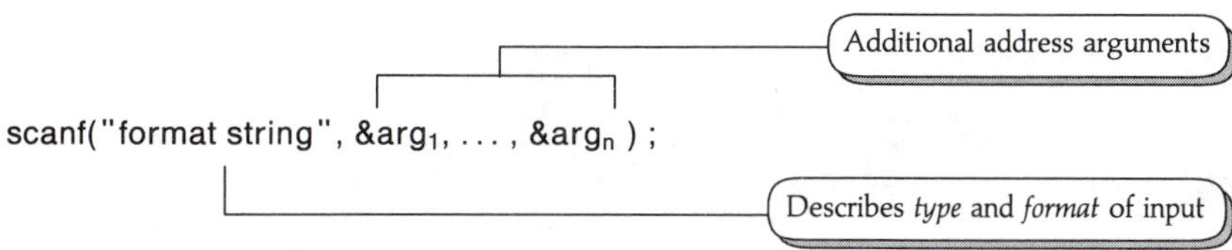
Additional address arguments
scanf("format string", &arg1, . . . , &argn) ;
Describes type and format of input

As you can see, scanf( ) expects all of its arguments to be addresses. These are the addresses of the variables into which scanf( ) will store the converted input for the program. Failure to supply scanf( ) with these addresses (which were not required with printf( )) is probably the single most common mistake the programmer is likely to make.

Each '%' formatter within the format string argument corresponds to one of the additional arguments. These implicitly tell scanf( ) the type of data to expect, and the way it is to be converted and stored. The use of multiple '%' formatters allows several items of data to be read, converted and stored with a single call to scanf( ).

As a simple example, we could read a decimal integer from the operator's keyboard and store it in the variable 'a', with the following call to scanf( ). Notice how '%d' was specified in the format string, indicating decimal integer format. The variable 'a' must of course be an integer, otherwise the operation is undefined and could lead to program crashes:

Address of *integer* 'a' matched with '%d'

```
scanf("%d", &a) ;
```

15.3.1 *Format indicators recognized by* scanf( )

Table 15.12 contains a full list of format indicators recognized by scanf( ). You will see that for the most part, they are similar to those recognized by printf( ) but with some important differences.

Notice how quite separate formatters are required by scanf( ) to differentiate between short ints and ints and also between floats and doubles. This is because scanf( ) stores a converted value directly *into* a variable, and must therefore be told how big that variable is so that it can cast it to the appropriate size prior to storage. It is *not* sufficient to simply state that the quantity is integral or real and expect scanf( ) to know the actual size of the variable from the address it has been given.

Study Table 15.12 again closely and compare scanf( )'s format indicators with those of printf( )'s in Table 15.1 and spot the differences.

Table 15.12 Format indicators recognized by scanf().

Format indicator	*Interpretation*
%d, %u, %x (%X), %o, %i	Read an int in the following formats: decimal, unsigned decimal, hexadecimal, octal and any recognized integer format, respectively
%ld, %lu, %lx (%lX), %lo, %li	Read a long int in the same formats as above
%hd, %hu, %hx (%hX), %ho, %hi	Read a short int in the same formats as above
%g (%G), %f, %e (%E)	Read a float in any recognized real format
%lg (%lG), %lf, %le (%lE)	Read a double in any recognized real format
%Lg (%LG), %Lf, %Le (%LE)	Read a long double in any recognized real format
%c	Read a single text character
%s	Read a string terminated by white space
%[char set]	Read a string composed of characters matching 'char set'
%[^ char set]	Read a string composed of characters *not* matching 'char set'
%*(format)	Ignore next entry matching (format), for example %*s
%p	Read an address/pointer value in system dependent format
%n	Record the number of characters read so far into the integer whose address is given as the corresponding argument
%%	Read a single '%' character

15.3.2 *Reading multiple items with* scanf()

scanf() is able to read and convert several items of data in much the same way that printf() is able to display several items, through the use of multiple '%' formatters in the format string. For example, we could read an integer followed by a floating point value using a single call to scanf() as shown in Program 15.4. Notice how a check was carried out to ensure that scanf() had performed the two conversions successfully.

Here, scanf() attempts to read and convert an integer value followed by a floating point value and store the result of the conversion directly into the variables 'a' and 'b'. The success or otherwise of the conversion depends entirely upon the operator, who must take care to ensure that:

(1) The response entered is recognizable and compatible with what scanf() has been told to expect.

(2) The integer and floating point entries supplied can be distinguished from each other, usually by separating each entry by a space or tab or by entering them on separate lines.

Program 15.4 Reading multiple items with scanf().

```
#include  <stdio.h>

int main( void )
{
   int    a ;
   float  b ;

   printf("Enter an integer value and then a floating point value: ") ;

   if( scanf("%d %f", &a, &b ) == 2)
      printf("a = %d, b = %f\n", a, b ) ;
   else
      printf("Error on input ... \n") ;
   return 0 ;
}
```

Check for two successful conversions

Try Program 15.4 and in response to the prompt, supply two items of data separated by a space character (make sure that they are integer and floating point values, respectively). What happens if only one value is entered or if no identifiable separator is used to distinguish one field from another? You should find that scanf() will wait until it thinks a second value has been entered.

You might also have noticed a very *unfriendly* act from scanf() if the type of response supplied by the operator does not match that which scanf() had been led to expect. For example, run Program 15.4 again, and this time enter your name in place of the integer value.

Because scanf() is expecting a numeric response, it will not be expecting alphabetic characters and will immediately abort if the operator's entry contains such characters. Thus, if the operator supplied the following response while executing Program 15.4:

```
Paul 123.0
```

scanf() would fail leaving both the text string "Paul" and the floating point value 123.0 unconverted. scanf() will not even attempt to search the remainder of the operator's entry for something that might resemble the response it is expecting.

This is important, since it places some of the burden of responsibility onto the operator to ensure that data is supplied in the correct format. However, by considering the value returned by scanf() – that is, the number of successful conversions – the program should be able detect this and do something about it by calling fflush(stdin) to flush the standard input streams buffer to remove the offending text and all other entered data.

15.3.3 *Reading a text string with* scanf()*: '%s'*

Text strings may be read using the '%s' format indicator. You will recall that the name of an array is simply a shorthand notation for the address of the first element, and thus the '&' operator is not required when passing the array as an argument to scanf(). Program 15.5 demonstrates how to read a text string using scanf().

Program 15.5 Reading a text string with scanf().

```
#include  <stdio.h>

int main( void )
{
   int    age ;
   char  name[ BUFSIZ ] ;

   printf("Enter your name: ") ;
   scanf("%s", name) ;
                                        No '&' operator required for an array
   printf("Enter your age: ") ;
   scanf("%d", &age) ;

   printf("Your Name is %s and you are %d years old", name, age ) ;

   return 0 ;
}
```

15.3.4 *White space in the operator's response: Field separation*

scanf() generally ignores white space characters when they precede an operator's entry, but does, however, use them as a field separator when reading multiple data. Therefore, if Program 15.5 were run, and an attempt were made to enter your full name, which might well include a space character, as shown below:

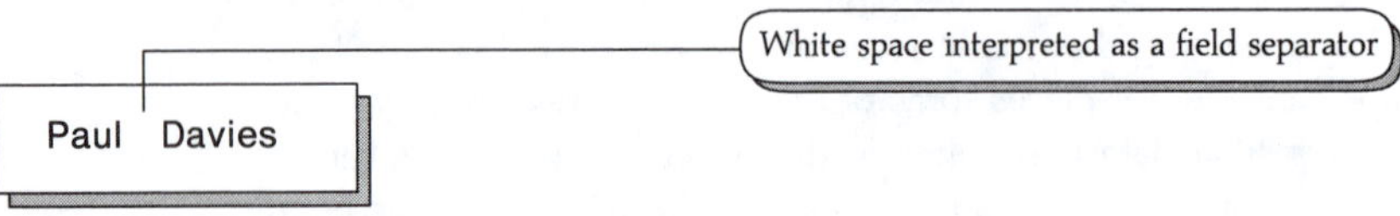
White space interpreted as a field separator
Paul Davies

scanf() would, unfortunately, interpret the space in the response as a field separator and would only extract the name 'Paul' from the operator's response.

The unconverted text, 'Davies', however, is not lost or discarded, but sits in the operating system's stream buffer, waiting to be read next time.

Unfortunately, when scanf( ) subsequently attempts to read the operator's 'age', as a decimal integer, it now reads the remaining text 'Davies', which leads to scanf( ) aborting (leaving the unconverted text still in the stream buffer). A call to fflush(stdin) may be used to remove any remaining text in the buffer.

15.3.5 *The effect of literal text in the format string:* scanf( )

If any literal text is specified in the format string, the operator will be expected to enter such text in exactly the same format character by character as it is described within the format string, otherwise scanf( ) will abort the conversion. If the operator's response matches that in the format string, such text is discarded and no attempt is made to convert it. As an example, suppose we wished to write a program to read data that we know will be entered in exactly the following format:

```
Radius = 3.0, Circumference = 18.849556, Area = 28.27433
```

scanf( ) could be called to extract the three floating point values from this string in the following way:

```
scanf("Radius = %lf, Circumference = %lf, Area = %lf", &radius,
                                                        &circum, &area) ;
```

It is unlikely that many operator driven programs would rely on this feature of scanf( ), since an operator's response is highly unpredictable, but as we mentioned before, a program may have had its input redirected from a device other than the keyboard, perhaps a disk file for example, which may contain text in a predictable format, and this feature of scanf( ) is particularly useful in those circumstances.

Note that white space characters in the format string (or in the operator's response), such as tabs, spaces and so on, are not expected to be matched. For example, the statement:

White space characters are *not* matched against operator's entry

```
scanf("%d   %d", &a, &b) ;
```

contains several spaces, which may or may not be supplied by the operator in his or her response.

15.3.6 *Ignoring a field entry: The '%*' format indicator*

scanf( ) may be requested to ignore a particular type of entry by placing a '*' in the format indicator. For example, given that a program's input has been redirected from a disk file which contains data in the following known format:

```
Radius 3.0 Circumference 18.849556 Area 28.27433
```

scanf( ) could be asked to extract the three floating point values in the following way, which relies on the space character in the read text acting as a field separator:

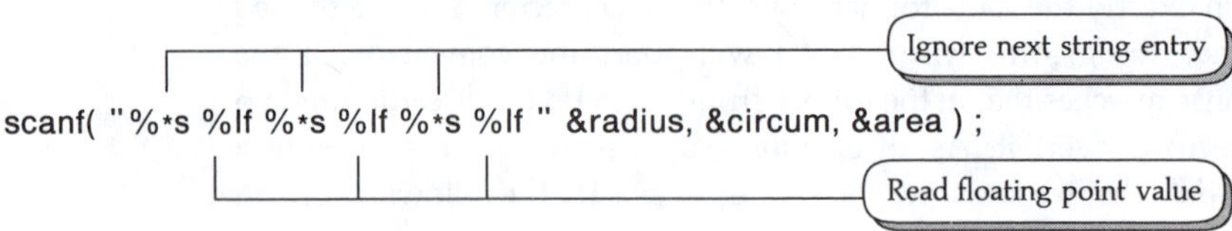

15.3.7 *Matching characters in a string entry: '%[char set]'*

The '%s' format indicator may be replaced by '%[char set]', in which case scanf( ) is forced to accept a text string containing only those characters that are a subset of 'char set'. For example, the statement:

Match response against these characters

```
scanf("%[abcdefghijklmnopqrstuvwxyz]", name) ;
```

requires scanf( ) to read a string containing only lower case letters. If a string is entered containing, for example, the digit '0', scanf( ) will abort, accepting only those legitimate characters that had been supplied up to that point. If the operator had replied at this point with the string:

```
hello world
```

then scanf( ) would accept only the string 'hello', since the space character was not included in the matching set. By including a space in 'char set', scanf( ) could be used to read a whole line of text and not treat the space as a field separator.

Note that character subsets can also be specified and that a character may appear more than once in 'char set'. For example, if scanf( ) were required to read a text string containing only letters (both upper and lower case) and digits, scanf( ) could be called in the following manner:

Character subsets

```
scanf("%[a-zA-Z0-9]", name) ;
```

If the hyphen '-' is also to be a matching character, then it may be included in char set as the first or last character, or used to separate character subsets not in ascending order, for example:

Hyphen here means match '-' in response

```
%[Z-A-]
```

a '\"' and '\\' may be used to represent the characters '"' and '\' in 'char set'.

15.3.8 *Excluding characters from a string entry:* '%[^char set]'

If the first character in 'char set' is '^' then scanf() rejects characters from the operator's entry that match 'char set'; thus the statement:

```
scanf("%[^a-z]", name) ;
```

forces scanf() to reject all lower case characters from the operator's response. Interestingly enough, acceptance of a string containing any character may be specified using the character set:

```
"%[^\n]"
```

which only rejects the new line character '\n', which was never matched anyway.

15.3.9 *Controlling input field width:* scanf()

scanf() also recognizes a field width specifier in the format string (but no precision specifier). For example, the following statement forces scanf() to read a four digit integer, followed by a six digit floating point number:

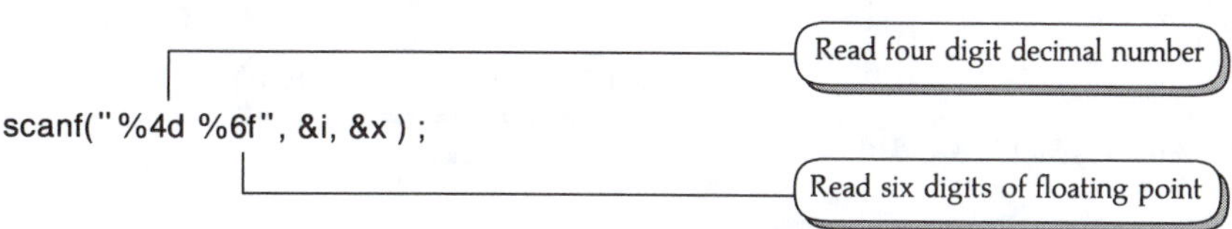

Care must be taken by the operator to ensure that each field entered contains the correct number of characters. For example, if the operator supplied the following data in response to the above scanf() statement:

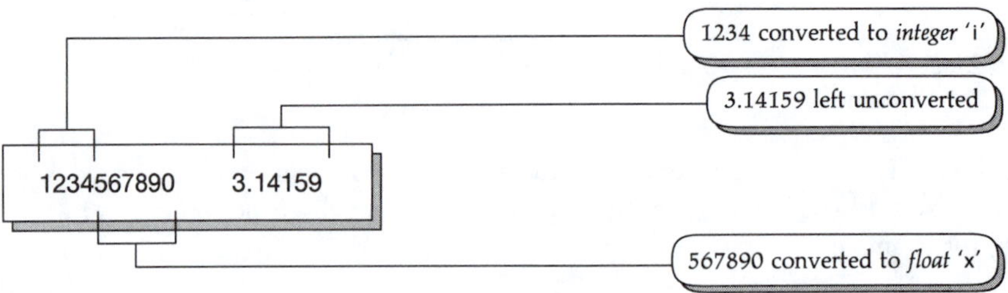
1234 converted to integer 'i'
3.14159 left unconverted
1234567890 3.14159
567890 converted to float 'x'

then scanf() would take the first four characters (the digits '1234'), convert and store the result in the variable 'i', leaving the remaining six digits from the first field (567890) to be converted and stored into the variable 'x'. The second field (3.14159) is left untouched by scanf() and will be read next time scanf() is called, possibly causing problems further down the line.

Again, these features of scanf() are more likely to be used when a program's input has been redirected from a disk file, whose format is known in advance.

15.3.10 *Why use* scanf() *at all?*

Unfortunately, the use of scanf() resembles in most cases a 'sledge hammer to crack a nut' approach to data input. There are so many possibilities for something to go wrong when reading data from the operator's keyboard that you may instead be tempted to use some of the simpler more predictable functions such as gets(), getchar(), atof() and so on. However, do not be put off, as the function scanf() closely resembles the function fscanf(), which is frequently used to read formatted data from disk files, and is covered in the next chapter.

scanf() is also useful if you know at compile time that your program's input will be redirected to come from a disk file whose contents and format may well be known.

Detecting errors and returned data: scanf()

scanf() returns the integer number of successful conversions, which *should* match the number of valid conversion formatters in the format string if the conversions have been performed successfully. For example, the following statement:

Two conversion formatters

```
i = scanf( "%*s %d %*s %d", &a, &b) ;
```

should assign the value 2 to 'i' if *both* integers had been *correctly* converted, or the value 1 if 'a' but *not* 'b' had been converted, or the value 0 if *neither* 'a' nor 'b' had been converted. The value of the symbolic constant EOF is returned if an end-of-input/file status is detected for the input device, before any successful conversions.

Other functions related to scanf( )

The functions sscanf( ), fscanf( ), vfscanf( ), vscanf( ) and vsscanf( ) are related to scanf( ).

15.4 Chapter summary

(1) printf( ) and scanf( ) cater for the mixed display and entry of data in a variety of different formats. A number of '%' formatters in conjunction with a format string control the type and format of the data.

(2) scanf( ) stores its converted data directly into a variable, rather than returning it back to the program. This means that scanf( ) is able to convert and store several items of data with a single call. It also means that scanf( ) requires the addresses of the variables into which it will store the converted data. scanf( ) returns the number of successful conversions performed, or EOF if end-of-file is detected.

(3) Failure to use the correct '%' formatter with printf( ) or scanf( ) is the most common cause of error when using either of these functions, because the compiler is unable to perform any checking.

(4) There are a number of subtle differences between the '%' formatters recognized by printf( ) and scanf( ), reflecting the fact that scanf( ) needs to know the exact size of the data that it must store.

(5) Because scanf( ) is easily confused by unpredicted input, its use should primarily be restricted to applications where input is likely to be redirected from a device such as a file, where the data is known to exist in a predefined format. The use of scanf( ) to read an operator's entry from the keyboard is fraught with problems.

15.5 Exercises

15.1 What is the default format of the display produced by printf( ) using the format indicators '%d', '%f', '%e' and '%g'? Why is it common to use '%g' in most programs in preference to '%f' or '%e'? Given the following calls to printf( ), what is displayed?

```
printf("%f %e\n", 2.0, 2.0 ) ;
printf("%f %e %g\n", 123.0000001, 123.0000001, 123.0000001 ) ;
printf("%d %x %o %c\n", 66, 66, 66, 66 ) ;
printf("%d %u\n", -3, -1, 23 ) ;
printf("%d %u %d\n", 34000, 34000 ) ;
```

15.2 What is meant by text justification and what default justification does printf() use? What other text justification does printf() support and how is it controlled?

15.3 What is meant by field width control in relation to printf()'s display? How is it specified? What happens if printf()'s output does not fit within a specified width? What do the following calls to printf() display?

```
printf("%12d %012d %12f %012f\n", 5, 5, 23.0, 23.0 ) ;
printf("%*d\n", atoi(gets(buff)), x) ;
```

15.4 How, using the '%f' or '%e' format indicators, is it possible for columns of floating point data to be displayed such that the decimal points are all aligned? Give two good reasons why this is difficult to achieve if the '%g' format indicator is used.

15.5 What effect does specifying a 'precision field' for the format indicators '%d', '%f', '%e', '%g' and '%s' have on printf()'s display?

15.6 What modified format indicator would be required to display tables of floating point values using left justified text, so that the decimal points align?

15.7 What does the following call to printf() display?

```
printf("%x %#x %o %#o %d %#d\n", 110, 110, 110, 110, 110, 110) ;
```

15.8 Using a loop in conjunction with a call to printf(), write a program to display the following data in exactly the format shown, where F = 1.8C + 32.0.

```
Celsius    Fahrenheit
+10.0        +50.00
 +5.0        +41.00
 +0.0        +32.00
 -5.0        +23.00
-10.0        +14.00
-15.0         +5.00
-20.0         -4.00
-25.0        -13.00
```

Using the output redirection operator '>' on the operating shell command line, redirect the output of the program to a disk file.

15.9 Why is it that scanf() requires separate format indicators to differentiate between floats and doubles, and between integers and short integers, while printf() does not?

15.10 The following call to scanf() attempts to read in an integer followed by a floating point value:

```
scanf("%d %f", &i, &f) ;
```

If this statement is executed, what happens to the values of 'i' and 'f'? What values are returned by scanf() if an operator replies with the following responses?

(a) An end-of-file (EOF) condition is immediately generated by pressing <Control-Z> (on an MS-DOS system) or <Control-D> (on a UNIX system).

(b) The values 23, <carriage return>, 34 <carriage return> are entered.

(c) The values 23, <carriage return>, 34 EOF are entered.

(d) The values 23, <space>, 34 <carriage return> are entered.

(e) The values <space> 23, <carriage return>, <carriage return>, 34 <carriage return> are entered.

(f) The value 2 followed by EOF.

(g) The value 2 followed by the text 'f = 34.0'.

15.11 Which of the following responses are acceptable to scanf() when it is asked to read a numeric point value using the '%f', '%e', '%g', '%d', '%x', '%o' and '%s' format indicators:

+1, –1, 1.2, +1.2e–3, –1.2e+0004, 0x34, .24, 24.2 Degrees.

15.12 If scanf() rejects an entry because it considers it to be incompatible with what it has been led to expect, what happens to that entry? Why is this a possible problem for the program later? How can it be overcome?

15.13 Making use of the input redirection operator ' < ', write a program to read and extract the Fahrenheit data saved on a disk file by Exercise 15.8 and recalculate and display the Celsius temperature.

15.14 What happens if literal text is included in the format string to scanf()? Making use of this knowledge, write a program to call scanf() as part of a loop to convert successive operator entries of the form shown below, such that the values for Celsius and Fahrenheit temperatures are extracted and stored in two floating point variables:

Celsius = 5.0, Fahrenheit = 41.00 Degrees

15.15 Write a program to ignore any operator's response that does not begin with a punctuation character. Write the program using only calls to scanf().

15.16 Write a program to accept a text string consisting entirely of lower case characters.

16 Stream and File Manipulation

Most of the examples so far have dealt principally with reading and displaying data from/to the user's terminal. However, with the improved performance of modern day personal computers, many programmers find themselves under increasing pressure to develop applications that are able to link to and access information from many diverse areas. A clear example of this can be seen in the trend towards offering network support and access to CD-ROMs, as shown in Figure 16.1.

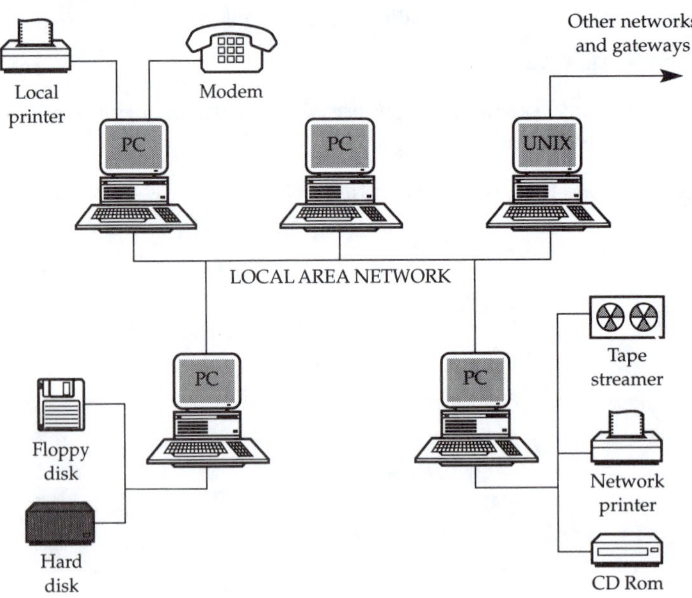

Figure 16.1 Some clip art images of networked computers/printers/CD-ROMs/disks.

To provide the programmer with the right support for developing such applications, most operating systems and compilers have developed flexible tools and program interfaces to promote the development of programs that are able to communicate with these widely differing devices in a **consistent** and **portable** manner.

One of the first operating systems to address this was UNIX, which laid the foundations for many of today's operating systems. The concepts used by UNIX are as relevant now as they were when originally conceived, and are reflected in many modern offerings, such as MS-DOS, which provide a similar, if somewhat less sophisticated, operating system environment.

One of the more influential features of UNIX was its adoption of a unified I/O structure, whereby all devices appeared to look and behave in the same way, from a programming point of view. This powerful feature enabled applications to be developed that were more or less independent of the physical characteristics of the device with which they were communicating.

This was an important issue for programmers, since it enabled them to develop their applications to be independent of the actual device with which the program itself communicated; in other words, the same input/output operations used to drive a terminal could also be used to drive any type of device, from a disk drive to a network or printer.

Such an approach was based around the concept of a **device driver**, consisting of a collection of primitive I/O routines, probably written by the device's manufacturer, that when integrated into the operating system provided a generic device independent interface between the operating system kernel and the physical device itself.

Routines within the device driver were invoked by the operating system in response to requests made by a program to communicate with the device, and would subsequently be responsible for transferring the actual data to and from the device in a manner completely transparent to both program and operating system. Thus the same application program that had previously written its output to a terminal could, with very minor modifications, involving perhaps only the name of the device, write its output to a disk, even though the two devices shared few common characteristics.

A useful by-product of this approach was that it enabled the program's operator to select the name of the device with which the program wished to communicate at *run time*, rather than have the program assume the device and have its name nested within the program's code.

Furthermore, even if the program did assume a specific output device such as the operator's terminal, by making use of the functions `printf()` and `scanf()`, this could be overridden at run time (as we saw in Chapter 1) using the input/output redirection operators such as '<' and '>', which is a concept mostly taken for granted these days when copying or listing files to a printer or VDU.

Where operating systems such as MS-DOS differ slightly from UNIX is that UNIX treats all devices in the system as if they were disk files; in fact, it is possible to perform a directory and see all of the devices known to the system.

MS-DOS and other operating systems have chosen a somewhat simpler, less generic approach.

The programmer should mostly be unaware of these differences and the two operating systems should still provide a consistent platform for most programs to access any device. With MS-DOS, devices such as the printer port and VDU may be accessed using the device names 'prn' and 'con', respectively. Thus the output from a program running under MS-DOS could be redirected to the printer with a command of the form:

```
c: prog_name >prn
```

This chapter deals with the development of C programs that need to communicate with external devices. It describes briefly the way in which a peripheral is interfaced to the operating system via its device driver and the effect this has on the operation of the device. No excuses are made for including this discussion, even though it is unrelated to the C language itself, since the author feels it offers a more complete treatment of the subject while at the same time providing valuable insight into the nature and characteristics of certain classes of device, which may occasionally need to be considered by the programmer.

A discussion of the C language **stream** interface and the stream manipulation functions in the standard library that facilitate the exchange of data between program and operating system is also provided, but before discussing either of these, let us introduce and talk briefly about the subject of streams and the role of the device driver.

16.1 Stream buffer and device interfaces

Program communication with a device is generally supported at one of two levels in C. The first, often referred to as **high level** or **buffered** I/O, makes use of stream manipulation functions from the standard library. The term 'buffered' relates to the operating system's use of **stream buffers** to queue incoming and outgoing data exchanged between program and device.

The second approach, often referred to as **low level** or **unbuffered** I/O, relies on functions that for the most part are integral parts of the operating system. These include library functions such as `open()`, `create()`, `read()` and `write()`, which are generally quite small and serve mostly to provide the required software **hooks** or links to the primitive I/O routines provided by the operating system and associated device driver.

As these low level functions are not standardized in C, and are likely to vary from one system to another, and because they offer very few facilities that cannot be achieved with high level functions they are not discussed any further in this book. The reader is referred to their C compiler library reference manual for details of these functions.

16.1.1 *Devices and device drivers*

To help promote and sell their hardware, manufacturers often provide a device driver for a particular operating system, consisting of a set of low level routines that provide basic primitive communications with a device. The driver often includes functions such as:

- Initialize and deinitialize the device;
- Read and write data characters/blocks from/to the device;
- Get and set the device status.

It is at the device driver level that the interface to specific hardware and the characteristics of the device are considered. The operating system, upon receiving a request from a program to use a device, might invoke the device's initialize routine, supplying it with parameters that might affect the operation of the device. For example, if the device were a serial communication port connected to a VDU, the parameter information might include information about baud rate, parity, number of bits per character and so on.

Read requests made by a program would be intercepted by the operating system, which in turn would direct the request to the read routine within the driver to accomplish whatever operations were required to read data from the device itself. For example, a request by a program to read 'N' bytes of data from a disk file might be translated by the device driver into a physical track and sector number on the disk, which would be located and read.

A device driver would frequently employ its own internal data buffering in order to queue data for or read from the device. Such buffers are often maintained independently of the operating system stream buffers. For example, a disk device driver might allocate its own internal buffer that reflects the size of a sector on the disk, perhaps 512 bytes, while a printer driver might simply allocate a buffer that can queue data on a line by line or even just a character by character basis.

One of the most important operations performed by the device driver is error detection and its possible correction within the associated device. Errors can occur for a number of reasons, such as reading bad disk sectors or writing to a full disk, or perhaps detecting parity errors in serial communications chips. The device driver will often interrogate the status of the hardware during read and write operations to detect these conditions and may, if appropriate, attempt to retry the operation and/or correct the error. If this is unsuccessful the condition is reported back to the operating system by the driver, which in turn is passed back to the program, which may take appropriate action.

16.1.2 *Device communication within C*

The C language, although not supporting device communication directly (that is, you cannot go and write to a specific sector of a disk or access the hardware devices controlling it), has nevertheless developed a number of generalized stream functions within the standard library that can be applied to a wide range of devices, and that often participate in the formatting and preparation of data in much the same way as `printf()` and `scanf()`.

It is at this point in the discussion that many texts on C choose to refer to devices within the system as 'files', since this is how they are treated under UNIX. This can be somewhat confusing for a new programmer because the terms 'file' and 'file manipulation function' imply or suggest that such functions are applicable only to the manipulation of disk based files, which is *not* necessarily the case. To clarify matters, this chapter uses the concept of a 'file' only in relation to disk based files. The more generic use of the term 'stream' can be applied to any device in the system, including a disk file.

A stream, as we shall see later, is primarily a software concept, and implies a buffered route or path for the exchange of data between a program and a physical device within the system. This device may well be a disk drive, in which case file manipulation can be performed appropriately, but the stream functions in the standard library may also be used to communicate with other devices, such as terminals, printers and networks.

16.1.3 *Text and binary streams*

In C, the programmer also has the choice of communicating with a device using one of two possible types of stream, as listed below:

- Text or character streams
- Binary streams

The **text** stream has evolved principally for use with character oriented devices such as terminals or printers, but may be applied equally to other types of device such as the type of disk file often created by text editors. Text streams usually contain data in the form of the host computer's character set, such as ASCII, so the data should be suitable for displaying on a terminal or printer.

With any text stream, some hidden (in the sense that it is performed transparently by the operating system/device driver) formatting of the data may take place during its passage between program and device. Characters may be translated, added or deleted from the stream by the operating system, to conform with conventions present on the host machine. Furthermore, an implementation dependent number of `NULL` characters may also be appended to a text stream's output.

For example, the new line character '\n', usually represented in C by a single character, may be translated during its passage into a carriage return *and* a line feed sequence, usually two characters. Thus, there is no guarantee of a one-to-one correspondence between the characters written to or read from a stream and those that are actually written to or read from a specific device.

A **binary** stream, on the other hand, does have a one-to-one correspondence, and no translation of data takes place. Binary streams are frequently employed by programs that wish to save and recover large amounts of data to disks, with the minimum of overheads, but are not concerned with how the data will physically be stored by the device itself, since it is unlikely to find that data being sent to a terminal or printer. Examples of binary files include executable programs stored on disk. Some operating systems, such as UNIX for example, do not differentiate between the two types of stream and treat all streams as if they were binary.

16.2 The C language stream interface

Before discussing the stream functions in detail, it is worth pausing at this point to consider the stream interface provided by the C language to connect a program and its data to the operating system. If you take the time and trouble to locate and examine the header file <stdio.h> that came with your compiler, you will probably find the declaration of a structure template, often called _buffer, that is not too dissimilar to the one shown in Program 16.1.

Program 16.1 The FILE structure.

```
#define MAX_FILE_NUM 20          Maximum of 20 streams may be open at any one time

struct _buffer  {                Structure template _buffer
   int       level ;          /* full or empty level of stream buffer */
   unsigned  flags ;          /* Stream status flags */
   char      path ;           /* Stream descriptor */
   unsigned  char hold ;      /* To hold any ungetc char if no buffering used */
   int       bsize ;          /* Size of buffer for stream */
   unsigned  char *buffer ;   /* Pointer to stream buffer */
   unsigned  char *nextc ;    /* Pointer to next character in buffer */
   unsigned  tempfile ;       /* Temporary file flag */
}
                                 FILE is a new data type based on structure template _buffer
typedef struct   _buffer FILE ;
                                 External array of 20 elements of type FILE
extern FILE      _iob[ MAX_FILE_NUM ] ;
```

The contents of the structure and the variable names shown are likely to differ from one compiler/operating system to another. The example given in Program 16.1 is typical of that which can be found on an MS-DOS C compiler. Note how the new data type FILE has been created with a typedef statement using this structure template.

The header file also **declares** (not defines) the external array _iob[ ], since the array itself is allocated storage within the operating system, rather than the program. Each element of this array is of type FILE; that is, each element is a structure based around the template _buffer and as such contains the elements declared by that template.

The number of elements allocated to _iob[ ] by each operating system will vary but ultimately limits the number of streams that a program (or process in a multi-tasking system) may have open at any one time. In the above example, 20 were defined, as dictated by the symbolic constant MAX_FILE_NUM.

When a request is made by the program to use or 'open' a stream using the function fopen( ) (see later), an element from the array _iob[ ] is allocated for use by that stream; its address is returned to the program in the form of a FILE pointer and a stream buffer is allocated at the same time, as shown in Figure 16.2. If the program requests the simultaneous use of several streams, then further elements

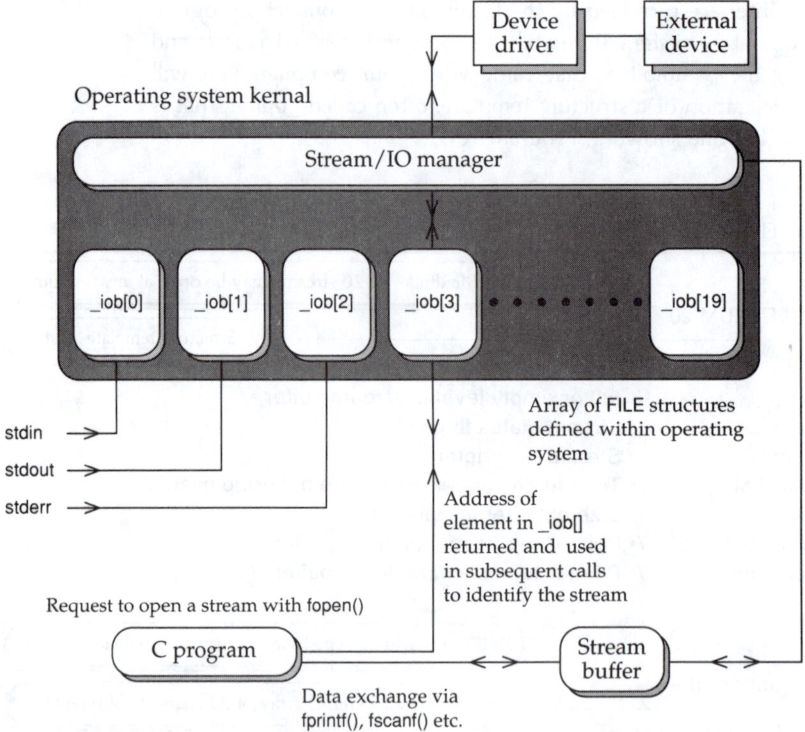

Figure 16.2 The stream mechanism.

within _iob[ ] are allocated, on the basis of one per stream. Once a program has finished using a stream, it may choose to close the stream, thus freeing the respective FILE structure within _iob[ ] for use by another stream.

You can also see from Figure 16.2 that the first three elements of _iob[ ] are reserved for the operating system default input, output and error message streams, and thus the FILE pointers stdin, stdout and stderr (see Chapter 1) point to them. Thus _iob[0], _iob[1] and _iob[2] are associated with the program's terminal (unless I/O has been redirected).

The elements described in the structure template _buffer from which FILE is derived, although largely irrelevant for most purposes, are used by the stream functions, and the operating system to locate and synchronize the passage of data between the operating system stream buffer and the user's program. For example, the structure contains information about the size, location and free space available in the stream buffer as well as **condition flags** that log any error or end-of-file conditions that might be associated with the stream.

Fortunately, the interface to and use of this structure is largely transparent since the programmer is not expected to access and manipulate the structure directly; this is largely the job of the stream functions so programmers need not concern themselves too much with its contents. Once some experience has been gained, the reader might find it informative to examine how the variables within the FILE structure are modified by operations such as reading or writing.

16.2.1 *The stream buffer*

When a stream is initially opened by a program, a stream buffer is usually allocated by the operating system, which is designed in some circumstances to reduce the amount of device activity required in response to program read and write requests. The size of the stream buffer is largely system dependent, being defined by the symbolic constant BUFSIZ in <stdio.h>, but is typically 256, 512 or 1024 bytes.

The type of the stream buffering adopted, its size and even its location are determined initially by the operating system, but the programmer is free to change these parameters after the stream has been opened, with the function setvbuf( ). Three modes of stream buffering are catered for:

- Line buffering;
- No buffering;
- Full buffering.

The physical characteristics of the device influence the mode of buffering initially adopted by the operating system. For example, streams connected to printers and terminals may well use line or no stream buffering, while disk drives would probably make use of full stream buffering.

Line buffering simply means that data is transferred between the stream and the device driver on a line by line basis, with the end of a line indicated by the new line character '\n'. This explains why the function **getchar()**, for example, only returns the character entered at the keyboard when the operator supplies a carriage return and why output may not appear on the operator's terminal when using **printf()**, unless a new line is present in the output. With no stream buffering, data is transferred between program and device driver as soon as there is data/space available at the device.

With full stream buffering, the operating system will attempt to fill the stream buffer with data from a device during a read operation, even though such data has not been and may not be requested by the program. It would also ensure that any written data is only physically transferred to the device driver when the stream buffer is full, and helps to reduce the amount of physical device activity.

If the size of the stream buffer is made representative of the size of a **sector** on the disk, say 1024 bytes, then reading data from a file might only require the disk drive to be accessed once in every 1024 bytes of data read or written. These modes are discussed in more detail under the description of the function **setvbuf()** in Section 16.7.

Note that the issue of stream buffering *may* be further complicated by the actions of the device driver, which maintains its own device buffers independently of any stream buffer. This is shown in Figure 16.3. The operation of these device driver buffers is for the most part not user controllable but may be customized for a particular device. Such customizing is usually carried out by the system's manager or the originator of the device driver.

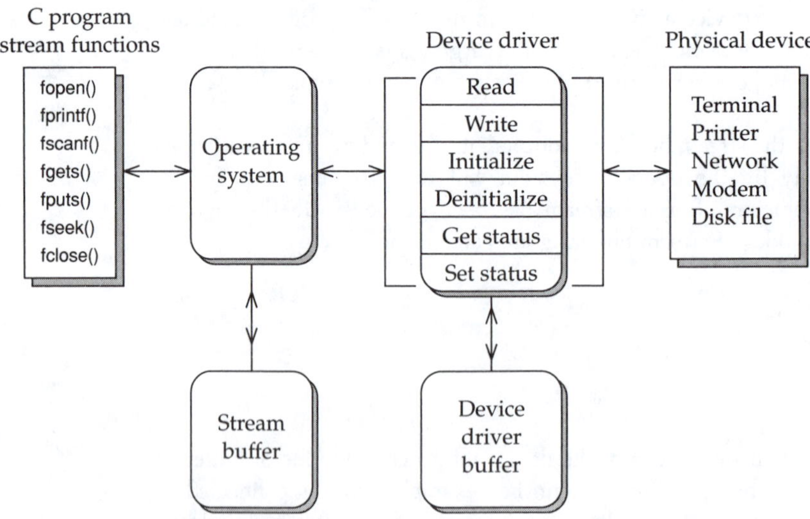

Figure 16.3 The device driver buffer and interface.

16.2.2 *Identifying devices via a pathlist*

Identification of devices within a system is commonly performed using a **pathlist**. Every device in the system, including the default terminal, printer and any disk drives and files, possesses a unique pathlist, which may be referred to when requesting communication with that device/file. The pathlist name is specified when initially establishing a link with the device.

However, pathlist naming conventions are not standardized and thus vary from one operating system to another. For example, under MS-DOS a disk file pathlist of the form 'c:\dos\include\fred.c' would locate the file 'fred.c' on disk 'c:' within the subdirectories '\dos\include', while a UNIX pathlist of the form '/usr/p.davies/fred.c' locates the file 'fred.c' in the 'usr' partition in the directory 'p.davies'. Note that because MS-DOS is a single user system, a program is permitted to access non-sharable devices such as the printer (and screen/keyboard) directly, using the device/pathlist names 'prn' and 'con', respectively.

16.2.3 *Stream errors and end-of-file status*

An important issue for the programmer concerns the detection of errors associated with a device/stream. Although not that common, device errors can occur for a variety of reasons. Electrical noise, for example, may interfere with serial communications or networks, while disk files can become corrupted.

Normally, the task of identifying these errors lies with the device driver, which may, where appropriate, attempt to correct them or retry the operation, but if the error still persists, the driver may inform the program (via the operating system and stream function), which is then left with the sometimes difficult task of deciding what, if anything, to do about it.

Another more frequent condition arises during a read operation when all of the data from a stream/file has been read by the program. In this situation, the program would have to be able to detect the end-of-file (EOF) status for a stream, which could even include the operator's terminal. An EOF status is a fairly straightforward concept to grasp in relation to disk files, but for other devices, such as the operator's terminal, it may not at first be so obvious.

However, if you consider that a program could have had its input redirected from a disk file, it may have to be written to detect the EOF status in a generic way, if the same program is to be used to read data from a number of alternative devices.

We saw at the end of Chapter 1 that many operating systems such as MS-DOS or UNIX permit the operator to *simulate* an EOF condition at the terminal's keyboard by pressing <Control-Z> or <Control-D>, respectively. The operating system recognizes this condition and returns an EOF status to the program, which may be used to terminate any further read requests. The UNIX shell, for example, often uses the EOF condition to log-out the operator.

16.2.4 *Detecting error and EOF status within a C program*

When a read or write operation is performed on a stream, its success or otherwise is indicated to the program via the appropriate stream function's returned value. If an error or EOF condition is detected for a stream, then flags associated with the stream's FILE structure are set and remain asserted until specifically cleared by the program; thus further read/write operations on the stream continue to return the same status. Two stream functions, ferror() and feof(), exist to permit the program to test the error and EOF status of a stream, perhaps after many read and/or write operations have been performed.

Cautionary note: The header file <stdio.h> defines the symbolic integer constant EOF (usually with the value −1), which is frequently returned by stream functions to indicate the failure of their operation. Do not assume that the value EOF implies that the failure is due to an end-of-file condition; it could equally well result from an error condition with the device/file. The program will have to establish the exact cause of failure for itself using ferror() and/or feof().

When a stream error is detected, the value of the external int errno (declared in <errno.h>) is generally set to a value indicating the reason for the failure, such as invalid file name/directory, read error and so on. By interrogating the value of errno immediately after a stream failure, the program should be able to determine the *exact* cause of failure. Note, however, that the value assigned to errno in these circumstances is not standardized and may give rise to portability problems if the absolute value of errno is used in any expression.

In most cases, the program itself is generally not interested in the actual value of errno, and is probably more interested in displaying a suitable error message on the operator's terminal. The functions perror() and strerror() may thus be used to perform this operation in a portable and system independent manner. Note, however, that the value of errno is updated each time an error occurs, so its value may not be representative of the original error unless it is read immediately after the error is detected.

16.3 The C stream library

The following sections describe the contents and operation of the functions in the stream library. Briefly, these functions fall into five categories:

- Stream creation and control: fopen(), freopen(), fclose(), fflush(), setbuf(), setvbuf(), tmpfile();
- Stream read and write: fprintf(), fputs(), fputc(), fscanf(), fgets(), fgetc(), ungetc(), fread() and fwrite();
- Stream positioning: fgetpos(), fsetpos(), fseek(), rewind(), ftell();

- Error functions: feof(), ferror(), clearerr(), strerror() and perror();
- Miscellaneous functions: rename(), remove(), tmpnam().

These functions are now discussed in detail.

16.3.1 *Creating and/or opening a stream:* fopen()

The stream library defines the function fopen() which enables a program to connect or associate a stream with a physical device. The function expects to be supplied with two arguments identifying the pathlist of the physical device and the intended mode of operation.

The mode argument specifies whether the device (perhaps a disk file) should be created or simply opened, and whether data is to be read from or written to the device or perhaps both. The choice of a binary or text stream is also specified here.

The operating system usually determines the capabilities of the device – disk file, VDU and so on – by considering the pathlist argument supplied, or alternatively by interrogating the device type via its driver software. This information will influence the type of stream buffering adopted for the device.

If the program requests the creation of a disk file, then assuming the disk is formatted and the program has the required authority to perform this operation, an empty file is created on the disk. However, if a request is made to open an *existing* device/file the operating system will probably check the file/device's **permission attributes** to assess whether the device supports that mode of operation.

When a stream is opened, a stream buffer and an element from the array _iob[] are allocated to the program, and a pointer to this element is returned by fopen() in the form of a FILE pointer. This pointer is crucial since it will be used subsequently by all other stream related functions to reference that particular stream. It is, if you like, the key to accessing the opened stream. This is shown in Figure 16.4.

Function prototype: fopen()

The function prototype for fopen() can be found in the header file <stdio.h> and is given below:

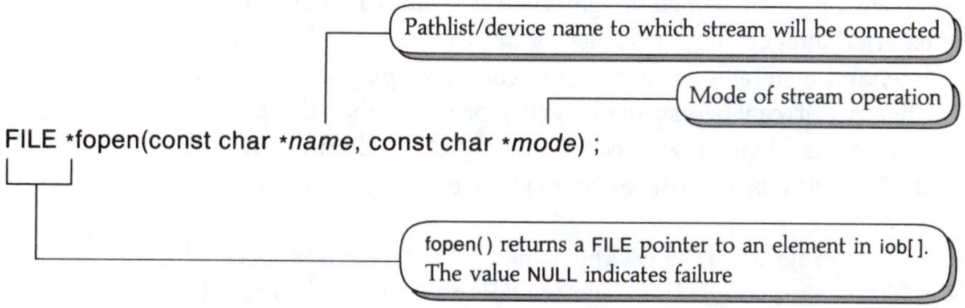
Pathlist/device name to which stream will be connected
Mode of stream operation
FILE *fopen(const char *name, const char *mode) ;
fopen() returns a FILE pointer to an element in iob[].
The value NULL indicates failure

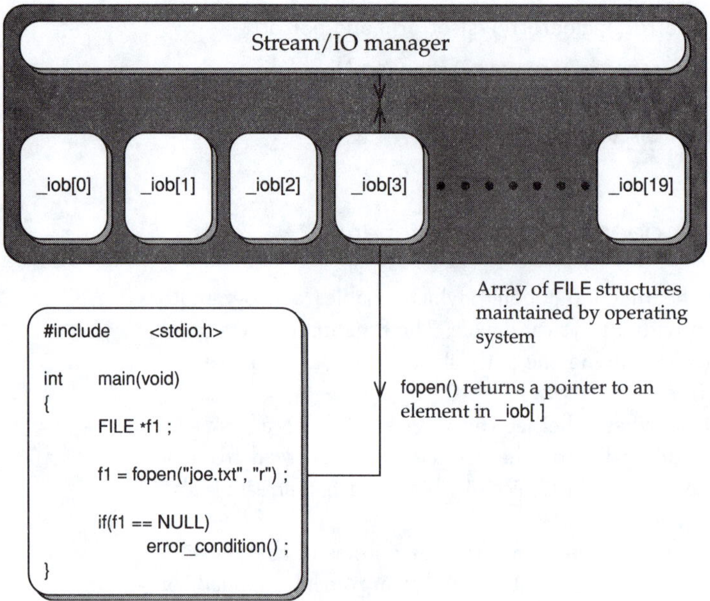

Figure 16.4 Opening a stream with fopen( ).

where 'name' is the pathlist name for the device and 'mode' specifies the way in which the program intends to manipulate the device. These modes are described in Table 16.1.

Notice how the type specifier for fopen( ) is declared as returning a pointer to the new data type FILE. This pointer must be saved by the program so that the stream can be referenced later. A suitable definition for such a pointer is shown below:

'fp' is a FILE pointer

```
FILE *fp ;
```

Error considerations and returned values: fopen( )

If fopen( ) fails to create/open the named stream, then it returns a NULL pointer. The value of the external integer errno will then be set to a value indicating the reason for the failure, and a suitable error message can be displayed if required using perror( ). Otherwise it can be assumed by the program that the pointer contains the address of the element within the array _iob[ ] allocated to that stream. Program 16.2 illustrates the use of fopen( ) in opening a disk file for reading.

You will notice in Program 16.2 how the name of the device was specified using an MS-DOS file naming convention. The operating system is thus able to

Table 16.1 Valid mode parameters for `fopen()`.

Mode	*Explanation*
"r"	Open an existing TEXT device/file for reading.
"w"	Truncate an existing TEXT device/file or, if not present, create it and then open it for writing.
"a"	Open a TEXT device/file for appending at the end or create it if it does not exist.
"r+"	Open an existing TEXT device/file for reading and writing.
"w+"	Truncate an existing TEXT device/file or, if not present, create it and then open it for reading and writing.
"a+"	Open TEXT device/file for appending in both read and write mode, or create it if it does not exist.
"rb"	Open existing BINARY device/file for reading.
"wb"	Truncate an existing BINARY device/file or, if not present, create it and then open it for writing.
"ab"	Open a BINARY device/file for appending at the end or create it if it does not exist.
"rb+"	Open an existing BINARY device/file for reading and writing.
"wb+"	Truncate an existing BINARY device/file or, if not present, create it and then open it for reading and writing.
"ab+"	Open a BINARY device/file for appending in both read and write mode, or create it if it does not exist.

Note 1: The mode parameters "rb+", "wb+" and "ab+" can also be written as "r+b", "w+b" and "a+b". Some compilers may permit the inclusion of the letter 't' to indicate a text stream, for example "rt", "wt+".
Note 2: When a stream is opened in append mode, for example a disk file, then data is always appended to the *end* of the file even if the file is randomly accessed (see Section 16.6.1).

determine that the program has requested use of a disk file and can then determine if the mode of operation 'r', to be interpreted as reading, is appropriate for use with that file.

Table 16.1 summarizes the valid modes of operation/access that are recognized by `fopen()`. Some of these imply creation, truncation, text or binary streams and read/write/append data. Some of the modes may only make sense when applied with due regard for the characteristics of the device.

In the following sections, much of the emphasis on stream usage is in relation to the manipulation of disk files since, other than the user's VDU, this is the most common form of stream I/O performed by a program. The reader is, however, encouraged to consider the application of these functions to other types of devices such as terminals and printers. Later sections in this chapter will attempt to relate the operation of the VDU functions `printf()`, `scanf()`, `puts()`, `gets()` and so on to the more generalized stream functions discussed here.

Program 16.2 Example use of fopen() to open a disk file.

```
#include   <stdio.h>          /* fn prototype for fopen() located here */
#include   <stdlib.h>         /* function prototype for exit() here */
#include   <errno.h>

int main( void )
{
/*
** Define a pointer to save address of FILE structure allocated to a stream
*/
                    'fp1' is a FILE pointer to save address returned by fopen()
  FILE *fp1 ;

/*
** Open an existing disk text file in read mode, if the returned pointer has the value
** NULL then print cause of error using function perror() and exit program. The
** pathlist supplied to fopen() assumes MS-DOS compatibility
*/
                                             Save returned address in 'fp1'
                                             MS-DOS pathlist for disk file
                                             Stream will be used for read mode
  if( (fp1 = fopen( "joe.c", "r")) == NULL )  {
     perror("Cannot open file joe.c") ;
     exit( EXIT_FAILURE ) ;
  }

/*
** Additional code to access the file here
*/
  ...
}
```

The reader is also asked to consider the device's inherent characteristics when applying these stream functions, since not all the devices to which they may be applied are capable of the operations specified and may generate errors if applied inappropriately.

16.3.2 *Stream position indicators and end-of-file markers*

For the purposes of this and further discussion in this chapter, it would be useful to visualize a stream as an array of characters with a **stream position indicator** (SPI), known as a **file position indicator** (FPI) on UNIX systems, pointing to the next character in the stream. The SPI moves forwards in the stream with successive read/write operations so that it is always pointing to the next available character or space to be read from or written to the stream. Such a concept is analogous to stepping a pointer through an array. An EOF (end of stream/file) marker can also be visualized as always pointing just beyond the last character/free space in the stream.

A read operation attempts to move the SPI successively on a character by character basis from its current position towards the end of the stream. The function fgetc( ), which we shall meet later, reads one character from the stream and moves the SPI one place closer towards the end-of-file marker. This operation can be performed repeatedly until the SPI reaches the end of the stream, upon which further read operations may generate an EOF condition for the stream.

Whether an actual EOF condition is raised when all data from the stream has been read depends upon the characteristics of the device to which the stream is attached. For example, a disk file, once its contents had been read, would certainly generate an EOF condition. However, a stream connected to a terminal might not, since the read operation would simply wait until the operator had satisfied the read request.

When a write operation is performed to a disk file, data present within the file may be overwritten (but not if opened in append mode), particularly if the SPI is positioned at a point prior to the end of the file. When the SPI encounters the EOF marker, the operating system will attempt to enlarge the file, making it progressively larger with each write operation. A terminal or printer operates in a similar manner to a disk file, except of course that it can be thought of as being infinitely large, able to accommodate any amount of data written to it.

A failure to enlarge the file, perhaps because it is attached to a disk that has become full, would generate an error condition for the stream. The function fseek( ) permits the current position of the SPI to be repositioned anywhere within a stream attached to a device that is capable of supporting random data access to data.

This is particularly useful for disk files, where the position of the SPI can be moved under program control (using the function fseek( )) to any place in the stream/file, allowing subsequent read or write operations to take place at that new position. This technique is frequently employed in database manipulation, where a record is read from a file, modified by an operator and then written back, thus overwriting the old record.

Note that positioning the SPI at a point in a disk file and then closing the file does not set the EOF at that position; in other words, a disk file *cannot* be shortened.

The initial position of the SPI for a disk file: Write mode

When an existing file is first opened the initial placement of the SPI within it is governed by the mode of operation specified with fopen( ). If one of the write modes "w", "wb", "w+" or "wb+" is specified, then the contents of the file will be lost. If, however, the file does not exist, it will be created. In both cases, the SPI and EOF indicators will therefore point to the start (and end) of an empty file/stream.

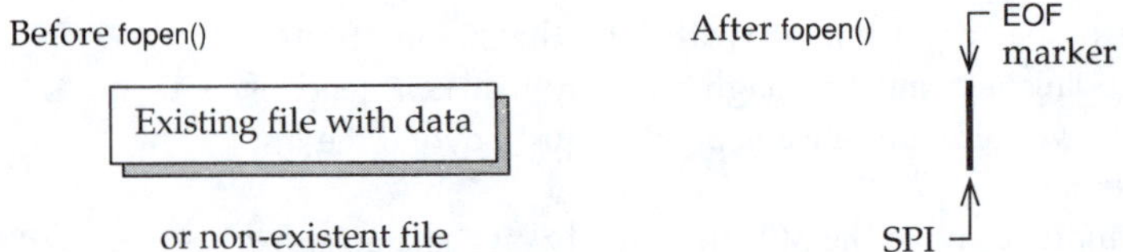

Figure 16.5 The effect on a file, SPI and EOF marker after a call to fopen( ) with modes "w", "w+", "wb" or "wb+".

A write operation at this point transfers data from the program to the stream buffer, and eventually to the file, which results in an increase in the size of that file (if possible), and both the SPI and EOF indicators are moved (conceptually) in the process. A read operation (permitted when the stream has been opened for reading and writing with modes "w+" or "wb+") without a call to an intervening function such as fseek( ) (which repositions the SPI) will produce an EOF condition, since there is no data to be read. This is illustrated in Figure 16.5.

Subsequent valid read or write operations

Table 16.2 gives a list of suggested stream read and write functions that may be used depending upon which write mode has been specified. These functions will be discussed later.

The initial position of the SPI for a disk file: Read mode

If a file is opened with the mode specified as either "r", "rb", "r+" or "rb+", then it is assumed that the named file must already exist, since no attempt will be made to create it. An error is returned by fopen( ) if the named device is found not to exist.

Once opened, the SPI is set to the start of the file/stream, for subsequent read and/or write operations. Write operations (permitted when the stream has been opened for reading and writing with modes "r+" and "rb+") at this point overwrite existing data in the file, while attempts to write beyond the EOF marker simply extend the size of the file (if possible), moving both markers. A read

Table 16.2 Suggested stream I/O functions for use with write modes.

Mode	*Stream read/write functions*
Text streams: "w"	fprintf( ), fputs( ), fputc( )
"w+"	fprintf( ), fputs( ), fputc( ), fscanf( ), fgets( ), fgetc( )
Binary streams: "wb"	fwrite( )
"wb+"	fread( ), fwrite( )

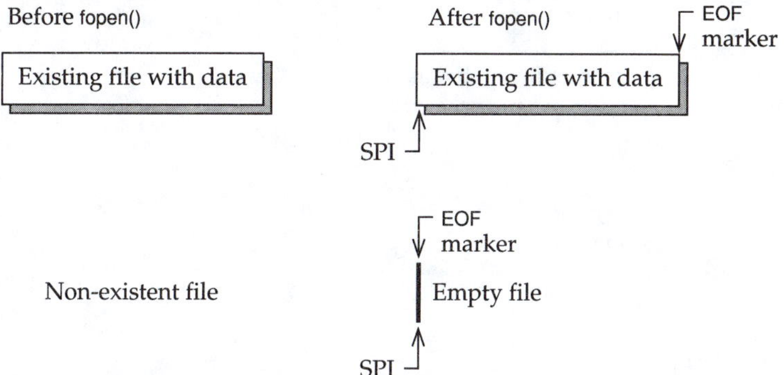

Figure 16.6 The effect on a file, SPI and EOF marker after a call to fopen( ) with modes "r", "r+", "rb" or "rb+".

operation permits the program to fetch data from the stream up to the point at which the EOF condition is encountered. This is illustrated in Figure 16.6.

Subsequent valid read or write operations

Table 16.3 gives a list of suggested read and write functions that may be used, depending upon which of the read modes have been specified.

Table 16.3 Suggested stream I/O functions for use with read modes.

Mode	*Stream read/write functions*
Text streams: "r"	fscanf( ), fgets( ), fgetc( )
"r+"	fprintf( ), fputs( ), fputc( ), fscanf( ), fgets( ), fgetc( )
Binary streams: "rb"	fread( )
"rb+"	fread( ), fwrite( )

The initial position of the SPI for a disk file: Append mode

If a file is opened with the mode specified as either "a", "ab", "a+" or "ab+", then the operating system will attempt to open an existing file for append mode, in which case, the data will *not* be truncated. If the file does not exist, it is created. In either case, the EOF and (usually) the SPI markers are placed initially at the end of the file/stream, as illustrated in Figure 16.7, although some operating systems arrange for the SPI to be initially positioned at the start of the file/stream. Consult your C compiler reference manual for details.

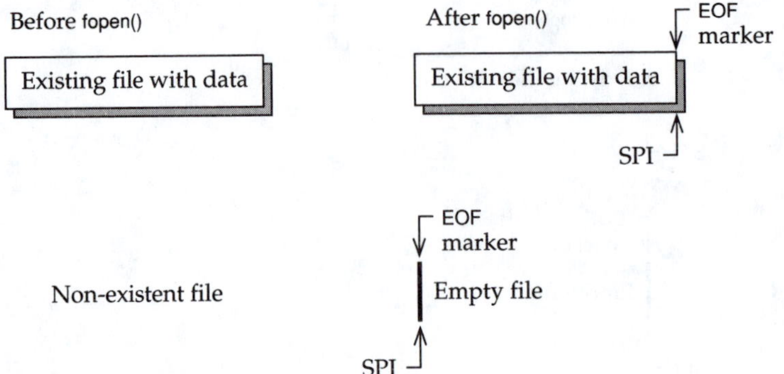

Figure 16.7 The effect on a file, SPI and EOF marker after a call to fopen( ) with modes "a", "a+", "ab" or "ab+".

A read operation at this point, depending upon the initial position of the SPI, might result in an EOF condition, while a write operation simply extends the size of the file (if possible) by appending data to the end of the file.

Subsequent valid read or write operations

Table 16.4 gives a list of suitable read and write functions that can be used depending upon which of the append modes have been specified.

Table 16.4 Suggested stream I/O functions for use with append modes.

Mode	Stream function name
Text streams: "a"	fprintf( ), fputs( ), fputc( )
"a+"	fprintf( ), fputs( ), fputc( ), fscanf( ), fgets( ), fgetc( )
Binary streams: "ab"	fwrite( )
"ab+"	fread( ), fwrite( )

We shall now consider some suitable stream functions that enable a program to read and write data to text streams. Binary streams will be dealt with later.

16.3.3 *Reading and writing text and numbers to disk files:* fprintf( ) *and* fscanf( )

The stream library defines the function fprintf( ), allowing formatted text and numeric output to be written as text to a previously opened stream. Its operation is almost identical to that of the standard terminal output function printf( ).

Function prototype: fprintf( )

The function prototype for fprintf( ) can be found in the header file <stdio.h> and is given below:

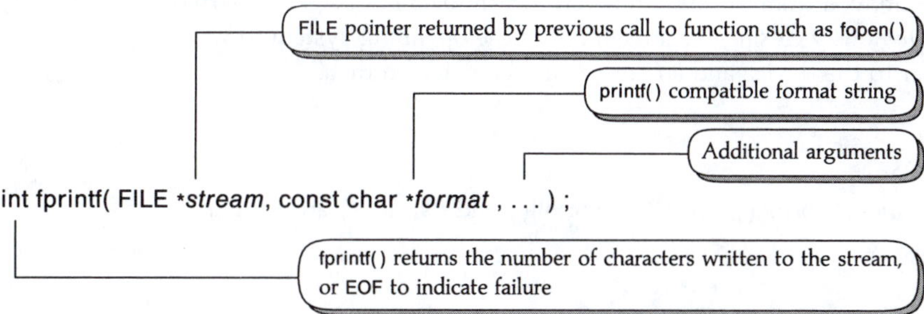
FILE pointer returned by previous call to function such as fopen( )
printf( ) compatible format string
Additional arguments
int fprintf(FILE *stream, const char *format , . . .) ;
fprintf( ) returns the number of characters written to the stream, or EOF to indicate failure

where stream is a FILE pointer identifying the stream, and can be obtained from a successful call to the functions fopen( ) or freopen( ), format is a literal text string describing the text and format of any data to be written and the ellipsis parameter (. . .) indicates the presence or otherwise of additional parameters that may, under the direction of the format string, be written to the stream.

The reader is directed to the discussion of the function printf( ) in Chapter 15 for a detailed description of the operation of the format string and ellipsis parameters.

Error considerations and returned values: fprintf( )

fprintf( ) returns the number of characters successfully written to the stream, or the value of the symbolic constant EOF defined in <stdio.h> if unsuccessful, perhaps because of an invalid stream argument, or perhaps if an error associated with the device has been detected, such as disk full. In which case the error flag in the FILE structure is also set, and can be tested with the function ferror( ) or cleared with the functions clearerr( ) or rewind( ). The value of the external integer errno will be set to a value indicating the cause of the failure, and a suitable error message can be displayed using perror( ).

Whether the data is transferred to the device successfully may not immediately be known, since the call to fprintf( ) (and other output functions that we shall meet later such as fputs( ), fputc( ) and so on) normally only results in the output being written to the stream buffer until such time as there is sufficient data to transfer to the physical device.

Therefore, a call to fprintf( ) may *appear* to work since fprintf( ) does not return EOF, but any actual error may only be detected later when the operating system attempts to transfer the contents of the stream buffer to the device, or if an attempt is made to close the stream with fclose( ). Only then can the operating system detect and flag the error to the program during a write operation.

For a disk file making use of full stream buffering, this may not occur until one sector's worth or more of data is present in the stream buffer. This is an important consideration for the programmer, since a successful write operation to the stream is no guarantee of a successful write to the device. Data could be lost if the power is removed from the system before stream data has been transferred to the device. Obviously closing the stream forces the operating system to write the stream buffer to the device and an error could be detected then.

Related functions

The functions sprintf( ), printf( ), vprintf( ), vfprintf( ) and vsprintf( ) are related to fprintf( ).

Application 16.1

Generate a program that writes the sine of all angles between 0 and PI in increments of 0.01 radians to the disk file 'sin.dat'.

Application 16.1 Example use of fprintf( ).

```
#include   <stdio.h>
#include   <stdlib.h>
#include   <errno.h>
#include   <math.h>          /* function prototype for sin( ) in here */

#define  PI  3.1415927

int main( void )
{
   FILE     *f1 ;
   double  count ;

/*
** Attempt to open the disk file 'sine.dat' for creation/truncation and write mode
** Exit with a suitable error message and status if unsuccessful
*/

    if( (f1 = fopen( "sine.dat" , "w")) == NULL)  {
       perror("Error cannot open file 'sine.dat' for writing ... " ) ;
       exit( EXIT_FAILURE ) ;
    }

/*
** If successful, start writing text to the device
** Test for error and exit with a suitable error message and status if unsuccessful
*/
```

```
    for( count = 0 ; count < PI ; count += 0.01 )  {
      if( fprintf( f1 , "Sine of %g radians = %g\n" , count, sin( count )) == EOF)  {
        perror("Error writing out file 'sine.dat' ... ") ;
        exit( EXIT_FAILURE ) ;
      }
    }

    if( fclose( f1 ) )
      perror("Error Closing File 'sine.dat' ... ") ;

    return 0 ;
  }
```

16.3.4 *Formatted text input:* fscanf()

Having written a mixture of both text and numeric output to a stream using fprintf(), the most efficient way to read such data back is generally via the function fscanf(). The operation of fscanf() is similar to that of the keyboard input function scanf() and the reader is directed to the discussion of that function in Chapter 15. Briefly, fscanf() will attempt to read and convert text read from a stream into a format that is appropriate for storing in other types of variables such as integers or floating point numbers. Such a stream might well include a disk file, or the operator's keyboard. The conversion may fail if text is encountered from a stream that is incompatible with the format expected.

Function prototype: fscanf()

The function prototype for fscanf() can be found in the header file <stdio.h> and is given below:

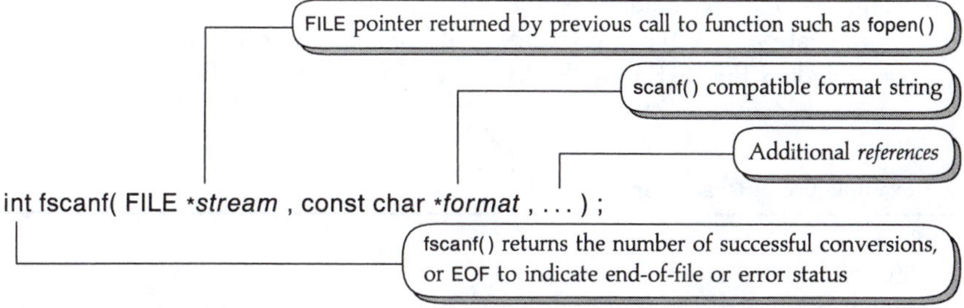

where 'stream' is a FILE pointer identifying the stream, and can be obtained from a successful call to fopen() or freopen(), 'format' is a text string that indicates the place and format of the data to be read from the stream, and the ellipsis parameter (...) indicates the presence of additional parameters that may or may not be required, as defined by the format parameter.

The reader is reminded that fscanf() stores the result of any successful conversions directly into a variable so a reference, address or pointer to the variable(s) must be supplied for any of the parameters controlled by the ellipsis.

Error considerations and returned values: fscanf()

If fscanf() detects an error or an end-of-file condition associated with the stream *before* any successful conversions, then it returns the value of the symbolic constant EOF defined in the header file <stdio.h> and sets the error or end of file flag appropriately for the stream, which can be tested with the function ferror() or feof() and cleared with the function clearerr() or rewind(). The value of the external integer errno is appropriately set to a value indicating the cause of any error, and a suitable error message can be displayed using perror().

If fscanf() successfully converts one or more – but not necessarily all – of its inputs, it returns an integer value equal to the number of successful conversions performed. This could also arise as a result of an error or premature EOF being encountered, or more likely that the input read from the stream is not compatible with the conversion specified. It follows from this, that if all 'n' conversions have been performed successfully, fscanf() returns the integer value 'n'.

In the event of an unsuccessful conversion due to an incorrect format, fscanf() will abort immediately, leaving any unconverted text in the stream, therefore attempting the same operation again with the same format indicator will result in the same failure; fflush() can be generally called to rid the stream of this data.

Related functions

The functions scanf(), sscanf(), vfscanf(), vscanf() and vsscanf() are related to fscanf().

Application 16.2

Write a program using fscanf() to read back the file 'sine.dat' created by Application 16.1 and generate a new file, 'sctan.dat', that contains the original angle and sine values excluding the text, plus the cosine and tangents of all the angles.

Application 16.2 Example use of fscanf() and fprintf().

```
#include  <stdio.h>
#include  <stdlib.h>
#include  <math.h>
#include  <errno.h>

int main( void )
{
   FILE    *fp1, *fp2 ;
   double  count, temp_sin ;
```

```
/*
** Attempt to open the disk file 'sine.dat' for reading
** Exit with a suitable error message and status if unsuccessful
*/

   if( (fp1 = fopen("sine.dat" , "r")) == NULL )  {
      perror("Error opening File 'sine.dat' ... ") ;
      exit( EXIT_FAILURE ) ;
   }

/* Open/create the file sctan.dat for writing */

   if( (fp2 = fopen("sctan.dat" , "w")) == NULL )  {
      perror("Error opening File 'sctan.dat' ... ") ;
      exit( EXIT_FAILURE ) ;
   }

/*
** If successful, start reading text from the device and check conversion
** No attempt is made by the program to determine the cause of the failure
*/

   while( 1 )  {
      if( fscanf( fp1 , "Sine of %lf radians = %lf\n" , &count, &temp_sin) != 2)
         break ;

/*
** Check for error writing file
*/

      if( fprintf( fp2 , "%f %f %f %f\n",
                              count, temp_sin, cos( count ), tan( count )) == EOF )
         break ;
   }

   if( ferror( fp1 ))
      perror("Error Reading File 'sine.dat' ... ") ;

   if( fclose( fp2 ))
      perror("Error Writing to File 'sctan.dat' ... ") ;

   return 0 ;
}
```

16.3.5 *Closing a stream:* fclose()

Under normal circumstances, the operating system ensures that all active streams associated with a program are closed automatically when the program terminates. However, there are occasions where programmers may wish to force the closure of a stream, perhaps because they wish to open another stream that would exceed the maximum permissible for the program under a given operating system.

Given this requirement, a program may call fclose() to force the operating system to release the stream buffer and FILE structure associated with the stream. Further operations on the stream will then not be permitted unless the stream is re-opened.

If the stream is currently being read from by the program, the operating system will discard any unread data left in the stream's buffer, otherwise any unwritten data still resident within an output stream buffer is written to the device. Any errors encountered in physically writing the data to the device at this point will be reported as an error.

Function prototype: fclose()

The function prototype for fclose() can be found in the header file <stdio.h> and is given below:

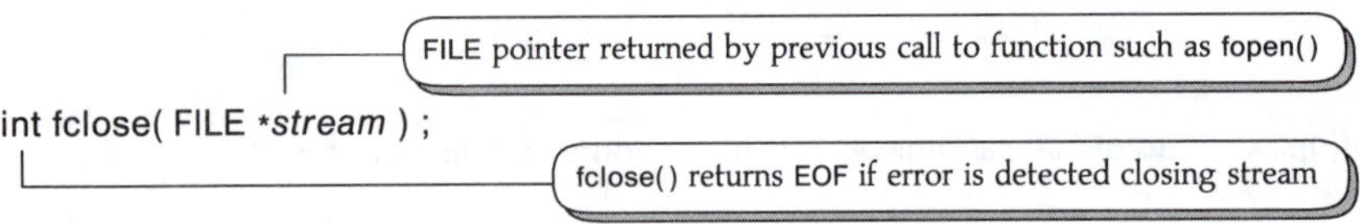

FILE pointer returned by previous call to function such as fopen()
int fclose(FILE *stream) ;
fclose() returns EOF if error is detected closing stream

where the parameter 'stream' is a FILE pointer identifying the stream, and can be obtained from a successful call to the functions fopen(), freopen() or tmpfile().

Error considerations and returned values: fclose()

If successful, fclose() returns zero. However, if for some reason the operation fails when the device driver attempts to write the contents of the stream buffer to the physical device, perhaps because a disk has become full, then the value of the symbolic constant EOF (defined in <stdio.h>) is returned and the value of the external integer errno is set to a value indicating the nature of the failure, which can be displayed on the operator's terminal with a call to perror().

It is here that many programmers fail to appreciate a particularly nasty problem. The write functions such as fprintf(), fputs(), fwrite() and so on, as we have seen, only transfer data to the operating system's stream buffer. It is only when that data is eventually written to the device itself that any *physical* errors, such as disk full for example, can be detected.

For example, suppose a program were involved in a series of write operations to a disk file. Because the programmer may have changed the type and size of buffering used by the stream (see Section 16.7.1), it is possible that the stream buffer could have been made sufficiently large that it could accommodate all of the data that the program ever intended to write to the file. Under these circumstances, the data in the stream would only be transferred to the physical device when the stream was closed.

It might therefore appear to the program as if all its write operations were being performed successfully, since any physical error that *might* occur would not be evident during the write operation to the stream. If that same program relied upon the operating system to automatically/implicitly close the stream on its behalf, any physical device error that may occur will not be evident to the program. An experienced programmer would therefore always check for errors closing a stream by explicitly calling fclose( ).

Note that this problem is more likely to occur if full stream buffering is used and the size of the buffer is larger than BUFSIZ (defined in <stdio.h>); see Section 16.7 for details. Program 16.3 illustrates this problem, where a write error due to the disk becoming full was only detected on the author's systems by the function fclose( ). Without this check the program would never have known that the error had occurred.

Program 16.3 Detecting write errors with fclose( ).

```
#include  <stdio.h>
#include  <stdlib.h>
#include  <errno.h>

char      buff[ 10000 ] ;        /* big stream buffer */

int main( void )
{
  FILE  *fp ;
  int     i ;

/*
** Open a disk file, note MS-DOS naming conventions
*/

  if( (fp = fopen("a:\\joe.txt", "wb")) == NULL)  {
    perror("Cannot open joe.txt") ;
    exit(EXIT_FAILURE ) ;
  }

/*
** Change buffer size to large user-defined one (see later)
*/

  if( setvbuf( fp , buff, _IOFBF, sizeof( buff )) != 0 )  {
    perror("Unable to set buffer for 'joe.txt' ") ;
    exit( EXIT_FAILURE ) ;
  }
```

```
/*
** Now perform a series of write operations, testing for errors
*/

   for( i = 0 ; i < 100 ; i++ )  {
      if( fprintf( fp, "%d\n" , i ) == EOF)  {
         perror("Error writing ... ") ;
         exit( EXIT_FAILURE ) ;
      }
   }

/*
** Now close the stream and detect if an error occurs now
*/

   if( fclose( fp ) )
      perror("Error closing file ... ") ;

   return 0 ;
}
```

16.3.6 *Flushing a stream:* fflush()

The function fflush() may be called to flush the contents of a stream buffer. For an input stream all unread data in the stream buffer is simply discarded.[†] This function can be particularly useful when called after a function such as scanf() or fscanf(), which might have failed to convert its input data and thus would have left that data in the input stream waiting to be read next time.

Calling fflush() for an output stream forces the operating system to transfer any data in the stream buffer to the device driver, whereupon it *may* be written to the device, which in turn largely depends upon the characteristics of the device itself. If the device were character based, such as a terminal, then calling fflush() might enable the stream data to be written to the device immediately without having to wait for the end of a line. However, if the device were a disk file, the driver may not write the data to the disk file until it has filled its own buffer with perhaps one sector's worth of data.

Note: An automatic call to fflush() is performed by the operating system between changes of direction of data for those streams that have been opened for both read and write modes and fflush() has no effect when a stream is unbuffered.

Function prototype: fflush()

The function prototype for fflush() can be found in the header file <stdio.h> and is given below:

[†] Strictly speaking the operation of fflush() for an input stream is not defined and this may not work consistently on all machines. However, both UNIX and MS-DOS honour the request.

```
int fflush( FILE *stream) ;
```

FILE pointer returned by previous call to function such as fopen()

fflush() returns EOF if error is detected flushing stream

where the parameter 'stream' is a FILE pointer identifying the stream, and can be obtained from a successful call to the functions fopen(), freopen() or tmpfile().

Finally, note that if the parameter 'stream' has the value NULL (zero), then *all* streams in use by the program are flushed.

Error considerations and returned values: fflush()

If fflush() fails, due for example to a disk becoming full, then it returns the value of the symbolic constant EOF defined in <stdio.h>, and the value of the external integer errno will be set to a value indicating the cause of the failure. A suitable error message can be displayed using perror(). Otherwise, upon success zero is returned. An example use of the function fflush() is shown in Application 16.3.

Application 16.3

Write a program to read two floating point numbers from the operator's terminal, multiply them together and display them back. You can assume for the moment that the FILE pointer stdin declared in <stdio.h> can be used for reading data from the keyboard with fscanf().

Note that the function fflush() can be generally applied to the operator's terminal to flush both input and output streams using the calls fflush(stdin) and fflush(stdout), respectively, where stdin and stdout are defined in <stdio.h>.

Application 16.3 Example use of fflush().

```
#include  <stdio.h>
#include  <stdlib.h>
#include  <errno.h>

double  num[2] ;
int     flag, i ;

int main( void )
{
  while( 1 )  {

    i = 0 ;

/*
** Start a loop to read two numbers
*/

    while( i < 2 ) {
```

```
/*
** If fscanf() does not return the correct number of conversions, then check if
** this was the result of EOF condition, if not, must be
** incompatible data read from stream so flush it and try again.
*/

            if(( flag = fscanf( stdin , "%lf" , &num[ i ])) != 1 )  {

/*
** If failure was due to EOF then exit, otherwise flush stdin
*/

                if( flag == EOF )
                    return 0 ;

                else  {
                    printf("Unrecognized Data ... Flushing input ... \n") ;
                    fflush( stdin ) ;
                    continue ;
                }
            }
            i++ ;
        }
        printf("%g * %g = %f\n", num[0], num[1], num[0] * num[1] ) ;
    }
}
```

16.3.7 *Dealing with errors and EOF status:* feof() *and* ferror()

The stream library provides two functions to facilitate the detection of errors or end of file conditions associated with a stream. When functions such as fprintf() or fscanf(), or others that we shall meet later, encounter an error condition an error flag is set within the FILE structure associated with that stream; similarly, those functions likely to encounter an end of file condition set an appropriate EOF flag when it occurs. These flags then remain asserted until specifically cleared.

Although a function such as fscanf() can indicate that something has gone wrong during the input/conversion phase, it is unable to indicate the nature of the problem. The functions feof() and ferror() therefore permit the program to interrogate the error and end of file flags associated with a stream to determine the cause of the problem.

Function prototypes: feof() *and* ferror()

The function prototypes for both of these functions can be found in the header file <stdio.h> and are given as:

FILE pointer returned by previous call to function such as fopen()

```
int feof( FILE *stream )
int ferror( FILE *stream )
```

Both functions return non-zero if an error or end-of-file status, respectively, has been logged for the stream

where the parameter 'stream' is a FILE pointer identifying the stream and can be obtained from a successful call to the functions fopen(), freopen() or tmpfile(). The implementation of these two functions is usually defined in the header file <stdio.h> using a pre-processor macro and may look something like this:

```
#define  feof( fp )    ((( fp ) -> flags & _E_EOF) != 0 )
#define  ferror( fp )  ((( fp ) -> flags & _E_ERROR) != 0 )
```

Error considerations and returned values: feof() *and* ferror()

Both functions return a non-zero value if they determine that the EOF or error flags, respectively, are set for the stream. The value zero is returned otherwise.

Both flags can be cleared by the functions clearerr() and rewind(), which are discussed later. Repositioning the SPI for the stream with the function fseek() may also clear (and set if the move is inappropriate) the EOF flag. Program 16.4 illustrates the use of these two functions in determining the cause of a read problem with fscanf().

Program 16.4 Example use of feof() and ferror().

```
#include  <stdio.h>
#include  <stdlib.h>
#include  <errno.h>

int main( void )
{
  char  buff[ BUFSIZ ] ;
  FILE  *fp ;

/*
** Open a disk file for reading, exit with a suitable status value if it cannot be found
*/

  if( ( fp = fopen("joe.txt", "r")) == NULL )  {
    perror( "Cannot open file joe.txt");
    exit( EXIT_FAILURE );
  }

/*
** Read a string using fscanf(), while conversion is successful
*/
```

```
    while( fscanf( fp, "%s", buff ) == 1 )
      puts( buff ) ;

  /*
  ** Now test to see whether the loop terminated because fscanf()
  ** encountered the natural end of the file, or because an error was detected
  */

    if( feof( fp ) )
      puts("End of file encountered ... ") ;

    if( ferror( fp ) )
      puts("Error reading data from file ... ") ;

    return 0 ;
}
```

16.3.8 *Clearing the error and end-of-file flags:* clearerr()

Once an error or EOF condition has been logged for the stream, these conditions will persist until they are cleared by the program, or the stream is closed. The function clearerr() will clear the error and EOF flags for a stream.

This function might be found useful if an error or EOF has occurred for a device but the program wishes to manipulate the device further, rather than simply exit. For example, a program might wish to read the data from a file until the EOF condition is raised before attempting to overwrite some or all of the information in the file. A call to clearerr() could be made to clear the EOF condition raised by attempting to read beyond the end of the file.

Function prototype: clearerr()

The function prototype for clearerr() can be found in the header file <stdio.h> and is given below:

FILE pointer returned by previous call to function such as fopen()

```
void clearerr( FILE *stream ) ;
```

where the parameter 'stream' is a pointer to a FILE structure identifying the stream, and can be obtained from a successful call to fopen(), freopen() or tmpfile(). No data is returned by this function, since it is only the values of two flags that are cleared.

16.3.9 *Generating an error message:* perror( ) *and* strerror( )

Although the use of these two functions is not really restricted to or associated with stream manipulation, a discussion of them is included here since they are frequently used in this context. We have already seen that, upon detection of a stream error, the external integer errno is set to a value indicating the reason for the error. Under these circumstances, the program often chooses to display a suitable error message on the operator's terminal.

Until the advent of standard C, the program was pretty much responsible for interrogating the value of errno and generating that error message itself. Unfortunately, there was little standardization among operating systems as to the interpretation of errno's value, leading to programs that were difficult to 'port' to other environments.

For this reason the standard now provides the functions perror( ) and strerror( ), which provide a mechanism for the interpretation of errno and the subsequent display (if required) of a suitable error message in a system independent and thus portable manner.

perror( ) accepts a string argument supplied by the program and writes this to the default error stream, stderr (usually the operator's terminal unless error messages have been redirected to an alternative device). A colon ':' and a space character are then written to the same stream, followed by an *internally* generated error message, based on the value of errno, and finally the new line character '\n'.

The function strerror( ) may be invoked to create an error message based on the value of an integer supplied as its parameter (usually the value of errno). The message is held in a static storage area within the function, and a pointer to it is returned. The message generated is of the same form as perror( ).

strerror( ) is useful in situations where the generated error message may need to be manipulated by the program, perhaps with additional text appended to it before being written by the program to the default error stream.

Function prototype: perror( ) *and* strerror( )

The function prototypes for perror( ) and strerror( ) can be found in the header file <stdio.h> and are given below:

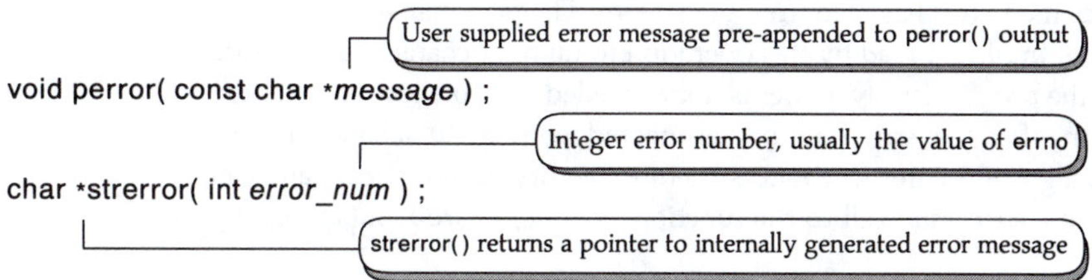
User supplied error message pre-appended to perror( ) output
void perror(const char *message) ;
Integer error number, usually the value of errno
char *strerror(int error_num) ;
strerror( ) returns a pointer to internally generated error message

where the parameter 'message' is a text string that will be displayed exactly as presented and error_num is an integer value (usually the value of errno) for which strerror( ) will attempt to generate a system dependent error message.

Error considerations and returned values: perror( ) *and* strerror( )

A pointer to the generated error message string is returned by strerror( ). No data is returned by perror( ). Note that successive calls to strerror( ) will overwrite the message held in the static storage area allocated by strerror( ).

16.4 Reading and writing text strings: fgets( ) and fputs( )

The stream library defines the function fgets( ) to enable a line of text, terminated by the new line character '\n', to be read from a stream. The text is placed directly into a suitably defined buffer, typically an array of characters. This function operates in a similar manner to the terminal input function gets( ) but differs slightly, in that gets( ) *replaces* the operator generated new line character '\n' with a NULL, while fgets( ) preserves the new line character and appends a NULL character '\0' onto the end.

Function prototype: fgets( )

The function prototype for fgets( ) can be found in the header file <stdio.h> and is given below:

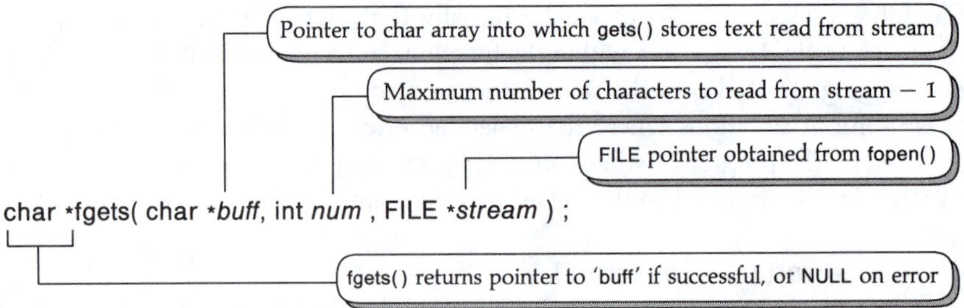
Pointer to char array into which gets( ) stores text read from stream
Maximum number of characters to read from stream – 1
FILE pointer obtained from fopen( )
char *fgets(char *buff, int num , FILE *stream) ;
fgets( ) returns pointer to 'buff' if successful, or NULL on error

where 'buff' is a pointer to the start of a program allocated char array into which fgets( ) will place the text it has read from the stream. The parameter 'num' is used to restrict the length of text read by this operation to num – 1 characters to ensure that the end of the program array/buffer is not exceeded and to allow space at the end of the buffer for the string to be terminated with a '\0' character. The parameter 'stream' is a pointer to a FILE structure identifying the stream and can be obtained from a successful call to the functions fopen( ) or freopen( ).

Error considerations and returned values: fgets( )

fgets( ) returns a pointer to the start of the buffer into which it has placed the text read from the stream, should it be useful, for example, as the subsequent argument to one of the string manipulation functions.

In the event of an error or EOF condition being encountered, fgets() returns a NULL pointer, and the error and/or EOF flags in the FILE structure are set accordingly. The value of these flags can be tested with the functions ferror() and feof() and cleared by calling the functions clearerr() or rewind(). The external int errno is also set for an error condition and a suitable error message can be displayed using the function perror().

Why restrict the length of a line with fgets()*?*

Because there are no restrictions imposed on the length of a line of text that can be written to a device such as a disk file, the programmer may find, when he or she comes to read the text back, that the line could consist of many thousands of characters. In fact there is nothing to prevent the whole file existing as one line of text. The programmer, in calling fgets() to read back the text, would have to take care to ensure that the allocated buffer used to hold the data read from the stream was sufficiently large to accommodate any sized line of text, or corruption of the program could take place.

Of course, at run time there is no way for a program to know this length in advance, so fgets() includes the parameter 'num' to restrict the length of a line of text read from a stream. The parameter 'num' is usually obtained from the sizeof operator in conjunction with the name of the char array used to hold the read text.

Note that if fgets() is used to read a line of text from a stream which is larger than the size of the parameter 'num' then only part of the line will be read, and a NULL character '\0' will be appended to the end of the program's copy of it. This does *not* mean that the remainder of the line of text is lost; it simply means that only the first num − 1 characters are read with that call to fgets(). A subsequent call will read some or all of the remaining characters in that line.

Application 16.4

Write a program that displays the contents of a text file on the user's terminal, such that the name of the file is passed as a command line argument, for example:

```
list joe.txt
```

Application 16.4 Example use of fgets() to display a file.

```
#include  <stdio.h>
#include  <stdlib.h>
#include  <errno.h>

int main( int argc , char *argv[ ] )
{
   static char array [ 10 ] ;
   FILE  *f1 ;
```

```
    if( argc != 2 ) {
        printf("Usage: List <filename>\n") ;
        return 0 ;
    }

    if( (f1= fopen( argv[ 1 ] , "r" )) == NULL )  {
        perror( "Cannot open file for reading" ) ;
        exit( EXIT_FAILURE ) ;
    }

/*
** Read text until an error or EOF is encountered
*/

    while( fgets( array , sizeof( array ) , f1 ) != NULL )
        printf( "%s", array ) ;

/* Now test for an error */

    if( ferror( f1 ) )
        perror("Error reading text from file ... ") ;

    return 0 ;
}
```

Note how printf( ) was called to display the line of text read from the file, since the use of puts( ) would issue a new line character '\n', which might duplicate one that was already present in the string read from the disk file (since these are preserved by fgets( )). Also note that the output was displayed using the call to printf( ) as printf("%s", array) and not printf(array), since the text might contain percentage characters '%' which would be interpreted as format indicators.

Application 16.5

Write a program to compare the contents of two text files. If the files are the same, the program should say so. If they differ, then it should list the lines in each file where a difference is found, along with a line number. The program should stop after at most 10 differences have been found.

Application 16.5 Example use of fgets( ) to compare files.

```
#include  <stdio.h>
#include  <stdlib.h>
#include  <errno.h>
#include  <string.h>
```

```
int main( int argc, char *argv[] )
{
   FILE  *f1, *f2 ;
   int     line_count = 1;
   int     diff_count = 0 ;

   char  *p1, *p2 ;
   char  buff1[ BUFSIZ ], buff2[ BUFSIZ ] ;

/*
** File names are passed as command line arguments
** so check for correct number of args
*/

   if( argc != 3 )  {
      printf("Incorrect Usage: compare <file 1>  <file 2>") ;
      exit( 0 ) ;
   }

/*
** Open both files for reading and check for errors
*/

   f1 = fopen( argv[1], "r") ;
   f2 = fopen( argv[2], "r") ;

   if((f1 == NULL) || (f2 == NULL ))  {
      perror("Cannot Open Files ... ") ;
      exit( EXIT_FAILURE ) ;
   }

   do  {

/*
** Read a line from each file
*/

      p1 = fgets( buff1, sizeof( buff1 ), f1 ) ;
      p2 = fgets( buff2, sizeof( buff2 ), f2 ) ;

/*
** Compare each line and display them if found to be different
*/

      if( strcmp( p1, p2 ) != 0 )  {
         printf("Differences: Line [ %d ] \n", line_count) ;
         printf("\tFile [ %s ]: %s", argv[1], p1 ) ;
         printf("\tFile [ %s ]: %s\n", argv[2], p2) ;
```

```
/*
** If 10 differences found then stop
*/
        if( ++diff_count > 10 )
          break ;
      }

      line_count ++ ;

/*
** Stop when the end of either file has been reached
*/

   } while((p1 != NULL) && (p2 != NULL) ) ;

   if( diff_count == 0 )
      printf("File [ %s ] and File [ %s ] are IDENTICAL ... \n", argv[1], argv[2]) ;

   else if( diff_count > 0 )
      printf("File [ %s ] and File [ %s ] are DIFFERENT ... \n", argv[1], argv[2]) ;

   if( ferror( f1 ) || ferror( f2 ))
      perror("Error reading files ... ") ;

   return 0 ;
}
```

16.4.1 *Writing a line of text:* fputs()

The function fputs() permits a line of text, terminated with a NULL character '\0', to be written to a stream. Its operation is similar to that of the VDU function puts(), except that fputs() does not automatically issue a new line character '\n' at the end of the line.

Function prototype: fputs()

The function prototype for fputs() can be found in the header file <stdio.h> and is given below:

```
int fputs( const char *array , FILE *stream ) ;
```

- *array*: Pointer to char array containing text to be written to stream
- *stream*: FILE pointer obtained from fopen()
- return value: fputs() returns the value of the integer constant EOF on error

where the parameter 'array' is a pointer to a char array containing the text to be written to the stream. The parameter 'stream' is a pointer to a FILE structure identifying the stream to be written to and can be obtained from a successful call to the functions fopen() or freopen().

Error considerations and returned values: fputs()

fputs() returns the value zero upon success. However, in the event of an error condition being encountered, fputs() returns the value of the symbolic integer constant EOF (defined in <stdio.h>) and the error flag in the FILE structure is set. The value of this flag can be tested using the function ferror() and cleared by calling the functions clearerr() or rewind(). The external int errno is also set to a value indicating the reason for the error, and a suitable error message can be displayed using the function perror().

Application 16.6

Write a program using fgets() and fputs() to copy the contents of one disk file to another. Assume that the file names are supplied as command line arguments. What would be the effect of using an alternative device in place of the file name pathlist, for example 'con' or 'prn', on an MS-DOS system?

Application 16.6 Example use of fputs() and fgets() to copy a file.

```
#include  <stdio.h>
#include  <stdlib.h>
#include  <errno.h>

int main( int argc , char *argv[ ] )
{
  FILE  *f1 , *f2 ;                       /* two file pointers */
  char  array[256] ;                      /* array to hold characters */

/*
** Check argument numbers and abort on error
*/

  if( argc != 3)  {
    printf("Error : Usage Copy <pathlist 1>  <pathlist 2>\n" ) ;
    exit( 0 ) ;
  }

  printf("Copying '%s' to '%s' ... \n", argv[1], argv[2]) ;

/*
** Open source and destination streams and check for errors
*/
```

```
    f1 = fopen( argv[1] , "r" ) ;
    f2 = fopen( argv[2] , "w" ) ;

    if( (f1 == NULL) || ( f2 == NULL) )          /* check opened OK */
      exit( 0 ) ;

/*
** Read a line and write to destination until
** end of source file or an error occurs with either stream
*/

    while( ( fgets( array , sizeof( array ) , f1 )) != NULL)   {
      if( fputs( array , f2 ) == EOF )   {
        perror("Error writing out file: Copy Failed ... ") ;
        exit( EXIT_FAILURE ) ;
      }
    }

/*
** Check that read operation did not abort due to read error
*/

    if( ferror( f1 ) )
      perror("Error reading source file: Copy Failed ... ") ;

    if( fclose( f2 ) )
      perror("Error Writing Destination File: Copy Failed ... ") ;

    return 0 ;
}
```

16.5 Reading and writing characters: fgetc( ) and fputc( )

The function fgetc( ) reads an unsigned char from a stream and returns it to the program, without sign extension, as an int.

Function prototype: fgetc( )

The function prototype for fgetc( ) can be found in the header file <stdio.h> and is given below:

```
int fgetc( FILE *stream ) ;
```

FILE pointer obtained from fopen( )

fgetc( ) returns the value of the integer constant EOF on *error* or EOF

where 'stream' is a pointer to the FILE structure identifying the stream and can be obtained from a successful call to the functions fopen( ) or freopen( ). Note that the header file <stdio.h> usually defines the macro getc( ), which performs a similar operation to fgetc( ), and the two are usually interchangeable.

Error considerations and returned values: fgetc( )

In the event of an error or EOF condition being encountered, fgetc( ) returns the value of the symbolic integer constant EOF (defined in <stdio.h>) and the error and/or EOF flags in the FILE structure are set accordingly. The value of these flags can be tested with the functions ferror( ) and feof( ) and cleared by calling the functions clearerr( ) or rewind( ). For an error condition the external int errno is set to a value indicating the reason for the error and a suitable error message can be displayed using the function perror( ).

Why does fgetc( ) *return an* int *and not a* char*?*

To see why fgetc( ) returns an integer, consider the following loop, which reads characters from the stream pointed to by 'fp' until the EOF or error condition is encountered:

```
while ( fgetc( fp ) != EOF )
   ;
```

If fgetc( ) were defined as returning just a char instead of an int and chars were by default unsigned quantities, then upon detecting the end of the file, fgetc( ) would return the value of the symbolic constant EOF (usually −1) as an unsigned char – that is, an 8 bit value which in two's complement binary would be represented as [11111111].

However, the above program, in comparing the 8 bit char returned by fgetc( ) with the signed integer quantity EOF (represented in binary as [11111111 11111111]), would have to promote the char to an int, and because the char may be unsigned, no sign extension would take place and thus the program would be left to compare the integer values:

```
11111111 11111111      integer constant EOF
00000000 11111111      unsigned char constant EOF returned by fgetc( )
```

Thus the program could never detect the EOF status for the stream. If, however, the compiler assumed signed chars (which cannot be guaranteed), this problem would not occur, since sign extension would then be carried out on the char value returned from fgetc( ). To solve this dilemma, fgetc( ) is declared as returning an int. Any normal character read from the stream is present in the lower 8 bits of this returned value.

16.5.1 *Writing characters to a stream:* fputc( )

The function fputc( ) writes a character to a stream. The function prototype for fputc( ) can be found in the header file <stdio.h> and is given below:

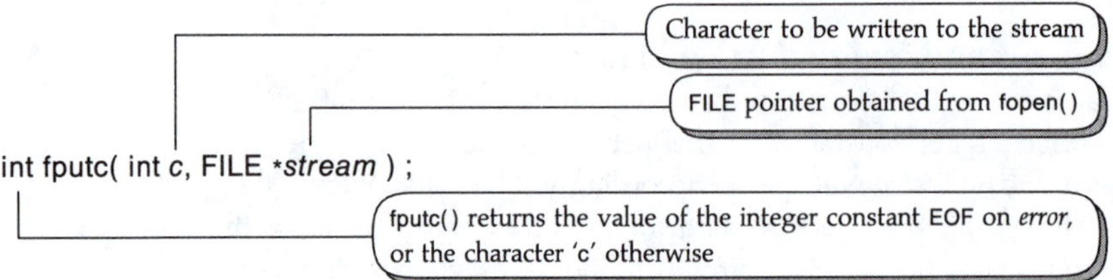
Character to be written to the stream
FILE pointer obtained from fopen( )
int fputc(int c, FILE *stream) ;
fputc( ) returns the value of the integer constant EOF on error, or the character 'c' otherwise

where 'stream' is a FILE pointer identifying the stream and can only be obtained from a successful call to the functions fopen( ) or freopen( ), and 'c' contains the character to be written to the stream. Note that the header file <stdio.h> usually defines the macro putc( ), which behaves in a similar manner to fputc( ), and the two are usually interchangeable.

Error considerations and returned values: fputc( )

fputc( ) returns the value of the character 'c' written to the stream. In the event of an error condition being encountered, fputc( ) returns the value of the symbolic integer constant EOF (defined in <stdio.h>) and the error flag in the FILE structure is set. The value of this flag can be tested using the function ferror( ) and cleared by calling the functions clearerr( ) or rewind( ). The external int errno is also set and a suitable error message can be displayed using the function perror( ).

Application 16.7

Write a program using fgetc( ) to display the contents of a text file on the operator's VDU, where the name of the file is present as a command line argument.

Application 16.7 Example file display program using fgetc( ).

```
#include  <stdio.h>
#include  <stdlib.h>
#include  <errno.h>

int main( int argc , char * argv[ ] )
{
  FILE  *f1 ;
  int    c ;

  if( argc != 2 )  {
    printf("Error: Usage List <pathlist>\n") ;
    exit( 0 ) ;
  }
```

```
/*
** Open the file in read mode, exit with a suitable error message and status if not able
*/

   if( (f1 = fopen(argv[ 1 ] , "r" )) == NULL )  {
      perror("Cannot open file") ;
      exit( EXIT_FAILURE ) ;
   }

/*
** Read a character from the file and save in 'c', while EOF is not returned by fgetc()
** Then display on the user's VDU using putchar(). Note that fgetc() returns EOF when
** an error is encountered, not just on end-of-file, so a check is made using ferror()
*/

   while( (c = fgetc( f1 )) != EOF )
      putchar( c ) ;

   if( ferror( f1 ) )
      perror("Error reading data from file" ) ;

   return 0 ;
}
```

Application 16.8

Write a program using fgetc() and fputc() to copy the contents of one file into another. Assume that the file names are supplied as command line arguments. What would happen if the names of alternative devices such as 'con' and 'prn' on an MS-DOS system were used in place of file names?

Application 16.8 Example file copy program using fgetc() and fputc().

```
#include <stdio.h>
#include <stdlib.h>
#include <errno.h>

int main( int argc , char *argv[ ] )
{
   FILE  *f1 , *f2 ;
   int     c ;

   if( argc != 3 )  {
      printf("Error: Usage Copy <pathlist 1>  <pathlist 2>\n") ;
      exit( 0 ) ;
   }
```

```
/* Now open device names and check for errors */

   f1 = fopen( argv[ 1 ] , "r" ) ;
   f2 = fopen( argv[ 2 ] , "w" ) ;

   if( (f1 == NULL ) || (f2 == NULL )) {
      printf("Error: Cannot open device %s and %s\n", argv[1] , argv[2] ) ;
      exit( EXIT_FAILURE ) ;
   }

/*
** Read a character from the file and save in 'c', while EOF is not returned by fgetc( )
** Then write the character to a second file using fputc( ).
** Note that fgetc( ) and fputc( ) may also return EOF when an error is encountered,
** so a check is made using ferror( )
*/

   printf("Copying file [ %s ] to [ %s ]\n", argv[1], argv[2]) ;

   while( (c = fgetc( f1 )) != EOF ) {
      if( fputc( c , f2 ) == EOF ) {
         perror("Error copying file: Copy Failed") ;
         exit( EXIT_FAILURE ) ;
      }
   }

/* Check that no error occurred during read */

   if( ferror( f1 ) )
      perror("Error Reading Source File: Copy Failed") ;

   if( fclose( f2 ))
      perror("Error Writing Destination File . . . ") ;

   return 0 ;
}
```

Application 16.9

Write a program that reads the contents of one text file and converts lower case characters to upper case and vice versa, before writing to a second file. The file names are to be supplied as command line arguments. The program should also convert spaces to underscores.

Application 16.9 Converting a text file to upper and lower case.

```
#include  <stdio.h>
#include  <stdlib.h>
#include  <errno.h>
#include  <ctype.h>

int main( int argc, char *argv[] )
{
  FILE  *f1, *f2 ;
  int     c ;

/* Check for correct number of arguments */

  if( argc != 3 )  {
    printf("Incorrect Parameters: Usage Progname <Source>  <Destination> ") ;
    exit( 0 ) ;
  }

/* Open/create both files and check for errors */

  f1 = fopen( argv[1], "r") ;
  f2 = fopen( argv[2], "w") ;

  if((f1 == NULL) || (f2 == NULL ))  {
    perror("Cannot Open Files . . . ") ;
    exit( EXIT_FAILURE );
  }

/* Repeatedly reads chars from the source file until unable to read any more */

  do  {
    c = fgetc( f1 ) ;

/* Perform text conversion, upper to lower and lower to upper */

    if( islower( c ) )
      c = toupper( c ) ;

    else if( isupper( c ) )
      c = tolower( c ) ;

/* Convert spaces to underscores */

    else if( c == ' ' )
      c = '_' ;
```

```
/* Write new character to destination device and check for error during read or write */

    } while( c != EOF && fputc( c, f2) != EOF ) ;

/* Check for any errors reading source and closing destination files */

    if( ferror( f1 ))
      puts("Error reading source file ... ") ;

    if( fclose( f2 ))
      perror("Error Writing Destination File ... ") ;

    return 0 ;
}
```

16.5.2 *Returning a character to a stream:* ungetc()

The function ungetc() can be used to return or push back a character to the stream from which it has previously been read. Only one character at most is guaranteed to be returned successfully. A subsequent read operation will return the pushed back character. Note that:

(1) The character itself is not *written* back to the device from which it originated, rather, the operating system accepts the character back into the stream buffer ready to be read again;

(2) If a call to fseek(), rewind() or fsetpos() is performed, after a character has been pushed back with ungetc() and prior to it being read again, the pushed back character is discarded.

Function prototype: ungetc()

The function prototype for ungetc() can be found in the header file <stdio.h> and is given below:

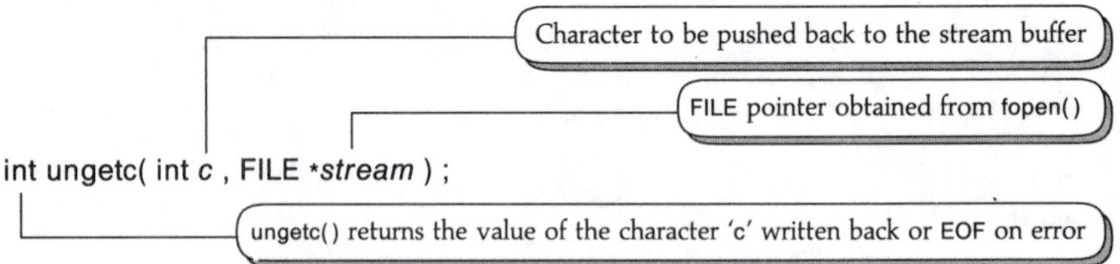

where 'c' is the value of the character to be pushed back to the stream and 'stream' is a pointer to the FILE structure identifying the stream and can only be obtained from a successful call to the functions fopen() or freopen().

Error considerations and returned values: ungetc( )
ungetc( ) returns the value of the character it pushed back to the stream or, if the character was not accepted back successfully, the value of the symbolic constant EOF defined in <stdio.h> is returned. This implies that EOF cannot be returned to the stream.

Applications of ungetc( )
ungetc( ) is most often used in applications where it is desirable to test the next character available on an input stream, prior to returning it for reading with another function. For example, a program may wish to test that the next character to be read is an acceptable numeric character prior to reading a number from the stream. In fact, the functions scanf( ) and fscanf( ) probably make use of ungetc( ).

16.6 Random access streams

Thus far, it has been assumed that a stream is connected to a **sequential** device. In other words, if a program wished to read a particular character from a device or file, then all preceding characters in the stream have to be read first. When the stream is attached to a disk file, however, this approach is often inconvenient and time consuming.

To speed up the access to data within a file, or other device supporting random access, the function fseek( ) may be called to allow a program to dynamically reposition its SPI anywhere within the stream and thus the file. The function ftell( ) exists to allow a program to determine the current position of its SPI. Note that not all classes of devices support random access; in particular, it is considered inappropriate to use fseek( ) with a stream attached to a terminal or printer.

The function rewind( ) is also defined to reset the position of the SPI back to the start of the file, although this is an operation that can easily be achieved with fseek( ). Two further functions fgetpos( ) and fsetpos( ) are also defined to save and restore the position of a stream's SPI.

16.6.1 *Stream repositioning:* fseek( )

The function fseek( ) permits an SPI to be moved to a specified position within the stream. The new position is defined in terms of a **relative offset** from one of three fixed positions for the stream, namely the start, end or current position of the SPI within the stream.

Function prototype: fseek( )
The function prototype for fseek( ) can be found in the header file <stdio.h> and is given below:

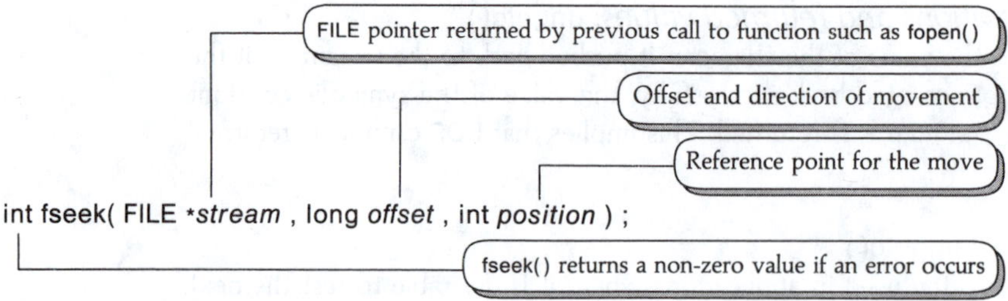
FILE pointer returned by previous call to function such as fopen()
Offset and direction of movement
Reference point for the move
int fseek(FILE *stream , long offset , int position) ;
fseek() returns a non-zero value if an error occurs

where 'stream' is a pointer to the FILE structure identifying the stream and can only be obtained from a successful call to the functions fopen(), freopen() or tmpfile(), and 'offset' specifies the direction and number of bytes that the SPI will be moved, relative to 'position'.

Positive values for 'offset' imply a move towards the *end* of the stream/file, while negative values imply a move towards the *start*. The parameter 'position' specifies the reference point for the move and can be described in terms of one of the three symbolic constants SEEK_SET, SEEK_CUR or SEEK_END described in Table 16.5.

Note that a long int is required for the parameter 'offset' to allow movements of greater than ±32k in each direction where an integer might only be represented by a 16 bit quantity.

Three symbolic constants are defined within the header file <stdio.h>, any of which may be used as the parameter 'position', to reference one of three possible starting points for the move. These symbols are shown in Table 16.5, while Table 16.6 contains some example calls to fseek() and their effect.

Table 16.5 Symbolic constants for use with fseek() as parameter 'position'.

Symbol	*Value*	*Reference point*
SEEK_SET	Usually 0	Beginning of a stream
SEEK_CUR	Usually 1	Current position in a stream
SEEK_END	Usually 2	End of a stream

Table 16.6 Example calls to fseek().

Example fseek() calls	*Interpretation*
fseek(fp, 0L, SEEK_SET)	Move to start of stream
fseek(fp, 100L, SEEK_SET)	Move 100 characters forward from start of stream
fseek(fp, 0L, SEEK_END)	Move to end of stream
fseek(fp, –100L, SEEK_END)	Move 100 characters backwards from end of stream
fseek(fp, –10L, SEEK_CUR)	Move back 10 characters in stream
fseek(fp, (long)(sizeof(array)), SEEK_CUR)	Move forwards by size of array
fseek(fp, –(long)(sizeof(struct p)), SEEK_CUR)	Move backwards by size of struct 'p'

Note that moving the current SPI for the stream either forwards or backwards using fseek( ), rewind( ) or fsetpos( ) and then closing the stream with fclose( ) does *not* set the EOF marker at that position. In other words, disk files can only grow in size, or be truncated to zero length when they are opened/created:

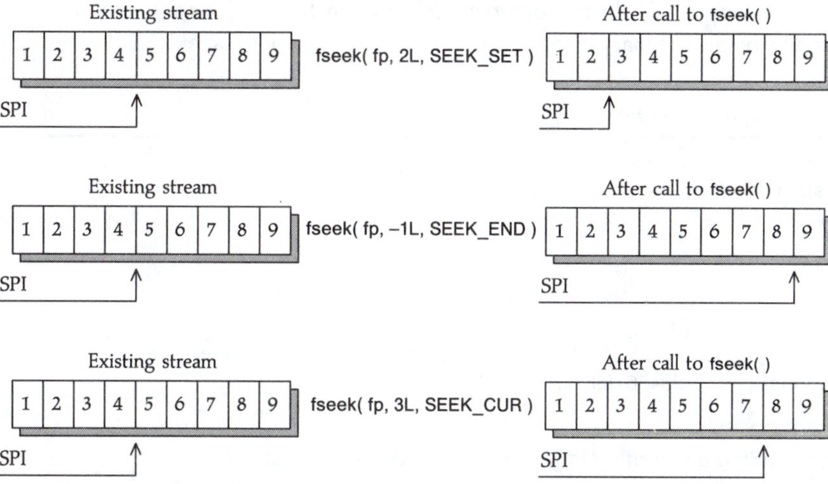

Finally, note that a file opened in append mode will always cause data written to the stream to be appended to the end of the file, even if fseek( ), rewind( ) or fsetpos( ) is used to reposition the SPI to a point other than the end of the file, prior to the write operation.

Error considerations and returned values: fseek( )

The function fseek( ) returns a non-zero value upon detection of an error and the value of the external int errno will then be set to a value indicating the cause of the failure. A suitable error message can be displayed using perror( ).

Note that an invalid offset which would attempt to place the SPI in front of the start of the file *should* be reported as an error (but at least one popular operating system does not do so). However, an attempt to place the SPI beyond the end of the stream is quite legal and is frequently employed with a subsequent write operation to set the size of a disk file. This is useful in applications where it is important to know that there will be sufficient space available on a disk before commencing a series of write operations. Note that the size of the file is only set when a write operation is performed at the new position. Once the size of the file has been set, fseek( ), rewind( ) or fsetpos( ) can be used to reset the stream position indicator to the start of the file. There may be alternative ways of achieving this with other non-standard library functions so check your C compiler manual for details.

Note that as a precaution when working with text streams (as opposed to binary streams), movements within the stream should be restricted to offsets of zero from the start, end or current position in the files, because of the different ways in which binary and text data may be represented within the stream and the fact that there may not be a one-to-one correspondence between data written to the stream and that written to the file. Alternatively, a value returned by the function ftell() may be used in place of 'offset', in which case 'position' must be relative to the start of the stream.

No restrictions are imposed on the use of fseek() for a binary stream. Some operating systems such as UNIX do not differentiate between text and binary streams and treat all streams as binary. Program 16.5 illustrates the use of fseek().

Program 16.5 Example use of fseek().

```
#include  <stdio.h>
#include  <stdlib.h>
#include  <errno.h>

int main( void )
{
  FILE  *f1 ;
  char  name[ ] = "Paul" ;
  char  telephone[ ] = "123456789 " ;

/*
** Open file for reading and writing in text mode and write data out
*/

  if( (f1 = fopen("personal.dat " , "w+" ) )==NULL)  {
    perror("Error opening 'personal.dat' " ) ;
    exit( EXIT_FAILURE ) ;
  }

  fprintf( f1 , "Name [ %s ], Telephone [ %s ] ", name , telephone ) ;

/*
** Seek backwards to the start of the stream and Read name and telephone
** data back. Note because this is a text stream, offsets of zero are used.
*/

  fseek( f1 , 0L , SEEK_SET ) ;
  fscanf( f1, "Name [ %s ], Telephone [ %s ] %s ", name, telephone ) ;

/*
** Just check for an error or EOF condition
*/

  if( ferror( f1 ) || ferror( f1 ))
    perror("Error reading back data ... ") ;

  puts( name ) ;
  puts( telephone ) ;

  return 0 ;
}
```

16.6.2 *Moving the SPI to the start of a stream:* rewind()

The function rewind() repositions the SPI to the beginning of the stream and clears any error or EOF conditions that may be associated with it. The function prototype for rewind() can be found in the header file <stdio.h> and is often defined in terms of a call to the functions fseek() and clearerr(), as shown below. No data is returned by rewind():

```
void rewind( FILE *stream )
{
  fseek( stream, 0L, SEEK_SET ) ;
  clearerr( stream ) ;
}
```

FILE pointer returned by function such as fopen()

Move to start of stream

Clear EOF and *error* flags for stream

Program 16.6 shows an application of the function rewind().

Program 16.6 Example use of rewind().

```
#include   <stdio.h>
#include   <stdlib.h>
#include   <errno.h>

int main( void )
{
  FILE  *fp ;
  int    c ;

/* Now create or truncate existing file for reading and writing text */

  if( (fp = fopen("joe.txt", "w+")) == NULL )  {
    perror("Cannot open file joe.txt for writing ") ;
    exit( EXIT_FAILURE ) ;
  }

/* Set mode to write by writing text to file */

  fprintf(fp, "Hello World\n") ;

/* Move to the start of file and clear any error and EOF flags */

  rewind( fp ) ;

/* Display contents of file */

  while ((c = fgetc( fp ) ) != EOF )
    putchar( c ) ;

  return 0 ;
}
```

16.6.3 *Determining the position of the SPI in a stream:* ftell()

The function ftell() returns the position of the SPI for the stream, in terms of the number of bytes into the stream that the SPI is positioned. The function returns a long int to cater for systems where an integer might only be implemented as a 16 bit quantity.

Function prototype: ftell()

The function prototype for ftell() can be found in the header file <stdio.h> and is given below:

```
long ftell( FILE *stream ) ;
```

FILE pointer returned by previous call to function such as fopen()
ftell() returns position of SPI on success or EOF cast to a long on failure

where 'stream' is a pointer to a FILE structure identifying the stream and can only be obtained from a successful call to the functions fopen(), freopen() or tmpfile().

Error considerations and returned values: ftell()

The function ftell() returns the current value of the SPI associated with the stream or, if an error occurs, the value (long)(EOF), which is defined in <stdio.h>, in which case the value of the external int errno is set to a value indicating the cause of the failure.

Application 16.10

Write a program that displays the size of a file in bytes on the operator's terminal. The file name is to be supplied as a command line argument.

Application 16.10 Example use of ftell() to determine the size of a file.

```
#include  <stdio.h>
#include  <stdlib.h>
#include  <errno.h>

int main( int argc, char *argv[ ] )
{
  FILE  *fp ;

  if( argc != 2 )  {
    printf("Error: Usage Len <filename> ... ") ;
    exit( 0 ) ;
  }
```

```
    if(( fp = fopen(argv[ 1 ] , "r" )) == NULL ) {
      perror("Error cannot open fred.txt for reading") ;
      exit( EXIT_FAILURE ) ;
    }

/* Seek to end of file */

    if( fseek( fp , 0L , SEEK_END ) ) {
      perror("Cannot seek to end of file . . . ") ;
      exit( EXIT_FAILURE ) ;
    }

/*  Display current position of SPI */

    printf("File size of file %s is %ld bytes \n" , argv[ 1 ], ftell( fp )) ;
    return 0 ;
}
```

16.6.4 *Saving and restoring stream positions:* fgetpos( ) *and* fsetpos( )

The function fgetpos( ) may be used to save the current position of the stream's SPI, while fsetpos( ) may be used to restore the value of SPI to a value previously obtained with fgetpos( ). Their function prototypes can be found in the header file <stdio.h> and are given below:

FILE pointer returned by previous call to function such as fopen( )

Pointer to an object of type fpos_t into which current value of SPI is saved

```
int fgetpos( FILE *stream , fpos_t *ptr ) ;
int fsetpos( FILE *stream , const fpos_t *ptr ) ;
```

Both functions return zero on success or non-zero on failure

where 'stream' is a pointer to a FILE structure identifying the stream and may be obtained from a successful call to the functions fopen( ), freopen( ) or tmpfile( ) and 'ptr' is a pointer to an object of type fpos_t that can be used to hold the value of the SPI. The data type fpos_t is usually type defined (within <stdio.h>) as a long integer on a small or medium sized system.

If the programmer wishes to introduce a variable into which the value of the SPI could be saved, that variable should, for reasons of portability, be defined as being of type fpos_t, rather than long int. This is because fpos_t might be implemented in a way that allowed it to hold more than 32 bits of data, which would be useful in applications where access to disk files greater than 4 Gbytes in size were necessary.

Error considerations and returned values: fgetpos() *and* fsetpos()

Both functions return zero upon success. If an error occurs, the error flag for the stream will be set and the value of the external int errno is set to indicate the source of the error. Note that these functions are often implemented on small systems using fseek() and ftell(), as shown below:

```
int fgetpos(FILE *stream, fpos_t *pos)
{
   return ((*pos = ftell(stream)) == -1) ? -1 : 0 ;
}

int fsetpos(FILE *stream, const fpos_t *pos)
{
   return ( fseek(stream, *pos, SEEK_SET) ) ;
}
```

so the same comments relating to offsets used by fseek() within text streams may also apply here. The reader is also referred to the notes relating to append modes in Section 16.6.1. Program 16.7 illustrates the use of these functions.

Program 16.7 Example use of fsetpos() and fgetpos().

```
#include  <stdio.h>
#include  <stdlib.h>
#include  <errno.h>

int main( void )
{
   FILE    *f1 ;
   char    buff[ BUFSIZ ] ;
   fpos_t  x ;

   if( (f1 = fopen("joe.txt", "w+" ) ) == NULL )  {
      perror("Cannot open joe.txt ... ") ;
      exit( EXIT_FAILURE ) ;
   }

/* Save file position */
```

```
    if( fgetpos( f1 , &x ) )  {
        perror("Cannot get File position ... ") ;
        exit( EXIT_FAILURE ) ;
    }

/* Write out text */

    if( fprintf( f1 , "Hello\n") == EOF )  {
        perror("Cannot write to file position ... ") ;
        exit( EXIT_FAILURE ) ;
    }

/* Restore file position */

    if( fsetpos( f1 , &x ) )  {
        perror("Cannot set File position ... ") ;
        exit( EXIT_FAILURE ) ;
    }

/* Read back the text and display it on terminal */

    if( fscanf( f1, "%s", buff ) != 1 )  {
        perror("Cannot read data ... ") ;
        exit( EXIT_FAILURE ) ;
    }

    printf("%s\n", buff) ;

    return 0 ;
}
```

16.7 Manipulating the stream buffer

We have already seen how high level stream manipulation functions such as fgets( ) and fprintf( ) make use of automatic stream buffers to queue incoming and outgoing data between device and program. Most of the time this approach works fine, with the operating system allocating and choosing a size and mode of operation for the buffer in accordance with the characteristics of the device. Thus, programmers are generally not too concerned by its operation.

There are, however, occasions when the size and mode of buffering adopted by the operating system may not be the most appropriate for the application. That is not to say that it will not work; it simply means that the buffer size or location may not suit the needs of the application. For this reason the standard library defines the function setvbuf( ) to permit the program to define the type, size and location of the stream buffer used. The function prototype can be found in the header file <stdio.h> and is given below:

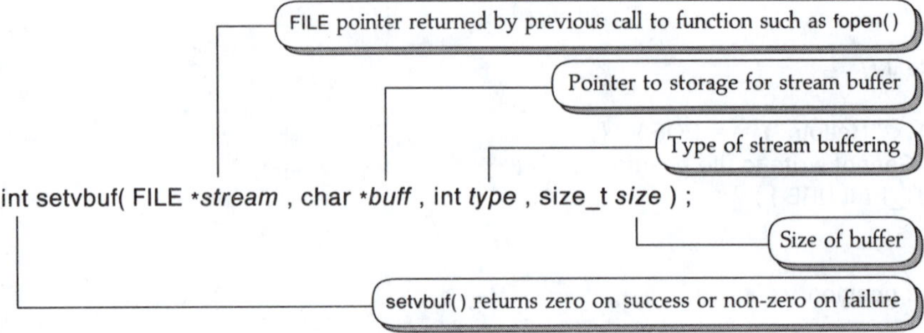
FILE pointer returned by previous call to function such as fopen()
Pointer to storage for stream buffer
Type of stream buffering
int setvbuf(FILE *stream , char *buff , int type , size_t size) ;
Size of buffer
setvbuf() returns zero on success or non-zero on failure

where 'stream' is a pointer to a FILE structure identifying the stream and can be obtained from a successful call to the functions fopen(), freopen() or tmpfile(), and 'type' defines the mode of buffering used by the stream. The parameters 'buff' and 'size' define the buffer's location and size.

Storage for the stream buffer can be allocated internally by the operating system, if the parameter 'buff' is a NULL pointer, otherwise it is assumed that 'buff' points to the start of a program allocated stream buffer, which is typically an array or an area of memory allocated by malloc() or calloc().

Three modes of stream buffering are offered and three symbolic constants are defined in the header file <stdio.h>, which can be used as arguments for the parameter 'type'. These are shown in Table 16.7.

Note that the header files <stdio.h> and <stddef.h> define the new data type size_t as an unsigned integral quantity. Should the programmer wish to introduce a variable into a program to hold, for example, the 'size' argument to setvbuf(), it should be declared for reasons of portability as size_t and not simply as int. Note the sizeof operator also yields a result of type size_t, making this an ideal way of determining the size of an array that could be used as a stream buffer.

Table 16.7 Symbolic constant for use as the parameter 'type' to setvbuf().

Symbol	*Explanation*
_IOFBF	The stream is fully buffered. The next input operation will attempt to fill the buffer, while outgoing operations wait until the buffer is full. This is the normal default mode for disk type devices on many operating systems.
_IOLBF	Line buffering. The next input operation will attempt to fill the buffer. Outgoing data is written to the device – that is, the buffer is flushed – when a new line is sent. Terminal and printer buffering is often implemented using this mode.
_IONBF	No buffering. Parameters 'buff' and 'size' are ignored and transfer of data between device and program is carried out on a character by character basis.

Note also that stream buffering can only be altered *before* any read and write operations have been performed on it, or after a call to the function fseek( ).

Error considerations and returned values: setvbuf( )

setvbuf( ) returns zero if the function was called successfully. Make sure, if you are allocating your own storage for the stream buffer, that you do not deallocate this before the stream is closed.

16.7.1 *Manipulating the stream buffer:* setbuf( )

The function setbuf( ) is simply a variation on the function setvbuf( ). The function prototype can be found in the header file <stdio.h> and is given below:

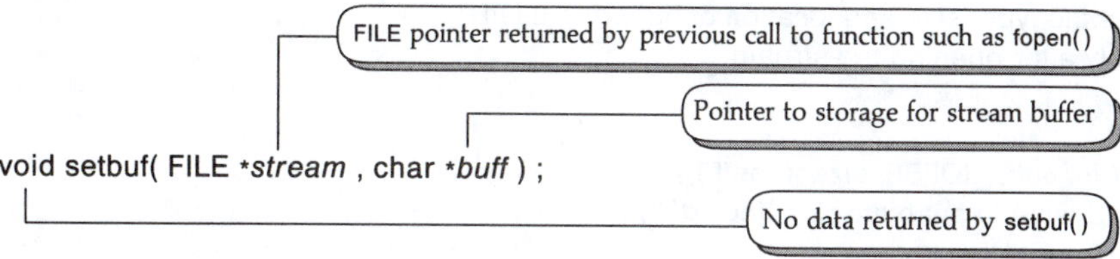
FILE pointer returned by previous call to function such as fopen( )
Pointer to storage for stream buffer
void setbuf(FILE *stream , char *buff) ;
No data returned by setbuf( )

where 'stream' is a FILE pointer that identifies the stream and can be obtained from a successful call to the functions fopen( ), freopen( ) or tmpfile( ) and 'buff' defines the buffer's location.

The operation of setbuf( ) is simple. If the parameter 'buff' is NULL, then no stream buffering is used and the following two statements are equivalent:

```
setbuf( fp, NULL ) ;
setvbuf( fp, NULL, _IONBF, 0 ) ;
```

If, however, the parameter 'buff' is *not* NULL, it is assumed to be the address of a buffer that can be used in mode _IOFBF (see Table 16.6) and must be at least BUFSIZ bytes in size; thus the following two statements are equivalent, where array has been defined as char array[BUFSIZ].

```
setbuf( fp , array ) ;
setvbuf( fp, array , _IOFBF, BUFSIZ ) ;
```

Program 16.8 attempts to open a disk file and set the type of buffering to line buffering and the buffer size to 2000 bytes.

Program 16.8 Example use of setvbuf().

```
#include   <stdio.h>
#include   <stdlib.h>
#include   <errno.h>

int main( void )
{
    FILE  *fp ;
    char  buff[ 2000 ] ;

    if( (fp = fopen("joe.txt", "w+")) == NULL )  {
        perror("Cannot open file 'joe.txt' ") ;
        exit( EXIT_FAILURE ) ;
    }

/*
** Now define the type, size and location of buffering used
** immediately after opening the stream
*/

    if( setvbuf( fp, buff, _IOFBF, sizeof( buff ))) {
        perror("Unable to set buffer for 'joe.txt' ") ;
        exit( EXIT_FAILURE ) ;
    }

    ...
    ...
}
```

16.8 File removal and renaming: rename() and remove()

The standard library defines the functions rename() and remove() which permit the renaming or removal of disk files from a specified disk/directory. Good programming practice would dictate that the file is closed prior to renaming or removing it. Other functions may be supported by the standard library to include the creation and removal of directories and the changing of directories, but these are not standardized so check your C compiler manual for details.

Note that some operating systems permit files of zero length to remain in existence, and remove() is the only easy way to get rid of such files. The function rename() allows files to be moved from one location to another, if the old and new file names contain different disk/directory names in their pathlist.

Function prototypes: rename( ) *and* remove( )

Both function prototypes can be found in the header file <stdio.h> and are given below:

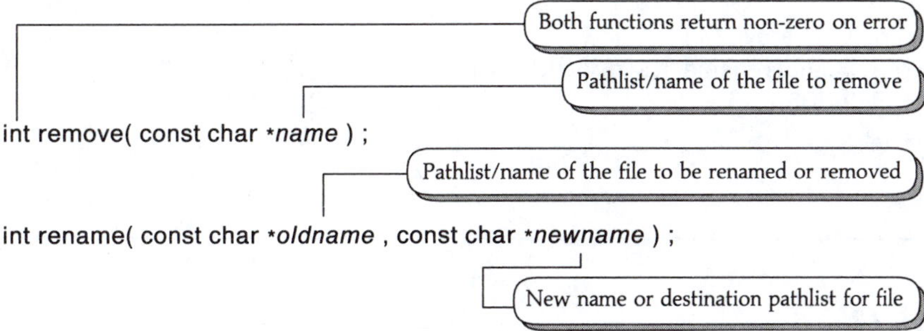

where all parameters are text strings that conform with the standard disk file pathlist naming conventions for the host operating system and are thus a possible source of non-portable code unless well-documented.

Error considerations and returned values: rename( ) *and* remove( )

Both functions return non-zero if their operation is unsuccessful. Note that renaming or moving a file where another file already exists with that name is not considered an error, and will result in the loss of the original file with that name. Note that the low level function access( ) (not defined by the standard but commonly available) may be called to check for the existence of a file perhaps prior to renaming or removing it.

Application 16.11

Write a program that renames and/or moves a file from one source/file name to another, using pathlists supplied as command line arguments, the command line format being of the form:

```
rename oldfile newfile
```

Application 16.11 Example use of rename( ).

```
#include    <stdio.h>
#include    <stdlib.h>
#include    <errno.h>

int main( int argc, char *argv[ ] )
{
```

```
    if( argc != 3 )  {
        puts("Insufficient arguments: rename <oldname>  <newname>") ;
        exit( 0 ) ;
    }

    if( rename( argv[1 ] , argv[ 2 ] ) )  {
        printf("Error: cannot rename %s to %s\n", argv[1], argv[2] ) ;
        exit( EXIT_FAILURE ) ;
    }
    return 0 ;
}
```

Application 16.12

Write a program that deletes a file using pathlists supplied as command line arguments. The program should work with wildcards of the form *.*, p???.* and so on. The command line format should be of the form:

```
del filename
```

Application 16.12 Example use of remove().

```
#include  <stdio.h>
#include  <stdlib.h>
#include  <errno.h>
#include  <ctype.h>

int main( int argc, char *argv[ ] )
{
    int i =1 ;

    if( argc  < 2 )  {
        puts("Insufficient arguments: del <filename>") ;
        exit( 0 ) ;
    }

/*
** Step through each of the file names present on the command line
** Note that wildcards such as *.* will be expanded by the shell into separate
** command line argument within argv[ ]
*/

    while( i <= argc )  {
        printf("Delete file ... [ %s ] ?", argv[ i ] ) ;
```

```
/*
** If the operator is sure he or she wants to delete the file
*/

        if( toupper( getchar()) == 'Y' )  {
          if( remove( argv[ i ] ) )  {
            printf("Error: Cannot Delete File %s ... \n", argv[ i ] ) ;
            exit( EXIT_FAILURE ) ;
          }

/*
** Remove CR from keyboard path
*/

          fflush( stdin ) ;
        }
        i ++ ;
    }

    return 0 ;
}
```

16.9 Creating temporary files and file names

It is often desirable within a program to be able to create a temporary 'scratch' file perhaps to hold temporary data read from a disk. The problem for the programmer comes in generating the name for the temporary file in such a way that:

(1) It is portable between different operating systems with different naming conventions and syntax;

(2) It does not conflict with the name of any file currently in the directory.

The functions tmpfile() and tmpnam() described below are designed to overcome these problems.

16.9.1 *Creating a temporary file:* tmpfile()

The function tmpfile() may be used to create and open a unique file in the current directory in **binary update** mode using the function fopen() in conjunction with the mode argument "wb+". If successful, a FILE pointer is returned to the program, which can be saved for use with subsequent read/write operations to the file.

Function prototype: tmpfile()

The function prototype for tmpfile() can be found in the header file <stdio.h> and is given below:

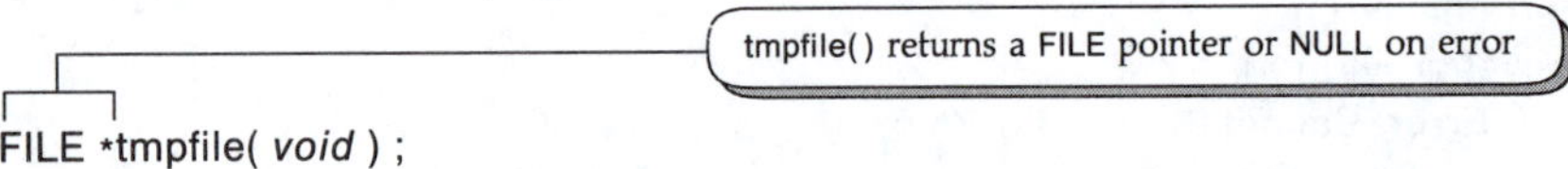
tmpfile() returns a FILE pointer or NULL on error
FILE *tmpfile(void) ;

Note that such files are automatically deleted either when the program terminates or when the file is closed. If the file cannot be created (due to the media being write protected, for example), then tmpfile() returns a NULL pointer and errno is set to a value indicating the source of the error.

16.9.2 *Generating a temporary file name:* tmpnam()

The function tmpnam() is designed to generate a uniquely portable file name. Note that tmpnam() does *not* create the file, only a name. The file can subsequently be created with a call to the function fopen(), which gives the programmer more control over the mode of operation, rather than simply assuming "wb+".

Function prototype: tmpnam()

The function prototype for tmpnam() can be found in the header file <stdio.h> and is given below:

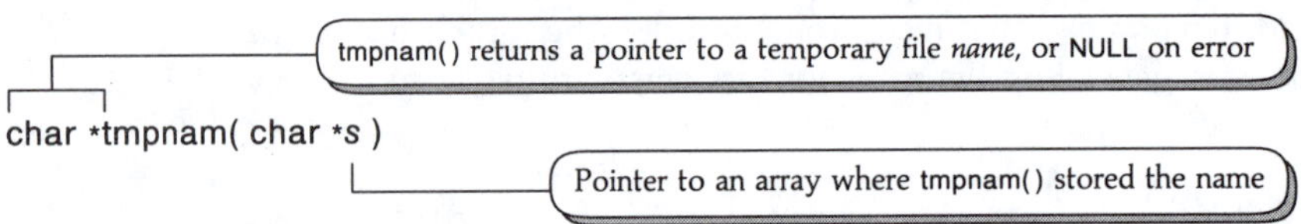
tmpnam() returns a pointer to a temporary file *name*, or NULL on error
char *tmpnam(char *s)
Pointer to an array where tmpnam() stored the name

where 's' is a pointer to a char array into which tmpnam() will store the ('\0' terminated) name it has generated, provided 's' is not a NULL pointer. It is the programmer's responsibility to ensure that sufficient storage has been allocated to hold the file name. Regardless of this, tmpnam() also saves the file name internally in static storage defined by the function, and a pointer to this internally stored name is always returned by tmpnam(), assuming one can be generated.

Note that if the program relies on the static storage area allocated by tmpnam() to save the file name, rather than copying it to another area allocated by the program, subsequent calls to tmpnam() will overwrite this name.

Note also that the function tmpnam() may be called successfully at most TMP_MAX times within a program to allow at most TMP_MAX temporary unique file names to be created. Each name is guaranteed to be no greater than L_tmpnam characters in length. Both symbols are defined within the header file <stdio.h>.

Also note that the **removal** of any temporary files created subsequently by the program using names generated by tmpnam() is the responsibility of the programmer.

Error considerations and returned values: tmpnam()

tmpnam() returns a NULL pointer if the name cannot be created, or a pointer to the name if successful. Program 16.9 demonstrates the use of both tmpnam() and tmpfile().

Program 16.9 Example use of tmpnam() and tmpfile().

```
#include   <stdio.h>
#include   <stdlib.h>

int main( void )
{
   char  buff [ L_tmpnam ] ;
   FILE  *fp1, *fp2 ;

/* Generate temporary filename and save in array 'buff' */

   if( tmpnam( buff ) == NULL )  {
      perror("Cannot generate temporary file name ... ") ;
      exit( EXIT_FAILURE ) ;
   }

/* Now attempt to generate a temporary file with tmpnam() */

   if( (fp1 = fopen( buff , "w+")) == NULL )  {
      perror("Cannot open temporary file ... ") ;
      exit( EXIT_FAILURE ) ;
   }

/*
** Now attempt to generate a temporary file with tmpfile(), if this fails, then we must
** remove the file generated by tmpnam(), since this is not automatic
*/

   if( (fp2 = tmpfile( )) == NULL)  {
      printf( "Cannot generate temporary file (tmpfile()) ... \n") ;
      fclose( fp1 ) ;
      remove( buff ) ;
      exit( EXIT_FAILURE ) ;
   }

/* Rest of program to manipulate the file here */
   ...
   ...
}
```

16.10 Binary streams

Thus far, our discussions have centred primarily upon the use and applications of text streams, that is to say, streams where data is written to the stream/device in the form of text characters. As such, text streams are ideal for connecting programs to character based devices such as terminals or printers, where the overheads in converting the data stored in memory in binary form into an equivalent text form are insignificant, since the speed of the device is often more limiting than the speed at which such data can be converted.

Unfortunately, this is not the case when large amounts of data, such as the contents of arrays or structures, have to be rapidly saved and recovered from a disk file. Here the binary to text conversion could significantly slow down the rate at which data can be exchanged between program and file. If, however, the data could be stored to disk in its natural binary form, then the conversion to text characters would be unnecessary and the transfer could proceed more rapidly. For this reason, C supports binary streams, where data can be written to and recovered from a device without the need to convert it to an alternative text form.

To understand why binary streams are more efficient than their textual equivalents, let us consider the example of writing a long int variable 'a' (assumed to be 32 bits in size) to a text stream attached to a printer. Since the variable is probably represented in two's complement binary, a format that would not be understood by a printer, we must call upon the services of fprintf() to perform a binary to text conversion of 'a', so that it can be written to the stream as a sequence of characters (probably ASCII) with the following statement:

```
fprintf( stream , "%d\n" , a ) ;
```

Now, although just 4 bytes of data were originally required to represent the variable 'a' in memory, converting this to an equivalent text form, where each character is represented by one byte, generally yields an output that is considerably larger than the storage requirements of the original variable. For example the integer value '−2000000000' could be represented in binary form as a signed 4 byte (32 bit) value. The equivalent text representation requires 11 characters (bytes), nearly three times the size.

Consider, now, a program faced with the prospect of saving an array of 1000 such long ints to a disk file. Using fprintf() to save each one individually could introduce considerable overheads, as the value of each long int is converted to its equivalent text form, resulting in perhaps 11 000 characters having to be transferred to the file. Then, of course, there is the time consuming job of recovering that data using fscanf().

Imagine what improvements could be gained, if the data could simply be **dumped** from memory in its binary form directly onto a disk file, without *any* conversion. Three obvious benefits would be gained by this:

- The speed of the operation would increase dramatically, since no conversion and interpretation of the data would need to be performed;
- The amount of disk space required to store the data would be exactly equivalent to the amount of memory required to hold that data in the first place; in other words, there would be no wastage;
- More than one element could be written to the file with one operation. Perhaps the contents of a whole array could be saved or recovered with one single operation.

The only drawback to this approach is that the file would then not be suitable for listing to a screen or printer, but provided this is understood, it should not present a problem.

To support the manipulation of binary streams, two additional functions, fread() and fwrite() are provided to permit the reading and writing of binary data. In addition, fopen() recognizes modified mode arguments to indicate that a binary stream is being opened/created. These modes were summarized in Table 16.1 and are similar to their text mode except for the inclusion of the letter 'b', for example "wb", "rb", "ab", "wb+", "rb+" and "ab+".

These modes are important, since they indicate that a one-to-one correspondence between stream and device data is required and that no translation of, for example, the new line character '\n' into a carriage return line feed sequence is to be performed.

16.10.1 *Writing binary data:* fwrite()

The function fwrite() permits the writing of binary data to a stream. Any data, ranging in size from a single char to perhaps a whole array or structure, can be written with just one single operation.

Function prototype: fwrite()

The function prototype for fwrite() can be found in the header file <stdio.h> and is given below:

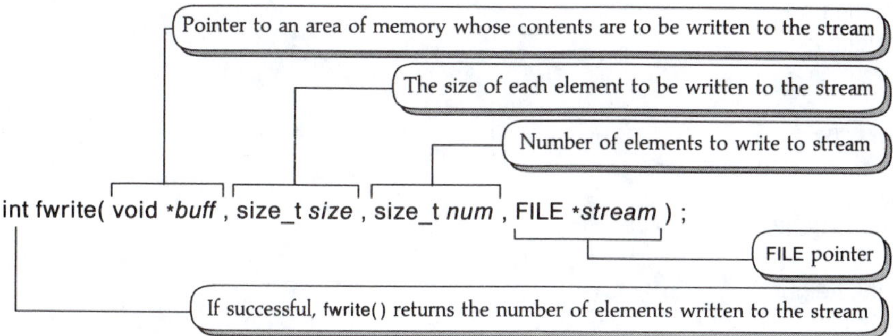
Pointer to an area of memory whose contents are to be written to the stream
The size of each element to be written to the stream
Number of elements to write to stream
int fwrite(void *buff , size_t size , size_t num , FILE *stream) ;
FILE pointer
If successful, fwrite() returns the number of elements written to the stream

where 'stream' is a FILE pointer identifying the device and can be obtained from a successful call to the functions fopen(), freopen() or tmpfile(). The pointer 'buff' points to the start of an area of memory whose contents are to be written to the stream. Note that because 'buff' is a void pointer, it is permissible for it to point to any type of data.

The parameter 'size' is the size in bytes of each element stored at the address pointed to by 'buff', while 'num' indicates the number of elements to be written to the stream. Note that the standard defines the type of 'size' and 'num' as size_t, defined in the header files <stdio.h> and <stddef.h>, generally as an unsigned int. For reasons of portability , the sizeof operator should be used to determine the size of these two quantities.

Note that the product of the parameters 'size' and 'num' indicates the total number of bytes to be written to the stream starting at the address supplied in the parameter 'buff'. It is up to you how you express this product in terms of the two parameters 'size' and 'num' (see examples below).

Error considerations and returned values: fwrite()

The function fwrite() returns the number of elements written to the stream; that is, the value of the parameter 'num' if the operation is performed successfully. If the returned value differs from 'num', then an error has occurred. The error flag will be set within the FILE structure and will persist until cleared by a call to the function clearerr() or rewind(). The value of this flag can be tested with the function ferror(), while the external int errno will be set to a value indicating the cause of the error.

Application 16.13

Write a program to allow an operator to enter details about the name, age, weight and height of 20 individuals. This data should be saved to disk in binary format.

Application 16.13 Example use of fwrite().

```
#include <stdio.h>
#include <stdlib.h>
#include <errno.h>

#define NUM 20

struct details {
    char name[ BUFSIZ ] ;
    int  age ;
    float weight, height ;
} people[ NUM ] ;
```

```
int main( int argc, char *argv[ ] )
{
  FILE  *fp ;
  int    i ;
  char  buff[ BUFSIZ ] ;

/* Check file name supplied on command line */

  if( argc != 2 )  {
    printf("Error: Usage progname <pathlist>\n") ;
    exit( 0 ) ;
  }

/* Open/create file in binary mode */

  if( (fp = fopen(argv[ 1 ], "wb")) == NULL )  {
    printf("Error: Cannot Open file [ %s ] for Binary Write ... ", argv[ 1 ] ) ;
    exit( EXIT_FAILURE ) ;
  }

/* Now read details */

  for ( i = 0; i < NUM ; i++ )  {
    printf("Enter Name ... ") ; gets( people[ i ].name ) ;
    printf("Enter Age ... ") ; people[ i ].age = atoi( gets( buff )) ;
    printf("Enter Weight ... ") ; people[ i ].weight = atof( gets( buff )) ;
    printf("Enter Height ... ") ; people[ i ].height = atof( gets( buff )) ;
    putchar('\n') ;
  }

/*
** Now write out the contents of the array 'people'. Note we could have
** saved the array with a statement such as
** if( fwrite( people, sizeof( struct details), NUM) != NUM) { etc.
*/

  if( fwrite( people , sizeof( people ) , 1 , fp ) != 1 )  {
    perror("Error Saving Data to File ... ") ;
    exit( EXIT_FAILURE ) ;
  }

  if( fclose( fp ) )
    perror("Error Writing Data to File ... " ) ;

  return 0;
}
```

Application 16.14

Application 16.14 is typical of that frequently seen in simple data acquisition systems, where samples of data have been gathered from an analog to digital converter and stored in two arrays prior to saving to a disk file.

Application 16.14 Example use of fwrite().

```
#include  <stdio.h>
#include  <stdlib.h>
#include  <errno.h>

/*
** Two arrays that hold sampled data from channel 0 and 1
** from the 16 bit analog to digital converter
*/

unsigned short adc0[ 1024 ] ;                         /* A to D data */
unsigned short adc1[ 1024 ] ;

int main( void )
{
  FILE  *fp ;
  int    a1 , a2 ;
  void  gather_data( unsigned short *, int ) ;   /* function prototype*/

/* Now open a disk file to save results in binary mode */

  if( (fp = fopen("adcdat.bin" , "wb" )) == NULL )  {
     perror("Error opening binary file for writing ") ;
     exit( EXIT_FAILURE ) ;
  }

/*
** Go and Gather 1024 samples from channels 0 and 1 of the ADC
** The function gather_data( ) is assumed to exist in a library that is linked
** in at run time
*/

  gather_data( adc0, 1024 ) ;
  gather_data( adc1, 1024 ) ;

/*
** Save the contents of the two arrays to the disk. Note the two different ways
** used to specify the size of the data and each element
*/

  a1 = fwrite( adc0 , sizeof( short ) , 1024 , fp ) ;
  a2 = fwrite( adc1 , sizeof( adc1) , 1 , fp ) ;
```

```
/* Now check to see if data saved correctly */

    if( ( a1 != 1024) || ( a2 != 1 ) )  {
        perror("Error writing to file ... ") ;
        exit( EXIT_FAILURE ) ;
    }

    if( fclose( fp ) )
        perror( "Error closing file ... ") ;

    return 0 ;
}
```

16.10.2 *Reading binary data:* fread()

The function fread() performs the converse operation of fwrite() and can be used to read large quantities of binary data from a stream. The data read is stored directly into memory with no conversions being performed.

Function prototype: fread()

The function prototype for fread() can be found in the header file <stdio.h> and is given below:

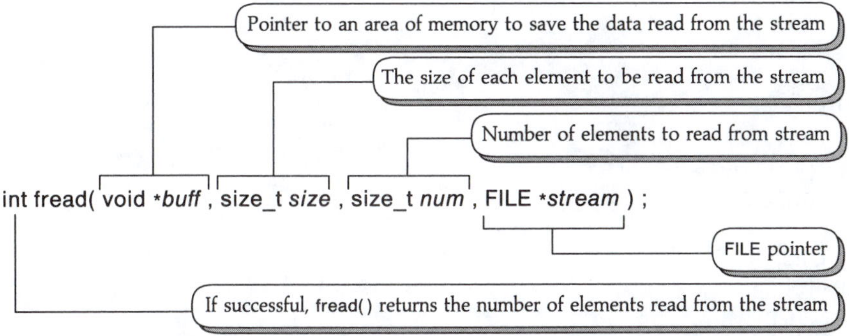
Pointer to an area of memory to save the data read from the stream
The size of each element to be read from the stream
Number of elements to read from stream
int fread(void *buff , size_t size , size_t num , FILE *stream) ;
FILE pointer
If successful, fread() returns the number of elements read from the stream

where 'stream' is a FILE pointer identifying the device and can only be obtained from a successful call to the functions fopen(), freopen() or tmpfile(). The pointer 'buff' points to the start of an area of memory where the read data will be stored. Because 'buff' is a void pointer, it is permissible for it to point to any type of data.

The parameter 'size' is the size in bytes of each element to be read from the stream, while 'num' is the total number of elements to be read. Note that the standard defines the type of 'size' and 'num' as size_t, which is defined in the header files <stdio.h> and <stddef.h>, generally as an unsigned int.

For reasons of portability, the sizeof operator should be used to determine the size of these two objects. The elements read from the stream will be stored in memory at successive bytes commencing at the address supplied by the parameter 'buff'.

Note that the product of the parameters 'size' and 'num' indicates the total number of bytes to be read from the stream. It is up to you how you choose to express this product in terms of the two parameters (see examples below).

Error considerations and returned values: fread()

fread() returns the number of elements read from the stream; that is, the value of the parameter 'num', if all goes well. If this returned value differs from the parameter 'num', then an error or EOF condition has occurred. The error or EOF flag will be set within the FILE structure and will persist until cleared by a call to the function clearerr() or rewind(). The values of these two flags can be tested with the functions ferror() and feof(), while the external int errno may, in the event of an error, be set to a value indicating the cause of the error.

Application 16.15

Write a program that reads back the information about individuals' details saved to disk by Application 16.13.

Application 16.15 Example use of fread().

```
#include  <stdio.h>
#include  <stdlib.h>
#include  <errno.h>

#define   NUM 20

struct details  {
   char  name[ BUFSIZ ] ;
   int    age ;
   float  weight, height ;
} people[ NUM ] ;

int main( int argc, char *argv[ ] )
{
   FILE  *fp;
   int    i ;

/* Check file name supplied on command line */

   if( argc != 2 )  {
      printf("Error: Usage progname   <pathlist>\n") ;
      exit( 0 ) ;
   }
```

```
/* Open/create file in binary read mode */

    if( (fp = fopen(argv[ 1 ] , "rb")) == NULL )  {
        printf("Error: Cannot Open File [ %s ] for Binary Read ... ", argv[ 1 ] ) ;
        exit( EXIT_FAILURE ) ;
    }

/*
** Now read back the contents of the array 'people'.
** Note we could have saved the array with a statement
** such as if( fread( people, sizeof( struct details), NUM) != NUM) { etc.
*/

    if( fread( people , sizeof( people ) , 1 , fp ) != 1 )  {
        if( ferror( fp ) || feof( fp ))  {
            perror("Error: Could not read back all the Data ... ") ;
            exit( EXIT_FAILURE ) ;
        }
    }

/* Now display details */

    for ( i = 0; i < NUM ; i++ )  {
        printf("Name ... [ %s ]\n", people[ i ].name ) ;
        printf("Age ... [ %d ]\n", people[ i ].age ) ;
        printf("Weight ... [ %f ]\n", people[ i ].weight ) ;
        printf("Height ... [ %d ]\n\n", people[ i ].height ) ;
    }

    return 0 ;
}
```

Application 16.16

Write a program to read back the analog to digital converter data saved to disk by Application 16.14.

Application 16.16 Reading back analog to digital converter data.

```
#include   <stdio.h>
#include   <stdlib.h>
#include   <errno.h>

unsigned short adc0[ 1024 ] ;  /* A to D data */
unsigned short adc1[1024 ] ;
```

```
int main( void )
{
  FILE  *fp ;
  int    a1 , a2 ;

/* Now open a disk file to read data in binary mode */

  if( (fp = fopen("adcdata.bin" , "rb" )) == NULL )  {
    perror("Error opening binary file for reading ... ") ;
    exit( EXIT_FAILURE ) ;
  }

/* Read the contents of the two arrays from the disk file */

  a1 = fread( adc0 , sizeof( short ) , 1024 , fp ) ;
  a2 = fread( adc1 , sizeof( adc1) , 1 , fp ) ;

/* Now check to see if performed correctly */

  if( ( a1 != 1024) || ( a2 != 1 ) )  {
    perror("Error reading from file ... ") ;
    exit( EXIT_FAILURE ) ;
  }

  return 0 ;
}
```

16.11 A unified I/O structure

Many operating systems have what is commonly known as a **unified I/O structure** that enables the operating system to access all devices within the system in the same manner using the same stream library functions. Such devices might include:

- Disk storage: floppy, optical and fixed disks.
- Terminals/printers: serial link based.
- Pipelines: interprocess communication.
- Network: Ethernet, MAP and so on.
- Specialized: A/D and D/A converters IEEE-488.

If your operating system supports this unified approach, you may be wondering why the functions getchar( ) and putchar( ) were specifically written to work with the user's terminal and cannot be used to communicate with other devices. Likewise, how is the operating system able to redirect a program's input and output to an alternative device in a way that is transparent to the program? These issues will now be discussed.

When a program is run, three text streams are assumed to have been automatically opened by the operating system. These streams are known as the standard input, output and error message streams and are normally connected to the operator's terminal unless the program's I/O has been redirected to another device.

16.11.1 *The file pointers* stdin, stdout *and* stderr

The three FILE pointers generated as a result of the operating system having automatically opening these three streams are given the symbolic names stdin, stdout, and stderr, for input, output and error messages streams, respectively. The program may assume that these FILE pointers exist the moment the program is run and may be used in place of any FILE pointer parameter used by the stream functions in the stream library.

An extract from the contents of the header file <stdio.h> supplied with a typical MS-DOS compatible C compiler is shown below; it identifies the three FILE pointers:

Addresses of the first three FILE structure elements within _iob[]

```
#define  stdin   ( &_iob[0] )    /* default input stream */
#define  stdout  ( &_iob[1] )    /* default output stream */
#define  stderr  ( &_iob[2] )    /* default error stream */
```

As you can see, they are in fact the addresses of the first three elements in the array _iob[] (see Figure 16.2). In other words, the first three elements in _iob[] are reserved by the operating system for attachment to the system's default I/O device. In fact, MS-DOS opens two other streams that are attached to the computer's auxiliary and printer ports. These additional FILE pointers are referred to as stdaux and stdprn and are shown below:

```
#define  stdaux  ( &_iob[3] )    /* default auxiliary port stream */
#define  stdprn  ( &_iob[4] )    /* default printer port stream */
```

Now, as we have already seen, if a program wished to write the simple message "Hello World" to the operator's terminal, it could obviously call printf() to perform the task. However, the same operation could be performed with a call to fprintf() using the FILE pointer stdout, as shown below:

Write "Hello World\n" to default *output* stream

```
fprintf( stdout , "Hello World\n" ) ;      /* write to default output stream */
```

Similarly, the same message could be written to the error message stream or, if you are using an MS-DOS system, the auxiliary or printer ports, with any of the following statements:

Write "Hello World\n" to default *error, auxiliary* and *printer* streams

```
fprintf( stderr , "Hello World\n" ) ;     /* write output to error stream */
fprintf( stdaux , "Hello World\n" ) ;     /* write output to auxiliary port stream */
fprintf( stdprn , "Hello World\n" ) ;     /* write output to printer stream */
```

Similarly, a character could be read from the operator's keyboard or from the auxiliary port with statements such as:

Read a character from default *input* (keyboard) and *auxiliary* streams

```
c = fgetc( stdin ) ;                      /* read char from default input stream */
c = fgetc( stdaux ) ;                     /* read char from auxiliary port */
```

16.11.2 *Tying together the stream and default I/O functions*

To understand how functions such as getchar() and putchar() work, you only need examine the header file <stdio.h>, where you may well see the following, or similar **macros** created with the C pre-processor directive #define:

```
#define  getchar()    fgetc( stdin )
#define  putchar( c ) fputc( c , stdout )
```

This means that any calls to getchar() and putchar() are replaced at compile time by calls to fgetc() and fputc() in association with the FILE pointers stdin and stdout. Similarly, the functions gets(), scanf(), puts() and printf() have been written to call the generic functions fgets(), fscanf(), fputs() and fprintf() in conjunction with the appropriate FILE pointers stdin and stdout.

This means that program error messages can be written independently of program output to a separate stream/device, using fprintf() in conjunction with the FILE pointer stderr, as shown below, although example programs so far in this book have not done so:

```
if( ferror( fp ) != 0)
  fprintf( stderr, "Error: Cannot read from disk file %s\n", name) ;
```

16.11.3 *Redirection of program I/O and error messages*

Many operating systems, including UNIX and MS-DOS, allow the streams stdin, stdout and stderr to be redirected at run time to an alternative device, such as a disk file or printer. This can be particularly useful in a multi-tasking environment, such as UNIX, where several programs may be running concurrently and might otherwise be fighting to access the same device; that is, the operator's terminal.

Such redirection is accomplished transparently, by the operating system, which acts upon command line operators supplied when the program is invoked. For example, program output could be redirected to a printer under MS-DOS with a shell command such as:

```
c: prog1 >prn
```

where the operator '>' is used to redirect the output of the program prog_name to the device 'prn'. Note that the '>' operator is intercepted by the operating system shell and is *not* presented to the C program as one of the arguments to argv[].

Operating system redirection is actually accomplished through the use of the function freopen() described below, which permits the closure of a specified stream and subsequent re-opening with an attachment to an alternative device. In the previous example, where the program output was redirected to the device 'prn', the default output stream, stdout, would have been closed and re-opened by the operating system attached to the printer port.

16.11.4 *Using* freopen() *within a program*

The programmer can also make use of freopen() to allow the program to redirect its own I/O independently of any redirection that may have been specified on the command line. A description of freopen() is given below.

Function prototype: freopen()

The function prototype for freopen() can be found in the header file <stdio.h> and is given below:

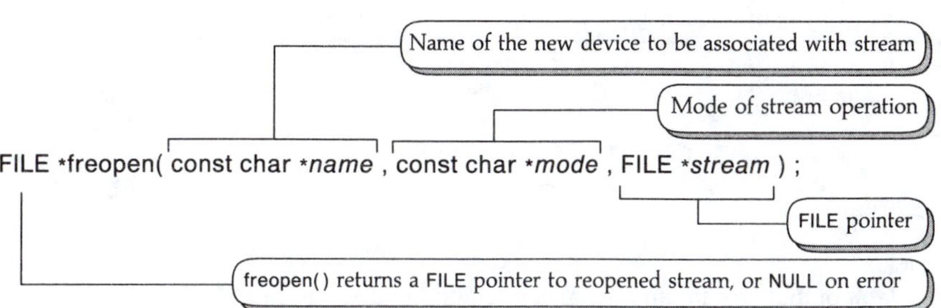
Name of the new device to be associated with stream
Mode of stream operation
FILE *freopen(const char *name , const char *mode , FILE *stream) ;
FILE pointer
freopen() returns a FILE pointer to reopened stream, or NULL on error

where 'stream' is a FILE pointer that is currently associated with an open stream, such as stdin, stdout or stderr, or any other FILE pointer that the program may have obtained via a successful call to the functions fopen( ), freopen( ) or tmpfile( ). 'name' is the name/pathlist of the new device to which the re-opened stream will be attached. The parameter 'mode' describes the way in which the program intends to use the newly opened stream, for example "r", "w" and so on.

Error considerations and returned values: freopen( )

If freopen( ) fails, then a NULL pointer is returned, and the value of the external int errno will be set to a value indicating the cause of the failure, otherwise freopen( ) returns a valid FILE pointer to the re-opened stream. Note, however, that if freopen( ) fails the stream could be left in a closed state, leaving the program with the possibility of having no access to the original stream.

As an example, let us examine a program that wishes to redirect some, but not all, of its output to a disk file. This effectively rules out the output redirection operator ' > ' on the command line, since this would redirect *all* output for the program. Of course, the program could use fopen( ) to open a disk file and subsequently use fprintf( ) to write some of its output to that device, while using printf( ) to display the rest to the terminal.

An alternative solution would be to close the stream referenced by stdout and re-open it connected to another device, in this case a disk file. All output generated by statements such as printf( ) or fprintf(stdout, ...) would then be written to that file. Once the required output to the file had been accomplished, the default output stream could once more be closed and re-opened, with the connection to the original terminal.

Program 16.10 uses just such an approach to redirect some of the program's output to the disk file 'joe.txt', before redirecting the remainder of the output to the default terminal. Note that this example below assumes a number of pathlist naming conventions unique to MS-DOS, such as the disk pathlist 'a:\joe.txt' and the name of the terminal 'con'. These may have to be altered for other operating systems.

Note that a useful by-product of this approach is that any redirection of the program's output specified on the command line will be overridden with the first call to freopen( ).

Program 16.10 Example use of freopen( ).

```
#include  <stdio.h>
#include  <stdlib.h>
#include  <errno.h>

int main( void )
{

/* Close the default output stream and associate it with the disk file "joe.txt" */
```

```
    if( freopen("a:\\joe.txt", "w", stdout ) == NULL)  {
      perror("Error cannot open a:\joe.txt") ;
      exit( EXIT_FAILURE ) ;
    }

    printf("Hello Disk File ... ") ;            /* Output sent to disk file */

/*
** Close the default output stream (currently connected to the disk file ) and
** associate it once more with the terminal "con"
*/

    if( freopen("con", "w", stdout ) == NULL)  {
      perror("Error cannot open a:\joe.txt") ;
      exit( EXIT_FAILURE ) ;
    }

/* Send the following message to the terminal */

    printf("Hello Terminal ... ") ;
    return 0 ;
}
```

16.12 Chapter summary

(1) A program may communicate with a device using either high or low level library functions, commonly referred to as buffered and unbuffered I/O, respectively. High level communication is achieved through operating system streams and buffers, while low level communication is accomplished via direct read and write calls.

(2) High level streams may be opened in text or binary mode and separate functions exist to manipulate each. With a text stream some translation of characters may occur between device and program, which does not occur with a binary stream.

(3) The name of the device is identified via a pathlist such as "prn" or "c:\\file.c" on an MS-DOS system.

(4) The program may have to detect various errors for a stream, to ensure that operations have been performed correctly, as well as detecting an end-of file status for an input stream. This is achieved through the use of the functions ferror( ) and feof( ).

(5) Streams may be opened with a call to fopen( ), which identifies the device and the mode of operation to be used, for example reading, writing, text or binary, and closed with a call to fclose( ).

(6) Stream buffer size and mode of operation may be adjusted by calls to setvbuf( ) and setbuf( ), while the stream may be flushed or emptied with a call to fflush( ).

(7) Some streams may be randomly accessed. The functions fseek( ) and fsetpos( ) permit the program to reposition the stream's SPI. The function ftell( ) determines the position of the SPI for a given stream, while fgetpos( ) saves the position of a stream's SPI. The function rewind( ) repositions the SPI to the start of the stream.

(8) Temporary files and file names may be generated by calls to the functions tmpfile( ) and tmpnam( ), while rename( ) and remove( ) permit a file to be renamed/moved to another location or to be removed altogther.

(9) A binary stream may be manipulated with calls to the functions fread( ) and fwrite( ). These two functions permit large quantities of unformatted binary data to be read from/written to a stream with a single function call.

(10) The streams stdin, stdout and stderr refer to the operator's input, output and error message streams, respectively and are associated with the operator's terminal unless they have been redirected. Thus, the following function calls behave in an equivalent manner:

```
fprintf(stdout, "Hello") ;
printf( "Hello") ;
```

16.13 Exercises

16.1 Examine your compiler documentation and/or the header file <stdio.h> and determine the following:

- **(a)** The maximum number of files that may be open simultaneously.
- **(b)** The default size of a stream buffer.
- **(c)** The maximum length of a file name and the maximum number of file names produced by tmpnam( ) and tmpfile( ).

16.2 Write example calls to the function fopen( ) to open/create the text file joe.txt and the binary file joe.bin in the following specified modes:

- **(a)** Reading only.
- **(b)** Reading and writing but no creation.
- **(c)** Reading and writing with file creation/truncation.

(d) Appending for reading and writing.

(e) Writing with no truncation/creation.

What is the difference between the modes "r+" and "w+"?

16.3 Write a program to create a text file for writing. Using the function fprintf(), write a simple text message such as "hello\n" to the file and close it. Now re-open it for read mode and, using the functions ftell() and fseek(), determine the following:

(a) Whether or not your operating system performs translation of the '\n' character into a carriage return/line feed sequence.

(b) Whether the SPI is positioned at the start or end of the file when an existing file is opened in append mode.

(c) Whether the operating system permits empty files of zero length to remain in existence after they have been closed.

16.4 Write a program to allow the operator to enter the ages of a number of students in a class. Upon detection of the EOF condition generated by the program's operator (<Control-D> for UNIX, <Control-Z> for MS-DOS), close the file and re-open it in read mode. Now use fscanf() to read back the ages and display the number of students in the class and their average age.
Rewrite the program to use fgets() and atof() in place of fscanf().
Rewrite the program to use fgets() and scanf() (see Section 18.12).

16.5 Write a program to generate and save a table of temperatures expressed in Celsius to a disk file. Using this file as the input to further programs read back the table of temperatures and generate a second file containing a table of equivalent Fahrenheit temperatures. The program should be written such that it prompts for the source and destination file names. What modifications would be required to the program if the input and output redirection operators '<' and '>' in conjunction with two other file names were used on the operating system command line?

16.6 Write a program to analyse a text file and display the following statistics:

(a) The number of lines.

(b) The number of blank or empty lines.

(c) The number of words.

(d) The number of characters.

16.7 A 'filter' program is required to replace all occurrences of the character 'x' within a disk file with the character 'y' (where 'x' and 'y' are supplied by the operator when the program is run). Write a program to accept the file name along with the characters 'x' and 'y' from the command line and update the file.

16.8 Write a program to read lines of text from a file and display them on the operator's terminal preceeded by a six digit line number plus a space character. Modify the above program such that it pauses after 'n' lines have been displayed, where 'n' is a command line argument of the form '–n=6'. The display may be resumed by pressing the <return> key.

16.9 Modify the program in Exercise 16.8 such that the operator may, with the addition of further command line arguments, format the display to include optional left, right, top and bottom margins, page size in terms of width and length expressed in characters, and headings and page numbers for inclusion at the top and/or bottom of the page. The program should assume defaults for each parameter if not expressly given.

16.10 Write a program to search a number of files whose names are supplied as command line arguments, for occurrences of the *text* string "xyz". If found, the file name, line and line number are to be displayed.

Hint: Use the function strstr( ) (see Section 18.14).

16.11 Modify the program in Exercise 16.10 such that all occurrences of the string "xyz" are replaced by the string "abc" in the file.

Hint: Generate a second intermediate file (use tmpfile( ) or tmpname( ) to generate this) to hold the result of the converted text before the original file is deleted and replaced by the updated file.

16.12 Use the program in Exercise 16.11 to implement a simple mail merge utility where a personalized letter is generated from a 'standard' letter by replacing all occurrences of the text string '< < <name> > >' with a name supplied at run time via the keyboard. The program should now be enhanced to read a second file containing a list of 'n' names and thus generate 'n' personalized letters. The program should now be further enhanced to replace occurrences of the string '< < <address> > >' with an address read from the second file.

16.13 Joe's supermarket has just installed the latest bar code readers to improve efficiency at their checkouts. The bar code reader is linked to a computer database, which contains the bar codes, product descriptions and unit prices of each product sold by the supermarket. This information is stored within the database in the following format:

- Barcode: an integer value followed by a space character.
- Product description: a text string stored in a field of 30 characters.
- Unit price: a floating point value followed by a new line character.

Assuming that the bar codes are, for the purposes of this program, entered via the keyboard, write a program to look up the product description and unit price and produce a bill and receipt for all products bought by an individual.

16.14 Modify the program in Exercise 16.13 such that the database also keeps a record of the quantity of each item in stock. As purchases are made, that entry in the database is updated. When the level of stock reaches less than 10, new stock is to be ordered by writing the bar code number of the product to a second file, which is printed at the end of the day and used to order more goods.

16.15 Using a binary file and the function `fwrite()`, write a program to save the value of 200 random integral values generated by the function `rand()` (see Section 18.13). Now enhance the program to sort the file in ascending order, using modified versions of the following algorithms, and compare the relative performance of the two algorithms:

(a) The bubble sort presented in Chapter 7.

(b) The quicksort presented in Chapter 8.

Note that the program should sort the data *on disk* and should not read it into an array and sort it there, neither should it use any additional disk files in the process.

Hint: Write a function that allows the file's SPI to be positioned to point to the nth record (integer) within the file. Now modify the program to implement a binary search for data on the sorted file.

16.16 A car dealer maintains computerized records of all transactions made. The information recorded includes:

- Name, address, sex and age of purchaser.
- Make, model and colour of vehicle sold and whether estate, saloon or hatchback.
- Vehicle registration number, recorded mileage, price paid and date of purchase.

Write a simple database program to allow the dealer to perform the following operations:

(a) Record a sale.

(b) Search for details of a previous transaction using vehicle registration as a key.

(c) Amend details of a transaction.

(d) Delete details of a transaction.

(e) Count the number of transactions recorded.

(f) Wipe all records in the database (password protected).

17 Dynamic Data Structures

It is often said that the true test of a programming language is the ease with which it is able to support the creation and manipulation of complex dynamic data structures. Although the subject is worthy of a book in itself, and indeed several texts exist, this chapter is set aside for a discussion of some of the most popular data structures in the form of the **linked list** and the **binary tree**. An implementation of the software **stack** and **queue** are also presented, based around the linked list.

It is not recommended that any reader tackle this chapter unless they feel completely at ease with all aspects relating to the use and application of pointers and structures. The chapter is included mainly to demonstrate the applications of C in solving complex real-world problems. As such, no 'new' features of the language are introduced here; only the application of existing ones.

To understand how and why the need for linked lists arose, consider for a moment that most basic and fundamental data structure, the array. We have seen in previous chapters that any array can be thought of as a collection of related objects sharing a common type (an array of `int`s, `char`s, `float`s and so on), which are stored sequentially in memory to provide a simple table or list. Access to each element is via an integer index/subscript, which is both fast and efficient.

The array, however, suffers from a number of drawbacks when used in more advanced applications. Firstly, because the size of the array is generally defined at compile time, a sometimes severe restriction is imposed on the programmer, who may be asked to estimate the size of the array at compile time, which may not always be possible. For example, if the programmer were developing a CAD package that would enable an operator to draw several simple objects such as points, lines, circles and squares, which were then used subsequently as the building blocks for a more complex object, it would be unrealistic to suggest that the programmer could predict at compile time the complexity and thus the number of objects an operator might choose to enter.

Even if the programmer attempts to 'play safe' and use dynamic memory allocation functions such as `malloc()` and `realloc()` to dynamically request storage for the array as new objects are inserted, the program might not be very efficient for several reasons. Firstly, the insertion of a new object at a specific point within such an array, perhaps because the data needs to be kept sorted, requires that all objects above it in the array be shifted up to create space for the new element, while deletion of an object requires other elements to be moved down to fill the space.

Furthermore, resizing the array may not always be practical since the operation is relatively slow, particularly if `realloc()` has to copy the existing data to a new memory block, and may not always be possible if memory fragmentation results in many small blocks of non-contiguous memory. Let us, then, take a look at how all of these problems can be overcome by introducing a linked list.

17.1 The basic/single linked list

The linked list is based upon the principle of requesting and releasing memory from/to the operating system as required by the program at run time. A linked list can be thought of as a number of separate objects, stored within **nodes**. Each node contains a pointer, which points to the next node in the list, thus forming a chain of nodes and their related data, as shown in Figure 17.1. The last node in the list is marked by a NULL pointer; that is, a pointer to the address 0.

The application itself need only maintain a pointer to the first node in the list to allow access to any element in the list. The operation of inserting data into the list requires only that storage for a new node be allocated, and that the appropriate links in the chain be manipulated to accommodate them. Deletion of a node is accomplished in the reverse manner. Neither operation requires that any existing data/node in the list be moved.

In reality, a linked list is often a little more sophisticated than this. For example, although inserting data at the start of the list is fairly straightforward, inserting data at the end, particularly in a long list, requires that the program **traverse** the list to locate the address of the last node. Its 'next' pointer can then

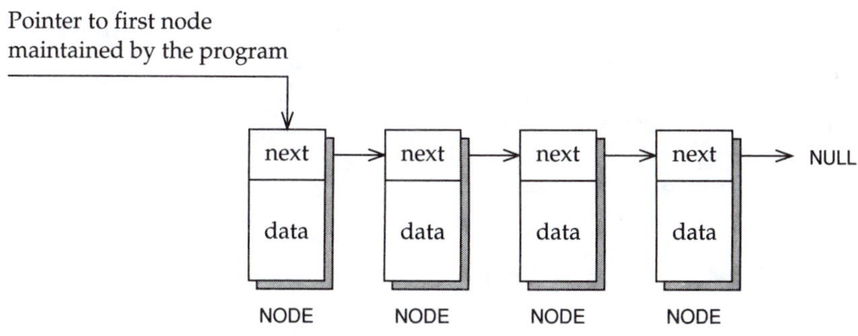

Figure 17.1 A simple linked list.

be set to point to the new node. From this point of view, a real application program might also choose to maintain a pointer to the last node in the list, and in the process record the number of nodes in the list.

Obviously such information could easily be recorded by the program, but when several lists are maintained it becomes a little tricky to keep track of the pointers for each list, so an implementation that stores this information as part of the list itself is often chosen. Figure 17.2 shows how this is achieved.

You will see that a ROOT data structure has been included, which maintains pointers to the first and last nodes in the list, and the integral number of nodes within the list. The node itself now contains pointers to the next node in the list, and to the data stored at (but not in) that node.

Provided the programmer maintains his or her own ROOT pointer (rather than a pointer to the first node in the list), it should be possible to write several **generic** functions to manipulate linked lists, such as insertion, deletion, searching and so on. With a little thought these can be written such that they are independent of the data stored within the list. This is ideal, since it will then be possible to create a library of list manipulation functions that may be used within any program to manipulate data.

As you might imagine, the manipulation of any linked list is heavily dependent upon the use of structures and pointers. Most of the functions developed in this section involve multi level indirection and make heavy use of void pointers (for their generic properties) and pointers to functions. If you can follow and understand these functions, then you should have nothing to worry about when it comes to more advanced applications.

To create a linked list of the type shown in Figure 17.2, we must first describe two structure templates for the ROOT and NODE type objects. These are presented in Program 17.1. Note how the NODE structure contains the void pointer 'data', which you will recall is a generic pointer, able to assume the address of any type of object. Note also how the NODE structure contains the self-referential pointer 'next' to record the address of the next node in the list. The ROOT structure contains two NODE pointers, which point to the first and

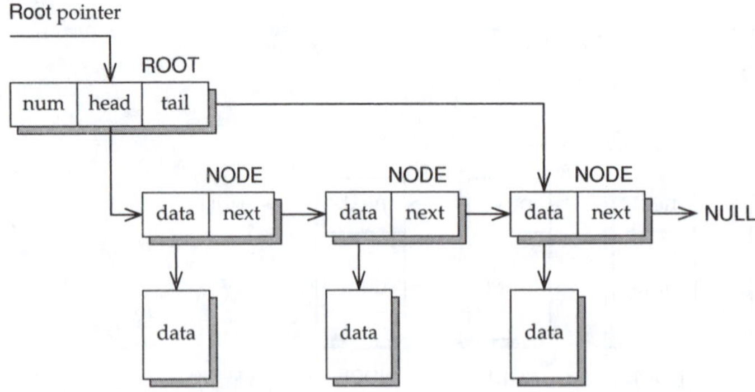

Figure 17.2 A typical linked list implementation.

Program 17.1 The ROOT and NODE data structures for a linked list.

```
/*
** The ROOT and NODE data structures for a linked list
*/

typedef struct node {
    void         *data ;        /* pointer to data at this node */
    struct       node *next ;   /* pointer to next node in list */
} NODE ;                        /* a generic pointer to any type of data */

typedef struct {
    long   num ;                /* number of nodes in list */
    NODE   *head ;              /* pointer to first node in list */
    NODE   *tail ;              /* pointer to last node in list */
} ROOT ;
```

last nodes in the list, as well as the variable num to record the number of nodes in the list.

We are now in a position to develop some simple functions to enable us to create and initialize these two types of object. The function make_root( ) shown in Program 17.2 allocates storage for a new object of type ROOT using the library

Program 17.2 Making a root node in a linked list.

```
/*
** The macro 'NEW()' allocates storage for and yields a pointer to a object of type x
*/

#define  NEW( x )  (x *)malloc( sizeof( x ))

/*
** Make a new ROOT and set the head and tail pointers to invalid (NULL) and set 'num'
** to zero, since there cannot be any nodes in the list. Then return a pointer to the newly
** created ROOT structure, or return a NULL pointer if it cannot be created.
*/

ROOT  *make_root( void )
{
    ROOT *root ;

    if((root = NEW( ROOT )) != NULL )  {
        root->head = root->tail = NULL ;    /* mark head and tail pointers as invalid */
        root->num = 0 ;                     /* no nodes yet */
    }
    return root ;                           /* return a pointer to new ROOT structure */
}
```

function malloc() and returns a pointer to it. When a ROOT object is created, its 'head' and 'tail' pointers are marked as invalid by setting them to NULL and num is set to zero until such time as a node is first inserted into the list.

Inserting data into the list involves the creation of a NODE. The data pointer within that node can then be adjusted to point to its data, before it is inserted into the list. In this particular implementation, the responsibility for allocating and initializing the storage for the node's data rests with the user's program. This enables the function make_node() shown in Program 17.3 to be independent of the type of data stored at the node.

The address of the storage allocated by the program for the node's data must be supplied to make_node() as the argument data. This address is then assigned to the new node's data pointer. Finally, the node's next pointer is set to NULL (which is useful if the node is ever inserted at the end of the list).

Program 17.3 Making a node in a linked list.

```
/*
** Make a new node and point it to the data whose address is supplied in the call.
** A pointer to the new node is returned or NULL on error.
*/

NODE  *make_node( void *data )
{
   NODE  *node ;                          /* a temporary NODE pointer */

   if((node = NEW( NODE )) != NULL )  {
      node->data = data ;                 /* point new node to its new data */
      node->next = NULL ;                 /* mark next node as invalid */
   }
   return node ;                          /* return pointer to new node or NULL if error */
}
```

17.1.1 *Inserting data into a list*

The two most common positions for inserting data into a list are at the head and the tail, although it is also possible to insert a node between two existing nodes. Figure 17.3 illustrates the mechanics of insertion at the head, which requires that the head pointer in the ROOT structure be adjusted to point to the new node, and that the *new* node is set to point to what was previously the first node.

Inserting a new node at the tail requires that the existing tail node and the tail pointer in the root structure be adjusted to point to the new tail node. This is illustrated in Figure 17.4.

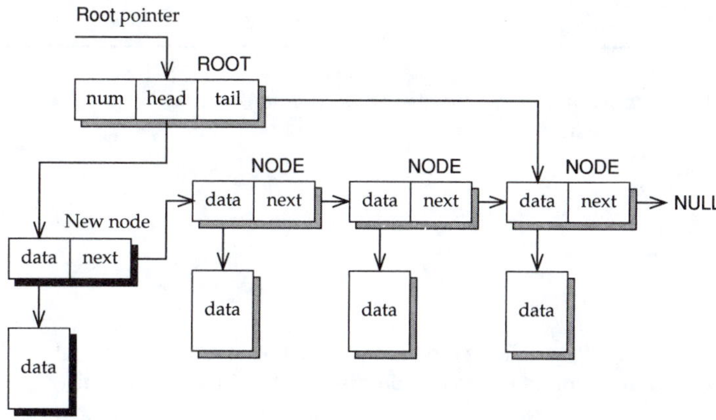

Figure 17.3 Inserting a new node at the head of a linked list.

The function insert_data() in Program 17.4 permits an object to be inserted either at the head or tail of a list, based upon the value of the argument position. Note that the user's program must have previously defined a pointer to the ROOT structure of the list, which *must* have been initialized to NULL prior to the insertion of the first node. The address (not the value) of this root pointer is supplied to insert_data() to identify the list (as there may be several in operation in complex applications).

The value of the root pointer is examined by the function and, if found to be NULL (indicating an invalid or empty list), the root structure for a new list is automatically created, and a node is created and inserted. If successful, the program's root pointer is adjusted to point to the new ROOT structure for the list.

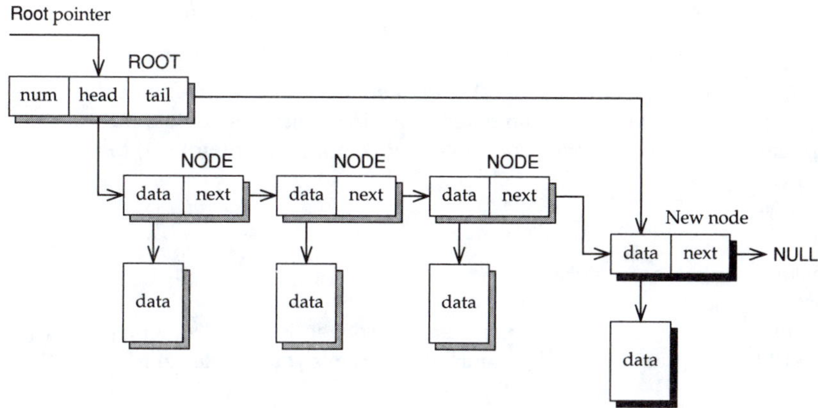

Figure 17.4 Inserting a new node at the tail of a linked list.

Program 17.4 Inserting data into a linked list.

```
/*
** A simple macro to test if the program's ROOT pointer is valid, and one to access
** the number of nodes in the linked list.
*/

#define  VALID( x )  ((*x) != NULL )
#define  NUM( x )    ((*x)->num)

/*
** The following function creates and inserts a new node into a list. If 'position' is equal
** to 0, the new node is inserted at the head of the list, otherwise, it will be inserted at
** the tail.
**
** If the list does not exist when the first item is inserted, then the root structure will
** be created, and the program's 'root' pointer set to point to it. Upon success, 0 is
** returned.
*/

int insert_data( ROOT **root, void *data, int position )
{
  NODE  *new ;                          /* temporary NODE pointer */

/*
** If the program's root pointer is NULL, then the list does not exist, so attempt to
** create the list's root structure. If successful the address of the new root structure is
** assigned to the program's root pointer.
*/

  if( !VALID(root))
    if((*root = make_root( )) == NULL)
      return (-1) ;

/*
** If root exists, OR root has just been made (above), then make a new node. If new
** node cannot be created AND there are no other nodes in the list, then delete the
** root structure and assign NULL to the program's root pointer, then return (-1) to
** indicate the error.
*/

  if((new = make_node( data )) == NULL)  {
    if(NUM(root) == 0)  {
      free( *root ) ;                   /* release the root structure if list is empty */
      *root = NULL ;                    /* and set program's root pointer to NULL */
    }
    return (-1);                        /* return fail */
  }
```

```
/*
** If this node is the first node to be inserted into the list, then set both
** 'head' and 'tail' pointers in the ROOT structure to point to this new node
*/

    if( NUM(root) == 0)
        (*root)->head = (*root)->tail = new ;


/*
** Otherwise (because a node must already exist in the list), if 'position' is equal to 0,
** the newly created node will be inserted at the head of the list
*/

    else  {
      if( position == 0 )  {
        new->next = (*root)->head ;      /* point new node to existing head node */
        (*root)->head = new ;            /* make new node the head node */
      }

/* Else insert the new node at the tail and point the existing tail node to it */

      else  {
        (*root)->tail->next = new ;      /* point existing tail node to new node */
        (*root)->tail = new ;            /* make new node the new tail node */
      }
    }

    (NUM(root)) ++ ;                     /* increment node count for list */
    return 0 ;                           /* return success */
}
```

Having written these few generic routines, we can now write a simple program, shown in Program 17.5, to insert several elements of type DATA (a user defined type, which in this example is simply an integer) into the list, and then display the contents of the list. Note that a type specific function to display data stored within a node will be required for complete genericity.

Program 17.5 Inserting integral data into a linked list.

```
#include  <stdio.h>
#include  <stdlib.h>

#define   NEW( x )  (x *)malloc( sizeof( x ))

typedef   int  DATA ;                  /* data to be stored in list is an integer */
```

```
/*
** The following is a user supplied function to display the data stored at a node
** The function expects to be passed the address of the node's data, which in
** this instance it casts to a DATA pointer before extracting the data (an integer)
*/

void display_DATA( void *data )
{
   printf("%d ", *(DATA *)(data)) ;
}

/*
** The following function displays the data stored at each node in the list. Note how the
** list is traversed with a simple loop until the last node is found.
** Note also how the function expects to be given a pointer to a display function
** which is later called to display the data in a node
*/

void display_list( ROOT **root, void (*disp)( void *data ))
{
   NODE  *node ;

   if( VALID(root))  {                    /* if the list is valid; that is, 'root' is not NULL */
      node = (*root)->head ;              /* point 'node' to first node in list */

/* Traverse the list, displaying the data at each node until the end of the list is found */

      do {
         disp( node->data) ;              /* call display function */
         node = node->next ;              /* move to next node */
      }while( node != NULL ) ;
   }
   putchar('\n') ;
}

int main( void )
{
   ROOT  *root = NULL ;                   /* program ROOT pointer set to NULL */
   DATA  *data ;                          /* create a pointer to object of type DATA */
   int      i ;

   for( i = 0; i < 5 ; i ++ )  {                 /* Now insert five elements into the list */
      data = NEW( DATA ) ;                       /* allocate storage for new DATA */
      *data = i ;                                /* copy i to new storage */
      printf("Inserting data = %d at head of list : ", i ) ;
      insert_data( &root, data, 0 ) ;            /* insert at head of list */
      display_list( &root, display_DATA ) ;      /* Display data at each node */
   }
```

```
    for( i = 10; i < 15 ; i ++ )  {                /* Now insert five elements into the list */
        data = NEW( DATA ) ;                       /* allocate storage for new DATA */
        *data = i ;
        printf("Inserting data = %d at tail of list : ", i ) ;
        insert_data( &root, data, 1 ) ;            /* insert at tail of list */
        display_list( &root, display_DATA ) ;      /* Display data at each node */
    }
    return 0 ;
}
```

When Program 17.5 is run, the following display is produced:

```
Inserting data = 0 at head of list : 0
Inserting data = 1 at head of list : 1 0
Inserting data = 2 at head of list : 2 1 0
Inserting data = 3 at head of list : 3 2 1 0
Inserting data = 4 at head of list : 4 3 2 1 0
Inserting data = 10 at tail of list : 4 3 2 1 0 10
Inserting data = 11 at tail of list : 4 3 2 1 0 10 11
Inserting data = 12 at tail of list : 4 3 2 1 0 10 11 12
Inserting data = 13 at tail of list : 4 3 2 1 0 10 11 12 13
Inserting data = 14 at tail of list : 4 3 2 1 0 10 11 12 13 14
```

17.1.2 *Insertion at a fixed point in a list*

From the point of view of maintaining a sorted list, it might be desirable to insert a new node between two existing nodes. Figure 17.5 illustrates the operation.

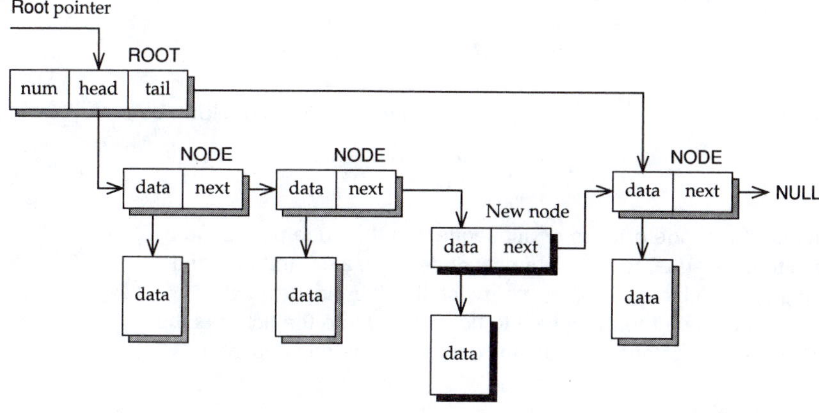

Figure 17.5 Inserting a new node between two existing nodes.

The function insert_at_position( ) shown in Program 17.6 permits a node to be inserted into a list at a specified position. The argument this_node must contain the address of an *existing* node within the list (a check is performed to ensure this), while position dictates whether the new node will be inserted prior to or subsequent to this node.

Program 17.6 Inserting data at a specified position.

```
/*
** The following function searches a linked list to obtain and return the address
** of the node prior to that pointed to by 'this_node' If 'this_node' cannot
** be located in the list, then NULL is returned to indicate an error.
**
** If 'this_node' exists in the list, then the address of its previous
** node is returned, or, in the case where the node is the
** first node in the list, then the address of that first node is returned.
*/

NODE  *find_previous_node( ROOT **root, NODE *this_node )
{
  NODE  *previous_node, *current_node ;

  current_node = previous_node = (*root)->head ;      /* point to head node in list */

/*
** while 'current_node' is not pointing to the node we have asked it to search for
** and it is not pointing to the last node in the list then move 'current_node'
** on to the next node, saving the address of the previous node
*/

  while((current_node != this_node) && (current_node->next != NULL ))  {
    previous_node = current_node ;
    current_node = current_node->next ;
  }

  return (previous_node) ;                          /* return address or NULL on error */
}

/*
** This function inserts a node prior to or subsequent to the node pointed to by
** 'node'. If 'position' is equal to 0, then a new node is created and inserted
** prior to the node pointed to by 'node', otherwise it will be inserted after
** that node. 'data' must point to the object to be inserted into the list. It is the
** program's responsibility to ensure that storage for this data is allocated.
**
** Upon success, 0 is returned
*/
```

```
int insert_at_position( ROOT **root, NODE *node, void *data, int position )
{
  int      flag = 0 ;
  NODE  *new, *prev ;

  if( !VALID(root) )
    return (-1) ;                                    /* if invalid list, return error */

/*
** If the node is the first node and the insertion is to take
** place prior to that node, then simply insert the data at the head of the list
*/

  if(((*root)->head == node) && (position == 0))       /* if inserting before head */
    flag = insert_data( root, data, 0 ) ;              /* insert at head */

/*
** Otherwise, if the node is the last node and the insertion is to take
** place after that node, then simply insert the data at the tail
*/

  else if(((*root)->tail == node) && (position == 1))  /* if insert after tail node */
    flag = insert_data( root, data, 1 ) ;              /* insert at tail */

/*
** Otherwise, we must be inserting a new node at a point that does not affect the
** 'head' or 'tail' pointers in the ROOT structure, so obtain the address of node's
** previous node. If successful, 'prev' is set to the address of the node prior to the
** specified node or if unsuccessful, 'prev' is set to NULL, and the insert is aborted.
*/

  else  {
    if(( prev = find_previous_node( root, node )) == NULL )
      return (-1) ;

    if((new = make_node( data )) == NULL)
      return (-1) ;

/*
** If we are inserting after the specified node, then point new node to where the
** specified node is pointing, and then point the specified node to the new node.
*/

    if( position == 1 )  {
      new->next = node->next ;
      node->next = new ;
    }

/*
** Otherwise we are inserting prior to the specified node, so make the previous node
** point to the new node and make the new node point to the specified node.
*/
```

```
    else {
      new->next = prev->next ;
      prev->next = new ;
    }
    NUM(root) ++ ;                          /* increment node count in root structure */
  }
  return flag ;
}
```

17.1.3 *Deleting a node from a list*

Deleting a node involves the opposite sequence of operations to inserting a node. The node to be deleted and its previous node are located in the list. The deleted node's link to its 'next' node will be saved in its previous node, thus by-passing the deleted node and ensuring the integrity of the list. The storage occupied by the node can then be released and the node count in the root structure decremented by one.

If the deleted node was the first or last node, or both if there was only one node in the list, then the head and tail pointers in the ROOT structure are adjusted. Finally, if the node count becomes zero, this particular implementation chooses to release the storage occupied by the ROOT structure, and set the program's root pointer to NULL, thus marking it as invalid.

Note that as the user's program was responsible for the allocation of the storage for the node's data, the function delete_node() shown in Program 17.7 returns a pointer to the storage at the deleted node, so that the program may release it. Of course the function could easily be modified to do this for itself, but this would sacrifice the generic nature of the list and would affect its use in other applications such as the stack and the queue (see later).

Program 17.7 Deleting a node from a linked list.

```
/*
** This function deletes a node from the list and returns a pointer to the data that was
** (and still is) stored there. NULL is returned upon failure.
**
** Note: If all nodes have been deleted, then the ROOT structure is released
** and the program's 'root' pointer is set to NULL.
*/

void *delete_node( ROOT **root, NODE *node)
{
  NODE  *prev ;
  void  *data_ptr ;              /* pointer to data in node to be deleted */

/* Check that list exists, if not return NULL to indicate error */
```

```
    if( !VALID(root))
        return (NULL) ;

/*
** If list does exist then attempt to locate the address of the previous node
** and save in 'prev'. If 'node' does not exist in the current list
** then NULL is returned, and the delete operation is aborted.
*/

    if((prev = find_previous_node( root, node)) == NULL )
        return (NULL) ;

/*
** If the node is at the head node of the list, then point 'head' in root structure to next
** node in list (which will be NULL if there is only one node). Likewise, if the
** node to be deleted is the last node then point 'tail' to previous node.
*/

    if((*root)->head == node)
        (*root)->head = node->next ;

    if((*root)->tail == node)
        (*root)->tail = prev ;

/*
** Now point the previous node to the node subsequent to the node being deleted, then
** release the storage occupied by the node.
*/
    prev->next = node->next ;
    data_ptr = node->data ;            /* save address of data in this node */
    free( node ) ;                     /* release storage occupied by node */

/*
** Now decrement the number of nodes in the list and if zero, free the root
** structure and set program's root pointer to NULL
*/

    if( --NUM(root) == 0)  {
        free(*root) ;                  /* release storage occupied by root */
        *root = NULL ;
    }
    return (data_ptr) ;                /* return address of data from deleted node */
}
```

17.1.4 *Deleting a complete list*

Deleting a complete linked list is accomplished by traversing the list from head to tail, releasing the storage occupied by each node *and* its data. Finally, the storage occupied by the root data structure is released and the program's root pointer set to NULL (invalid), as shown in Program 17.8.

Program 17.8 Deleting a complete linked list.

```
/*
** The following function releases the storage occupied by an entire list. Upon
** success, the program's 'root' pointer is set to NULL and 0 is returned.
*/

int  delete_list(ROOT **root)
{
   NODE  *this ;                        /* pointer to the node to be deleted */
   NODE  *next ;                        /* pointer to the next node to be deleted */

   if( !VALID(root))                    /* check validity of list */
      return (-1) ;

   this = (*root)->head ;               /* point 'this' to the first node in list */

/* Now traverse the list from start to end releasing each node and its data */

   do  {
      next = this->next ;               /* pointer to the next node in the list (or NULL) */
      free( this->data ) ;              /* free storage occupied by DATA */
      free( this ) ;                    /* free storage occupied by NODE */
      this = next ;                     /* go to next node in list */
   } while( this != NULL ) ;            /* repeat until all nodes free */

/* Now free the root node and set the program's root pointer to NULL */

   free( *root ) ;                      /* free storage occupied by root structure */
   *root = NULL ;                       /* mark program's root pointer as invalid */
   return 0 ;                           /* return success */
}
```

17.1.5 *Searching a list*

Searching a list for a specified item of data is again a matter of traversing the list, comparing the data at each node with that to be located until a match is found or the end of the list is reached. Because we require a generic search function that is independent of the type of data stored by the program we must supply the search function with a pointer to a type specific 'comparison' function (as we saw with the function bsearch( ) in Chapter 10). The search function can then invoke this comparison function to compare two items of generic list data.

A different version of this function will ultimately be required for each type of data stored in a list. The example function given in Program 17.9 compares two integer values.

Program 17.9 Searching a linked list.

```
/*
** The following function compare( ) will be called later by search( ). Its purpose
** is to determine if two items of DATA (in this case integers) are identical, if so, 0 is
** returned or non-zero if they are not.
*/

int  compare_DATA( void *d1, void *d2 )
{
  if( *(DATA *)(d1) == *(DATA *)(d2))        /* cast both d1 and d2 to 'DATA pointers */
    return 0 ;                               /* both identical */
  else
    return 1 ;                               /* both differ */
}

/*
** The function search( ) locates a node containing identical data to that pointed to by
** 'data'. If found, a pointer to the node containing the data is returned, or NULL if the
** list does not exist or if the data cannot be found.
**
** Note how search( ) requires a pointer 'cmp' to a function
** that expects two 'void' pointers and returns 0 if they are identical
*/

NODE  *search(ROOT **root, void *data, int (*cmp)( void *, void *))
{
  NODE  *node = NULL ;

/*
** Check that list is valid, if so, set 'node' to the head of the list, then begin a
** comparison of the data in the first node with key data. If found, 'node' is left
** pointing to the first node containing data matching 'data', otherwise 'node' is
** incremented to point to the next node
*/

  if( VALID(root))  {
    node = (*root)->head ;                   /* go to first node */

    while((node != NULL ) && (cmp( node->data, data ) != 0))
      node = node->next ;                    /* traverse list comparing data at each node */
  }
  return (node) ;
}
```

The function search_and_delete() shown in Program 17.10 searches for and deletes a particular node from the list. Again, if the list becomes empty, the root structure is released, and the program's root pointer is set to NULL (invalid).

Program 17.10 Searching for and deleting a node.

```
/*
** The following function searches for the specified data in the list and deletes it.
** Zero is returned upon success.
**
** search_and_delete() requires a pointer 'cmp' to a comparison function
** that expects two void pointers and returns an int result. This enables any two
** objects to be compared regardless of their type.
*/

int search_and_delete( ROOT **root, void *data, int (*cmp)( void *, void *) )
{
  NODE  *node ;
  void   *p1 ;

  if( VALID(root))
    if((node = search( root, data, cmp )) != NULL )
      if((p1= delete_node( root, node )) != NULL )  {  /* release the node */
        free( p1 ) ;                                   /* release the data at node */
        return 0 ;                                     /* return success */
      }
  return (-1) ;                                        /* return error if any problem */
}
```

Program 17.11 demonstrates the use of the search_and_delete() functions (which exercise the functions search(), compare() and delete_node()). The program begins by inserting several integer objects into a list. The list is displayed, and the program prompts the operator for integer data. That data is located in the list, and then removed, prior to the list being redisplayed. This is repeated until the list is empty.

Program 17.11 Example use of search and delete functions.

```
#include  <stdio.h>
#include  <stdlib.h>

#define  NEW(x)  (x *)malloc( sizeof( x ))

typedef   int        DATA ;                  /* DATA in a node is an integer */
```

```
int main(void)
{
   ROOT  *root = NULL ;
   DATA  *data , d1;
   char   buff[ BUFSIZ ] ;
   int      i = 0 ;

/* Insert 10 nodes into the list */

   for( i = 0; i < 10 ; i ++ )  {
      data = NEW( DATA ) ;                  /* allocate storage for new data, an integer */
      *data = i ;                           /* copy value of 'i' to it */
      printf("Inserting data = %d at head of list : ", i ) ;
      insert_data( &root, data, 0 ) ;       /* add data to list */
      display_list( &root, display_DATA ) ; /* display whole list */
   }

   printf("Deleting a Node . . . \n") ;

/* Now prompt and remove nodes from list until list is empty */

   while( VALID( &root ) )  {               /* while list is still valid; that is, contains data */
      printf("Enter data : ") ;
      d1 = atoi( gets( buff )) ;

/* Find first node with matching data and delete it, then redisplay list */

      if( search_and_delete( &root, &d1, compare_DATA ) == 0)  {
         printf("Deleted data %d from list . . . \n", d1) ;
         display_list( &root, display_DATA ) ;
      }
      else
         printf("Could not delete data %d from list . . . \n", d1) ;
   }
   return 0 ;
}
```

17.2 Doubly linked lists

A particularly common requirement of a linked list is the ability to traverse it in both directions. Moving forwards through a list, as we have seen, is relatively straightforward, since each node contains a pointer to the next node in that list. However, moving backwards presents some difficulty, and unfortunately this makes certain operations, such as inserting or deleting a node, rather inefficient as the address of the previous node may have to be located.

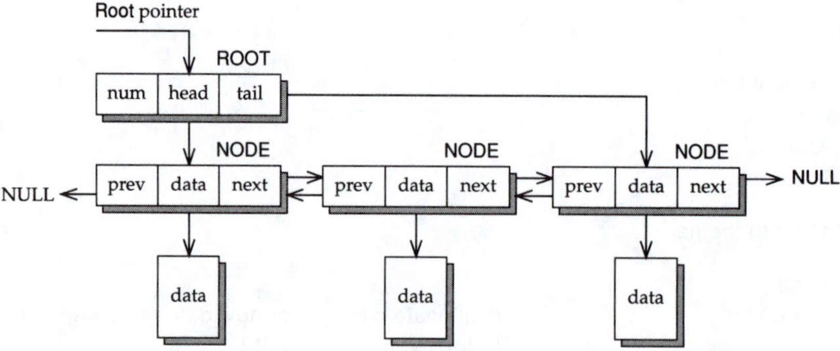

Figure 17.6 A typical doubly linked list implementation.

Faced with such a situation, the programmer might choose to modify the NODE structure of the (singly) linked list developed in the previous section, to include an additional pointer. This pointer could be used to point to the *previous* node in the list, as shown in Figure 17.6. Such a list is referred to as a doubly linked list and overcomes the limitations discussed above.

Of course some changes will be required to several of the list manipulation functions, but many work equally well with singly and doubly linked lists. Those functions requiring modifications are presented below. Firstly, however, the NODE structure will have to be modified to support a pointer to a previous node, as shown in Program 17.12.

Program 17.12 Making a node for a doubly linked list.

```
/*
** New data type NODE for a doubly linked list
*/

typedef struct  node  {
   struct node  *next ;                    /* pointer to next node in list */
   struct node  *prev ;                    /* pointer to previous node in list */
   void         *data ;                    /* pointer to data at this node */
} NODE ;                                   /* new data type is NODE */

/*
** Now modify make_node() to initialize the new 'prev' pointer to NULL
*/

NODE  *dbl_make_node( void *data )
{
   NODE  *node ;
```

```
    if((node = NEW( NODE )) != NULL )  {
      node->data = data ;                  /* point new node to its new data */
      node->next = NULL ;                  /* mark next node as invalid */
      node->prev = NULL ;                  /* mark previous node as invalid */
    }
    return node ;                          /* return a pointer to new node or NULL on error */
  }
```

Inserting a node now requires that the 'prev' pointer in a new node be initialized to point to its previous node, or NULL if the node is the first in the list, as shown in Program 17.13.

Program 17.13 Inserting data into a doubly linked list.

```
/*
** The following function creates and inserts a new node into a doubly linked list.
** If 'position' is equal to 0, the new node is inserted at the head of the list, otherwise
** it will be inserted at the tail. 0 is returned upon success.
*/

int  dbl_insert_data( ROOT **root, void *data, int position )
{
  NODE  *new ;

/*
** If root pointer in user's program is NULL, then list does not exist, so attempt to
** create it. If successful the address of the newly created root structure is assigned
** to the program's root pointer, otherwise it is left as NULL and (–1) is returned.
*/

  if( !VALID( root))
    if((*root = make_root( )) == NULL)
      return (–1);

/*
** If root exists, OR root has just been made (above), then make a new node.
** If new node cannot be created AND there are no other nodes in the
** list, then delete the root itself and assign NULL back to the program's root
** pointer and return (–1) to indicate the error.
*/

  if((new = dbl_make_node( data )) == NULL)  {
    if(NUM(root) == 0)  {
      free( *root ) ;
      *root = NULL ;
    }
    return (–1) ;
  }
```

```
/*
** If this is the first node, then set both 'head' and 'tail' in
** root structure to point to new node regardless of 'position'
*/

  if(NUM(root) == 0)
    (*root)->head = (*root)->tail = new ;

  else {
    if( position == 0 ) {                    /* insert at head */
      new->next = (*root)->head ;            /* point new node to existing head node */
      (*root)->head->prev = new ;            /* point existing head node to new node */
      (*root)->head = new ;                  /* make new node the head node */
    }
    else {                                   /* else insert at tail */
      (*root)->tail->next = new ;            /* point old tail node to new node */
      new->prev = (*root)->tail ;            /* point new node to old tail node */
      (*root)->tail = new ;                  /* make new node the tail */
    }
  }
  NUM(root) ++ ;                             /* increment node count for list */
  return 0 ;                                 /* return success */
}

/*
** The following function inserts a node prior to or after the node pointed to by
** node. If position is equal to 0, then the node is inserted
** prior to the node pointed to by 'node', otherwise it will be inserted after
** that node. 0 is returned upon success.
*/

int dbl_insert_at_position( ROOT **root, NODE *node, void *data, int position )
{
  int     flag = 0 ;
  NODE  *new, *prev ;

  if(!VALID(root) )
    return (-1) ;

  if(((*root)->head == node) && (position == 0))      /* if inserting before head node */
    flag = dbl_insert_data( root, data, 0 );            /* insert at head */


  else if(((*root)->tail == node) && (position == 1))  /* if inserting after tail node */
    flag = dbl_insert_data( root, data, 1 ) ;           /* insert at tail */

/*
** Otherwise, we must be inserting at a point that does not affect head or tail
** so obtain the address of its previous node.
*/
```

```
    else  {
        prev = node->prev ;                          /* get address of previous node */
        if((new = dbl_make_node( data )) == NULL)
            return -1 ;

/*
** If we are inserting after the specified node, then point new node to where the
** specified node is pointing, and point specified node to new node.
*/

        if( position == 1 )  {
            new->next = node->next ;                 /* point new node to next node */
            new->next->prev = new ;                  /* point next node to new node */
            node->next = new ;                       /* point specified node to new node */
            new->prev = node ;                       /* point new node to specified node */
        }

/*
** Otherwise inserting prior to current node, so make previous node point to new
** node and new node point to current node.
*/

        else  {
            new->next = node ;                       /* point new node to specified node */
            node->prev = new ;                       /* point specified node to new node */
            prev->next = new ;                       /* point previous node to new node */
            new->prev = prev ;                       /* point new node to previous node */
        }
        NUM(root) ++ ;                               /* increment node count */
    }
    return flag ;
}
```

17.2.1 *Deleting a node from a doubly linked list*

On the face of it, the function to delete a node from a doubly linked list, shown in Program 17.14, appears rather more complicated than that of its singly linked counterpart, but in fact it is far more efficient, since the address of the previous node is directly accessible from the deleted node.

Program 17.14 Deleting a node from a doubly linked list.

```
/*
** This function deletes the node pointed to by 'this' from a list. A pointer to the data
** stored at the deleted node is returned to the program, or NULL if the node cannot
** be deleted. Note that if all nodes have been deleted, then the ROOT structure is
** released and the program's root pointer is set to NULL.
*/
```

```
void  *dbl_delete_node( ROOT **root, NODE *this)
{
  void  *data_ptr ;                        /* pointer to data at node to be deleted */
  if( !VALID(root))
    return (NULL) ;                        /* return Error if list invalid */

/*
** If there are at least two nodes in the list and if the node to be deleted is at the head,
** then adjust the 'head' pointer in the 'root structure' to point to next node.
*/

  if(NUM(root) > 1 )  {
    if((*root)->head == this )  {
      (*root)->head = this->next ;
      this->next->prev = NULL ;
    }

/*
** If there are at least two nodes in the list and if the node to be deleted is at the tail,
** then adjust the 'tail' pointer in the 'root structure' to point to previous node.
*/

    else if((*root)->tail == this )  {
      (*root)->tail = this->prev ;
      this->prev->next = NULL ;
    }

/*
** If the else below is taken, there must be at least three nodes and the one to be
** deleted is neither at the head nor the tail of the list so there must be a node on
** either side of it.
**
** Therefore make the next node (that is, the one after the node to be deleted)
** point to the previous node (that is, the one before the node to be deleted) and
** vice versa.
*/

    else  {
      this->next->prev = this->prev ;
      this->prev->next = this->next ;
    }
  }

  data_ptr = this->data;                   /* save address of data at node to be deleted */
  free( this ) ;

/*
** Now decrement node count, and if it is zero, delete root structure
** and set program root pointer to NULL.
*/
```

```
    if(--NUM(root) == 0)  {
        *root = NULL ;
        free(*root) ;
    }

    return (data_ptr) ;                          /* return address of deleted node's data */
}
```

As we no longer require the use of the function find_previous_node( ), it now becomes the programmer's responsibility to validate the node address, although in practice the node address would probably be obtained by traversing the list in the first place and is therefore unlikely to be invalid.

Traversing a doubly linked list backwards is demonstrated by the function shown in Program 17.15, which displays the data in all nodes of the list, commencing with the last and moving towards the first.

Program 17.15 Example traversal of a doubly linked list.

```
/*
** This function displays the data in every node in the list. A pointer to a function
** that can be called to display the data at each node is required.
*/

void display_list_tail(ROOT **root, void (*disp)( void *data ))
{
    NODE  *node ;

    if( VALID(root))  {
        printf("Backwards: ") ;
        node = (*root)->tail ;

        do  {
            disp( node->data) ;                   /* call display function */
            node = node->prev ;                   /* move to previous node */
        }while( node != NULL ) ;
    }
}
```

17.2.2 *Saving and recovering a linked list to/from a file*

Often, the contents of a linked list may have to be saved to and recovered from a disk file. Such an operation is easily achieved by traversing the list from head to tail, saving the data stored at each node.

It is important to appreciate that neither the nodes themselves nor the root structure or pointer need to be saved, and in fact must *not* be saved, since there is no guarantee that upon recovery of the list from disk the addresses contained in these objects will be valid. To recover the list, successive items of data must be read from the file and re-inserted at the end of the (non-) existing list to preserve the original order. The latter will be more efficient with a doubly linked list. The functions save_list() and recover_list() shown in Program 17.16 illustrate how this might be achieved.

Program 17.16 Functions to save and recover a doubly linked list.

```
/*
** The following function saves the data stored in the linked list whose ROOT is
** pointed to by 'root', to the file given by 'filename'. Each item of data in the list
** is assumed to be 'datasize' bytes in size. The list and its contents are unaffected
** by this operation.
**
** Upon success, 0 is returned, or (-1) if the disk file cannot be opened or written to.
*/

int  save_list( const char *filename, ROOT **root, size_t datasize)
{
  FILE   *fp ;
  NODE  *node = (*root)->head ; /* point to first node at head of list */

  if(VALID( root ))  {                 /* check that list has at least one node in it */

    if((fp = fopen(filename, "wb")) == NULL)
      return (-1) ;                    /* return error if cannot create/open file for writing */

/*
** Now write the data in successive nodes to the disk in binary form
** until the end of the list is encountered (or a write error occurs) then close file.
*/

    do  {
      if(fwrite( node->data, datasize, 1, fp) != 1)
        return (-1) ;                  /* error writing to disk */

      node = node->next ;              /* go to next node */
    }while( node != NULL ) ;           /* while not at end of list */
    return( fclose( fp )) ;            /* return 0 on success or -1 on failure */
  }
  return 0 ;                           /* success */
}

/*
** This function recovers the data for a linked list from a disk file and appends it to
** an existing doubly linked list pointed to by root. If root is NULL, then a new list
** is created.
```

```
** On success 0 is returned. (-1) is returned on a memory allocation error, (-2) for a
** disk read error, or (-3) for a list insertion error.
*/

int recover_list( const char *filename, ROOT **root, size_t datasize)
{
  FILE  *fp ;
  void  *dptr ;

  if((fp = fopen(filename, "rb")) == NULL )  /* open named file for reading */
    return (-1) ;                           /* return -1 on error */

  do  {
    if((dptr = malloc( datasize )) == NULL)  /* allocate storage for each item of data */
      return (-1) ;                         /* return (-1) on memory allocation error */

    if(fread( dptr, datasize, 1, fp) != 1) {  /* read one item of data */
      if( feof( fp))                        /* if failure, was it due to end-of-file */
        return 0 ;                          /* return success */
      else  {                               /* otherwise must have been due to error */
        free( dptr ) ;                      /* yes, release storage for data just requested */
        return (-2) ;                       /* return (-2) on read error */
      }
    }

/*
** Now try and insert new data at the end of the list. If unsuccessful, return an error.
*/

    if(dbl_insert_data( root, dptr, 1 ) != 0)  /* insert data at tail of list */
      return (-3) ;                         /* return (-3) on insertion error */

  } while( 1 );                             /* repeat until EOF or error */
}
```

17.3 The software stack

Another extremely useful data structure is the **stack**. Applications for stacks arise routinely in applications where there is a need to store temporary data. Virtually every modern microprocessor employs a **hardware** or 'silicon' stack specifically to save the program counter's 'return' address when a function is called. Temporary variables, such as arguments to functions and automatic variables, are also pushed/created on the stack by the compiler, as we saw in Chapter 6.

From a conceptual point of view, a stack can be thought of as a linked list, with a number of imposed limitations. Firstly, data may only be inserted at one end of the list (usually the head, but the tail is also acceptable) with a 'push'

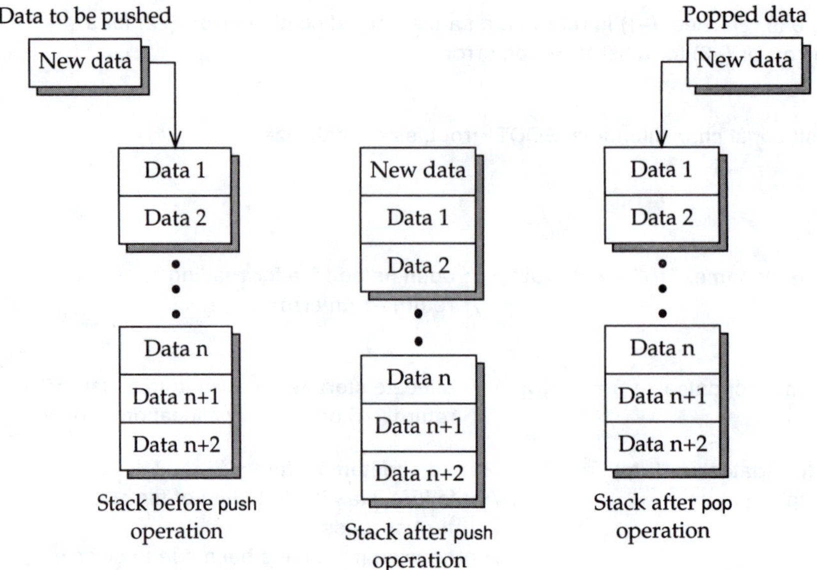

Figure 17.7 The operation of a typical software stack.

operation. That data can subsequently be recovered with a 'pop' operation, which removes the last item of data previously 'pushed' on the stack (Figure 17.7).

Because a stack limits the insertion and retrieval of data to just one position, a simple stack can be, and often is, implemented using an array, especially when the storage requirements of the stack can be predicted at compile time, but such an approach still raises the possibility of a **stack overflow**, should the bounds of the array be exceeded. The stack implementation developed here overcomes this limitation through the use of a linked list.

Recalling that a 'push' operation simply adds data to the top of a stack a generic push( ) function or even a macro could be written as shown in Program

Program 17.17 Pushing data onto a stack.

```
/*
** The following function pushes the data pointed to by 'data' onto the stack pointed to
** by 'stack'. 0 is returned upon success. Note that it is the programmer's responsibility
** to ensure that storage for the data is allocated, and that it has been initialized.
*/

typedef   ROOT   STACK ;                    /* create new data type 'STACK' */

int push( STACK **stack, void *data )
{
   return( dbl_insert_data( stack, data, 0 ) ) ;
}
```

17.17. For readability, the new data type STACK has been created, based upon the data type ROOT developed for the linked list.

Likewise, **popping** the stack recovers the data from the node at the head of the list and returns a pointer to it back to the calling program, before the storage occupied by its node is released. Note that the implementation of 'pop' in Program 17.18 returns a generic pointer to the data at the top of the stack, *not* the data itself. It is therefore the programmer's responsibility to release the storage occupied by this data.

Program 17.18 Popping data from a stack.

```
/*
** 'pop' data from the top of a stack. A pointer to the data is returned, or NULL on error.
*/

void *pop(STACK**stack)
{
   return( dbl_delete_node( stack, (*stack)->head) ) ;
}
```

Program 17.19 demonstrates these two functions in relation to the manipulation of an integer stack. The program assumes the existence of the doubly linked list functions described in Section 17.2.

Program 17.19 Pushing integer data onto a stack.

```
#include  <stdio.h>
#include  <stdlib.h>

#define   NEW(x)     (x *)malloc( sizeof( x ))
#define   VALID(x)   ((*x) != NULL)

int main( void )
{
   STACK   *root = NULL ;     /* program 'STACK' pointer must be initialized to NULL */
   int     *data, d1, i ;     /* create a pointer 'data' to an object of type int */

/* Now push 10 integers onto the stack */

   printf("Pushing : ") ;

   for( i = 0; i < 10 ; i ++ )  {
      data = NEW( int ) ;     /* allocate storage for an int */
      *data = i ;             /* copy data to new storage */
      printf("%d ", i ) ;
      push(&root, data ) ;    /* push onto stack */
   }
```

```
    putchar('\n') ;

/* Now pop data off stack until empty */

    printf("Popping : ") ;

    while( VALID( &root)) {
        data = pop( &root ) ;        /* pop data off stack */
        d1 = *data ;                 /* copy data to permanent variable */
        free( data ) ;               /* release storage held by data */
        printf("%d ", d1) ;          /* display data popped off stack */
    }
    return 0 ;
}
```

When Program 17.19 is run, the operator will observe the following output displayed on the terminal, demonstrating how the stack behaves as a last-in, first-out (LIFO) buffer. That is to say, the last item of data pushed onto the stack is the first to be popped off:

```
Pushing : 0 1 2 3 4 5 6 7 8 9
Popping : 9 8 7 6 5 4 3 2 1 0
```

The benefit of using a linked list rather than an array is that the size of the stack can easily be adjusted to accommodate any amount of data. Basing the stack implementation around a linked list also has the benefit that other linked list functions may be called upon to perform other (non-standard) actions upon a stack. Functions such as delete_list( ), for example, can be used to tidy up or delete a stack when the program has finished with it.

Although the push( ) and pop( ) functions developed above are simple, they rely upon the programmer to allocate, initialize and release the storage occupied by each item of stack data. An alternative, but less generic, solution might call an intermediate function, such as push_int( ), which could allocate storage for an int, initialize it with the data and then call push( ) to add it to the stack. Likewise, a function such as pop_int( ) could act as an interface to extract and release the storage occupied by an int on the stack.

The only drawback to such an approach is that unique push and pop functions would be required for each type of data to be stacked. However, where the number of different types of data to be stacked is limited, it can prove worthwhile. Such an approach is used in the example in Program 17.20, which implements a simple four function calculator using a stack. The operator is expected to supply both data and operators using the postfix or 'reverse polish'

Program 17.20 A simple four function calculator using a stack.

```
#include  <stdio.h>
#include  <stdlib.h>
#include  <ctype.h>                          /* for isdigit() */
#include  <string.h>                         /* for strcmp() */

#define   NEW( x )    (x *)malloc( sizeof( x ))
#define   VALID( x )  ((*x) != NULL )
#define   NUM( x )    ((*x)->num)

typedef   ROOT        STACK ;               /* new data type called STACK for readability */

/*
** This function pushes data of type 'double' onto the stack
** The storage is allocated automatically and initialized with the data
** pointed to by 'data'. 0 is returned upon success.
*/

int push_double( STACK **stack, double *data )
{
  double  *ptr ;

  if((ptr = NEW( double )) != NULL )  {     /* allocate storage for data on stack */
    *ptr = *data ;                           /* copy data to new storage and insert at head */
    return( dbl_insert_data( stack, ptr, 0)) ;
  }
  return (-1) ;
}

/*
** This function pops a 'double' from the top of the stack and stores it at the address
** held by 'data'. The storage for the node and its data is released. 0 is returned
** upon success.
*/

int pop_double( STACK **stack, double *data )
{
  if( !VALID(stack))
    return (-1) ;

/*
** Get data from top of stack and store at address pointed to by 'data', then release the
** storage and delete the node.
*/

  *data = *(double *)((*stack)->head->data) ;
  free((*stack)->head->data) ;

  if( dbl_delete_node( stack, (*stack)->head ) == NULL)
    return (-1) ;
```

```
  else
    return 0 ;
}

int main( void )
{
  STACK  *stack = NULL;                       /* mark stack as initially invalid */
  double  d1, d2, d3;                         /* variables to hold arguments and result */
  char    buff[ BUFSIZ ] ;

  while( 1 )  {
    gets( buff ) ;                            /* read operator entry */

    if( buff[ 0 ] == NULL )
      continue ;                              /* ignore CR entries */

    if( buff[ 0 ] == 'c')  {
      delete_list( &stack) ;                  /* Clear calculator stack */
      printf("Calculator Cleared . . . \n") ;
      continue ;
    }

/* If the entry is not a digit and not CR, must be an operator */

    if( !isdigit( buff[0] ) && strlen(buff) == 1 )  {

/*
** Check that there are sufficient arguments on stack as each operation requires two.
** If so, pull two arguments off the stack.
*/

      if( !VALID( &stack) || NUM( &stack ) < 2 )  {
        printf("NOT enough arguments . . . \n") ;
        continue ;
      }

      pop_double( &stack, &d1 ) ;
      pop_double( &stack, &d2 ) ;

/* Decide which operation to perform */

      switch( buff[ 0 ] )
      {
/* Addition */        case '+' :  d3 = d2 + d1 ;
                                  printf("%g + %g = %g\n", d2, d1, d3 ) ;
                                  push_double( &stack, &d3) ;
                                  break ;

/* Subtraction */     case '-' :  d3 = d2 - d1 ;
                                  printf("%g - %g = %g\n", d2, d1, d3 ) ;
                                  push_double( &stack, &d3 ) ;
                                  break ;
```

```
/* Multiplication */    case '*' :  d3 = d2 * d1 ;
                                    printf("%g * %g = %g\n", d2, d1, d3 ) ;
                                    push_double( &stack, &d3 ) ;
                                    break ;

/* Division */          case '/' :  if( d1 == 0.0 )
                                    printf("Divide by zero ... \n") ;
                                    else  {
                                      d3 = d2 / d1 ;
                                      printf("%g / %g = %g\n", d2, d1, d3 ) ;
                                      push_double( &stack, &d3 ) ;
                                    }
                                    break ;

      }
    }
    else  {                         /* must be data so push it on stack */
      d1 = atof(buff ) ;
      push_double( &stack, &d1 ) ;
    }
  }
  return 0 ;
}
```

notation, which was once very popular with some of the first generation handheld calculators. Table 17.1 shows how an expression expressed conventionally (using infix notation) can be converted to postfix notation.

Program 17.20 reads data from an operator. If the entry is numeric, the data is pushed onto a stack. Otherwise, if the entry is an operator, such as '+', '–', '*' or '/', then the last two entries on the stack are popped and the appropriate operation is performed on them. The result is then pushed back onto the stack.

A feature to clear the calculator (that is, to remove any data on the stack) has also been incorporated, along with a test to ensure that at least two items of data exist on the stack before an operator can be applied.

Table 17.1 Infix to postfix conversion.

Infix expression	*Postfix expression*
2 + 3	2 3 +
2 – 3	2 3 –
(2 + 3) – 4	2 3 + 4 –
2 + (3 – 4)	2 3 4 – +

17.4 The software queue

A queue, like a stack, can also be constructed around an array or a linked list. It differs from a stack only in the sense that data is retrieved from a queue in the *same* order in which it is inserted. It thus behaves as a first-in, first-out buffer or FIFO, or, looking at it in another way, as a last-in, last-out buffer. Figure 17.8 illustrates the insertion and retrieval of data in/from a queue.

Applications for queues are many and varied. Multi-tasking computer systems frequently employ a queue to facilitate interprocess communication using a 'pipeline'. Process communication with external devices such as terminals often uses a queue to buffer incoming and outgoing data between device and program.

Two functions/macros are required to manipulate a queue; in Program 17.21 both are based around the doubly linked list. The first function, `insert()`, will add an item of data to the head of a queue, and is thus identical to the function `push()` developed for a stack. The second function, `retrieve()`, returns a pointer to the data at the end of the queue and releases the storage for its node.

If Program 17.19 was modified such that the calls to `push()` and `pop()` were replaced by calls to `insert()` and `retrieve()`, and the messages `"Pushing"` and `"Popping"` replaced by `"Inserting"` and `"Retrieving"`, then the following display

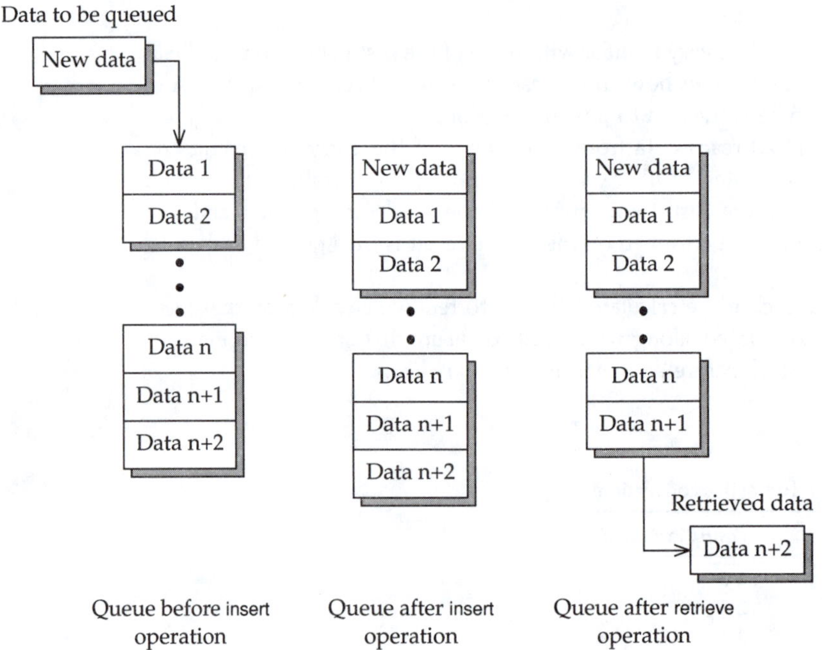

Figure 17.8 The operation of a typical software queue.

Program 17.21 Inserting and retrieving data from a queue.

```
/*
** The following function inserts a node at the head of the queue pointed to by 'queue'
** and associates the data pointed to by 'data' with that node. 0 is returned upon
** success. It is the programmer's responsibility to ensure that storage for the data is
** allocated, and that it has been initialized with the appropriate data.
*/

typedef ROOT QUEUE ;

int insert( QUEUE **queue, void *data )
{
    return( dbl_insert_data( queue, data, 0 )) ;
}

/*
** This function retrieves the data from the end of a queue and returns a pointer to it.
** The storage occupied by the node is released. It is the programmer's responsibility
** to ensure that the storage occupied by this data is released later.
*/

void *retrieve(QUEUE **queue)
{
    return( dbl_delete_node( queue, (*queue)->tail) ) ;
}
```

would be observed on the operator's terminal, demonstrating the first-in, first-out nature of the queue:

```
Inserting : 0 1 2 3 4 5 6 7 8 9
Retrieving : 0 1 2 3 4 5 6 7 8 9
```

17.5 The circular queue

A simple variation on the basic queue is the circular queue, which is often used by operating system schedulers. Here, the node at the tail of the queue is set to point to the node at the head (and the head node is set to point to the tail node in the case of a doubly linked list), thus creating a circular list of nodes, as shown in Figure 17.9.

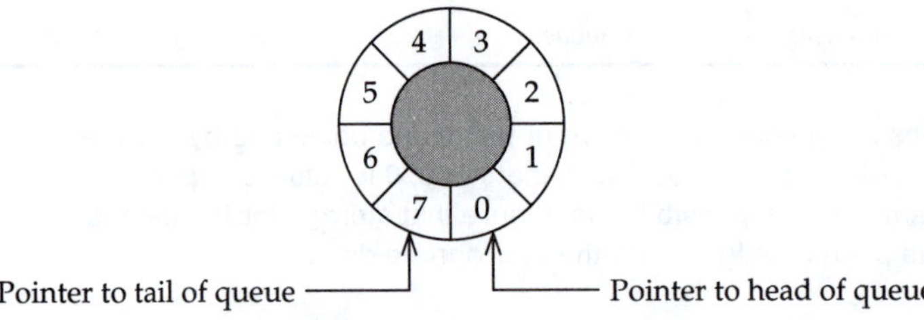

Figure 17.9 The circular queue.

Figure 17.10 shows how a circular queue might be implemented using a doubly linked list.

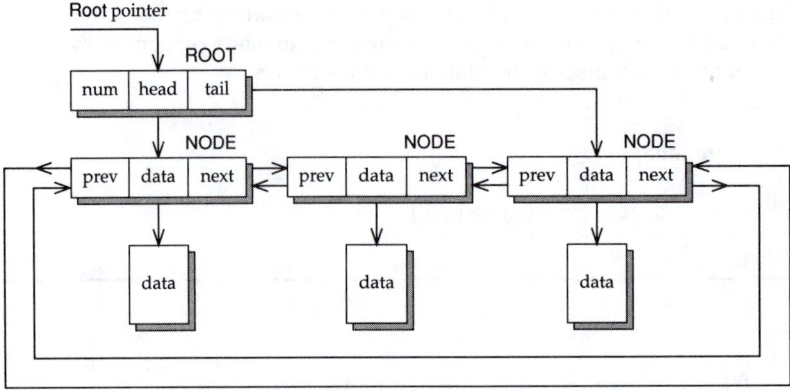

Figure 17.10 The circular queue using a doubly linked list.

17.5.1 *Inserting data into a circular queue*

Data is easily inserted into a circular queue by creating a new node and inserting it either as the new head node or the new tail node. The next and prev pointers of the head and tail nodes are then adjusted to point to each other. The head and tail pointers in the root structure serve only as a reference point for the insertion, and one or other may need adjusting after the insertion.

The function insert_circ_queue(), shown in Program 17.22, inserts a new node at the head or tail of a circular queue, under the direction of the argument position. The next and prev pointers of the head and tail nodes are then adjusted to point to each other to maintain the circular nature of the queue.

As before, the calling program must take responsibility for the allocation and initialization of the storage for any data to be inserted into the queue. The address of this storage should be given in the argument data. For readability, the

Program 17.22 Inserting data into a circular queue.

```
/*
** Insert an object into a circular queue. If 'position' is equal to 0, the new node will
** become the head node, otherwise it will become the tail. The queue will be created
** if it does not exist. Upon success, 0 is returned
*/

typedef  ROOT  CQUEUE ;                /* New data type CQUEUE for readability */

int insert_circ_queue( CQUEUE **queue , void *data, int position )
{
  if( dbl_insert_data( queue, data, position ) != 0 )
    return (-1) ;

/*
** Adjust both the head and tail nodes pointers to keep queue circular
*/

  (*queue)->tail->next = (*queue)->head ;
  (*queue)->head->prev = (*queue)->tail ;

  return 0 ;
}
```

new data type CQUEUE has been created based upon the ROOT data type developed for doubly linked lists.

17.5.2 *Deleting data from a circular queue*

Deleting data from a circular queue requires that the storage for the corresponding node be released, and that a pointer to the data be returned to the program (should it be required). The next and prev pointers in the head and tail nodes are then adjusted to maintain the circular nature of the queue. These actions are demonstrated in the function delete_circ_queue( ), in Program 17.23. The user's program must take responsibility for releasing the storage held by the deleted node's data at a suitable point in the program.

Program 17.23 Deleting data from a circular queue.

```
/*
** Delete a node from the head of a circular queue. A pointer to the deleted node's
** 'data' is returned if successful, or NULL if not.
*/
```

```
void *delete_circ_queue( CQUEUE **queue )
{
   void *p1 ;                          /* pointer to data at the deleted node */

   if((p1 = dbl_delete_node( queue, (*queue)->head )) == NULL )
        return NULL ;

/*
** Check in case the queue no longer exists then adjust pointers to head and tail nodes
*/

   if( VALID( queue )) {
      (*queue)->tail->next = (*queue)->head ;
      (*queue)->head->prev = (*queue)->tail ;
   }
   return p1 ;                         /* return pointer to data */
}
```

17.5.3 *Extracting and replacing data in a circular queue*

Many applications of circular queues require that the program be able to 'extract' or make a copy of the data stored within a node, preferably without having to delete the node in the process. Similarly, the program may wish to update or replace the data in a node, without having to re-insert it.

The macro extract( ) shown below copies the data held by the node at the head of a queue into the object pointed to by 'dptr', while the macro replace( ) copies the data pointed to by 'dptr' into the node at the head of the queue:

```
#define extract(queue, dptr, type) ((*dptr) = *(type *)((*queue)->head->data))
#define replace(queue, dptr, type) (*(type *)((*queue)->head->data) = (*dptr))
```

Note that both macros are generic and are independent of the type of data stored in the queue. This is accomplished through the use of the macro argument type which must be a proper C data type such as int, double and so on.

17.5.4 *Rotating a circular queue*

Rotating a circular queue is easily accomplished by moving the head and tail pointers in the root structure, forwards or backwards one node. The function rotate( ) in Program 17.24 demonstrates this, where the direction of rotation is controlled by the argument direction.

Program 17.24 Rotating a circular queue.

```
/*
** Function to rotate a circular queue forwards or backwards by one node
*/

int rotate( CQUEUE **queue, int direction )
{
  if( !VALID( queue ))
    return (-1) ;

  if( direction == 0)                              /* Rotate forwards */
    (*queue)->head = (*queue)->head->next ;        /* move 'head' to next node */
  else                                             /* Rotate backwards */
    (*queue)->head = (*queue)->head->prev ;        /* move 'head' to previous node */

  (*queue)->tail = (*queue)->head->prev ;          /* move 'tail' to node prior to head */

  return 0 ;
}
```

17.5.5 *Traversing a circular queue*

Traversing a circular queue from head to tail, perhaps for the purpose of deleting or listing the data contained within its nodes, requires a different approach to that of traversing a linked list, since the queue has no obvious end. Testing for a NULL valued next pointer within each node will thus not work. However, as any node pointer used to traverse the queue will eventually wrap around and end up pointing to the node it started with, this can be used to terminate the loop, as shown in Program 17.25.

Program 17.25 Traversing a circular queue.

```
/*
** Function to traverse a circular queue
*/

void traverse( CQUEUE **queue )
{
  int  count = 0 ;
  NODE  *node = (*queue)->head ;            /* start from node at head of queue */

  do  {
    printf("Visiting Node %d\n", count++ ) ;
    node = node->next ;                     /* move to next node */
  } while( node != (*queue)->head ) ;       /* until head node encountered again */
}
```

The circular queue is important since it forms the basis of the 'scheduler' found in many multi-tasking operating systems. Such a scheduler usually maintains a circular queue of process descriptors containing information about each eligible process, such as the value of the CPU registers, the process's priority, current processing state, memory requirements and so on.

A new process is normally initiated by invoking the scheduler via a software primitive such as fork( ). The scheduler creates a descriptor for the process, which is then inserted into the circular queue. Should a process terminate itself, then by definition it must be executing at the time and thus the descriptor at the head of the queue is deleted.

Forced process swaps are generally effected by means of a hardware real-time clock (RTC) interrupting the CPU at periodic intervals, typically in the range of 10 and 50 ms. These interrupts are intercepted by the scheduler, which records the state of the current process within the corresponding process descriptor (currently at the head of the queue), then the queue is rotated. The descriptor now at the head of the queue is extracted and the state of the CPU restored to its previous value. The process is then allowed to resume.

Program 17.26 demonstrates these concepts by simulating processes using functions that are called in rotating sequence by the scheduler. A process descriptor is created for each process, and is inserted into the scheduler's circular queue. Time-slicing is simulated by the functions themselves, using software time delays, after which they return to the scheduler. Process termination is simulated by the process returning a value of 0 back to the scheduler.

Program 17.26 A mini operating system scheduler.

```
#include <stdio.h>
#include <stdlib.h>
#include <time.h>                    /* for clock( ) function and 'clock_t' data type */

/*
** Now define the data to be stored in the circular queue. It will take the form
** of a simple 'process descriptor'
*/

typedef struct data {
    int        process_id ;          /* process identification number */
    int        num_ticks ;           /* number of ticks received by the process */
    int        (*function)(void) ;   /* pointer to a function that simulates the process */
    clock_t time ;                   /* total time received by the process */
} PROCESS ;                          /* new data type PROCESS */

#define VALID(x)  ((*x) != NULL )
#define NEW(x)    (x *)malloc(sizeof(x))

/*
** Some simple macros to make the program more readable
*/
```

```
#define  ADD_JOB          insert_circ_queue
#define  KILL_JOB         delete_circ_queue
#define  SHOW_JOBS        display_circ_queue
#define  SWAP_JOB         rotate
#define  UPDATE_PROCESS   replace
#define  GET_NEXT_JOB     extract

#define  MAX_JOBS         1    /* maximum number of processes to simulate */

/*
** This is the basic template for a 'function' that will simulate a process in our scheduler.
** Many of these can be created to simulate a multi-process simulation.
*/

int func0( void )
{
/*
** This 'process' will run for five time periods before terminating. This can be
** altered to simulate a process that runs for longer
*/

  static int count = 5 ;
  long i ;

/*
** A software delay to simulate the time between ticks
** from the real-time clock. Delay may be adjusted to suit
*/

  for( i = 0; i < 2000000L; i ++ )
    ;

  return (--count ) ;              /* Return 0 when process wishes to terminate for good */
}

/* The following is a user supplied function to display the ID number of a process */

void display( void *data )
{
  printf("%d ", ((PROCESS *)(data))->process_id ) ;
}

/*
** The following function displays the process ID numbers
** of all processes in the circular queue. It requires a pointer
** to a function that can be called to display the data within
** an object of type PROCESS, such as the function display( ) above.
*/
```

```
void display_circ_queue( CQUEUE **queue, void (*disp)( void *data ) )
{
  NODE  *node, *head ;

  printf("Process Queue = [ ") ;

  if( VALID( queue ))  {
    head = node = (*queue)->head ;
    do  {
      disp( node->data) ;                 /* call display function */
      node = node->next ;                 /* move to next node */
    } while( node != head ) ;             /* until all nodes visited */
  }
  printf("]\n") ;
}

int main( void )
{
  CQUEUE    *c_queue = NULL ;             /* new pointer to a circular queue */
  PROCESS   pd, *process;                 /* a new process descriptor and pointer */
  clock_t   t1, t2 ;                      /* two objects to record CPU time */
  int       i ;

/*
** Introduce an array of pointers to functions initialized with the addresses of those
** functions that will simulate processes.
*/

  int (*ptr[ ])( void ) = { func0 } ;     /* other functions can be added to this list */

/* Now create a process descriptor and submit it to the scheduler for running */

  for( i = 0; i < MAX_JOBS; i++ )  {
    process = NEW( PROCESS ) ;
    process->process_id = i;              /* set process ID to 'i' */
    process->function = ptr[ i ] ;        /* call this function to simulate process */
    process->time = 0 ;                   /* set total CPU time to zero */
    process->num_ticks = 0 ;              /* number of ticks set to zero */
    ADD_JOB( &c_queue, process, 1 ) ;     /* submit job for scheduling */
    SHOW_JOBS( &c_queue, display) ;       /* show list of jobs in queue */
  }

/*
** While there are process descriptors in the scheduler
** queue, then let the process at the head of the queue run
*/

  while( VALID( &c_queue ))  {
    GET_NEXT_JOB( &c_queue, &pd , PROCESS) ;
    printf("Running Process [%d] : ", pd.process_id) ;
    SHOW_JOBS( &c_queue, display ) ;
```

```
/*
** Record how many ticks and how much CPU time the process has received
** during this 'time-slice' and add this to the total CPU time given to the process.
*/

     t1 = clock( ) ;                              /* record current time */
     i = pd.function( ) ;                         /* call function to simulate a process */
     t2 = clock( ) ;                              /* record new time */

     pd.time += (t2 – t1) ;                       /* record total CPU time used by process */
     pd.num_ticks ++ ;                            /* record number of ticks allotted to process */

/*
** If function returned 0, this indicates that it now wishes to be terminated, so remove
** it from the scheduler queue and free its storage, otherwise, update its process
** descriptor, swap the process out and get the next process to run
*/

     if( i == 0 )  {
       free( KILL_JOB( &c_queue )) ;
       printf(" ... Process %d Died after %g seconds of CPU time and %d ticks\n",
                                       pd.process_id, pd.time/CLK_TCK, pd.num_ticks) ;
     }
     else  {
       UPDATE_PROCESS( &c_queue, &pd, PROCESS ) ;
       SWAP_JOB( &c_queue, 0 ) ;          /* rotate circular queue */
     }
   }

/* Stop when all processes have run to completion */

   printf("Process Queue is Empty ... \n" ) ;
   return 0 ;
}
```

When Program 17.26 was run with a three process queue, which would be simulated for two, four and five time slices, respectively, the following example display was produced:

```
Process Queue = [ 0 ]
Process Queue = [ 0 1 ]
Process Queue = [ 0 1 2 ]
Running Process [ 0 ] : Process Queue = [ 0 1 2 ]
Running Process [ 1 ] : Process Queue = [ 1 2 0 ]
Running Process [ 2 ] : Process Queue = [ 2 0 1 ]
Running Process [ 0 ] : Process Queue = [ 0 1 2 ]
Running Process [ 1 ] : Process Queue = [ 1 2 0 ]
... Process 1 Died after 1.20879 seconds of CPU time and 2 ticks
```

```
Running Process [ 2 ] : Process Queue = [ 2 0 ]
Running Process [ 0 ] : Process Queue = [ 0 2 ]
Running Process [ 2 ] : Process Queue = [ 2 0 ]
Running Process [ 0 ] : Process Queue = [ 0 2 ]
Running Process [ 2 ] : Process Queue = [ 2 0 ]
... Process 2 Died after 2.41758 seconds of CPU time and 4 ticks
Running Process [ 0 ] : Process Queue = [ 0 ]
... Process 0 Died after 3.13187 seconds of CPU time and 5 ticks
Process Queue is Empty ...
```

17.6 Binary trees

For many applications, the linked list offers a versatile and expandable structure that can form the core of other more complex data structures, with few or no modifications. However, the basic linked list suffers from two fundamental weaknesses. Firstly, because there is no fixed relationship between the position of nodes stored in memory within a linked list (the operating system allocates memory to malloc( ) wherever it is available), it will not be possible to search the list using a binary search algorithm (see Chapter 8). Any search operation will thus have to take the form of a rather inefficient linear search, traversing the list from head to tail until the required data is located. For large lists this can be particularly slow.

Secondly, because of the random distribution of nodes in memory, any sorting algorithm designed to sort linked lists will also be inefficient. Even if the programmer were to design his or her application such that new data was always inserted in a 'sorted' order, such an operation would rely upon a (linear) search to locate the correct point for the insertion.

Thus, when an application calls for the versatility of a linked list, coupled with the ability to rapidly search and sort the data it maintains, the structure of the linear linked list is often modified into the form of a binary tree, as shown in Figure 17.11. In this illustration, each node in the tree stores a unique integer as its data.

A binary tree is thus a **hierarchical** structure based on a modified form of a linked list. Each node in the tree maintains two further node pointers, known as 'left' and 'right', which point to left and right **sub-trees** of that node.

Absent sub-trees are marked by a NULL-valued left or right pointer within their corresponding node. A node with neither left nor right sub-trees is known as a **leaf** node, while the node at the top of the tree is called the **root** node.

Figure 17.11 illustrates what is known as a 'balanced' tree, where there is, at most, a one node difference in the depth of nodes that lie between any two leaf nodes. For optimum performance during searching and sorting, this is a highly desirable feature. A data structure and a function to support the creation of a tree node are given in Program 17.27.

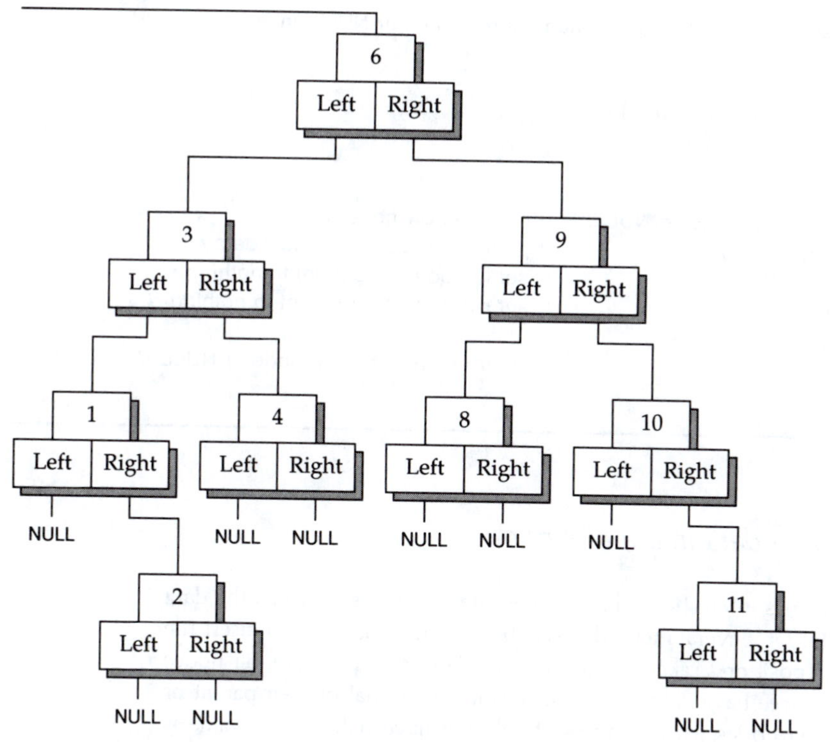

Figure 17.11 The structure of a typical binary tree.

Program 17.27 Data structure and make_node() function for a binary tree.

```
/*
** Data structure for the creation of a binary tree
*/

#define NEW( x )   (x *)malloc( sizeof( x ))

typedef struct tnode {
    void   *data ;                  /* pointer to this node's data */
    struct tnode *left ;            /* pointer to this node's left sub-tree */
    struct tnode *right ;           /* pointer to this node's right sub-tree */
} TNODE ;                           /* new data type is TNODE */

/*
** The following function makes a new tree node and associates with it
** the program's data, whose address is held in the argument 'data'. It is the
** program's responsibility to ensure that storage has been allocated for the
** data at this node, and that 'data' points to it. The left and right
** sub-tree pointers are initialized to invalid (NULL).
```

```
**
** Upon success, a pointer to the new node is returned, or NULL on failure
*/

TNODE   *make_node( void *data )
{
   TNODE   *root ;

   if((root = NEW( TNODE)) != NULL) {  /* make a new node */
      root->data = data ;              /* point new node to its new data */
      root->left = NULL ;              /* set left pointer to point to nothing */
      root->right = NULL ;             /* set right pointer to point to nothing */
   }
   return (root) ;                     /* return pointer to new node or NULL */
}
```

17.6.1 *Inserting data into a binary tree*

A binary tree becomes interesting when we consider the ways in which the data may be inserted into it. Several methods exist, but the most useful is to insert the data in its sorted position. Take another look at Figure 17.11. Here, all nodes within any left sub-tree have data whose value is less than that of their parent or root node, while all nodes within any right sub-tree have data whose value is greater than that of their parent or root node. This analysis is true for any node at any level in the tree.

Insertion of data in a sorted binary tree is simply a matter of comparing that data with that stored at the root node. If the former is less than or greater than the latter, then the data must be inserted, respectively, within the left or right sub-tree of the root node. The insert routine then moves to the node at the head of the chosen sub-tree and again compares the insert data with the data in this node.

This process is repeated until finally a node is encountered with a NULL pointer, marking the end of a chosen path through the tree. This node then represents the correct place to hang or insert a new node and its data. For example, inserting the value '5' into the tree shown in Figure 17.11 would result in a new right node and sub-tree being created for node '4'. Using this approach it is easy to see that an insertion routine requires at most 'n' comparisons, where 'n' is the depth of hierarchy, or number of levels within the tree, 4 for Figure 17.11.

This insertion algorithm is important, since the order in which data is inserted into the tree dramatically affects its shape and depth. For example, if the integer data 9, 4, 6, 8, 2, 1, 3, 11, 10 were inserted in that order into an empty tree, a tree of the shape shown in Figure 17.12 would result.

It is interesting to observe the effect on the shape of the tree if data is inserted in ascending or descending order. Here the tree **degenerates** into a

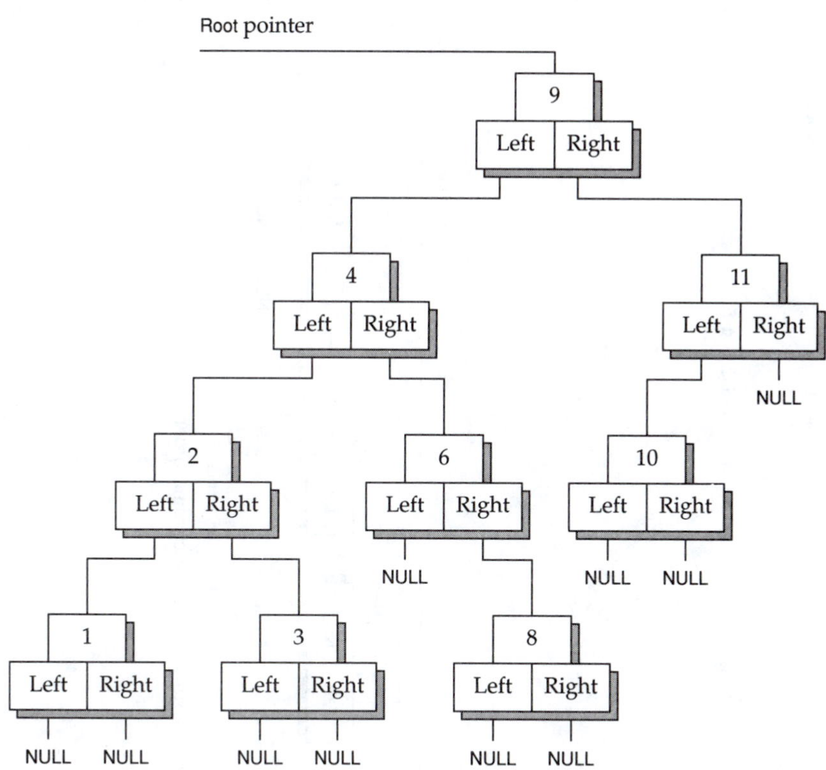

Figure 17.12 Shape of the tree when inserting data in the order 9, 4, 6, 8, 2, 1, 3, 11, 10.

simple linear linked list, as shown in Figures 17.13 and 17.14 with either the left or right pointers at each node simply set to NULL. In these instances, searching a degenerate tree becomes no more effective than searching a linked list.

The function insert_data() shown in Program 17.28 facilitates the creation and insertion of generic data into a binary tree. Note how a user supplied comparison function is required to enable insert_data() to compare two items of generic data stored within the tree. Also note that insert_data() requires a pointer to the program's root pointer (which must be initialized to NULL if the tree is empty) so that it may be adjusted to point to the first node to be inserted into the tree.

Note that in the interests of maintaining generic tree functions, the tree's data has been separated from its node, thus the programmer must assume responsibility for its allocation and initialization. The address of this storage must be present within the argument data to insert_data(). The newly created node will then be initialized to point to that data.

Note how the function follows a particular route down the tree until it finds a suitable place to hang the new node. This is slightly tricky, since the

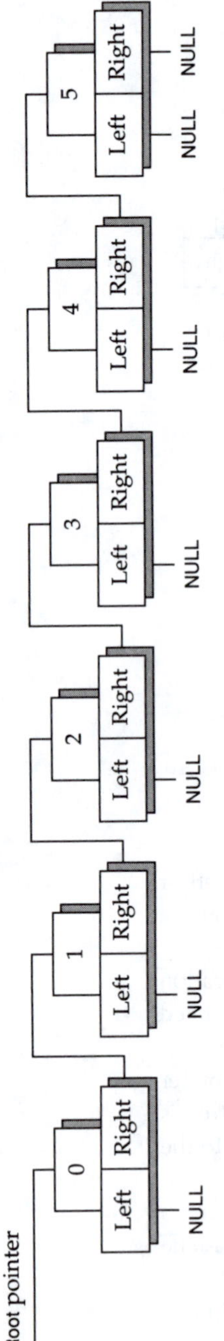

Figure 17.13 Shape of the tree when inserting data in ascending order: 0 1 2 3 4 5.

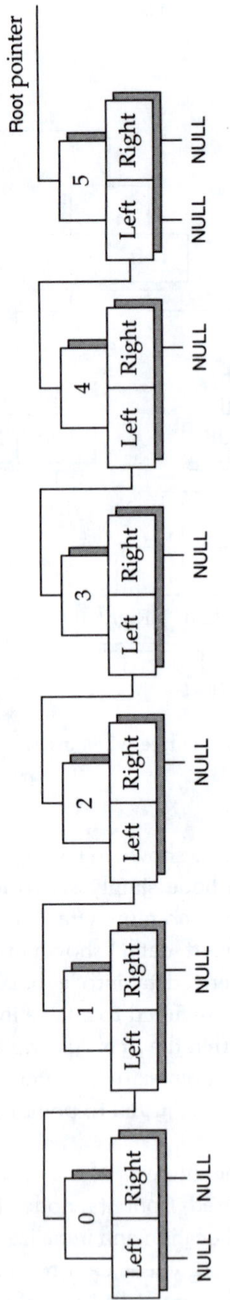

Figure 17.14 Shape of the tree when inserting data in descending order: 5 4 3 2 1 0.

Program 17.28 Inserting data into a binary tree.

```
/*
** The insert_node( ) function searches a binary tree attempting to find
** a point at which it can insert a new node. If an identical item of data
** already exists in the tree, or a memory allocation error occurs, then an
** error is returned to the program. Otherwise storage for a new
** node is allocated and the data and left and right pointers are initialized
**
** The following values are returned by insert_node( )
**
** 0   if successful in inserting the data
** 1   if the item of data already exists in the tree
** 2   if there is insufficient memory to allocate space for the data
*/

int insert_node( TNODE **root, void *data, int (*cmp)( void *, void *))
{
  int result ;

/*
** While the current root pointer is pointing to a node
** if the current node contains the data we are inserting
** return 1 to indicate that data already exists.
*/

  while(*root != NULL )  {
    if((result = cmp((*root)->data, data)) == 0 ) /* call user written compare function */
      return 1 ;                                 /* data exists */

/*
** If the data we are inserting into the tree is greater than that
** stored in the current node, then we must insert it somewhere in the right
** sub-tree so take the address of the current node's 'right' pointer.
** Otherwise take the address of the current node's 'left' pointer
*/

    if( result > 0 )
      root = &(*root)->right ;
    else
      root = &(*root)->left ;
  }

/*
** At this point, 'root' should contain the address of a left or right pointer
** within a parent node (or the address of the program's 'root pointer',
** if this is the first node to be inserted) onto which a new node should be
** 'hung'.
```

```
**
** Now allocate storage for a new node and initialize it to point to its data, and set the
** parent's left or right pointer to point to it. If memory allocation error occurs, then
** return 2
*/

   if((*root = make_node( data )) == NULL)
      return 2 ;                                /* memory allocation error */

   return 0 ;                                   /* success */
}
```

program must record the address of the left or right node pointer of the parent sub-tree it has chosen to follow. This will enable the program to hang the new node off that parent node, when it is eventually inserted.

An example user supplied integer comparison function is given in Program 17.29. The function has been written to receive two void pointers to the data to be compared and should return an integer value of 0, less than 0 or greater than 0, if the data pointed to by 'd2' is respectively equal to, less than or greater than the data pointed to by 'd1'. Note how each void pointer is cast to an appropriate int pointer before the data it points to is accessed.

Program 17.29 A user supplied comparison function.

```
/*
** A user supplied integer comparison function
*/

int compare_int( void *d1, void *d2 )
{
   return(*(int *)(d2) – *(int *)(d1)) ;
}
```

17.6.2 *Searching a binary tree*

Studying Figure 17.12 more closely, it becomes apparent that the data has been inserted into the tree in such a way that at each level in the hierarchy, the tree has been partitioned into left and right sub-trees, all of whose sub-nodes contain data that is, respectively, less than or greater than that stored in the parent node. This is important, since it enables a much faster search than would be possible with a simple linked list.

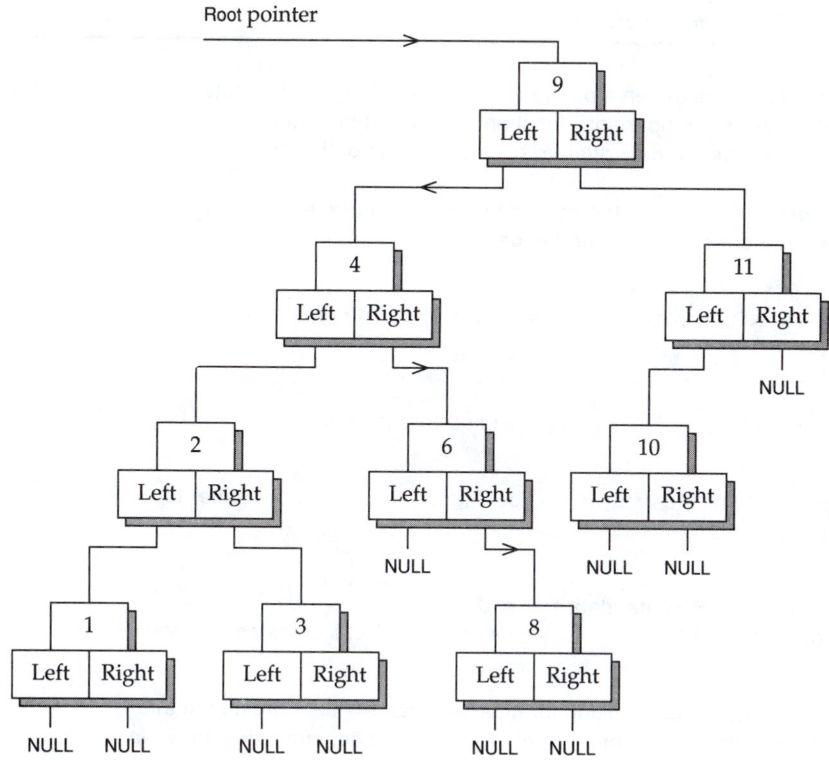

Figure 17.15 Searching a binary tree for the integer value '8'.

To locate a given item of data within the tree, a search function need only compare the data present in the 'parent' node, to determine whether the data (if it exists at all) lies somewhere in the left or right sub-tree and a further search resumes there. The data is considered not to exist if its pursuit eventually leads to a NULL left or right pointer blocking any further progress along that sub-tree. This approach is illustrated in Figure 17.15, when searching for the integer data '8'.

It is easy to see that searching for data in a tree of depth 'n', as with insertion, requires at most 'n' comparisons, and provided that the tree is not degenerate this operation is generally faster than searching a simple linked list, where 'm' (the number of nodes in the list) comparisons may be required.

The function search_tree() shown in Program 17.30 uses this algorithm to locate specified data within the tree. If found, a pointer to the data within the tree is returned, or NULL if it is not present. Note that unlike the function insert_data(), which may have to modify the program's root pointer (when inserting the first node), and was thus given the *address* of the program's root pointer, search_data() only requires a *copy* of that pointer.

Program 17.30 Searching a binary tree.

```
/*
** The following function searches a binary tree for the data given by 'data'
** A pointer to the user's 'comparison' function is required to enable
** a generic search routine to be written to be independent of the tree's data
**
** If the data is found, a pointer to the data in the tree is returned
** or NULL if the tree does NOT contain the data.
*/

void *search_tree( TNODE *root, void *data, int (*cmp)( void *, void *) )
{
   int result ;

   while(root != NULL)  {                     /* sub-tree is valid */

/*
** If current node contains the data we are looking for, then return a pointer to
** current data
*/

      if((result = cmp(root->data, data )) == 0 )
         return (root->data) ;                /* return address of matching data */

/*
** Otherwise, if the data we are looking for is larger than the data present in this
** node, then move to the RIGHT sub-tree of the current node, otherwise, move to
** its LEFT sub-tree.
*/

      if( result > 0 )
         root = root->right ;                 /* Move down right sub-tree */
      else
         root = root->left ;                  /* Move down left sub-tree */
   }

/*
** Only get this far if a node is encountered with no sub-tree in the direction
** we wish to travel. Therefore the data does not exist.
*/

   return NULL ;                              /* Data not found */
}
```

17.6.3 *Traversing a binary tree*

Having inserted several items of data into a tree, the program may now wish to traverse the tree, perhaps to display the data contained within each node. There are three ways in which a tree may be traversed using the 'pre-order', 'post-order' or 'in-order' algorithms. All three are beautifully expressed using recursion and are described below.

Pre-order traversal

The pre-order traversal algorithm visits the parent node first, followed by the left and right sub-tree nodes, respectively. The function preorder_tree_display() shown in Program 17.31 uses this algorithm to display the data in each node of a binary tree.

Program 17.31 Traversing a binary tree using pre-order algorithm.

```
/*
** The following function traverses a binary tree using the pre-order algorithm and
** displays the data in each node. The parameter 'disp' is a pointer to a user
** supplied display function that can be called upon to display the data stored in a node.
*/

void preorder_tree_display(TNODE *root, void (*disp)( void *) )
{
   if( root != NULL ) {
      disp(root->data) ;
      preorder_tree_display( root->left, disp ) ;
      preorder_tree_display( root->right, disp ) ;
   }
}
```

If the tree in Figure 17.15 were traversed in a pre-order manner, then the following data would be displayed:

```
9 4 2 1 3 6 8 11 10
```

Post-order traversal

The post-order traversal algorithm visits each sub-tree first (in this case the left followed by the right), followed lastly by the parent node. The function postorder_tree_display() shown in Program 17.32 uses the post-order traversal algorithm to display the data in each node of a binary tree.

Program 17.32 Traversing a binary tree using post-order algorithm.

```
/*
** The following function traverses a binary tree using the post-order algorithm and
** displays the data in each node. The parameter 'disp' is a pointer to a user supplied
** display function that can be called upon to display the data stored in a node.
*/
```

```
void postorder_tree_display(TNODE *root, void (*disp)( void *) )
{
  if( root != NULL )  {
    postorder_tree_display( root->left, disp ) ;
    postorder_tree_display( root->right, disp ) ;
    disp(root->data) ;
  }
}
```

If the tree in Figure 17.15 were traversed post-order, the following data would be displayed:

```
1 3 2 8 6 4 10 11 9
```

In-order traversal

The in-order traversal method is the most interesting and useful of the three. Here, one sub-tree is visited first, (usually the left) followed by the parent node, followed lastly by the other sub-tree. The function inorder_tree_display( ) shown in Program 17.33 uses the in-order traversal algorithm to display the data in each node of a binary tree.

Program 17.33 Traversing a binary tree using in-order algorithm.

```
/*
** The following function traverses a binary tree using the in-order algorithm and
** displays the data in each node. The parameter 'disp' is a pointer to a user
** supplied display function that can be called upon to display the data stored in a node.
*/

void inorder_tree_display(TNODE *root, void (*disp)( void *))
{
  if( root != NULL )  {
    inorder_tree_display( root->left, disp ) ;
    disp(root->data) ;
    inorder_tree_display( root->right, disp ) ;
  }
}
```

If the tree in Figure 17.15 were traversed in-order, then the following data would be displayed:

```
1 2 3 4 6 8 9 10 11
```

As you can see, provided the data has been inserted into the tree using the correct algorithm, traversing the tree using the in-order algorithm visits each node in the correct ascending order.

17.6.4 *Deleting a binary tree*

The post-order traversal algorithm may be put to another use when deleting a binary tree. The function delete_tree( ) in Program 17.34 visits each sub-tree node in turn followed finally by the parent node, releasing the storage occupied by both node and data.

Program 17.34 Deleting a complete binary tree.

```
/*
** Function to traverse a tree post-order to release the storage occupied by node
** and data
*/

void delete_tree( TNODE **root )
{
  if( *root != NULL )
  {
    delete_tree(&(*root)->left) ;     /* visit left sub-tree */
    delete_tree(&(*root)->right) ;    /* visit right sub-tree */
    free((*root)->data) ;             /* visit and release parent data and node */
    free( *root ) ;
  }
}
```

17.6.5 *Deleting data from a binary tree*

Deleting data from a binary tree is considerably more complex than insertion, since each node *could* be the parent of zero, one, or two other sub-trees. When a node is removed, its sub-tree(s) may have to be relocated and attached to the node of another sub-tree. Let us consider each possibility in turn.

Deleting a leaf node (that is, a node with no sub-trees) is straightforward, since the parent's left or right pointer need only be set to NULL and the storage for the deleted node released. This is illustrated in Figure 17.16. Many programs often omit this test for a leaf node deletion, since it is caught by default by that part of the algorithm that deals with the deletion of a node with one sub-tree (see below).

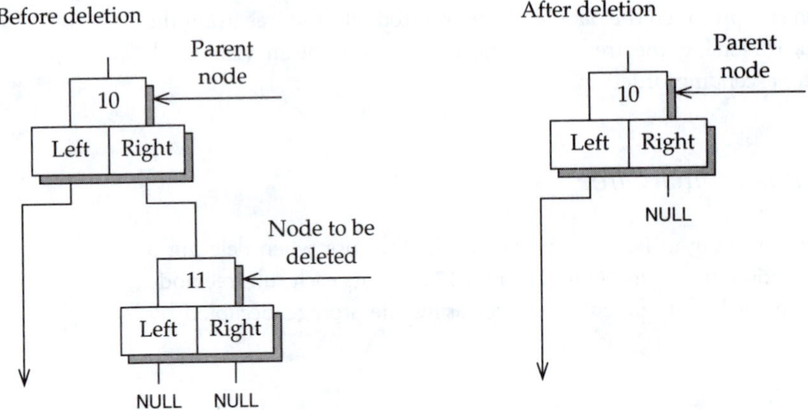

Figure 17.16 Deleting a node with no sub-trees.

If, however, a node possesses one or other (but not both) sub-trees then its parent node's corresponding left or right pointer can be set to point to the single sub-tree of the node to be deleted, before the storage occupied by that node is released. This is illustrated in Figure 17.17 for a node with a right sub-tree only, but the principle is the same for a left sub-tree.

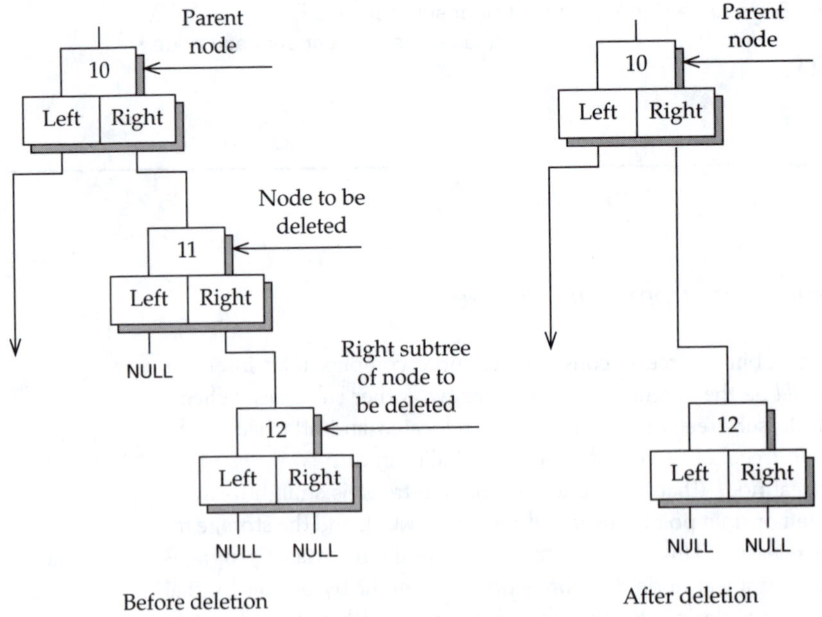

Figure 17.17 Deleting a node with only one sub-tree.

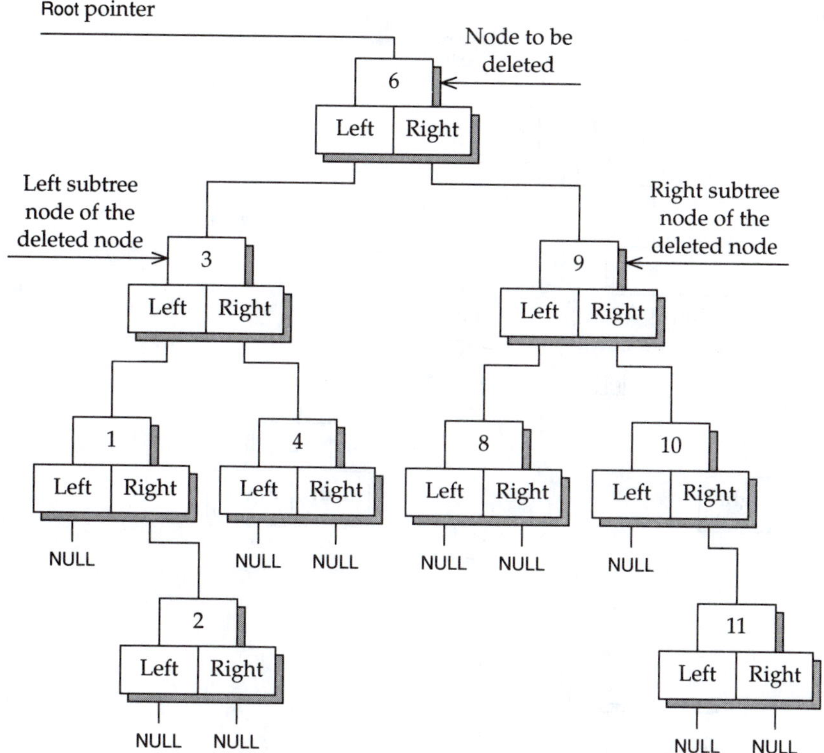

Figure 17.18 Before deletion of root node.

Lastly, if a node possesses both left and right sub-trees, a radical adjustment to the shape of the tree may be required. For example, consider the tree shown in Figure 17.18.

If, in the worst case, the root node (with data '6') were to be deleted, this would leave two separate sub-trees headed by the nodes with data '3' and '9'. These will now have to be merged to form a single tree. The simplest approach, but not one that necessarily gives rise to a 'balanced' tree, is to choose the node at the head of either the left or right sub-tree to become the new root node for the tree itself. The remaining sub-tree (from the deleted node) can then be hung off a suitable point on the new tree.

Figure 17.19 illustrates this by promoting the right sub-tree node (data = 9) of the deleted node (data = 6) to become the new root node for the whole tree, while the left sub-tree node (data = 3) is then hung off the leftmost node (data = 8) on the new tree. This approach maintains the integrity of the tree and ensures that any in-order traversal algorithm still visits each node in the 'correct' order.

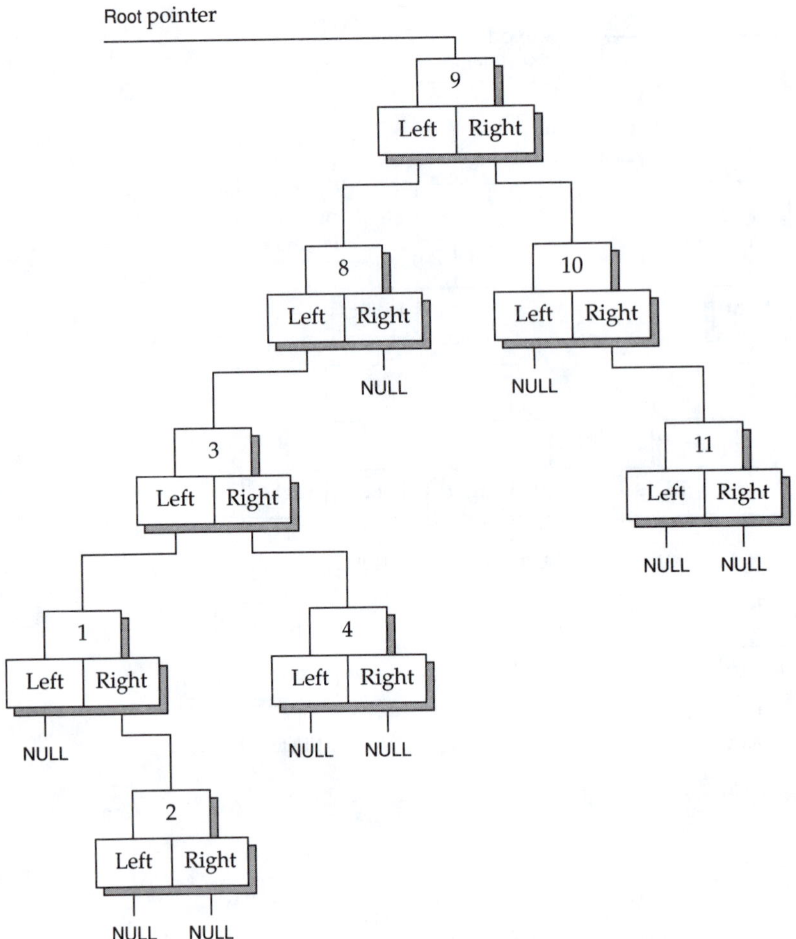

Figure 17.19 After deletion of the root node.

The function delete_node( ) shown in Program 17.35 applies these ideas to the deletion of any node (and its data) from a binary tree.

Program 17.35 Deleting a node from a binary tree.

```
/*
** This function deletes a node from the tree, and returns 0 upon success. If the
** tree becomes empty, then the program's root pointer is set to NULL.
*/

int delete_node( TNODE **root, void *data, int (*cmp)(void *, void *))
{
```

```
  int   result ;

/*
** 'subtree' points to either the left or right pointers in the parent
** node of the node to be deleted, or, in the case where the root node
** is being deleted, it points to the program's root pointer.
*/

  TNODE   **subtree = root ;
  TNODE   *left_sub_tree,   *right_sub_tree,   *left_most_node ;

/*
** Search the tree for the node to be deleted. 'sub-tree' will then be left pointing to the
** left or right pointer of the parent node of the node to be deleted. Or, if the node to be
** deleted is the root node, 'subtree' will be pointing to the program's root pointer.
*/

  while(1)  {

/*
** If 'subtree' points to NULL either the tree was invalid to start with, or the
** search failed to find the node. In either case return an error.
*/

     if(*subtree == NULL )
        return ( -1 ) ;                         /* not found or invalid tree */

/*
** If we have found the node to be deleted, break from loop, and leave 'sub-tree'
** pointing to the left or right pointer of its parent node.
*/

     if((result = cmp((*subtree)->data, data)) == 0 )
        break ;

/*
** Otherwise, decide whether the node lies in the left or right sub-tree of
** current node and save the address of its parent's left or right pointer.
*/

     if( result > 0)
        subtree = &(*subtree)->right;          /* move down right sub-tree */
     else
        subtree = &(*subtree)->left ;          /* move down left sub-tree */
  }

/*
** Having found the node to be deleted, point 'left' to the left sub-tree node of the node
** to be deleted, point 'right' to the right sub-tree node of the node to be deleted
** Free the storage occupied by the node and its data
*/
```

```
    left_sub_tree = (*subtree)->left ;
    right_sub_tree = (*subtree)->right ;

    free((*subtree)->data) ;                    /* free data at this node */
    free(*subtree) ;                            /* delete the node */

/*
** If the node contains no sub-trees or its right sub-tree is NULL, then set its parent's
** appropriate pointer to either NULL, or to the deleted node's left sub-tree
*/

    if(right_sub_tree == NULL )                 /* if right sub-tree is empty */
        *subtree = left_sub_tree ;              /* set parent's right pointer to NULL */

    else if( left_sub_tree == NULL )            /* if left sub-tree is empty */
        *subtree = right_sub_tree ;             /* set parent's left pointer to NULL */

/*
** However, if the node to be deleted possesses both a left and right sub-tree
** then save the address of the right sub-tree node in 'left_most_node' and then
** attempt to find the leftmost node within that sub-tree.
*/

    else {
        left_most_node = right_sub_tree ;       /* point to right sub-tree of deleted node */

        while( left_most_node->left != NULL )
            left_most_node = left_most_node->left ;    /* move down left node in right */
                                                        /* sub-tree */

/*
** Now attach the left sub-tree of the node to be deleted onto the
** leftmost node of the right sub-tree.
*/

        left_most_node ->left = left_sub_tree ;
        *subtree = right_sub_tree ;             /* update the parent's left/right pointer */
    }
    return 0 ;                                  /* return success */
}
```

Program 17.36 demonstrates the use of these primitive functions by inserting and deleting integer data supplied by an operator into a binary tree.

Program 17.36 Exercising a binary tree.

```
#include <stdio.h>
#include <stdlib.h>

typedef int DATA ;              /* data stored in the tree is an integer */
```

```
/*
** Following macro values are returned by insert_node()
*/

#define  SUCCESS        0      /* successful insertion of data */
#define  EXIST          1      /* could not insert data as it already existed in tree */
#define  ALLOC_ERROR  2      /* could not allocate storage for a new node */

/*
** A user modifiable function to display the data in a node
*/

void display_DATA( void *d1 )
{
  printf("%d ", *(DATA *)(d1) ) ;
}

int main( void )
{
  TNODE  *root= NULL ;          /* initialize root to NULL to indicate no tree */
  DATA   *dptr ;                /* pointer to DATA */
  char   buff[ BUFSIZ ] ;
  int    reason, d ;

  while ((d = atoi( gets( buff ))) != -999)  {
    dptr = NEW( DATA ) ;        /* allocate storage for new data */
    *dptr = d ;                 /* copy data to new storage area */

    if((reason = insert_node( &root, dptr, compare_int )) != SUCCESS )  {
      if( reason == EXIST)
        printf("%d already exists in the tree ... \n", d) ;
      else  {
        printf("Memory Allocation Error ... ") ;
        break ;
      }
    }
  }

/*
** Now display the contents of the tree using the in-order technique
** and ask the operator which node to delete
*/

  while( root != NULL )  {
    inorder_tree_display( root, display_DATA ) ;

    printf("\nEnter node to delete: " ) ;
    d = atoi( gets( buff )) ;

    if( d == -999)              /* break on '-999' entry */
      break ;
```

```
/*
** Make sure node exists in tree, if so, delete it and its data
*/

        if(delete_node( &root, &d, compare_int ) == 0 )
            printf("Deleted ... ") ;
        else
            printf("%d does not exist in tree ... \n", d) ;
    }

/*
** Now tidy up by deleting what is left of the tree
*/

    delete_tree( &root ) ;
    root = NULL ;                       /* mark tree as empty */
    return 0 ;
}
```

17.7 Chapter summary

(1) The linked list is a flexible, generic data structure whose size may be adjusted dynamically by the program. It caters for the rapid insertion and deletion of data although sorting and searching are not performed very efficiently. Each node in a linked list contains a pointer to its data and a pointer to the next node in the list, or NULL for the last node.

In the case of a doubly linked list, a pointer to the previous node in the list is also maintained, where the first node also points to NULL. The linked list often forms the heart of more complex data structures, such as the stack and queue.

(2) The stack is a last-in, first-out buffer. The operation 'push' adds an item of data to the stack, while 'pop' removes and returns the last item of data 'pushed' on to the stack. Stacks may be designed around arrays if the depth of the stack can be predicted at compile time, or around a linked list if a dynamically sizeable stack is required.

(3) The queue is a first-in, first-out buffer. The operation 'insert' adds an item of data to the 'tail' or end of a queue, while the operation 'retrieve' returns and removes the data at the head or front of a queue. Queues may also be designed around arrays if the size of the queue can be predicted at compile time, or around a linked list if a dynamically sizeable queue is required.

(4) The circular queue is a variation on the basic queue, where the head and tail of the queue are joined to form a complete loop. A single marker is used to indicate the position of the data at the 'notional' head and tail of the queue. Data may be inserted into and removed from a circular queue using the marker as the reference position, while rotation of a circular queue is achieved by advancing the marker in either direction.

(5) A binary tree is a hierarchical, essentially recursive data structure based around a modified linked list. Searching for and inserting data is much faster using a binary tree than is generally possible using a linear linked list. A binary tree may be traversed using the 'in-order', 'pre-order' or 'post-order' algorithms. The 'in-order' traversal is most commonly used because this gives the data in its *sorted* order.

17.8 Exercises

17.1 List the principal advantages of using a linked list for dynamic storage, rather than using the memory allocation functions `malloc()`, `calloc()` and so on to create a dynamically sizeable array.

17.2 Why is the introduction of a ROOT data structure, maintained as part of the list itself, more effective than the program simply maintaining a pointer to the first node in the list? Why is it more useful to have each item of DATA stored in the list kept separate from its associated NODE structure, even though this places an extra burden on the application program, which now has to allocate and release such storage for itself?

17.3 Why are insert and delete operations more efficient with a doubly linked list than with a singly linked list?

17.4 In order to help you with the remaining exercises in this chapter, create a source file `list.c` containing the definitions of those functions that manipulate a doubly linked list, stack and queue. Compile this source file down to its relocatable object form so that it may be linked in with other application programs at compile time. Create also the header file `list.h` containing any relevant function prototypes, type definitions and macros that may be needed by an application that manipulates doubly linked lists, stacks and queues.

17.5 Write a program to construct a memory resident database based around a doubly linked list to record the following details about an individual:

- Name
- Address
- Age

The program should provide a menu driven interface to allow the program's operator to select the following operations:

(a) Enter and record an individual's details.

(b) Search (by name) and display an individual's details.

(c) Delete an individual's details.

(d) Save and restore the entire list to/from a disk file.

17.6 Create and add the following functions to your source and header files list.c and list.h:

(a) A function to merge two linked lists into one.

(b) A function to split a linked list into two separate linked lists.

(c) A function index() that accepts an integral argument 'i' and returns a pointer to the data stored in the ith node of a linked list. This function should permit array-like operations on a linked list such as *index(5) = *index(10) and so on.

(d) A function to sort, using the bubble sort algorithm, the contents of a list. Consider whether or not it is feasible to sort a linked list using an implementation of the quicksort algorithm.

17.7 Given that the linked list functions presented in this chapter have been generic and independent of the type of data stored in a list, think about the design of a data structure to record a two-dimensional linked list; that is, one where each node in a primary list points to the 'root' data structure of one or more secondary linked lists.

Now write a function index2() to accept two integral arguments 'i' and 'j' and return a pointer to the data stored in the jth node (of the secondary list) of the ith node (in the primary list) and thus implement a two-dimensional linked list.

Consider how such a data structure could be employed in the design of a spreadsheet where x and y coordinates are used to reference a cell containing data.

17.8 Write a program that generates (using rand()) and inserts in the correct ascending order up to 32 000 items of random integer data (or less if your computer cannot allocate sufficient memory) into both a linked list and a binary tree. Compare the performance of the search, insert and delete operations of both these data structures.

17.9 Modify the program resulting from Exercise 17.5 to use a binary tree rather than a linked list. Take care that the data is saved to disk in the correct order so that a degenerate tree does not result upon its recovery.

17.10 Write a function to merge two binary trees into one.

17.11 Discuss ways in which the concept of a binary tree could be applied to the database problem from Chapter 16 (Exercise 16.16) to speed up the search operation.

18 The C Standard Library and Header Files

In this final chapter we take a brief look at each of the library functions, macros, header files and data types defined by the standard. It is not intended to be a definitive reference to these topics for three reasons. Firstly, one chapter is not sufficient space to do them complete justice. Secondly, the library reference manual that comes with your compiler (probably a complete book in itself) will describe each function (and its possible idiosyncrasies) in far more detail than there is space to describe them here. Thirdly, the on-line help facility provided by many excellent compilers such as Borland's Turbo C provides a far more convenient means of accessing and cross-referencing material than could be provided by a book.

In conclusion, then, this chapter sets out to achieve two things: firstly, to discuss the contents of the 15 header files defined by the standard, and secondly to describe (briefly) the use and application of each function defined within the standard library. Note, however, that where a function has been covered in detail in a previous chapter, only a simple summary and cross-reference to that material are provided.

18.1 The header file <assert.h>

The header file <assert.h> contains the definition of the assert() macro. For further details the reader is referred to Section 13.9.

18.2 The header file <ctype.h>

This header file <ctype.h> contains the definition of a number of parameterized macros, such as isalpha(), isupper(), islower() and so on, which may prove useful when determining the classification of a particular character, such as determining whether it is alphabetic, upper or lower case and so on. Each macro is also present as a function within the standard library.

Each macro/function returns a non-zero value (that is, boolean true) if the character argument passes that particular classification. These macros/functions should be independent of the host computer's character set such as ASCII and thus their use should be completely portable. The reader is referred to Section 9.6 for a list and description of these macros along with a sample program demonstrating their use.

Also declared in <ctype.h> are the function prototypes for the two character translation functions shown below. If the character argument 'c' is suitable, each function returns that character converted to its upper or lower case equivalent; otherwise, the argument 'c' is returned unchanged:

- int toupper(int c) ;
- int tolower(int c) ;

The reader is referred to Section 9.7 for a description of these two functions.

18.3 The header file <errno.h>

The header file <errno.h> contains the declaration for the external integer errno, as shown below:

```
extern volatile int errno ;
```

The value of errno is always set to zero at the start of the program's execution. Many of the functions in the standard library, upon detecting an error, set errno to an appropriate value before returning an error status back to their calling program. By interrogating the value of errno (whose value is system dependent for a given failure condition) the program can determine the reason for the failure. Also of interest and relevant to the discussion of errno is the function perror() (see Section 16.3.9), which may be used to interpret the value of errno and write a suitable error message to the default error message stream (usually the operator's terminal unless error messages have been redirected).

Also defined in <errno.h> are a number of system dependent, integer macros/constants relating to error conditions that may arise within the host computer's operating environment, such as illegal path name for a device/file, or file not found. These are often the values that are assigned to errno when a particular error condition is recognized. A few of these are given below; all begin with the letter 'E'. The exact contents vary from one machine to another, so check out the header file <errno.h> on your compiler.

```
#define  ENOFILE        2      /* Unable to find FILE */
#define  EINVALFORMAT 11       /* Invalid format */
#define  EINVALCODE    12      /* Invalid access code */
#define  EINVDRIVE     15      /* Invalid drive specified */
```

The following two macro names should be common to all <errno.h> header files, although the actual integer values defined for them may vary:

```
#define  EDOM    33            /* Maths function argument */
#define  ERANGE  34            /* Result of math function too large */
```

The value of errno is set to EDOM if a maths function (see Section 18.7) is supplied with an argument which lies outside the domain for which the function is defined, for example attempting to take the arc sine of the value '1.2' or the square root of a negative number.

The value of errno is set to ERANGE if a maths function is unable to represent the result of its calculation within its returned data type. For example, attempting to evaluate the expression '$e^{1000.0}$' using the library function exp() would, with many compilers, result in a domain error, since the result is most likely to be too large to be accommodated by the double that exp() returns.

18.4 The header file <float.h>

The header file <float.h> defines a number of system dependent macros representing the maximum and minimum floating point values for the real data types implemented by that compiler – that is, floats, doubles and long doubles. Some typical examples are given in Program 18.1, in which a long double is assumed to be 10 bytes in size. Check out the header file <float.h> on your compiler. Program 2.2 demonstrates some of these macros in action.

Program 18.1 The contents of a typical <float.h> header file.

```
/* Minimum values representable by a double, float and long double quantity */

#define  DBL_MIN    2.2250738585072014e-308
#define  FLT_MIN    1.17549435e-38
#define  LDBL_MIN   3.3621031431120935 1e-4932

/* Maximum values representable by a double, float and long double quantity */

#define  DBL_MAX    1.7976931348623157e+308
#define  FLT_MAX    3.40282347e+38
#define  LDBL_MAX   1.189731495357231 76e+4932
```

```
#define  DBL_MAX_10_EXP   +308     /* Maximum exponent value for a double */
#define  FLT_MAX_10_EXP   +38      /* Maximum exponent value for a float */
#define  LDBL_MAX_10_EXP  +4932    /* Maximum exponent value for a long double */

#define  DBL_MIN_10_EXP   -307     /* Minimum exponent value for a double */
#define  FLT_MIN_10_EXP   -37      /* Minimum exponent value for a float */
#define  LDBL_MIN_10_EXP  -4931    /* Minimum exponent value for a long double */

#define  DBL_DIG   15              /* Precision of a double is 15 digits */
#define  FLT_DIG   6               /* Precision of a float is 6 digits */
#define  LDBL_DIG  19              /* Precision of a long double is 19 digits */

/*
** Smallest value that may be added to a double, float or long double resulting in a
** change of value
*/

#define  DBL_EPSILON   2.2204460492503131e-16
#define  FLT_EPSILON   1.19209290E-07
#define  LDBL_EPSILON  1.084202172485504e-19

#define  FLT_ROUNDS    1   /* Floating point calculations are rounded up (or down if 0) */
#define  FLT_RADIX     2   /* The radix of exponent representation */
```

18.5 The header file <limits.h>

The header file <limits.h> serves a similar purpose to <float.h> but defines a number of macros/symbolic constants relating to the maximum and minimum values that may be assumed by all integral data types – that is, char, short, int and long – with that compiler. Some examples are shown in Program 18.2, in which it is assumed that a char is a signed quantity and that two's complement binary representation is used. Check out the <limits.h> header file on your compiler. Program 2.2 demonstrates some of these macros in action.

Program 18.2 A subset of a typical <limits.h> header file.

```
#define  CHAR_BIT    8          /* Size of a char in bits */

#define  CHAR_MAX    127        /* Max value of a char (assumed to be signed) */
#define  SCHAR_MAX   127        /* Max value of a signed char */
#define  UCHAR_MAX   255        /* Max value of an unsigned char */

#define  SHRT_MAX    0x7FFF     /* Max value of a short (signed by default) */
#define  USHRT_MAX   0xFFFF     /* Max value of an unsigned short */

#define  INT_MAX     0x7FFF     /* Max value of an int (signed by default) */
#define  UINT_MAX    0xFFFFU    /* Max value of an unsigned int */
```

```
#define  LONG_MAX   0x7FFFFFFFL     /* Max value of a long int (signed by default) */
#define  ULONG_MAX  0xFFFFFFFFUL    /* Max value of an unsigned long int */

#define  CHAR_MIN   (-128)          /* Min value of a char (assumed to be signed) */
#define  SCHAR_MIN  (-128)          /* Min value of a signed char */

#define  SHRT_MIN   (int)(0x8000)   /* Min value of a short */
#define  INT_MIN    ((int)0x8000)   /* Min value of an int */
#define  LONG_MIN   0x80000000L     /* Min value of a long */
```

18.6 The header file <locale.h>

The standard has attempted to take account of what are referred to as 'cultural differences' in an attempt to cater for the different local environments (or locales) in which a program may be run. For example, in many European countries, a comma is sometimes used in preference to a decimal point when displaying currency values, while the format for date and time displays differs from that used in, for example, the USA. Currency symbols also vary depending upon the current locale, such as $, £, DM and so on. The header file <locale.h> contains a number of function prototypes and macro definitions that permit a program to select its own locale.

The function setlocale() provides the program with the means to select its own locale, which may affect the operation of certain other standard library functions. The general format for setlocale() is shown below:

- `char *setlocale( int category, const char *locale ) ;`

The following six macros (others may also be defined, so check your compiler documentation) expand to integer constants and may be used as arguments for the parameter 'category' in a call to setlocale(). A typical definition for these macros is given below:

```
#define  LC_ALL       0  /* Sets entire locale */
#define  LC_COLLATE   1  /* Modifies the behaviour of library function */
                         /* strcoll() (see <string.h> */
#define  LC_CTYPE     2  /* Modifies the behaviour of the character */
                         /* manipulation functions */
#define  LC_MONETARY  3  /* Affects the monetary display */
#define  LC_NUMERIC   4  /* Modifies numeric decimal point in formatted */
                         /* output */
#define  LC_TIME      5  /* Modifies the behaviour of strftime() */
                         /* (see <time.h>) */
```

Two values for the locale parameter are also defined as shown below and should be recognized by every setlocale() function, although others may also be recognized depending upon the compiler:

"C" Selects a minimalist environment suitable for C translation.
" " Selects the host system's 'native' environment, which is system dependent.

At run time, the environment behaves as if a call to setlocale() of the form:

```
setlocale( LC_ALL, "C" ) ;
```

had been made. By selecting an appropriate 'LC_' value and environment, that part of the locale can be affected. For example, a call to setlocale() of the form:

```
setlocale( LC_ALL, "UK" ) ;
```

where the locale "UK" was supported (there is no guarantee of this) might select all of the settings appropriate for running the program in the United Kingdom, such as a specific date and time format and a '£' for the currency symbol. Likewise, a call of the form:

```
setlocale( LC_MONETARY, "USA" ) ;
```

might select a monetary environment suitable for the USA, such as a '$' sign for currency. Upon completion, setlocale() returns a pointer to a string defining the new current locale ("C", "UK" or "USA", for example). If an error occurs, such as non-recognition or lack of support for the specified locale, then a NULL pointer is returned.

If a NULL locale string is given as the argument to setlocale() then the current locale is *not* altered, but a pointer to a string defining the current locale is returned. For example, the following call might display the current locale as "C":

```
printf("%s\n", setlocale(LC_ALL, ""))
```

Also declared within <locale.h> is a structure of the form shown below. The exact contents will vary from one compiler to another depending upon the support for different locales.

```
struct lconv
{
  char  *decimal_point ;
  char  *thousands_sep ;
  char  *currency_symbol ;
  char  *mon_decimal_point ;
  char  *mon_thousands_sep ;
} ;
```

This structure contains a number of char pointers to NULL terminated text strings. The function localeconv( ) whose prototype is given below:

- struct lconv *localeconv(void) ;

returns a pointer to a structure of type lconv from which information may be extracted about the *current* locale. For example, the entry 'decimal_point' in the above structure may point to the character string "." or ",", while the entry 'currency_symbol' may point to the strings "$", "£" or "DM", depending upon what locale is currently in effect.

18.7 The header file <math.h>

The header file <math.h> defines and declares a number of mathematical constants and function prototypes. In the case of all maths functions, the external int errno (declared in <errno.h>) is set to the value of EDOM if a function is given an argument outside the domain for which that function is defined, such as attempting to take the arc sine of 1.2 or the square root of a negative number. In such cases, the result returned by the function will be implementation defined.

If a maths function attempts to return a value that cannot be represented by its returned data type (a double) , then an error will occur. If the value is too large to represent, then the value of the symbolic constant ±HUGE_VAL (see below) is returned, which is the largest double precision real number representable by the compiler, and errno is set to ERANGE. If the value is too small to return, then 0.0 is returned and the value of errno is implementation defined.

```
#define  HUGE_VAL  1.797693134862315e+308
```

Many <math.h> header files often define a number of useful macros, such as the value of 'PI' or 'e'. A typical selection is shown below. Check out your header file for details.

```
#define  M_E     2.71828182845904523536L    /* value of e */
#define  M_PI    3.14159265358979323846L    /* value of PI */
#define  M_PI_2  1.57079632679489661923L    /* value of PI / 2.0 */
#define  M_PI_4  0.78539816339744830961 6L  /* value of PI / 4.0 */
```

Mathematical functions

The following mathematical functions are defined by the standard and their prototypes should be declared in <math.h>:

- double sin(double x) ;
- double cos(double x) ;
- double tan(double x) ;

which, respectively, return the sine, cosine and tangent of the angle 'x' expressed in radians. Likewise the functions:

- `double asin( double x ) ;`
- `double acos( double x ) ;`
- `double atan( double x ) ;`

return the inverse or arc sine, arc cosine and arc tangent, respectively, of the argument 'x', which must lie in the range [-1 <= x <= 1] or a domain error will occur. The range of the returned values are: asin[$-\pi/2$ to $+\pi/2$ radians], acos[0 to π radians] and atan[$-\pi/2$ to $+\pi/2$ radians].

- `double atan2( double y, double x ) ;`

atan2( ) returns the arc tangent of the expression '(y/x)' in the range [$-\pi$ to $+\pi$ radians] and at the same time determines the correct quadrant by considering the signs of the arguments 'x' and 'y'. For correct operation, the expression '(y/x)' must be in the range [-1 <= x <= 1]. A domain error occurs if both 'x' and 'y' are zero, or if 'y/x' is not representable.

The hyperbolic functions shown below return, respectively, the hyperbolic sine, cosine and tangent of the argument 'x':

- `double sinh( double x ) ;`
- `double cosh( double x ) ;`
- `double tanh( double x ) ;`

The remaining commonly used mathematical functions are given below:

- `double log( double x ) ;`
- `double log10( double x ) ;`
- `double exp( double x ) ;`
- `double pow( double x, double y ) ;`
- `double sqrt( double x ) ;`

which, respectively, return the value of log to the base e and log to the base 10 of 'x', e raised to the power 'x', 'x' raised to the power 'y' and the square root of 'x'.

- `double frexp( double x, int *exponent) ;`

The function frexp( ) splits its argument 'x' into the form of (mantissa $\times$ 2^{exponent}), where mantissa is the value returned by frexp( ) and lies in the range 0.0 to 1.0 and the integer exponent is stored in the integer variable pointed to by the parameter 'exponent'. For example, the expression frexp(3.141592653, &i) would return the mantissa of 0.78539816 and store the exponent 2 in 'i'.

- double ldexp(double mantissa, int exponent) ;

The function ldexp( ) performs the opposite operation to frexp( ), calculating the value of the expression (mantissa $\times$ 2^{exponent}). Thus the value of ldexp(0.78539816, 2) results in the value of 3.141 592 653.

- double modf(double x, double *integer_ptr) ;

The function modf( ) splits the double precision argument 'x' into its integer and fractional parts. The fractional value is returned, while the integer value is stored (as a double precision value) in the variable pointed to by integer_ptr. Thus, a value of 3.141 breaks down into the integral value 3.0 and the fraction 0.141.

- double ceil(double x) ;
- double floor(double x) ;

The function ceil( ) returns the smallest integral value (as a double) not less than 'x'. In other words, it rounds up a floating point value to the next highest integral value, for example ceil(12.23) produces the result 13.0. The function floor( ) returns the smallest integer value (as a double) not greater than 'x'; that is, it rounds down a floating point value to the nearest integral value. For example, floor(12.23) produces the result 12.0.

- double fabs(double x) ;
- double fmod(double x, double y) ;

The function fabs( ) returns the absolute (positive) value of the floating point argument 'x', while the function fmod( ) returns the floating point remainder of the expression '((x)/(y))'. For example, fmod(7.0, 4.0) returns the answer 3.0.

18.8 The header file <setjmp.h>

You will recall from Section 5.8 that it was *not* permitted to use goto to jump directly between functions or blocks. The reason for this is that the compiler would find it very difficult to keep track of any automatic variables, arguments, return addresses and so on maintained on the computer's 'stack' if the code to clean up that stack at the end of the function/block were not correctly executed, which could occur if a premature jump occurred prior to the end of a function and could well lead to a subsequent program crash.

There are situations, however, when it might be desirable to perform a jump, if a problem is encountered deep in the hierarchy of a set of *nested function calls*. Rather than use a number of flags (as was suggested in Section 5.8.1 to escape from a set of nested loops) and a sequence of return statements to resume processing at some arbitrary starting point, C provides a means with a 'long jump' to return to a predetermined point in the program. Random jumps to one or more labels are still not permitted.

The explanation that follows is somewhat peculiar owing to the nature and operation of the two functions involved, coupled with the fact that they seem to fly directly in the face of almost all of the ideas expressed so far in this book and that of a structured programming approach. In the author's opinion any alternative to the use of the two functions discussed below is preferable and should be adopted wherever possible. However, once some experimentation has been performed, the 'trick' becomes obvious.

Let us begin by taking a look at the mechanisms involved. The header file <setjmp.h> declares the function prototypes for the functions setjmp() and longjmp(), which are given below:

- int setjmp(jmp_buf jmpb) ;
- void longjmp(jmp_buf jmpb, int retval) ;

Also defined in <setjmp.h> is the new data type jmp_buf, usually created with a typedef statement and often based around a structure declaration. Before any long jump operation can be performed, the program must introduce a variable of type jmp_buf, which will be used to save and subsequently restore the current state of the program, prior to performing the jump itself.

A call to setjmp() saves the current program state within the user defined jmp_buf variable. At this instant, setjmp() returns 0, indicating that the progam status has been successfully saved. The program may then proceed to call a number of nested functions within the program.

When a call to longjmp() is later encountered in the program (to restore the program's status), it resumes execution with the statement immediately following the initial call to setjmp() (the one that saved the current program status in the first instance), and it thus appears as if setjmp() has returned for a second time! The argument retval in longjmp(), which must be a value other than 0, *becomes* the new value returned by setjmp() on this second occasion. Program 18.3 demonstrates this.

Program 18.3 Example use of setjmp() and longjmp().

```
#include  <stdio.h>
#include  <setjmp.h>
#include  <stdlib.h>

void sub1( void) ;              /* function prototypes */
void sub2( void ) ;

jmp_buf jump_buffer ;           /* variable to store the current state of the program */

int main(void)
{
   int value ;
```

```
/*
** Now call setjmp() to save the current state of the program in 'jump_buffer'.
** This is the first time that setjmp() returns and on this occasion returns 0. If a call is
** made to longjmp() later in the program then setjmp() will return again with a
** non-zero value
*/

   if((value = setjmp(jump_buffer)) != 0 )   {
      printf("Longjmp() returned with value %d\n", value) ;
      exit(0) ;
   }

/* Having saved the current state, we now call several nested functions, in this case 2 */

   sub1() ;
   return 0 ;
}

void sub1( void )
{
   printf("Within function sub1()...\n") ;
   sub2() ;
}

void sub2( void )
{
   printf("Within function sub2() ... \n") ;

/*
** Now we 'return' to the point in main() where setjmp() was first run, restoring the
** current program state saved in jump_buffer, thus setjmp() now returns for a second
** time, returning in this instance the value 3.
*/

   longjmp(jump_buffer, 3) ;

/* Any statements here are never reached since longjmp() can never return directly */
}
```

18.9 The header file <signal.h>

From time to time, during the execution of a program, certain asynchronous 'exceptions' may arise which cannot be foreseen by the program. Many of these exceptions occur accidentally and are often detected by the CPU. Examples include attempting to execute an illegal machine code instruction in the program code (perhaps if the programmer had embedded some illegal assembly language code) or a memory address bounds violation.

Other exceptions may occur as a result of the underlying hardware of the system, for example dividing by floating point zero (where a maths co-processor is available to detect and generate the exception) or attempting to access invalid memory locations where a memory management unit (MMU) exists. Alternatively, user generated exceptions can be raised by the program for a specific purpose.

Although there are no limits to the number of exception *types* that may occur within a program, the standard defines six exceptions that are common to most machines and, as such, a C compiler should be able to produce code enabling the application to deal with them should they arise. These common exceptions are:

(1) Abnormal program termination such as a call to abort();

(2) A floating point exception;

(3) An illegal instruction;

(4) An operator intervention such as Control-C;

(5) A memory access violation;

(6) A termination request made *to* the program, perhaps by the operating system.

When any of these six exceptions arises, a unique integer signal value is generated and 'sent' to the program, which normally results in the program's forced termination. However, by making use of the function signal() it is possible for the program to intercept the generated signal and deal with the exception for itself.

For example, rather than have the program simply terminate when a divide by zero occurs, it might be considered more useful if the program could perhaps recover the situation itself, if only to terminate the program in a more controlled manner. Let us see how this can be achieved using signal(). The function prototype for signal() is given below:

- void (*signal(int sig, void (*func) (int)))(int) ;

where the parameter func is a pointer to a function that will be called or invoked automatically whenever the exception type specified by 'sig' occurs. Such a function should be written to receive a single integer argument 'x' and return no data. The integer argument given to that function will be the integer value of the argument 'sig'. This last feature allows a single generic signal handler to be written to deal with many different types of exceptions.

signal() itself returns a pointer to the function that was previously dealing with that type of exception (before the new one is installed with signal()), and is probably a pointer to the function exit() or some such similar function. By saving this returned pointer it should be possible to re-install that function later to handle future occurrences of the exception. If the installation of the signal handler function fails, the value of SIG_ERR is returned.

The standard defines six symbolic constants within <signal.h> that may be used as the argument 'sig' in the call to signal( ). These are shown below along with their typical values:

```
#define  SIGABRT 22    /* Abnormal program termination (abort( )) */
#define  SIGFPE   8    /* Floating point exception such as divide by zero */
#define  SIGILL   4    /* Illegal instruction */
#define  SIGINT   2    /* Operator intervention such as Control-C */
#define  SIGSEGV 11    /* Memory access violation */
#define  SIGTERM 15    /* Termination request made to the program */
```

Two further macros are also defined in <signal.h>, as shown below, which may be used as the argument func in the call to signal( ):

SIG_DFL Install the *default* or initial exception handler function for that type of exception, typically exit( ).

SIG_IGN Ensures that a given type of exception will be *ignored* by the program should it arise.

With an exception handler installed, any exception arising during the execution of the program results in the installed exception handler being invoked, with its single integer argument set to a value identifying the type of exception. Upon completion, the exception handler returns (if that is how it was written) and the program resumes where the exception arose.

Caution must be observed when intercepting some exceptions, since the exception itself may give rise to undefined behaviour, from which it may not be sensible for the program to resume. Examples include an illegal instruction, in which case the exception handler would probably terminate the program. As an example, Program 18.4 demonstrates how a program could be written to intercept the two types of exception SIGFPE and SIGABRT.

Program 18.4 Intercepting exceptions.

```
#include  <stdio.h>
#include  <signal.h>
#include  <stdlib.h>

/* Function designed to catch all floating point exceptions; that is, SIGFPE */

void floating_point_exception_handler(int sig)
{
   printf("Signal Exception code is %d\n", sig) ;
   printf("Caught Floating Point exception ... \n");
}
```

```
/* Function designed to catch all calls to abort( ); that is, SIGABRT */

void abort_exception(int sig)
{
   printf("Signal Exception code is %d\n", sig) ;
   printf("Sorry ... All aborts have been interecepted\n");
}

int main( void )
{
   double a, c = 1.0 ;

/* Install functions to handle floating point and abort exceptions */

   signal(SIGFPE, floating_point_exception_handler) ;
   signal(SIGABRT, abort_exception) ;

/* Now divide by zero to force a floating point exception */

   a = c / 0.0 ;

/* Now call abort( ) and let this be intercepted */

   abort( ) ;
   return 0 ;
}
```

Program generated exceptions

The function raise( ), whose prototype is given below, can be invoked to generate a synchronous exception from within the program. For example, the statement raise(SIGFPE) ; would raise a floating point exception.

- int raise(int signal) ;

The header file <signal.h> also defines the data type sig_atomic_t, which is the largest integral data type that may be safely read or stored in the presence of an interrupt/exception on the host machine and is generally an int sized quantity, as shown below:

```
typedef int sig_atomic_t ;
```

This is of particular interest to programs that run in a multi-tasking environment where processes are often time-sliced under the control of a real-time multi-tasking clock (RTC), generating periodic interrupts or 'ticks' to the CPU, perhaps on a 10–50 ms basis.

These ticks force the current process to be de-scheduled and allow another process to resume execution, presenting the illusion that several programs are actually running in parallel. In such an environment, two or more processes often communicate with each other through the use of shared or process-wide variables. A problem can arise if one process is in the middle of updating such a variable while at the same time the operating system is attempting to de-schedule it. This could allow another process to access that incompletely updated variable, with possible dire consequences for the system.

If, however, the process is updating a variable of type sig_atomic_t then it is guaranteed that the variable will be updated correctly before the process is de-scheduled. No such guarantee holds true for any variable type bigger or more complex than sig_atomic_t.

18.10 The header file <stdarg.h>

You will recall from Section 6.1.5 that a compiler, with the exception of arrays, passes arguments to a function by value or copy. In other words, a copy of the original arguments in the calling function are made, and these copies are presented to and eventually become the parameters in the called function, which are stored on the stack. We also noted in Section 6.1.11 that it was possible, through the use of the ellipsis '...' in the function's parameter list, to define a function able to receive a *variable* number of function arguments of varying type and size. However, the discussion of how such a function could be written to extract those arguments from the stack was deferred until now.

The header file <stdarg.h> defines the new data type va_list and three macros that enable a function to extract the arguments it has been given. However, before this is possible, the function will obviously need to know both the number and type of the actual arguments that have been presented to it by the calling function.

For example, printf( ) is a classic example of a function written to receive a variable number of arguments of differing type. By examining the '%' formatters in the format string (which is always the first argument and is always a string), printf( ) is able to determine the number and type of any additional arguments it may have been given. In other words, there must be a mechanism whereby the called function can determine (or even assume) the number and type of the arguments passed to it by the calling function.

As an example, let us imagine that the function f1( ) has been written to receive a variable number of arguments. The programmer could, for example, assume that the first argument to that function describes the number of other arguments available to the function from the calling program. The function header for f1( ) might therefore look like this:

```
void f1( int num_arg, ... )
{
   ...
   ...
}
```

In order that f1() can extract the additional arguments from the stack, it must first introduce a variable of type va_list. This data type is type defined within <stdarg.h>, frequently as a char pointer, as shown below:

```
typedef char *va_list;
```

The macro va_start() initializes an object of type va_list to point to the address of the first additional argument presented to the function, currently stored on the stack. An example definition of this macro is given below, where 'vp' is an object of type va_list, and 'pn' is the first known argument in the function's parameter list and contains the number of actual arguments presented to the function:

```
#define va_start(vp, parmn) ((vp) = (va_list) &(pn) + sizeof(pn))
```

In the case of the function f1(), assuming it is called with three additional arguments of type int, double and int, 'vp' is set to point to the address of the first of those additional arguments, as shown below:

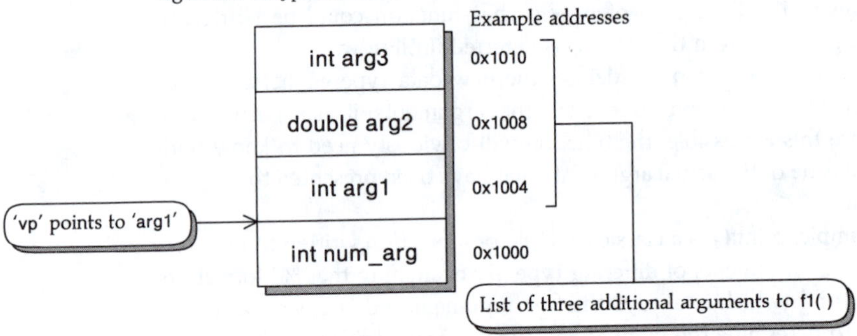

To extract successive arguments from the stack requires successive calls to the macro va_arg(), the typical definition of which is shown below. Using the pointer 'ap' and, unusually, the *type* of the parameter to be extracted, the function's arguments can be extracted off the stack, and 'vp' is then incremented to point to the next argument:

```
#define va_arg(vp,type) (*((type *)vp)++)
```

Once the arguments have all been extracted, a call to the macro va_end(), shown below, should be made to deinitialize 'ap', which, given the way that 'ap' was defined above, often performs no action:

```
#define va_end(ap)          /* no macro expansion for this implementation*/
```

As a trivial example, let us see how we could write the whole function f1() to receive and extract a variable number of arguments given to it by the calling function. It will be assumed that such arguments, should they be present, will be all doubles. Program 18.5 demonstrates this.

Program 18.5 Example variable argument function.

```
#include  <stdarg.h>

/*
** A function to calculate the combined total resistance of several resistors in
** parallel, given by the equation 1/rtot = 1/r1 + 1/r2 + ... + 1/rn
** This function extracts 'num_res' resistance values off the stack which, if present,
** are all assumed to be doubles, and returns the value of rtot
*/

double par_resistance( int num_res, ... )
{
   int      i ;
   double  temp, result = 0.0 ;

/* Introduce a variable of type 'va_list' */

   va_list  ap ;

/* Initialize 'ap' to point to the first additional argument; that is, the one after 'num_res' */

   va_start( ap, num_res ) ;

   for( i = 0; i < num_res; i++ )  {
      temp = va_arg( ap, double ) ;
      result += 1.0/temp ;
   }

/* Now deinitialize 'ap' and return result */

   va_end( ap ) ;
   return (1.0/result) ;

}
```

This function could be called in any of the following manners, among others:

```
par_resistance( 1, r1 ) ;
par_resistance( 2, r1, r2 ) ;
par_resistance( 3, r1, r2, r3 ) ;
par_resistance( 4, r1, r2, r3, r4 ) ;
```

A cautionary note on default argument promotions

You will recall from Section 6.1.12 that in the absence of a parameter list in the function prototype or for a parameter governed by the ellipsis '...', the compiler automatically promotes the corresponding arguments to the functions in accordance with the following rules:

(1) All arguments of type char and short are promoted to int.

(2) All arguments of type float are promoted to double.

From this we can deduce that if a variable of type float were presented as the second additional argument to the function f1(), then the compiler would automatically promote that float to a double and f1() should thus always be written in conjunction with the va_arg() macro to extract a float quantity as a double. Likewise, any char or short type arguments should be extracted as ints.

Structures and arrays may also be passed in this way, but it may be more convenient to pass them by *reference*; that is, by address. The called function could then extract a pointer to that type of object and access the object using pointer notation.

You may well conclude after a study of this section that for everyday programming applications, passing a variable number of arguments to a function is rather complicated, and, in many cases, unnecessary. For most applications, the author prefers to pass a variable number of arguments to a function within a structure or an array. The program can then extract whatever elements it likes from it. However, there are other functions in the standard library that make use of variable arguments, such as vprintf() (see Section 18.12), so an understanding of the mechanisms involved is useful.

18.11 The header file <stddef.h>

The header file <stddef.h> defines a number of macros and new data types, some examples of which are shown below, but they are likely to vary from one compiler to another:

```
typedef  long int      ptrdiff_t ;
typedef  short int     wchar_t ;
typedef  unsigned int  size_t ;


#define  NULL                         ((void *) 0))
#define  offsetof( s_type, member )  ( size_t)&(((s_type*)0) -> member )
```

The data type ptrdiff_t

You will recall from Chapter 8 that the storage requirements for a pointer are not strictly defined. On some machines a pointer may be represented by a 16 or 32 bit quantity. This poses a number of portability problems, particularly when calculating the difference between two pointer values. For example, would the result be a signed or unsigned quantity (important if used with other types of variables in an expression), and would the difference be representable within an int or would it require a long int?

To solve this dilemma the standard defines the new data type ptrdiff_t, able to represent the integral difference between two pointer values. Typically, ptrdiff_t is implemented as a (signed) long int.

The data type wchar_t

The data type wchar_t has been introduced to enable a **wide character** to be represented. Such characters exist on some computers, particularly those with extended character sets that require more than 8 bits to represent them. In such instances, the data type wchar_t would be represented perhaps by a short int. However, where the host computer/compiler does not support such an extended character set, wchar_t would typically be represented as a simple char.

Implicit wide character and string constants of type wchar_t are generated by preceding that character or string with the letter 'L', such as in the expression L'@' or L"Hello".

The data type size_t

The data type size_t is generally defined as an unsigned integral quantity and happens to be the type of the sizeof operator. Note that many of the standard library functions now declare their integral arguments as being of type size_t, particularly those functions such as fread(), fwrite(), calloc() and malloc() where such arguments are generally expected to have been generated by sizeof.

The macro offsetof()

The macro offsetof() may be used to determine the offset, in bytes, of a structure's member elements relative to the address of the structure itself, and yields a result of type size_t. The first argument to offsetof() must be the structure template's name, not the name of any structure variable based upon it. The second argument is the name of the member element within the structure. For example, given the structure template complex and the calls to printf() shown below:

```
struct complex  {
   double x ;
   double y ;
} ;

printf("Element x is offset %u bytes from the start of structure\n",
      (unsigned int )offsetof(struct complex, x )) ;
printf("Element y is offset %u bytes from the start of structure\n",
      (unsigned int )offsetof(struct complex, y )) ;
```

The operator might realistically expect to see the results 0 and 8 displayed, respectively.

The symbolic constant/macro NULL

Lastly, <stddef.h> defines the symbolic constant/macro NULL, which is defined as a (void) pointer to the address 0. Thus, the symbolic constant NULL may be assigned to or compared with any pointer to mark or compare it as invalid. An example is shown below:

```
#define  NULL  (void *)(0)
```

18.12 The header file <stdio.h>

This is probably the 'busiest' of all the header files, containing prototypes for all those functions in the standard library associated with any form of stream input or output. A number of macros are also defined in support of them. An extract from the contents of a typical <stdio.h> header file is given in Program 18.6.

Program 18.6 The contents of a typical <stdio.h> header file.

```
struct _buffer  {
   int            level ;        /* Full or empty level of stream buffer */
   unsigned       flags ;        /* Stream status flags */
   char           path ;         /* Stream descriptor */
   unsigned char  hold ;         /* To hold any ungetc char if no buffering used */
   int            bsize ;        /* Size of buffer for stream */
   unsigned char  *buffer ;      /* Pointer to stream buffer */
   unsigned char  *nextc ;       /* Pointer to next character in buffer */
   unsigned       tempfile ;     /* Temporary file flag */
}

/* Create a new data type called FILE based on the structure '_buffer' */

typedef  struct _buffer  FILE ;

/*
** Symbolic name for the maximum number of streams that may be open at any
** one time
*/

#define  MAX_FILE_NUM  30

/* Declare the array of FILE structures as external within operating system */

extern  FILE  _iob[ MAX_FILE_NUM ] ;

/* 'Fake' file pointers for the standard input, output and error message streams */

#define  stdin    ( &_iob[0])    /* standard input stream */
#define  stdout   ( &_iob[1])    /* standard output stream */
#define  stderr   ( &_iob[2])    /* standard error message stream */
```

```
/* The following 'fake' file pointers may be present on an MS-DOS machine */

#define  stdaux  ( &_iob[3] )    /* stream connected to auxiliary port */
#define  stdprn  ( &_iob[4] )    /* stream connected to printer port */

/* Definition of the file position type used by fgetpos( ) and fsetpos( ) */

typedef  long int  fpos_t ;

/* Symbolic constants to control the type of buffering used by setvbuf( ) */

#define  _IOFBF  0              /* Full buffering */
#define  _IOLBF  1              /* Line buffering */
#define  _IONBF  2              /* No buffering */

#define  EOF     (-1)           /* End of file constant */
#define  NULL    0              /* NULL defined as the integer constant 0 */

/*
** Default size of buffer used by setbuf( ). Typical values may be 512 or 1024 but
** should be at least 256
*/

#define  BUFSIZ  1024

/*
** The minimum size of any char array designed to hold a file name generated by
** tmpnam( )
*/

#define  L_tmpnam  20

/* Maximum number of unique file names that can be generated by 'tmpnam( )' */

#define  TMP_MAX  0xFFFF

/* Symbolic constants for use with function fseek( ). */

#define  SEEK_SET  0            /* seek from start of file */
#define  SEEK_CUR  1            /* relative to current position */
#define  SEEK_END  2            /* relative to end of file */

/* Typical predefined macros to perform character I/O to/from a stream */

#define  getchar( )   getc(stdin)
#define  putchar(c)   putc((c),stdout)

#define  getc(fp)     fgetc(fp)
#define  putc(c,fp)   fputc((c),(fp))

/*
** The following two macros define a unique 'bit' within the 'flag' variables defined
** within the structure '_buffer'. When set, they indicate that an 'end-of-file' or 'error'
** condition has been reached/detected for that stream
*/
```

```
#define  _IOEOF  0x10                          /* end of file has occurred */
#define  _IOERR  0x20                          /* error has occurred */

/* Typical macros for detecting error or EOF status for a stream */

#define  ferror(fp)     ((fp)->_flags&_IOERR)          /* test error bit in _flags */
#define  feof(fp)       ((fp)->_flags&_IOEOF)          /* test eof bit in _flags */
#define  clearerr(fp)  ((void)((fp)->_flags &= ~(_IOERR | _IOEOF)))
#define  rewind(fp)    ((void)(fseek(fp,0L,SEEK_SET) , ((fp)->_flags &= ~_IOERR)))
```

Function prototypes within <stdio.h>

- `int remove( const char *filename ) ;`

removes the disk file specified by filename (see Section 16.8).

- `int rename( const char *old_name, const char *new_name ) ;`

renames the disk file specified by old_name to the name specified by new_name (see Section 16.8).

- `char *tmpnam( char *s ) ;`

generates a unique temporary file name (see Section 16.9).

File creation and control

- `FILE *fopen( const char *name, const char *mode ) ;`

creates/opens a device/file and attaches it to a stream for communication in a specified mode (see Section 16.3.1).

- `FILE *freopen( const char *name, const char *mode, FILE *stream ) ;`

closes a stream and reopens it attached to another device (see Section 16.11.4).

- `int fclose( FILE *stream ) ;`

closes a stream (see Section 16.3.5).

- `FILE *tmpfile( void ) ;`

creates a temporary disk file (see Section 16.9).

Stream manipulation and control

- int setvbuf(FILE *stream, char *buf, int type, int size) ;

modifies the type of stream buffering in use (see Section 16.7).

- void setbuf(FILE *stream, char *buf) ;

modifies the type of stream buffering in use (see Section 16.7.1).

- int fflush(FILE *stream) ;

flushes the contents of a stream buffer (see Section 16.3.6).

Formatted stream I/O

- int printf(const char *format, ...) ;

writes formatted text and numeric output to the default output stream, stdout (usually the operator's terminal unless output has been redirected) (see Chapter 15).

- int sprintf(char *buffer, const char *format, ...) ;

sprintf( ) is similar to printf( ) except that the output is instead written into the array pointed to by buffer. A '\0' is then appended to the end of the output to terminate it.

- int fprintf(FILE *stream, const char *format, ...) ;

fprintf( ) is similar to printf( ), but writes formatted text and numeric output to a specified stream (see Section 16.3.3).

- int vprintf(const char *format, va_list arglist) ;

vprintf( ) is similar to printf( ) but uses a variable length parameter list given by the parameter arglist (the data type va_list has been type defined in <stdarg.h>) rather than a list of separate arguments. For details of the data type va_list and how to write and access functions with variable length parameter lists, see Section 18.10.

Such a function finds applications where it is necessary to write functions able to display a variable length list of data items, as demonstrated in Program 18.7.

Program 18.7 Example use of vprintf( ).

```
#include   <stdio.h>
#include   <stdarg.h>

/* Function to receive a format string and a variable number of arguments */

void print_valist(char *format, ... )
{
   va_list  data ;
   va_start(data, format) ;
   vprintf(format, data) ;
   va_end(data) ;
}

int main(void)
{
   char *format = "%d %d %g\n";

   print_valist(format, 1, 2, 3.0) ;
   return 0 ;
}
```

- int vsprintf(char *buffer, const char *format, va_list arglist) ;

vsprintf( ) is similar to vprintf( ) but writes its output into the array pointed to by buffer before a '\0' is appended to the end of the output to terminate it.

- int vfprintf(FILE *stream, const char *format, va_list arglist) ;

vfprintf( ) is similar to vprintf( ) except that the output is written to a specified stream.

- int scanf(const char *format, ...) ;

reads, converts and stores formatted text and numeric input from the default input stream, stdin (usually the operator's terminal unless input has been redirected). Upon detection of an end-of-file condition, and prior to any conversions, scanf( ) returns the value of the symbolic constant EOF defined in <stdio.h>, otherwise, the number of successful conversions performed by scanf( ) is returned (see Chapter 15).

- int sscanf(const char *buffer, const char *format, ...) ;

sscanf( ) is similar to scanf( ) except that the data is instead read from the char array pointed to by buffer. EOF is returned if sscanf( ) attempts to read beyond the '\0' marking the end of the text in the array.

- int fscanf(FILE *stream, const char *format, ...) ;

fscanf() is similar to scanf() but the data is read from the specified input stream (see Section 16.3.3).

- int vscanf(const char *format, va_list arglist) ;

vscanf() is similar to scanf() but uses a variable length parameter list specified by the parameter arglist (the data type va_list has been type defined in <stdarg.h>) rather than a list of separate argument addresses. For details of the data type va_list and how to write and access functions with variable length parameter lists, see Section 18.10. This function is useful where it is necessary to create a function to read in a variable length list of data items. For example, Program 18.8 demonstrates how vscanf() might be called.

Program 18.8 Example use of vscanf().

```
#include <stdio.h>
#include <stdarg.h>

/* Function to receive a format string and a variable number of arguments */

void read_valist(char *format, ... )
{
    va_list data ;

/*
** Now initialize data to the start of the first of the variable argument
** parameters contained on the stack
*/

    va_start( data, format ) ;

/*
** Call vscanf() and pass it the format string and the pointer
** to the start of the variable argument list
*/

    vscanf( format, data );
    va_end( data );
}

int main(void)
{
    char    *format = "%d%d%lg";
    int     a, b ;
    double  c ;

    read_valist(format, &a, &b, &c) ;
    printf("%d %d %g\n", a, b, c) ;
    return 0 ;
}
```

- int vsscanf(const char *buffer, const char *format, va_list arglist) ;

vsscanf( ) is similar to vscanf( ) except that the data is read from the char array pointed to by buffer rather than the standard input stream. EOF is returned if an attempt is made to read beyond the '\0' marking the end of the text in the array.

- int vfscanf(FILE *stream, const char *format, va_list arglist) ;

vfscanf( ) is similar to vscanf( ) except that the data is read from the specified input stream.

Character input and output

- int getchar(void) ;

getchar( ) is a macro defined in <stdio.h> (see Program 18.6) that reads a single character from the default input stream, stdin (usually the operator's terminal unless input has been redirected). Upon detection of an error, or the end-of-file condition, getchar( ) returns the value of the symbolic constant EOF defined in <stdio.h>.

- int getc(FILE *stream) ;

getc( ) is generally a macro defined in <stdio.h> (see Program 18.6) and operates in a similar manner to getchar( ), except that it reads a single character from a specified stream.

- int fgetc(FILE *stream) ;

fgetc( ) is generally implemented as a function, equivalent in operation to the macro getc( ) (see Section 16.5).

- int putchar(int c) ;

putchar( ) is a macro defined in <stdio.h> (see Program 18.6) that writes a single character to the default output stream stdout (usually the operator's terminal unless the program's output has been redirected). Upon detection of an error, putchar( ) returns the value of the symbolic constant EOF defined in <stdio.h>.

- int putc(int c, FILE *stream) ;

putc( ) is generally a macro defined in <stdio.h> (see Program 18.6) and operates in a similar manner to putchar( ), except that it writes a single character to a specified stream.

- int fputc(int c, FILE *stream) ;

fputc( ) is generally implemented as a function, equivalent in operation to the macro putc( ) (see Section 16.5).

String input and output

- char *gets(char *buffer) ;

gets( ) reads a string from the default input stream, stdin (usually the operator's terminal unless input has been redirected) and stores the characters read into the array pointed to by buffer. A pointer to the start of that array is then returned. Note that gets( ) replaces the <return> key entered by the operator with a '\0' to terminate the string. Upon detection of an error or the end-of-file condition, gets( ) returns a NULL pointer.

- char *fgets(char *buffer, int num, FILE *stream) ;

fgets( ) is similar to gets( ), but reads a string from a specified stream. At most 'num−1' characters are read. However, fgets( ) retains the <return> key and appends a '\0' onto the end (see Section 16.4).

- int puts(const char *buffer) ;

writes the '\0' terminated string in the array pointed to by buffer to the default output stream, stdout (usually the operator's terminal unless output has been redirected). A new line character '\n' is then appended to the output. Upon detection of an error, puts( ) returns the value of the symbolic constant EOF defined in <stdio.h>.

- int fputs(const char *buffer, FILE *stream) ;

fputs( ) is similar to puts( ), except that fputs( ) writes its output to a specified stream and does not append a new line character '\n' (see Section 16.4).

Direct or binary input/output functions

- int fread(void *ptr, size_t size, size_t num, FILE *stream) ;

reads binary data from the specified stream (see Section 16.10.2).

- int fwrite(const void *ptr, size_t size, size_t num, FILE *stream) ;

writes binary data to the specified stream (see Section 16.10.1).

Stream positioning functions

- int fseek(FILE *stream, long offset, int position) ;

permits the random repositioning of the specified stream's SPI for those devices that support random access (see Section 16.6.1).

- long ftell(FILE *stream) ;

returns the current position of the specified stream's SPI (see Section 16.6.3).

- int fgetpos(FILE *stream, fpos_t *pos) ;

saves the current value of the specified stream's SPI (see Section 16.6.4).

- int fsetpos(FILE *stream. const fpos_t *pos) ;

restores the value of the specified stream's SPI (see Section 16.6.4).

- void rewind(FILE *stream) ;

rewinds the specified stream's SPI to the start of the stream and clears the error and end-of-file status for the stream (see Section 16.6.2).

End-of-file and error detection

- int feof(FILE *stream) ;

returns a non-zero value if the program has attempted to read beyond the end of the specified stream (see Section 16.3.7).

- int ferror(FILE *stream) ;

returns a non-zero value if an error condition has been logged for the specified stream (see Section 16.3.7).

- void clearerr(FILE *stream) ;

clears the error and end-of-file status for a specified stream (see Section 16.3.8).

- void perror(const char *s) ;

generates and writes a system dependent error message to the default error stream (stderr) based on the value of the external int errno (see Section 16.3.9).

18.13 The header file <stdlib.h>

This header file contains a number of function prototypes for several loose and often unrelated functions that do not seem to fit conveniently into any of the other header files.

Dynamic memory allocation

- `void *calloc( size_t num, size_t size );`

calloc() requests an area of contiguous memory from the 'heap' large enough to hold num elements each of which is size bytes in size. calloc() ensures that all bytes in the allocated memory are set to 0 before a pointer to the start of the allocated block is returned. Failure to allocate the memory results in a NULL pointer being returned (see Section 8.4.2).

- `void *malloc( size_t size );`

malloc() requests an area of contiguous memory from the 'heap' large enough to hold one element of size bytes in size. A pointer to the allocated memory is returned or NULL if unsuccessful. Note that unlike calloc(), malloc() does not clear the allocated memory block to zero (see Section 8.4.2).

- `void *realloc( void *mem_ptr, size_t size );`

realloc() permits a block of previously requested memory to be adjusted to a new size. The argument mem_ptr is a pointer to the block of memory to be resized and can only be obtained by a successful call to calloc(), malloc() or realloc().

Where possible, realloc() will attempt to enlarge/reduce the size of the previously granted block of memory, but if this fails, a new area of memory will be allocated. realloc() will then copy all data from the previously granted memory into the new area and free the previous memory. A pointer to the resized or new block of memory is then returned, or a NULL pointer if the request cannot be met (see Section 8.4.2).

- `void free( void *mem_ptr );`

free() releases the block of memory pointed to by mem_ptr, whose address can only be obtained by a previous call to malloc(), calloc() or realloc() (see Section 8.4.2).

Sorting and searching

The functions bsearch() and qsort() provide a means of searching and sorting data in a table or array of arbitrary length. Both functions rely on a user supplied comparison function, which is called by each of these two functions to compare two elements in the table/array. The prototypes for both functions are given below:

- `void *bsearch( const void *key, const void *base, size_t num, size_t size, int (*fcompare)(const void *, const void *)) ;`

- `void qsort( void *base, size_t num, size_t size, int (*fcompare)(const void *, const void *) ) ;`

where key points to a copy of the item of data to be located within the array, base is a pointer to the first element in the array, size is the size of each element in the array and num contains the number of elements in the array. An example program demonstrating the use of both functions can be found in Section 10.3.2.

Random number generation

- `int rand( void ) ;`

returns a random integer number in the range 0 to RAND_MAX (defined in <stdlib.h>). The same sequence of random numbers is repeatedly generated each time the program is run. However, the pseudo-random sequencer that forms part of the function can be re-seeded to produce numbers from a different point in the sequence with the function srand() described below. Note that a random number between 0 and 'n – 1' can be generated with an expression such as rand() %n.

- `void srand( unsigned seed ) ;`

Calling srand() with a value of 1 re-initializes or re-seeds the pseudo-random sequencer to the start of a sequence so that the next 'n' subsequent calls to rand() produce the same sequence as the first 'n' calls when the program was initially run.

Any other value for seed forces rand() to generate random numbers from a different point in the sequence. Calling srand() with an argument obtained by rand(), or with a value returned by time(), randomly re-seeds the pseudo-random sequencer.

Communication with the host environment

- `char *getenv( const char *name ) ;`

searches the list of environment parameters supplied by the operating system for the environment parameter specified by name. If found a pointer to the full environment string is returned (see Section 9.4.2). Note that environment parameters are generally case sensitive.

- int system(const char *s) ;

allows the program to directly invoke a shell command for immediate processing, for example the statement system("dir c:\\dos") ; on an MS-DOS machine forces the host operating system to display a directory listing. A NULL value string 's' may be used to find out if the program is running in a hosted environment with a connection to a command line interpreter. If so, a non-zero value is returned.

- void abort(void) ;

forces the program to abort execution by raising the signal SIGABRT. Unless the program is written to intercept the signal (see Section 18.9), the program will terminate and write the message 'Abnormal program termination' to the standard error message stream (stderr). Whether any open streams/files are flushed and closed prior to the program termination is system dependent. The program then returns an unsuccessful termination status to the host environment.

- int atexit(void (*func)(void)) ;

atexit() forces the function pointed to by func to be 'registered' as an exit function. Up to 32 such functions may be registered by the program. Upon termination (not abortion) or completion of the program, all such registered functions are executed sequentially in the reverse order of their registration. This may be useful in performing any tidying up operation prior to the program terminating.

- void exit(int status) ;

forces the program to terminate 'normally', returning control and the value of status back to the host environment. Within <stdlib.h> the following two symbolic constants are defined, which may be used in place of the status argument to exit():

```
EXIT_SUCCESS  0                      /* program terminated successfully */
EXIT_FAILURE  (A Non zero value)     /* program failed */
```

When a call to exit() is made, all registered exit functions (see atexit() above) are executed, followed by the flushing and closure of all open streams. Lastly, any temporary files created by tmpfile() and still in existence are removed, and control is then passed to the host operating system. Note that exit() never returns to the program that calls it.

Integer arithmetic

- int abs(int i) ;

returns the absolute (positive) value of the integer argument 'i'.

- long labs(long i) ;

returns the absolute (positive) value of the long integer argument 'i'.

The following two functions, div() and ldiv(), divide the parameter numerator by the denominator and return a structure (which has been type defined in <stdlib.h>) containing the quotient and remainder of the division:

- div_t div(int numerator, int denominator) ;
- ldiv_t ldiv(long int numerator, long int denominator) ;

An example of how the two data types div_t and ldiv_t may have been defined is given below:

```
typedef struct {              typedef struct {
  int quot ;                    long int quot ;
  int rem ;                     long int rem ;
} div_t ;                     } ldiv_t ;
```

String to numeric conversion

- double atof(const char *s) ;
- int atoi(const char *s) ;
- long atol(const char *s) ;

These three functions search the '\0' terminated text string pointed to by 's', attempting to extract and return an equivalent numeric value for it. The general format of the string recognized by all three functions is given in Table 18.1. Also recognized by atof() are the strings "–INF", "+INF", "+NAN" and "–NAN". In the event of an overflow – that is, the extracted number cannot be represented by the returned data type – the result is undefined.

In Table 18.1 '[ ]' denotes an optional input and 'ddd' represents a number of digits/characters in the range '0–9'. Note that octal and hex notation are not recognized, but leading white space in the string is skipped. All three functions return the result of their conversion (as an int, long or double) up to the point where the end of the string or the first invalid character is encountered. None attempts to skip over invalid characters. Zero is returned if a number cannot be extracted. Note that there is no way using these three functions for the program to differentiate between the successful conversion of the value 0 and an unsuccessful conversion .

Table 18.1 Valid formats for atoi(), atol() and atof().

Function name	*Format*
atoi(), atol()	[white space] [sign] [ddd]
atof()	[white space] [sign] [ddd] [.] [ddd] [e or E[sign]ddd]

- double strtod(const char *s, char **endptr) ;
- long strtol(const char *s, char **endptr, int base) ;
- unsigned long strtoul(const char *s, char **endptr, int base) ;

These three functions are closely related to atof(), atoi() and atol(). Each will search the string pointed to by the argument 's', attempting to extract and return an equivalent numeric value. If any unrecognized/invalid character is detected within the string pointed to by 's', and endptr is *not* NULL, then the address of that unrecognized character is stored in the pointer pointed to by endptr. If no error occurs, that pointer will be set to NULL. This feature allows the programmer to check if an attempt has been made to convert an invalid string – that is, one not containing a numeric entry – a feature that is absent from atof(), atoi() and atol().

The functions strtol() and strtoul() extract a long and unsigned long, respectively, from their string. More interestingly, the programmer may control the numeric base of the number to be extracted through the use of the argument base which may assume a value in the range 2 (for binary) to 36. Characters in the range 0–9 and a–z or A–Z may then be recognized within the string where an appropriate base has been selected.

If base is set to 10, then the input is assumed to be in decimal and only the characters 0–9 in the string are recognized. A base of 16 permits hexadecimal input using the characters 0–9, a–f and A–F (a leading 0x or 0X in the string is optional and will be ignored). If base is set to 0, then a default base is assumed based upon the number contained in the string. For example, if the number begins with 0 or 0x (or 0X) then it is assumed to be in octal or hex format, respectively.

On underflow or overflow, each function sets the value of the external int errno (declared in <errno.h>) to the value ERANGE (declared in <math.h>), in which case each function returns the following value:

- strtod() returns ±HUGE_VAL (defined in <math.h>) on overflow, or 0 on underflow;
- strtol() returns LONG_MAX or LONG_MIN (defined in <limits.h>) on overflow;
- strtoul() returns ULONG_MAX (defined in <limits.h>) on overflow.

Program 18.9 demonstrates the use of the function strtol().

Program 18.9 Example use of the function strtol().

```
#include <stdlib.h>
#include <stdio.h>

int main(void)
{
   char string[BUFSIZ], *endptr;
   long lnumber;
```

```
/* Read a number and convert to a long decimal */

   gets(string);
   lnumber = strtol(string, &endptr, 10);

/* If an invalid character encountered display it */

   if( *endptr != NULL)
      printf("Error: Invalid character '%c'\n", *endptr) ;

   printf("Converted Number is = %ld\n", lnumber);
   return 0;
}
```

Multi-byte character and string functions

The standard has attempted to cater for situations where the host computer's operating environment supports an extended character set whose characters might require more storage than a char to represent them and to allow more than one character to be packed into a single storage unit (typically an integer), for example 'ab' or 'abcd'. Furthermore, the encoding of traditional characters such as 'a', 'b', 'c' and so on might not follow the usual conventions on such systems. The functions listed below are not commonly used, but permit conversion of multi-byte characters into characters of type wchar_t.

- `int mblen( const char *s, size_t num ) ;`

If 's' is a NULL pointer the function returns non-zero if a multi-byte character has what is referred to as a 'state dependent' encoding. Otherwise, if 's' is not a NULL pointer, it is assumed to point to a string and mblen( ) will examine at most num characters from that string and return the number of bytes that comprise the next character. If 's' does not point to a multi-byte character, −1 is returned.

- `int mbtowc( wchar_t *p, const char *s, size_t num ) ;`

mbtowc( ) is similar to mblen( ), except that if 'p' is not a NULL pointer, mbtowc( ) converts the next multi-byte character in 's' into a wide character and stores it in the object pointed to by 'p'.

- `int wctomb( char *s, wchar_t c ) ;`

If 's' is a NULL pointer the function returns non-zero if a multi-byte character has what is referred to as a 'state dependent' encoding. Otherwise, if 'c' is a wide character corresponding to a multi-byte character, then wctomb( ) stores the multi-byte character in 's' and returns the integer number of bytes required to represent it. Otherwise, −1 is returned.

- size_t mbstowcs(wchar_t *p, const char *s, size_t num) ;

converts the multi-byte character string pointed to by 's' into a wide character string, of which at most num characters are stored in the array pointed to by 'p', before that array is terminated by a '\0'. If successful, the number of wide characters written to the array will be returned. If an invalid multi-byte sequence is encountered, −1 is returned.

- int wcstombs(char *s, const wchar_t *p, size_t num) ;

converts the wide character array pointed to by 'p' into a multi-byte character sequence, which is then stored in the array pointed to by 's'. At most num wide characters are converted or until a NULL character is encountered in 'p'. If successful, the number of wide characters converted is returned, or −1 otherwise.

18.14 The header file <string.h>

This header file contains a number of function prototypes relating to the string and memory manipulation functions defined in the standard library. They are described below.

- char *strcat(char *dest, const char *source) ;

strcat( ) appends a copy of the string pointed to by source (including the '\0' termination character) to the end of the string pointed to by dest. A pointer to the start of the newly appended string (that is, the argument dest) is then returned, and this is often used as a further argument to other string manipulation functions (see Section 9.5.4).

Note that the '\0' string terminator character that initially marked the end of the dest string is overwritten by the first character from source. The length of the new string is given by strlen(dest) + strlen(source). Note also that it is the programmer's responsibility to ensure that sufficient storage has been allocated at dest to accommodate the new string (remember to allocate space for the '\0' terminator).

- char *strchr(const char *s, int c) ;

strchr( ) searches the string pointed to by 's' (up to and including the '\0' termination character) for the first occurrence of the character specified by 'c'. If found, a pointer to that character in the string 's' is returned; otherwise, if the string does not contain the character, a NULL pointer is returned. Note that a pointer to the end of the string can be obtained by setting the argument 'c' to '\0' (see Section 9.5.5).

- int strcmp(const char *s1, const char *s2) ;

strcmp( ) compares the two strings pointed to by 's1' and 's2' in a lexicographical order. The characters in both strings are treated as unsigned chars for the purposes of comparison. If the two strings are identical, then 0 is returned, otherwise a value of less than 0 or greater than 0 is returned depending upon whether the string pointed to by 's1' is considered to be less than or greater than the string pointed to by 's2' (see Section 9.5.3).

- int strcoll(const char *s1, const char *s2) ;

strcoll( ) is similar to strcmp( ) but compares the strings 's1' and 's2' according to the current locale (see Section 18.6).

- char *strcpy(char *dest, const char *source) ;

strcpy( ) copies the string pointed to by source to the area of memory pointed to by dest, overwriting whatever was at dest in the process. Note that it is the programmer's responsibility to ensure that sufficient storage has been allocated at dest to hold the string (remember to allocate space for the '\0' terminator) (see Section 9.5.2).

- size_t strcspn(const char *s1, const char *s2) ;

strcspn( ) searches for the first occurrence of any character that is common to both of the strings pointed to by 's1' and 's2'. If such a character is encountered, then strcspn( ) calculates and returns the length of the initial string segment in 's1' consisting entirely of characters *not* contained within the string 's2'. For example, the statement:

```
length = strcspn("abcdefghi", "fhijklmop") ;
```

assigns the value 5 to length, since the character 'f' at position 6 in 's1' is the first character common to both strings, thus the length of the initial substring in 's1' containing characters that are not common to 's2' is 5.

- char *strerror(int error_number) ;

generates a system dependent error message based on the value of the argument error_number and returns a pointer to the start of the internally allocated static storage area where the message is held (see Section 16.3.9).

- size_t strlen(const char *s) ;

strlen() returns the length or number of characters (excluding the '\0' terminator) in the string pointed to by 's' (see Section 9.5.1).

- char *strncat(char *dest, const char *source, size_t num) ;

strncat() is similar to strcat() except that at most num characters (not counting the '\0' character) from the string pointed to by source are appended to dest.

- int strncmp(const char *s1, const char *s2, size_t num) ;

strncmp() is similar to strcmp() except that at most num characters from both strings are compared.

- char *strncpy(char *dest, const char *source, size_t num) ;

strncpy() is similar to strcpy() except that at most num characters are copied.

- char *strpbrk(const char *s1, const char *s2) ;

strpbrk() returns a pointer to the first character in 's1' that is also in 's2'. If no characters are common to both strings, then a NULL pointer is returned. For example, the statement:

```
strpbrk("2 + 3 = 4", "+*-\=") ;
```

returns a pointer to the character '+' in the string "2 + 3 = 4", since this is the first occurrence of a character common to both strings.

- char *strrchr(const char *s, int c) ;

strrchr() searches for the last occurrence of the character 'c' in the string 's'. If found, a pointer to that character in that string is returned; otherwise, a NULL pointer is returned (see Section 9.5.6).

- size_t strspn(const char *s1, const char *s2) ;

strspn() searches for the first character in the string pointed to by 's1' that is not present in the string pointed to by 's2'. If such a character is encountered, then strspn() calculates and returns the length of the initial string segment in 's1' consisting entirely of characters from the string 's2'. It follows, therefore, that if 's1' consists entirely of characters from 's2', then stspn() returns the length of the string 's1'. For example, the expression:

```
strspn("C is such joy", "C is the one for me") ;
```

yields the value 6, since the character 'u' at position 7 in 's1' is not present in 's2'.

- char *strstr(const char *s1, const char *s2) ;

strstr() searches the string pointed to by 's1' for the first occurrence of the substring pointed to by 's2'. If found, a pointer to the start of that substring in 's1' is returned; otherwise, a NULL pointer is returned. For example, the statement puts(strstr("Oh what a beautiful morning", "what a")) ; would display the text 'what a beautiful morning'.

- char *strtok(char *s1, const char *s2) ;

strtok() provides a simple and convenient mechanism for breaking down a text string into a number of shorter components or substrings. The operation is somewhat peculiar at first since several calls to strtok() may be required to extract all of the substrings contained within it. Furthermore, the function actually modifies the string that it is breaking down, so do not attempt to decompose a constant or literal text string using this function.

For example, an operator may have supplied the text response "Sorry I don't know the answer" in response to a question posed to him or her by the program. Rather than deal with one long text string, the program might wish to decompose this string into the six substrings shown below:

```
"Sorry" "I" "don't" "know" "the" "answer"
```

The process of extracting these substrings from the operator supplied string commences with an initializing call to strtok() using two string arguments. The parameter 's1' points to the initial string to be broken down, while the second parameter 's2' points to a string containing a number of possible delimiter characters that can be used to separate the substrings. Using the previous example, such a string need only consist of the space character. strtok() then initiates a search of the string pointed to by 's1', attempting to locate the first occurrence of a character or 'token' within it that matches any of those characters specified by the string pointed to by 's2'. If found, that token in 's1' is replaced by a '\0' terminating character, thus extracting the first substring from within 's1'. For example, assuming that the array buff contained the text string "Sorry I don't know the answer" then the first call to strtok() of the form:

```
strtok( buff, " " ) ;
```

where the argument 's2' has been set to a string containing a single space character, modifies buff such that displaying its contents with a call to puts() results in the text 'Sorry' being displayed.

Extracting the remaining substrings is a little more difficult and requires repeated calls to strtok( ) with the argument 's1' set to NULL, upon which strtok( ) returns a pointer to the start of each further substring or NULL when no further substrings exist. An example is demonstrated in Program 18.10.

Program 18.10 Example use of strtok( ).

```
#include <stdio.h>
#include <string.h>

int main( void )
{
  char buff[ BUFSIZ ], *p1;
  char delimit[ ] = " " ;         /* delimiter is a space character */
  int  i = 1 ;

/*
** Now initialize the test string with several substrings. Note that
** since strtok( ) modifies its first argument, any literal or constant text
** must be copied to a char array first, as in this example
*/

  gets( buff ) ;

/* Now the initializing call to strtok( ) to extract the first string */

  strtok( buff, delimit) ;
  printf("First call to strtok leaves the string \" %s \" in buff\n", buff ) ;

/*
** Now a loop that repeatedly calls strtok( ) to extract subsequent substrings. Note how
** s1 has been replaced by a NULL and how the loop terminates when strtok( ) returns
** NULL.
** Note also that the set of delimiter characters present in the argument s2 can be
** changed if required with each call to strtok( ).
*/

  while(( p1 = strtok( NULL, delimit )) != NULL )
    printf("Sub string %d = \"%s\"\n", i++, p1) ;

  return 0 ;
}
```

- size_t strxfrm(char *dest, const char *source, size_t num)

strxfrm( ) is similar to strncpy( ) but provides the additional features that the copied string is transformed in the process in accordance with the user's current locale (see Section 18.6) and a '\0' is always appended to the end of the string. The transformation performed by strxfrm() is such that any two transformed strings compared with strcmp() produce the same result as if they had not been transformed and compared with strcoll().

Memory handling functions

- `void *memchr( const void *p, int c, size_t num ) ;`

searches the first num bytes of a block of contiguous memory pointed to by 'p', looking for the character 'c'. If successful a pointer to the character 'c' in 'p' is returned. The comparison is performed as if 'c' were an unsigned char.

- `int memcmp( const void *p1, const void *p2, size_t num ) ;`

compares the first num bytes of the block of memory pointed to by 'p1' and 'p2' as if each byte were an unsigned char. One of the following values is then returned based upon the comparison:

- 0 if both blocks of memory are the same;
- <0 if the block pointed to by 'p1' is considered to be less than the block pointed to by 'p2';
- >0 if the block pointed to by 'p1' is considered to be greater than the block pointed to by 'p2'.

Note: Do not attempt to use memcmp() to compare two structures as their member elements may be separated by spare bytes of padding, which will adversely affect such comparison.

- `void *memcpy( void *dest, void *source, size_t num ) ;`

copies at most num bytes of data from the block of memory pointed to by source to the block of memory pointed to by dest. A pointer to the start of the destination block is returned. Note that it is the programmer's responsibility to ensure that there is sufficient storage allocated at dest to hold the copied data; also, if the source and destination blocks overlap, the result is undefined.

- `void *memmove( void *dest, void *source, size_t num ) ;`

memmove() is similar to memcpy() except that memmove() is defined for overlapping blocks.

- `void *memset( void *p, int c, size_t num ) ;`

sets the first num bytes in the block of memory pointed to by 'p' to the value of (unsigned char)(c). A pointer to the start of the block is returned.

18.15 The header file <time.h>

The header file <time.h> contains various function prototypes, macros, data types and structure templates for various date and time manipulation and display functions, which may be expressed in a variety of ways. The fundamental time unit is measured in seconds. It is known as 'calendar time' and is the unit of time measurement used by many of the functions in the standard library. However, calendar time is not always the most useful way to express a given time, for example to be told that it is now 5324 seconds past midnight is not very helpful.

To ease the burden on the programmer of creating a more meaningful measure and display of time, several other functions exist that permit calendar time to be converted to and displayed as 'broken down time' expressed in terms of hours, minutes, seconds, days, months, years and vice versa. Other functions also exist to determine the time between two events and to convert between two different time zones.

The header file <time.h> defines the new data types clock_t and time_t as well as the symbolic constant CLOCKS_PER_SECOND, as shown below. Also declared is the structure template 'tm' which contains the member elements shown in Program 18.11 and allows the program to extract various components of a broken down time unit.

Program 18.11 The contents of a typical <time.h> header file.

```
struct  tm  {                        /* a structure to hold a broken down time unit */
    int   tm_sec ;
    int   tm_min ;
    int   tm_hour ;
    int   tm_mday ;
    int   tm_mon ;
    int   tm_year ;
    int   tm_wday ;
    int   tm_yday ;
    int   tm_isdst ;
} ;

typedef  long  clock_t ;
typedef  long  time_t ;

#define  CLOCKS_PER_SEC   18.2   /* note that this is a floating point constant */
```

- clock_t clock(void)

The function clock( ) returns the number of implementation dependent clock 'ticks' that have elapsed since the program began. By dividing this value by the symbolic floating point constant CLOCKS_PER_SEC the time is converted to seconds. If the time from the system clock is unavailable, −1 is returned.

- time_t time(time_t *tp) ;

Provided that 'tp' is not a NULL pointer, time() calculates and returns the current calendar time, in seconds, that have elapsed since 00:00:00 on 1st January 1970. That time is then stored to the memory location pointed to by 'tp'.

- char *ctime(const time_t *time_ptr) ;

ctime() converts the calendar time unit pointed to by time_ptr, which can be obtained from a successful call to time(), into a broken down time string suitable for display and of the same form as that produced by asctime(). The string so generated is held in a static storage area allocated by ctime() and a pointer to the start of that string is returned. Note that successive calls to ctime() will overwrite the string. Program 18.12 demonstrates the use of time() and ctime().

Program 18.12 Example use of time() and ctime().

```
#include <stdio.h>
#include <time.h>

int main( void )
{
  time_t t1 ;

/* Get current time in seconds elapsed since 00:00:00 1st January 1970 and store in t1 */

  t1 = time(NULL) ;

/* Convert time in t1 to a string and display it */

  puts( ctime(( &t1))) ;
  return 0 ;
}
```

- double difftime(time_t t2, time_t t1) ;

computes the difference t2 – t1 expressed in seconds between two calendar time units. Note that the arguments 't1' and 't2' may be obtained from successful calls to time().

- struct tm *gmtime(const time_t *time_ptr) ;

converts the calendar time pointed to by time_ptr and expressed in seconds that have elapsed since 00:00:00 1st January 1970 into a broken down time unit. The time unit is of the form described by the structure 'tm' (see Program 18.11) and is expressed relative to Greenwich Mean Time (GMT).

Note that gmtime() allocates its own static storage into which the broken down time is stored, which will be overwritten by a subsequent call to gmtime() or localtime(). A pointer to this structure is then returned to the program.

Note also that the function asctime() may subsequently be called to convert a broken down time unit into the form of an ASCII string suitable for display purposes (thus a call to gmtime() followed by a call to asctime() is equivalent to a call to ctime()). An example use of the functions gmtime() and asctime() is given in Program 18.13, which produces a display of the form:

```
Wed Jan 16 23:12:27 1993
```

Program 18.13 Example use of gmtime() and asctime().

```
#include  <stdio.h>
#include  <time.h>

int main( void )
{
  time_t  t1 ;

  t1 = time(NULL) ;
  puts( asctime(gmtime( &t1))) ;
  return 0 ;
}
```

- `time_t  mktime( struct tm *time_ptr ) ;`

converts a broken down time unit pointed to by time_ptr into a calendar time unit expressed as seconds that have elapsed since 00:00:00 on 1st January 1970, and is thus the complementary function to gmtime().

- `struct tm *localtime( const time_t *time_ptr ) ;`

localtime() is similar to gmtime() but expresses the broken down time relative to a pre-programmed local time zone. With Borland's Turbo C, for example, the external global variable 'timezone' is initialized to the difference in seconds between the time locally and GMT. This variable is used by localtime() to determine the correct time for the user's current time zone. Likewise, the function tzset() permits the program to alter 'timezone' and make adjustments for US daylight saving.

- char *asctime(const struct tm *tp) ;

converts a broken down time unit (generated by the functions gmtime() or localtime()) into an ASCII string of the form. 'DDD MMM dd hh:mm:ss YYY', where:

- DDD is the current day and is of the form Mon, Tue, Wed and so on;
- MMM is the current month and is of the form Jan, Feb, Mar and so on;
- dd is the current day of the month, between 1 and 31;
- hh is the current hour of the day, between 1 and 24;
- mm is the current minute of the hour, between 1 and 59;
- ss is the current second of the minute, between 1 and 59;
- YYYY is the current year.

For example:

```
Wed Jun 16 23:12:27 1993
```

The string so generated is held in a static storage area allocated by asctime() and a pointer to the start of that string is returned. Note that successive calls to asctime() overwrite the string. Note also that the related function ctime() performs a similar action using non-broken down or calendar time units. Note that the statements ctime(&t1) and asctime(gmtime(&t1)) are equivalent.

- size_t strftime(char *s, size_t num, const char *format_string,
  const struct tm *time_ptr) ;

This function is to the display of time what printf() is to the display of formatted text and numeric output. A broken down time unit (obtained by a call to time() in conjunction with a call to localetime() or gmtime()) pointed to by time_ptr is converted into a text string, under the control of format_string, and written to the char array pointed to by 's'. At most num characters are written before a '\o' is appended. Upon success, the number of characters written to 's' is returned. If the generated string is longer than num, zero is returned.

strftime() recognizes a number of '%' formatters included in its format string, which are summarized in Table 18.2. These formatters control the position in the generated string where strftime() will place data about the current time. Any constant or literal text included in the format string will be copied to the generated string.

The format string for strftime() consists of zero or more directives and ordinary characters. A directive consists of the '%' character followed by a character that determines the substitution or conversion that is to take place.

Table 18.2 '%' formatters recognized by strftime().

%%	Percentage character
%a	Abbreviated weekday name
%A	Full weekday name
%b	Abbreviated month name
%B	Full month name
%c	Date and time
%d	Two-digit day of the month
%H	Two-digit 24 hour time (00–23)
%I	Two-digit 12 hour time (01–12)
%j	Three-digit day of the year (001–366)
%m	Two-digit month (01–12)
%M	Two-digit minute (00–59)
%p	a.m. or p.m. displayed
%S	Two-digit second (00–59)
%U	Two-digit week number 00–52 beginning on a Sunday
%W	Two-digit week number 00–52 beginning on a Monday
%w	Weekday number (0 = Sunday, 6 = Saturday)
%x	Date
%X	Time
%y	Two-digit year (00–99)
%Y	Four-digit year (1900+)
%Z	Time zone name

Program 18.14 demonstrates the use of the function strftime().

Program 18.14 Example use of strftime().

```
#include  <time.h>
#include  <stdio.h>

int main( void )
{
  time_t  t1;
  char    array[100] ;          /* output array for strftime() */

  time( &t1 ) ;                 /* get time in seconds */

/* Convert and format the time */

  strftime( array , sizeof( array ) - 1 ,
     "The Time is now %H:%M and %S seconds (%Z) on"
     " %A %d of %B %Y",
     localtime( &t1 )) ;

  puts(array) ;                 /* display time */
  return 0 ;
}
```

On the author's system, Program 18.14 produced the following display:

```
The Time is now 20:26 and 51 seconds (EDT) on Wednesday 16 of June 1993.
```

Index to Functions by Association

Arithmetic/mathematical

abs() absolute integer value function 727
acos() inverse cosine function 45, 704
asin() inverse sine function 45, 704
atan() inverse tangent function 45, 704
atan2() inverse tangent function 704
ceil() rounding up function 705
cos() cosine function 45, 703
cosh() hyperbolic cosine function 45, 704
div() integer quotient and remainder function 728
exp() exponential function 45, 704
fabs() floating point absolute value function 45, 705
floor() rounding down function 705
fmod() floating point remainder function 705
frexp() floating point to mantissa/exponent conversion function 704
labs() absolute long integer value function 728
ldexp() mantissa/exponent to floating point conversion function 704–5
ldiv() long integer quotient and remainder function 728
log() natural or log to base **e** function 45, 704
log10() log to base 10 function 45, 704
modf() floating point to integer/fraction function 705
pow() power function 45, 704
sin() sine function 45, 703
sinh() hyperbolic sine function 45, 704
sqrt() square root function 45, 704
tan() tangent function 45, 703
tanh() hyperbolic tangent function 45, 704

Character processing and validation

isalnum() character test function/macro 370
isalpha() character test function/macro 370
isascii() character test function/macro 370
iscntrl() character test function/macro 370
isdigit() character test function/macro 370
isgraph() character test function/macro 370
islower() character test function/macro 37–8, 370
isprint() character test function/macro 370
ispunct() character test function/macro 370–1
isspace() character test function/macro 370
isupper() character test function/macro 37–8, 370
isxdigit() character test function/macro 370
tolower() case conversion function 37–8, 371, 698
toupper() case conversion function 37–8, 371, 698

Date and time manipulation

asctime() broken down time to string conversion function 740
clock() elapsed clock ticks time function 737

ctime() calendar to broken down time function 738
difftime() calendar time difference function 738
gmtime() calendar to broken down time conversion function 738
localtime() calendar to broken down local time conversion function 739
mktime() broken down to calendar time conversion function 739
strftime() formatted time display function 740–2
time() elapsed calendar time function 738

File and stream manipulation

clearerr() clear stream error and end-of-file condition function 584, 718
fclose() file/stream closure function 48, 578–80, 718
feof() file/stream end-of-file detection function/macro 564–5, 582–4, 718, 724
ferror() file/stream error detection function/macro 564–5, 582–4, 718, 724
fflush() file/stream flush function 184, 580–2, 719
fgetc() file/stream character read function 49–51, 592–8, 717, 722
fgetpos() file/stream position record function 605–6, 724
fgets() file/stream string read function 586–90, 723
fopen() file/stream creation function 46–53, 565–8, 718
fprintf() formatted file/stream write function 47–8, 572–5, 719
fputc() file/stream character write function 47, 49–51, 592–8, 717, 723
fputs() file/stream string write function 47, 590–1, 723
fread() file/stream binary read function 621–4, 723
freopen() file/stream open function 627–9, 718
fscanf() formatted stream read function 48–9, 575–577, 721
fseek() file/stream positioning function 599–602, 724
fsetpos() file/stream positioning function 605–6, 724
ftell() file/stream position function 604, 724
fwrite() file/stream binary write function 617–24, 723
remove() file removal function 610–13, 718
rename() file rename function 610–13, 718
rewind() file/stream positioning function/macro 603, 718, 724
setbuf() stream buffer manipulation function 609–10, 719
setvbuf() stream buffer manipulation function 607–10, 719
tmpfile() temporary file creation function 613–15, 718
tmpnam() temporary file name creation function 613–15, 718
ungetc() return character stream function 598–9
vfprintf() formatted text and numeric stream output function 720
vfscanf() formatted text and numeric stream input function 721

Input/output

getc() character read function/macro 717, 722
getchar() character read function/macro 37, 626, 717, 722
gets() string read function 36, 723
perror() error message display function 585–6, 724
printf() formatted text and numeric output function 6–7, 13, 33, 524–42, 719
putc() character output function/macro 717, 722
putchar() character output function/macro 37, 626, 717
puts() string output function 35–6, 723
scanf() formatted text and numeric input function 15–17, 542–51, 720
sprintf() formatted array output/write function 524, 719

Jump control

Locale

Memory allocation and manipulation

Miscellaneous

Multi-byte character and string manipulation

Program termination and control

Searching and sorting

Signal and exception generation and processing

String manipulation

atof() string to float conversion function 39–41, 728

atoi() string to int conversion function 39, 728

atol() string to long int conversion function 39, 728

strcat() string concatenation function 38–9, 366–8, 731

strchr() string search function 368–9, 731

strcmp() string comparison function 38–9, 363–6, 732

strcoll() string comparison according to locale function 732

strcpy() string copy function 38–9, 361–3, 732

strcspn() string segment length function 732

strerror() error message generator function 585–6, 732

strlen() string length function 38–9, 359–61

strncat() string concatenation function 733

strncmp() string comparison function 733

strncpy() string copy function 733

strpbrk() find common character function 733

strrchr() reverse search string function 369–70

strspn() find non-common character function 733

strstr() find substring function 734

strtod() string to double conversion function 729

strtok() string breakdown function 734

strtol() string to long int conversion function 729

strtoul() string to unsigned long int conversion function 729

strxfrm() string copy according to locale function 735

Variable parameter list processing

va_arg() variable parameter extraction macro 712–13

va_end() variable parameter termination macro 712–13

va_start() variable parameter commencement macro 712–13

General Index

A

B

C

D

E

F

J

K

L

M

N

O

P

Q

R

S

T

U

V

W

X

Y

Z